Lesson Plans

Dynamic Physical Education for Secondary School Students

Sixth Edition

Carole M. Casten

California State University, Dominguez Hills

D1737652

PEARSON
Benjamin Cummings

San Francisco Boston New York
Cape Town Hong Kong London Madrid Mexico City
Montreal Munich Paris Singapore Sydney Tokyo Toronto

Senior Acquisitions Editor: Sandra Lindelof
Associate Editor: Emily Portwood
Managing Editor: Wendy Earl
Production Editor: Leslie Austin
Cover Design: Riezebos Holzbaur Design Group
Manufacturing Buyer: Dorothy Cox
Marketing Manager: Neena Bali

Copyright © 2009 Pearson Education, Inc., publishing as Pearson Benjamin Cummings, 1301 Sansome St., San Francisco, CA 94111. All rights reserved. Manufactured in the United States of America. This publication is protected by Copyright and permission should be obtained from the publisher prior to any prohibited reproduction, storage in a retrieval system, or transmission in any form or by any means, electronic, mechanical, photocopying, recording, or likewise. To obtain permission(s) to use material from this work, please submit a written request to Pearson Education, Inc., Permissions Department, 1900 E. Lake Ave., Glenview, IL 60025. For information regarding permissions, call (847) 486-2635.

Many of the designations used by manufacturers and sellers to distinguish their products are claimed as trademarks. Where those designations appear in this book, and the publisher was aware of a trademark claim, the designations have been printed in initial caps or all caps.

Pearson Benjamin Cummings™ is a trademark, in the U.S. and/or other countries, of Pearson Education, Inc. or its affiliates.

PEARSON
Benjamin Cummings

ISBN 0-321-55702-6
ISBN 978-0-321-55702-5
3 4 5 6 7 8 9 10 V0CR 14 13 12 11 10
www.pearsonhighered.com

Contents

2 Day Units

Preface

Lesson Plans for Dynamic Physical Education for Secondary School Students is designed for use with the textbook *Dynamic Physical Education for Secondary School Students,* 6th Edition, *(DPESS)* by Robert P. Pangrazi and Paul W. Darst. Most of the activities in these lesson plans are covered in detail in the textbook and references to relevant chapters are noted in the lesson plans. These lesson plans provide a guide for teachers presenting lessons in a well-ordered, sequential manner, to students from 7th grade through 12th grade. These lesson plans should be regarded as an aid in curriculum and instructional planning, and can serve as a framework for developing a curriculum to meet the needs of the students being served and the teachers.

Many teachers take the activities from the lesson plans and write them on 3" x 5" index cards. Having notes helps teachers mentally organize a lesson and results in a more effective presentation. All lesson presentations should be mentally rehearsed to prevent wasted time and excessive use of written notes. Brief notes relieve the teacher of the burden of trying to remember the sequence of activities and the worry of forgetting the main elements of each lesson.

This edition of the Lesson Plans includes an indication of the National Standards for Physical Education met in each lesson. Additionally, a cognitive element has been added to each chapter covering the history of the activity or tips to communicate to students about the activity, and is indicated with the following icon: . Student review questions at the end of most lessons now incorporate the cognitive areas and the information presented during the lesson.

Format of the Lesson Plans

Three-week, two-week, one-week and two-day units are presented for numerous topics (see the Contents on the following pages for a detailed break-down). The movement experiences are for the beginning learner. Each lesson plan is divided into four instructional parts as described in Chapter 4 of *DPESS,* plus a concluding evaluation and a cheer. The instructional parts of the lesson plan and the major purposes of each are as follows:

1. **Introductory Activity:** Introductory activities are used to physiologically prepare youngsters for activity when entering the activity area. They can serve as a gross motor warm-up as well as a time to practice and reinforce class management skills. Descriptions of introductory activities can be found in *DPESS*, Chapter 14.

2. **Fitness Development Activity:** Fitness activities should be allocated 8–12 minutes in a 30–35 minute activity period. The length of the fitness section of class varies depending on the time frame of each scheduled class and the developmental level of the students. The activities should be personalized, progressive in nature, and exercise all parts of the body. Brief discussions should be included in the lessons about the values of fitness for a healthy lifestyle. A comprehensive discussion of physical activity and fitness principles and activities is found in *DPESS,* Chapters 15 and 16.

3. **Lesson Focus Activities:** The purpose of the lesson focus is to help youngsters attain major program objectives, body management competency, and fundamental specialized skills. The lesson focus uses 15–20 minutes of the daily lesson depending on the length of the teaching period. While the lesson plan activities are organized into three-week, two-week, and one-week units in this book, the instructor may adapt and expand the lessons to any length to fit the organizational needs of the school. The content of each unit is presented in a developmental sequence ensuring that students can be successful and that material will be presented in a progressive manner.

4. **Game Activity:** This part of the lesson uses the final 5–7 minutes of the period. Games can be used as the culminating activity for practicing skills presented in the lesson focus or can be unrelated to the lesson focus. This portion of the lesson is presented for the purpose of completing the lesson with a fun and enjoyable activity. The game portion of each lesson should leave students with positive feelings toward movement.

5. **Evaluation/Review:** Good instruction puts closure on a lesson by conducting an evaluation/review requiring active involvement of the students. The instructor should end each lesson asking students pertinent questions evaluating elements of the day's activities and an introduction to activities for the next period.

6. **Cheer:** Athletic teams build spirit and bonding by ending each practice or entering each competition with a cheer. This practice applied to physical education classes can have the same result. Ending the class with a cheer can produce enthusiasm, bonding, and spirit. While the lesson plans include cheers, students really enjoy creating them. Allow students the opportunity to demonstrate their creativity by creating their own cheers. Try to end the classes with a cheer and see the spirit and enthusiasm blossom.

Orientation and Class Management Games

During the first lesson with new students, the instructor should teach and reinforce class management rules and games. Following are elements of instruction you might find useful in establishing the class format, routines, and expectations.

1. **Class rules, format, objectives, and expectations:** Discuss class rules, format, objectives, and expectations with the class the first day you meet the students to assure their understanding. Explain what the consequences are when rules are not followed. Explain that the format of each lesson will include an introductory activity, fitness development, lesson focus, and will finish with a game activity.

2. **Grading:** Explain the course grading policies and grading scale the first day of each unit.

3. **Entry and exit behaviors:** Demonstrate and explain entry and exit behaviors for the physical education class. Establish a policy for obtaining equipment.

4. **Non-participation:** Explain how excuses for non-participation will be handled. Establish guidelines for making up missed material or lost points.

5. **Safety:** Describe safety procedures for physical education classes. Explain that each unit will have unique rules that you will explain at the onset of the unit.

6. **Distribution of equipment:** Make students responsible for acquiring equipment and returning it at the end or appropriate portion of the lesson. Place equipment around the perimeter of the teaching area for easy and safe distribution of equipment.

7. **Starting and stopping class:** In general, a whistle, a drum beat, and a raised hand are effective signals for stopping the class. A voice command should be used to start the class. Use the phrase: "When I say go", or "When I say begin" followed by what you want executed to assure that students do not begin before instructions are finished.

8. **Formations:** Practice various teaching formations such as scattered, moving into a circle, and grouping. Transitions between formations should be done while moving, i.e., jogging from scatter formation into a circular formation. Refer to *DPESS* Chapter 7 for class management details.

   - **Creating partners:** Use the Back-to-Back, or Elbow-to-Elbow, or Toe-to-Toe technique for creating groups of two. All students not finding an elbow to touch should move toward a marker in the center of the room and raise a hand to find a partner. Emphasis should be on finding a partner near them, not searching for a friend, and taking a different partner each time.

   - **Forming a circle:** Use the technique of moving around the room with a locomotor movement and direct students to follow the back of someone's neck and fall-in to a circle.

   - **Groups of 3 or more:** Use the Whistle Mixer to create groups of 3 or more. Students move around the area with a locomotor movement, the teacher whistles (or claps, etc.) a given number of times and raises the same number of fingers above their head to signal the group size. Students move together to create groups the size matching the number of whistles signaled. Groups not complete should raise arms identifying the need for additional members and move toward the center of the area. Students needing to join a group should move toward the center of the area toward the established marker and raise their hand to facilitate finding others needing a group. The goal is to find the correct number of students as quickly as possible.

9. **Freeze positions:** To establish and focus attention on instructions, it is valuable to establish a "freeze" position for students to assume whenever you signal a stop via whistle, drum, etc. A commonly used freeze position is that similar to the "ready" position in sports with the hands on the knees. Equipment is placed between the feet.

Notes of Appreciation

Acknowledgments and appreciation go to my husband, Rich, for his computer expertise, perfectionist nature, and endless hours spent on the compilation of this textbook. Sincere thanks are extended to Dr. Robert P. Pangrazi for his continued support, feedback, friendship, and confidence in my writing. Additional thanks are extended to Debbie Pangrazi for new ideas for the 6th edition lesson plans and both Dr. Pangrazi, professor emeritus, and Dr. Paul Darst, professor at Arizona State University, co-authors of the textbook *Dynamic Physical Education for Secondary Students* for the opportunity to write this lesson plan book. Emily Portwood and Sandy Lindelof, Benjamin Cummings, deserve special thanks for their support in the writing of this book.

Some of the information shared in this textbook was motivated or gathered from the innovative and creative thinking of a number of professors and teachers in the greater Los Angeles Area and graduate and senior students at California State University Dominguez Hills (CSUDH). Dr. Reginald Price, professor emeritus, California State University San Bernardino, contributed the lesson focus, task sheets, and exam portion of the Racquetball Unit. To him I owe sincere gratitude for his hard work in a timely manner. Thank you to all of the following people for contributing ideas or materials to the lesson plans: Janice Manion and Kathy Odorico–Tennis Unit; Nick Carr, and Dr. John Johnson, professor, CSUDH–Golf Unit; Anthony Quiarte contributed the “written lesson” and “programmed instruction”–Weight Training Unit; Diana Vance–Volleyball Unit; Joanna Enserro Natividad–Soccer Unit; Alicia Megofina and Eric Calhoun–Orienteering Unit; Barry Barnes and Alan Ransom–Rock Climbing Unit; Neftali Rivera and Wilma Uy–Team handball Unit; Grace Dacanay and Luis Gomez–Table Tennis Unit; John Noble and Arturo Gutierrez–Frisbee Golf; Irene Flores and Stephanie Rodriguez–Flag Football Unit; and Wendy Bogdanovich, Mike Cota, John Ramirez and Carrie Reeder–Softball Unit; Michelle Mara contributed to the Yoga Unit; Debby Martin contributed to the Bowling Unit; Rafael Hernandez contributed additional new ideas to the Golf, Racquetball and Orienteering units; Mutah Nasouf, Los Angeles Unified School District, contributed to the Pickleball unit; Kemberlee Zuniga for ideas for the Guided Discovery Frisbee Golf Task Sheet; Tracy Barrientos contributed to the softball unit; and Mallory Dominguez for some additions to the one-week units. Appreciation is given to Mary Dean, Kyrene School District, AZ and Sean Jonaitis, Gilbert School District, AZ, for ideas included in the Swim Unit. To Melissa Acosta, Kevin Geddes, and Lisa Goldschein, thank you for field-testing the lessons at the California Academy of Mathematics and Science. To the other teachers in the greater Los Angeles area, thank you for field-testing items from the textbook. To Beverly Francis, secretary, California State University Dominguez Hills, thank you for your continued encouragement.

To **all** the contributors to this textbook, I offer sincere gratitude and a big THANK YOU.

Badminton

This unit has been specifically designed to meet all six components of the NASPE National Standards for Physical Education.

OBJECTIVES:

The student will:

1. Juggle one, two, or three scarves as directed by the instructor.
2. Work cooperatively with peers during the High Five Introductory Activity.
3. Demonstrate agility and speed in the Triangle Tag Game
4. Demonstrate balancing in a variety of positions during the Balance Tag.
5. Demonstrate cooperation with peers during the Snowball Relay game.
6. Demonstrate agility, starting, stopping and stretching skills during the Move and Stretch Activity.
7. Demonstrate agility and dodging skills during the introductory activities.
8. Demonstrate cooperation and agility during the Pentabridge Hustle Introductory Activity.
9. Execute balancing positions, running, and dodging skills during the Balance Tag Introductory Activity
10. Participate strengthening and stretching exercises, in the Fitness Challenge Course Circuit, Fitness Obstacle course Parachute Rhythmic Activities, Interval Training Activities, Four Corners Fitness activities, Continuity Exercises, jump roping activities. To improve their overall fitness levels.
11. Participate in "Marking" demonstrating agility and quickness.
12. Play Tug-of-War challenge with a partner.
13. Participate in Back to Back Take Down with partner following the rules and playing cooperatively.
14. Execute forehand and backhand strokes
15. Execute proper form of the forehand clear shot demonstrated by teacher.
16. Demonstrate the forehand smash and drop shots using form demonstrated in class.
17. Execute the backhand clear shot on the court using form demonstrated in class.
18. Execute the backhand drop shot on the court using form demonstrated in class.
19. Execute the forehand shots on the court using form demonstrated in class.
20. Perform the Badminton Forehand Clear Shot as demonstrated by the instructor.
21. Demonstrate forehand net drop using form taught by instructor.
22. Demonstrate serving on the court aiming for the hoops on the floor and using form demonstrated in class.
23. Demonstrate the forehand drive and drop shot during a rally activity with classmates.
24. Read the Rules Handout distributed by the instructor.
25. Practice underhand, forehand and backhand shots on a court using appropriate task sheets.
26. Practice the forehand smash to a target on the court using appropriate task sheets.
27. Execute skills and knowledge of rules while playing Badminton Doubles.
28. Play Singles Badminton with a partner demonstrating knowledge of rules of the game.
29. Play Badminton in a Round Robin Tournament during class executing skills and rules demonstrated in class.
30. Complete a Badminton Written Knowledge Exam during class and scoring 70% or better.
31. Complete a Badminton Skills Test working cooperatively with a partner during the class period.

Academic Integration Areas

1. The Challenge Course activities can integrate Muscular Use Identification, Numeric Patterns and Contrasting Terms.
   The teacher can say:
   a. Tell me the main muscles that are used during your leaping and jumping fitness activities.
   b. What muscles are you using during crab walks, curl-ups, and push-ups?
   c. Create a pattern for moving through the Challenge Course. Reverse the pattern.
2. The Frisbee 21 game requires cooperation and responsibility between the students. It also can reinforce numeric patterning.
   a. What pattern did you notice developed to earn points? Were more points earned with the 2 handed catch or the 1-handed catch?

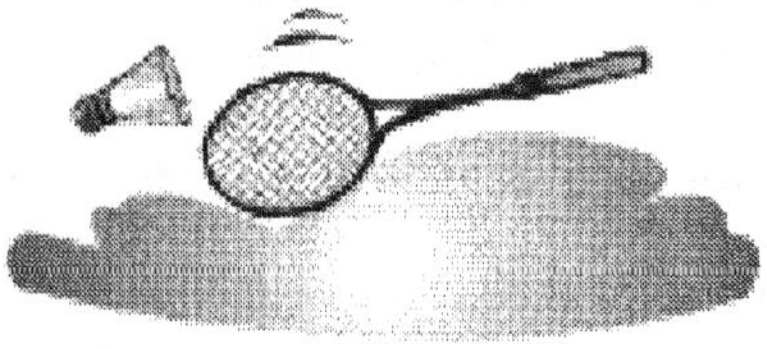

BADMINTON BLOCK PLAN
3 WEEK UNIT

Week #1	Monday	Tuesday	Wednesday	Thursday	Friday
Introductory Activity	Juggling Scarves	Weave Drill	Triangle Plus 1 Tag	Balance Tag	Running High Fives
Fitness	Challenge Course	4-Corners	Continuity Exercises	Challenge Course	General Movements
Lesson Focus	Forehand Grip Backhand Grip	Underhand Serve, Review Forehand & Backhand Grip	Forehand Clear Forehand Drop Forehand Smash	Backhand Shots, Clear and Drop Review Forehand	Review Skills Forehand Backhand Serve
Game	Frisbee 21	Partner Tug of War	Hoops on the Ground	Hoops and Plyometrics	Circle Hook On

Week #2	Monday	Tuesday	Wednesday	Thursday	Friday
Introductory Activity	Marking	Move and Stretch	Fastest Tag	Vanishing Bean Bags	Zipper
Fitness	Continuity Exercises	Interval Training	Challenge Course	4-Corners	Challenge Course
Lesson Focus	Review: Forehand Net Drop, Backhand Net Drop, Underhand Long Serve	Rules Skills Review Play Drive Rally	Play Doubles Badminton Games	Station Skill Review	Play Badminton Games
Game	Fetch Relay	Mixed Doubles Games	Snowball Relay	Over and Under Ball Relay	Frozen Tag

Week #3	Monday	Tuesday	Wednesday	Thursday	Friday
Introductory Activity	Pentabridge Hustle	Juggling Scarves	Move and Perform a Stretch	Eliminate today	Balance Tag
Fitness	Parachute Rhythmic Aerobic Activities	Stations	Continuity Exercises	Parachute Rhythmic Aerobic Activities	Four-Corners
Lesson Focus	Play Badminton Games	Play Badminton Games	Written Exam	Skills Partner Testing	Round Robin Tournament
Game	Partner Tug of War	Back to Back Take Down	Round Robin Tournament	Round Robin Tournament	Round Robin Tournament

Badminton Lesson Plan 1

EQUIPMENT:

1 Badminton racquet per student
2 Shuttlecocks per student
Music CD/Tape, CD/Cassette Player
3 Juggling scarves per student

OBJECTIVES:

The student will:

1. Demonstrate eye-hand coordination juggling scarves one, two, or three at a time using form demonstrated by the instructor.
2. Participate in Challenge Course during the fitness section of class to improve agility, flexibility, muscular strength and endurance.
3. Demonstrate the forehand and backhand grip during the lesson focus using form demonstrated by the instructor.
4. Demonstrate cooperative skills and eye-hand coordination by playing Frisbee 21 during the game portion of class.

National Standards Met in this Lesson: **1, 4, 5, 6**

INSTRUCTIONAL ACTIVITIES	TEACHING HINTS

INTRODUCTORY ACTIVITY (2 – 3 MINUTES)

Juggling Scarves

Scarves are held by the finger-tips near the center. To throw the scarf, it should be lifted and pulled into the air above eye level. Scarves are caught by clawing, a downward motion of the hand, and grabbing the scarf from above as it is falling.

See DPESS Chapter 18 for details.
Scattered formation
Place scarves along perimeter of teaching area.
Cascading Activities: One scarf; Two Scarves; Three Scarves

A juggling scarf is square of light nylon that slowly floats through the air. Juggling scarves are useful for teaching children since they slow down the juggling pattern, and are easy to catch. Juggling teaches eye-hand coordination.

FITNESS DEVELOPMENT (8 – 12 MINUTES)

Challenge Course

- Agility run between and around cones
- Hop through hula hoops
- Hurdle over 3 benches set up with space between them
- Leap/jump over ropes set up on a diagonal
- Crab walk (feet first) length of a mat
- Log roll down the length of a mat
- Jump rope 10 times using "Hot Peppers"
- Skip around cones set-up
- Crab walk (hands first) between markers/cones
- Curl-ups
- Jog around the area
- Push-ups
- Stretching activities

See DPESS Chapter 16 for details.

Use music to motivate moving through obstacle course.

A Challenge Course works all muscles in the body; it also helps improve agility, strength, flexibility, and aerobic endurance.

INSTRUCTIONAL ACTIVITIES	TEACHING HINTS

LESSON FOCUS (15 – 20 MINUTES)

Forehand Grip
Backhand Grip

- Demonstrate grips

Forehand Grip = thumb and forefinger should form a V. This points towards shoulder of opposite stroking arm when held in front of body.

Backhand Grip = thumb should be resting o the flat side behind the handle. The thumb is further up on the handle than the index finger.

See DPESS Chapter 19 for details.
No courts are needed for this lesson
Scattered formation
Direct students to pick up a racquet and return to space.
Practice grip using forehand grip, hit birdie with the palm of racquet face up. Bounce birdie on racquet into air 20 times.
Bounce birdie to self-20 times using backhand grip.
Bounce birdie using forehand grip while changing levels. Repeat with backhand.
Bounce birdie to self in air while walking.
In place, keep birdie in air switching alternately from forehand to backhand.
Direct students to bounce birdie at difference heights.

An early form of badminton was played in ancient Greece and Egypt. In Japan, the related game Hanetsuki was played as early as the 16th century. In the west, badminton came from a game called battledore and shuttlecock, in which two or more players keep a feathered shuttlecock in the air with small racquets. The game was called "Poona" in India during the 18th century, and British Army officers stationed there took a competitive Indian version back to England in the 1860's, where it was played at country houses as an upper class amusement

Holding the racket correctly will increase your stroke's power and accuracy.

GAME (5 MINUTES)

Frisbee 21
Players stand 10 yards apart and throw the disc back and forth. The throws must be accurate and catchable. One point is awarded for a 2-handed catch and 2 points for a 1-handed catch. A player must get 21 points and win by 2 points.

See DPESS Chapter 20 for details.
Use "elbow-to-elbow" to make pairs.

Direct students to area having 1 student pick up Frisbee before going.

EVALUATION/REVIEW AND CHEER

Ask students questions:

1. Reviewing elements of forehand and backhand grip.
2. Reviewing the history of badminton.
3. What is the value of a Challenge Course?
4. What is the early history of badminton?

2, 4, 6, 8. P.E. is really great!

Badminton Lesson Plan 2

EQUIPMENT:

1 Tug of War rope per 2 students
1 Badminton racquet per student
2 Shuttlecocks per student
Cones, beanbags, jumping boxes
Courts and nets
CD/Cassette player
Music CD/tape for fitness

OBJECTIVES:

The student will:

1. Participate in the Weave Drill to warm-up following the instructions of the instructor.
2. Participate in Four-Corners during the fitness section of class to improve agility, flexibility, muscular strength and endurance.
3. Demonstrate the underhand serve during the lesson focus using form demonstrated by the instructor.
4. Demonstrate the forehand and backhand grips during the lesson focus using form demonstrated by the instructor.
5. Demonstrate cooperative skills by participating in partner Tug-of-War activities 21 during the game portion of class.

National Standards Met in this Lesson: **1, 3, 4, 6**

INSTRUCTIONAL ACTIVITIES	TEACHING HINTS

INTRODUCTORY ACTIVITY (2 – 3 MINUTES)

Weave Drill

See DPESS Chapter 14 for details.

Students are in ready position. They will shuffle left, right, forward, backward, over, and around obstacles on signal by the teacher's hand motion.

Scattered formation in front of teacher. Mark area with cones.

FITNESS DEVELOPMENT (8 – 12 MINUTES)

Four-Corners

See DPESS Chapter 16 for details.

On signal, each student will move around the perimeter counter-clockwise. As students pass the corner they change the movement they are doing based on the instructions posted on each cone.

Set up a rectangle boundary with cones.

Use music for continuous motivation.

Examples of movements listed at each cone:
Crab walk, hopping, bear crawl, jogging, skipping, galloping, curl-ups, reverse curl-ups, push-ups, jump roping, etc.

LESSON FOCUS (15 – 20 MINUTES)

The first Badminton club was the Badminton Club of New York, formed in 1878. It became a weekend meeting place for New York's society leaders. Badminton gained popularity in the 1930's as educational institutions, YMCAs, and hundreds of new clubs offered badminton instruction.

Underhand Serve

See DPESS Chapter 19 for details.

- Scattered formation.
- Racquets and shuttlecocks around perimeter of teaching area.
- Direct students to pick up a racquet and a shuttlecock and return to demonstration area. Shuttlecock placed on floor between feet.

Demonstrate Serve

Students should use their shuttlecock and their partners to serve twice into the correct service court. Then change servers.

- Student practices serve motion in own space.
- Use management technique "back-to-back" to make partners; Assign 4 students to each serving area.
- Rotate positions on court.
- Each student should serve 8 times per service court.

INSTRUCTIONAL ACTIVITIES	TEACHING HINTS

Use the underhand serve during singles play to move an opponent as **far back in court** as possible, thus opening up the court. Be more cautious using this serve during doubles. Opponents with strong attacking abilities will work this serve to their advantage.

Review Forehand and Backhand Grips

Demonstrate and review

- Student bounces birdie to self-10 times using forehand and then backhand grip.
- Alternate bouncing to self-using forehand and backhand.

GAME (5 MINUTES)

Partner Tug of War Activities

- **Different Positions**
- **Pick-up and Pull**

See DPESS Chapter 18 for details.

- Create partners.
- 1 rope per 2 students

EVALUATION/REVIEW AND CHEER

Ask students "What are the important parts of the serve?"
"Where should you serve from?"
"Where do you serve to?"

P.E., P.E., What does it mean? Pretty exciting physical education!

Badminton Lesson Plan 3

EQUIPMENT:

1 Badminton Racquet per student
2 Shuttlecocks per student
Continuity Music CD/Tape, CD/Cassette Player
Hula-hoops for 1/2 class size

OBJECTIVES:

The student will:

1. Participate in the Triangle Plus 1 Tag to warm-up following the instructions of the instructor.
2. Participate in Continuity Exercises during the fitness section of class to improve agility, flexibility, muscular strength, endurance and aerobic endurance.
3. Demonstrate the forehand clear shot, drop shot, and the forehand smash during the lesson focus using form demonstrated by the instructor.
4. Demonstrate the forehand and backhand grips during the lesson focus using form demonstrated by the instructor.
5. Rally with a partner demonstrating skills previously learned and using form demonstrated by the instructor.
6. Demonstrate cooperative skills by participating in partner Hoops on the Ground activities during the game portion of class.

National Standards Met in this Lesson: **1, 2, 3, 5, 6**

INSTRUCTIONAL ACTIVITIES	TEACHING HINTS

INTRODUCTORY ACTIVITY (2 – 3 MINUTES)

Triangle Plus 1 Tag

Three students hold hands to form a triangle. One person in the triangle is the leader. The fourth person outside the triangle tries to tag the leader. The triangle moves around to avoid getting the leader tagged. Leader and tagger are changed often.

See DPESS Chapter 14 for details.

Use Whistle Mixer to make groups of 3.

FITNESS DEVELOPMENT (8 – 12 MINUTES)

Continuity Exercises

These exercises are a type of interval training. Create a CD/cassette tape with 30 – 35 seconds of music and 20 seconds of silence. During the music, the students will jump rope.

During each silence instruct the students to do a different exercise i.e. push-ups; curl ups; reverse push-ups; side leg lifts on each side; coffee grinder, arm circling, crab walks forward and backward, etc.

When the music resumes, the students jump rope again

See DPESS Chapter 16 for details.

Scattered formation

Direct students to pick up a rope and move to their own space.

1 Individual jump rope per student

LESSON FOCUS (15 – 20 MINUTES)

Forehand Clear Shot

See DPESS Chapter 19 for details.

Direct student to pick up racquet and 2 shuttlecocks. Return to demonstration area.

 Forehand Clear Shot: A shot hit deep into the opponent's court.

Demonstrate Forehand Clear Shot

Practice hit four shuttlecocks in a row to partner over net. Change roles. Repeat.

Student practices with shuttlecocks on floor.
Use elbow-to-elbow to create pairs.
Direct students to courts.

Demonstrate Forehand Drop Shot

Bring students together
Assign students to hit 4 drop shots over net to partner. Change roles. Repeat.

Demonstrate Forehand Smash

Bring students together.
Assign practice: Forehand clear/drop shot. Return with a smash.
Repeat

Rally

Use all strokes and keep the shuttlecock in place as much as possible.

Assign students to court

GAME (5 MINUTES)

Hoops on the Ground

Students run around the area where hoops are spread. When the teacher calls a number, that number of students must get inside 1 hoop in 5 seconds or less.

See DPESS Chapter 14 for details.

Spread hoops around floor.

Repeat and vary challenges.

EVALUATION/REVIEW AND CHEER

Name one forehand shot? Where should the shuttle land in a drop shot?
Where should the shuttle land on the court when using the forehand clear shot?

5, 4, 3, 2, 1,. Badminton is lots of fun!

Badminton Lesson Plan 4

EQUIPMENT:

1 hoop per person
2 Shuttlecocks per student
1 Badminton Racquet per student
Obstacle course markers
CD/Cassette Player
Music CD/Tape

OBJECTIVES:

The student will:

1. Participate in the Balance Tag to warm-up following the instructions of the instructor.
2. Participate in Challenge Course during the fitness section of class to improve agility, flexibility, muscular strength, endurance and aerobic endurance.
3. Demonstrate the backhand clear shot and the backhand drop shot during the lesson focus using form demonstrated by the instructor.
4. Rally with a partner demonstrating skills previously learned and using form demonstrated by the instructor.
5. Demonstrate cooperative skills by participating in partner Hoops and Plyometrics activities during the game portion of class.

National Standards Met in this Lesson: **1, 2, 3, 4, 5, 6**

INSTRUCTIONAL ACTIVITIES	TEACHING HINTS
INTRODUCTORY ACTIVITY (2 – 3 MINUTES)	
Balance Tag	**See DPESS Chapter 14 for details.**
To be safe, balance in a stipulated position.	Scatter formation; Select several "its."
FITNESS DEVELOPMENT (8 – 12 MINUTES)	
Challenge Course	**See DPESS Chapter 16 for details.**
Agility run between and around cones	Use Whistle Mixer to create groups of 3
Hop through hula hoops	Direct each group to begin at a different station
Hurdle over 3 benches set up with space between them	When the activity is completed at that station, they move to the next station.
Leap/jump over ropes set up on a diagonal	
Crab walk (feet first) length of a mat	
Log roll down the length of a mat	Use music to motivate moving through obstacle course.
Jump rope 10 times using "Hot Peppers"	
Skip around cones set up	
Crab walk (hands first) between markers/cones	
Curl-ups	
Jog around the area	
Push-ups	
Stretching activities	
LESSON FOCUS (15 – 20 MINUTES)	
Backhand Clear Shot	**See DPESS Chapter 19 for details.**
Demonstrate	Direct students to pick up racquet and 2 Shuttlecocks; then go to demonstration area.
Practice	Scattered formation.
Partner stands on same side of court and tosses shuttles to backhand side. Change roles after 4 shots. Repeat.	Shuttlecocks on floor between feet. Practice movement following demonstration. Use elbow-to-elbow to create pairs. Assign 2 pairs to each court.
Backhand Drop Shot	**See DPESS Chapter 19 for details.**
Demonstrate	
Practice	Same groups as in Clear Shot practice
Partner stands on same side of court and tosses shuttles to backhand side. Change roles after 4 shots. Repeat.	

INSTRUCTIONAL ACTIVITIES | **TEACHING HINTS**

Backhand: Stroke used to return balls hit to left of a right handed player and to right of a left handed player.

Review Forehand Shots

Bring students together to review all shots.
Assign students to play and keep shuttlecock in play using all strokes practiced.

GAME (5 MINUTES)

Hoops and Plyometrics
Student rolls or carries the hoop while jogging

See DPESS Chapter 14 for details.
On signal student drops hoop on floor
Challenge student to move in and out of as many hoops as possible during given time period. Change challenges frequently.

Plyometrics: Any exercise in which muscles are repeatedly and rapidly stretched ("loaded") and then contracted (as in jumping high off the ground or in push-ups with a clap between them). The aim of Plyometrics is to improve muscle power.

EVALUATION/REVIEW AND CHEER

Ask questions of the day's lesson.
1. Where is the hitting point during the Backhand Shots?
2. Where should the shuttlecock land when using the Backhand Drop?
3. What is the value of Plyometrics activities?

3, 2, 1. Badminton is really fun!

Badminton Lesson Plan 5

EQUIPMENT:

1 Badminton Racquet per student
2 Shuttlecocks for student
1 Clipboard and pencil per 3 students
CD/Cassette Player
Music CD/tape to direct fitness
1 Forehand Clear & 1 Serving Task Sheet per student.

OBJECTIVES:

The student will:
1. Demonstrate coordination and cooperation during Running High Five's during the introductory activity and following the instructions set by the instructor.
2. Participate in the Jump Rope fitness section of class to improve agility, flexibility, muscular strength and endurance.
3. Demonstrate the forehand clear shot and serve cooperating with a group on the Task Sheets and using form demonstrated by the instructor.
4. Demonstrate cooperative skills and agility by playing Circle Hook-On during the game portion of class.

National Standards Met in this Lesson: **1, 3, 4, 5, 6**

INSTRUCTIONAL ACTIVITIES | **TEACHING HINTS**

INTRODUCTORY ACTIVITY (2 – 3 MINUTES)

Running High Five's
Students use a locomotor movement (run, skip, slide, gallop) to move around. When whistle is blown, students run to a partner and jump in air and give each other a "high five" and then continue moving until whistle is blown again.

See DPESS Chapter 14 for details.
Scattered formation in area marked off by cones.

Alternate locomotor movements.

INSTRUCTIONAL ACTIVITIES	TEACHING HINTS
FITNESS DEVELOPMENT (8 – 12 MINUTES)	
Jump Rope	**See DPESS Chapter 20 for details.**
Students perform different styles of jump roping as instructed by teacher.	Scattered formation.
Forward in place and while traveling; Backward in place and traveling; Alternating feet/ leg swings; Hot peppers	Create a routine to music.
Stretching Exercises	**See DPESS Chapter 16 for details.**
Stretch entire body, particularly leg muscles worked.	
Strengthening Exercises	**See DPESS Chapter 16 for details.**
Focus on upper body development exercises	
LESSON FOCUS (15 – 20 MINUTES)	
Forehand Clear Shot and Serve Practice	**See DPESS Chapter 19 for details.**
Explain Reciprocal Task Sheet for Badminton Skills.	Use Whistle Mixer to create groups of 3. Identify a Doer, Tosser, and Observer in each group. Assign students to courts.

Serve: The stroke used to put the shuttlecock into play at the start of each rally; also called a "service".

Practice	Use task sheets.
GAME (5 MINUTES)	
Circle Hook-On	Use Whistle Mixer to create groups of 4.
1 student plays against 3 students with joined hands. Lone student tags a designated student in circle. The other 2 students maneuver to keep tagger away from designated student.	Rotate roles as players are tagged. Circle may move in any direction but must not release hands.

EVALUATION/REVIEW AND CHEER

Review main elements of shots practiced today. When is the Serve used?

Cheer: 2, 4, 6, 8. The weekends are really great!

BADMINTON RECIPROCAL TASK SHEET: FOREHAND CLEAR SHOT AND SERVE

Doer's Name: ____________________

Tosser's Name: ____________________

Observer's Name: ____________________

Directions: This task is performed in groups of three: Doer, tosser, and observer.
The tosser: Throw a high, clear service to the doer.
The observer: Read the below tasks to the does. Analyze the doer's form comparing the performance to the criteria listed below. Offer feedback about what is done well and what needs to be corrected. Rotate roles after the doer hits 2 Forehand Clear Shots and 2 Serves.
The doer: Perform the tasks read to you by the observer.

ROTATION: Doer → Tosser → Observer → Doer

Please note: Each person in your group needs a task sheet. 1 pencil and clipboard per group. If you hold the racket in your right hand, your right foot is dominant, vice versa.

TASKS	DATES										
(Record date of practice)											
A. Ready Position for Forehand Clear	**Y**	**N**	**Y**	**N**	**Y**	**N**	**Y**	**N**	**Y**	**N**	**Feedback**
1. Keep feet square.											
2. Keep toes straight.											
3. Feet are shoulder width apart.											
4. Knees are slightly bent.											
5. Weight on balls of feet.											
6. Hold racket in front of body.											
7. Hold racket with handshake grip.											
8. Keep your eyes on the shuttlecock.											
B. Foot Work for Forehand Clear											
1. Lead with dominant foot.											
2. Pivot on nondominant foot.											
3. Hit shuttlecock.											
4. Recover to ready position.											
5. Maintain balance.											
6. Transfer weight from non-dominant foot to dominant foot.											
C. Serving											
1. Ready position: dominant foot is behind nondominant foot.											
2. Use forearm rotation and wrist action.											
3. Contact shuttlecock below the waist.											
D. Change Roles											
E. Repeat											

Badminton Lesson Plan 6

EQUIPMENT:

Continuity Music CD/Tape
CD/Cassette Player
1 Individual jump rope per student
Station instructional cards
2 Shuttlecocks per student
Badminton courts and nets
1 Badminton racquet per student

OBJECTIVES:

The student will:

1. Demonstrate coordination and cooperation during Running High Five's during the introductory activity and following the instructions set by the instructor.
2. Participate in the Jump Rope fitness section of class to improve agility, flexibility, muscular strength and endurance.
3. Demonstrate the forehand clear shot and serve cooperating with a group on the Task Sheets and using form demonstrated by the instructor.
4. Demonstrate cooperative skills and agility by playing Circle Hook-On during the game portion of class.

National Standards Met in this Lesson: **1, 2, 3, 4, 5, 6**

INSTRUCTIONAL ACTIVITIES	TEACHING HINTS
INTRODUCTORY ACTIVITY (2 – 3 MINUTES)	
Marking	**See DPESS Chapter 14 for details.** Scattered formation
FITNESS DEVELOPMENT (8 – 12 MINUTES)	
Continuity Exercises Jump Rope Sit ups (15) Jump Rope Push-ups (15) Jump Rope Double Crab Kick (20) Side Leg Flex (12 ea. side) Jump Rope Reclining Partner Pull-up (10 times ea.) Jump Rope Curl-ups Jump Rope Reverse Curl-ups Jump Rope Stretch all body parts	**See DPESS Chapter 16 for details.** Scattered formation. Alternate jumping rope and performing two count exercises. Rope jumping is done to pre-recorded music (40 seconds) and exercise done on silence pre-recorded to 30 seconds.

INSTRUCTIONAL ACTIVITIES	TEACHING HINTS

LESSON FOCUS (15 – 20 MINUTES)

Stations:

1. Forehand Net Drop
   Demonstrate aiming to hoops
2. Backhand Net Drop
   Demonstrate aiming to hoops
3. Underhand Long Serve
   Demonstrate aiming to hoops set on court.
4. Forehand Clear Shot
   Demonstrate aiming to hoops set in backcourt.
5. Backhand Clear Shot
   Demonstrate aiming at hoops set in backcourt.
6. Forehand Clear, Smash Return
   Demonstrate skill.

6. Rally shuttlecock using all strokes.

See DPESS Chapter 19 for details.

- Hit over net aiming for hula-hoops placed across court, near net.
- Move students from station to station as you demonstrate.
- Can repeat Stations on courts if desire.
- Following all demonstrations, use "toe-to-toe" to make partners.
- 1 partner gets equipment.
- Assign other partner to court.
- Partners go to court to practice.
- Each student hits 4 shots and then changes roles.
- Signal when to rotate.

In 1949 David Freeman of Pasadena, California, became the first American men's singles world champion at the prestigious All-England Championships (considered the unofficial world championships until 1977 when World Championships were instituted). Americans, Clinton and Patsy Stevens, won the All-England mixed doubles title the same year.

GAME (5 MINUTES)

Fetch Relay

Squads line up and place 1 member at the other end of the playing area, 10 to 20 yards away. This person runs back to the squad and fetches the next person. The person who has just been fetched in turn runs back and fetches the next person. The pattern continues until all members have been fetched to the opposite end of the playing area.

See DPESS Chapter 18 for details.

Use Whistle Mixer to create groups of 4-5.

Create lines/squad formation with each group.

Identify first player to go to opposite end of playing area.

EVALUATION/REVIEW AND CHEER

Discuss skills necessary for accuracy.

Cheer: 2, 4, 6, 8. What do we appreciate? Drop shot!

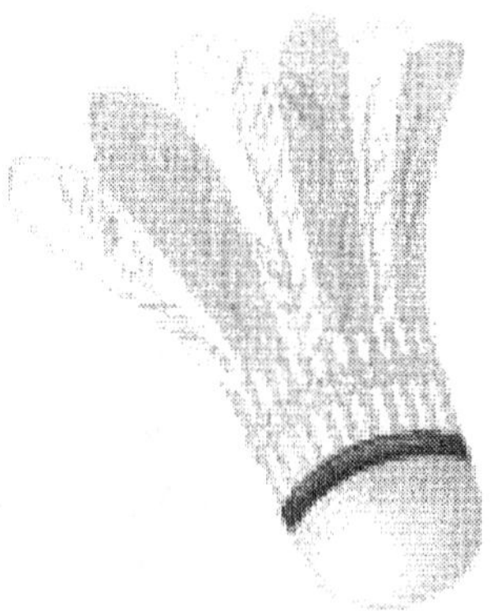

Badminton Lesson Plan 7

EQUIPMENT:

1 Badminton racquet per person
2 Shuttlecocks per person
Rules Handout

OBJECTIVES:

The student will:

1. Demonstrate coordination and cooperation during the introductory activity of Move and Stretch and follows the instructions set by the instructor.
2. Participate in the Interval Training fitness section of class to improve agility, flexibility, muscular strength and endurance.
3. Demonstrate the forehand clear shot and serve cooperating with a group on the Task Sheets and using form demonstrated by the instructor.
4. Demonstrate cooperative skills and agility by playing Circle Hook-On during the game portion of class.

National Standards Met in this Lesson: **1, 2, 3, 4, 5, 6**

INSTRUCTIONAL ACTIVITIES | **TEACHING HINTS**

INTRODUCTORY ACTIVITY (2 – 3 MINUTES)

Move and Stretch

Students run within set perimeter and perform stretches upon designated signal. Use flash cards to signal stretches.
Both Arms Up: stretch high
Touch Toes
Hamstring Stretch: Right leg forward left back with heal on ground. Hold 30 seconds and switch.
Standing Hip Bend: Both sides. Hold 20 seconds each side.
Wishbone Stretch: Hands clasped behind back and lean forward.

See DPESS Chapter 14 for details.

Scattered formation

FITNESS DEVELOPMENT (8 – 12 MINUTES)

Continuous Movement Activities:
Interval Training

Brisk Walk; Rope Jumping; Brisk Walking; Jog in Place; Brisk Walking; Jump Rope in Place; Brisk Walk; Hot Peppers Rope Jumping; Slow Jog; Jump Rope Quickly; Brisk Walking; Jog

See DPESS Chapter 16 for details.
Scattered formation.
Object is to monitor heart rate, first warming up to 120-140 beats per minute music. Then strenuous activity is alternated with rest interval; 45 seconds for strenuous activity followed by 30 seconds rest period. Heart rate is taken before and after rest period.

Interval training has proved to be an efficient training method for champion runners.

Strength Exercises
Curl-ups; Push-ups; Reverse Push-ups

See DPESS Chapter 16 for details.

Stretching
Lower Leg
Bear Hug
Hurdler's Stretch
Sitting Side Stretch
Back Bender
Stretch Arms Up Going Up on Toes

See DPESS Chapter 16 for details.

INSTRUCTIONAL ACTIVITIES | **TEACHING HINTS**

LESSON FOCUS (15 – 20 MINUTES)

Explain Badminton Rules and Strategies

See DPESS Chapter 19 for details.
Distribute rules handout

Badminton has a rich history in Europe. One of the early stars of the game was the English tennis star Kitty Godfree who was badminton champion three times in the 1920s. As other national badminton associations began appearing and the game picked up popularity around the world, in 1934 the International Badminton Federation (IBF) was born. The original members were England, Wales, Ireland, Scotland, Denmark, Holland, Canada, New Zealand and France.

Review skills by demonstration.

Doubles: A game where a team of two players play against another team of two.

Doubles Drop
Game played between the net and short service line. Keep track of the number of rallies and increase the number of hits.

See DPESS Chapter 19 for details.

Whistle Mixer to create groups of 4.

Assign to courts to play Lead-Up games using rules.

Drive Rally

```
      X    X
o--------------------o
      O    O
```

See DPESS Chapter 19 for details.

Played with 4 players; drive crosscourt and down the alley; if shot is too high, smash return it.

GAME (5 MINUTES)

Mixed Doubles Games

See DPESS Chapter 19 for details.
Using Whistle Mixer, create groups of 4.
Follow Rules while playing.

EVALUATION/REVIEW AND CHEER

Review and discuss rules and strategies.
Who was one of the early female stars of Badminton?
What muscles were used in class today?

Cheer: 2, 4, 6, 8. Badminton is Really Great!

BADMINTON RULES HANDOUT

Games and Match: Eleven points make a game in women's singles. All doubles and men's singles games are 15 points. A match constitutes two games out of three. As soon as a side wins two games, the match is over. The winner of the previous game serves the next game. Players change courts after the first and second games. In the third game, players change after 8 points in a 15-point game and after 6 points in an 11-point game.

Scoring: Only the serving side scores and continues to do so until an error is committed.

Setting: if the score becomes tied, the player or side first reaching the tied score may extend the game. In a 15-point game, the set may occur at 13-13 (setting to 5 points) or 14-14 (setting to 3 points). In an 11-point game, the score may be set at 10-10 (setting to 2 points) or 9-9 (setting to 3 points). A set game continues, but the score called is now 0-0, or "Love all." The first player or side to reach set score wins. If a side chooses not to set, the regular game is completed.

Singles Play: The first serve is taken from the right service court and received cross court (diagonally) in the opponent's right service court. All serves on 0 or an even score are served and received in the right-hand court. All serves on an odd score are served and received in the left service court.

Doubles Play: In the first inning, the first service is one hand only. In all other innings, the serving team gets to use two hands. At the beginning of each inning, the player in the right court serves first. Partners rotate only after winning a point.

Even and odd scores are served from the same court as in singles play. If a player serves out of turn or from the incorrect service court and wins the rally, a let will be called. The let must be claimed by the receiving team before the next serve.

If a player standing in the incorrect court takes the serve and wins the rally, it will be a let, provided the let is claimed before the next serve. If either of the above cases occurs and the side at fault loses the rally, the mistake stands, and the players' positions are not corrected for the rest of the game.

Faults: A fault committed by the serving side (in-side) results in a side out, while a fault committed by the receiving side (out-side) results in a point for the server. A fault occurs in any of the following situations.

1. During the serve, the shuttlecock is contacted above the server's waist, or the racquet head is held above the hand.
2. During the serve, the shuttlecock does not fall within the boundaries of the diagonal service court.
3. During the serve, some part of both feet of the server and receiver do not remain in contact with the court, inside the boundary lines, until the shuttlecock leaves the racquet of the server. Feet on the boundary lines are considered out-of-bounds.

Badminton Lesson Plan 8

EQUIPMENT:

1 Badminton Racquet per student
2 Shuttlecocks per student
CD/Cassette Player
Individual jump ropes for fitness
4 individual mats for fitness
Music for fitness circuit
Challenge Course station instruction signs
4 wands for challenge course
Cones
Balance bench

OBJECTIVES:

The student will:

1. Demonstrate coordination and cooperation during the introductory activity Fastest Tag and follow the instructions set by the instructor.
2. Participate in the Challenge Course Circuit fitness section of class to improve agility, flexibility, muscular strength and endurance.
3. Demonstrate knowledge of badminton skills, game rules, and strategies taught in class by playing doubles.
4. Demonstrate cooperative skills and agility by playing Snowball Relay during the game portion of class.

National Standards Met in this Lesson: **1, 2, 3, 4, 5, 6**

INSTRUCTIONAL ACTIVITIES	TEACHING HINTS
INTRODUCTORY ACTIVITY (2 – 3 MINUTES)	
Fastest Tag	**See DPESS Chapter 14 for details.**
Object is to tag other players without being tagged.	Scatter formation.
Players that get tagged must sit where they are and wait for 10 seconds. They can re-join game. If two people tag each other at the same time both must sit down.	Every player is a tagger.
FITNESS DEVELOPMENT (8 – 12 MINUTES)	
Challenge Course Circuit	**See DPESS Chapter 16 for details.**
Set up 3-4 parallel (side-by-side) courses in one-half of the area.	Movement should be continuous.
Course 1. Crouch jumps; pulls, or scooter movements or balance down a bench; agility hop through two hoops on floor. Skip, slide, or jog to a cone.	Arrange three or four courses with a group at each course. Students perform the challenges from start to finish and jog back to repeat the course. On signal, groups move to a new course.
Course 2. Weave in and out of four wands held upright by cones; Crab walk between two cones: lead with feet once, hands once. Gallop to a cone.	
Course 3. Do a tumbling activity length of mat; agility run through hoops; Leap frog over partner alternating roles between cones.	Rotate groups to each course after a specified time. Music can be used for motivation and to signal changes.
Course 4. Curl-ups and push-ups on a mat. Sitting stretches. Jump rope in place.	

Circuit training is an evolving training exercise program developed by R.E. Morgan and G.T. Anderson in 1953 at the University of Leeds in England. A variety of strength and agility stations are presented with aerobic work between the other stations. It's a fast, efficient method of training and improving your fitness levels.

INSTRUCTIONAL ACTIVITIES	TEACHING HINTS

LESSON FOCUS (15 – 20 MINUTES)

Play Doubles Badminton
Review Doubles rules and strategy.
Rotate positions on court after each point.

See DPESS Chapter 19 for details.
Use Whistle Mixer to make groups of 4.
Assign to courts.
Mix-up players on teams after each game.

GAME (5 MINUTES)

Snowball Relay
This relay is similar to the fetch relay, except that after 1 person has been fetched, both players run back and pick up another player. The pattern continues until the majority of squad members are running back and forth, picking up the remaining members. This relay can be exhausting for the first few people in line.

See DPESS Chapter 18 for details.
Use Whistle Mixer to create line/squads of 5-6.

Place lines at one end of area with one person opposite line at other end of area.

EVALUATION/REVIEW AND CHEER

Ask how games went and if there were any rule questions needing clarification.
What are some of the values of circuit training?
What muscles did you work during fitness today?

Cheer: Badminton, Cooooo-ol!

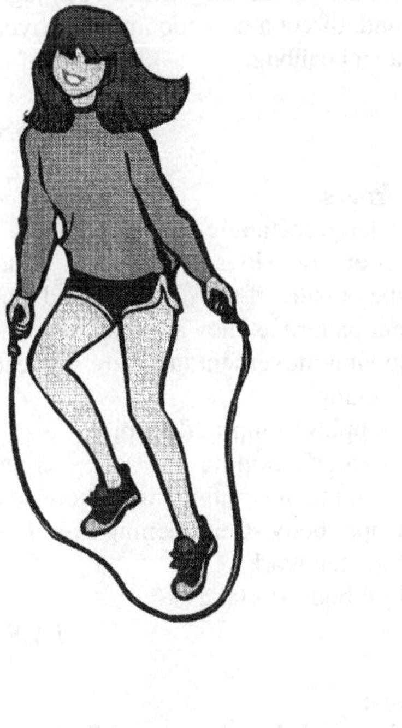

Badminton Lesson Plan 9

EQUIPMENT:

Task Sheets, 1 per student: Forehand/Backhand; Smash
1 Badminton racquet per student
2 Shuttlecocks per student
1 ball per 4 students for Game
Fitness station instructions
Mats
8 Cones
Station signs for Lesson Focus

OBJECTIVES:

The student will:

1. Demonstrate coordination and cooperation during the introductory activity Vanishing Bean Bags and follow the instructions set by the instructor.
2. Participate in the Four Corners fitness section of class to improve agility, flexibility, muscular strength and endurance.
3. Participate in the badminton skill stations using form demonstrated by the instructor.
4. Demonstrate cooperative skills and agility by playing the Over and Under Relay during the game portion of class.

National Standards Met in this Lesson: **1, 2, 3, 4, 5, 6**

INSTRUCTIONAL ACTIVITIES	TEACHING HINTS
INTRODUCTORY ACTIVITY (2 – 3 MINUTES)	
Vanishing Bean Bags Spread beanbags throughout the area to allow 1 per student. Students move around the area until a signal is given. On the signal, they find a beanbag and sit on each. Each round, direct a new locomotor movement task and take away a beanbag.	**See DPESS Chapter 14 for details.** Scatter formation
FITNESS DEVELOPMENT (8 – 12 MINUTES)	
Four Corners Outline a large rectangle with four cones. Place signs with tasks on both sides of the cones. Students move around the outside of the rectangle and change their movement pattern as they approach a corner sign. The following movement tasks are suggested: 1. Jogging 2. Skipping/Jumping/Hopping 3. Sliding/Galloping 4. Abdominal strengthening exercises 5. Upper body strengthening exercises 6. Side leg work 7. Full body stretches	**See DPESS Chapter 16 for details.** Use Whistle Mixer to create 4 equal groups. Assign each group a corner to begin at.
LESSON FOCUS (15 – 20 MINUTES)	
3 Stations: **1. Underhand, Forehand and Backhand Shot.** **2. Forehand Smash to Target Area.** **3. Singles Badminton** This lesson focus may take two class periods to complete.	**See DPESS Chapter 19 for details.** Review skills Explain task sheets Explain stations Review Singles rules Using a management game, divide the class into 3 groups. Assign each group to a station. Describe rotation procedures. Distribute equipment and task sheets

INSTRUCTIONAL ACTIVITIES	**TEACHING HINTS**

The first ladies team championship was in 1956 when the US won the Uber Cup. As more tournaments were being held, badminton became a demonstration sport at the 1972 Munich Olympic Games.

GAME (5 MINUTES)

Over and Under Ball Relay	**See DPESS Chapter 18 for details.**
Distribute 1 ball per group	Use Whistle Mixer to create lines/squads of 5-6.
	Assign spaces for lines leaving room between lines.

EVALUATION/REVIEW AND CHEER

Discuss singles rules and any questions that may have arisen.
Review elements of skills taught in class today.
What muscles were used during class today?

Cheer: P.E. is great for me!

RECIPROCAL TASK SHEET: UNDERHAND SHOT – FOREHAND

Name of Doer: ______________________________

Directions:	You will work with two partners on this task sheet. The roles are:
Doer:	Using the Forehand hit the shuttle 6 times in a row between the two lines on the wall.
Score Keeper:	Count how many times the shuttle lands in the target area. Report score to recorder.
Recorder:	Observe doer and record elements performed.

	DATES											
(Record date of practice)												
	Y	**N**	**Y**	**N**	**Y**	**N**	**Y**	**N**	**Y**	**N**	**Y**	**N**
1. Stand 6' from the wall. Drop the shuttle and hit it underhand to the target area.												
2. Shuttlecock held at chest height.												
3. Shuttle contacted below waist level.												
4. Racquet head below wrist level.												
5. Wrist cocked throughout the stroke.												
6. Repeat until hit wall 6 times.												
7. Accuracy: Hit in target area.												
8. Change roles: Doer →Recorder → Scorekeeper → Doer												

RECIPROCAL TASK SHEET: UNDERHAND SHOT – BACKHAND

Name of Doer: ______________________________

Directions:	You will work with two partners on this task sheet. The roles are:
Doer:	Using the Backhand hit the shuttle 6 times in a row between the two lines on the wall.
Score Keeper:	Count how many times the shuttle lands in the target area. Report score to recorder.
Recorder:	Observe doer and record elements performed.

(Record date of practice)	Dates											
	Y	N	Y	N	Y	N	Y	N	Y	N	Y	N
1. Stand 6' from the wall. Drop the shuttle and hit it underhand to the target area.												
2. Shuttlecock held at chest height.												
3. Shuttle contacted below waist level.												
4. Racquet head below wrist level.												
5. Wrist cocked throughout the stroke.												
6. Repeat until hit wall 6 times.												
7. Accuracy: Hit in target area.												
8. Change roles: Doer →Recorder → Scorekeeper → Doer												

RECIPROCAL TASK SHEET: FOREHAND SMASH TO TARGET

Name of Doer: ______________________________

Directions: You will work with two other people on this task sheet. One will be the Doer, one the Recorder-Observer, and the third the Tosser/Hitter.

Tosser/Hitter:	Hit 4 high serves to your partner
Doer:	Stand between the centerline and the short service line. Smash the serves into your partner's court. Try and call the location you are aiming towards.
Observer:	Check the doer for the elements listed below.
Rotation:	Doer → Tosser → Observer → Doer

(Record date of practice)	DATES							
	Yes	No	Yes	No	Yes	No	Yes	No
1. Shuttle hit with racquet face square to shuttle's flight.								
2. Shuttle contacted 12-18" in front of body.								
3. Arm straight at impact.								
4. Continual racquet acceleration throughout swing, impact and follow through.								
5. Did the smash land where doer called it.								
6. Change roles after 4 tries.								

Badminton Lesson Plan 10

EQUIPMENT:

Task Sheets, 1 per student; Forehand/Backhand; Smash
1 Badminton racquet per student
2 Shuttlecocks per student
Challenge Course instructions
CD/Cassette Player
Music CD/tape for fitness
Mats, Cones, Benches
Station instruction signs used in Lesson 9

OBJECTIVES:

The student will:

1. Demonstrate coordination and cooperation during the introductory activity Zipper and follow the instructions set by the instructor.
2. Participate in the Challenge Course fitness section of class to improve agility, flexibility, muscular strength and endurance.
3. Participate in the badminton skill stations using form demonstrated by the instructor.
4. Demonstrate cooperative skills and agility by playing the game Frozen Tag during the game portion of class.

National Standards Met in this Lesson: **1, 2, 3, 4, 5, 6**

INSTRUCTIONAL ACTIVITIES	TEACHING HINTS

INTRODUCTORY ACTIVITY (2 – 3 MINUTES)

Zipper Each student bends over, reaches between the legs with the left hand, and grasps the right hand of the person to the rear. This continues on down the line until all hands are grasped. On signal, the last person in line lies down, the next person backs over the last person and lies down, and so forth until the last person lies down, and then immediately stands and reverses the procedure. The first team to zip and unzip the zipper is declared the winner.	**See DPESS Chapter 14 for details.** Divide class into lines of 7-9. Players make a single-file line. Space lines out in area.

FITNESS DEVELOPMENT (8 – 12 MINUTES)

Challenge Course	**See DPESS Chapter 16 for details.** See Lesson 1 this unit for details Use music to motivate moving through obstacle course. Create a CD/ tape with 30 seconds of music and 5 seconds of no sound to indicate a change of stations. Or, just use music and allow students to progress around the Challenge Course at their own pace.

LESSON FOCUS (15 – 20 MINUTES)

Continue with stations, wherever students left off after previous lesson.

GAME (5 MINUTES)

Frozen Tag When tagged, the person must freeze with the feet in straddle position. To be able to resume play, 3 people must move under and through a "frozen" person's legs.	**See DPESS Chapter 14 for details.** Scatter formation. Select several "its" to start the tag game.

EVALUATION/REVIEW AND CHEER

What part of the Challenge Course was the most difficult?
Badminton, F – U – N !

Badminton Lesson Plan 11

EQUIPMENT:

Parachute
1 partner tug of war rope per 2 students
Round Robin Tournament Chart
1 Badminton racquet per student
2 Shuttlecocks per student

OBJECTIVES:

The student will:

1. Demonstrate coordination and cooperation during the introductory activity Pentabridge Hustle and follow the instructions set by the instructor.
2. Participate in the Parachute Rhythmic Aerobic Activity during the fitness section of class to improve agility, flexibility, muscular strength and endurance.
3. Participate in the badminton tournament in class following set badminton rules and cooperating with classmates in a positive manner.
4. Demonstrate cooperative skills and agility by participating in Partner Tug-of-War activities during the game portion of class.

National Standards Met in this Lesson: **1, 2, 3, 4, 5, 6**

INSTRUCTIONAL ACTIVITIES	TEACHING HINTS
INTRODUCTORY ACTIVITY (2 – 3 MINUTES)	
Pentabridge Hustle	**See DPESS Chapter 14 for details.** Use Whistle Mixer to create groups of 4 – 5. Students move continuously under bridges made by group.
FITNESS DEVELOPMENT (8 – 12 MINUTES)	
Parachute Rhythmic Aerobic Activity • Skip both directions • Slide both directions • Run both directions • Jump to center • Hop backward • Lift parachute overhead • Lower parachute to toes • Repeat above • Run CW with chute overhead • Make a dome • Strengthening and stretching exercises	**See DPESS Chapter 16 for details.** Direct locomotor movements while holding parachute. Use music to motivate. Alternate locomotor movements with seated strength and stretching exercises.
LESSON FOCUS (15 – 20 MINUTES)	
Round Robin Badminton Tournament	Explain tournament Explain how chart is used Students not interested in the tournament can play singles or doubles.

The 1996 Olympic games in Atlanta improved the visibility and interest in Badminton in the U.S.

GAME (5 MINUTES)	
Partner Tug-of-War	**See DPESS Chapter 18 for details.** Use management game to create pairs. 1 rope per 2 students

EVALUATION/REVIEW AND CHEER

What muscles were used in class today?
When did the interest increase in Badminton in America?
Discuss tournament play. Review rules.

Cheer: 2, 4, 6, 8, Badminton is really great!

Badminton Lesson Plan 12

EQUIPMENT:

Music for fitness
CD/Cassette Player
1 Badminton racquet per student
Station Fitness Signs
2 Shuttlecocks per court
Round Robin Tournament Chart
3 juggling scarves per person

OBJECTIVES:

The student will:

1. Demonstrate coordination, focus and eye-hand coordination during the introductory activity Juggling Scarves and follow the instructions set by the instructor.
2. Participate in the Station Fitness to improve agility, flexibility, muscular strength and endurance.
3. Participate in the badminton tournament in class following set badminton rules and cooperating with classmates in a positive manner.

National Standards Met in this Lesson: **1, 2, 3, 4, 5, 6**

INSTRUCTIONAL ACTIVITIES	TEACHING HINTS

INTRODUCTORY ACTIVITY (2 – 3 MINUTES)

Juggling Scarves

Scarves are held by the finger-tips near the center. To throw the scarf, it should be lifted and pulled into the air above eye level. Scarves are caught by clawing, a downward motion of the hand, and grabbing the scarf from above as it is falling.

See DPESS Chapter 18 for details.
Scattered formation
Place scarves along perimeter of teaching area.
Cascading Activities: One scarf; Two Scarves; Three Scarves

FITNESS DEVELOPMENT (8 – 12 MINUTES)

Station Fitness

1. Partner resistance exercises
2. Jump Rope
3. Crab walks and Body Twist
4. Curl-ups, push-ups, reverse curl-ups
5. Stretching
6. Treadmills
7. Jumping Jacks
8. Running in Place

See DPESS Chapter 16 for details.

Make Station Signs
Use management game to divide class into 8 groups.
Assign each group to a station to begin.
Explain stations.
Explain rotation.
Use music to motivate and musical silences to signal station rotation.

LESSON FOCUS (15 – 20 MINUTES)

Continue Round Robin Tournament.

GAME (5 MINUTES)

Continue Tournament or Play Back to Back Take Down

See DPESS Chapter 18 for details.

EVALUATION/REVIEW AND CHEER

Which stations in the fitness were the most challenging?
Thumbs up if you discovered what fitness areas you need to work on more.
What was the most challenging activity you tried today using Juggling Scarves? Why?
What was the most challenging part of the tournament?

Cheer: Badminton, ... FUN!

Badminton Lesson Plan 13

EQUIPMENT:

Continuity Exercise Music CD/Tape
CD/Cassette Player
1 Written exam per student
1 Racquet pr student
2 Shuttlecocks per court

OBJECTIVES:

The student will:

1. Demonstrate coordination and agility n during the introductory activity Move and Perform a Stretch while following the instructions set by the instructor.
2. Participate in the Continuity Exercises to improve agility, flexibility, muscular strength, muscular endurance and cardiovascular endurance.
3. Complete a written exam during the class period and earn a passing grade.
4. Participate in the badminton tournament in class following set badminton rules and cooperating with classmates in a positive manner.

National Standards Met in this Lesson: **1, 2, 3, 4, 5, 6**

INSTRUCTIONAL ACTIVITIES	TEACHING HINTS
INTRODUCTORY ACTIVITY (2 – 3 MINUTES)	
Move and Perform a Stretch	**See DPESS Chapter 14 for details.** See Lesson Plan 7, this unit: Introductory Activity
FITNESS DEVELOPMENT (8 – 12 MINUTES)	
Continuity Exercises	**See DPESS Chapter 16 for details.** See Lesson Plan 6, this unit: Fitness Development.
LESSON FOCUS (15 – 20 MINUTES)	
Written Exam	
GAME (5 MINUTES)	
Play Badminton Singles or Doubles	Allow students to play or rally upon completion of written exam.

Badminton returned as an exhibition sport in the 1988 Seoul Olympics and was given full medal status at the 1992 Barcelona Olympics. Mixed doubles was introduced at the 1996 Atlanta Games.

EVALUATION/REVIEW AND CHEER

Discuss questions from exam.
Discuss game strategies and issues that might have arisen during the tournament.

Cheer: 3, 2, 1, Badminton is fun!

BADMINTON KNOWLEDGE TEST

NAME: ______________________________

Part I. **True-False.** If the statement is true mark it with a +. If it is false mark it with a 0.

_____ 1. A women's singles game consists of 11 points, a doubles game is 15 points.
_____ 2. After the serve is made, either side can score a point.
_____ 3. The backhand grip is different than the grip for the forehand.
_____ 4. The server serves five times and alternating courts for each serve.
_____ 5. In men's singles, if the score is 14 all, it may be set at 3 points.
_____ 6. In doubles, after the serve is returned, the partner can cross the mid-court line.
_____ 7. In doubles play, the up and back formation is weak in covering side line shots.
_____ 8. In singles, the server will serve from the right hand court when his score is an odd number.
_____ 9. In singles play, the long service line is not used.
_____10, If the shuttlecock is struck above the waist on the serve, it is a fault.

Part II. **Best Answer.** Select the best answer for the statement.

_____11. If the serving side touches the net during play it is
a. a point for the server c. a let
b. a side out d. played over

_____12. In general, when playing a backhand stroke, the best position is to have the
a. left side toward the net c. body face the net
b. right side toward the net d. none of the above

_____13. In doubles, the most effective defensive formation is the
a. up-and-back position c. combination
b. rotation d. side-by-side

_____14. In doubles, the basic serve is the
a. high clear c. drive
b. smash d. low and short

_____15. The around-the-head stroke is used as a
a. substitute for all backhand strokes c. in place of a high backhand stroke
b. drop shots d. a recovery stroke

_____16. If the shuttlecock flight is high and it falls sharply near the baseline it is a
a. high clear c. drop
b. smash d. drive

_____17. In doubles, the combination formation should be changed from a up-and-back to a side-by-side formation if the shuttlecock is returned by a
a. clear c. drop
b. smash d. drive

_____18. The best stroke for returning a shuttlecock, if you are in doubt during singles play is the
a. drive c. lob
b. drop d. smash

_____19. In doubles, when the serving team is playing in the up-and-back formation, the short serve is returned with
a. drive cross the court c. clear to the backhand corner of the court
b. down the side boundary line d. drop to the server's backhand

_____20. If the receiver steps out of his receiving court after the shuttle is served and before it crosses the net, it is
a. a point for the server c. a side out
b. a let d. served over

Part III. **Matching**. Match the statements in Column B to the terms in Column A.

		Column A Strokes		**Column B Bird Flight**
______	21.	Smash	a.	Upward and back to the baseline.
______	22,	Hairpin	b.	Flat flight and very near to the top of the net.
______	23.	Drop shot	c.	Straight up and straight down over the net.
______	24.	High clear	d.	Falls close to the net between the net and short service line.
______	25.	Drive	e.	Sharply downward.

BADMINTON KNOWLEDGE TEST ANSWERS

I. True-False

1.	+	6.	+
2.	0	7.	+
3.	+	8.	0
4.	0	9.	+
5.	+	10.	+

II. Best Answer

11.	b	16,	a
12.	b	17.	a
13.	d	18.	c
14.	d	19.	b
15,	c	20.	a

III. Matching

21.	e
22.	c
23.	d
24.	a
25.	b

Badminton Lesson Plan 14

EQUIPMENT:

1 Skills Test Score Sheet per student
1 Badminton racquet per student
1 Clipboard and pencil per 3 students
5 Shuttlecocks per group
Music for fitness (optional)
CD/Cassette Player for fitness (optional)

OBJECTIVES:

The student will:

1. Participate in the Rhythmic Aerobic Activities to improve agility, flexibility, muscular strength, muscular endurance and cardiovascular endurance.
2. Complete a partner skills test during the class period and earn a passing grade.
3. Participate in the badminton tournament in class following set badminton rules and cooperating with classmates in a positive manner.

National Standards Met in this Lesson: **1, 2, 3, 4, 5, 6**

INSTRUCTIONAL ACTIVITIES	TEACHING HINTS
INTRODUCTORY ACTIVITY (2 – 3 MINUTES)	
Eliminate today to allow extra time for skill tests.	
FITNESS DEVELOPMENT (8 – 12 MINUTES)	
Parachute Rhythmic Aerobic Activities	**See DPESS Chapter 16 for details.** See Lesson Plan 11, this unit for details.
LESSON FOCUS (15 – 20 MINUTES)	
Partner Skills Test	Use Whistle Mixer and create groups of 3. Explain Skills Test Task Sheets.

The first World Badminton Championships, including singles events, were held in 1977. Over the next decade the sport was dominated by Asians, most notably China's top women Li Lingwei and Han Aiping. Morten Frost of Denmark was one exception, winning over 70 international titles during the 1980s.

INSTRUCTIONAL ACTIVITIES	TEACHING HINTS
GAME (5 MINUTES)	
Badminton Play Singles or Doubles	Allow students to play upon completion of exam.
EVALUATION/REVIEW AND CHEER	
Discuss element of skills test. When were the first world championships held? **Students create cheer.**	

Badminton Lesson Plan 15

EQUIPMENT:

Four Corners Fitness Instruction Signs
Cones
Mats
Music for fitness
CD/Cassette Player
1 Badminton racquet per student
2 Shuttlecocks per court
Tournament Chart

OBJECTIVES:

The student will:

1. Demonstrate cooperation and agility while participating in Balance Tag during the Introductory phase of class.
2. Participate in the Four Corners fitness activity to improve agility, flexibility, muscular strength, muscular endurance and cardiovascular endurance.
3. Complete a partner skills test during the class period and earn a passing grade.
4. Participate in the badminton tournament in class following set badminton rules and cooperating with classmates in a positive manner.

National Standards Met in this Lesson: **1, 2, 3, 4, 5, 6**

INSTRUCTIONAL ACTIVITIES	TEACHING HINTS
INTRODUCTORY ACTIVITY (2 – 3 MINUTES)	
Balance Tag	**See DPESS Chapter 14 for details.** See Lesson Plan 4, this unit: Introductory Activity.
FITNESS DEVELOPMENT (8 – 12 MINUTES)	
Four Corners	**See DPESS Chapter 16 for details.** See Lesson Plan 9, this unit: Fitness Development.
LESSON FOCUS AND GAME (15 – 25 MINUTES)	
Round Robin Badminton Tournament	

Badminton now has the glory of being the fastest racket sport (the fastest smash was clocked at 260 kilometres per hour by Great Britain's Simon Archer) as well as one of the most widely played sports in the world, and is growing in popularity all the time.

EVALUATION/REVIEW AND CHEER

Review unit.
Discuss results of playing in a tournament.
Introduce next unit.

Cheer: The Weekend's here. Yeah! -Or-
Badminton was fun!

BADMINTON SKILLS TEST

Name of Doer, Partner,
Recorder____

Directions: Work with two other people on this self-test: **Doer:** Complete elements on exam; **Partner:** Toss/Hit to doer as listed; **Recorder**: Read instructions, observe doer, and record results.

Equipment: Clipboard and pencil; 2 Badminton racquets per group; 1 Skill Test per person; 5 Shuttlecocks per group

Serves	**Score Out of 5**
1. Standing behind the short service line on the right side of the court, serve the shuttlecock crosscourt over the net 5 times.	
2. Standing behind the short service line on the left side of the court, serve the shuttlecock crosscourt over the net 5 times.	
3. Standing behind the short service line, next to the centerline in the right court, serve the shuttlecock crosscourt over the net, between the net and a rope 1 foot above it. Repeat 5 times in a row from the right.	
4. Standing behind the short service line, next to the centerline in the right court, serve the shuttlecock crosscourt over the net, between the net and a rope 1 foot above it. Repeat 5 times in a row from the left.	
Underhand Clears: Forehand and Backhand	
5. Standing between the net and the short service line, drop the shuttlecock and underhand clear on the forehand side. 5 clears in a row to the back 4 feet of the court marked for doubles.	
6. Standing between the net and the short service line, drop the shuttlecock and underhand clear on the backhand side, 5 clears in a row to the back 4 feet of the court marked for doubles.	
7. Standing 6 feet behind the short service line, underhand clear on the forehand side 5 clears in a row to the back 4 feet of the doubles court.	
8. Standing 6 feet behind the short service line, underhand clear on the backhand side 5 clears in a row to the back 4 feet of the doubles court.	
Drops	
9. Standing just behind the short service line on the right court, underhand drop on the forehand side a tossed shuttlecock from your partner. Return 5 drops in a row from the forehand side.	
10. Standing just behind the short service line on the right court, underhand drop on the forehand side a tossed shuttlecock from your partner. Return 5 drops in a row from the backhand side.	
Long Serves	
11. Standing to the right of and next to the centerline, 12 feet from the net, serve 5 long serves in a row to the opposite court.	
12. Standing to the left of and next to the centerline, 12 feet from the net, serve 5 long serves in a row to the opposite court.	
Overhead Clears: Forehand	
13. Standing within 12 feet of the net, a partner underhand clears the shuttlecock. Return 5 shuttlecocks in a row with an overhead forehand clear into the doubles court, at least 10 feet from the net.	
14. Standing within 12 feet of the net, a partner underhand clears the shuttlecock. Return 5 shuttlecocks in a row with an overhead forehand clear into the doubles court, to the back 4 feet of the doubles court.	
15. A server sets up short, high shots 6 to 8 inches from the net. Standing 6 feet from the short service line, smash 5 in a row within 15 feet of the net.	
16. Standing within the last 5 feet of the backcourt, overhead drop opponent's clears to you. Drop 5 shuttlecocks to the right courtside between the net and the short service line.	
17. Standing within the last 5 feet of the backcourt, overhead drop opponent's clears to you. Drop 5 shuttlecocks to the left courtside between the net and the short service line.	
18. Stand on the centerline, 6 feet from the short service line. Partner set up low, flat serves down the forehand alley. Hit 5 forehand drives in a row down that alley.	
19. Stand on the centerline, 6 feet from the short service line. Partner set up low, flat serves down the forehand alley. Hit 5 forehand drives in a row down that alley.	
20. Standing within 12 feet of the net, from a high clear set-up by a partner, backhand 5 overhead clears in a row to the back 6 feet of the doubles court.	

Basketball

This unit has been specifically designed to meet all six components of the NASPE National Standards for Physical Education.

OBJECTIVES:

The student will:

1. Participate in the Over, Under and Around #1, and Hula Hoop Circle Pass activities demonstrating cooperation and agility.
2. Execute scarf juggling skills juggling 2 or 3 scarves using skills demonstrated in class.
3. Demonstrate cooperation developing partner stunts during the Introductory Activity.
4. Demonstrate agility and cooperation during the Vanishing Bean Bags activity.
5. Play Addition Tag demonstrating dodging and sprinting skills.
6. Participate in Blob Tag demonstrating cooperation with classmates, dodging, and starting and stopping skills.
7. Participate in partner mirroring activities demonstrating cooperation and creativity.
8. Improve her cardiovascular and physical fitness levels during the Continuity Exercise fitness activities.
9. Execute a variety of fitness exercises and aerobic movements during the Rhythmic Parachute Activities.
10. Improve their fitness levels while participating in the Fitness Scavenger Hunt activities as demonstrated by the instructor.
11. Complete the Fitness Challenge Course to improve all levels of fitness.
12. Jump rope to improve cardiovascular endurance.
13. Participate in Circuit Training to improve his overall fitness.
14. Participate in dribbling and passing drills using skills demonstrated by the instructor.
15. Execute defensive dribbling activities.
16. Demonstrate defensive footwork using techniques demonstrated by the instructor.
17. Perform the following footwork: jump stop pivot, v-cuts, inside turns, defensive slide with head up and good balance.
18. Perform the Chest pass and the Overhead pass with accuracy and follow through.
19. Demonstrate lay-up shots from the center and each side of the basket five times.
20. Perform five jump shots fifteen feet from the center and the sides of the court.
21. Demonstrate offensive basketball skills using form demonstrated in class by her instructor.
22. Perform dribbling skills during the Dribble Relay game.
23. Demonstrate an understanding of Basketball rules strategy while playing Basketball in class.
24. Participate in the Round Robin Tournament executing cooperation, teamwork, and basketball skills learned during the unit.
25. Execute basketball skills of dribbling, shooting, passing, offense and defense as demonstrated throughout the unit during the skill testing.
26. Complete a written exam scoring 70 % or better.

BASKETBALL BLOCK PLAN
3 WEEK UNIT

Week #1	Monday	Tuesday	Wednesday	Thursday	Friday
Introductory Activity	Move and Change Direction	Juggling Scarves	Over, Under and Around #1	Parachute Activities	Run and Lead
Fitness	Rope Jumping	Aerobic Workout	Fitness Scavenger Hunt	Jog and Stretch	Continuity Exercises
Lesson focus	Ball Handling Dribbling	Dribbling Passing	Dribbling Passing	Shooting Rebounding Dribbling	Passing Shooting
Game	Triangle Plus One Tag	Spider Tag	Hula Hoop Pass	Wand Activities	Hoops and Plyometrics

Week #2	Monday	Tuesday	Wednesday	Thursday	Friday
Introductory Activity	Individual Stunts	Jog Around Obstacles	Vanishing Bean Bags	Pentabridge Hustle	Blob tag
Fitness	Parachute Activities	Stretch and Strengthening Exercises	Continuity Exercises	Circuit Training	Fitness Scavenger Hunt
Lesson focus	Defensive Footwork and Skills	Stations: Lay-Ups; Free Throws; Dribbling; Guarding; Rebounding	Stations: Footwork; Dribbling; Passing; Shooting; Guarding	Offensive Skills Jump Stop Pivoting Dribbling and Stopping	Rules and Strategy Player Positions
Game	Horse	Individual Tug of War	Dribble Relay	Sideline Basketball	5 on 5 Half Court Basketball

Week #3	Monday	Tuesday	Wednesday	Thursday	Friday
Introductory Activity	Mirroring	Musical Hoops	Addition Tag	Eliminate allowing time for Tournament	Move and Perform Stretch
Fitness	Challenge Course	Walk, Jog, Sprint	Aerobic Workout	Challenge Course	Walk, Jog, Sprint
Lesson focus	Play Basketball	Skill Testing	Written Exam	Round Robin Tournament	Round Robin Tournament (Cont.)
Game	Play Basketball	Dribble Relay	Play Basketball	Tournament (Cont.)	Tournament (Cont.)

Basketball Lesson Plan 1

EQUIPMENT:

Basketball Courts
1 Basketball per student
1 Individual Jump Rope per student
CD/Cassette player
Rope Jumping Exercise Music CD/Tape

OBJECTIVES:

The student will:

1. Demonstrate cooperation and agility while participating in Move and Change Direction during the Introductory phase of class.
2. Participate in the Rope Jumping fitness activity to improve agility, flexibility, muscular strength, muscular endurance and cardiovascular endurance.
3. Demonstrate ball handling skills presented by the instructor during the Lesson Focus of class.
4. Participate in Triange Plus One Tag demonstrating cooperative and agility skills during the game portion of class and following the instructions established by the instructor.

National Standards Met in this Lesson: **1, 2, 3, 4, 5, 6**

INSTRUCTIONAL ACTIVITIES	TEACHING HINTS
INTRODUCTORY ACTIVITY (2 - 3 MINUTES)	
Move and Change Direction	**See DPESS Chapter 14 for details.**
Students run in any direction; change directions on signal	Scattered formation Reverse; 45 degrees; Left turns
FITNESS DEVELOPMENT (8 - 12 MINUTES)	
Rope Jumping	**See DPESS Chapter 20 for details.**
Students jump rope until command given to change activities. Create a music CD/tape with 1-minute music, 30 seconds blank. Alternate jumping with exercise.	Push-ups; Bend and Stretch; Curl-ups; Reverse Curl-ups Treadmill
LESSON FOCUS (15 - 20 MINUTES)	
Drills handle ball comfortably in place	**See DPESS Chapter 19 for details.**
Ball around waist Ball around right, left knee Ball around right, left ankle Figure 8 around legs both directions Ball between legs switching arm from front to back	Scattered formation Demonstrate 1 ball per student for practice
Walking and passing alternately under each front leg	Demonstrate
Dribbling In place; Walk; Jog; Stop and go	Practice length of court 1 ball per student

Dr. James Naismith is known world-wide as the inventor of basketball. In 1891, Dr. Naismith invented the indoor game of basketball using a soccer ball and peach baskets as the goals. Naismith wanted to create a game of skill for the students instead of one that relied solely on strength. His rules required throwing the ball to teammates. No dribbling was involved in his first games.

INSTRUCTIONAL ACTIVITIES	TEACHING HINTS
GAME (5 MINUTES)	
Triangle Plus 1 Tag	**See DPESS Chapter 14 for details.**
Person outside triangle tries to tag leader. Leader and tagger change places when tagged.	Create groups of 4 using management game. 3 make triangle formation holding hands. Select leader in group.

INSTRUCTIONAL ACTIVITIES	TEACHING HINTS

EVALUATION/REVIEW AND CHEER

Review elements of dribbling and ball handling.
Who invented basketball?
In what year was basketball invented? In what ways did the original game differ from today's game?

Cheer: Yea, Basketball is here this year!

Basketball Lesson Plan 2

EQUIPMENT:

1 Basketball per student
3 Juggling Scarves per student
Aerobic workout music CD/tape
CD/Cassette player

OBJECTIVES:

The student will:

1. Demonstrate eye-hand coordination and concentration performing juggling scarf activities during the Introductory phase of class.
2. Participate in the Aerobic Workout fitness activity to improve agility, flexibility, muscular strength, muscular endurance and cardiovascular endurance.
3. Demonstrate ball handling skills presented by the instructor during the Lesson Focus of class.
4. Participate in Spider Tag demonstrating cooperative and agility skills during the game portion of class and following the instructions established by the instructor.

National Standards Met in this Lesson: **1, 2, 3, 4, 5, 6**

INSTRUCTIONAL ACTIVITIES	TEACHING HINTS
INTRODUCTORY ACTIVITY (2 - 3 MINUTES)	
Juggling Scarves Column juggling; Cascading	**See DPESS Chapter 18 for details.** Scattered formation; 3 scarves per student
FITNESS DEVELOPMENT (8 - 12 MINUTES)	
Aerobic Workout	**See DPESS Chapter 16 for details.** See Lesson 7, Racquetball Unit for details
LESSON FOCUS (15 - 20 MINUTES)	
Review Dribbling Skills **Passing Skills** Bounce pass; Chest pass; Overhead pass	**See DPESS Chapter 19 for details.** Scattered formation for reviewing dribbling. Set up passing activities in lines or scattered formation

In 1892, the physical education teacher at the all-female Smith College, Senda Berenson, used a modified game of basketball in her classes. The purpose of the game was for physical fitness for her ladies. Ms. Berenson changed some of Dr. Naismith's rules to strive for teamwork development and cooperation, rather then competition. She broke the court into 3 zones and 9 players would play on each team. Each zone would have 3 players. No player could leave her zone. The player could only hold the ball 3 seconds and dribble the ball 3 times before passing. This reduced the ability for single players to become stars and required the effort of all.

INSTRUCTIONAL ACTIVITIES	TEACHING HINTS
GAME (5 MINUTES)	
Spider Tag Pairs work together to tag other pairs When tagged, they become "its"	**See DPESS Chapter 14 for details.** Using a management game, create partners Select on pair to be the "its"

EVALUATION/REVIEW AND CHEER

Discuss important elements of passing skills.
When was basketball introduced to women's play? Where? How did it differ from the original game developed by Dr. Naismith?
Have students create the cheer.

Basketball Lesson Plan 3

EQUIPMENT:

1 Basketball per student
1 Hula Hoops per five students
Fitness Scavenger Hunt Instruction Cards
Music and CD/Cassette Player for Fitness Activities

OBJECTIVES:

The student will:

1. Participate in Over, Under and Around #1 demonstrating agility and cooperative skills during the Introductory phase of class.
2. Participate in the Fitness Scavenger Hunt to improve agility, flexibility, muscular strength, muscular endurance and cardiovascular endurance.
3. Demonstrate dribbling and passing skills using form demonstrated by the instructor during the Lesson Focus of class.
4. Participate in the Hula Hoop Circle Pass demonstrating cooperative and agility skills during the game portion of class and following the instructions established by the instructor.

National Standards Met in this Lesson: **1, 2, 3, 4, 5, 6**

INSTRUCTIONAL ACTIVITIES	TEACHING HINTS
INTRODUCTORY ACTIVITY (2 - 3 MINUTES)	
Over, Under and Around #1	**See DPESS Chapter 14 for details.** Using toe-to-toe, create groups of 2.
FITNESS DEVELOPMENT (8 - 12 MINUTES)	
Fitness Scavenger Hunt See Golf, Lesson 7 for details	**See DPESS Chapter 16 for details.**
LESSON FOCUS (15 - 20 MINUTES)	
Dribbling **Two hand V; One hand V** **Dribbling with: Crab turn; Crab slide; V-Cut; Reverse pivot**	**See DPESS Chapter 19 for details.** Demonstrate each skill followed by practice in scattered formation Practice in formations
Keep the ball close to your body and away from your opponent. You can even use your back to shield the ball and bump.	
Reviewing Passing Skills	Demonstrate each skill followed by practice Practice in scattered formation then in set formations
GAME (5 MINUTES)	
Hula Hoop Circle Pass	**See DPESS Chapter 14 for details.** See Golf Unit, Lesson 2 for details. Use Whistle Mixer to make 4 groups of students.

EVALUATION/REVIEW AND CHEER

Review major elements of dribbling skills presented in class.
How can you shield the ball from your opponent?

Cheer: 3, 6, 8, Basketball is great!

Basketball Lesson Plan 4

EQUIPMENT:

1 Basketball per student
1 Large parachute
1 Wand per student

OBJECTIVES:

The student will:

1. Participate in Parachute Activities demonstrating cooperative skills during the Introductory phase of class.
2. Participate in Jog and Stretch to improve agility, flexibility, muscular strength, muscular endurance and cardiovascular endurance during the Fitness portion of class.
3. Demonstrate free throws, shooting, lay-ups, jump shot, set shot and rebounding skills using form demonstrated by the instructor during the Lesson Focus of class.
4. Participate in the Wand Activities demonstrating cooperative and agility skills during the game portion of class and following the instructions established by the instructor.

National Standards Met in this Lesson: **1, 2, 3, 4, 5, 6**

INSTRUCTIONAL ACTIVITIES	TEACHING HINTS

INTRODUCTORY ACTIVITY (2 - 3 MINUTES)

Parachute Activities	**See DPESS Chapter 16 for details.**

FITNESS DEVELOPMENT (8 - 12 MINUTES)

Jog and Stretch Lower leg stretch (Stand facing a wall with feet shoulder width apart) Achilles tendon stretch; Bear hug stretch; Hurdlers stretch; Groin stretch, Ankle stretch; Standing hip bend; Elbow puller; Wishbone stretch; Push ups; Curl-ups; Reverse Curl-ups	**See DPESS Chapter 16 for details.** Scattered formation Jog around Gym several times, then stretch

An important reason to participate in fitness activities is to warm up muscles for activity and avoid injury.

LESSON FOCUS (15 - 20 MINUTES)

Shooting **Free Throws** **Lay-ups; Jump Shots; Set Shot** **Rebounding** **Dribbling challenge drills**	**See DPESS Chapter 19 for details.** Demonstrate each shot then practice first without ball and then with one at courts. Assign to baskets. Set up challenging drills for small groups of students

The ball rests on your fingertips and your wrist is bent back 90 degrees in jump shot preparation. You should see a wrinkle at the back of your hand in this position. The ball is at least shoulder height for jump shots.

GAME (5 MINUTES)

WAND ACTIVITIES	**See DPESS Chapter 18 for details.**
Wand Whirl Stand wand in front of body. Balance it with 1 finger. Release, turn, and catch the wand.	Scattered formation
Wand Kick over Begin same as Whirl, but leg kick over the wand before turning.	Work with a partner.
Wand Wrestle Goal: move the wand to a horizontal plane.	Wand is held in vertical position by opponent.

EVALUATION/REVIEW AND CHEER

Review main points presented in basketball shooting.
Explain your hand, wrist, and fingertip position for a jump shot.

Cheer: We love basketball!

Basketball Lesson Plan 5

EQUIPMENT:

Basketball Courts
1 Basketball per student
1 Individual Jump Rope per student
CD/Cassette player
Continuity Exercise Music CD/Tape
1 Hoop per student

OBJECTIVES:

The student will:

1. Participate in Run and Lead demonstrating cooperative skills during the Introductory phase of class.
2. Participate in Continuity Exercises to improve agility, flexibility, muscular strength, muscular endurance and cardiovascular endurance during the Fitness portion of class.
3. Demonstrate chest and overhead passing skills using form demonstrated by the instructor during the Lesson Focus of class.
4. Participate in Hoops and Plyometrics demonstrating cooperative and agility skills during the game portion of class and following the instructions established by the instructor.

National Standards Met in this Lesson: **1, 2, 3, 4, 5, 6**

INSTRUCTIONAL ACTIVITIES	TEACHING HINTS

INTRODUCTORY ACTIVITY (2 - 3 MINUTES)

Run and Lead (Similar to File Running)	**See DPESS Chapter 14 for details.**
Students jog in formation. Last person sprints to front of line to become leader.	Line or circle formation

FITNESS DEVELOPMENT (8 - 12 MINUTES)

Continuity Exercises	**See DPESS Chapter 16 for details.**
See Badminton Unit, Lesson 3 for complete details.	Scattered formation

Continuity Exercises are a form of interval training. Interval training helps prevent the injuries associated with repetitive endurance exercise. Interval training allows you to increase your training intensity without overtraining or burn-out. In this way, adding intervals to your workout routine is a good way to cross train.

LESSON FOCUS (15 - 20 MINUTES)

Passing Skills Review • **Chest** • **Overhead**	**See DPESS Chapter 19 for details.** Create Task Sheets covering these passing skills. Allow students to work together and check form on Task Sheets.

Avoid passing over or around the defender. Pass fake in opposite direction. Watch the defender's hands and make a quick, accurate pass away from them. When the defender plays with his/her hands up, fake high and pass under their arm pit. When the defender holds his/her down, fake low and pass over their shoulder between their arm and head.

GAME (5 MINUTES)

Hoops and Plyometrics	**See DPESS Chapter 14 for details.**
Spread hoops around the area and give directions to move around using locomotor movements and freeze inside a hoop.	Scattered formation.

EVALUATION/REVIEW AND CHEER

Review elements of passing skills taught.
What type of training style are continuity exercises?
Why is interval training a good way to cross train?
When passing in basketball, what are some cues to successful passing?

Cheer: 2, 4, 6, 8, Basketball is really great!

Basketball Lesson Plan 6

EQUIPMENT:

1 parachute
Music CD/tape for fitness activities
1 Basketball per student
CD/Cassette player

OBJECTIVES:

The student will:

1. Participate in Individual Stunts demonstrating creativity and agility during the Introductory phase of class.
2. Participate in Rhythmic Parachute Activities to improve agility, flexibility, muscular strength, muscular endurance and cardiovascular endurance during the Fitness portion of class.
3. Demonstrate defensive skills using form demonstrated by the instructor during the Lesson Focus of class.
4. Participate in Horse demonstrating cooperative and shooting skills during the game portion of class and following the instructions established by the instructor.

National Standards Met in this Lesson: **1, 2, 3, 4, 5, 6**

INSTRUCTIONAL ACTIVITIES	TEACHING HINTS
INTRODUCTORY ACTIVITY (2 - 3 MINUTES)	
Individual Stunts Leg dip; Behind Back Touch; Double Heel Click	**See DPESS Chapter 18 for details.** Scattered formation Explain stunts and student practices
FITNESS DEVELOPMENT (8 - 12 MINUTES)	
Rhythmic Parachute Activities See Lesson 11, Badminton for details	**See DPESS Chapter 16 for details.** Use a music CD/tape for added motivation and enthusiasm.

Most physical activities have an inherent rhythm (e.g., tennis, swimming, running, or basketball). By participating in activities that focus on rhythm students sharpen their kinesthetic awareness of the body in space as well as the length of time required to perform the individual components of a movement or skill.

INSTRUCTIONAL ACTIVITIES	TEACHING HINTS
LESSON FOCUS (15 - 20 MINUTES)	
Defensive Footwork **Jump stop pivots; V-Cuts; Defensive slides**	**See DPESS Chapter 19 for details.** Body position; Good footwork; Balanced pivot
One on One Defense Defensive player keeps offensive player in front of her using defensive slides.	Create pairs Student with ball is defensive player.
GAME (5 MINUTES)	
Horse	**See DPESS Chapter 19 for details.** Use a management game to create groups of 4.

EVALUATION/REVIEW AND CHEER

Review defensive skills taught during the class.
Why is it important to develop rhythm skills?

Cheer: Playing Basketball is Great!

Basketball Lesson Plan 7

EQUIPMENT:

1 Basketball per student
16 Cones
1 Individual Tug of War rope per 2 students

OBJECTIVES:

The student will:

1. Participate in the Light Jog Around Cones demonstrating agility and following instructions during the Introductory phase of class.
2. Participate in directed exercises to improve agility, flexibility, muscular strength, muscular endurance and cardiovascular endurance during the Fitness portion of class.
3. Demonstrate lay-ups, rebounding, dribbling, and free throw shooting using form demonstrated by the instructor during the Lesson Focus of class.
4. Participate in Partner Tug of War Activities demonstrating cooperative and shooting skills during the game portion of class and following the instructions established by the instructor.

National Standards Met in this Lesson: **1, 2, 3, 4, 5, 6**

INSTRUCTIONAL ACTIVITIES	TEACHING HINTS
INTRODUCTORY ACTIVITY (2 - 3 MINUTES)	
Light Jog Around Cones	**See DPESS Chapter 14 for details.** Allow students to "fall in" line behind a leader moving around cones.
FITNESS DEVELOPMENT (8 - 12 MINUTES)	
Calf Stretch; Hamstring Side Stretch; Jump in place; Groin stretches; Jog, Sprint, Jog; Curl-ups; Push-ups; Reverse curl-ups	**See DPESS Chapter 16 for details.** Scattered formation. Instructor leads activities. Use music CD/tape for interest and fun.
LESSON FOCUS (15 - 20 MINUTES)	
Station Work: **Lay-ups; One on one rebounding; Dribbling Review; Free Throws**	**See DPESS Chapter 19 for details.** Create stations Demonstrate movements of each station Assign groups of 4 - 5 to each station

The best shooters in the world hit only about 40% of their long-range shots in real games. That's 4 out of 10. That's why it's good to work on lay-ups and rebounding.

INSTRUCTIONAL ACTIVITIES	TEACHING HINTS
GAME (5 MINUTES)	
Partner Tug of War Activities • **Different Positions** • **Pick-up and Pull**	**See DPESS Chapter 18 for details.** • Create partners using Back-to-Back with someone your own size. • 1 rope per 2 students

EVALUATION/REVIEW AND CHEER

Ask questions regarding skills used in lay-ups and free throws.
What is the average percentage of success in long-range shots in a game?

Students create cheer.

Basketball Lesson Plan 8

EQUIPMENT:

1 Basketball per student
Continuity Exercise Music CD/Tape
Station Instruction Charts
Cones to mark Stations

OBJECTIVES:

The student will:

1. Participate in the Vanishing Bean Bags demonstrating agility and following instructions during the Introductory phase of class.
2. Participate in Continuity Exercises to improve agility, flexibility, muscular strength, muscular endurance and cardiovascular endurance during the Fitness portion of class.
3. Demonstrate dribbling, passing, guarding, and shooting skills using form demonstrated by the instructor during the Lesson Focus of class.
4. Participate in the Dribble Relay demonstrating cooperative and dribbling skills during the game portion of class and following the instructions established by the instructor.

National Standards Met in this Lesson: **1, 2, 3, 4, 5, 6**

INSTRUCTIONAL ACTIVITIES	TEACHING HINTS

INTRODUCTORY ACTIVITY (2 - 3 MINUTES)

Vanishing Bean Bags

See DPESS Chapter 14 for details.
See Lesson 3, Golf Unit for complete details

FITNESS DEVELOPMENT (8 - 12 MINUTES)

Continuity Exercises
These exercises are a type of interval training.

See DPESS Chapter 16 for details.
See Lesson Plan 3, Golf Unit for complete details.

LESSON FOCUS (15 - 20 MINUTES)

5 Station Practice:
Write instructions for each station on Station Cards.
Demonstrate activities for each station.

See DPESS Chapter 19 for details.
Use Whistle Mixer to create even groups to distribute to each station.

- **Footwork Review Activities**
- **Dribbling Review Activities**
- **Passing Review Activities**
- **Shooting Review Activities**
- **Guarding Activities Introductory Skill Station:**
  Demonstrate skills as each group comes to the station

Assign groups to begin at each station.
Explain rotation procedures.

GAME (5 MINUTES)

Dribble Relay

See DPESS Chapter 19 for details.
Create even groups of 5 - 6.

Students dribble around cone and return to line.
When all have dribbled, group sits down.
Can vary dribbling challenge each round.

Assign to starting position.

EVALUATION/REVIEW AND CHEER

Review elements of each station. Discuss areas of difficulty or concern.
Was there any area of the continuity exercises that was very difficult?
What muscles were used in today's lesson?

Cheer: 2, 4, 6, 8, Basketball is great!

Basketball Lesson Plan 9

EQUIPMENT:
1 basketball per student
CD/Cassette player and music CD/tape for Circuit Training

OBJECTIVES:
The student will:
1. Participate in the Pentabridge Hustle demonstrating agility and following instructions during the Introductory phase of class.
2. Participate in Circuit Training to improve agility, flexibility, muscular strength, muscular endurance and cardiovascular endurance during the Fitness portion of class.
3. Demonstrate offensive footwork skills using form demonstrated by the instructor during the Lesson Focus of class.
4. Participate in the Sideline Basketball demonstrating cooperative, dribbling and shooting skills during the game portion of class and following the instructions established by the instructor.

National Standards Met in this Lesson: **1, 2, 3, 4, 5, 6**

INSTRUCTIONAL ACTIVITIES	TEACHING HINTS
INTRODUCTORY ACTIVITY (2 - 3 MINUTES)	
Pentabridge Hustle Students move continuously under bridges created by group members.	**See DPESS Chapter 14 for details.** Using Whistle Mixer, create groups of 5. 4 members of group make bridges that 1 must go under. Movement flows continuously.
FITNESS DEVELOPMENT (8 - 12 MINUTES)	
Circuit Training Create 9-10 different fitness circuit stations. Make the station cards for each station. Use a music CD/tape for interest and motivation.	**See DPESS Chapter 16 for details.** Distribute students evenly throughout circuit. Explain rotation. Give a locomotor movement to execute between stations.
LESSON FOCUS (15 - 20 MINUTES)	
Offensive Footwork and Skills Demonstration followed by practice in scattered formation.	**See DPESS Chapter 19 for details.** Scattered formation.
To be a good basketball player, you must be able to accelerate from a stationary position. By paying attention to the fundamentals, you can improve your speed and quickness.	
Jump Stop • **Jump stop and hold**	Create groups of 4 for line drills. Assign group a line placement on courts. Two foot jump stop jog forward, take short jump, land on both feet. Hands up read to receive ball. Call out ball when landed.
Pivoting • **Jump stop front pivot each foot** • **Jump stop back pivot each foot**	Pivoting, jog forward, jump stop pivot backward (180 degrees), then pivot forward on same foot. Continue down practice area.
Dribbling and Stopping	Dribble forward until hear whistle, stop. Dribble again on signal.
GAME (5 MINUTES)	
Sideline Basketball	**See DPESS Chapter 19 for details.** Divide class into two teams per court. Select 4 players for center court work. Sideline players pass to court players. Game continues until a team scores a point.

EVALUATION/REVIEW AND CHEER

Review elements of skills taught.
What are some elements of a good basketball player?

Cheer: Let students create the cheer for the day.

Basketball Lesson Plan 10

EQUIPMENT:

Fitness Scavenger Hunt Cards
Basketball rules information handout
1 Basketball per student
CD/Cassette player and music CD/tape for exercising

OBJECTIVES:

The student will:

1. Participate in Blob Tag demonstrating agility and following instructions during the Introductory phase of class.
2. Participate in the Fitness Scavenger Hunt to improve agility, flexibility, muscular strength, muscular endurance and cardiovascular endurance during the Fitness portion of class.
3. Demonstrate knowledge of basketball skills and game rules using during the Lesson Focus of class.
4. Participate in a game of 5 on 5 Half Court Basketball demonstrating cooperative, dribbling and shooting skills during the game portion of class and following the instructions established by the instructor.

National Standards Met in this Lesson: **1, 2, 3, 4, 5, 6**

INSTRUCTIONAL ACTIVITIES | **TEACHING HINTS**

INTRODUCTORY ACTIVITY (2 - 3 MINUTES)

Blob tag
Person at end of line tags and holds hand of those tagged.

See DPESS Chapter 14 for details.
Using a management game, create pairs. Select several "its". "Its" hold hands.

FITNESS DEVELOPMENT (8 - 12 MINUTES)

Fitness Scavenger Hunt
Have cards made directing groups to a particular fitness activity area. Each area has fitness activity/ exercise instructions.

See DPESS Chapter 16 for details.
Create groups of 4 - 5 using Whistle Mixer. Direct each group to begin at a particular area for the Scavenger Hunt.

Why is participating in fitness activities important? Exercise can reduce the risk for developing cancer, diabetes, heart disease, obesity, and high blood pressure. Staying fit can also boost self-esteem. Working on fitness and physical activity improvements will also increase personal self-image and help develop a desire to set personal goals.

LESSON FOCUS (10 - 15 MINUTES)

Basketball Rules, Strategy, Player Positions
Have handouts ready for homework reading assignment.

See DPESS Chapter 19 for details.
Explain and demonstrate rules, player positions, and game strategy. Have students set up situations you direct and practice player positions and rules.

Focus is an important part of a successful game: This is absolutely necessary to have any real success in basketball. You need to have the ability to concentrate fully on what you're working on.

GAME (10 MINUTES)

Play 5 on 5 Half Court Basketball
Use regulation rules.

See DPESS Chapter 19 for details.
Using Whistle Mixer, create groups of 5. Assign to courts for 1/2-court games.

EVALUATION/REVIEW AND CHEER

Discuss rules and situations needing clarification.
Explain upcoming Round Robin Tournament.
Why is participating in Fitness activities important in your life?
What element is necessary to have real success in basketball?

Cheer: 4, 3, 2, 1 Basketball is Really Fun!!!

Basketball Lesson Plan 11

EQUIPMENT:

Obstacle course instruction sheets
Mats
Cones
Music CD/tape and CD/cassette player
1 Basketball per person

OBJECTIVES:

The student will:

1. Participate in the Mirror Drill in Place demonstrating agility and following instructions during the Introductory phase of class.
2. Participate in the Challenge Course to improve agility, flexibility, muscular strength, muscular endurance and cardiovascular endurance during the Fitness portion of class.
3. Participate in a game of 5 on 5 Half Court Basketball demonstrating knowledge of game rules, cooperative, dribbling and shooting skills during the game portion of class and following the instructions established by the instructor.

National Standards Met in this Lesson: **1, 2, 3, 4, 5, 6**

INSTRUCTIONAL ACTIVITIES	TEACHING HINTS

INTRODUCTORY ACTIVITY (2 - 3 MINUTES)

Mirror Drill in Place	**See DPESS Chapter 14 for details.** Students work with a partner.

FITNESS DEVELOPMENT (8 - 12 MINUTES)

Challenge Course	**See DPESS Chapter 16 for details.** See Badminton Unit, Lesson 1 for details.

You should accumulate at least 60 minutes of physical activity per day; however, several hours of activity would be even better.

Daily activity should include 10 to 15 minute periods of vigorous exercise.

LESSON FOCUS AND GAME COMBINED (20 - 25 MINUTES)

Play 5 on 5 Half Court or Full Court Basketball Use regulation rules. Groups that are ready can play full court basketball.	**See DPESS Chapter 19 for details.** Using Whistle Mixer, create groups of 5. Assign to courts for 1/2-court games.

EVALUATION/REVIEW AND CHEER

Review rules of Basketball. Ask questions regarding rules application of the rules you observed during game.
How many minutes of physical activity is recommended per day?
You should be trying to participate in how many minutes of vigorous activity per day?
Cheer: 1, 2, 3, We All Agree on PE!

Basketball Lesson Plan 12

EQUIPMENT:
Music CD/Tape
CD/Cassette Player

1 clipboard and pencil per 2 students
1 Basketball per student
1 Skill test sheet per student

OBJECTIVES:
The student will:
1. Participate in Musical Hoops demonstrating rhythmic awareness and cooperative skills while following instructions during the Introductory phase of class.
2. Participate in Walk, Jog, Sprint to improve agility, flexibility, muscular strength, muscular endurance and cardiovascular endurance during the Fitness portion of class.
3. Demonstrate skills mastered during the unit by completing the skills test.
4. Participate in Dribble Relay demonstrating cooperative and dribbling skills during the game portion of class and following the instructions established by the instructor.

National Standards Met in this Lesson: 1, 2, 3, 4, 5, 6

INSTRUCTIONAL ACTIVITIES	TEACHING HINTS

INTRODUCTORY ACTIVITY (2 - 3 MINUTES)

Musical Hoops (Variation of Hoops on the Ground)

Create a music CD/tape with 10-second pauses.
Have 1 less hoop than number of students
Call out a different locomotor movement after each pose.

See DPESS Chapter 14 for details.

When music stops, students must be in a hoop. Call out positions they must stop/pose in during each break of the music.

FITNESS DEVELOPMENT (8 - 12 MINUTES)

Walk, Jog, Sprint

See DPESS Chapter 16 for details.
See Golf Unit, Lesson 12 for details

Interval training is a period of hard exercise followed by a period of easy exercise or recovery. The Walk, Jog, Sprint activity is a form of Interval Training. Intervals can improve your training because they: Create mental toughness; Provide confidence; Train speed; Reset the central brain governor allowing greater skeletal muscle recruitments during maximum exercise (see Lore of Running by Timothy Noakes, MD); Enhance the muscular activity of Type II muscle fibers to make you faster.

LESSON FOCUS (15 - 20 MINUTES)

Skill Testing

See DPESS Chapter 19 for details.
Use "Core Objectives" to create a skill exam.
Students can work in partners and test each other.

GAME (5 MINUTES)

Dribble Relay

See Lesson 8 for details

EVALUATION/REVIEW AND CHEER

Review material for written exam.
Explain the value of Interval Training.

What activity did we do today that is a type of Interval Training?

Cheer: 1, 2, 3, 4, Give me more of Basketball!

Basketball Lesson Plan 13

EQUIPMENT:

CD/Cassette player
Aerobic Exercise Music CD/Tape
1 Written Exam per student
1 basketball per student

OBJECTIVES:

The student will:

1. Participate in Addition Tag demonstrating agility and cooperative skills while following instructions during the Introductory phase of class.
2. Participate in the Aerobic workout to improve agility, flexibility, muscular strength, muscular endurance and cardiovascular endurance during the Fitness portion of class.
3. Complete a written exam passing with a score of 70% or better.
4. Participate in a game of Basketball during the game portion of class and following the instructions established by the instructor and demonstrating good sportsmanship skills.

National Standards Met in this Lesson: **1, 2, 3, 4, 5, 6**

INSTRUCTIONAL ACTIVITIES	TEACHING HINTS
INTRODUCTORY ACTIVITY (2 - 3 MINUTES)	
	See DPESS Chapter 14 for details.
Addition Tag Select 2 - 3 "its". They run and try to tag others. Each line grows as outside person tags and picks up other line "members". The longest line at the end is the winner.	
FITNESS DEVELOPMENT (8 - 12 MINUTES)	
	See DPESS Chapter 16 for details.
Aerobic workout	See Racquetball Unit, Lesson 7 for details
LESSON FOCUS (15 - 20 MINUTES)	
	Exam follows.
Written Exam	
GAME (5 MINUTES)	
Full Court Basketball	Allow students to play upon completion of exam.

EVALUATION/REVIEW AND CHEER

Discuss Round Robin Tournament
What muscles were worked today during the Aerobic Workout?
Are there any areas of the body that you noticed you will need more work?
What muscles continued to be worked during your games of Basketball?

Cheer: Basketball, yes!

BASKETBALL EXAM

Directions: Fill in the letter matching the most appropriate response on your answer sheet. True = A; False = B

True/False

1. There are 7 players plus substitutes on an official basketball team.
2. A field goal is worth 2 points.
3. A free throw is worth 2 points.
4. After making a field goal, the team that made the goal takes the ball out at the end line.
5. Blocking is stopping the progress of a person with or without the ball.
6. Faking or feinting is a defensive technique.
7. A bounce pass is rarely effective near the goal.
8. A player should use the dribble to cover the ground.
9. Man-to-man defense means that the guards move with the ball.
10. It is legal to hand the ball to another player.
11. On a jump ball, a player may <u>not</u> tap the ball until it reaches its highest point.
12. A jump ball is taken in the center-restraining circle <u>only</u> at the beginning of each quarter.

Multiple Choice

13. ___ is called by the referee if while dribbling you drop the ball, stop and pick it up, and then begin dribbling again.
    a. traveling
    b. double dribbling
    c. free throw
    d. a & b
    e. all of the above
14. How long may a player of the offensive team stand in the free throw lane?
    a. indefinitely
    b. 5 seconds
    c. 3 seconds
    d. 10 seconds
15. The penalty for two players on opposite teams holding the ball at the same time is
    a. a free throw for the first player that got the ball
    b. a jump ball for the two players involved in the tie ball
    c. the ball is taken out of bounds at the sideline
    d. all of the above
16. After 5 team fouls, the penalty for unnecessary roughness or over guarding is
    a. ball taken out of bounds at the sidelines by the team that was fouled
    b. free throw for the team making the foul
    c. free throw for the team that was the victim of a foul
    d. all of the above
17. Which of the following is the easiest to intercept?
    a. long pass
    b. low bounce
    c. dribble
    d. any of the above
18. How long may a player in bounds hold the ball when <u>not</u> being closely guarded?
    a. 3 seconds
    b. 5 seconds
    c. indefinitely
    d. 10 seconds
19. Which of the following is illegal?
    a. striking the ball with the fists
    b. holding the ball for six seconds when closely guarded
    c. using both hands on the first dribble
    d. all of the above
20. How long may a player stand in the free throw lane if her team does not have possession of the ball?
    a. 3 seconds
    b. 5 seconds
    c. 10 seconds
    d. indefinitely

Basketball Lesson Plan 14

EQUIPMENT:

Fitness Challenge Course Instructions (see Badminton Unit, Lesson 1 for details)
Round Robin Tournament chart
1 ball per court

OBJECTIVES:

The student will:

1. Participate in the Challenge Course workout to improve agility, flexibility, muscular strength, muscular endurance and cardiovascular endurance during the Fitness portion of class.
2. Participate in a game of Basketball during the game portion of class and following the instructions established by the instructor and demonstrating basketball and sportsmanship skills learned during the unit.

National Standards Met in this Lesson: **1, 2, 3, 4, 5, 6**

INSTRUCTIONAL ACTIVITIES	TEACHING HINTS
INTRODUCTORY ACTIVITY AND FITNESS COMBINED (15 MINUTES)	
Challenge Course	**See DPESS Chapter 16 for details.** See Badminton Unit, Lesson 1 for details
LESSON FOCUS AND GAME COMBINED (20 MINUTES)	
Round Robin Tournament	Create teams and chart for tournament.

In a round-robin schedule, each participant plays every other participant once. If each participant plays all others twice, this is frequently called a double round-robin.

EVALUATION/REVIEW AND CHEER

Discuss issues that may have arisen during tournament.
What is the difference between a round-robin tournament and a double round-robin tournament?
Students create cheer.

Basketball Lesson Plan 15

EQUIPMENT:

Round Robin Tournament Chart
1 basketball per court

OBJECTIVES:

The student will:

1. Move and Perform a Stretch during the Introductory Activities.
2. Participate in Walk, jog, Sprint workout to improve muscular strength, muscular endurance and cardiovascular endurance during the Fitness portion of class.
3. Participate in a game of Basketball during the game portion of class and following the instructions established by the instructor and demonstrating basketball and sportsmanship skills learned during the unit.

National Standards Met in this Lesson: **1, 2, 3, 4, 5, 6**

INSTRUCTIONAL ACTIVITIES	TEACHING HINTS
INTRODUCTORY ACTIVITY (2 - 3 MINUTES)	
Move and Perform a Stretch	**See DPESS Chapter 14 for details.** See Lesson 13, Badminton for details.
FITNESS DEVELOPMENT (8 - 12 MINUTES)	
Walk, Jog, Sprint	**See DPESS Chapter 16 for details.** See Lesson 12 for details
LESSON FOCUS AND GAME COMBINED (20 - 25 MINUTES)	
Round Robin Tournament Conclusion	
EVALUATION/REVIEW AND CHEER	
Discuss Tournament and introduce next unit.	Students create cheer.

Golf

This unit has been specifically designed to meet all six components of the NASPE National Standards for Physical Education.

OBJECTIVES:

The student will:

1. Participate in gross motor movements, isometrics, Plyometrics and cardiovascular activities.
2. Cooperate with group members during the fitness scavenger hunt as directed by the instructor.
3. Participate in Continuity Exercise Activities to increase cardiovascular endurance, strength, and flexibility.
4. Execute Formation Rhythmic Running to increase the circulation and generally warm the body up while reinforcing the following of a beat while moving.
5. Demonstrate starting, stopping, running skills in Bean Bag Touch and Go and Ball Activities.
6. Read the class safety rules hand out and sign the cover sheet indicating understanding.
7. Demonstrate and use the proper grip 100% of the time.
8. Demonstrate the proper address of the ball 100% of the time.
9. Execute the chip, pitch and drive shots using form demonstrated in class.
10. Demonstrate the stance, grip, and address routine used in putting a golf ball.
11. Putt the ball on the practice greens.
12. Demonstrate the basics of the full swing.
13. Review chipping using a self check task sheet.
14. Identify etiquette and rules on Task Sheets 15 – 17.
15. Demonstrate the golf full swing using the 5 iron and skills demonstrated in class.
16. Using the full swing, practice hitting into a net and at targets.
17. Improve sand trap shot technique as demonstrated by the instructor.
18. Execute form taught in class for Sand Trap Shots.
19. Complete a written exam covering rules, etiquette, and skills techniques scoring at least 70%.
20. Work with a partner and complete the "Golf Rating Scale" to receive a skill exam grade.
21. Play Frisbee Keep Away demonstrating throwing, catching and jumping skills.
22. Play Tug of War with a team.
23. Demonstrate dodging, running, and agility during Push-Up Tag.
24. Play "Frisbee 21" with a partner demonstrating one and two hand catching and throwing accuracy.
25. Play a game of simulated golf demonstrating skills, rules and etiquette studied during the unit.

GOLF BLOCK PLAN
3 WEEK UNIT

Week #1	Monday	Tuesday	Wednesday	Thursday	Friday
Introductory Activity	Blob tag	Parachute Routine	Vanishing Bean Bags	Parachute Locomotor Routine	Ball Activities
Fitness	Continuity Exercise	Parachute Activities	Continuity Exercises	Parachute Fitness Activities	Walk, Jog, Sprint
Lesson Focus	Putting	Chip Shot	Chip Shot Review Pitch Shot	Full Swing	Review Address Routine Swings
Game	Frisbee Catch	Hula Hoop Pass	Football Pass Relay	Reverse Hula Hoop Spin	Pentabridge Hustle

Week #2	Monday	Tuesday	Wednesday	Thursday	Friday
Introductory Activity	Over, Under, Around	Formation Rhythmic Running	Bean Bag Touch and Go	Mirror Drill in Place	Partner Tug of War
Fitness	Continuity Exercise	Fitness Scavenger Hunt	Continuity Exercise	Stretching Four Corners Partner Resistance	Circuit Training
Lesson Focus	Full Swing	Pitch Shot Chip Shot Full Swing	Sand Trap Stunts Full Swing	Putting	Full Swing
Game	Frisbee Keep Away	Team Tug of War		Frisbee Freedom	Nine Lives

Week #3	Monday	Tuesday	Wednesday	Thursday	Friday
Introductory Activity	**Mirror Drill in Place**	Follow the Leader	Flag Chase	Eliminate Today	Formation Rhythmic Running
Fitness	Exercise to Music	Walk, Jog, Sprint	Fitness Challenge Course	Stretching	Golf Game
Lesson Focus	Pitch Shot	Pitch and Run Putting	Pitching Rules and Etiquette	Written and Skill Exam	Golf Game
Game	Musical Hoops	Frozen Tag	Frisbee 21	Putting Practice	Golf Game

Golf Lesson Plan 1

EQUIPMENT:

1 Putter per student
5 Golf balls per student
1 Putting green per 2 students
1 Whistle
1 Clipboard and pencil per green
1 Frisbee per 2 students
1 Individual jump rope per student
1 CD/Cassette player
Continuity music CD/tape
2 Putting Task Sheets per pair placed on clipboard

OBJECTIVES:

The student will:

1. Participate in the Blob Tag demonstrating cooperative skills and agility
2. Participate in Continuity Exercises to improve fitness.
3. Demonstrate the putting stance as demonstrated by the instructor.
4. Demonstrate the putting grip as demonstrated by the instructor.

National Standards Met in this Lesson: 1, 2, 4, 5, 6

INSTRUCTIONAL ACTIVITIES	ORGANIZATION TEACHING HINTS
INTRODUCTORY ACTIVITY (2 – 3 MINUTES)	
Blob tag Select 2 – 3 it's	**See DPESS Chapter 14 for details.** Change it's 1 or 2 times during activity.

A Scottish term for tag is "tig."

INSTRUCTIONAL ACTIVITIES	ORGANIZATION TEACHING HINTS
FITNESS DEVELOPMENT (8 – 12 MINUTES)	
Continuity Exercises These exercises are a type of interval training. Create a CD/cassette tape with 30 – 35 seconds of music and 20 seconds of silence. During the music the students will jump rope.	**See DPESS Chapter 16 for details.** When the silence begins, instruct the students to do an exercise i.e. push-ups; curl ups; reverse push-ups; etc. When the music resumes, the students jump rope. During each silence direct a difference exercise.
Stretching During the last silence, conduct stretching exercises to stretch the areas worked i.e. calves; quadriceps; etc.	**See DPESS Chapter 16 for details.** Slower and lower volume music should be added to this portion of the CD/tape for enjoyable stretching.
Bear Hug	**See DPESS Chapter 16 for details.**
Lunge Forward: Achilles and calf stretch Lunge forward and extend rear leg straight back.	Attempt to place the rear foot flat on the floor. Hands on front thigh for support. Back flat and on upward diagonal.
Hamstring Stretch-Reverse Lunge: From the lunge position, shift lunge and weight to rear leg, extend front leg. Keep heel on ground, toe flexed and pointing to sky.	Hold stretch for 30 seconds. Change legs. Hands on front thigh for support, back flat but on upward diagonal.
Standing Hip Bend (Both sides) Hold the position for 20 – 20 seconds.	**See DPESS Chapter 16 for details.**
Elbow Puller and Pusher (Both sides)	**See DPESS Chapter 16 for details.**
Wishbone Stretch Hold position for 10 – 20 seconds	**See DPESS Chapter 16 for details.**

One muscle that makes up a hamstring muscle is biceps femoris.

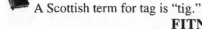

INSTRUCTIONAL ACTIVITIES	ORGANIZATION TEACHING HINTS

LESSON FOCUS (15 – 20 MINUTES)

Putting
Teach putting at a carpeted green. Use the "green" for your demonstration area.

Reverse Overlap Grip
Stance
Aiming
Address Routine
Practicing putting

Putting Task Sheet

If students complete Task Sheet quickly, they can play a putting game. See how many points can be earned when a person earns 1 point for each putt made.

See DPESS Chapter 20 for details.
Direct each student to pick up a putter and bring it to the demonstration area.
Scattered formation around demonstration area.
Demonstrate then students practice the grip.
Demonstrate then have students practice the stance.
Line up sight line with club. Imagine a line to the hole.
Demonstrate then practice Address Routine.
Direct students to get elbow to elbow to select a partner.
Ask each pair to pick up 5 golf balls and then go to a putting green.
Students practice putting 5 balls and then change roles.
Repeat.
Direct students to pick up a clip board with attached Task Sheet 1 and a pencil and come to the demonstration area.
Explain the Task Sheet. One student is the "doer". One student is the "observer". Observer reads task sheet to doer, records results, and offers feedback. Change roles as directed on task sheet.

A "putt" means to play a stroke where the ball doesn't leave the ground.

GAME (3 – 5 MINUTES)

Frisbee Catch
Partners can keep score or just free throwing and catching.
1 hand catch = 2 points
2 hand catch = 1 point
Keep score to 20 points and then start over.

See DPESS Chapter 20 for details.
Demonstrate throwing and catching a Frisbee.
Use back to back with a new person to create partners.
One person puts a hand on their head. The person with his hand on his head is to go and get a Frisbee for the pair and return to the partner.

Frisbee came about by throwing and catching empty pie tins from the Frisbie baking company. The game later was trade marked Frisbee.

EVALUATION/REVIEW AND CHEER

Evaluation
Have students take home "Golf Safety Rules", read it, sign it and return "cut off" to class on the next day.

- Name a muscle that makes up the Hamstring muscle.
- What muscles were used today?
- Describe a putt shot.
- How did the Frisbee develop?
- What is a Scottish term for "tag?"

Cheer: **2, 4, 6, 8, playing golf is really great!**

Bring students together and review learning experiences of the day.

RECIPROCAL TASK SHEET 1: ADDRESSING AND PUTTING THE BALL

Name: ______________________________

Name: ______________________________

Directions: Work with a partner. Place both of your names on each task sheet. One person is the "doer" while the other person is the "observer". Observer reads information/instructions to the doer, offers verbal feedback and places a check in the "yes" or "no" column recording the performance of their partner. Record the date of the practice. Complete the task sheet until you are directed to "change roles". Then, the "doer" becomes the "observer". Each person has his/her own task sheet.

ADDRESS ROUTINE	**DATES**							
(Record date of practice)								
	Yes	**No**	**Yes**	**No**	**Yes**	**No**	**Yes**	**No**
1. Assume the grip you have selected to use.								
2. Stand behind the ball and sight the hole.								
3. Move up to the side of ball, with arms extended place the club head down directly behind the ball so the clubface is "square" to the intended line of the putt.								
4. Place your feet so the ball is in front of the left foot about one putter blade length in front of the toe. Feet about 12" apart.								
5. Knees slightly bent.								
6. Weight mainly on left foot.								
7. Head over the ball. Eyes on ball.								
PUTTING								
8. Partner should place his club right above toes of partner making a straight line toward the target.								
9. Point both elbows out slightly.								
10. Swing the club back 12" – 18". Swing forward and through the ball. The follow through should be about the same distance as the BACKSWING. Accelerate through the ball in a smooth motion.								
11. BACKSWING and follow through make a straight line parallel to partners club.								
12. Change roles.								
13. Repeat 1 – 12								

GOLF SAFETY RULES

1. Follow all rules set by your instructor.
2. Do not swing a golf club until you have been instructed to do so. Always look around to see that no one is close by and within range of your swing.
3. Be careful where you walk while other people are taking practice swings.
4. Stand well away and out of range of a player taking a swing.
5. Do not swing a golf club so the follow through of the swing is traveling toward anyone.
6. If you hit a golf ball that is traveling toward someone, call "FORE".
7. Wait for the signal from your instructor before retrieving balls.
8. Accidents occur because of carelessness, lack of awareness, or lack of knowledge. Always look around and practice safely.

Please cut off at the dashed line, sign, date, and return below to your instructor.

CUT OFF AND RETURN TO INSTRUCTOR

I, ______________________________, have read and understand the golf safety rules. I agree to follow the rules of the class.

____ Date ____________________

(Signature)

Golf Lesson Plan 2

EQUIPMENT:

Whistle
6 Whiffle balls per student
Individual jump ropes
1 Parachute
Bag of golf tees, 5 of each color
Easel chalkboard or diagram of setups on field
#7 Iron
5 Hula-hoops
15 Beanbags
CD/Cassette Player
6 Cones

OBJECTIVES:

The student will:

1. Perform quality parachute movements as demonstrated by the instructor.
2. Demonstrate proper chip shot grip and stance as demonstrated by the instructor.

National Standards Met in this Lesson: 1, 2, 4, 5, 6

INSTRUCTIONAL ACTIVITIES	ORGANIZATION TEACHING HINTS
INTRODUCTORY ACTIVITY (2 – 3 MINUTES)	
Parachute (Locomotor) Routine with Music	**See DPESS Chapter 16 for details.**
Define: clockwise & counter clockwise	Explain routine. Turn on music.
Ask "What are locomotor movements?"	
Parachute in French means "fall protection."	
Routine example:	Locomotor Routine to a popular Tape/CD:
16 Runs clockwise	"Run left"
16 Runs counter-clockwise	"Run right"
16 Jumps to center	"Jump to center!"
16 Jumps back	"Jump back and tighten chute!"
8 count lift overhead	"Lift overhead!" (8 Counts.)
8 count lower to toes	"Lower to toes"
4 count lift	"Again!" "Up! Down!"
4 count lower	"Hold overhead and run left!" (32 Counts.)
	"Hold at waist and run right!"
Repeat all, but increase difficulty by holding chute overhead on CW run	"Lift overhead!" (16 Counts.) "Lower to toes!"
Release on last lift.	"Lift & Release!"
FITNESS DEVELOPMENT (8 – 12 MINUTES)	
Parachute Fitness Activities	**See DPESS Chapter 16 for details.**
Toe Touches Explain isometrics. Lift chute taut to chin. Bend forward and touch grip to toes. Hold taut to chin.	Hold parachute sitting while in extended leg position around the parachute. 16 repetitions.
Curl Ups: Curl-up, bend knees, lie back, extend legs. Repeat 16 times.	Hold Parachute sitting position in a circle. Curl up, bent knees. Extended legs under chute and lie on back.
Dorsal Lifts	Lying prone head toward chute arms straight chest taut. Lift arms and chest, lower, repeat 8 times.
Sitting leg lift: Sit – legs under chute, on signal lift a leg off ground for 6 to 10 seconds. Try to keep leg straight. Alternate legs.	When Blow whistle: Freeze. Try variation: Side leg lefts. Lie on side. Lift top leg and lower.
Jump rope in place	Scattered formation.
Travel while rope jumping	Move around carefully while rope jumping.
Hot Peppers	Jump as fast as you can until I blow the whistle.
Skip rope at a comfortable pace.	

Jump rope is an excellent way to perform an aerobic exercise.

INSTRUCTIONAL ACTIVITIES	ORGANIZATION TEACHING HINTS
LESSON FOCUS (15 – 20 MINUTES)	
Chip Shot	**DPESS page 472**
Each student gets a 7 iron	Explain purpose
Demonstrate grip.	Practice grip
Demonstrate stance: Forward foot open toward target	Practice stance
Demonstrate swing	Have students spread out to safe location to swing.
Practice swing aiming at target	Set cones approximately 10' from chipping area. Cones mark the target.
Hit balls to target	Have students get balls.
Repeat practice	Signal to retrieve balls.
Count # balls stopping close to target	Try to have ball stop rolling close to cone.
Complete activity.	Collect equipment.

Typically, golf courses have 18 holes and involve shots that require the full swing, chipping, and putting.

GAME (5 MINUTES)

Hula Hoop Circle Pass	**DPESS page 314**
Place a hula-hoop over the clasped hands of two members of each circle. On signal – pass the hoop around the circle without releasing handgrips.	Use Whistle Mixer to form groups formed in circles. Approximately 5 per group. Members of each group hold hands.

Hula hoops used to be made out of grapevines and stiff grasses.

EVALUATION/REVIEW AND CHEER

Review elements of the swing.
What does the word Parachute mean?
Name one aerobic exercise performed today.
What was the hula hoop made out of before plastic?
Students create cheer

Golf Lesson Plan 3

EQUIPMENT:

Self-check task sheets	Whistle
Clipboards	Pencils
Parachute	15 Hula-hoops
6 Whiffle balls per student	90 Beanbags
4 Chip nets	#7 Irons
Rope	1 Football per 5 students
CD/Cassette Player	Continuity Music CD/Tape

OBJECTIVES:

The student will:

1. Perform proper pitch shot swings technique as demonstrated by the instructor.
2. Incorporate football skills during the game activity as directed by the instructor.

National Standards Met in this Lesson: 1, 2, 4, 5, 6

INSTRUCTIONAL ACTIVITIES	ORGANIZATION TEACHING HINTS
INTRODUCTORY ACTIVITY (2 – 3 MINUTES)	
Vanishing Bean Bags	**See DPESS Chapter 14 for details.**
Another type of equipment that is similar to bean bags is the hacky sack.	Spread beanbags out in area. Begin with 1 bag/student. Have students begin by moving around the area until you give a signal.

INSTRUCTIONAL ACTIVITIES	ORGANIZATION TEACHING HINTS

FITNESS DEVELOPMENT (8 – 12 MINUTES)

Continuity Exercises	**See DPESS Chapter 16 for details.**
Stretch	**See DPESS Chapter 16 for details.**
Bear Hug	**See DPESS Chapter 16 for details.**
Standing Hip Bend. Be sure not to bounce.	**See DPESS Chapter 16 for details.** Hold the position for 10 – 20 seconds
Arm and Shoulder Stretch	**See DPESS Chapter 16 for details.**
Elbow Puller and Pusher	**See DPESS Chapter 16 for details.** Both sides in each exercise.
Wishbone stretch	**See DPESS Chapter 16 for details.** Hold position for 10 – 20 seconds.

Jump rope is an excellent way to perform an aerobic exercise. Intermittent exercise, such as Continuity Exercises, can greatly improve aerobic fitness levels.

LESSON FOCUS (15 – 20 MINUTES)

Review Chip Shot
Review basic elements.

See DPESS Chapter 20 for details.
Have students complete the Self Check Task Sheet: Golf Chip Shot.

Pitch Shot
Demonstrate grip.
Practice grip
Demonstrate stance
Practice stance
Demonstrate swings:
1/2 swing
3/4 swing
Full swing

See DPESS Chapter 20 for details.
Demonstrate and discuss difference in loft of 9 iron, 7 iron and pitching wedge. Describe purpose and effectiveness of each club in reach the green or getting out of bunkers. Student pick up a club. Spread students out to practice swings Use hula hoops and "chip nets" as targets

Hint: Long jump ropes can be stretched to indicate swing area.

Direct student s to the practice area. 6 balls per student are needed.

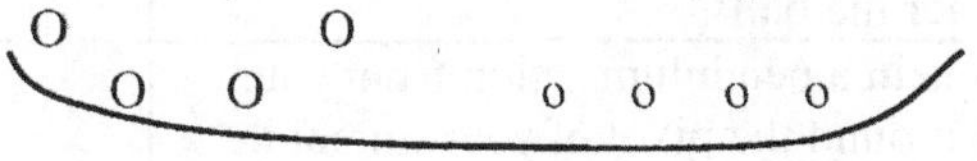

Safety Reminder

Practice each type of swing 6 times before trying to aim at the target.

Whistle to indicate when to retrieve balls and when practice can resume. Return equipment.

The first stroke in each hole is hit from a tee. The Chip Shot and Pitch Shots are not hit from a tee.

GAME (5 MINUTES)

Football Pass Relay Leader hands off football turning right with torso rotation similar to the "take away" of the golf club.	Organize lines of 5 – 6 students using Whistle Mixer Explain that students freeze when they hear the whistle.
Each student receives the pass and hands off. Last person runs with ball to the head of the squad.	Repeat relay until all have finished. Then group sits down.

In football, a touchdown gives the team 6 points.

EVALUATION/REVIEW AND CHEER

Review main elements of pitch and chip shots.
Which exercises performed today can improve your aerobic fitness level?
Which golf shot is hit from a tee?
When are the Chip and Pitch Shots used?
What is the name of another piece of equipment that can be used similarly to a Bean Bag?
How many points do you earn for a touchdown?

Cheer: 2, 4, 6, 8 Golf is really, really great!

SELF-CHECK TASK SHEET: GOLF CHIP SHOT

Name: ____________________________________

Objective: The student will demonstrate the grip, the stance, the ball alignment and the chipping stroke.

Directions: Record date of practice. Record all components followed for each section: grip, stance, ball alignment and stroke.

1st:	Two Shots	Chip 15'
2nd:	Two Shots	Chip 30'

(Record date of practice)	DATES							
GRIP	**Yes**	**No**	**Yes**	**No**	**Yes**	**No**	**Yes**	**No**
1. The most common grip is started with the palm of right hand facing the target								
2. The back of the left hand faces the target with the left thumb on top of the club (for left handers the reverse is done).								
STANCE								
1. Place feet on both ends of 12" strip set parallel to target line.								
2. Knees are bent.								
3. Eyes on ball.								
BALL POSITION								
1. Ball slightly in front of left foot.								
STROKE								
1. Keep your head perfectly still and your eyes directly over the ball.								
2. Swing arms in a pendulum action from your shoulders around the pivot of your immobile head.								
3. Point both elbows outward slightly.								
4. Club should end facing in the direction you are hitting the ball.								

Golf Lesson Plan 4

EQUIPMENT:

CD/Tape
1 Weighted scarf per student
Tees for each student
10 Whiffle balls per student
Rope
Bucket of 10 hard golf balls
CD/Cassette Player
#9 Iron for each student
8 Hoops
3 Chipper nets
2 Cones
Parachute

OBJECTIVES:

The student will:

1. Increase cardiovascular strength during the fitness development as directed by the instructor.
2. Demonstrate group cooperation by participating in the activities in the lesson as directed by the instructor.

National Standards Met in this Lesson: **1, 2, 3, 4, 5, 6**

INSTRUCTIONAL ACTIVITIES	ORGANIZATION TEACHING HINTS
INTRODUCTORY ACTIVITY (2 – 3 MINUTES)	
Parachute Locomotor Routine	**See DPESS Chapter 16 for details.**
Popular music	Whistle to change action
16 runs CW	"Tighten 'chute!"
16 runs CCW	Hold 'chute overhead on CW run.
8 jumps in place	
16 skips forward	
8 count lift overhead	
8 count lower to toes	
4 count lift	
4 count lower to toes	
Repeat all	
Face chute and hold with 2 hands:	Whistle to signal direction change.
Slide CW; Slide CCW	
Sebastien Lenormand, a French man, established the word parachute.	
FITNESS DEVELOPMENT (8 – 12 MINUTES)	
Parachute Fitness Activities	**See DPESS Chapter 16 for details.**
	Hold chute with left hand
Skip forward CCW; Skip CW; Run CCW; Run CW	Change hands on 'chute to change directions. Whistle signals "stop". Give directions.
Slide right, Slide left	Place two hands on 'chute; Hold 'chute tautly. Put 'chute down Sprint around room Whistle to return to spot around 'chute.
Stretching exercises	**See DPESS Chapter 16 for details.**
Overhead; Standing hip bend; Wishbone stretch	
Toe Toucher	**See DPESS Chapter 16 for details.**
Lift to taut – chin level	Sitting, legs under 'chute. Bend to touch grip to toes; Lift to taut – chin level Repeat 16 times
Curl ups	Taut to chin. Hold. Curl up – bend knees. Touch edge of 'chute to toes.
Legs under 'chute – lie on back, curl up – bend knees, lie back – extend legs. Repeat total 4 times.	
Parachute Drills	Lying prone.
Dorsal Lifts	Head toward 'chute.

INSTRUCTIONAL ACTIVITIES	ORGANIZATION TEACHING HINTS
Lift arms and chest, hold, lower.	Arms straight
Repeat 8 times total.	Keep parachute taut
Sitting Leg Lifts	Sit, legs under 'chute
Lift legs straight Hold 6-8 sec. Variation: lying supine lift torso and straight legs to a "V" sit position, hold.	Whistle; "Lift & Hold" Whistle; "Lower"
Sitting Pulls	Sit with back to 'chute.
Hold 'chute overhead on signal try to pull to knees.	Whistle "Up and Hold"
All Fours Pull Hold overhead, 6-8 sec to eye level, 6-8 sec to waist, etc.	Sitting facing chute hands and knees hold chute with one hand.
On signal, pull and hold 6-10 sec. Repeat other hand.	Whistle "Pull and Hold"
Roll parachute tightly	Everyone walks to center to fold up 'chute.
Sprint-Jog File Run	**See DPESS Chapter 16 for details.**
All students in each line jog around area. Last runner in each line sprints to weave in and around each of the people in the line until he gets to front. Then last person in line repeats.	Organize groups of 5 using Whistle Mixer. Make lines.

Lenormand created the first the parachute in 1783 in France. He was also the first person witnessed using a parachute.

LESSON FOCUS (15 – 20 MINUTES)

Full Swing	**See DPESS Chapter 20 for details.**
Demonstrate grips: Baseball, Overlapping, Interlocking.	Direct student to pick up a club. #9 or #7 iron.
	Practice grips.
Address the ball: Body position; Weight; Knees; Shoulders and Arms; Lining up club head and feet	Practice
Demonstrate Full Swing	Review safety rules.
Practice 3/4 swing and full swing 10 times without ball.	Direct students to go to practice area and place club down. Pick up practice balls.
Practice full swing with Whiffle balls.	Direct starting and ball collection.
Use of the tee	Practice with hard golf balls and tee.
When used?	Change balls.
How high is ball on tee?	Put equipment away.

If the ball is put in the hole on the first stroke, it is called a "hole in one."

GAME (5 MINUTES)

Reverse Hula-Hoop Spin	**See DPESS Chapter 18 for details.**
Squad Leaders: Roll hoop forward with a reverse spin – when it returns – pass it over your body to the ground – step out of it and pass it to the next person in squad line. (Winning squad is first to finish.)	Squads of 5-6 people. Leader takes a hoop. Leader collects hoops.

The 100-millionth hula hoop was sold in 1959.

EVALUATION/REVIEW AND CHEER

Review elements of the full swing.
What is a "hole in one?"
Who invented the first parachute and in what year? From what country was this inventor?
In what year was the 100-millionth hula hoop sold?

Students create cheer

Golf Lesson Plan 5

EQUIPMENT:

1 Rubber ball per student
1 Nine Iron per student
6 Whiffle golf balls per student
1 Clipboard per 2 students
Reciprocal Task Sheets 2 – 4
15 Hula-hoops for shooting targets

OBJECTIVES:

The student will:

1. Increase Cardiorespiratory endurance during the fitness development section as directed by the instructor.
2. Practice grips and stances using the reciprocal task sheet as directed by the instructor.
3. Demonstrate cooperative skills playing Pentabridge Hustle.

National Standards Met in this Lesson: **1, 2, 4, 5, 6**

INSTRUCTIONAL ACTIVITIES	ORGANIZATION TEACHING HINTS
INTRODUCTORY ACTIVITY (2 – 3 MINUTES)	
Ball Activities	**See DPESS Chapter 14 for details.** Scattered formation.
FITNESS DEVELOPMENT (8 – 12 MINUTES)	
Walk, Jog, Sprint 1 Whistle = Walk 2 Whistles = Jog 3 Whistles = Sprint	**See DPESS Chapter 16 for details.** Direct moving around track and varying activity with whistle signal for 10 minutes. Watch students response to vigorous movement and adjust directions accordingly.
Strength Exercises Push-ups; Inclined wall push-ups; Curl-ups; Curl-ups with twist; Reverse push-ups Push-ups are performed in the prone position.	**See DPESS Chapter 16 for details.**
LESSON FOCUS (15 – 20 MINUTES)	
Review following skills Grips Addressing Ball Review safe practice techniques. Practice will take place with task sheets.	**See DPESS Chapter 20 for details.** Scattered formation. Have student practice without ball following each review. Demonstration. Direct students to get "Toe to Toe", with someone to create partners.
Explain each Task Sheet	Direct students to get a 7 or 9 iron, a clipboard with pencil and Task Sheets 2, 3, and 4.
Demonstrate swings: 1/2 swing 3/4 swing Full swing	Student picks up a #9 iron and 6 Whiffle balls. Scattered formation directed by teacher. Practice each swing without ball following demonstration. Practice each swing with each set of balls at practice area.
Review/Demonstrate Pitch Shot	Direct students to re-group for demonstration. Assign to practice alone with 6 balls and then re-group.
Review/Demonstrate Chip Shot	Following demonstration, assign to practice alone with 6 balls.

The first recorded golf game took place in Scotland in 1456.

INSTRUCTIONAL ACTIVITIES	ORGANIZATION TEACHING HINTS
GAME (5 MINUTES)	
Pentabridge Hustle	**See DPESS Chapter 14 for details.** Play Whistle Mixer to create groups of 5. 4 students make bridges that the others go under. As soon as a student exits the last bridge they form a new one. Then the first "bridge" becomes the "hustler". You can add locomotor challenges before creating a new bridge.

EVALUATION/REVIEW AND CHEER

Discuss main elements of swings practiced during the class period.
In what position are push-ups performed?
In what year was the first recorded game of golf played?

Cheer: Give me a "G"; Give me an "O"; Give me an "L"; Give me an "F"; What does that spell? Golf! Yea!

RECIPROCAL TASK SHEET 2: GRIPS

Name: ______________________________

Name: ______________________________

Directions: Work with a partner. Your partner will read the task sheet to you. Record dates and check appropriate response for each checkpoint for the grip. Complete the grip practice with your partner a minimum of five times.

GRIPS* Check hand positions	**DATES**							
(Record date of practice)								
BASEBALL GRIP								
LEFT HAND	**Yes**	**No**	**Yes**	**No**	**Yes**	**No**	**Yes**	**No**
1. Hand placed so only cap of club is extended beyond palm.								
2. Club head is resting flat on its sole and is squarely aligned with target.								
3. Back of hand facing toward target.								
4. Fingers gripped around club so the grip of the club lies diagonally across the second joint of the index finger.								
5. No spaces between fingers.								
6. Thumb positioned slightly to right of the top of the grip.								
7. V formed by thumb and index finger points to right shoulder when club placed squarely in front of body.								
RIGHT HAND								
1. Place right hand on grip as though you were slapping grip (palm facing target).								
2. Grip fingers around club so left thumb fits snugly in palm of right hand.								
3. Little finger touches index finger of left hand.								
4. No spaces between fingers.								
5. V formed by thumb and index finger points to right of chin.								
OVERLAPPING OR VARDON GRIP See photo to right. * The check points refer to right handed golfers.	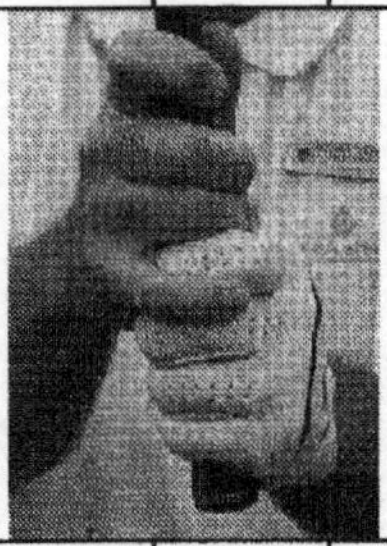							
1. Little finger of right hand overlaps the index finger of left hand.								
INTERLOCKING GRIP (Same as 10 finger or baseball grip except:)								
1. Little finger of right hand interlocks the index finger of left hand.								

RECIPROCAL TASK SHEET 3: ADDRESS

Name: ________________________________

Name: ________________________________

Directions: Work with a partner. Your partner will read the task sheet to you as you perform the address. Record the dates and check the appropriate response for each checkpoint for the address. Execute the address by yourself and with your partner reading to you a minimum of five times. Rotate after five times.

ADDRESS ROUTINE	**DATES**							
(Record date of practice)								
ADDRESS (Address routine)	**Yes**	**No**	**Yes**	**No**	**Yes**	**No**	**Yes**	**No**
1. Assume correct grip. (Review Task Sheet)								
2. Stand behind ball and sight target. (Choose a tree, post, etc. to act as target)								
3. Move up to side of ball, with arms extended place the club head down directly behind the ball so the club head is perpendicular or "square" to the intended line of flight.								
4. Place your feet so the ball is opposite the center of your stance.								
5. Weight is evenly distributed through feet.								
6. Knees relaxed – not hyper-extended.								
7. Body bent slightly forward from hips.								
8. Shoulders relaxed so arms hang freely from body.								
9. Arms and shoulders form triangle with hands as the apex of the triangle.								
10. Feel comfortable.								

Do you look like this?

RECIPROCAL TASK SHEET 4: STANCES

Name: ________________________________

Directions: Work with a partner. Partner reads task sheet as you perform. Record the dates and check the appropriate response for each check point for the stances. Perform each task 5 times alternating practice turns with your partner.

STANCE	**DATES**							
(Record date of practice)								
SQUARE OR PARALLEL	**Yes**	**No**	**Yes**	**No**	**Yes**	**No**	**Yes**	**No**
1. Feet approximately shoulder width apart.								
2. Weight evenly distributed.								
3. Knees relaxed – not hyper-extended.								
4. Toes pointed toward intended line of flight.								
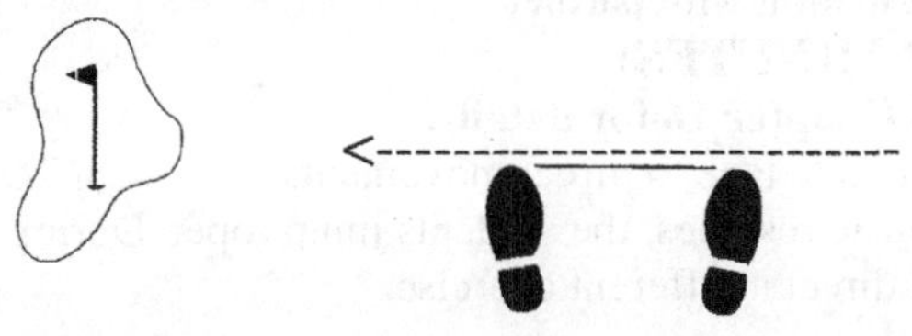 Square								
OPEN								
1. Feet 8-10 inches apart.								
2. Weight evenly distributed.								
3. Knees relaxed – not hyper-extended.								
4. Toes appointed toward intended line of sight.								
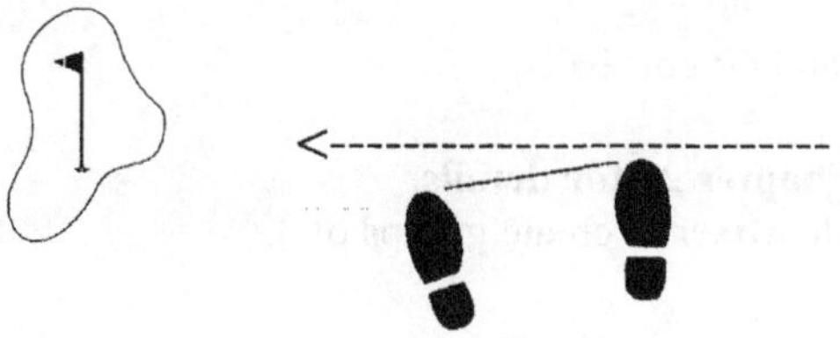 Open								
CLOSED								
1. Feet slightly more than shoulder width apart.								
2. Weight evenly distributed.								
3. Knees relaxed – not hyper-extended.								
4. Toes pointed toward intended line of flight.								
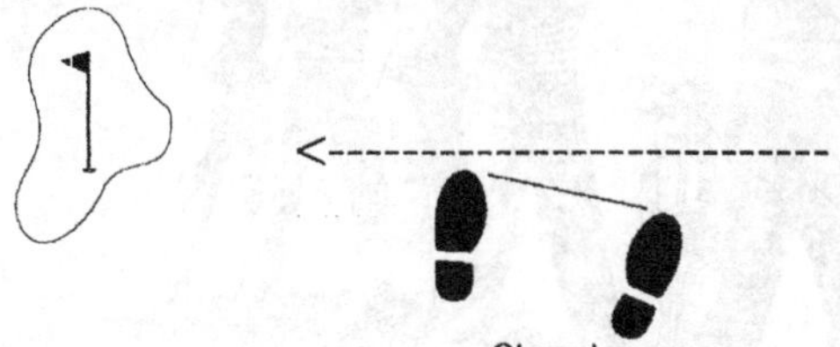 Closed								

Golf Lesson Plan 6

EQUIPMENT:

1 Frisbee per student
1 nine iron per student
1 five iron per student
CD/Cassette Player
Continuity exercise CD/tape
Reciprocal Task Sheet 5
5 Whiffle balls per student

OBJECTIVES:

The student will:

1. Demonstrate jump roping for 30 seconds as demonstrated by the instructor.
2. Demonstrate proper Frisbee keep away as demonstrated by the instructor.

National Standards Met in this Lesson: **1, 2, 4, 5, 6**

INSTRUCTIONAL ACTIVITIES	ORGANIZATION TEACHING HINTS

INTRODUCTORY ACTIVITY (2 – 3 MINUTES)

Over, Under and Around

See DPESS Chapter 14 for details.
Use elbow-to-elbow or back-to-back to form partners.
Scattered formation with partner.

FITNESS DEVELOPMENT (8 – 12 MINUTES)

Continuity exercises

Create a CD/cassette tape with 30 – 35 seconds of music and 20 seconds of silence. During the music, the students will jump rope. When the silence begins, instruct the students to do an exercise i.e. push-ups; curl ups; etc.

See DPESS Chapter 16 for details.
Use a CD/cassette tape to direct movements.
When the music resumes, the students jump rope. During each silence direct a different exercise.

If you jump rope for an hour, you can burn about 1300 calories.

LESSON FOCUS (15 – 20 MINUTES)

Reciprocal Task Sheet Activities
For Full Swing

Distribute task sheets.

There are driving ranges where players can go to practice their swing and hit golf balls.

GAME (5 MINUTES)

Frisbee Keep Away

Change places when center player catches Frisbee or on the teacher's signal.

See DPESS Chapter 20 for details.
Use the Whistle Mixer to create groups of 3.

There over a dozen different versions of Frisbee games.

EVALUATION/REVIEW AND CHEER

Discuss elements of the full swing.
How many calories can you burn jumping rope for one hour?
What is a driving range?
What muscles were used in class today?

Cheer: We Love to Golf

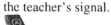

RECIPROCAL TASK SHEET 5: FULL SWING

Name: ____

Directions: Work with a partner. Record the dates and check the appropriate response for each checkpoint for the full swing. Have your partner check you a minimum of 5 – 10 times. See your instructor for additional task sheets. Each person needs his or her own task sheet. Partner (observer) – try to observe no more than two checkpoints at one time.

	DATES							
(Record date of practice)								
BACKSWING (As club begins to move back:)	**Yes**	**No**	**Yes**	**No**	**Yes**	**No**	**Yes**	**No**
1. Head – head down, eyes on ball.								
2. Club – brushes back against ground in an arc.								
3. Arms – left arm straight, right elbow begins to bend, wrists begin to cock.								
4. Trunk – inclined forward, gives naturally in direction of BACKSWING.								
5. Legs – left knee turns inward, right leg straight.								
TOP OF BACKSWING								
1. Head – head down, eyes looking over left shoulder at ball.								
2. Arms – left elbow remains extended (relaxed) while right elbow is pointing down, wrists are cocked.								
3. Trunk – inclined forward, rotated to right from hips.								
4. Feet – most weight is on right foot and only left heel has lifted slightly.								
5. Grip – firm grip maintained – last 3 fingers of left hand squeezed around club grip.								
DOWNSWING								
1. Head – head down.								
2. Arms – left arm remains extended, right elbow coming into side, wrists remain cocked as trunk uncoils.								
3. Trunk – uncoils and turns to left, weight shifting to left foot.								
4. Legs – left knee straightens and right knee begins to turn inward.								
CONTACT								
1. Head – head down and eyes on ball.								
2. Arms – elbows straight.								
3. Trunk – rotated slightly left.								
4. Club – clubface contacting ball squarely.								
FOLLOW-THROUGH								
1. Head – head down until right shoulder hits chin.								
2. Arms – right arm is extended and left arm bent, hands high.								
3. Trunk – body remains balanced as hips and shoulders (center of waist) turn to face target.								

RECIPROCAL TASK SHEET 6: FULL SWING – #5 IRON WITH PLASTIC BALLS

Name: ______________________________

Directions: You and your partner each need your own task sheets to write on. Go to the field together and take a #5 iron and 10 plastic balls. You will take turns hitting 10 balls. Record the number of balls you hit up in the air out of 10. Each day you and your partner should hit a minimum of 30 shots each. If you swing and miss you need not count it. Each person needs his or her own task sheet. You may record your progress or have your partner record this.

Date	# Out of 10	# Out of 10	# Out of 10	# Out of 10	# Out of 10	# Out of 10	# Out of 10	Total
1.								
2.								
3.								
4.								
5.								
6.								
7.								
8.								
9.								
10.								

BE CAREFUL WHERE YOU WALK------------------------------PEOPLE ARE SWINGING!

NO ONE RETRIEVES BALLS UNTIL EVERYONE HAS HIT AND SIGNAL IS GIVEN

Golf Lesson Plan 7

EQUIPMENT:
1 Nine iron per student
6 Whiffle golf balls per student
15 Hula-hoops
Scavenger Hunt Instructions
2 large team Tug of War ropes

OBJECTIVES:
The student will:
1. Cooperate with group members during the fitness scavenger hunt as directed by the instructor.
2. Demonstrate proper full swing technique as demonstrated by the instructor.

National Standards Met in this Lesson: **1, 2, 4, 5, 6**

INSTRUCTIONAL ACTIVITIES	ORGANIZATION TEACHING HINTS

INTRODUCTORY ACTIVITY (2 – 3 MINUTES)

Formation Rhythmic Running

See DPESS Chapter 14 for details.
Scattered formation.

FITNESS DEVELOPMENT (8 – 12 MINUTES)

Fitness Scavenger Hunt
Each group is given a list directing them to designated areas to find directions for exercise/activity at that location.

The original scavenger hunt was created by Elsa Maxwell in the modern era.

See DPESS Chapter 16 for details.
Use Whistle Mixer to create groups of 3.
Each group is assigned a different starting point.
Each station lists exercises that work the entire body.

LESSON FOCUS (15 – 20 MINUTES)

Practice:
- Pitch Shot
- Chip Shot
- Full Swing

See DPESS Chapter 20 for details.
Scattered along safe zone
Set up targets to hit towards:
- Hoops
- Flags
- Ropes
- Cones

Par is the number of strokes that a skilled golfer should require to complete the hole.

GAME (5 MINUTES)

Team Tug of War

See DPESS Chapter 18 for details.
Use management game to create 4 teams. Two teams share one large Tug of War rope.

Tug-of-War was part of the Olympic Games from 1900 to 1920.

EVALUATION/REVIEW AND CHEER

Review elements of chip, pitch, and full swing.
Discuss Tug of War games. Student created cheer.

Golf Lesson Plan 8

EQUIPMENT:

Task Sheets: Sand Traps, Full Swing
Pencils
9 Iron or pitching wedge for 1/2 class
Continuity Exercise CD/Tape
Clipboards
5 Iron or wood for 1/2 class
CD/Cassette Player
Distance Markers/Flags

OBJECTIVES:

The student will:

1. Increase cardiovascular endurance during the fitness development as directed by the instructor.
2. Improve sand trap shot technique as demonstrated by the instructor.

National Standards Met in this Lesson: **1, 2, 3, 4, 5, 6**

INSTRUCTIONAL ACTIVITIES | **ORGANIZATION TEACHING HINTS**

INTRODUCTORY ACTIVITY (2 – 3 MINUTES)

Bean Bag Touch and Go
On signal, run to beanbag, touch it and run again.
Increase challenges with instructions during Freeze.

See DPESS Chapter 14 for details.
Scattered formation. Establish "Freeze".
Examples: Touch 5 blue bean bags and sprint; Touch 3 bean bags and skip; etc

Bean bags are commonly used for juggling.

FITNESS DEVELOPMENT (8 – 12 MINUTES)

Continuity Exercises

See DPESS Chapter 16 for details.

This activity will increase cardiovascular strength and endurance.

LESSON FOCUS AND GAME COMBINED TODAY (20 MINUTES)

Sand Trap Shots
Full Swing Review

Demonstrate hitting from sand using "Running Long Jump Area"

See DPESS Chapter 20 for details.
Divide group in half.
Group 1: Use Reciprocal Task Sheet 7: Full Swing 5 iron. Explain Task Sheet. Direct to area set up.
Group 2: Use Sand Trap Reciprocal Task Sheet 8 working in pairs.

Sand Traps are also called "bunkers."

EVALUATION/REVIEW AND CHEER

Review Sand Trap techniques.

Cheer: Sand Traps... Oh, Dear!

RECIPROCAL TASK SHEET 7: FULL SWING #5 IRON

Name: ______________________________ **Date** ________________

Directions: You and your partner each need your own task sheets to write on. Go to the field together and take a #5 iron and 10 balls. You will take turns hitting 10 balls and recording the spot where the ball hit for each shot. Designate where the ball hits by placing the number of the shot on the task sheet. Each day you and your partner should hit a minimum of 20 shots each so numbers 1-20 should show on your task sheet. If you swing and miss you need not count it.

120 yards ____

100 yards ____

80 yards ____

60 yards ____

40 yards ____

20 yards ____

Hitting line ____

BE CAREFUL WHERE YOU WALK ------------------------------------PEOPLE ARE SWINGING!

NO ONE RETRIEVES BALLS UNTIL EVERYONE HAS HIT AND SIGNAL IS GIVEN

RECIPROCAL TASK SHEET 8: SAND TRAPS

Name: ______________________________

Directions: Work with a partner. Each person has his or her own task sheet. One person is the "doer" while the other person is the "observer". Observer reads information/instructions to the doer, offers verbal feedback and places a check in the "yes" or "no" column recording the performance of their partner. Record the date of the practice. Complete the task sheet until you are directed to "change roles". Then, the "doer" becomes the "observer". Each person has his/her own task sheet.

	DATES							
(Record date of practice)								
	Yes	**No**	**Yes**	**No**	**Yes**	**No**	**Yes**	**No**
1. Use open stance.								
2. Keep hands ahead of ball at Address.								
3. Hit down on ball, do not scoop it up.								
4. Execute chip shot with arms and shoulders – no body motion.								
5. Ball hit out of trap on first contact.								
6. Change roles with partner.								

Golf Lesson Plan 9

EQUIPMENT:

Putting greens
1 Putter per student
1 golf ball per student
1 Task Sheet per student
4 Cones
Exercise Station Task Sheets for Cones
1 Clipboard and pencil per 2 students

OBJECTIVES:

The student will:

1. Increase flexibility during the fitness development as directed by the instructor.
2. Perform putting technique using the reciprocal task sheet as demonstrated by the instructor.

National Standards Met in this Lesson: **1, 2, 3, 4, 5, 6**

INSTRUCTIONAL ACTIVITIES	ORGANIZATION TEACHING HINTS
INTRODUCTORY ACTIVITY (2 – 3 MINUTES)	
Mirror Drill in Place	**See DPESS Chapter 14 for details.** Scattered formation with a partner.
FITNESS DEVELOPMENT (8 – 12 MINUTES)	
Stretching Lower Leg Stretch Achilles Tendon Stretch Balance Beam Stretch Side Leg Stretch Groin Stretch Cross-Legged Stretch Body Twist Standing Hip Bend Elbow Grab Stretch	**See DPESS Chapter 16 for details.** Students scattered. Place arms on wall or fence for support Make task sheet for each cone

The Achilles tendon is attached to the gastrocnemius and soleus muscles to the calcaneus bone.

INSTRUCTIONAL ACTIVITIES	ORGANIZATION TEACHING HINTS
Aerobic Activity **Four Corners** Skipping Jogging Sliding Running backwards Jumping Leaping Hopping Galloping	**See DPESS Chapter 16 for details.** Set up 4 cones creating a square. Each cone should list two locomotor activities on a Task Sheet. Student executes the movement listed on the task sheet on the cone until she gets to next cone. Music CD/tape directs length of aerobic exercising.
Stretch Activities Partner Resistance Exercises	**See DPESS Chapter 16 for details.**

INSTRUCTIONAL ACTIVITIES | **ORGANIZATION TEACHING HINTS**

LESSON FOCUS (15 – 20 MINUTES)

Putting

See DPESS Chapter 20 for details.

The direction of growth of individual blades of grass often affects the roll of a golf ball and is called the "grain." This is important to know when putting.

Review technique
Grip; Stance
Address; Aiming
Explain Putting Task Sheet

Scatter formation

Use Management Game (i.e. Back to Back/Elbow to Elbow) to make pairs.

The slope of the green is called the "break."

GAME (5 MINUTES)

Putting Challenge

With partner on putting carpet/green.

1. Pick a spot to putt from.
2. Challenge your partner and see who can get the ball into the hole in the least number of putts.
3. Let your partner select a point to put from. Same rules.
4. Repeat.
5.

High 5 your partner upon completion.

Return equipment.

Frisbee Freedom
Play Frisbee toss with partner.

See DPESS Chapter 20 for details.
Select a safe place to play.

EVALUATION/REVIEW AND CHEER

Review elements involved in proper putting technique.

Cheer: Golf swings!

RECIPROCAL TASK SHEET 9: PUTTING

Name: ________________________________

Name: ________________________________

Objective: The student will putt the ball from various distances using technique demonstrated in class.

Instructions:
1. You will work with a partner and check each other off on this task sheet.
2. Read the instruction to your partner.
3. Give your partner verbal feedback on the task.
4. Change roles upon completion of each task.
5. Go to a putting green for your practice.

TASKS	PARTNER 1		PARTNER 2	
	Yes	No	Yes	No
1. Address the ball.				
2. Aim at hole. Begin each shot with #1 and #2.				
3. Stand 5 feet from the hole and putt. Repeat 5 times. Record number of times ball goes into hole on 1 putt.				
4. Stand 10 feet from hole and putt. Record how many holes you make in 3 or less putts.				

Turn in Task Sheet and Clip Board.

Golf Lesson Plan 10

EQUIPMENT:

1 Partner Tug of War Rope per 2 students
1 #9 iron per student
1 Clipboard, pencil per 2 students
Continuity CD/Tape for Circuits (35 seconds music, 15 seconds silence)
CD/Cassette Player
10 Golf balls per student
Task Sheets 10 and 11 per student

OBJECTIVES:

The student will:

1. Increase muscular and cardiovascular strength during the fitness development as directed by the instructor.
2. Utilize the 9 iron and 3 woods properly as demonstrated by the instructor.

National Standards Met in this Lesson: 1, 2, 4, 5, 6

INSTRUCTIONAL ACTIVITIES | **ORGANIZATION TEACHING HINTS**

INTRODUCTORY ACTIVITY (2 – 3 MINUTES)

Partner Tug of War Activities
Partner pulls: Side to side; Facing; Crab position hooked on foot; Back to back.

See DPESS Chapter 18 for details.

Use elbow-to-elbow to make pairs.

Tug-of-War was practiced in ancient Egypt and China. It was used as a way to strengthen warriors.

FITNESS DEVELOPMENT (8 – 12 MINUTES)

Circuit Training
Activities include:
Jump rope
Chair Squats
Posterior Shoulder Stretch
Should Extension
Trunk Rotation Stretch
Shoulder Abduction/Flexion/Rotation
Trunk Forward Flexion Stretch
Push-ups
Back Arch and Sag
Abdominal Crunches
Hamstring Stretch
Bent-over Row
Jogging

See DPESS Chapter 16 for details.

Use Whistle Mixer to create groups of 4-5.

Continuity CD/tape to signal the duration of exercise at each station. Station work: 1 minute of exercise followed by 10-second interval for rest and preparation for the next station.

It is important if circuit training is to be effective that quality exercise be performed at each station.

This circuit is designed specifically for golf.

Abdominal crunches work primarily the rectus abdominis muscle.

LESSON FOCUS (15 – 20 MINUTES)

Full Swing
Go over instructions on each task sheet.
Have students take: Two golf clubs (9 iron and 3 wood), a clipboard, task sheets, and 10 golf balls each. Go to the practice area.

See DPESS Chapter 20 for details.
Explain Reciprocal Task Sheets 10 and 11.
Review elements of full swing. Demonstrate with the wood.
Use "Back to Back" to create pairs.

While practicing the Full Swing, make sure that no one is behind you.

INSTRUCTIONAL ACTIVITIES	ORGANIZATION TEACHING HINTS

GAME (5 MINUTES)

Nine Lives
Any number of fleece balls can be used-the more the better. At a signal by the instructor, players scramble for a ball and hit as many people below the waist with it as possible. Once a player has been hit nine times, he/she leaves the game and stands out of bounds for a count of 25.

Scatter formation.
Cone off 50' area. Place 10 fleece balls around perimeter of area.
Remind the students about fair play and the importance of keeping an accurate count of the number of hits they have received. Compare the experience to keeping a golf score.
A player may have only one ball at a time.
A hit above the shoulders eliminates the thrower.

EVALUATION/REVIEW AND CHEER

Discuss:

1. What muscles do abdominal crunches work?
2. Importance of a one piece take-away.
3. What may happen if the swing goes past parallel at the top of the full swing?
4. Safety procedures when practicing full swing.

Cheer: 2...4...6...8...Hitting a golf ball can be great.

RECIPROCAL TASK SHEET 10: FULL SWING #9 IRON

Name: ______________________________

Directions: You and your partner take a task sheet for yourself and go to the field with a #9 iron and 10 balls. You will take turns hitting 10 balls and recording the spot where the ball hit for each shot. Designate where the ball hits by placing the number of the shots on the task sheet. Each day you and your partner should hit a minimum of 20 shots each so numbers 1-20 should show on your task sheet. If you swing and miss you need not count it.

Dates			
125 yards			
90 yards			
80 yards			
70 yards			
60 yards			
50 yards			
40 yards			
30 yards			
20 yards			
10 yards			
Hitting line			

BE CAREFUL WHERE YOU WALK -----------------------------------PEOPLE ARE SWINGING!

NO ONE RETRIEVES BALLS UNTIL EVERYONE HAS HIT AND A SIGNAL IS GIVEN BY THE TEACHER

Signature of partner: ______________________________

RECIPROCAL TASK SHEET 11: FULL SWING #3 WOOD

Name: ______________________________

Directions: Use your own task sheet and have your partner watch you and record the results. You and your partner go to the field and take a #3 wood and 10 balls. You will take turns hitting 10 balls and recording the spot where the ball hit for each shot. Designate where the ball hits by placing the number of the shot on the task sheet. Each day you and your partner should hit a minimum of 20 shots each so numbers 1-20 should show on your task sheet. If you swing and miss you need not count it.

120 yards ______________________________

100 yards ______________________________

80 yards ______________________________

60 yards ______________________________

40 yards ______________________________

20 yards ______________________________

Hitting line ______________________________

BE CAREFUL WHERE YOU WALK ----------------------------------PEOPLE ARE SWINGING!

NO ONE RETRIEVES BALLS UNTIL EVERYONE HAS HIT AND A SIGNAL IS GIVEN

Signature of partner: ______________________________

Golf Lesson Plan 11

EQUIPMENT:

1 Clipboard and pencil per 2 students
1 9 and 7 iron per 2 students
Marked area for "Pitch and Run" Station
CD/Cassette Player
Task Sheet 12 and 13 for each student
5 Balls per student
Marked area for "Pitch Shot"
12-minute music CD/tape 120-150 beats per min.
Music CD/Tape 5 minutes long with 10 seconds of silence following 30 seconds of music.

OBJECTIVES:

The student will:

1. Demonstrate the pitch shot with the safety rules in mind as directed by the instructor.

National Standards Met in this Lesson: **1, 2, 4, 5, 6**

INSTRUCTIONAL ACTIVITIES / **ORGANIZATION TEACHING HINTS**

INTRODUCTORY ACTIVITY (2 – 3 MINUTES)

Mirror Drill in Place

See DPESS Chapter 14 for details.
Use a management game to make pairs. Identify first leader/follower. Signal time for leader and follower to change roles after approximately 30-40 seconds.

FITNESS DEVELOPMENT (8 – 12 MINUTES)

Rhythmic Aerobic Exercise to Music

Standing Hip Bend	40 seconds
Trunk Twist	30 seconds
Slides each direction	30 seconds
Skip around cones	30 seconds
Jumping Jacks	30 seconds
Triceps Push-Ups	30 seconds
Curl-Ups	30 seconds
Knee Touch Curl-Ups	30 seconds
Push-Ups	30 seconds
Gallop around cones	30 seconds
Jump Rope	1 minutes
Lower Leg Stretch	30 seconds
Balance Beam Stretch	30 seconds
Rocking Chair	30 seconds
Carioca around cones	1 minutes
Jog in place	
Calf Stretch	

See DPESS Chapter 16 for details.
Create a music CD/tape 120-150 beats per minute or use Aerobic Exercise CD/Tape.

Scatter formation within a coned area in the teaching area.

See DPESS Chapter 16 for details.

Jumping jacks are also called side straddle hop in the military.

LESSON FOCUS (15 – 20 MINUTES)

Pitch Shot
Review the Pitch Shot
Review safety rules.
Instruct students how and when to change stations.

Collect Task Sheets upon completion of activity.

See DPESS Chapter 20 for details.
Use management game to divide class in half. Assign group 1 to begin with Task Sheet 12. Group 2 should begin with Task Sheet 13.
Direct students to take 9 and 7 irons, 10 balls, Task Sheets 12 and 13 and clipboard to their assigned area.

Most major championships courses have a par of 70 or 71.

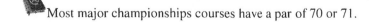

INSTRUCTIONAL ACTIVITIES	ORGANIZATION TEACHING HINTS

GAME (5 MINUTES)

Musical Hoops (Variation of Hoops on the Ground)
Hoops, one fewer than the number of students, placed on the floor. Players are given a locomotor movement to do around the hoops while the music is played.

See DPESS Chapter 14 for details.
Scattered formation.
When the music stops, the students step inside and empty hoop. One student per hoop. Repeat with another locomotor movement. Examples are: slide, gallop, run, skip, leap, and carioca.

Musical Hoops derived from the game of "musical chairs."

EVALUATION/REVIEW AND CHEER

Discuss:
What muscles were used today?
What did the military call Jumping Jacks?
Were you successful during Pitch and Run Activities? What activities need more practice?
What is the par on most championship golf courses?
From where was musical hoops derived?

Cheer:
Give me a par, par, par; Give me a birdie, birdie, birdie; Give me an Eagle, Eagle, Eagle; Give me an H, O, L, E, (2 times) I, N, ONE
Hole in One (clap, clap)
All of us.
(Baseball Cheer Take-Off)

RECIPROCAL TASK SHEET 12: PITCH AND RUN – #7 IRON

Name: ______________________________ **Date:** ______________

Directions: You and your partner go to the area marked for the "Pitch and Run" and take a #7 iron and 10 balls. Stand anywhere around the 30 foot circle (starting line) and record where the ball comes to rest by writing the number of the shot on the target. Each practice must consist of a minimum of 20 shots for each person.

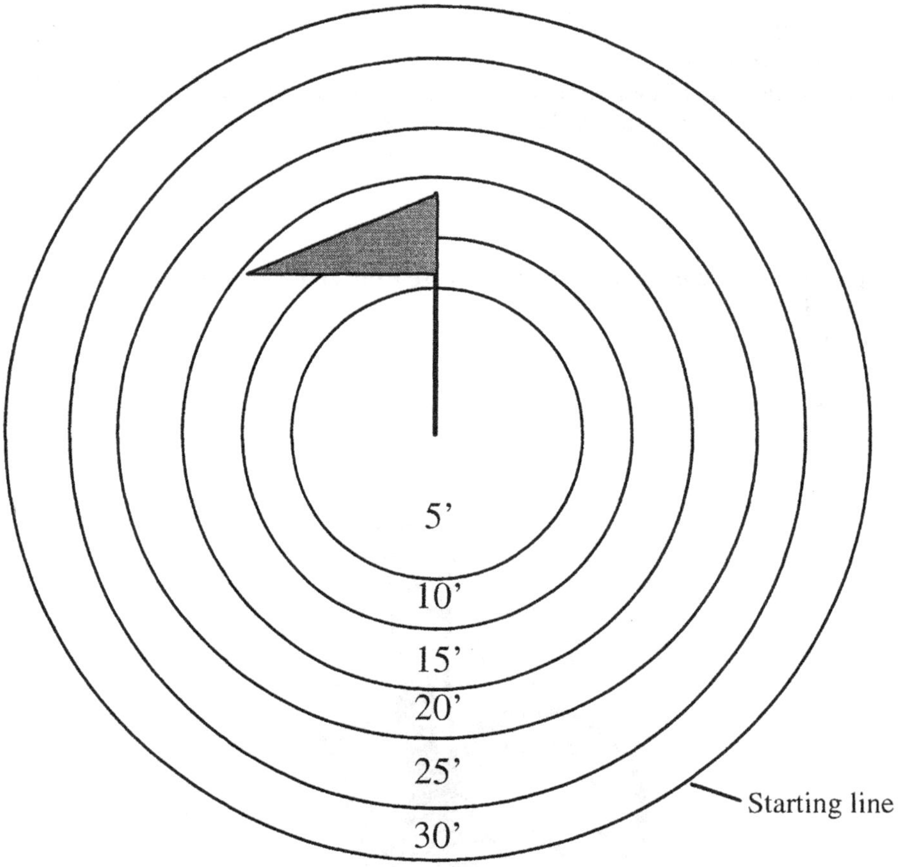

NO ONE RETRIEVES BALLS UNTIL EVERYONE HAS HIT

Partner's signature: ______________________________

RECIPROCAL TASK SHEET 13: PITCH SHOT #9 IRON

Name: ______________________________ **Date:** ________________

Directions: You and your partner go to the area marked for the "Pitch Shot" and take a #9 iron and 10 balls. Stand anywhere around the 75 foot circle (starting line) and record where the ball comes to rest by writing the number of the shot on the target. The ball must carry in the air to the 50 foot restraining line before it is considered a pitch shot

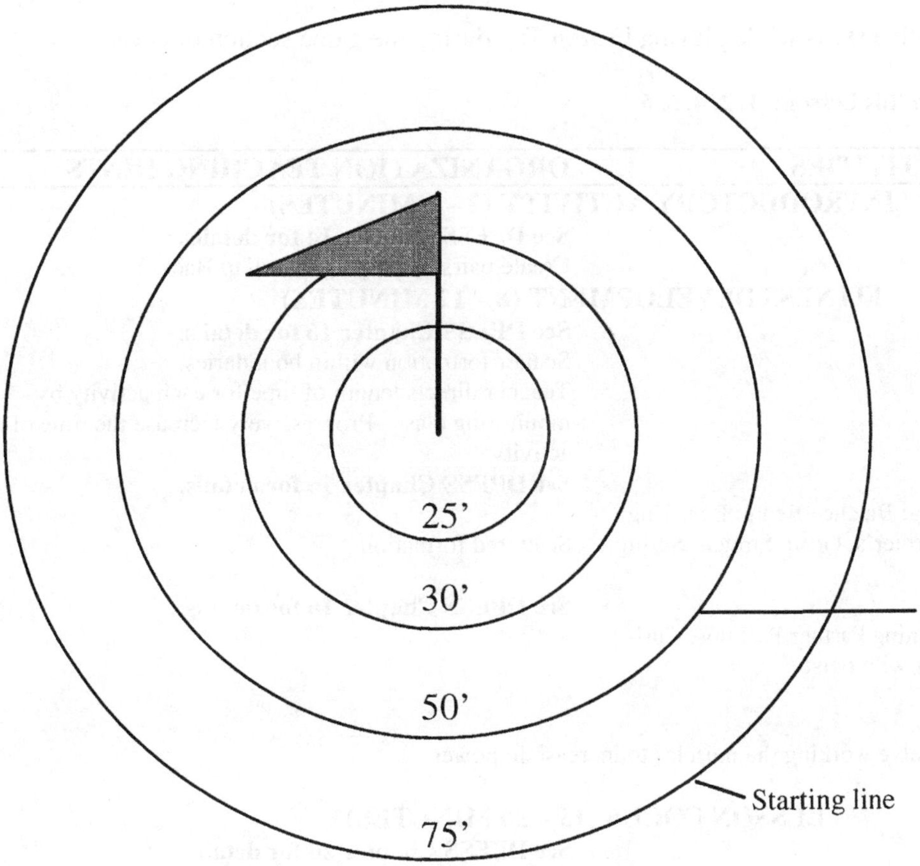

BE CAREFUL THAT NO ONE IS ON THE OPPOSITE SIDE OF THE TARGET WHEN HITTING. YOU MAY GET HIT.

NO ONE RETRIEVES BALLS UNTIL EVERYONE HAS HIT!

Partner's signature: ______________________________

Golf Lesson Plan 12

EQUIPMENT:

1 7 iron per 2 student
Clipboard and pencil per 2 students
5 balls per student

1 Putter per 2 students
Task Sheets 14, 15, and 16 for each student
Whistle

OBJECTIVES:

The student will:

1. Participate in walk-jog-sprint to improve aerobic capacity.
2. Execute stretching and strengthening activities to improve fitness in those areas.
3. Improve putting accuracy by practicing strokes with the use of the task sheet as directed by the instructor.
4. Demonstrate cooperative skills while playing Frozen Tag during the game section of class.

National Standards Met in this Lesson: 1, 2, 4, 5, 6

INSTRUCTIONAL ACTIVITIES	ORGANIZATION TEACHING HINTS
INTRODUCTORY ACTIVITY (2 – 3 MINUTES)	
New Leader	**See DPESS Chapter 14 for details.**
	Create pairs by playing "Back to Back."
FITNESS DEVELOPMENT (8 – 12 MINUTES)	
Walk-Jog-Sprint	**See DPESS Chapter 16 for details.**
1 Whistle = Sprint	Scatter formation within boundaries.
2 Whistle = Walk	Teacher directs length of time for each activity by
3 Whistle = Jog	monitoring class. Progressively increase the time of each activity.
Stretch	**See DPESS Chapter 16 for details.**
Achilles Tendon; Lower Leg; Balance Beam; Bear Hug; Leg Pick-Up; Side Leg; Hurdler's; Groin Stretch; Sitting Toe Touch; Body Twist	Scattered formation
Strength	**See DPESS Chapter 16 for details.**
Crab Walk; Push-ups; Reclining Partner Pull-ups; Curl-ups; Reverse curls; Curl-ups with twist	

 Strength exercises involve working the muscles to increase in power.

LESSON FOCUS (15 – 20 MINUTES)

Pitch and Run Game	**See DPESS Chapter 20 for details.**
Putting Station	Stations
Explain Task Sheets 14 and 15 and Score Card.	Using management technique to divide class in half.
Pitch and Run Game Equipment	Play Elbow to Elbow to create pairs in each group.
10 balls per 2 students	
1 7 iron per 2 students	Assign groups to begin at Putting or Pitch and Run Game.
2 Task Sheet 14's, clipboard and pencil	Explain how and when to change stations. Explain Score
Putting	Card.
10 balls	
1 putter per 2 students	Direct students to pick up equipment needed for their first
Task Sheet 12 and 13 for each student	station.
Clipboard and pencil	

 A handicap is a numerical measure of an amateur golfer's ability to play golf over 18 holes

INSTRUCTIONAL ACTIVITIES	ORGANIZATION TEACHING HINTS

GAME (5 MINUTES)

Frozen Tag	**See DPESS Chapter 14 for details.** Scatter formation. Select several "its".
Freeze tag is called "Koori Oni" in Japan.	

EVALUATION/REVIEW AND CHEER

Discuss results of day's activities.
Describe what strengthening exercises do for your body.
What does "handicap" mean in golf?
What is Freeze Tag called in Japan?

Cheer: 2, 4, 6, 8 Playing Golf is Really Great!

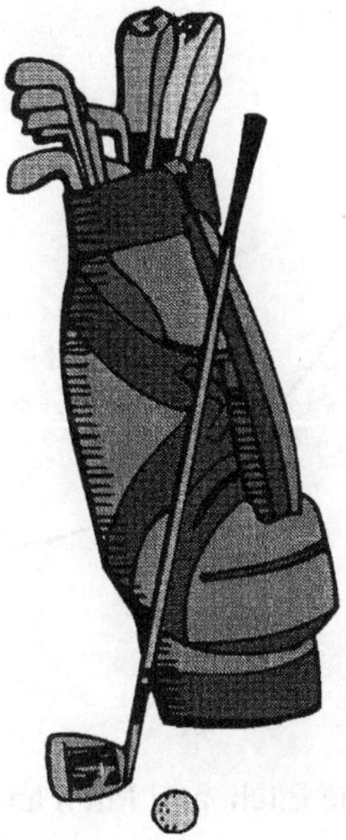

TASK SHEET 14: PITCH AND PITCH & RUN GAME

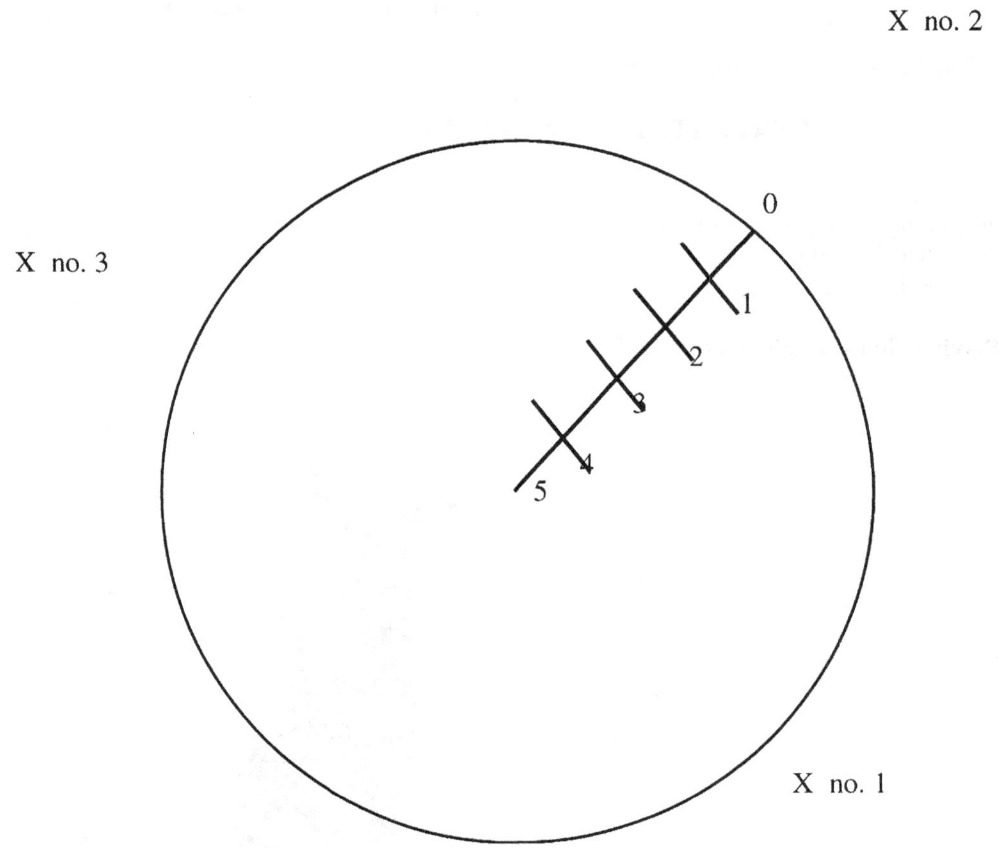

Instructions: Report to the Pitch, and Pitch and Run game station on the field with your partner. Standing at position number 1 (no. 1), each person hits ten balls and partner records scores. Standing at position number 2 (no. 2), each person hits ten balls and partner records scores. Stand at position number (no. 3). Each person hits ten balls and records the scores. To score, your partner takes rope around to each ball hit, and measures the distance from the stake to decide your score. Scores are 5 points, 4 points, 3 points, 2 points, 1 point, 0 points, successively, from each stake. The highest score of all ten balls wins the round for that position.

SCORE CARD

Name: ______________________________

Directions: Check the appropriate column for the number of points you score on each ball. Do this for each position.

	Trials	5 pts.	4 pts.	3 pts.	2 pts.	1 pt.	0 pts.
		Points					
	1						
	2						
	3						
	4						
	5						
Position No. 1	**6**						
	7						
	8						
	9						
	10						
	Total						
	1						
	2						
	3						
	4						
	5						
Position No. 2	**6**						
	7						
	8						
	9						
	10						
	Total						
	1						
	2						
	3						
	4						
	5						
Position No. 3	**6**						
	7						
	8						
	9						
	10						
	Total						
	Grand Total						

Winner's Name ______________________________

Partner's Name ______________________________

RECIPROCAL TASK SHEET 15: PUTTING
SHORT PUTTS

Directions: You and your partner go to the area set up for short putts and take 5 balls and a putter with you. Take 10 trials each from a distance of 1', 3', 5', 7', and 10' and record the number made.

		1'	3'	5'	7'	10'	Total
1st trial	**(1 out of 10)**						
2nd trial	"						
3rd trail	"						
4th trial	"						
5th trial	"						
6th trial	"						
7th trial	"						
8th trial	"						
9th trial	"						

RECIPROCAL TASK SHEET 16: PUTTING
LONG PUTTS

Directions: You and your partner go to the indoor area set up for long putts and take 5 balls and a putter with you. Take 10 trials each and record the number of putts it took you to get the ball into the cup from a distance of 15 feet, 20 feet, 25 feet, and 30 feet.

Distance	1	2	3	4	5	6	7	8	9	10
15'										
20'										
25'										
30'										

Golf Lesson Plan 13

EQUIPMENT:

Flag "Football" belts for 1/2 class
CD/Cassette Player
Long Rope and 2 standards
Low balance beam/bench
Station instructions for Challenge Course
10 golf balls for 1/2 class
15 minutes music CD/tape for fitness Challenge Course activities
Clipboard and pencils for 3/4 class
10 Hoops
Horizontal climbing ladder
Cones
7 irons for 1/2 class
Task Sheets 17 – 20 for each student

OBJECTIVES:

The student will:

1. Pull flags only during the introductory activity as directed by the instructor.
2. Increase pitch shot with each attempt as demonstrated by the instructor.

National Standards Met in this Lesson: **1, 2, 4, 5, 6**

INSTRUCTIONAL ACTIVITIES	ORGANIZATION TEACHING HINTS

INTRODUCTORY ACTIVITY (2 – 3 MINUTES)

Flag Grab and Chase

One team wears flags positioned in the back of the belt. On signal, the chase team captures as many flags as possible within a designated amount of time. The captured flags are counted. The teams switch positions and the team that captures the most flags wins.

See DPESS Chapter 14 for details.

Scatter formation inside large boundary area.
Split class into using a management game such as back-to-back; toe-to-toe; or elbow-to-elbow to make two groups by then directing one in the group to put hand on hips. Then separate the two groups into teams.
Direct one team to pick up belts with flags attached.

FITNESS DEVELOPMENT (8 – 12 MINUTES)

Fitness Challenge Course

Design a course using the following components:

- Agility run through hoops
- Log rolls
- Run and weave through a coned course
- Leap over a taut rope
- Cross a horizontal ladder (or hang for 5-10 seconds)
- Power jump onto and off of three jumping boxes
- Walk the length of a balance beam
- Run high knees for 50 yards
- Curl-ups
- Crab Walks from one cone to another
- Stretching exercises
- Rope jumping
- 10-20 push-ups

One of the muscle groups that push-ups work are triceps brachii.

See DPESS Chapter 16 for details.

Divide class into groups of 4 – 5 using Whistle Mixer. Assign each group a starting point on the Challenge Course. Use music to motivate.

Course should be created to exercise all parts of the body
All students should be able to run the Challenge Course 3 times
Allow students to develop new challenges for the course
Music can be used for fun and to motivate students
Students will travel the course at their own pace. Have a passing lane to the right.

LESSON FOCUS (15 – 20 MINUTES)

Pitching Practice

Task Sheet 17
Explain organization to switch stations.
Explain Task Sheets 18-20

See DPESS Chapter 20 for details.

Use a management technique to create 2 groups. Within the groups play "Back-to-Back" to create partners.
Assign one group to the Pitching Practice area. Direct them to take a clipboard with pencil, 2 copies of Pitching Task Sheet 17, a 7 iron, and 10 balls.
The other group picks up a clipboard for each person with a pencil and Task Sheets 18 - 20.

In 2005, there were nearly 32,000 golf courses in the world.

INSTRUCTIONAL ACTIVITIES	ORGANIZATION TEACHING HINTS

GAME (5 MINUTES)

"Frisbee 21"

Game Rules:

- Players stand 10 yards apart
- Throw disc back and forth. Throws must be catchable.
- 1 point = 1 hand catch
- 2 points = 2 hand catch

A game that combines golf and Frisbee is "disc golf."

See DPESS Chapter 20 for details.

Create partners using "elbow-to-elbow" technique. Have 1 person kneel. The standing partner gets a Frisbee from perimeter of area and brings to partner.

Player must get 21 points to win and win by 2 points.

EVALUATION/REVIEW AND CHEER

Review rules and etiquette of golf.
What muscles were used during fitness?
What are elements of the Pitch Shot that you practiced?
About how many golf courses are there in the world?
What game combines Frisbee and golf?

Students create cheer.

RECIPROCAL TASK SHEET 17: PITCH SHOT

Name: ______________________________

Directions: You and your partner go to the marked area. Stand anywhere behind the starting line and record where the ball comes to rest by writing the number of the shot on your chart. The ball must carry in the air 50 feet to be considered a pitch shot.

75'

50'

30'

25'

Starting Line

TASK SHEET 18: RULES AND ETIQUETTE

Name: ______________________________

Unplayable Lie

One of these four options is illegal:

a) Two club-lengths from the ball

b) Point on extension of line from ball to cup ten yards away

c) Anywhere on line from tee to ball

d) Spot from which original ball was hit

Which one of the above is illegal? (See diagram below)

Circle the correct answer.

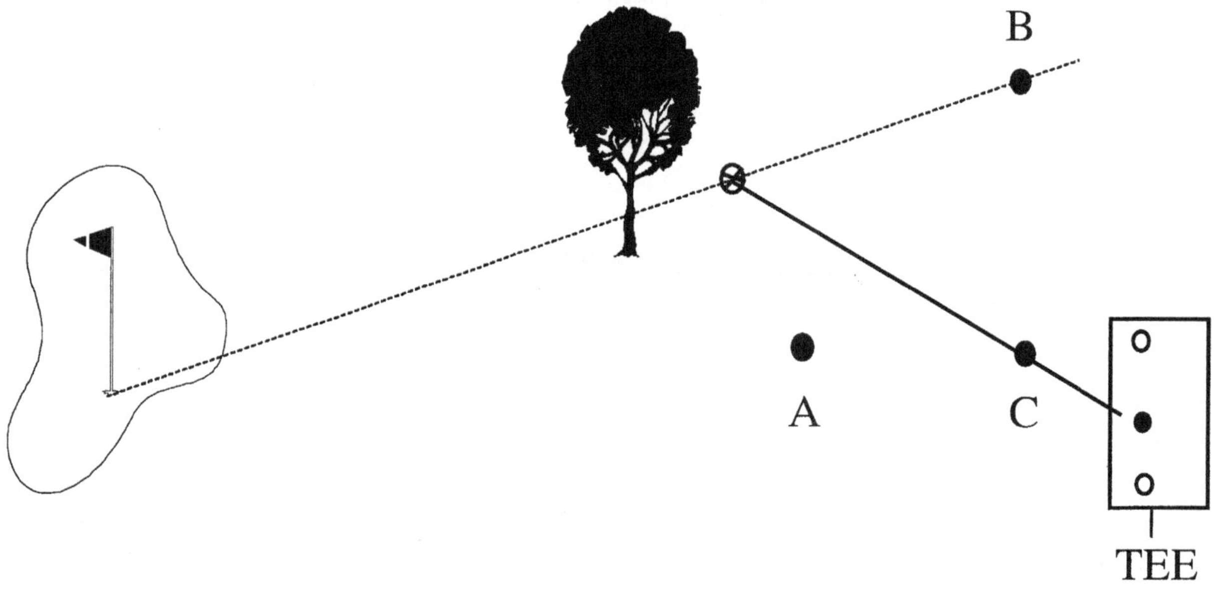

TASK SHEET 19: RULES AND ETIQUETTE

Name: ________________________________

Lateral Water Hazard

Four options are given below as possible points from which to play a ball entering a lateral water hazard:

a) Teeing ground

b) Within five feet of the margin of the water where the ball entered

c) Within three feet of the margin of the water on the other side of the hazard opposite where the ball entered

d) 30 feet in the adjacent fairway, on a line drawn between the point where the ball crossed the margin of the water and the hole

How many of the above choices are legal? Which one(s)? Circle legal choices.
(See diagram below)

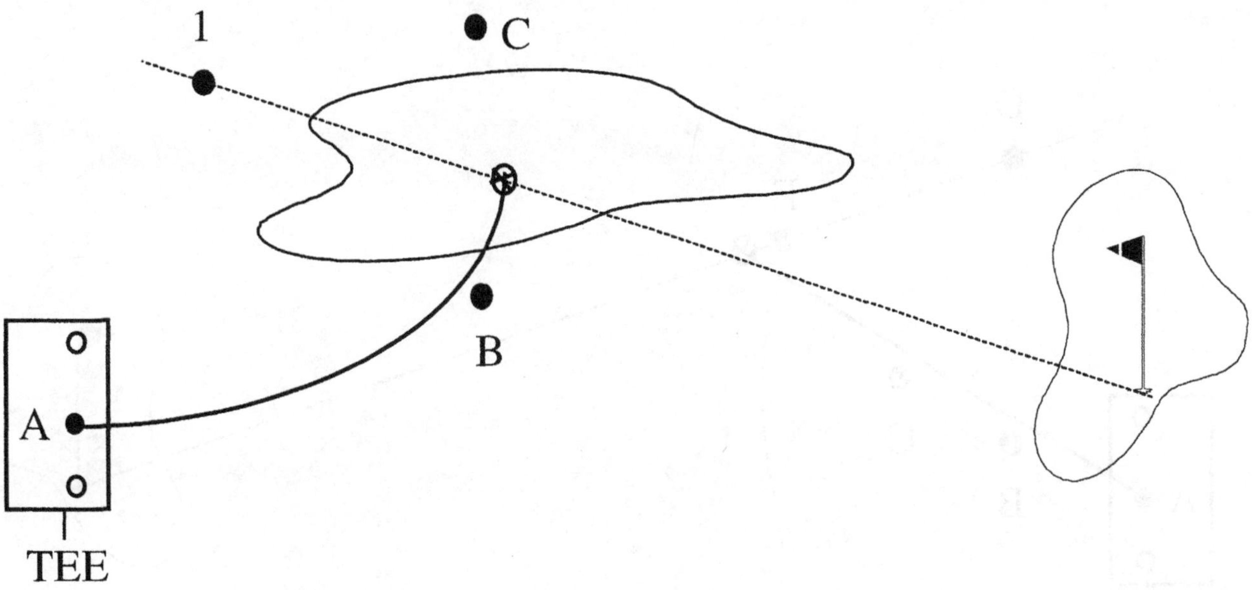

TASK SHEET 20: RULES AND ETIQUETTE

Name: ______________________________

Direct Water Hazard

Only two of the five options described below are points from which a ball entering a water hazard from the tee may be played:

a) From teeing ground

b) 45 yards in front of the tee in line of entry

c) 90 yards in front of the tee in line of entry

d) 75 yards behind water on line from entry to hole

e) Five feet from point of entry in line to hole

Which are the two alternatives? (See diagram below)
Circle the two alternatives.

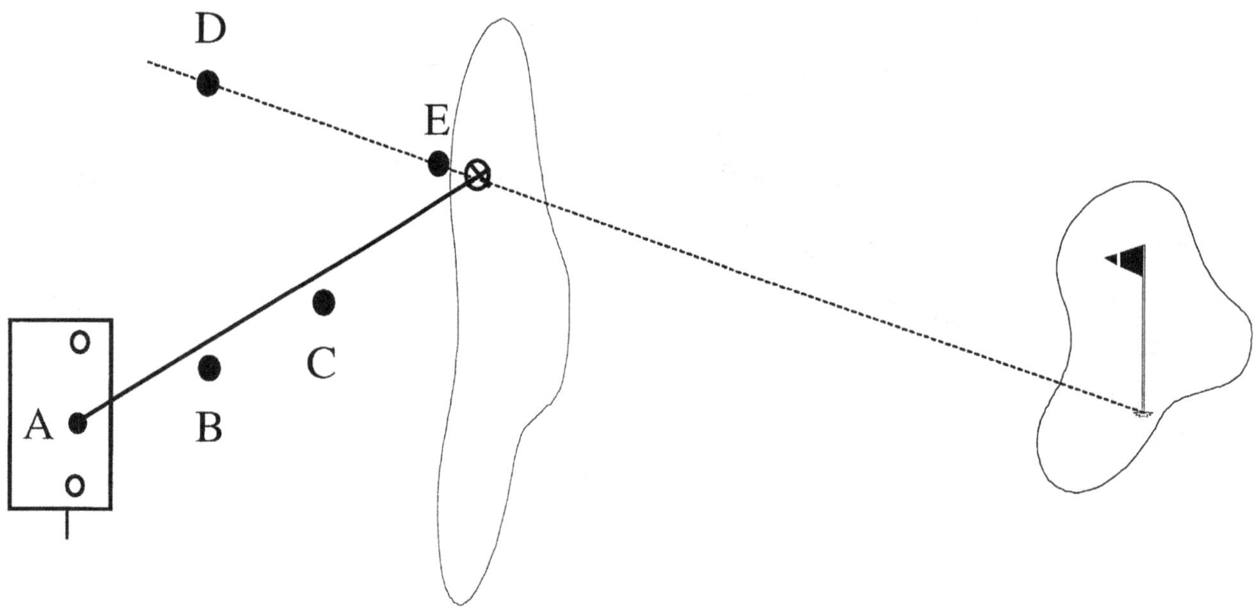

Golf Lesson Plan 14

EQUIPMENT:

1 nine iron per student
Whiffle golf balls
6 Flag markers
Golf Rating Scale Skill Exam (**DPESS page 474**)
Golf Score Cards
15 Hula-hoops
Written Exam

OBJECTIVES:

The student will:

1. Demonstrate stretches used during the Golf unit to date.
2. Apply golf knowledge into the written exam as directed by the instructor.

National Standards Met in this Lesson: 1, 2, 4, 5, 6

INSTRUCTIONAL ACTIVITIES	ORGANIZATION TEACHING HINTS
INTRODUCTORY ACTIVITY (5 MINUTES)	
Eliminate today to allow time for Game and Exam.	
FITNESS DEVELOPMENT (5 MINUTES)	
Student directed stretching	
LESSON FOCUS (15 – 20 MINUTES)	
Distribute Written Exam. Give instructions. When exam is completed, student should begin the Golf Rating Scale activity.	Distribute Golf Rating Scale Assign student a partner to complete rating scale. Turn in rating scale upon completion.

GOLF RATING SCALE (See DPESS Chapter 20 for details.)

Name: ____________________ Class Period: ____________________

1. **Grip** (4 points -- 1 each)
   - _____ Right-hand V is straight up or slightly right
   - _____ Two knuckles of left hand showing
   - _____ Grip tension is correct
   - _____ Hands completely on grip of club
2. **Stance** (4 points -- 1/2 each)
   - _____ Feet proper width apart
   - _____ Standing proper distance from ball
   - _____ Weight even over feet (ask)
   - _____ Knees bent properly
   - _____ Proper bend from waist
   - _____ Arms hanging naturally
   - _____ No unnecessary tension in arms and hands
   - _____ No unnecessary tension in legs
3. **Alignment** (3 points -- 1 each)
   - _____ Not left of target
   - _____ Not right of target
   - _____ Proper sequence of address. (Draw imaginary line and pick a spot on the line. Set club square, feet together. Place right foot first on parallel line. Take last look at target.)
4. **Swing** (10 points -- 1 each)
   - _____ One piece take away
   - _____ Head did not move up and down
   - _____ Head did not move back and forth
   - _____ Left arm extended
   - _____ A complete coil is present
   - _____ Club toe up to target -- BACKSWING -- at parallel level
   - _____ Club toe up to target -- forward swing -- at parallel level
   - _____ Club accelerates through ball
   - _____ Club continues after contact
   - _____ Facing target at the finish

Points	Performance
10	Good contact, good trajectory, good direction
9	Good contact, good trajectory, fair direction
8	Good contact, fair trajectory, fair direction
6	Fair contact, fair trajectory, fair direction
4	2 items fair, 1 item barely acceptable
2	1 item fair, 2 items barely acceptable
0	Miss or near miss

Golf Lesson Plan 15

EQUIPMENT:

1 nine iron per student
Whiffle golf balls
6 Flag markers
Drum/Tambourine
Golf Score Cards
15 Hula-hoops
Written Exam

OBJECTIVES:

The student will:

1. Participate in Formation Rhythmic Running as directed by the instructor to warm-up for the activities in the lesson.
2. Demonstrate golf etiquette on the field as demonstrated by the instructor.

National Standards Met in this Lesson: **1, 2, 4, 5, 6**

INSTRUCTIONAL ACTIVITIES	ORGANIZATION TEACHING HINTS
INTRODUCTORY ACTIVITY (2 – 3 MINUTES)	
Formation Rhythmic Running	**See DPESS Chapter 14 for details.**
Run 3 times	Give instructions to "fall in" to a circle or lines.
Run in a small circle 4 times	Play drum or tambourine to set rhythm.
Jump in place 8 times	
Run 8 times and clap on counts 1, 4, 5, 7, and 8	
Repeat above	Increase tempo.

This activity uses both upper and lower body extremities at different portions of the activity.

Format change for this lesson to allow time for game.
LESSON FOCUS/GAME (35 – 40 MINUTES)

INSTRUCTIONAL ACTIVITIES	ORGANIZATION TEACHING HINTS
Golf Game on Field	**See DPESS Chapter 20 for details.**
	Use whistle Mixer to create teams of 4 – 5
Explain Golf Game	Distribute score cards for each group
	Start groups at different holes

Golf was dominated by British golfers before WWI.

The biggest tour in the game is the PGA TOUR.

GOLF GAME SETUP ON FIELD

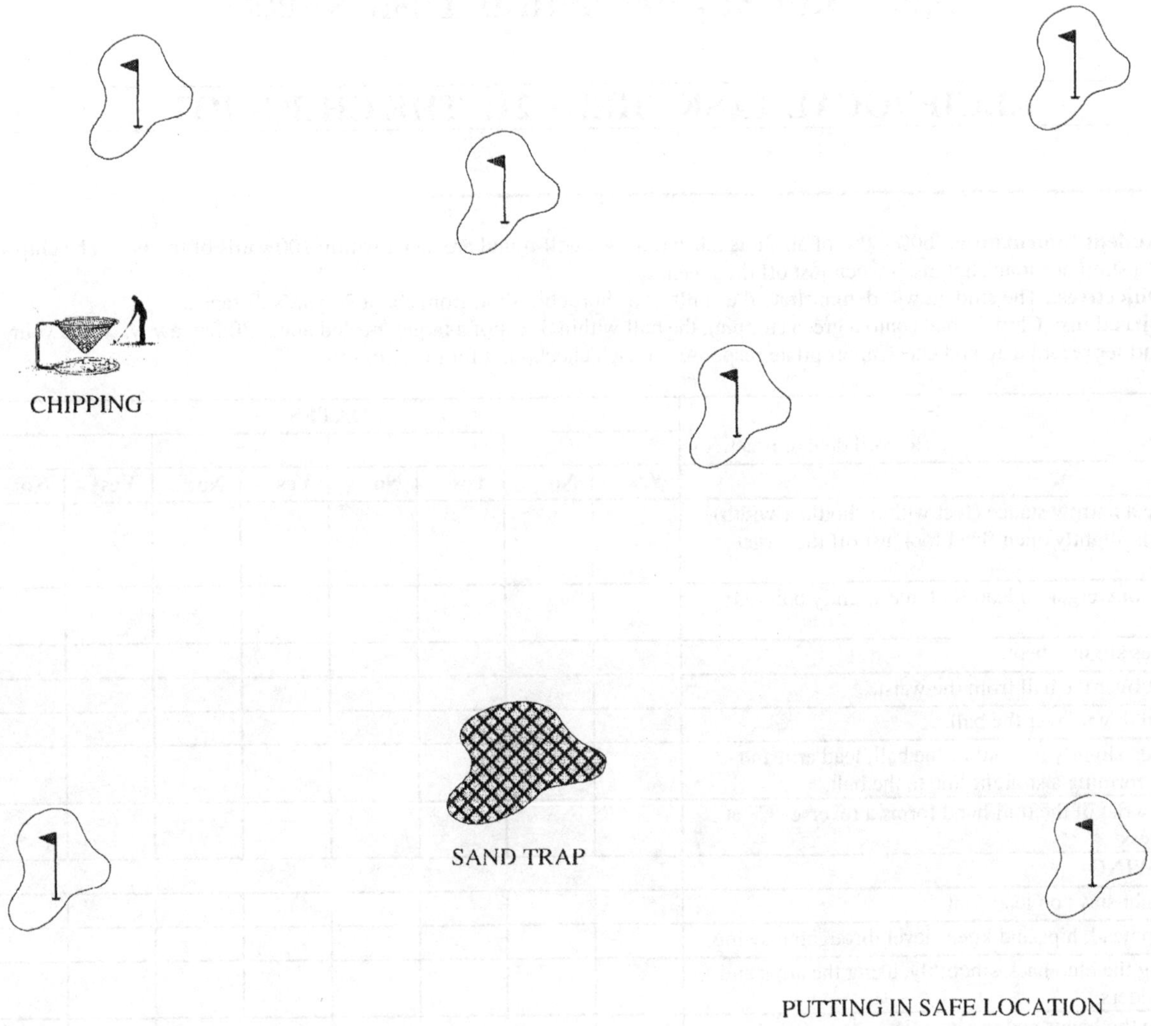

GOLF GAME SCORE CARD

Names	Holes					
	1	2	3	4	5	6

Exam and Supplemental Task Sheets

RECIPROCAL TASK SHEET 21: THE CHIP SHOT

Name: ______________________________

1. **Student Information**: 60%-70% of all shots taken during a golf round are taken within 100 yards of the pin. The chip shot is a short accurate shot, used when just off the green.
2. **Objectives**: The student will demonstrate the skills of a short chip shot, from about 20 yards distance.
3. **Directions**: Chip 20 balls onto a green stopping the ball within 3 feet of a target located about 30 feet away. Have your partner record date and check appropriate response for each checkpoint for the chip shot.

	DATES							
(Record date of practice)								
Address	**Yes**	**No**	**Yes**	**No**	**Yes**	**No**	**Yes**	**No**
1. Take a narrow stance (feet within shoulder width), that is slightly open (lead foot just off the target line).								
2. 60% of weight on lead foot, toe slightly pointed out.								
3. Knees slightly bent.								
4. Bent over the ball from the waist.								
5. Head down, over the ball.								
6. Hands slightly in front of the ball, lead arm and club forming a straight line to the ball.								
7. The wrist of the trail hand forms a reverse "C" at address.								
BACKSWING								
1. Weight stays on lead foot.								
2. Keep head, hips and knees level throughout swing.								
3. Bring the club back smoothly, using the arms and shoulders.								
4. Keep the hands and wrists quiet.								
5. Preserve the reverse "C" in the wrist of the trail hand.								
6. Make a compact swing. The club head should stay below the knees.								
Downswing								
1. Weight stays on lead foot through impact.								
2. Keep head, hips and knees level throughout swing.								
3. Control the club using arms and shoulders through impact.								
4. Keep hands and wrists quiet.								
5. Preserve the reverse "C" in the wrist of trail hand.								
6. Brush the grass through impact.								

	DATES							
(Record date of practice)								
Follow-Through	**Yes**	**No**	**Yes**	**No**	**Yes**	**No**	**Yes**	**No**
1. Weight stays on lead foot.								
2. Keep head, hips and knees level.								
3. Preserve the reverse "C" in the wrist of the trail hand.								
4. Change roles with partner.								
5. Repeat until you complete all three columns on this task sheet.								

RECIPROCAL TASK SHEET 22: SCORING

Directions: Two girls, Jane and Nancy, were playing a game of golf. The scores for each hole are listed as follows. Fill in the score card completely, on the answer sheet; Jane is keeping score.

Hole 1 - Jane shot a 4 and Nancy took a bogey.
2 - Jane made a 6 and Nancy a 7.
3 - Jane shot ladies' par for the hole and Nancy made a birdie.
4 - Jane and Nancy both shot a 6.
5 - On the drive, Jane swung at the ball and missed it. Her second attempt was good and after 6 more strokes, her ball was in the cup. Nancy made the hole in 7.
6 - Both players made the hole in even par.
7 - Jane made an eagle. Nancy sliced her drive; her second shot was short of the green, but with two approach shots and two putts the ball was in the cup.
8 - Jane had a lot of hard luck and ended up with a 13. Nancy took 6 strokes.
9 - Jane made a 6 and Nancy a 7.

SCORE CARD

Hole	Yards	Men's Par	Women's Par	Handicap	Jane	Nancy			W + L-H O
1	345	4	4	10					
2	410	4	5	1					
3	474	4	5	6					
4	229	3	4	14					
5	396	4	4	4					
6	159	3	3	16					
7	552	5	5	5					
8	316	4	4	13					
9	367	4	4	17					
Out	3218	35	38						

1. What is Jane's medal score?
2. What is Nancy's medal score?
3. Who is the winner by medal play?
4. Who is the winner by match play?
5. What is the score by match play for Jane?
6. What is the score by match play for Nancy?

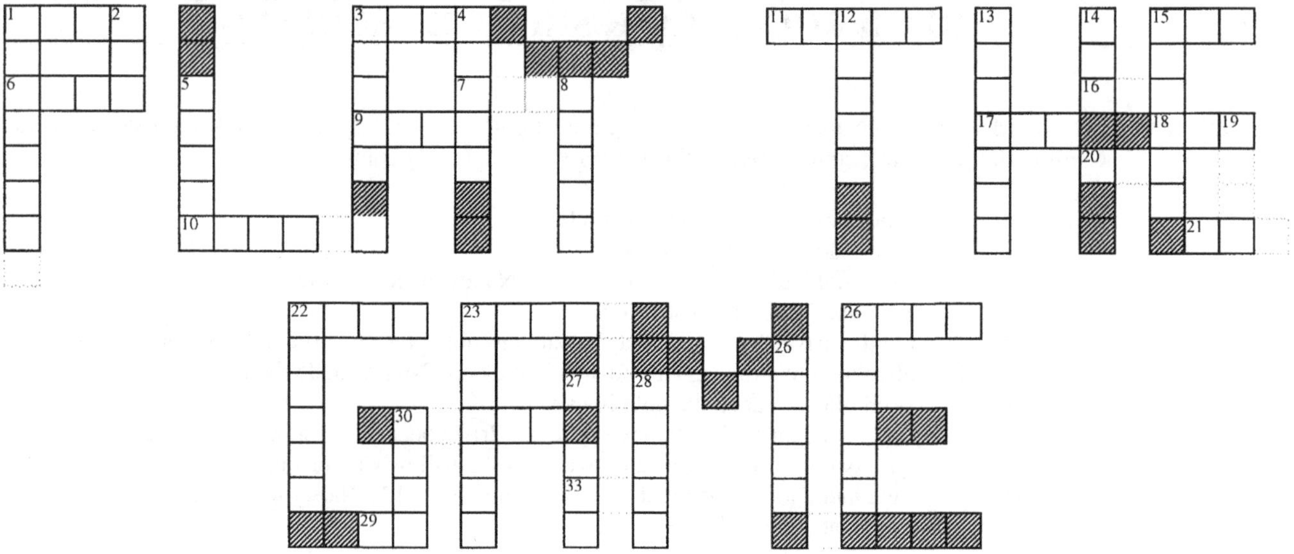

Across

1. Players should tee up within two _____ lengths behind the tee markers.
3. The player farthest from the _____ should shoot first during play.
6. Footprints in the _____ should be smoothed over with the club head.
7. The _____ of a coin may be used to decide who shoots first off the first tee.
9. Symbol for out-of-bounds.
10. The person with _____ score on the preceding hole tees off first.
11. Divots should be replaced immediately _____ the shot.
15. The reason _____ most beginners play too slowly is that they place their bag too far from the ball.
16. Each golfer must have his _____ set of clubs.
17. If there is a clear hole ahead, the group behind should be waved through by an _____ motion.
18. _____ practice swings before a shot during play is one too many.
20. The player should begin play from between _____ markers.
21. Beginners should _____ to speed up their play without rushing.
22. The basic _____ in golf is to play the ball where it lies.
23. Before teeing off, the golfer may practice at the driving _____.
24. One rule is that the player may not _____ the club in a sand trap.
27. The high side of a bunker is the _____.
29. The golfer may choose to leave the flagstick _____ the cup.
33. On the green, a golfer must _____ another player to mark his ball.

Down

1. There is no penalty for listing a ball from _____.
2. Playing too slowly is a _____ habit for a golfer.
3. Playing first off the tee is call the _____.
4. Player should _____ and leave a bunker at a spot level with the fairway.
5. In _____ play, a golfer does not return to the original spot to shoot another ball if his is lost because it slows play.
8. Part of the etiquette of golf is knowing where to _____ when others shoot.
12. The person whose ball is closest to the cup _____ the pin.
13. A _____ of one stroke is counted when a ball is hit into a pond.
14. An unplayable lie may be a ball which is _____ close to fence.
15. Preferred summer and _____ rules are the same.
19. A golfer should not shoot a ball _____ again while playing.
22. To _____ a ball during play is not good etiquette.
23. One should _____ a divot immediately.
24. A good golfer _____ the following group to play through if his group is slow.
26. If a player does not _____ his tracks in a sand trap he is not following proper etiquette.
28. On the tee a player may _____ a spot from which to shoot.
30. Whether or not he wants his score recorded depends _____ each player.
32. Usually there is a snack shop in the clubhouse where the golfer may _____ and drink.

ANSWER SHEET

Across

1. Players should tee up within two club lengths behind the tee markers.
3. The player farthest from the hole should shoot first during play.
6. Footprints in the sand should be smoothed over with the club head.
7. The toss of a coin may be used to decide who shoots first off the first tee.
9. Symbol for out-of-bounds. Rope
10. The person with lowest score on the preceding hole tees off first.
11. Divots should be replaced immediately after the shot.
15. The reason why most beginners play too slowly is that they place their bag too far from the ball.
16. Each golfer must have his own set of clubs.
17. If there is a clear hole ahead, the group behind should be waved through by an arm motion.
18. Two practice swings before a shot during play is one too many.
20. The player should begin play from between tee markers.
21. Beginners should try to speed up their play without rushing.
22. The basic rule in golf is to play the ball where it lies.
23. Before teeing off, the golfer may practice at the driving range.
24. One rule is that the player may not drop the club in a sand trap.
1. The high side of a bunker is the rim.
29. The golfer may choose to leave the flagstick in the cup.
33. On the green, a golfer must ask another player to mark his ball.

Down

1. There is no penalty for listing a ball from casualty
2. Playing too slowly is a bad habit for a golfer.
3. Playing first off the tee is call the honor.
4. Player should enter and leave a bunker at a spot level with the fairway.
5. In medal play, a golfer does not return to the original spot to shoot another ball if his is lost because it slows play.
8. Part of the etiquette of golf is knowing where to stand when others shoot.
12. The person whose ball is closest to the cup takes the pin.
13. A penalty of one stroke is counted when a ball is hit into a pond.
14. An unplayable lie may be a ball which is too close to fence.
15. Preferred summer and winter rules are the same.
19. A golfer should not shoot a ball over again while playing.
22. To remove a ball during play is not good etiquette.
23. One should replace a divot immediately.
24. A good golfer directs the following group to play through if his group is slow.
26. If a player does not smooth his tracks in a sand trap he is not following proper etiquette.
28. On the tee a player may mark a spot from which to shoot.
30. Whether or not he wants his score recorded depends upon each player.
32. Usually there is a snack shop in the clubhouse where the golfer may eat and drink.

GLOSSARY OF TERMS

Address: Taking the grip, stance, and proper body position in preparation to making a stroke.
Approach shot: A stroke played to approach putting green, i.e. pitch, chip.
Apron: the grass area around green.
Away: The ball farthest from hole.
Birdie: A score of one under par for a hole.
Bogey: A score of one over par for a hole.
Break of green: The slant of the green.
Bunker: A hazard, usually a depressed area covered with sand or a grassy mound.
Bye: The holes remaining to be played to determine the winner of the match.
Caddie: A person who carried the golfer's clubs and who can give her advice in regard to the course.
Casual water: Water, which accumulates on a course after a storm, not always present--not part of a hazard.
Chip shot: A short, low shot played to the green.
Closed Stance: The left foot slightly in advance of the right--the player tends to face slightly away from the line of flight of the ball.
Club: The implement with which the ball is struck.
Course: The area within which play is permitted.
Cup: The hole sunk in the green into which the ball must be played in order to terminate play on that hole.
Dead: A ball is said to be "DEAD" when it lies so near the hole that the putt is a dead certainty. A ball is also said to "FALL DEAD" when it does not run after slighting.
Divot: A piece of turf removed by the club in making a shot.
Dogleg: A hole in which the fairway curves to the right or to the left.
Double bogey: Two strokes over par for a hole.
Driver: #1 wood
Drop the Ball: The player stands facing the hole and drops the ball over her shoulder.
Eagle: A score of two under par for the hole.
Face: The striking surface of the club.
Fade: A shot that slightly curves to the right in flight.
Fairway: The mowed grassy area between the tee and the putting green.
Flag: Marks the spot on the green where the cup is located.
Flagstick: The marker indicating the location of the hole.
Flight: Division of players according to ability for tournament; also, the path of the ball in the air.
Fore: A warning cry to any person in the line of the play.
Four-Ball Match: Two players play their better ball against the better ball of their opponents.
Foursome: Two players playing one ball on each side; partners alternate hitting the ball.
Green: The putting surface.
Grip: That part of the club that is grasped and the grasp itself.
Gross score: The total number of strokes taken to complete a round of golf.
Grounding the club: Placing the sole of the club on the turf in preparation for making the stroke.
Half-Shot: A stroke that is less than a full swing.
Halved: Each side makes the same score on a hole.
Handicap: The approximate number of strokes one shoots over par, or the allowance of strokes to equalize players of different ability.
Hanging Lie: The ball lies on a downward slope.
Hazard: Any obstacle that interferes with the free flight or roll of the ball, (National; trees, natural water, rocks and so forth; made hazards; bunkers, sand traps; and so forth).
Head of the Club: The heavy part of the club, used for striking the ball.
Heel of the Club: The part of the club head below the point where the shaft and the head meet.
Hole: One unit of the course including the playing tee, fairway, hazards, green, and cup.
Holing Out: Sinking the ball in the cup.
Honor: The privilege of playing first, acquired by winning the preceding hole.
Hook: A flight of the ball curves to the left.
Impact: The contact of the club with the ball.
Irons: A graded series of metal-headed clubs.
Lie: The position of the ball on the ground.
Like: A player is playing "the like" when she makes an equal number of strokes to that just played by her opponent.
Links: The golf course.

Loft: To elevate the ball; also, the angle of pitch of the face of the club.
Loft of the club: The angle of pitch of the clubface.
Loose impediments: Objects such as dead grass, fallen leaves, pebbles, worms, fallen twigs, etc.
Mashie: A five iron used in golf.
Match Play: Competition by holes; the player winning the most holes wins the match.
Match: The game itself.
Medal Play: A competition by total scores for all holes; the player with the lowest total score wins the match.
Medallist: The low score player in a medal tournament.
Nassau: A system of scoring awarding one point for the winning of each "nine" and an additional point for the match.
Net score: The score resulting from subtracting handicap from gross score.
Niblick: An iron-headed golf club with the face slanted at a greater angle than any other iron except a wedge; a nine iron.
Nook: The point at which the shaft joins the head of the club.
Obstruction: An artificial object on the course, which may be movable or fixed.
Odd: A player is playing "odd" when on a given hole she is making a stroke one more in number than that last played by her opponent
Open Stance: The left foot is drawn back so that the player tends to face somewhat in the direction of the flight of the ball.
Out-of-Bounds: The area outside the proper course, from which balls may not be played.
Par: An arbitrary standard of scoring excellence based on the length and difficulty of a hole.
Pitch shot: A shot played to a putting green that travels in a high trajectory.
Press: Trying to hit the ball beyond one's normal power.
Provisional ball: A second ball played in case it is undetermined if the first ball is lost or out of bounds.
Pull: A ball that travels in a straight line to the left of the intended line of flight.
Push: A shot that travels in a straight line to the right of the intended line of flight.
Rough: The areas to the right or left of the fairway in which weeds and grass are allowed to grow.
Slice: A shot that curves in flight to the right, caused by the ball spinning in a horizontal, clockwise manner.
Stance: The position of feet in addressing the ball.
Stroke: Any forward motion of the club head made with intent to strike the ball.
Stroke play: Competition based on the total number of strokes taken.
Tee: The starting place for the hole or the peg on which the ball is placed for driving.
Tee markers: The markers placed on the tee to indicate limits of the teeing area.
Trajectory: The line of flight the ball takes when hit.
Whiff: When you swing and miss the ball.

GOLF QUIZ

TRUE-FALSE SECTION: Mark an A on the answer sheet if the statement is true. If the statement is false or partially false, mark B on the answer sheet.

1. A ball is said to have "hooked" when it curves off to the right.
2. The body should be facing the target at the end of the follow-through.
3. If a divot is taken, the player should not take the time to replace it.

MULTIPLE CHOICE: Place the corresponding letter of the best answer on the answer sheet.

4. What term is used to refer to the first shot on each hole?
   a. The drive
   b. The pitch and run
   c. The approach
5. In order to best sight the line of a putt, how should the player stand?
   a. With eyes to the right of the ball
   b. With eyes directly over the ball
   c. With eyes to the left of the ball
6. What is the last stroke necessary to reach the green called?
   a. Approach shot
   b. The drive
   c. The putt
7. What determines the amount of height a club gives to a ball?
   a. Length of the club
   b. Slant of the club head
   c. Weight of the head
8. In the grip, the little finger of the right hand overlaps or interlocks with what other finger?
   a. The forefinger of the left hand
   b. The middle finger of the left hand
   c. The little finger of the left hand
9. The part of the swing that allows the golfer to assume a comfortable position in relation to the ball is
   a. The follow-through
   b. The downswing
   c. The address
10. What do you call out loudly if there is any chance that your ball may hit someone?
   a. Fore
   b. Look-out
   c. Heads-up

TRUE AND FALSE: Read each question carefully and circle the correct answer. Good Luck!

11. The part of the club between the grip and the head is known as the shaft.	T	F
12. The club head should rest on the ground on the sole of the club rather than the heel.	T	F
13. Golf clubs, classified as woods and irons, vary primarily in loft angle and shaft length.	T	F
14. As loft increases shaft length decreases.	T	F
15. In regulation play, the golfer is allowed to carry 14 clubs: #2 through #9 irons; 1, 2, 3, and 4 woods, a putter and a wedge.	T	F
16. A pitching and sand wedge is used primarily to hit out of a sand trap.	T	F
17. All golf holes are the same length, but bunkers, sand traps, etc. are used to create variety.	T	F
18. After the drive, the person whose ball is farthest from the hole should play first.	T	F
19. One should not play an approach shot to the green until the players ahead have left it.	T	F
20. A ball that falls off the tee may not be re-teed without a penalty stroke.	T	F
21. Whenever a player hits a ball that he feels may hit or come close to another golfer, he should yell "fore"!	T	F
22. At the beginning of the swing, the club should be drawn back slowly rather than rapidly.	T	F
23. Rhythm in the golf swing is more important than speed	T	F
24. The stance has much to do with the direction the ball takes when hit.	T	F
25. The center of your waist should be facing the target at the end of the follow-through.	T	F
26. A ball is said to have "hooked" when it curves off to the right.	T	F

MULTIPLE CHOICE: Circle the best answer.

27. What term is used to refer to the first shot on each hole?
    a. The drive
    b. The pitch and run
    c. The approach
28. What is the last stroke necessary to reach the green called?
    a. The putt
    b. The approach shot
    c. The fairway shot
29. What is the standard of scoring excellence based on the length of a hole and allowing two putts on the putting green called?
    a. Birdie
    b. Bogey
    c. Par
30. What is the mowed grassy area between the tee and putting green called?
    a. The fairway
    b. The rough
    c. The green
31. The term "foursome" refers to:
    a. The number of strokes taken on the fairway
    b. Four players playing together
    c. The only number of players allowed to play together on a golf course
32. What term refers to the position of the ball on the ground?
    a. Flat
    b. Lie
    c. Set
33. What is the starting place for a hole or the peg on which the ball is placed for driving?
    a. Tee
    b. Marker
    c. Pin
34. In finishing the swing, where should the weight be?
    a. On the right foot
    b. On the heels
    c. On the left foot
    d. On the toes
35. What will lifting one's head on a swing cause?
    a. Topping ball
    b. Lifting ball
    c. Hooking ball
    d. Slicing ball
36. Which is common to all stances?
    a. Weight on toes
    b. Weight back toward heels
    c. Weight on whole foot
37. In the interlocking or overlapping grip, the little finger of the right hand interlocks or overlaps with which finger?
    a. Index or forefinger of the left hand
    b. Middle of left
    c. Little finger of left

RECIPROCAL TASK SHEET 23: SCORING

Directions: Two girls, Jane and Nancy, were playing a game of golf. The scores for each hole are listed as follows. Fill in the scorecard completely, on the answer sheet; Jane is keeping score.

Hole 1 - Jane shot a 4 and Nancy took a bogey.
2 - Jane made a 6 and Nancy a 7.
3 - Jane shot ladies' par for the hole and Nancy made a birdie.
4 - Jane and Nancy both shot a 6.
5 - On the drive, Jane swung at the ball and missed it. Her second attempt was good and after 6 more strokes, her ball was in the cup. Nancy made the hole in 7.
6 - Both players made the hole in even par.
7 - Jane made an eagle. Nancy sliced her drive; her second shot was short of the green, but with two approach shots and two putts the ball was in the cup.
8 - Jane had a lot of hard luck and ended up with a 13. Nancy took 6 strokes.
9 - Jane made a 6 and Nancy a 7.

SCORE CARD

Hole	Yards	Men's Par	Women's Par	Handicap	Jane	Nancy			W + L- H O
1	345	4	4	10					
2	410	4	5	1					
3	474	4	5	6					
4	229	3	4	14					
5	396	4	4	4					
6	159	3	3	16					
7	552	5	5	5					
8	316	4	4	13					
9	367	4	4	17					
Out	3218	35	38						

1. What is Jane's medal score?
2. What is Nancy's medal score?
3. Who is the winner by medal play?
4. Who is the winner by match play?
5. What is the score by match play for Jane?
6. What is the score by match play for Nancy?

GOLF ETIQUETTE

1. On Tee:
   a. Observe tee markers.
   b, Player with honor drives first.
   c. Don't talk or move around when another player is driving.
   d. In general, be still while person is driving.
   e. Stand diagonally in front to the right of player.

2. Fairway
   a. Player who is away plays first.
   b. Never stand in line of player's shots.
   c. Keep quiet when another player is shooting.
   d. Ball list, signal other players to go ahead.
   e. Wait until preceding players are off green before making approach shots.
   f. Replace and press down with foot all sods.
   g. Call, "FORE", if ball goes near other players.

3. Sand Trap
   a. Leave bag on edge of trap.
   b. Enter and leave at nearest point.
   c. Smooth out footmarks and club marks.
4. Green
   a. Leave bag on edge
   b. Place flag at the edge of green.
   c. Player away putts first.
   d. Keep away, out of line, or others putting.
   e. Keep still when player is putting.
   f. Avoid stepping on turf at edge of cup.
   g. Replace flag in cup.
   h. Leave green immediately after completing shots.
5. In General
   a. Only wear flat heels.
   b. When playing slowly, motion players behind to go ahead. Then wait until they are out of range before playing.

EQUIPMENT

CLUBS

Names and Uses:

1. Woods
   a. (#1) – driver – 120-180 yards, tee-off.
   b. (#2) – brassie – 150-170 yards, tee-off, fairway-good lie.
   c. (#3) – spoon – 145-160 yards, tee-off, on short holes; fairway.
2. Irons
   #1 – driving iron
   #2 – mid-iron, 140-150 yards, fairway long shots--poor lie, fairway long iron shots, low rough.
   #3 – Mid-mashie, 125-135 yards.
   #4 – Mashie iron, 115-125 yards, often used by women for tee shots on very short holes, long approach club, short roll-up approaches; more distance and less loft than mashie.
   *5 – Mashie, 105-115 yards, and less; most popular approach club; rough and bed lies where distance is greater than can be obtained from lofted clubs; occasionally tee shots on very short holes.
   #6 – Spade mashie; bad rough – greater distance than niblick.
   #7 – Mashie niblick, 95-105 yards.
   *8 – Pitching niblick, 85-95 yards.
   #9 – Niblick
   *10 – Putter

Woods and Iron Uses

1. The woods and first three irons are used for distance.
2. #4, 5, 6 irons are approach shots of medium distance; the ball will have a roll.
3. #7, 8, and 9 irons are used in hazards, bad rough, short approaches, and sand traps, and high pitch shots.
4. #10, the putter is used on the green.
5. Clubs marked (*) are essential for minimum set.

Racquetball

This unit has been specifically designed to meet all six components of the NASPE National Standards for Physical Education.

OBJECTIVES:

The student will:

1. Demonstrate agility, creativity, and cooperation while participating in the Introductory Activities.
2. Execute various locomotor movements called out by the instructor during the Rubber Band Introductory Activity.
3. Demonstrate cooperation with a partner during the Spider Tag Introductory Activity.
4. Perform locomotor movements to a beat while following the movements of a leader during the Introductory Activity.
5. Demonstrate dodging skills and the push-up position during the Introductory, Push-Up Tag Activity.
6. Demonstrate mirroring and cooperation skills while working with a partner.
7. Demonstrate leg, upper body strength, and teamwork skills while playing Crab Cage ball.
8. Demonstrate the ability to follow instructions, remember movement patterns and simultaneously run, bend, and recover during the Introductory Activity.
9. Participate in the Fitness Cookie Jar Activities to improve all components of fitness.
10. Participate in the Partner Fitness Racetrack to improve fitness.
11. Perform the Continuity Exercises as directed by the instructor to improve his fitness level.
12. Participate in the Four Corners Fitness Activity to improve his overall fitness levels.
13. Participate in Aerobic workouts to improve her endurance, strength, and flexibility.
14. Improve her fitness level by participating in the Fitness Obstacle Course.
15. Demonstrate hoop-rolling ability while running.
16. Demonstrate agility, creativity and cooperation during the Over, Under and Around activity.
17. Participate in the Parachute Rhythmic Aerobic activity to improve fitness and demonstrate moving to a beat.
18. Practice the ready position and the forehand stroke as demonstrated in class by the instructor.
19. Practice the backhand stroke using form demonstrated by the instructor.
20. Practice half-lob served using form demonstrated by the instructor in class.
21. Practice the fault and out serves using form demonstrated by the instructor.
22. Practice the back-wall return shot using form demonstrated by the instructor.
23. Practice the Power and “2” Serves using form demonstrated by the instructor.
24. Demonstrate the Pinch Shots using the Drop Hit Ball Drill demonstrated by the instructor.
25. Complete the Written Exam on Racquetball scoring 70% or better.
26. Cooperate with other students while participating in the Mass Stand Up Game.
27. Demonstrate cooperation and agility during the game “Entanglement.”
28. Demonstrate agility, cooperation, and speed and dodging during the Addition Tag Game.
29. Participate in the Wheelbarrow relay demonstrating cooperation with a partner.
30. Demonstrate Frisbee throwing and catching skills during the Frisbee 21 Game.
31. Participate in Wand balancing and agility activities directed by the instructor.
32. Demonstrate skills learned in class during the Skills Test to the satisfaction of the instructor.
33. Play singles games up to 5 points using skills demonstrated in class.
34. Play racquetball demonstrating the rules and skills taught by the instructor.
35. Play in the Round Robin Racquetball Tournament using skills and rules taught by the instructor.

RACQUETBALL BLOCK PLAN
3 WEEK UNIT

Week #1	Monday	Tuesday	Wednesday	Thursday	Friday
Introductory Activity	Seat Roll and Jog	Hoops and Plyometrics	Over, Under and Around	New Leader	Over, Under and Around
Fitness	Fitness Scavenger Hunt	Partner Racetrack Fitness	Continuity Exercises	Parachute Rhythmic Aerobic Activity	Challenge Course
Lesson Focus	Ready Position Forehand Stroke	Court Orientation Forehand Stroke Drop Hit Ball Drill	Backhand Stroke Drop Hit Drill	Half Lob Serve	Fault and Out Serves Back Wall Return
Game	Entanglement	Mass Stand Up	Wheelbarrow Relay	Addition Tag	Frisbee 21

Week #2	Monday	Tuesday	Wednesday	Thursday	Friday
Introductory Activity	Rubber Band	Spider Tag	Formation Rhythmic Running	Push-Up Tag	Mirror Drill In Place
Fitness	Circuit Training	Aerobic (Dance) Exercises	Four Corners	Continuity Exercises	Partner Racetrack Fitness
Lesson Focus	Dead Ball Hinders Serves	Back Corner Return Shot	Passing Shots	Power Drive and "2" Serves	Shot Pinch
Game	Over and Under Ball Relay	Crab Cage ball	Addition Tag	Wand Activities	Crab Cage ball

Week #3	Monday	Tuesday	Wednesday	Thursday	Friday
Introductory Activity	Bean Bag Touch and Go	Eliminate to allow time for games	Eliminate to allow time for games	Eliminate to allow time for Tournament	Eliminate to allow time for Tournament
Fitness	Fitness Cookie Jar Exchange	Challenge Course	Continuity Exercises	Aerobic Workouts	Parachute Rhythmic Aerobic Activity
Lesson Focus	Racquetball Record of Sheets Games	Skills testing	Written Exam	Round Robin Tournament	Round Robin Tournament
Game	Play Racquetball	Play Racquetball	Play Racquetball	Round Robin Tournament	Round Robin Tournament

Racquetball Lesson Plan 1

EQUIPMENT:

1 Racquet and racquetball per person
Fitness Scavenger Hunt Cards
Cones for stations
Station instruction cards
Music CD/Tape
CD/Cassette Player
6 Individual jump ropes
2 Clipboards task sheets and pencils per court

OBJECTIVES:

The student will:

1. Demonstrate the forehand stroke grip as demonstrated by the instructor.
2. Demonstrate agility and cooperation during the scavenger hunt as demonstrated by the instructor.

National Standards Met in this Lesson: **1, 2, 3, 4, 5, 6**

INSTRUCTIONAL ACTIVITIES	TEACHING HINTS

INTRODUCTORY ACTIVITY (2 - 3 MINUTES)

Seat Roll and Jog

Direct students to seat roll right/left with hand signal.
Alternate rolls with jogging in place.

See DPESS Chapter 14 for details.

Scattered formation.
Student begins on "all fours" with head up looking at teacher for instructions.

FITNESS DEVELOPMENT (8 - 12 MINUTES)

Fitness Scavenger Hunt

Ideas for Fitness Hunt Cards:

1. Run to each corner of the Gym and perform 15 curl-ups at each corner.
2. Run to the bleachers and perform step-ups.
3. Carioca to cones set up and touch each cone.
4. Jog to the tumbling mats and perform stretches listed on the station cards.
5. Jog to the jump rope station, start the music tap during the entire CD/tape.
6. Jog backwards to touch 2 walls.
7. Jog forwards and touch 4 colored lines on the courts.
8. Skip to the sit-up, push-up station. Follow station card instructions.
9. Slide to the jumping jack station.
10. Skip to the jump rope station.

See DPESS Chapter 16 for details.

Use Whistle Mixer to create groups of 5.
Direct students to work as a team to "hunt" for the exercise space/area.
Assign each group a different starting point.
Give each group a "Fitness Hunt" Card.

- Additional instructions can be added.

The scavenger hunt game was created by Elsa Maxwell, an American gossip columnist, in the mid 1900's. The University of Chicago Scavenger Hunt (or Scav Hunt) is an annual four-day team-based scavenger hunt held at the University of Chicago in May. It is often called the largest scavenger hunt in the world. During Scav Hunt, teams compete to acquire items off a list of approximately 300 items. The Scav Hunt began in 1987 and is an annual tradition now.

INSTRUCTIONAL ACTIVITIES	TEACHING HINTS

LESSON FOCUS (15 - 20 MINUTES)

Racquetball

Overview of the game of Racquetball: Court dimensions

- Types of games: Singles, Cut-throat, Doubles

See DPESS Chapter 20 for details.

Direct each student to pick up a racket, ball, and eye guards and bring them to the demonstration court. Explain the parts of the racket and how it is to be held when not striking the ball.

Joe Sobek created the sport in 1950. He had been a professional tennis player.

Ready Position

Forehand Stroke

Demonstrate forehand grips and position for hitting.

Demonstrate the ready position.

Demonstrate the movement pattern from ready position to forehand position.

Demonstrate the back swing, forehand stroke and follow through. Without a ball.

Practice: Explain the Task Sheet.

Direct four students to go to each court. Equipment is arranged around the perimeter of each court.

GAME (5 MINUTES)

Entanglement

Each group makes a tight circle with their arms.

See DPESS Chapter 18 for details.

EVALUATION/REVIEW AND CHEER

Review elements of the Ready Position and Forehand Stroke.

Who invented the scavenger hunt?

What university now has an annual scavenger hunt?

Who created the sport of Racquetball? When?

Cheer: Racquetball is cool!

RECIPROCAL TASK SHEET 1

Name: Student "A":

Name: Student "B": ______________________________

Directions: Two students will work together. Place both of your names on each task sheet. One individual is the "doer" while the other individual is the "observer". The "observer" reads information/instructions to the "doer", offers verbal feedback, and places a check in the "yes" or "no" columns recording the performance of their partner. When the "doer" has completed an item, the "doer" becomes the "observer" and the "observer" becomes the "doer".
<u>Note:</u> For this lesson, one pair of students will be working in one-half of the racquetball court while the other pair of students will be working in the other half of the court. In essence, the court will be divided into TWO long narrow areas. Each item is to be done five times before moving to next item.

	Student "A"		Student "B"	
	Yes	No	Yes	No
1. Demonstrate the Ready Position				
2. Demonstrate the Forehand Grip you plan to use when hitting a forehand shot.				
3. Demonstrate the Forehand Position for hitting the ball.				
4. Demonstrate the movement pattern from the Ready Position to Forehand Position.				
5. Demonstrate the back swing, forehand stroke and follow through. "NO Ball!!"				

When both students have completed this Task Sheet, you are to return to the demonstration court and submit your Task Sheet to the Instructor.

RACQUETBALL SAFETY RULES

1. Follow all rules set by your instructor.
2. Wear protective eye wear at all times while in a racquetball court.
3. Make sure the racket wrist thong is on your wrist before swinging the racket.
4. Before swinging racket for practice drills, look around to see that no one is within range of your swing.
5. Do not stand near a player that is involved in a practice drill.
6. Limit swing of the racket to an arc of 180 degrees - half circle.
7. Do not walk into front court area to retrieve a ball while another player is involved in a practice drill.
8. Do not enter a court while players are involved in practice drills and/or a game. When play has stopped, knock on the door and wait until invited to enter the court.
9. During a game, do not turn around and look for the ball when it is behind you.
10. Do not push an opposing player during a game in order to reach the ball.
11. Accidents occur because of careless, lack of awareness, or lack of knowledge. Always follow safety rules when involved in practice drills and games.

Please cut off at the dotted line, sign, date, and return below to your instructor.

CUT OFF AND RETURN THIS SLIP TO INSTRUCTOR

I, ______________________________, the undersigned, have read and understand the Racquetball Safety Rules. Furthermore, I agree to follow the rules of the class.

NAME: ______________________________ DATE:

(Printed)

NAME:

(Signature)

Racquetball Lesson Plan 2

EQUIPMENT:

1 Hula Hoop per student
Station instruction cards
1 Racquetball and racquet per student
2 Clipboards, Task Sheets and pencils per court
1 Pair protective eye guards per student

OBJECTIVES:

The student will:

1. Demonstrate the forehand stroke form as demonstrated by the instructor.
2. Demonstrate cooperative group participation as directed by the instructor.

National Standards Met in this Lesson: **1, 2, 3, 4, 5, 6**

INSTRUCTIONAL ACTIVITIES | **TEACHING HINTS**

INTRODUCTORY ACTIVITY (2 - 3 MINUTES)

Hoops and Plyometrics

Each student rolls the hoop while running. On signal, the hoops are dropped. Challenge students to move in and out of a given number of hoops specified by color. State locomotor movement to use. Student then picks up the hoop and resumes rolling it.

See DPESS Chapter 14 for details.
Scatter formation.
Each student has a hoop and listens for instructions..

Plyometrics is a type of exercise that uses explosive movements to develop muscular power.

FITNESS DEVELOPMENT (8 - 12 MINUTES)

Partner Racetrack Fitness

On signal 1 partner begins the first activity on station card while other jogs around perimeter. Switch roles, then perform next task alternating positions until they complete all tasks at the station. Rotate to next station. Task suggestions: Strengthening and stretching exercises i.e. sit-ups, push-ups, upper and lower body stretches, etc.

See DPESS Chapter 16 for details.
Use Back-to-Back to create partners.
Assign partners to a station to begin.
Explain station rotation.

LESSON FOCUS (15 - 20 MINUTES)

Court Orientation

Explain court markings:

- Service zone area (Service line, Short line, Drive Serve lines)
- Service Boxes for doubles play; Receiving lines
- Front Court Area; Back Court Area

See DPESS Chapter 20 for details.
Scattered formation

The game is normally played by two opposing players, though variations involving three and four players are also commonly played.

Review Forehand Stroke

Demonstrate drip hit ball drill - 3 contact areas.
Demonstrate rally drill - forehand only

Demonstrate ball contact areas:

1. Center of body
2. Front of lead leg
3. Back of lead leg

Demonstrate hitting off the lead leg.

Practice

When students complete Task Sheet, they are to continue practicing the drop hit drill and the rally drill.

Direct four students to go to each court and follow the task sheet instructions.

GAME (5 MINUTES)

Mass Stand Up

Start with 3 people sitting back to back. Lock elbows and try to stand up. Increase the number to 4 people, then 5, and so forth. See how many people can stand up simultaneously.

See DPESS Chapter 18 for details.
Use a management game i.e. Whistle Mixer to create group of 3.
Spread groups out in area.

While participating in this activity you'll be using core and leg muscles.

RECIPROCAL TASK SHEET 2

Name: Student "A": ____________________________________

Name: Student "B": ____________________________________

<u>Directions:</u> Two students will work together. Place both of your names on each task sheet. One individual is the "doer" while the other individual is the "observer". The "observer" reads information/instructions to the "doer", offers verbal feedback, and places a check in the "yes" or "no" columns recording the performance of their partner. When the "doer" has completed an item, the "doer" becomes the "observer" and the "observer" becomes the "doer".

<u>Note:</u> For items 1-5, one pair of students will be working in one-half of the racquetball court while the other pair of students will be working in the other half of the court. In essence, the court will be divided into TWO long narrow areas. Students must stay on their side of the court during item 5.

Items 2-5 are to be done five times before moving to next item.

	Student "A"		**Student "B"**	
	Yes	**No**	**Yes**	**No**
1. Point out the following court markings: Service line, Short line, Receiving line.				
2. Demonstrate movement pattern to Forehand Position, back swing, forehand stroke and follow through.				
3. Complete the drop hit ball drill from the Forehand Position.				
4. Using drop hit ball drill, demonstrate hitting the Forehand Stroke off the lead leg.				
5. Participate in the Rally drill. Forehand Strokes only! "Doer" hits the ball to font wall on their side of the court. When the ball rebounds from the front wall the "doer" hits the ball again (rallies) and continues to do so as long as the ball can be hit with a forehand stroke.				

When all items on Task Sheet have been completed by both students, repeat item 5 if time permits. Submit your completed Task Sheet to the Instructor.

Racquetball Lesson Plan 3

EQUIPMENT:

CD/Cassette Player
Exercise CD/Tape
1 Individual jump rope per student
1 Racquetball and racquet per student and Continuity eye guards
2 Clipboards, 2 Task Sheets and 2 pencils per court

OBJECTIVES:

The student will:

1. Increase fitness level by performing the continuity exercises as demonstrated by the instructor.
2. Demonstrate proper backhand stroke grip as demonstrated by the instructor.

National Standards Met in this Lesson: **1, 2, 3, 4, 5, 6**

INSTRUCTIONAL ACTIVITIES | **TEACHING HINTS**

INTRODUCTORY ACTIVITY (2 - 3 MINUTES)

Over, Under, and Around

One person gets in position on all fours while the other stands alongside, ready to begin the movement challenge. Challenge is to move over, go under, and run around partner a certain number of times. For example, move over your partner 5 times, go under 8 times, and run around 13 times.

See DPESS Chapter 14 for details.

Use "elbow-to-elbow" management technique to create partners.

When the task is completed, partners change positions and the challenge is repeated.

FITNESS DEVELOPMENT (8 - 12 MINUTES)

Continuity Exercises

See DPESS Chapter 16 for details.

Jump rope strengthens the arms, shoulders, legs and cardiovascular system.

LESSON FOCUS (15 - 20 MINUTES)

Backhand Stroke

Demonstrate backhand grips (Eastern & Continental).
Backhand position for hitting the ball.

Demonstrate ball contact areas:

1. Center of body
2. Front of lead leg
3. Back of lead leg

See DPESS Chapter 20 for details.

Demonstrate the movement pattern from the ready position to the backhand position.
Demonstrate the back swing, backhand stroke and follow through. No ball!
Review hitting off lead leg.
Demonstrate drop hit ball drill - 3 contact areas.
Demonstrate rally drill - backhand only.
Demonstrate cross-court rally drill-forehand/backhand.

Games involving two players are called singles.

Practice

Upon completion of the Task Sheet, two students at a time are to practice the cross-court rally drill. One student hits a forehand while the other hit a backhand. The two other students are to stand outside the court.

Direct four students to go to each court and follow the task sheets.
Students change roles after five rallies.

GAME (5 MINUTES)

Wheelbarrow Relay

See DPESS Chapter 18 for details.

Use "elbow-to-elbow" to create pairs. Then combine pairs to make lines/squads of 4 or 6.
Identify race area.

This relay requires the person holding the legs not to walk faster than the person walking on their hands.

EVALUATION/REVIEW AND CHEER

Review elements of the backhand stroke.
What parts of the body does jump rope work on?
What kind of a racquetball game is played that involves two players?

Students create cheer.

RECIPROCAL TASK SHEET 3

Name: Student "A": ______________________________

Name: Student "B": ______________________________

<u>Directions</u>: Two students will work together. Place both of your names on each task sheet. One individual is the "doer" while the other individual is the "observer". The "observer" reads information/instructions to the "doer", offers verbal feedback, and places a check in the "yes" or "no" columns recording the performance of their partner. When the "doer" has completed an item, the "doer" becomes the "observer" and the "observer" becomes the "doer".

<u>Note</u>: For items 1-5, one pair of students will be working in one-half of the racquetball court while the other pair of students will be working in the other half of the court. In essence, the court will be divided into TWO long narrow areas. Students must stay on their side of the court during item 5.

Items 2-5 are to be done five times before moving to next item.

	Student "A"		Student "B"	
	Yes	**No**	**Yes**	**No**
1. Demonstrate the Backhand Grip you plan to use when hitting a backhand shot.				
2. Demonstrate the Backhand Position for Hitting the ball.				
3. Demonstrate the movement pattern from the Ready Position to Backhand Position.				
4. Demonstrate back swing, backhand stroke and follow through. "NO Ball!"				
5. Complete the drop hit ball drill from the Backhand Position.				
6. Using drop hit ball drill, demonstrate hitting the Backhand Stroke off the lead leg.				
7. Participate in the Rally drill. Backhand Strokes only! "Doer" hits the ball to front wall on their side of the court. When the ball rebounds from the front wall the "doer" hits the ball again (rallies) and continues to do so as long as the ball can be hit with a backhand stroke.				

When all items on Task Sheet have been completed by both students, repeat item 5 if time permits. Submit your completed Task Sheet to the Instructor.

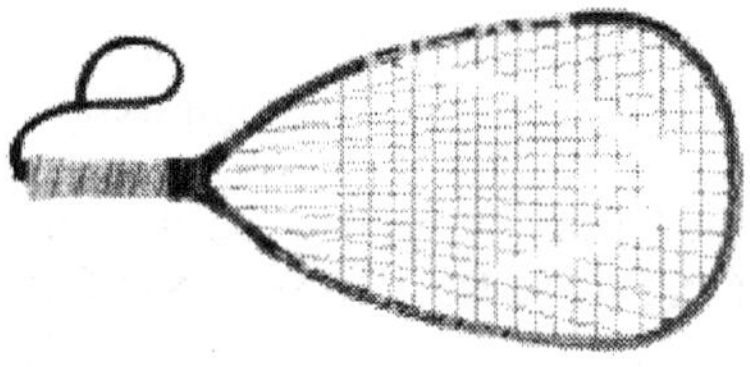

Racquetball Lesson Plan 4

EQUIPMENT:

1 Parachute
1 Racquetball, eye guards and racquet per student
2 Clipboards, 2 task sheets, and 2 pencils per court
CD/Cassette Player
Music CD/Tape

OBJECTIVES:

The student will:

1. Demonstrate the half lob serve as demonstrated by the instructor.
2. Participate in Addition Tag with the rest of the class as directed by the instructor.

National Standards Met in this Lesson: **1, 2, 3, 4, 5, 6**

INSTRUCTIONAL ACTIVITIES	TEACHING HINTS

INTRODUCTORY ACTIVITY (2 - 3 MINUTES)

New Leader

The task is to continuously move in a productive fashion that will warm up the group. One person begins as the leader. When a signal is given, a new leader steps up and leads the next activity.

See DPESS Chapter 14 for details.
Use Whistle Mixer to create groups of 3-5.

FITNESS DEVELOPMENT (8 - 12 MINUTES)

Parachute Rhythmic Aerobic Activity

See DPESS Chapter 16 for details.
See Badminton Unit, Lesson Plan 11 for details.

Parachutes are used by civilian and military personnel as well as children in school settings.

LESSON FOCUS (15 - 20 MINUTES)

Serve: Half Lob

Demonstrate the following:

- Position in service zone from which serve is delivered.
- Stroke action when delivering (hitting) the serve.
- Flight patterns (possible) of the ball during serve.
- Follow through action after stroking the serve.
- Movement pattern to center court position after served ball crosses Short Line.

Demonstrate Serve Drill

- The role of the individual serving.
- The role of the individual receiving/returning the served ball.

See DPESS Chapter 20 for details.
Scattered position on court near service area.

Fault and Out Serves

Describe a Fault Serve and an Out Serve.

Practice

Direct four students to go to each court. Students are to follow the instructions on the task sheets.

Out of Class Assignment

Handout: Fault Serves and the types of Out Serves.

Distribute handout at end of class. Students are to read information on the handout by next class period.

GAME (5 MINUTES)

Addition Tag

The "its" hold hands and can tag only with their outside hands. When they tag someone, that person must hook on. This continues and the tagging line becomes longer and longer. Regardless of the length of the line, only the hand on each end of the line is eligible to tag.

See DPESS Chapter 14 for details.
Scattered formation in area.
Select several "its".
Change its after each tag game.

In some parts of Australia, the game tag is called "tiggy", "chasey", "tips" or "tip".

EVALUATION/REVIEW AND CHEER

Review elements of faults and half lob serves.
Cheer: 2, 4, 6, 8, Tag games are great!

RACQUETBALL UNIT: FAULT SERVES HANDOUT

Service Faults: Result in an out if any two occur in succession.

A. Foot Faults
B. Short Service
C. Three-Wall Service
D. Ceiling Serve
E. Long Serve
F. Out-of-Court Serve
G. Bouncing Ball Outside Service Zone
H. Illegal Drive Serve
I. Screen Serve
J. Serving before the receiver is ready

Note: When the first serve is a fault serve, the server receives a second opportunity to place the ball in play by serving.

RACQUETBALL UNIT: OUT SERVES

Out Serves: Result in loss of serve (out).

A. Two Consecutive Fault Serves
B. Failure to Serve Promptly
C. Missed Serve Attempt
D. Touched Serve
E. Fake or Balk Serve
F. Illegal Hit
G. Non-Front Serve
H. Crotch Serve
I. Out-of-Order Serve
J. Ball Hits Partner
K. Safety Zone Violation

Note: When an out serve occurs, the server loses serve. They do not receive a second opportunity to place the ball in play by serving.

RACQUETBALL RECIPROCAL TASK SHEET 4

Name: Student "A": ______________________________

Name: Student "B": ______________________________

Directions: Two students will work together. Place both of your names on each task sheet. One individual is the "doer" and one is the "observer". Then they reverse roles.

Note: For items 1-3, one pair of students will be working in one-half of the racquetball court while the other pair of students will be working in the other half of the court. Students must stay on their side of the court. Items 2-3 are to be done five times before moving to next item. For safety, only two individuals can be in the court for item 4: Service Drill. One pair of individuals is to wait outside the court while the other pair of individuals complete one phase of this drill then individuals switch places.

	Student "A"		Student "B"	
	Yes	**No**	**Yes**	**No**
1. Demonstrate the position in the service zone from which Half Lob is delivered.				
2. Demonstrate stroke and follow through action for Half Lob serve.				
3. Demonstrate movement pattern to center court position after served ball crosses Short Line.				
4. Complete Serve Drill: Doer becomes *"Server"* and Observer becomes *"Receiver"*				
Phase 1: *Server:* Serve ball and watch rebound pattern *Receiver:* Move to served ball and catch it				
Phase 2: *Server:* Serve ball and move to center court position *Receiver:* Return served ball				
Phase 3: *Server:* Serve, center court position, rally return of serve *Receiver:* Return serve and move to center court area				
Phase 4: *Server:* Serve, center court position, rally return of serve to play out serve *Receiver:* Return serve, move to center court area and play out serve				

Submit your completed Task Sheet to the Instructor.

Racquetball Lesson Plan 5

EQUIPMENT:

Cones to mark obstacle course
Instruction cards for each station
3 Mats
Benches
Hoops
Music CD/Tape
CD/Cassette Player
1 Racquetball and racquet per student

OBJECTIVES:

The student will:

1. Demonstrate proper back-wall return shot as demonstrated by the instructor.
2. Catch a Frisbee with one or two hands as demonstrated by the instructor.

National Standards Met in this Lesson: **1, 2, 3, 4, 5, 6**

INSTRUCTIONAL ACTIVITIES	TEACHING HINTS
INTRODUCTORY ACTIVITY (2 - 3 MINUTES)	
Over, Under, and Around	**See DPESS Chapter 14 for details.**
FITNESS DEVELOPMENT (8 - 12 MINUTES)	
Challenge Course	**See DPESS Chapter 16 for details.** See Badminton Unit, Lesson Plan 1 for details.

During the Challenge Course activities, muscles in the whole body are utilized. The main muscles in the calf muscle are called the gastrocnemius and soleus.

INSTRUCTIONAL ACTIVITIES	TEACHING HINTS
LESSON FOCUS (15 - 20 MINUTES)	
Fault and Out Serves Demonstrate the above types of serves	**See DPESS Chapter 20 for details.** Scattered formation.
Shot: Back-wall Return Demonstrate the following: • Forehand Shot; Backhand Shot: Demonstrate back wall drill for: • Forehand shot; Backhand shot.	**See DPESS Chapter 20 for details.** A. Movement pattern from center court area to back court area. B. Forehand stroke ready position. C. Movement pattern during forehand stroke. D. Movement pattern after hitting forehand shot.

Points are scored only by the server, or in the case of a doubles match, the server's team.

INSTRUCTIONAL ACTIVITIES	TEACHING HINTS
Practice Explain task sheets.	Direct four students to go to each court and follow task sheet instructions and activities.
Out of Class Assignment: Direct students to read the information on the handout by the next class period.	At the end of class, distribute a handout on the different types of Dead-Ball Hinders.
GAME (5 MINUTES)	
Frisbee 21 Throw and catch Frisbee. Keep score: 2 handed catch = 1 point 1 hand catch = 2 points	**See DPESS Chapter 20 for details.** Create partners using "toe-to-toe" Students stand 10 yards apart. • Must win by 2 points.

Official Frisbee sizes range from 20 to 25 cm.

EVALUATION/REVIEW AND CHEER

Review elements of faults and out serves.
What is the name of the calf muscle?
Describe the shot: back –wall return.

Cheer: 2, 4, 6, 8, Racquetball is great!

RACQUETBALL UNIT HANDOUT: DEAD-BALL HINDERS

Dead-Ball Hinders: Result in the rally being replayed.

A. Court Hinders
B. Ball Hits Opponent
C. Body Contact
D. Screen Ball
E. Back swing Hinder
F. Safety Holdups
G. Other Interference

Note:

1. Play stops when either player calls "hinder".
2. Five of the seven types can be placed into one of the following categories:
   a. Contact
   b. Stroke
   c. Visual
   In some instances, it is easier to remember the 3 categories.
4. Hinder calls have been incorporated in the game of racquetball as a measure of safety.

RECIPROCAL TASK SHEET 5

Name: Student "A": ______________________________
Name: Student "B": ______________________________

Directions: Two students will work together. Place both of your names on each task sheet. One individual is the "doer" and one is the "observer". Then they reverse roles.

Note: For items 1-2, one pair of students will be working in one-half of the racquetball court while the other pair of students will be working in the other half of the court. Students must stay on their side of the court. Items 1-4 are to be done five times before moving to next item. For safety, only two individuals can be in the court for item 3-4: Back-Wall Return Drill. One individual from each pair is to wait outside the court while the other individual completes one phase of this drill then individuals switch places.

	Student "A"		Student "B"	
	Yes	**No**	**Yes**	**No**
1. Back-wall Return: Forehand shot. Demonstrate the following positions: A. Movement pattern from center court area to back court area B. Forehand stroke ready position C. Movement pattern during forehand Stroke D. Movement pattern after hitting forehand shot				
2. Back-wall Return: Backhand shot. Repeat Items A-D above for Backhand shot				
3. Complete Back-Wall Drill: From forehand ready position: A. Toss ball onto back wall, on rebound let ball bounce on the floor then catch. B. Toss ball onto back wall. On the rebound let the ball bounce on the floor then hit it toward the front wall. C. Toss ball so it hits the floor then hits the back wall and rebounds into the court. During the flight of the rebound from the back wall, hit the ball toward the front wall before it bounces on the floor.				
4. From Backhand Ready Position: Repeat Items 3 A - 3 C.				

Racquetball Lesson Plan 6

EQUIPMENT:

1 Rubber Ball per 5-6 students
Circuit Training Instructions
1 Racquetball, eye guard and racquet per student
2 Clipboards, 2 pencils, 2 task sheets per court

OBJECTIVES:

The student will:

1. Demonstrate proper lob serve form as demonstrated by the instructor.
2. Participate in circuit training to improve fitness level as demonstrated by the instructor.

National Standards Met in this Lesson: **1, 2, 3, 4, 5, 6**

INSTRUCTIONAL ACTIVITIES — **TEACHING HINTS**

INTRODUCTORY ACTIVITY (2 - 3 MINUTES)

Rubber Band

On signal, the students move away from the instructor using a designated movement such as a jump, run, hop, slide, carioca, or walk. On the second signal, students sprint back to the instructor's position where the activity originated. The cycle is repeated with different movements. As a variation students can perform 1 or 2 stretching activities when they return to the teacher.

See DPESS Chapter 14 for details.
Scattered formation near teacher/leader.

FITNESS DEVELOPMENT (8 - 12 MINUTES)

Circuit Training

See DPESS Chapter 16 for details.
See Golf Unit, Lesson Plan 10 for details.

Circuit training is an excellent way to increase strength and agility.

LESSON FOCUS (15 - 20 MINUTES)

Dead-Ball Hinders

Demonstrate the different types.

See DPESS Chapter 20 for details.
Scattered in safe location on court for demonstration.

Serve: Lob

Demonstrate the following:

- Position in service zone from which serve is delivered.
- Stroke action when delivering (hitting) the serve.
- Flight patterns of the ball during the serve.
- Follow through action after stroking the serve.
- Movement pattern to center court position after served ball crosses Short Line.

Serving, receiving/returning the served ball.
Fault Serves and Out Serves.

Review Serving

Practice

Direct four students to go to each court and follow the instructions on the task sheets.

GAME (3 - 5 MINUTES)

Over and Under Ball Relay:

See DPESS Chapter 18 for details.

EVALUATION/REVIEW AND CHEER

Review elements of the back corner return shot.
What form of fitness training helps to improve strength and agility?

Cheer: "Lob serves!"

Racquetball Lesson Plan 7

EQUIPMENT:

1 Cage ball
Aerobic Exercise Music CD/Tape
CD/Cassette Player
1 Racquetball, eye guards and racquet per student
2 Clipboards pencils, and task sheets per court

OBJECTIVES:

The student will:

1. Participate in Spider Tag to demonstrate cooperation skills as demonstrated by the instructor.
2. Participate in an Aerobic Workout to improve fitness levels.
3. Demonstrate the back corner drill as demonstrated by the instructor.
4. Play Crab Cageball demonstrating cooperative skills.

National Standards Met in this Lesson: **1, 2, 3, 4, 5, 6**

INSTRUCTIONAL ACTIVITIES — **TEACHING HINTS**

INTRODUCTORY ACTIVITY (2 - 3 MINUTES)

Spider Tag

Students stand back-to-back with a partner with the elbows hooked. The "its" chase the other pairs. If a pair is tagged (or becomes unhooked), they become "it."

See DPESS Chapter 14 for details.
Create partners using "Back-to-Back."
Select one pair to be "it."

In Finland, "tag" is "Hippa," which is also what the chasing person is called.

FITNESS DEVELOPMENT (8 - 12 MINUTES)

Aerobic Workout

See DPESS Chapter 16 for details.
Scattered formation.

Sample 8 Count Aerobic Exercise Phrases of Movement

Instructional Activities	Teaching Hints
• Jump in place 8 times	• Hit the sides of thighs with straight arms.
• Walk in place 16 times.	• On toes performing 16 steps moving arms down and up on the sides or in the front of the body.
• Run in place 8 times.	• Lift feet high in the rear.
• Run in place 8 times	• Lift knees high in front.
• Perform 8 jumping jacks.	• Arms move down and up with leg movements
• Perform 8 jumping jacks.	• Arms move down and up to shoulder level
• Mountain Climber	• Jump and land with feet separated forward and backward. Alternate which foot lands in front and in back on each jump. Arms swing high in opposition to legs.
• Run in place 8 times.	• Lift knees high in the front.
• Run in place 8 times.	• Lift feet high in the rear.
• Perform 4 slides to the right.	• Repeat to the left. Repeat whole phrase.
• Hop on one foot and lift up the opposite knee.	• Reverse
• Hop and swing kick the opposite foot forward.	• Alternate
• Charleston Bounce Step	• Step L, kick R foot forward, step back, and touch L toe back. Repeat 8 times. Reverse.
• Schottische step 4 times in a row (Run R, L, R, Hop L. Alternate 4 X.)	• Run 3 times in place or while traveling then hop (clap simultaneously).
• Grapevine	• Step to R, cross L foot over R, step to R on the R foot, cross L behind the R, and step on R while traveling to R. Repeat phrase 4 times moving to R.
• Grapevine Schottische. 4 times	• Step to R on R, cross L behind R, step on R-to-R and hop on R. Reverse. Repeat 4 times.
• Run 3 times in place.	• Kick and clap on 4th count. Alternate. Repeat 4 X.
• Twist the body using a bounce landing.	• Swing arms in opposition overhead on each twist.
• Walk in place	• To cool down
• Leg Stretches & Upper Body Stretches	**See DPESS Chapter 16 for details.**

INSTRUCTIONAL ACTIVITIES | **TEACHING HINTS**

The Schottische is a partnered country dance, Bohemian in origin.

LESSON FOCUS (15 - 20 MINUTES)

Shot: Back Corner Return

Demonstrate the following:

- Right Back Corner:
- Left Back Corner:

See DPESS Chapter 20 for details.

A. Movement pattern from center court area to corner area.
B. Ready position while facing the corner (junction of side wall and back wall).
C. Movement pattern, including an adjustment step, for stroking a ball that rebounds from the back wall/side wall.
D. Movement pattern, including an adjustment step, for stroking a ball that rebounds from the side wall/back wall.
E. Movement pattern after hitting return shot.

The player hitting the ball doesn't get a point if the ball does not reach the front wall on the fly.

Demonstrate Back Corner Drill:

A. Down-the Line return.
B. Cross-Court return.

Practice. Explain the task sheets.

Direct four students to go to each court

GAME (5 MINUTES)

Crab Cage Ball

See DPESS Chapter 18 for details.

Use Whistle Mixer to create 4 teams. Assign each team to a side of the square. Delineate square with cones in each corner. Assign each team a number.

This game can improve foot/eye coordination.

EVALUATION/REVIEW AND CHEER

Review elements of the back corner return shot.
Under what condition will the server receive a point?
You performed the schottische step during fitness. From what country did that step originate?
What is one of the benefits of playing Crab Cage Ball?
In Finland, what is the game of tag and the tagger called?

Cheer: "Serving scores!"

Racquetball Lesson Plan 8

EQUIPMENT:

Cones and Station Instruction Cards
Drum and beater
CD/Music CD/Tape
CD/Cassette Player
1 Racquetball, eye guards and racquet per person
2 Clipboards, 2 pencils, 2 task sheets per court

The student will:

1. Demonstrate the cross court shot as demonstrated by the instructor.
2. Demonstrate proper passing shots as demonstrated by the instructor.

National Standards Met in this Lesson: **1, 2, 3, 4, 5, 6**

INSTRUCTIONAL ACTIVITIES	**TEACHING HINTS**
INTRODUCTORY ACTIVITY (2 - 3 MINUTES)	
Formation Rhythmic Running	**See DPESS Chapter 14 for details.**

INSTRUCTIONAL ACTIVITIES	**TEACHING HINTS**
FITNESS DEVELOPMENT (8 - 12 MINUTES)	
Four Corners	**See DPESS Chapter 16 for details.** See Badminton Unit, Lesson Plan 9 for details.
LESSON FOCUS (15 - 20 MINUTES)	
Shot Demonstrations: **Passing** **Forehand Stroke** **Backhand Stroke**	**See DPESS Chapter 20 for details.** A. Down-the-Line shot B. Cross Court shot C. Wide Cross Court shot
Explain the purpose of Passing Shots	A. Winning the point on the shot OR B. Creating a weak return from your opponent Demonstrate practice drill for Passing Shots using drop hit ball drill. Drop hit ball drill was in Lesson 2.
Practice Explain practice with the task sheets.	Direct four students to go to each court.
Switching hands during a rally may cause you to lose the rally.	
Out of Class Assignment Handout: Avoidable Hinders	Students are to read the handout by next class period.
GAME (5 MINUTES)	
Addition Tag	**See DPESS Chapter 14 for details.** See Lesson Plan 4 this unit for details.

EVALUATION/REVIEW AND CHEER

Describe the three shots practiced today. What is the purpose of each shot?
Why is switching hands while rallying discouraged?
What muscles were used today during the lesson?

Cheer: 3, 2, 1, Racquetball is fun!

RACQUETBALL HANDOUT: AVOIDABLE HINDERS

Avoidable Hinders: Result in loss of rally.

A. Failure to Move
B. Stroke Interference
C. Blocking
D. Moving into the Ball
E. Pushing
F. Intentional Distractions
G. View Obstruction
H. Wetting the Ball
I. Apparel or Equipment Loss

Note:

1. In recreational type racquetball, few "avoidable hinder" situations arise.
2. Avoidable hinders are not replayed.

Racquetball Lesson Plan 9

EQUIPMENT:

Continuity Exercise Music CD/Tape
CD/Cassette Player
1 Racquetball and racquet per student

OBJECTIVES:

The student will:

1. Demonstrate push-up form during Push-Up Tag as demonstrated by the instructor.
2. Demonstrate backhand and forehand strokes as demonstrated by the instructor.

National Standards Met in this Lesson: **1, 2, 3, 4, 5, 6**

INSTRUCTIONAL ACTIVITIES	TEACHING HINTS
INTRODUCTORY ACTIVITY (2 - 3 MINUTES)	
Push-Up Tag	**See DPESS Chapter 14 for details.**
FITNESS DEVELOPMENT (8 - 12 MINUTES)	
Continuity Exercises	**See DPESS Chapter 16 for details.** See Lesson Plan 3 from the Badminton Unit for details.
Name a sport where jump rope is often used for training? Boxing	
LESSON FOCUS (15 - 20 MINUTES)	
Avoidable Hinders:	**See DPESS Chapter 20 for details.** Demonstrate the different types. Place students in safe area on court for demonstration.
Serves: Power (Drive) "2" • Position in service zone from which serve is delivered. • Stroke action when delivering (hitting) the serve. • Flight patterns of the ball during the serve. • Follow through action after stroking the serve. • Movement pattern to center court position after served ball crosses Short Line.	
Never aim your shot a person, it can be dangerous.	
Practice Explain task sheets	Use a management game to make groups of four. Assign four students to go to each court.
GAME (5 MINUTES)	
Wand Activities: Wand Whirl. Wand Kick Over Thread the Needles.	**See DPESS Chapter 18 for details.** Scattered formation. Direct students to pick up a wand and bring it to their space.

Racquetball Lesson Plan 10

EQUIPMENT:

Partner Fitness Racetrack Instructions
Station Markers
Music
CD/Cassette Player

OBJECTIVES:

The student will:

1. Demonstrate the reverse pinch shot form as demonstrate by the instructor.
2. Participate in Crab Cage ball as directed by the instructor.

National Standards Met in this Lesson: **1, 2, 3, 4, 5, 6**

INSTRUCTIONAL ACTIVITIES	TEACHING HINTS

INTRODUCTORY ACTIVITY (2 - 3 MINUTES)

Mirror Drill In Place

Student faces partner. One person is leader and makes a quick movement with the hands, head, legs, or body. Partner tries to mirror and perform the exact movement. Leader must pause briefly between movements. Leader and partner exchange places after 30 seconds.

See DPESS Chapter 14 for details.
Create partners using "Toe-to-Toe" technique.
Spread groups out in space.
Identify the first "leader."

FITNESS DEVELOPMENT (8 - 12 MINUTES)

Partner Racetrack Fitness

See DPESS Chapter 16 for details.
See Lesson Plan 2 this unit for details.

LESSON FOCUS (15 - 20 MINUTES)

Pinch Shot

- **Forehand Stroke**
- **Backhand stroke**

Reverse Pinch Shot

- **Forehand Stroke**
- **Backhand stroke**

Review Drop Hit Ball Drill
See Lesson 2 for details

Practice
Explain Pinch Shot Drill Task Sheets

Always wear goggles when playing this game.

See DPESS Chapter 20 for details.
Place students on court in safe place.
Demonstrate the following:

1. Forehand side of court
2. Backhand side of court

Explain the values of Pinch Shots and when they should be incorporated into a player's game.
Demonstrate practice drill for Pinch Shots using drop hit ball drill.
Direct four students to go to each court.

GAME (5 MINUTES)

Crab Cage ball

See DPESS Chapter 18 for details.
See Lesson Plan 7 for details.

This game will increase muscular strength in the triceps brachii.

EVALUATION/REVIEW AND CHEER

What muscles were used today?
Review elements of the Pinch Shot and Reverse Drop Hit.

"2, 4, 6, 8, Racquetball is really great!"

Racquetball Lesson Plan 11

EQUIPMENT:

20-30 Bean bags of several colors
Fitness Cookie Jar Instructions
1 Racquetball, eye guards and racquet per student
2 Clipboards, 2 pencils, 2 Task Sheets per court; Station markers

OBJECTIVES:

The student will:
1. Demonstrate various activities according to the station card suggestion as demonstrated by the instructor.
2. Demonstrate the passing shot as demonstrated by the instructor.
3. Demonstrate serving the ball using form demonstrated by the instructor.

National Standards Met in this Lesson: **1, 2, 3, 4, 5, 6**

INSTRUCTIONAL ACTIVITIES / TEACHING HINTS

INTRODUCTORY ACTIVITY (2 - 3 MINUTES)

Beanbag Touch and Go

See DPESS Chapter 14 for details.

FITNESS DEVELOPMENT (8 - 12 MINUTES)

Fitness Cookie Jar Exchange: Card suggestions:
1. Jog around the Gym.
2. Crab walk forward and backward between cones.
3. Jog and shake hands with 8 different people.
4. Carioca (grapevine) step around a court going each direction.
5. Jog backwards around the Gym and "high 5" 4 other people.
6. Perform a mirroring activity with your partner.
7. Execute maximum number of curl-ups/push-ups.
8. Perform the coffee grinder on each side.
9. Execute maximum reverse push-ups.
10. Jump rope at a Hot Peppers rate.

See DPESS Chapter 16 for details.
Use management game to create partners.
Direct each partner set to pick a card from the "Cookie Jar."
Create a music CD/tape with 35 seconds of music for activity followed by a 10 second silence for picking a new card and changing activities.

Jogging backwards utilizes your quadriceps more than hamstrings.

LESSON FOCUS (15 - 20 MINUTES)

Record of Games Sheets

Explain the Record of Games sheet.
See DPESS Chapter 20 for details.

Practice
Drills: (6-8 minutes)
Students practice the following and change after 5 tries:
1. Two types of serves
2. Back-wall or Back Corner return shot
3. Passing or Pinch shot

Use a management game to create groups of 4.
Direct four students to go to each court to practice drills explained.

Ceiling ball shot is a shot that strikes the ceiling and then the front wall to bounce high and make the opponent shoot from deep in the court.

GAME (5 MINUTES)

Modified Racquetball
Two students (doers) play a 3-point singles game. The other two students (observers) stand outside the court. Students change roles at the end of each 3-point game. Explain Records of Game Sheets

Direct students to return to same courts for games.
Each student is responsible for completing their Record of Games sheet and submitting it to the Instructor at the end of class.

A high Z is a shot ten feet high or higher into the front corner.

EVALUATION/REVIEW AND CHEER

Review racquetball rules and the Records of Games Sheets.
Students create cheer.

RACQUETBALL RECORD OF GAMES SHEET

NAME: ____

Game #1: **Date**________

Opponent: ______________________________________

Score: _________ - _________ Circle Your Score

Game #2: **Date**________

Opponent: ______________________________________

Score: _________ - _________ Circle Your Score

Game #3: **Date**________

Opponent: ______________________________________

Score: _________ - _________ Circle Your Score

Racquetball Lesson Plan 12

EQUIPMENT:

Obstacle course markers
Station instructions
1 Clipboard and pencil per 2 students
1 Skills Test Sheet per student

OBJECTIVES:

The student will:

1. Demonstrate all skills acquired through the Skills Test as directed by the instructor.
2. Participate in single games up to 5 points as directed by the instructor.

National Standards Met in this Lesson: **1, 2, 3, 4, 5, 6**

INSTRUCTIONAL ACTIVITIES — TEACHING HINTS

INTRODUCTORY ACTIVITY (2 - 3 MINUTES)

Eliminate to allow more time for Skill Test.

FITNESS DEVELOPMENT (8 - 12 MINUTES)

Challenge Course

See DPESS Chapter 16 for details.
See Badminton Unit, Lesson Plan 1 for details.

This activity will increase cardiovascular strength and endurance.

LESSON FOCUS (15 - 20 MINUTES)

Skill Test
Explain Skill Test.

Use Whistle Mixer to create groups of 4.
Direct four students to go to each court.
When the Skill Test sheets are completed, students submit them to the Instructor.

GAME (5 MINUTES)

Modified Games
Play singles games to 5 points.

Upon completion of Skills Test, students are to play.
Students change roles after each 5-point game.

The round-the-world shot is hit high into the side wall first so the ball then hits the front wall and then the other side wall, effectively circling the court.

EVALUATION/REVIEW AND CHEER

Discuss exam and how it went. Introduce upcoming class activities.
In what way will a Challenge Course help improve your fitness level?
What muscles did you use in the Challenge Course and then again while playing the games?
What is the name of the shot that is hit high into the side wall first?

Cheer: Racquetball is fun!

RACQUETBALL SKILL TEST

Name: Student "A": ________________________________

Name: Student "B": ________________________________

Directions: Two students will work together. Place both of your names on the Skill Test sheet. One individual is the "doer" while the other individual is the "observer". The "observer" reads the skill to be demonstrated to the "doer", and places a check in the "yes" or "no" columns recording the performance of the doer. When the "doer" has completed the Skill Test, the "doer" becomes the "observer" and the "observer" becomes the "doer".

Note: Students will drop hit/toss ball to demonstrate the skills listed. Two attempts can be utilized to demonstrate each skill. If the skill is not demonstrated in the two attempts, the "NO" column is to be marked.

	Student "A"		**Student "B"**	
	Yes	**No**	**Yes**	**No**
1. *Demonstrate Serves*: Select two of the following: A. Lob Serve				
B. Half Lob Serve				
C. Power (Drive)				
2. *Demonstrate the following shots:* A. Back wall Return: Forehand stroke				
B. Down-the-Line Pass: Backhand stroke				
C. Cross Court Pass: Forehand stroke				
D. Back Corner Return: Forehand stroke				
E. Back-wall Return: Backhand stroke				
F. Traditional Pinch: Backhand stroke Backhand side of Court				
G. Reverse Pinch: Forehand side of court				
H. Back-wall Return: Backhand stroke				
Totals:				

Racquetball Lesson Plan 13

EQUIPMENT:

1 Written exam and pencil per student
Continuity Exercise Music CD/Tape
CD/Cassette Player
1 Individual jump rope per person
1 Racquetball, racquet, and protective eye guard per student

OBJECTIVES:

The student will:

1. Increase fitness levels while participating in the continuity exercises as demonstrated by the instructor.
2. Participate in a game of racquetball as demonstrated by the instructor.

National Standards Met in this Lesson: **1, 2, 3, 4, 5, 6**

INSTRUCTIONAL ACTIVITIES	TEACHING HINTS

INTRODUCTORY ACTIVITY (2 - 3 MINUTES)

Eliminate to allow more time for exam and playing.

FITNESS DEVELOPMENT (8 - 12 MINUTES)

Continuity Exercises	**See DPESS Chapter 16 for details.** See Badminton Unit, Lesson Plan 3 for details.

Continuity exercises will increase cardiovascular strength and endurance.

LESSON FOCUS (15 - 20 MINUTES)

Written Exam Explain Exam Instructions.	Distribute a copy of the exam and a pencil to each student. Students complete the exam and return it and the pencil to the instructor.

GAME (5 MINUTES)

Play Racquetball Use 5 points as a game.	Allow students to set up games upon completion of exam. Change opponents after each 5-point game.

The first Racquetball World Championships were held in 1981.

EVALUATION/REVIEW AND CHEER

In what way do Continuity Exercises help your body?
When were the first World Championship games in racquetball held?
Review areas students were concerned about on the written exam.
Discuss how each of the games went.

Students create their own cheer.

RACQUETBALL ROUND ROBIN TOURNAMENT: SINGLES

GROUP: ____________ **CLASS**: ______________

PLAYERS:

1.______________________________

2.______________________________

3.______________________________

4.______________________________

5.______________________________

Play one (1) game to 7 points.

When the game has been played between two players,
circle the pairing numbers of the players.

1 vs 5	2 vs 4	5 vs 4
3 vs 1	4 vs 3	5 vs 2
3 vs 2	2 vs 1	1 vs 4
3 vs 5		

RACQUETBALL UNIT: EXAM

Name: ______________________________

TRUE - FALSE: Completely cover the T with a "dot" if the statement is TRUE or completely cover the F with a "dot" if the statement is FALSE.

T F 1. The game of racquetball experienced tremendous growth during the 1970's and became very popular.
T F 2. In a regulation game of racquetball, the first player to score 15 points (and ahead by 1 points) is the winner.
T F 3. The server should move to the center court area immediately after serving the ball.
T F 4. Short serves and long serves are the most common types of fault serves.
T F 5. Two types of passing shots are cross-court and down the line or wall.
T F 6. The individual receiving can score points.
T F 7. AARA rules require individuals to wear protective eye guards while playing.
T F 8. The player serving or the player receiving can call a hinder.
T F 9. A non-front serve is one type or example of a service fault.
T F 10. The "side-by-side" formation used in doubles play is the easier to master than the "I" formation.

FILL-IN-THE-BLANKS: Place the correct response or term in the appropriate blank(s).

1. There are three different types of games that can be played in racquetball. These involve the number of players. Name the three types of games.

   ______________ ______________ ______________

2. Various types of serves should be used in playing the game of racquetball. Name four types of serves that have been introduced and explained during this course.

   ______________ ______________
   ______________ ______________

3. Name four types of fault serves.

   ______________ ______________
   ______________ ______________

4. There are seven types of Dead-Ball Hinders, which can occur during a game. Name four of these:

   ______________ ______________
   ______________ ______________

5. Name four types of out serves.

   ______________ ______________
   ______________ ______________

MATCHING: Place the letter of the best response in the blank next to the statement that best describes said response.

A. Kill Shot	B. Dead-Ball Hinder	C. Service Zone
D. Short Serve	E. Play Continues	F. Passing Shot
G. Loss of Service	H. Point	I. Long Serve
J. Ceiling Serve	K. Doubles	L. Non-Front Serve

_____ 1. Player A serves the ball, B's return of service strikes A in the back of the leg.
_____ 2. Player B attempts to serve, but the ball contacts the side wall before hitting the front wall and rebounding into the backcourt area.
_____ 3. The area bordered by the service line and the short line.
_____ 4. During play, Player A, who has served, hits a return, which rebounds off the front wall and strikes their racket.
_____ 5. Player B's serve rebounds from the front wall, bounces on the floor back of the short line and contacts the left side wall before Player A attempts to return the ball.
_____ 6. Following a legal serve by Player A, Player B's return bounces on the floor on the way to the front wall.
_____ 7. Player A serves the ball, but the rebound is not long enough to carry the ball over the short line on the fly.

_____ 8. An offensive shot which is hit low on the front wall so the rebounding will ball bounce two times very quickly.

_____ 9. A game in which the players can utilize the "side-by-side" formation.

_____ 10. Player B's serve rebounds from the front wall and contacts the sidewall and back wall before bouncing on the floor.

Racquetball Lesson Plan 14

EQUIPMENT:

Round Robin Tournament Chart
1 Clipboard and pencil and score sheet per 2 students
Dance Exercise Music CD/Tape
1 Racquetball, eye guard and racquet per student
1 Record of Games Sheet per student from lesson 11.
CD/Cassette Player

OBJECTIVES:

The student will:

1. The student will participate in an aerobic workout to improve their overall fitness.
2. Participate in Round Robin Tournament using skills demonstrated by the instructor.

National Standards Met in this Lesson: **1, 2, 3, 4, 5, 6**

INSTRUCTIONAL ACTIVITIES	TEACHING HINTS

INTRODUCTORY ACTIVITY (2 - 3 MINUTES)

Eliminate to allow time for tournament play.

FITNESS DEVELOPMENT (8 - 12 MINUTES)

Aerobic Workout

See DPESS Chapter 16 for details.
See Lesson Plan 7 this unit for details.

LESSON FOCUS AND GAME (15 - 25 MINUTES)

2 Day Round Robin Tournament
All tournament games will be to 7 points.
Each student will record the results of their games on their Record of Games sheet and submit it to the instructor at the end of each class period.

Divide students into groups of 5 based on skill level. Each student will play a 7-point game against each student in his group. (Each student will end up playing four different opponents during the 2-day tournament.)

EVALUATION/REVIEW AND CHEER

Discuss how each of the tournament games is going.
Clarify questions regarding rules/ Records of Games Sheets.
What muscles were used during fitness today?
Was anything particularly challenging during the Aerobic Workout?

Teams create cheers.

Racquetball Lesson Plan 15

EQUIPMENT:
Round Robin Tournament Chart
1 Clipboard and pencil and score sheet per 2 students
Dance Exercise Music CD/Tape
1 Racquetball, eye guard and racquet per student
1 Record of Games Sheet per student
CD/Cassette Player

OBJECTIVES:
The student will:
1. Participate in Parachute Rhythmic Aerobics to improve strength, endurance, flexibility, and coordination.
2. Participate in the Round Robin Tournament and demonstrate all skills in racquetball learned during the instructional unit.

National Standards Met in this Lesson: **1, 2, 3, 4, 5, 6**

INSTRUCTIONAL ACTIVITIES	TEACHING HINTS

INTRODUCTORY ACTIVITY (2 - 3 MINUTES)
Eliminate to allow time for Tournament.

FITNESS DEVELOPMENT (8 - 12 MINUTES)
Parachute Rhythmic Aerobic Activity

See DPESS Chapter 16 for details.
See Badminton Unit, Lesson Plan 11 for details.

The first use of parachute in the military took place in WWI.

LESSON FOCUS AND GAME (15 - 25 MINUTES)
Complete Round Robin Tournament.

Continue Round Robin Tournament

Carrying or slinging the ball with the racquet results in the loss of the rally.

Pickup Games

Students that complete the tournament before the end of the class period can play 5-point singles games against any other student in the class.

This game was invented by Joe Sobek in 1948 incorporating rules from squash and handball.

EVALUATION/REVIEW AND CHEER
Discuss how each of the tournament games went.
Introduce the next unit.

Students create cheer.

Soccer

This unit has been specifically designed to meet all six components of the NASPE National Standards for Physical Education.

OBJECTIVES:

The student will:

1. Demonstrate changing from walking, to sprinting quickly when given a signal by the instructor.
2. Participate in the Four Corners Fitness Activities to improve her overall fitness levels.
3. Demonstrate proper tagging skills demonstrating safety rules explained by the instructor.
4. Demonstrate the ability to perform locomotor movements on command.
5. Rapidly change movements and count the number of repetitions performed during the Magic Number Challenge.
6. Form a variety of pyramids and demonstrate the proper points of support while performing them.
7. Demonstrate a smooth rhythmic run during the Formation Rhythmic Running Activity.
8. Space himself safely while running during Racetrack Fitness and Formation Rhythmic Running.
9. Participate in Circuit Training exercises and movements working towards performing at a higher intensity than previously.
10. Demonstrate the ability to work in groups and properly perform various exercises at each station.
11. Participate in Aerobic Exercises to improve overall fitness.
12. Perform Continuity Exercises including rope jumping for 30 seconds to improve her overall fitness levels.
13. Demonstrate the skills and techniques of passing a soccer ball in the air on the laces, as demonstrated by the teacher.
14. Demonstrate the correct techniques for dribbling a soccer ball with both inside and outside of both feet.
15. Demonstrate the ability to dribble a soccer ball for speed using outside of the foot.
16. Demonstrate control of her body and the ball while dribbling the around cones.
17. Develop ball foot and eye hand coordination using a soccer ball.
18. Demonstrate the proper techniques for passing a soccer ball short and long distances with both the inside and outside of both feet.
19. Demonstrate one and two touch passing skills using both inside and outside of both feet as demonstrated by the teacher.
20. Demonstrate the proper skills and techniques for collecting a soccer ball to themselves using their head.
21. Demonstrate quick reactions while playing soccer with classmates in a game situation.
22. Demonstrate the ability to work with a partner using a task sheet and during all class activities.
23. Demonstrate dribbling, passing, trapping and heading skills using form demonstrated by the instructor during the skill test.
24. Demonstrate proper dribbling techniques in a game of Dribblerama.
25. Participate in the Soccer Tournament demonstrating skills practiced during the unit.

SOCCER BLOCK PLAN
3 WEEK UNIT

Week #1	Monday	Tuesday	Wednesday	Thursday	Friday
Introductory Activity	Fastest Tag	Move and Assume Pose	Formation Rhythmic Running	Number Challenges	Combination Movements
Fitness	Circuit Training	Mini Challenge Course	Partner Racetrack Fitness	Fitness Scavenger Hunt	Parachute Fitness Exercises
Focus	Dribbling Kick and Trap	Dribbling Kicking	Dribbling with a Defender	Dribbling High Trapping Skills	Throw-ins Instep Kick and Trap
Game	Frisbee 21	Chain Tag	Team Tug of War	Parachute Activities	Hacky Sack Juggling

Week #2	Monday	Tuesday	Wednesday	Thursday	Friday
Introductory Activity	Blob Tag	Hoops on the Ground	Walk, Trot, Sprint	New Leader	Move and Freeze on Signal
Fitness	Circuit Training	Aerobic Workout	Four Corners	Continuity Exercises	Parachute Fitness Activities
Focus	Passing and Trapping	Passing Combination Skills	Passing	Heel Pass Heading Dribbling	Heading Goal Kicking Goalie Defense
Game	Frisbee Keep Away	Flag Chase	Half Court Sideline Soccer	Soccer Keep Away	Dribblerama

Week #3	Monday	Tuesday	Wednesday	Thursday	Friday
Introductory Activity	Group Tag	Run, Stop, Pivot	Vanishing Bean Bags	Mini Pyramids	Ball Gymnastics
Fitness	Hexagon Hustle	Challenge Course Circuit	Parachute Aerobic Activity	Circuit Training	Fitness Scavenger Hunt
Focus	Rules Soccer Game	Play Soccer	Soccer Skill Test	Round Robin Tournament	Continue Tournament
Game	Dribbling Relays	Continue Soccer Games	Heading Game	Tournament	Tournament

Soccer Lesson Plan 1

EQUIPMENT:

20 cones
Continuity music CD/tape
1 task sheet per 2 students
1 pen/pencil and clipboard per 2 students
1 ball per student
CD/Cassette player
Whistle

OBJECTIVES:

The student will:

1. Demonstrate proper tagging skills demonstrating safety rules explained by the instructor.
2. Demonstrate the ability to work in groups and properly perform various exercises at each station.
3. Demonstrate the correct techniques for dribbling a soccer ball with both inside and outside of both feet.
4. Demonstrate the correct techniques for trapping a soccer ball using form demonstrated by the instructor.
5. Demonstrate the ability to work with a partner when playing Frisbee 21 and use form demonstrated in class.
6. Describe the history of the game and activity now known as Frisbee.

National Standards Met in this Lesson: **1, 2, 3, 4, 5, 6**

INSTRUCTIONAL ACTIVITIES	TEACHING HINTS

INTRODUCTORY ACTIVITY (2 - 3 MINUTES)

Fastest Tag Everyone is "it".	**See DPESS Chapter 14 for details.** Scattered formation See Lesson 8, Volleyball Unit for details.

Student will demonstrate effective safety skills while playing game.

FITNESS DEVELOPMENT (8 - 12 MINUTES)

Stations: Circuit Training When music starts, students begin activity at the station. At pause in music they switch. Stations consist of push-ups, lunges, sit ups, flyers, etc.. Include stations for aerobic activity.	**See DPESS Chapter 16 for details.** Using Whistle Mixer, create groups of 7 students. Assign each group to begin at a different station. Go through all stations once then begin again.

Students perform correct techniques while performing strengthening exercises to maintain maximum level of proficiency.

LESSON FOCUS (15 - 20 MINUTES)

Dribbling using inside and outside of both feet. Explain Task Sheets and rotation. The doer will dribble the ball 10 times each with the inside, outside, left and right feet to the cone and back, then switch	**See DPESS Chapter 19 for details.** Place cones on field 10 feet apart for practice areas. Use Back- to - Back to create partners. Assign one partner to pick up equipment: 1 Ball, 1 Clipboard, pencil and Task Sheet Work with same partner.
Inside Kick and Trap: Demonstrate skill and drill.	

A form of soccer was originally developed in England in 1863. Soccer, as we know it today, however, was molded during the 1960s.

GAME (5 MINUTES)

Frisbee 21	**See DPESS Chapter 20 for details.** See Golf Unit, Lesson 13 for details.

The game of Frisbee originated in the mid 1800's when a group of Yale University students tossed a "Frisbie Baking Company" empty pie tin around for fun. In 1948, in Los Angeles, a plastic version of the Frisbee was invented by Walter Fredrick Morrison and his partner Warren Franscioni. In 1957 Wham-O began producing the Frisbee. In 1967, high school students in Maplewood, New Jersey, invented Ultimate Frisbee, a recognized sport that is a cross between football, soccer and basketball. Ten years later, a form of Frisbee golf was introduced, complete with professional playing courses and associations.

EVALUATION/REVIEW AND CHEER

Ask students what techniques they worked on in class.
Cheer: Soccer, Soccer, Let's Play!

Soccer Lesson Plan 2

EQUIPMENT:

20 cones
1 soccer ball per 2 students
1 task sheet per 2 students
1 pen/pencil, clipboard per 2 students
CD/Cassette Player
Continuity Music Exercise CD/Tape
Poster board for course
Whistle

OBJECTIVES:

The student will:

1. Demonstrate dribbling the ball for speed as demonstrated by the teacher.
2. Demonstrate kicking and trapping skills using form taught by the instructor.
3. Demonstrate the proper skills and techniques for dribbling, passing and trapping a ball using form demonstrated by the instructor.
4. Participate in the game of Chain Tag following instructions set by the instructor and cooperating safely with classmates.

National Standards Met in this Lesson: **1, 2, 3, 4, 5, 6**

INSTRUCTIONAL ACTIVITIES	TEACHING HINTS
INTRODUCTORY ACTIVITY (2 - 3 MINUTES)	
Move and Assume Pose Students will move doing a variety of locomotor movements. Freeze on signal and assume balancing poses on various body parts.	**See DPESS Chapter 14 for details.** Scattered formation.
FITNESS DEVELOPMENT (8 - 12 MINUTES)	
Mini Challenge Course The course will consist of crab walk, weave in and out of cones, and hop over cones, skip, and jog backward.	**See DPESS Chapter 16 for details.** See Lesson 6, Volleyball for details Students will be in groups and each group will start at different times to allow for space.

INSTRUCTIONAL ACTIVITIES	TEACHING HINTS
LESSON FOCUS (15 - 20 MINUTES)	
Dribbling for speed The student will run and dribble ball between 2 cones 10 times. Both partners can practice at once with adequate spacing.	**See DPESS Chapter 19 for details.** Set cones up 20 feet apart. Using a management technique, create partners. 1 ball per person
Kicking and Trapping Repeat drill used yesterday, but increase distance.	Use same partners.
Combination Dribbling and Kicking Drill Student dribbles toward partner 1/2 distance between the cones set up, then passes to partner who must trap the ball and begin the drill himself. Alternate turns.	Use same partners and cones set up for dribbling drill.

Soccer was originally called football and is still called futbol in some countries.

GAME (5 MINUTES)

Chain Tag Two parallel lines 20 feet apart. 3 people in center between the lines form a chain. The players on the end can tag people. On signal the center says "come" and the 2 lines run across, if tagged they join the chain.	Select 3 to be in center

EVALUATION/REVIEW AND CHEER

Talk about skills practiced today. Ask if there were any particular areas needing clarification.

Cheer: 2-4-6-8 "Dribblin's great!"

Soccer Lesson Plan 3

EQUIPMENT:

20 cones
1 soccer ball per person
Music tape
Poster board for course
Team Tug of War rope
CD player
Whistle
1 pen and clipboard per 2 students

National Standards Met in this Lesson: **1, 2, 3, 5, 6**

INSTRUCTIONAL ACTIVITIES	TEACHING HINTS

INTRODUCTORY ACTIVITY (2 - 3 MINUTES)

Formation Rhythmic Running
Run on signal, run in direction led.

See DPESS Chapter 14 for details.
Scattered formation inside a coned off area.
See Lesson 5, Volleyball Unit for complete details.

FITNESS DEVELOPMENT (8 - 12 MINUTES)

Partner Racetrack Fitness

See DPESS Chapter 16 for details.
See Lesson 6, Tennis Unit for complete details.

LESSON FOCUS (15 - 20 MINUTES)

Dribbling through cones
Stations set up with cones simulating defenders.
Each station will have more cones than the previous with a tighter area. Each student will dribble through each station 2 times once with left foot and once with right foot.
Object is to not knock down cones

See DPESS Chapter 19 for details.
Use Whistle Mixer to create groups of 3 - 4.
Assign groups of 3 - 4 to each station.
On signal, change stations. Keep head up and the ball close to body.
Use both inside and outside of foot. Maintain control.

Dribbling with a defender
Demonstrate methods of "stealing" ball from dribbler.
Dribble toward defender who tries to take ball away.

Same groups.
1 dribbler to 1 defender or 2 dribblers to 1 defender if in groups of 3.

Soccer is the most popular sport in the world played by people of all ages.

GAME (5 MINUTES)

Team Tug of War
There are 2 even teams each team on each half of the rope. On signal teams begin pulling and first team to pull the other over the line wins.

See DPESS Chapter 18 for details.
Use a management game i.e. back-to-back to create two groups.

Students should maintain caution balanced along with a positive attitude.

EVALUATION/REVIEW AND CHEER

Review skills taught by asking questions.
What muscles were used in today's fitness activities?
What is the name of a popular sport played by people of all ages all over the world?

Cheer: We Love Soccer!

Soccer Lesson Plan 4

EQUIPMENT:

Magic number cards
1 jump rope per student
1 soccer ball per student
30 cones
Whistle
Parachute

OBJECTIVES:

The student will:

1. Participate in the introductory activity Number Challenges demonstrating cognitive focus and memory skills.
2. Participate in the Fitness Scavenger Hunt following the directions and cooperating with teammates.
3. Demonstrate defensive dribbling skills using form demonstrated by the instructor
4. Perform high trapping skills as demonstrated by the instructor.
5. Participate in the parachute game activities demonstrating cooperation and the ability to follow instructions given by the instructor.

National Standards Met in this Lesson: **1, 2, 3, 4, 5, 6**

INSTRUCTIONAL ACTIVITIES	TEACHING HINTS
INTRODUCTORY ACTIVITY (2 - 3 MINUTES)	
Number Challenges Hold up a card with 3 numbers on it (i.e. 8,10,5). The students must then perform 3 selected movements the specified number of times.	**See DPESS Chapter 14 for details.** Scattered formation Students put together a series of movements based on the magic numbers given.
FITNESS DEVELOPMENT (8 - 12 MINUTES)	
Fitness Scavenger Hunt	**See DPESS Chapter 16 for details.** See Golf Unit, Lesson 7 for details.
LESSON FOCUS (15 - 20 MINUTES)	
Dribbling with Defensive Pressure First each student will dribble in coned area with 1 defender using skills learned, then 2 defenders. After going through coned area once, change roles. Repeat 3 X per student.	**See DPESS Chapter 19 for details.** Using Whistle Mixer, create groups of 3. Identify coned off area.
High Trapping Skills Demonstrating trapping with thigh. Practice: Toss ball toward thigh of partner. Trap with thigh and dribble 5 feet forward, Soccer games are played with 11 players on each team.	Use same groups as above, or switch to groups of 2 for this practice. Can rotate roles if groups of 3 used and 2 balls.
GAME (5 MINUTES)	
Parachute Activities	**See DPESS Chapter 16 for details.** See Weight Training Unit, Lesson 15 for details.

EVALUATION/REVIEW AND CHHER

Review elements involved in trapping and defense.
What muscles were used during the Fitness Scavenger Hunt?
How many players are on a soccer team?

Cheer: 2, 4, 6, 8, Soccer's Great!

Soccer Lesson Plan 5

EQUIPMENT:

1 parachute
1 Hacky Sack/ bean bag per student
Whistle
1 Soccer ball per student
2 cones per 2 students

OBJECTIVES:

The student will:

1. Participate in the Combination Movements activities following the steps directed by the teacher.
2. Participate in Parachute Fitness Exercises involving locomotor, strength, and flexibility activities as directed by the instructor.
3. Be able to throw the ball in and thigh trap 10 times with a partner as demonstrated by the instructor.
4. Demonstrate foot juggling skills with a Hacky Sack during the game portion of class.

National Standards Met in this Lesson: **1, 2, 3, 4, 5, 6**

INSTRUCTIONAL ACTIVITIES	TEACHING HINTS
INTRODUCTORY ACTIVITY (2 - 3 MINUTES)	
Combination movements Teacher will call out movements and students will follow. Movement suggestions: hop turn around and shake; jump make shape in air balance; skip, collapse and roll; curl, roll, jump with 1/2 turn; whirl skip sink slowly; hop collapse creep; kneel sway jump to feet.	**See DPESS Chapter 14 for details.** ("Move and Change the Type of Locomotion") Scattered formation. After each movement phrase, student will skip while waiting for next instruction.
FITNESS DEVELOPMENT (8 - 12 MINUTES)	
Parachute Fitness Exercises Student will hold a handle and begin either running, hopping, skipping, etc. On 1 whistle signal they will change directions. On 2 whistles they will lower chute quickly and do the exercise specified by teacher.	**See DPESS Chapter 16 for details.** Scattered around parachute, holding edge of chute.
LESSON FOCUS (15 - 20 MINUTES)	
Throw-in, Thigh Trap Demonstrate overhand throw-in. Demonstrate thigh trap, to foot trap.	**See DPESS Chapter 19 for details.** Use Elbow-to-Elbow technique to create partners. Direct students to practice throw in and trapping skills.
Throw-in, Thigh Trap, and Dribble Demonstrate skill and practice drill a given distance.	Same partners. Both partners practice.
Instep Kick and Trap Demonstrate Instep Kick to partner, foot trap.	Same partners. Alternate roles. Each person practices 10 times.

The most prestigious soccer competition is called the World Cup and is held every 4 years

GAME (5 MINUTES)	
Hacky Sack/ Bean Bag Juggling Student juggles bag on knees, thighs, and feet only. Strives to keep bag in action.	Scattered formation. Can challenge to count how many repetitions are possible before losing control. Identify class champion.

Hacky Sack juggling develops foot-eye coordination and juggling skills similar to those used in soccer.

EVALUATION/REVIEW AND CHEER

Review trapping and throw in skill elements.
What game was played today that develops similar skills to soccer?

Cheer: 2, 4, 6, 8, Jugglin's really great!

Soccer Lesson Plan 6

EQUIPMENT:

2 cones per 3 students
1 soccer ball per 3 students
1 task sheet per student
1 pencil and clipboard per 3 students
Continuity Music Exercise CD/Tape
CD/Cassette Player
6 Hula Hoops
6 Jump Ropes

OBJECTIVES:

The student will:

1. Participate in Blob Tag cooperating with classmates and following the safety and game instructions given by the teacher.
2. Participate in Circuit Training Activities involving locomotor, strength, and flexibility activities as directed by the instructor.
3. Be able to perform passing and trapping skills using task sheets in a group of 3.
4. Demonstrate the ability to play Frisbee Keep Away cooperating with teammates during the game portion of class.

National Standards Met in this Lesson: **1, 2, 3, 4, 5, 6**

INSTRUCTIONAL ACTIVITIES	TEACHING HINTS

INTRODUCTORY ACTIVITY (2 - 3 MINUTES)

Blob Tag

See DPESS Chapter 14 for details.

Students will exercise safety habits while playing Blob Tag. Students will also exhibit positive team play attitudes.

FITNESS DEVELOPMENT (8 - 12 MINUTES)

Circuit training

See DPESS Chapter 16 for details.
See Lesson 5, Golf Unit for details.

Students will demonstrate proper strength and flexibility techniques to avoid injury.

LESSON FOCUS (15 - 20 MINUTES)

Passing and Trapping Skills using Task Sheets
Explain Task Sheets and demonstrate skills to practice
Each group will be at a cone with another cone 10 ft. away.

Using Whistle Mixer, make groups of 3.
Direct students to take 1 clipboard, pencil and 1 Task Sheet per person to assigned areas.

Soccer games consist of two halves, yet the time per half varies with the league.

GAME (5 MINUTES)

Frisbee Keep Away

See DPESS Chapter 20 for details.
See Lesson 1, Golf Unit for details

EVALUATION/REVIEW AND CHEER

Discussion on skills practiced today.
What muscles were used during Circuit Training?

Cheer: PE's great!

RECIPROCAL TASK SHEET: SOCCER PASSING

Name: ____

Directions: Work with two other people. One person is the "doer", one person is the pass receiver, while the other person is the "observer". The observer reads the information/instructions to the doer, offers verbal feedback and places a check in the "yes" or "no" column recording the performance of the "doer". Record the date of the practice. After 5 practices, rotate roles. The "doer" becomes the "observer", the "observer" becomes the receiver. Each person has his/her own task sheet.

PASSING	**DATES**							
(Record date of practice)								
	Yes	**No**	**Yes**	**No**	**Yes**	**No**	**Yes**	**No**
1. Use the inside of your foot and pass the ball to your partner standing 10' away from you. Partner returns ball to you. Repeat 5 times.								
2. Use the outside of your foot and pass the ball to your partner standing 10' away from you. Repeat 5 times.								
ROTATE ROLES								
FOOT TRAPPING	**Yes**	**No**	**Yes**	**No**	**Yes**	**No**	**Yes**	**No**
1. Repeat # 1 above and foot trap the ball.								
2. Repeat # 2 above and foot trap the ball.								
ROTATE ROLES								
THROW IN, THIGH TRAP, FOOT TRAP	**Yes**	**No**	**Yes**	**No**	**Yes**	**No**	**Yes**	**No**
1. Throw-in ball to partner, trap with thighs, drop ball to foot trap. Repeat 5 times.								
ROTATE ROLES								
Turn Completed Task Sheets in to Instructor								

Soccer Lesson Plan 7

EQUIPMENT:

Cones to mark off dribbling area
1 soccer ball per 2 students
CD/Cassette player
Aerobic Exercise Music CD/Tape
1 flag for each student
1 Hula Hoop per 2 students

OBJECTIVES:

The student will:

1. Participate in Hoops on the Ground cooperating with classmates and following the instructions given by the teacher.
2. Participate in an Aerobic Workout presented by the teacher involving locomotor, strength, and flexibility activities.
3. Pass the ball with the top of the foot 5 times to a partner.
4. Demonstrate combining dribbling and passing skills throughout the lesson focus using form demonstrated by instructor.
5. Demonstrate the ability to cooperate with teammates during the game Flag Chase during the final portion of class.

National Standards Met in this Lesson: **1, 2, 3, 4, 5, 6**

INSTRUCTIONAL ACTIVITIES	TEACHING HINTS

INTRODUCTORY ACTIVITY (2 - 3 MINUTES)

Hoops on the Ground

Students run around the area where hoops are on ground. Teacher calls a number and that number of students must fit inside a hoop in 5 seconds or less.

See DPESS Chapter 14 for details.
Scattered formation.

FITNESS DEVELOPMENT (8 - 12 MINUTES)

Aerobic Workout

See DPESS Chapter 16 for details.
See Lesson 7, Racquetball Unit for details.

LESSON FOCUS (15 - 20 MINUTES)

Passing: Top of Foot

Demonstrate passing the ball in the air with top of foot Head should be down, toe down, and ankle locked.

See DPESS Chapter 19 for details.
Use elbow to elbow to create pairs.
1 ball per two students.

Combination Drills:

Dribbling, Instep Pass

Demonstrate dribbling down the field 15', instep pass to lead partner. Continue.

Toss ball to partner at foot. Partner passes using top of foot. Have doer face a fence so pass won't go too far. Repeat 5 times then switch roles (contact the ball with laces).

Throw in, Top of Foot Pass

Demonstrate throw in, top of foot pass to partner.

Pass ball to lead partner down field.

Dribbling, Outside Foot Pass

Repeat drill used performing with the Instep pass.

If a game ends in a tie, the game will go into overtime. If the games remains tied at the end of overtime, the game will go into a shootout. Teacher will explain shootout.

GAME (5 MINUTES)

Flag chase (Variation of Flag Grab)

On signal students run around and try to pull flags off. If flag is pulled you sit down. The one with the most flags after a given short period wins. Repeat.

See DPESS Chapter 14 for details.
Scattered formation.
Each student has a flag tucked into his or her shorts.

EVALUATION/REVIEW AND CHEER

Ask questions regarding the proper form used for passing the ball in the air.
What happens when a game ends in a tie score?

Cheer: Exercise...yeeaa

Soccer Lesson Plan 8

EQUIPMENT:

2 Cones per 2 students
Whistle
Signs for Four Corners
Pinnies
1 soccer ball per 2 students
Poster board

OBJECTIVES:

The student will:

1. Participate in Walk, Trot, Sprint cooperating with classmates and following the instructions given by the teacher.
2. Participate in an Four Corners fitness activities presented by the teacher involving locomotor, strength, and flexibility activities.
3. Demonstrate passing the ball to a partner while moving using form demonstrated by the instructor.
4. Demonstrate the soccer skills of dribbling, passing, and trapping and the ability to cooperate with teammates during the game Half Court Sideline Soccer during the final portion of class.

National Standards Met in this Lesson: **1, 2, 3, 4, 5, 6**

INSTRUCTIONAL ACTIVITIES	TEACHING HINTS
INTRODUCTORY ACTIVITY (2 - 3 MINUTES)	
Walk, Trot, Sprint 1 whistle = run; 2 whistles = trot; 3 whistles = sprint; 4 whistles = stop and perform a stretch demonstrated. If the teacher claps = change directions.	**(Similar to Walk, Jog, Sprint)** Scattered formation. Teacher directs the changes.
FITNESS DEVELOPMENT (8 - 12 MINUTES)	
Four corners There will be groups of students at each corner, with a sign with different movements on it at each corner. On signal students begin activity, on second signal they skip, jog, etc. to next station.	**See DPESS Chapter 16 for details.** See Lesson 9, Golf Unit for complete details. Use Whistle Mixer to create even numbers of people to begin at each corner.
LESSON FOCUS (15 - 20 MINUTES)	
Passing (1 touch, 2 touch passing) Students will be 5 yards apart. On each signal students will continue passing but move back to be next cone. On signal they will move back to last cone marker while still passing the ball. They will do the same thing with the 2 touch (start at 1 ft. and move to 20). **2 touch**: Same techniques but stop the ball with the inside of the foot first, then pass it back. Repeat drill.	**See DPESS Chapter 19 for details.** Use Toe to Toe to create partners. 1 ball per 2 students Partners stand opposite each other at cone markings.
GAME (5 MINUTES)	
Half Court Sideline Soccer Divide field in half. Follow rules of Sideline Soccer, but on 1/2 of field.	**See DPESS Chapter 19 for details.** Create even teams using a management game.
EVALUATION/REVIEW AND CHEER	
Discuss skills practiced during the day and Sideline Soccer game. What muscles were mainly used in class today? **Cheer: We Love Soccer!**	

Soccer Lesson Plan 9

EQUIPMENT:

1 jump rope per student
1 soccer ball per 2 students
Continuity Exercise Music CD/Tape
20 cones
CD/Cassette Player
Whistle

OBJECTIVES:

The student will:

1. Participate in New Leader activities cooperating with classmates and following the instructions given by the teacher.
2. Participate in an Continuity Exercises during the Fitness portion of class as presented by the teacher involving aerobic, agility, strength, and flexibility activities.
3. Demonstrate the Heel Pass technique to pass the ball to a partner using form demonstrated by the instructor.
4. Demonstrate the soccer skills of dribbling, passing, and trapping and the ability to cooperate with teammates during the lesson focus portion of class.
5. Demonstrate previously taught soccer skills and cooperation with teammates while playing Soccer Keep Away.

National Standards Met in this Lesson: **1, 2, 3, 4, 5, 6**

INSTRUCTIONAL ACTIVITIES	TEACHING HINTS
INTRODUCTORY ACTIVITY (2 - 3 MINUTES)	
New Leader The first person in line is the first leader. On signal leader executes a movement, the rest of the line must follow. On the next signal the leaders switch.	**See DPESS Chapter 14 for details.** Use Whistle Mixer to create groups of 3 - 5.
FITNESS DEVELOPMENT (8 - 12 MINUTES)	
Continuity Exercises See Lesson 1, Golf for complete details.	**See DPESS Chapter 16 for details.** Scattered formation.

Continuity Exercises are a form of interval training. Interval training is an exercise strategy that is intended to improve performance with short training sessions.

INSTRUCTIONAL ACTIVITIES	TEACHING HINTS
LESSON FOCUS (15 - 20 MINUTES)	
Heel Pass Demonstrate the heel pass. Goal: pass to a player behind you. Toe up and ankle are up and you pass the ball with the heel to a person behind you.	**See DPESS Chapter 19 for details.** Partner formation with a ball. Students will be 10 'apart and pass. This is a blind pass.
Heading Demonstrate heading to a partner. May use rubber balls to begin.	Same partner formation.
Dribble Through Cones (Review)	Same partners. Use drill taught on previous day.
GAME (5 MINUTES)	
Soccer Keep Away Use all skills taught to keep ball from middle person. Rotate when middle person intercepts ball or after a given time limit.	**See DPESS Chapter 19 for details.** Use Whistle Mixer to create groups of 3.

EVALUATION/REVIEW AND CHEER

Ask students which passing skill worked best for them and why.

Cheer: 3, 2, 1, Soccer is Really Fun!

Soccer Lesson Plan 10

EQUIPMENT:

Whistle
20 cones
Parachute
1 soccer ball per student

OBJECTIVES:

The student will:

1. Participate in Move and Freeze activities cooperating with classmates and following the instructions given by the teacher.
2. Participate in Parachute Fitness Activities during the Fitness portion of class as presented by the teacher involving locomotor, strength, and flexibility activities.
3. Demonstrate the Heading skills to pass the ball to a partner using form demonstrated by the instructor.
4. Demonstrate the soccer skills of goal kicking and goalie defensive moves during the lesson focus portion of class.
5. Demonstrate previously taught soccer skills and cooperation with teammates while playing Soccer Dribblerama.

National Standards Met in this Lesson: **1, 2, 3, 4, 5, 6**

INSTRUCTIONAL ACTIVITIES | **TEACHING HINTS**

INTRODUCTORY ACTIVITY (2 - 3 MINUTES)

Move and Freeze on Signal (Variation of Change, Move, and Quickly Stop)

Students move throughout the area using a variety of locomotor movements, on signal they freeze quickly.

See DPESS Chapter 14 for details.
Object is to try to reduce the response latency.
Scattered formation.

Students will demonstrate safety while performing locomotor movements in their own space.

FITNESS DEVELOPMENT (8 - 12 MINUTES)

Parachute Fitness Activities

See DPESS Chapter 16 for details.
See Lesson 4, Golf Unit for details.

LESSON FOCUS (15 - 20 MINUTES)

Heading

Drill: toss ball 10 times and partner will head it back, then switch.
Repeat trying to increase distance. Switch after 10 X.
Demonstrate power obtained by bending legs and jumping, to push the ball high and long.

See DPESS Chapter 19 for details.
Students will be in pairs with a ball.

Students will demonstrate proper technique using the forehead to head the ball.

Goal Kicking and Goalie Defense

Demonstrate skills.

Use Whistle Mixer to make groups of 3.
Assign 3 students to areas on field with cones marked simulating goals.

GAME (5 MINUTES)

Soccer Dribblerama

On signal students will dribble using skills learned and try to kick others balls out of the area. If ball goes out person must retrieve it. 1 point per ball intercepted and kicked out of boundaries.

Each student will have a ball and be inside a coned area.

EVALUATION/REVIEW AND CHEER

Discuss heading, goal kicking and defense skills.

Cheer: Soccer, yes!

Soccer Lesson Plan 11

EQUIPMENT:

20 cones
1 ball per 2 students
Music CD/tape for fitness activities
Signs for Hexagon Hustle
Poster board
CD/Cassette Player
Whistle
Game rules handout 1 per student

OBJECTIVES:

The student will:

1. Participate in Group Tag cooperating with classmates and following the instructions given by the teacher.
2. Participate in Hexagon Hustle during the Fitness portion of class as presented by the teacher involving locomotor, strength, and flexibility activities.
3. Play soccer using skills taught in class, follow the game rules, and cooperate with teammates during the lesson focus portion of class.
4. Participate in dribbling relay games using skills demonstrated by the instructor and following the rules of the game.

National Standards Met in this Lesson: **1, 2, 3, 4, 5, 6**

INSTRUCTIONAL ACTIVITIES | **TEACHING HINTS**

INTRODUCTORY ACTIVITY (2 - 3 MINUTES)

Group Tag (Variation of Blob Tag)

There are 3 students designated "it". They try and tag others, if you are tagged you help the group. Last one not tagged wins.

See DPESS Chapter 14 for details.

Scattered formation.

Students will exercise safety and positive attitudes while playing game.

FITNESS DEVELOPMENT (8 - 12 MINUTES)

Circuit Training: Hexagon Hustle

Make a hexagon with 6 cones. Place signs with directions on both sides of cone. The signs identify the hustle activity.

Assign groups to begin at each cone.
Use music for activity during silence perform flexibility, stretching and strengthening activities.

Students will perform exercise on cards using the correct technique to avoid injury.

LESSON FOCUS (15 - 20 MINUTES)

Soccer Game and Rules

Show a videotape of soccer and explain rules.

See DPESS Chapter 19 for details.

Give students a rules handout to read.

Play Soccer

Create teams ahead of time.
Assign students to playing field.

Students will demonstrate a positive and encouraging attitude while playing a soccer game.

GAME (5 MINUTES)

Dribbling relays

1. Dribble the ball with speed to the cone and back; then next person goes.
2. Dribble in and out of the cones and back to the line, then next person goes, sit when done.
3. Dribble to cone; leave ball at cone and run back. The next person runs to cone and dribbles ball back and so on. First line done wins.

Use Whistle Mixer to create groups of 5 - 6.
Lines of 5 - 6 students.

EVALUATION/REVIEW AND CHEER

Discuss how short Soccer Games went. Ask if any questions over the rules.

Cheer: Soccer's great

Soccer Lesson Plan 12

EQUIPMENT:

Cones for marking boundaries and stations
6 - 10 jump ropes for Circuit
1 soccer ball per student
Pinnies for 1/2 class
Soccer Goals
Instructions for Challenge Course Stations
CD/Cassette Player for Fitness Music
Music CD/tape Fitness Stations
Whistle or Drum

OBJECTIVES:

The student will:

1. Participate in Run, Stop, Pivot cooperating with classmates and following the instructions given by the teacher.
2. Participate in the Challenge Course Circuit during the Fitness portion of class as presented by the teacher involving locomotor, strength, and flexibility activities.
3. Play soccer using skills taught in class, follow the game rules, and cooperate with teammates during the lesson focus portion of class.
4. Be able to combine skills learned throughout unit and implement them into a game.

National Standards Met in this Lesson: **1, 2, 3, 4, 5, 6**

INSTRUCTIONAL ACTIVITIES	TEACHING HINTS

INTRODUCTORY ACTIVITY (2 - 3 MINUTES)

Run, Stop, Pivot (Similar to Move, Stop, Pivot)

Students run, stop then pivot on signal. Vary activity by directing pivot on alternate feet and to increase the circumference of the pivot.

See DPESS Chapter 14 for details.

Scattered formation.

Students will exhibit caution when performing introductory activity movements.

FITNESS DEVELOPMENT (8 - 12 MINUTES)

Challenge Course Circuit

Arrange three or four courses with a group at each course.

See DPESS Chapter 16 for details.

See Lesson 8, Badminton Unit for complete details.

Students will maintain safe strengthening exercises by using the correct techniques to avoid injury.

LESSON FOCUS (15 - 20 MINUTES)

Play Soccer

Review rules.

Use same teams as yesterday, but rotate opponents.

Students will maintain a positive and encouraging environment in which to play a soccer game.

GAME (5 MINUTES)

Continue games.

Rotate after each game won.

EVALUATION/REVIEW AND CHEER

Discuss how games went.
Ask questions to review important rules.

Cheer: We Love Soccer!

Soccer Lesson Plan 13

EQUIPMENT:

1 Bean Bag per student
1 soccer ball per student
1 Reciprocal Task Sheet Skill Test per student
1 Clipboard, pencil per 2 students
1 Parachute
Music CD/Tape for Fitness
CD/Cassette Player

OBJECTIVES:

The student will:

1. Participate in Vanishing Bean Bags cooperating with classmates and following the instructions given by the teacher.
2. Participate in the Parachute Aerobic Activity during the Fitness portion of class as presented by the teacher involving locomotor, strength, and flexibility activities.
3. Complete the Soccer Skill Test using the Reciprocal Exam Form and demonstrating integrity and honesty.
4. Be able to combine skills learned throughout unit and implement them into a Soccer Heading game.

National Standards Met in this Lesson: **1, 2, 3, 4, 5, 6**

INSTRUCTIONAL ACTIVITIES	TEACHING HINTS
INTRODUCTORY ACTIVITY (2 - 3 MINUTES)	
Vanishing Bean Bags Have students begin by moving around the area until you give a signal.	**See DPESS Chapter 16 for details.** Spread beanbags out in area. Begin with 1 bag/student.
FITNESS DEVELOPMENT (8 - 12 MINUTES)	
Parachute Rhythmic Aerobic Activity	**See DPESS Chapter 16 for details.** See Lesson Plan 11, Badminton Unit for complete details.
LESSON FOCUS (15 - 20 MINUTES)	
Soccer Skill Test Explain Task Sheet for Reciprocal Exam.	Create groups of students. Distribute Clipboards, Pencils, and Task Sheets. Assign students to areas for testing.

Student will combine movements learned throughout unit and maintain a positive attitude while completing the skills test.

INSTRUCTIONAL ACTIVITIES	TEACHING HINTS
GAME (5 MINUTES)	
Soccer Heading Game Object of game: pass the ball with hands to teammates who try to score by heading the ball into the goal. No goalie. Can take only 2 steps with the ball. If ball hits the ground during passing it becomes the other teams ball. First to score 3 goals wins	**See DPESS Chapter 19 for details.** to create teams. Use Soccer Field with goals at each end of field.

EVALUATION/REVIEW AND CHEER

Discuss skill exam, Heading Game, and upcoming tournament.
Cheer: Tournament play, HOORAY!

RECIPROCAL TASK SHEET: SOCCER SKILLS TEST

Name: ____

Observer's Name: ____________________________________

Directions: Work with 2 partners. Place the name of your observer on your task sheet. One person is the "doer", one-person rolls, tosses, or retrieves the ball, while the other person is the "observer". Observer reads information/instructions to the doer, offers verbal feedback and places a check in the "yes" or "no" column recording the performance of their partner. Complete the task sheet and then "change roles" within your group. Then, the "doer" becomes the "observer", the "observer" becomes the "retriever" and the "retriever" becomes the "observer". Each person has his/her own task sheet.

DRIBBLING	**Yes**	**No**	**Yes**	**No**	**Yes**	**No**	**Yes**	**No**
1. Dribble the ball using both feet through the cones and back to starting point.								
2. Repeat # 1.								
3. Dribble and inside pass ball to partner.								
4. Repeat using other foot.								
ROTATE POSITIONS								
PASSING								
1. Inside foot pass ball to partner.								
2. Repeat with other foot.								
3. Outside foot pass ball to partner.								
4. Repeat pass with other foot.								
ROTATE POSITIONS								
TRAPPING								
1. Trap passed/rolled ball with sole of foot.								
2. Repeat on other foot.								
3. Trap tossed ball with chest.								
4. Trap tossed ball with thigh.								
5. Repeat # 4 with other thigh.								
6. Repeat # 1 but dribble after trapping.								
HEADING								
1. Head tossed ball to target identified by instructor.								
ROTATE POSITIONS								
THROW-IN								
1. Throw ball to partner as demonstrated by instructor.								
GOAL KICKING								
1. Demonstrate an instep goal kick.								
2. Demonstrate a penalty kick								
ROTATE POSITIONS								

TURN IN THIS EXAM TO YOUR INSTRUCTOR WHEN YOU HAVE COMPLETED TAKING IT.

Soccer Lesson Plan 14

EQUIPMENT:

Cones for Circuit Training markers
Whistle
1 soccer ball per student
Circuit Training instructions
Music CD/tape for fitness
CD/Cassette player

OBJECTIVES:

The student will:

1. Participate in Mini Pyramids cooperating with classmates and following the instructions given by the teacher.
2. Participate in Circuit Training during the Fitness portion of class as presented by the teacher involving locomotor, strength, and flexibility activities.
3. Play soccer using skills taught in class, follow the game rules, and cooperate with teammates during the lesson focus portion of class.
4. Be able to combine skills learned throughout unit and implement them into a game.
5. Demonstrate a positive team spirit while playing soccer.

National Standards Met in this Lesson: **1, 2, 3, 4, 5, 6**

INSTRUCTIONAL ACTIVITIES | TEACHING HINTS

INTRODUCTORY ACTIVITY (2 - 3 MINUTES)

Mini Pyramids

On signal they find a partner and build a simple pyramid (table, statue). On the next signal, pyramids are quickly and safely dismantled and students move again.

See DPESS Chapter 18 for details.
Scattered formation.
Students move throughout the area until signal is given.

Students will demonstrate a safety awareness while making pyramids.

FITNESS DEVELOPMENT (8 - 12 MINUTES)

Circuit Training

See DPESS Chapter 16 for details.
Whistle Mixer to create groups of 4-5.
See Lesson 10, Golf Unit for complete details.

LESSON FOCUS (15 - 20 MINUTES)

Round Robin Soccer Tournament

Explain Tournament, chart and teams.

Assign teams to field areas.

Students will play a game in a positive, encouraging environment to promote team play.

GAME (5 - 10 MINUTES)

Continue Soccer Tournament Play

EVALUATION/REVIEW AND CHEER

Discuss how tournament games are going.
Cheer: We Love Playing Soccer!

Soccer Lesson Plan 15

EQUIPMENT:

20 cones
Whistle
Fitness Scavenger Hunt instruction cards
1 soccer ball per student

OBJECTIVES:

The student will:

1. Participate in Ball Gymnastics cooperating with classmates and following the instructions given by the teacher.
2. Participate in a Fitness Scavenger Hunt during the Fitness portion of class as presented by the teacher involving locomotor, strength, and flexibility activities.
3. Play soccer using skills taught in class, follow the game rules, and cooperate with teammates during the lesson focus portion of class.
4. Be able to combine skills learned throughout unit and implement them into a game.
5. Demonstrate a positive team spirit while playing soccer.

National Standards Met in this Lesson: **1, 2, 3, 4, 5, 6**

INSTRUCTIONAL ACTIVITIES	TEACHING HINTS

INTRODUCTORY ACTIVITY (2 - 3 MINUTES)

Ball Gymnastics

On signal begin activity directed by teacher. Activities: tap ball with feet; jump over ball side to side; jump over ball front and back. On signal, get with a partner and have 1 ball (back to back). Hand ball over and under, around the sides, etc.

Every student will have a ball.
Scattered formation.

FITNESS DEVELOPMENT (8 - 12 MINUTES)

Fitness Scavenger Hunt

Each group is given a list directing them to designated areas to find directions for exercises/activities at that location. Create exercises at each station work entire body.

See DPESS Chapter 16 for details.
Use Whistle Mixer to create groups of 3.
Each group is assigned a different starting point.

LESSON FOCUS AND GAME COMBINED (15 - 25 MINUTES)

Continue Round Robin Soccer Tournament

Students will demonstrate a positive attitude to ensure team play.

EVALUATION/REVIEW AND CHEER

Discuss tournament games.
Introduce next unit.

Students create cheer.

Tennis

This unit has been specifically designed to meet all six components of the NASPE National Standards for Physical Education.

OBJECTIVES:

The student will:

1. Demonstrate agility while shuffling between cones set up on a court and by participating in the Running Weave Drill during the Introductory phase of class.
2. Demonstrate movement control by changing movement patterns from skipping, to running, to galloping to side shuffles.
3. Participate in static stretching activities demonstrated in class.
4. Participate in the Flash Drill.
5. Participate in grass drills and strengthening exercises including push-ups, curl-ups, reverse push-ups, etc. for cardiovascular fitness, agility, and strength development
6. Participate in an Aerobic Rhythmic Exercise Routine to develop cardiovascular fitness and upper body strength.
7. Improve strength and fitness by participating in the Partner Resistance Exercises and the Knee High Running
8. Demonstrate agility and quick responses to instructions during the Quick Draw McGraw activity.
9. Demonstrate jump-roping skills during a variety of fitness activities such as Continuity Exercises.
10. Complete a Task Sheet on the Forehand Stroke while working with a partner.
11. Demonstrate a forehand drive stroke with follow through with and without a ball.
12. Demonstrate the volley across the net to a partner.
13. Identify parts of the tennis racquet when asked to point at their location.
14. Demonstrate the grip used for the volley and forehand stroke.
15. Demonstrate the ready position.
16. Perform backhand ground strokes using proper technique.
17. Demonstrate the volley to a partner while in the service box.
18. Demonstrate Forehand and Backhand Lob Shots and Forehand and Backhand Ground strokes.
19. Demonstrate the overhead smash, lob, and ground strokes using form demonstrated by the instructor.
20. Execute serving and ground strokes following the instructions on the Task Sheets using form demonstrated by the instructor.
21. Practice accuracy while hitting the tennis ball into hoops on the court.
22. Study the rules and etiquette of the game by reading the handout and listening to the lecture given by the instructor.
23. Rally the ball on the court using the ground strokes, lob, overhead, and serve demonstrated in class by the instructor.
24. Play Tennis Doubles using rules learned and skills demonstrated by the instructor during the unit
25. Participate in the Round Robin Tournament playing Tennis Doubles using rules learned and skills demonstrated by the instructor during the unit.

TENNIS BLOCK PLAN
3 WEEK UNIT

Week #1	Monday	Tuesday	Wednesday	Thursday	Friday
Introductory Activity	Lateral Shuffle	Square Drill	Flash Drill	Running Weave Drill	Individual Rope Jumping
Fitness	Astronaut Drills	Continuity Exercises	Partner Resistance	Aerobic Workout	The 12 Ways of Fitness
Focus	Grip, Stance Ready Position Volley	Forehand Drive Stroke	Short Court Volley Forehand Volley	Forehand Stroke	Backhand Stroke Forehand Stroke
Game	Back to Back	Midnight	Blob Tag	Frisbee Toss	Circle Bowling

Week #2	Monday	Tuesday	Wednesday	Thursday	Friday
Introductory Activity	Red Light Bean Bag Catch	Knee High	Quick Draw McGraw	Move, Stop, Pivot	Flash Drill
Fitness	Partner Racetrack Fitness	Partner Resistance Exercises	Continuity Exercises	Partner Resistance	Aerobic workout
Focus	Forehand Task Sheet Backhand Task Sheet	Lob Shot	Overhead Shot	Serve Lob Review Overhead	Station Review: Serve, Lob Overhead, Ground Strokes
Game	Over & Under	Fugitive Tag	Tennis Horse	Blob Tag	Alley Rally

Week #3	Monday	Tuesday	Wednesday	Thursday	Friday
Introductory Activity	In the Hoop	Eliminate	Eliminate	Eliminate	Eliminate
Fitness	Exercise Routine	Continuity Exercises	Exercise Routine	Aerobic Workout	Exercise Routine
Focus	Rules Rally and Play	Play Doubles Tennis	Written and Skills Exam	Round Robin Tennis Tournament	Round Robin Tennis Tournament
Game	Four Player Figure 8 Rally	Play Doubles Tennis	Continue Exams	Continue Tournament	Continue Tournament

Tennis Lesson Plan 1

EQUIPMENT:

20 cones	2 tennis balls per student
Whistle	1 racquet per student

OBJECTIVES:

The student will:

1. Demonstrate agility and cooperation during the Lateral Shuffle activity as demonstrated by the instructor.
2. Participate in Partner Resistance Exercises to improve fitness.
3. Demonstrate the stance, ready position and forehand stroke grip as demonstrated by the instructor.
4. Demonstrate the volley across the net to a partner using form demonstrated by the instructor.
5. Demonstrate cooperative skills by playing Back to Back.

National Standards Met in this Lesson: **1, 2, 3, 4, 5, 6**

INSTRUCTIONAL ACTIVITIES	TEACHING HINTS
INTRODUCTORY ACTIVITY (2 - 3 MINUTES)	
Lateral Shuffle Shuffle between the cones.	**See DPESS Chapter 14 for details.** "See how many times you can touch the cones." Stay low to the ground by bending your knees.
FITNESS DEVELOPMENT (8 - 12 MINUTES)	
Partner Resistance Exercises	**See DPESS Chapter 16 for details.** Use back-to-back finding someone the same size to create partners.
LESSON FOCUS (15 – 20 MINUTES)	
Grip, Stance, Ready Position	**See DPESS Chapter 20 for details.** Shake hands with racquet hands technique. Weight on balls of feet, knees bent. Racquet gripped with dominant hand and neck. Cradled with non-dominant hand.
The Volley (no bounce) Drill Begin next to the net and hit tennis ball over the net to partner without letting the ball bounce. X X X __________ Net X X X	Tennis Courts. Four people to a court, if not enough courts, then 6 students to a court. Ready position, knees bent, wrists ready to rotate, and eyes on the ball.
The Volley (with bounce)	Same drill, except with one bounce in the serving court, while standing near the serving court line.

Tennis can be played either by singles or doubles. It was in France that the game as we know it today really came into being. During the 16th, 17th and 18th centuries it became the highly fashionable sport of kings and noblemen and was called ' Jeu de paumme' - the game of the palm. Early French players would begin a game by shouting 'tenez' i.e. 'Play!' and the game soon became known as Royal, or Real Tennis.

GAME (3 - 5 MINUTES)	
Back-to-Back	Scattered formation. Students jog around randomly, when signal is given, they will quickly get with someone back to back. The one left out will call the next activity, such as skipping, hopping, jogging, galloping.

EVALUATION/REVIEW AND CHEER

What is different between a Volley and forehand drive shots?
What muscles did you use in Partner Resistance Exercises today?

Cheer: 2, 4, 6, 8 Volleying is really great!

Tennis Lesson Plan 2

EQUIPMENT:

1 Tennis racquet per student
2 Tennis balls per student
Cones with movement instruction cards
CD/Cassette Player
Continuity Music CD/Tape
1 Individual jump rope per student

OBJECTIVES:

The student will:

1. Demonstrate agility and cooperation during the Square Drill using movements demonstrated by the instructor.
2. Participate in Continuity Exercises to improve strength, endurance, and flexibility.
3. Demonstrate the forehand stroke while rallying the ball to a partner as demonstrated by the instructor.
4. Demonstrate cooperative skills, listening, responsibility and running while play Midnight using rules explained by the instructor.

National Standards Met in this Lesson: **1, 2, 3, 4, 5, 6**

INSTRUCTIONAL ACTIVITIES — **TEACHING HINTS**

INTRODUCTORY ACTIVITY (2 - 3 MINUTES)

Square Drill

When signal is given student will begin moving in one direction. At each cone will be a sign listing movement to perform to next cone:
1 = Skipping; 2 = Running; 3 = Galloping;
4 = Side shuffle

See DPESS Chapter 14 for details.
Play whistle mixer to make 4 even groups.
Cones in large square.

FITNESS DEVELOPMENT (8 - 12 MINUTES)

Continuity Exercises

Create a music CD/tape with 45 seconds of music and 30 seconds of blank for 10 minutes. During silence, instruct students to perform an exercise i.e. push-ups, curl-ups, reverse push-ups, side leg lifts, arm circling, crab walks, coffee grinder, etc.

See DPESS Chapter 16 for details.
Scattered formation.
Follow routine on page 322.
End music CD/tape with slower paced music appropriate for static stretches to stretch the muscles used.

Continuity Exercises are a form of interval training. Interval training helps prevent the injuries associated with repetitive endurance exercise. Interval training allows you to increase your training intensity without overtraining or burn-out. In this way, adding intervals to your workout routine is a good way to cross train.

LESSON FOCUS (15 - 20 MINUTES)

Toss ball to a partner

See DPESS Chapter 20 for details.
Forehand drive practice. Partner receives 4 tossed balls and they change roles.

Rally ball over net to partner

Rally ball over net with partner.

In tennis, we need to know some elements of biomechanics. In this sport we transfer the energy from our body to the ball via a tennis racket to create for velocity and spin.

GAME (5 MINUTES)

Midnight (Fox in the den)

The chickens need to stay away from the foxes.
Chickens approach den asking, "What time is it?" The fox may answer any clock time. When she answers "midnight" the chickens are chased.

Select several "foxes" and "mark" them with pennies.
The rest of the classes are "chickens."
At the signal the chickens run for safety. The chickens are safe when they reach a specified area or goal line at the opposite end of the play area. Anyone caught is taken to the den and then assists in helping the fox.

EVALUATION/REVIEW AND CHEER

What form of training is Continuity Exercises?
What element of biomechanics did you learn about today?

Cheer: 2, 4, 6, 8 Rallying is fun!

Tennis Lesson Plan 3

EQUIPMENT:

1 Tennis racquet per student
2 Tennis balls per student
Music CD/tape for grass drills
CD/Cassette player

OBJECTIVES:

The student will:

1. Demonstrate agility and cooperation during the Flash Drill using movements demonstrated by the instructor.
2. Participate in Partner Resistance Exercises to improve fitness.
3. Demonstrate the forehand volley stroke using form demonstrated by the instructor.
4. Demonstrate cooperative skills, listening, responsibility and running while play Blob tag using rules explained by the instructor.

National Standards Met in this Lesson: **1, 2, 3, 4, 5, 6**

INSTRUCTIONAL ACTIVITIES	TEACHING HINTS
INTRODUCTORY ACTIVITY (2 - 3 MINUTES)	
Flash Drill	**See DPESS Chapter 14 for details.**
FITNESS DEVELOPMENT (8 - 12 MINUTES)	
Partner Resistance Exercises (See Lesson 7 for details)	**See DPESS Chapter 16 for details.** Use back-to-back to select a partner the same size.
LESSON FOCUS (15 - 20 MINUTES)	
Forehand Volley **Demonstrate volley and practice drills**	**See DPESS Chapter 20 for details.** Play whistle mixer to create groups of 4-6. Assign 4-6 students to each court.
Short Court Volley **Forehand Volley from Service Line** Short court - from the service square, students will volley the ball to one another. Play all 4 balls before retrieving. Then start again.	Bring students together to demonstrate. Demonstrate. Explain each of the follow cues: • Set up with the side of the body to the net. • Contact the ball even with the front foot. • Make sure you run to meet the ball. • Early backswing - get the racquet back as soon as possible. • Keep the knees bent throughout swing.
Forehand Sideline Drill	Demonstrate using the forehand stroke and aiming to hit between the singles and doubles boundaries. Use Whistle Mixer to create groups of 4 - 6. If 6 students to a court, rotate pairs from left to right on the court.

At ball contact only medium grip pressure is needed to guide and stabilize the racket. This is because the forward momentum will carry the racquet through the ball without much effort. After contact the shoulder and torso and hips naturally rotate towards the non dominant side following the path of the racquet. This will result in a stretch of the opposite side musculature which will decelerate the racquet.

INSTRUCTIONAL ACTIVITIES	TEACHING HINTS
GAME (5 MINUTES)	
Blob tag Explain that two people begin by being "it." When they tag someone, they hold hands. As a number of people are tagged, the chain becomes long, and only those at the ends are eligible for tagging. The team(s) with the longest line wins.	**See DPESS Chapter 14 for details.** Scatter formation on 1 side of tennis net. Select 2 "its." (Can select 4) Repeat with new "its" if time permits.

EVALUATION/REVIEW AND CHEER

Evaluate skills practiced during the lesson
Cheer: 3, 2, 1 Tennis is Really Fun!

Tennis Lesson Plan 4

EQUIPMENT:

1 Tennis racquet per student
2 Tennis balls per student
4 cones per group of 4 students for Running Weave Drill
1 Task sheet on Forehand Stroke per student
1 Clipboard with pencil attached per 2 students

OBJECTIVES:

The student will:

1. Demonstrate agility and cooperation during the Running Weave Drill using movements demonstrated by the instructor.
2. Participate in an Aerobic Workout to improve fitness.
3. Demonstrate the forehand volley stroke using task sheets and form demonstrated by the instructor.
4. Demonstrate cooperative skills and focus while playing Frisbee Toss using rules explained by the instructor.

National Standards Met in this Lesson: **1, 2, 3, 4, 5, 6**

INSTRUCTIONAL ACTIVITIES	TEACHING HINTS

INTRODUCTORY ACTIVITY (2 - 3 MINUTES)

Running Weave Drill

Leader first runs through maze and others follow. Leader can change the locomotor movement used.

See DPESS Chapter 14 for details.

Create groups of 4 using the Whistle Mixer. Assign each group to a set of cones arranged in a maze.

FITNESS DEVELOPMENT (8 - 12 MINUTES)

Aerobic Workout

See DPESS Chapter 16 for details.

Create an Aerobic Rhythmic Exercise Routine lasting 8 - 10 minutes. The CD/tape you make should be 120 to 150 beats per minute. A pre-recorded Aerobic Dance Exercise CD/tape allowing the last two minutes to be used for a short cool down activity and approximately 5 minutes for abdominal and upper body strengthening, as well as stretching.

You don't have to be a dancer to create an enjoyable, high-energy routine. An example of 4 phrases of movement identified as A, B, C, D is described.
The A, B, C, D phrases can be performed first as listed, then combined in any order that works well with the movement and the music. A simple way to add variety to the routine you have created is to add different arm movements each time you repeat the phrase. Then the original 4 phrases of movement can be repeated as originally choreographed.

A: Hop on the left foot 8 times while pointing and tapping the right foot forward and then to the side (e.g., forward, side, forward, side, forward, side). Repeat the entire phrase while hopping (bouncing) on the right foot 8 times and tapping the left foot forward and to the side as described.
B: Run in place 8 times and clap on each run.
C: 8 jumping jacks using full arm movements.
D: Slide to the right 8 times and clap on the 8th slide. Repeat to the left.

INSTRUCTIONAL ACTIVITIES | **TEACHING HINTS**

LESSON FOCUS (15 - 20 MINUTES)

Forehand Stroke Review

Explain Task Sheets.
Pairs who complete the task sheets can turn materials in and rally using the Ready Position and Forehand Stroke.

See DPESS Chapter 20 for details.
Using the elbow-to-elbow, or back-to-back technique create pairs of students.
Have one person kneel. The person standing should pick up a clipboard with pencil and task sheets. The person kneeling should pick up a racquet and two tennis balls and return to partner. Assign students to courts to work on Task Sheets.

Sometimes Tennis is called Lawn Tennis. The name Lawn Tennis was given in the 19th Century when Victorian prosperity in England prompted a significant revival. Courts were built in many famous country houses and the first tennis clubs providing facilities for members began to appear. In was during this period that the game of Lawn Tennis began to emerge.

GAME (5 MINUTES)

Frisbee Toss to Partner

See DPESS Chapter 20 for details.
Play "toe to toe" to select new partners.
Students should be directed to safe direction to toss Frisbee to partner and toss and catch the Frisbee over the Tennis net.

EVALUATION/REVIEW AND CHEER

Bring students together to review and discuss elements of the lesson
When was tennis known as Lawn Tennis?

Cheer: Tennis, yes!

TENNIS RECIPROCAL TASK SHEET: FOREHAND STROKE

Name: ________________________________

Name: ________________________________

Directions: Work with a partner. Place both of your names on each task sheet. One person is the "doer" while the other person is the "observer". Observer reads information/instructions to the doer, offers verbal feedback and places a check in the "yes" or "no" column recording the performance of their partner. Record the date of the practice. Complete the task sheet until you are directed to "change roles". Then, the "doer" becomes the "observer". Each person has his/her own task sheet.

READY POSITION	**DATES**							
(Record date of practice)								
	Yes	**No**	**Yes**	**No**	**Yes**	**No**	**Yes**	**No**
1. Assume the handshake grip.								
2. Non-dominant hand supports neck of racquet.								
3. Knees bent.								
4. Weight on balls of feet and ready to move.								
5. Eyes looking across net at imaginary opponent..								
FOREHAND STROKE								
6. Side to net.								
7. Drop ball in front of foot closest to net.								
8. Racquet moves back into back swing of stroke.								
9. Steps forward toward direction of net while swinging.								
10. Follows through with swing and weight change.								
11. Repeat 1 - 10 above, pick up balls and change roles.								

Tennis Lesson Plan 5

EQUIPMENT:

1 Jump rope per student
1 Tennis racquet per student
2 Tennis balls per student
1 Hoop per student
4 Cones
Clubs
Rubber balls
Whistle

OBJECTIVES:

The student will:

1. Participate in individual rope jumping and The 12 Ways of Fitness to improve fitness.
2. Demonstrate the backhand stroke using form demonstrated by the instructor.
3. Demonstrate the forehand stroke, then ready position, then backhand stokes on the court while rallying with a partner.
4. Demonstrate cooperative skills and focus while Circle Bowling using rules explained by the instructor.

National Standards Met in this Lesson: **1, 2, 3, 4, 5, 6**

INSTRUCTIONAL ACTIVITIES	TEACHING HINTS
INTRODUCTORY ACTIVITY (2 - 3 MINUTES)	
Individual Rope Jumping	**See DPESS Chapter 14 for details.**
Tell the students to begin traveling while rope jumping when the music begins. When music stops - freeze.	Set up cones marking the boundaries. Scattered position. Emphasize jump roping as a tool that athletes use to achieve fitness.
FITNESS DEVELOPMENT (8 - 12 MINUTES)	
The 12 Way of Fitness	**See DPESS Chapter 16 for details.**
Explain singing tune to lead the exercise. Explain add-on fitness instructions. Execute 2-3 times through.	Using Whistle Mixer, create groups of 12. Scattered formation Identify the first student leader through the twelfth.
LESSON FOCUS (15 - 20 MINUTES)	
Backhand Stroke	**See DPESS Chapter 20 for details.**
Grip	Scattered formation
Ready position, grip change, and backhand stroke.	
Student Trial of Backhand	Direct students to pick up a racquet and bring to area. Practice ready position to grip without ball. Practice side to net, back swing and follow through.
Practice Backhand on Court	Use elbow-to-elbow technique to create pairs. Assign pairs to an area. Let each student hit 2 balls over net, then retrieve balls.
Forehand to Backhand	Demonstrate ready position, to forehand, to ready position, to backhand. Students practice. Students go to court and rally using this technique.

A player wins a set when they have won at least 6 games.

GAME (5 MINUTES)	
Circle Bowling	
Four clubs or bowling pins are placed in center of circle. A guard is chosen for each club. Two of the players in the circle have a ball. The object is to knock down one of the other person's clubs. If successful then the person may change places with the one guarding it.	Circle formation. Select several "its" to be first guards of clubs. Switch places if club knocked down.

EVALUATION/REVIEW AND CHEER

Review major elements of backhand stroke and other skills covered in class.
Students create cheer.

Tennis Lesson Plan 6

EQUIPMENT:

1 Tennis racquet per 3 students
4 Tennis balls per 3 students
Clipboard with pencil and task sheets per 3 students
6-8 Rubber balls

OBJECTIVES:

The student will:

1. Participate in Red Light, Bean Bag Catch, and Partner Racetrack Fitness to improve agility, eye-hand coordination and fitness.
2. Demonstrate the backhand stroke using form demonstrated by the instructor.
3. Demonstrate the forehand stroke and backhand stokes on the court while rallying with a partner and completing the Task Sheet.
4. Demonstrate cooperative skills and focus while Over and Under Ball Relay using rules explained by the instructor.

National Standards Met in this Lesson: **1, 2, 3, 4, 5, 6**

INSTRUCTIONAL ACTIVITIES / **TEACHING HINTS**

INTRODUCTORY ACTIVITY (2 - 3 MINUTES)

Red Light

Scattered formation.
Each student balances a beanbag or a tennis ball on his or her racquet. On "Green Light" students move in general space around other people. On "Red Light" each student stops without dropping object off racquet.

Bean Bag Catch

See DPESS Chapter 18 for details.
Play "racquet to racquet" or toe-to-toe to make pairs.
Toss bean bag/ball to partner 3 times in a row. If successful take a large step away from partner. Repeat.

FITNESS DEVELOPMENT (8 - 12 MINUTES)

Partner Racetrack Fitness

Set up 5-6 stations in working area. Each station has a Task Card listing 6-8 exercises to perform. List the locomotor movement to be performed by partner during each exercise.

See DPESS Chapter 16 for details.
Use Whistle Mixer to create groups of 6-10. Then use elbow to elbow within the group to make pairs.

Example Task Card

10	Jumping Jacks
	Jog around perimeter of area
20-30	Curl-Ups
	Slide around perimeter of area
15-20	Reverse Push-Ups
	Skip around perimeter
10-25	Push-Ups
	Gallop around perimeter of room
30-40	Treadmills alternating feet
	Run backwards around perimeter
30-40	Treadmills moving feet simultaneously
	Jog around perimeter
15	Second standing hip bend/stretch each side
	Skip
15-30	Second Lower Leg Stretch

Use a music CD/tape to make fitness fun and motivated movement.

Partner Racetrack Fitness activities use muscles in the entire body: core muscles, biceps, triceps, quadriceps, hamstring, and cardiovascular respiratory muscles.

INSTRUCTIONAL ACTIVITIES	TEACHING HINTS

LESSON FOCUS (15 - 20 MINUTES)

Forehand and Backhand Stoke Using Task Sheets Can rally in groups when complete Task Sheets.	**See DPESS Chapter 20 for details.** Play Whistle Mixer to create groups of 3. Direct students to pick up a Clipboard and Pencil with 3 Forehand and Backhand Task Sheets, 1 racquet 4 balls per group. Identify first Doer, Tosser and Observer. Explain Task Sheets. Assign groups to courts.

Biomechanics is important in tennis. It is a necessity in tennis in the need to be able to change your balance, recover and be in position to effectively hit the next shot. The concept of Economy of Movement is essential in this respect.

GAME (5 MINUTES)

Over and Under Ball Relay	**See DPESS Chapter 18 for details.**

EVALUATION/REVIEW AND CHEER

What were the main points to remember in the forehand ground stroke? How do you quickly switch from a forehand to a backhand?

Cheer: Tennis is the game to play!

TENNIS RECIPROCAL TASK SHEET: FOREHAND

Doer's Name: ______________________________

Observer's Name: ______________________________

Directions: Work in a group of 3. One student is the "doer;" one person is the "observer;" one is the ball tosser.

Doer: Complete tasks read to you.

Observer: Read Task Sheet to partner and place a check in the appropriate box looking at 1-2 points at a time. Offer feedback.

Tosser: Toss the ball to the forehand side of "doer."

FOREHAND	**DATES**							
(Record date of practice)								
	Yes	**No**	**Yes**	**No**	**Yes**	**No**	**Yes**	**No**
1. Assume ready position.								
2. Execute an early backswing getting racquet back as soon as possible.								
3. Quickly move to ball.								
4. Set up with the side of the body to the net.								
5. Step onto left leg (R handed players) before contact. Transfer weight to that leg.								
6. Contact the ball in front of the left leg.								
7. Contact the ball with the racquet perpendicular to the ground.								
8. Strong follow through. Right shoulder should almost touch your chin.								
9. Recover to ready position to receive another ball.								
10. Repeat task sheet hitting 4 balls in a row.								
11. Rotate. Tosser to Observer Observer to Doer Doer to Tosser								
12. After everyone in your group completes the Task Sheet, move on to the Backhand Task Sheet.								

TENNIS RECIPROCAL TASK SHEET: BACKHAND

Doer's Name: ______________________________

Observer's Name: ______________________________

Directions: Work in a group of 3. One student is the "doer;" one person is the "observer;" one is the ball tosser.
Doer: Complete tasks read to you.
Observer: Read Task Sheet to partner and place a check in the appropriate box looking at 1-2 points at a time. Offer feedback.
Tosser: Toss the ball to the backhand side of "doer."

BACKHAND	**DATES**							
(Record date of practice)								
	Yes	**No**	**Yes**	**No**	**Yes**	**No**	**Yes**	**No**
1. Assume ready position.								
2. Execute an early backswing getting racquet back as soon as possible.								
3. Quickly move to ball.								
4. Set up with the side of the body to the net.								
5. Step onto right leg (R handed players) before contact. Transfer weight to that leg.								
6. Contact the ball in front of the right leg.								
7. Contact the ball with the racquet perpendicular to the ground.								
8. Strong follow through.								
9. Recover to ready position to receive another ball.								
10. Repeat task sheet hitting 4 balls in a row.								
11. Rotate. Tosser to Observer Observer to Doer Doer to Tosser								
12. After everyone in group completes the Task Sheet, rally with your group on the court.								

Tennis Lesson Plan 7

EQUIPMENT:

1 Tennis Racquet per student
2 Tennis Balls per student

OBJECTIVES:

The student will:

1. Participate in Knee High Running and Partner Resistance Exercises to improve agility, eye-hand coordination and fitness.
2. Demonstrate the lob shot using form demonstrated by the instructor.
3. Demonstrate the backhand lob shot on the court while rallying with a partner and using form demonstrated by the instructor.
4. Demonstrate cooperative skills, running and agility while playing Fugitive Tag and using rules explained by the instructor.

National Standards Met in this Lesson: **1, 2, 3, 4, 5, 6**

INSTRUCTIONAL ACTIVITIES	TEACHING HINTS
INTRODUCTORY ACTIVITY (2 - 3 MINUTES)	
Knee High Running Students will run in place knee high and alternate with jogging in place.	**See DPESS Chapter 16 for details.** Scattered formation. Use verbal or whistle signal "knees high;" "knees low."
FITNESS DEVELOPMENT (8 - 12 MINUTES)	
Partner Resistance Exercises **Arm Curl-Ups** **Forearm Flex** **Fist Pull-Apart** **Butterfly** **Back builder**	**See DPESS Chapter 16 for details.** Play "elbow to elbow" with someone to make pairs. Scatter formation, standing next to partner.
Stretch and Pull Seated straddle position while facing partner with feet touching ankles of partner. Hold hands and very slowly one student will lean back while the other student is being pulled forward. Reverse directions.	Explain importance of stretching.
Scissors **Bear Trap** **Knee Bender** **Resistance Push-Up**	May use a carpet square to lie on.
Reverse Push-Up Sit with feet flat on ground near buttocks, knees bent. Place hands beneath shoulders, fingers facing heels. Support body weight on hands and feet. Bend at elbows to lower body near ground. Straighten arms. Repeat.	Both partners can perform this simultaneously or resistance can be placed by partner press down on shoulders as doer straightens arms.
Jog	Jog around the area several times. Use music to motivate fitness section.

While participating in Partner Resistance Exercises the partner applies pressure to offer exercise resistance similar to what one experiences while using resistance machines or bands. This makes the work-out more challenging.

INSTRUCTIONAL ACTIVITIES	TEACHING HINTS

LESSON FOCUS (15 - 20 MINUTES)

INSTRUCTIONAL ACTIVITIES	TEACHING HINTS
Lob Shot Practice: Toss balls to partner's forehand lob side Complete activity using all 4 balls. Change starter. Repeat 3 times. **Demonstrate**: Forehand Ground stroke; Backhand Ground stroke Lob	**See DPESS Chapter 20 for details.** The teacher will explain and demonstrate the lob. Create pairs using "toe-to-toe." Direct each student to pick up racquet and 2 balls. Assign students to courts. Bring students together. Practice rallying with forehand, to backhand, to lob as demonstrated.
Backhand Lob Practice by tossing ball to partner's backhand side 4 times in a row. Change roles.	Bring group together for demonstration.
Rally	Students rally using the 4 skills practiced in class.

The Law of Inertia is important to understand in tennis: The body will stay at rest or motion until acted upon by an outside force. It is the resistance of a body to move or to stop moving. When in ready position: The body has "resting inertia." To move as you need to do in rallying, you need to overcome the resting inertia by using force (muscular contraction) or gravity and push against the ground with your muscles and feet to move.

GAME (5 MINUTES)

INSTRUCTIONAL ACTIVITIES	TEACHING HINTS
Fugitive Tag One person is identified as fugitive and is given head start. Switch roles when tagged.	**See DPESS Chapter 14 for details.** Create partners using management game. Scattered formation.

EVALUATION/REVIEW AND CHEER

What angle should the racquet be held at to perform a lob?
What will the trajectory of the ball be at that angle?

Students create cheer.

Tennis Lesson Plan 8

EQUIPMENT:

Continuity Exercise Music CD/Tape
CD/Cassette Player
1 Tennis Racquet per student
2 Tennis balls per student

OBJECTIVES:

The student will:

1. Participate in Quick Draw McGraw to improve agility, eye-hand coordination and warm-up the body.
2. Participate in Continuity Exercises during the fitness section of class to improve strength, agility, flexibility and endurance levels.
3. Demonstrate the overhead and lob shot using form demonstrated by the instructor.
4. Demonstrate cooperative skills, running and agility and tennis skills while playing Tennis Horse using rules explained by the instructor.

National Standards Met in this Lesson: 1, 2, 3, 4, 5, 6

INSTRUCTIONAL ACTIVITIES	TEACHING HINTS
INTRODUCTORY ACTIVITY (2 - 3 MINUTES)	
Quick Draw McGraw Instructor faces student in "Ready Position." Instructor holds tennis ball at "gun belt" level and performs dramatic gestures with ball to right or left side. Students respond by demonstrating forehand or backhand stroke.	Scattered formation with imaginary racquet.
FITNESS DEVELOPMENT (8 - 12 MINUTES)	
Continuity Exercises	**See DPESS Chapter 16 for details.**
LESSON FOCUS (15 - 20 MINUTES)	
Overhead Practice by tossing ball high to self and execute overhead stroke.	**See DPESS Chapter 20 for details.** Scattered formation Demonstrate Arranges students on court facing fence. Student works alone and practices self-toss and overhead into fence 10 times.
Lob Skill Review **Drill:** Partner hits overhead shot from net, return with lob. Each person practices 4 times in a row.	Create partners using management game. Assign groups to courts.
Review Ground strokes	Rally with 1 or 2 other students on court.

When playing tennis, you need to aspire to hit the ball with smooth efficiency. Proper timing and a relaxed, fluid motion is essential to playing well and to prevent injury.

INSTRUCTIONAL ACTIVITIES	TEACHING HINTS
GAME (5 MINUTES)	
Tennis Horse Player 1 calls hit and attempts to hit it there. Others in line try to duplicate shot. If miss shot, player gets an "H', etc. until HORSE is spelled. If fail to make shot player assigned an "H." Second failure = "O." Last to spell "HORSE" is the winner.	**See DPESS Chapter 19 for details.** Create groups of 4 in lines at baseline. As soon as 1 person spells "HORSE," game starts over.

EVALUATION/REVIEW AND CHEER

Review the elements of all strokes played today.

What must be remembered to play well and prevent injury?
Students create cheer.

Tennis Lesson Plan 9

EQUIPMENT:

1 Tennis racquet per student
2 Tennis balls per student
Music for fitness
CD/ cassette tape player

OBJECTIVES:

The student will:

1. Participate in Move, Stop, Pivot to improve agility, eye-hand coordination and warm-up the body.
2. Participate in Partner Resistance Exercises during the fitness section of class to improve strength, agility, flexibility and endurance levels.
3. Demonstrate the tennis serve using form demonstrated by the instructor.
4. Demonstrate the overhead lob on the court using form demonstrated by the instructor.
5. Demonstrate cooperative skills, running and agility and tennis skills while playing Blob Tag using rules explained by the instructor.

National Standards Met in this Lesson: **1, 2, 3, 4, 5, 6**

INSTRUCTIONAL ACTIVITIES	TEACHING HINTS

INTRODUCTORY ACTIVITY (2 - 3 MINUTES)

Move, Stop, Pivot	**See DPESS Chapter 14 for details.**
Teacher blows whistle: once = jog twice = stop and pivot	Scatter formation.

This activity demonstrates the theory of momentum. Objects in motion are said to have a momentum. Then when you stop and pivot, you have to exert force to regain your jogging momentum.

FITNESS DEVELOPMENT (8 - 12 MINUTES)

Partner Resistance Exercises	**See DPESS Chapter 16 for details.**
Arm Curl-Ups Forearm Flex Fist Pull-Apart Butterfly Back builder	Play "elbow to elbow" with someone to make pairs. Scattered formation, standing next to partner. Use music to motivate fitness section.
Seated Stretch and Pull	See Lesson 7 for complete details.
Scissors	May use a carpet square to lay on.
Bear Trap	
Knee Bender	
Resistance Push-Up	
Reverse Push-Up	

Sit with feet flat on ground near buttocks, knees bent. Place hands beneath shoulders, fingers facing heels. Support body weight on hands and feet. Bend at elbows to lower body near ground. Straighten arms. Repeat. Both partners can perform this simultaneously or resistance can be placed by partner press down on shoulders as doer straightens arms.

Jog	Jog around the area several times.

INSTRUCTIONAL ACTIVITIES	TEACHING HINTS
LESSON FOCUS (15 - 20 MINUTES)	
Serve Motion Demonstrate serve	**See DPESS Chapter 20 for details.** Student picks up racquet Students practice motion spread out safely in area without a ball.
Serve Toss Demonstrate the toss	Direct students to bring 2 balls to area. Practice toss and catch several times.
Serve With Toss Demonstrate serve with toss.	Assign students to areas facing fence. Serve practice-using balls.
Serve Into Serve Box Demonstrate serving into service area.	Create Partners and assign to courts. Serve into service box 2 times then partner serves. Allow 10 practices per person.
Lob-Overhead Review Demonstrate Lob and Overhead Return.	**See DPESS Chapter 20 for details.** Scatter formation Practice

In serving you use the theory of opposite forces. For every action, there is an equal and opposite reaction. Stroke and movement are initiated from the legs by pushing against the ground. The ground pushes the player back up with the same amount of force.

Server needs to serve inside opposite box to avoid a "fault"; server gets 2 tries.

GAME (5 MINUTES)

Blob tag	**See DPESS Chapter 14 for details.** Scatter formation Select several "its."

EVALUATION/REVIEW AND CHEER

What are the similarities between the overhead and the serve?
What is the name of the scientific theory that is applied in serving?
What activities were done today that demonstrate the theory of momentum?

Students create cheer.

Tennis Lesson Plan 10

EQUIPMENT:

1 Task Sheet per person
Clipboard and pencil per 2 students
1 Tennis racquet per student
2 Tennis balls per student

OBJECTIVES:

The student will:

1. Participate in the Flash Drill to improve agility, eye-hand coordination and warm-up the body.
2. Participate in an Aerobic Workout during the fitness section of class to improve strength, agility, flexibility, aerobic and muscular endurance levels.
3. Demonstrate the tennis ground strokes using form demonstrated by the instructor and following the items on the task sheet.
4. Demonstrate the serve on the court using the task sheet and form demonstrated by the instructor.
5. Demonstrate cooperative skills, running and agility and tennis skills while playing Alley Rally using rules explained by the instructor.

National Standards Met in this Lesson: **1, 2, 3, 4, 5, 6**

INSTRUCTIONAL ACTIVITIES	TEACHING HINTS
INTRODUCTORY ACTIVITY (2 - 3 MINUTES)	
Flash Drill Teacher uses hand signals to direct movements.	**See DPESS Chapter 14 for details.** Scatter formation. Students jog in place or "stutter" while waiting for hand signal.
FITNESS DEVELOPMENT (8 - 12 MINUTES)	
Aerobic Workout	**See DPESS Chapter 16 for details.** See Lesson 4, this unit for details.
LESSON FOCUS (15 - 20 MINUTES)	
Skill Review Task Sheets **Serve** **Ground strokes** Explain Task Sheets.	**See DPESS Chapter 20 for details.** Create groups of 3 using Whistle Mixer. Assign 2 groups per court. Determine first doer, tosser and observer. Explain rotation. Assign each group to pick up a clipboard and pencil plus task sheets for each person.
Sides are switched each time you are going to serve the ball over the net.	
GAME (5 MINUTES)	
Alley Rally Each student must alternate forehand and backhand shots over net. Each player is responsible for making calls on balls that land on his or her side of the net. The hitter is not allowed to question the calls that the opponent makes.	Explain game. Use Whistle Mixer to create groups of 4. Assign groups to courts. Alley Rally over Net (Alternate Forehands and Backhands).
EVALUATION/REVIEW AND CHEER	
Discuss elements of skills practiced. When do players switch sides? **Cheer: Rallying is really fun!**	

TENNIS RECIPROCAL TASK SHEET: FOREHAND AND BACKHAND STROKE

Name: ______________________________ **Name:** ______________________________

Directions: Work with a partner. Place both of your names on each task sheet. One person is the "doer" while the other person is the "observer". Observer reads information/instructions to the doer, offers verbal feedback and places a check in the "yes" or "no" column recording the performance of their partner. Complete the task sheet until you are directed to "change roles". Then, the "doer" becomes the "observer". Each person has his/her own task sheet. Practice this task sheet once using Forehand, once using Backhand - ten change roles with your partner.

	Forehand		**Backhand**		**Forehand**		**Backhand**	
I. SET POSITION	**Yes**	**No**	**Yes**	**No**	**Yes**	**No**	**Yes**	**No**
A. Grip 1. Shaking hands (forehand) Palm on top (backhand) 2. Fingers spread								
B. Stance 1. Feet spread; knees bent 2. Weight on balls of feet								
C. Racquet 1. Parallel to ground 2. Standing on edge 3. Left hand, cradling racquet								
II. BACKSWING								
A. Pivot 1. Step promptly toward ball with nearest foot 2. Side turned completely								
B. Racquet 1. Backswing; begun early 2. Racquet head back first, with firm writs (left hand helps backhand)								
C. Run to Ball 1. Move quickly to ball 2. Sets on rear foot								
III. FORWARD SWING								
A. Ready position 1. Racquet head drops below point of contact 2. Racquet nearly parallel to ground, extends toward back fence								
B. Weight Transfer 1. Front foot steps into line of shot 2. All weight on ball of front foot 3. Knees bent; good balance								
C. Point of Contact 1. Ball contacted well in front of body 2. Wrist firm; racquet parallel								
D. Follow-Through 1. Racquet head continues out through line of shot 2. Racquet standing on edge 3. Forehand: wrist eye level; looking over elbow 4. Backhand: wrist above head; racquet nearly vertical to ground 5. Pose								
Repeat Task Sheet								

TENNIS RECIPROCAL TASK SHEET: THE SERVE

Name: ____________________ **Name:** ____________________

Directions: Work with a partner. Place both of your names on each task sheet. One person is the "doer" while the other person is the "observer". Observer reads information/instructions to the doer, offers verbal feedback and places a check in the "yes" or "no" column recording the performance of their partner. Complete the task sheet until you are directed to "change roles". Then, the "doer" becomes the "observer". Each person has his/her own task sheet. Practice serving four times in a row and then change roles. Observer: Watch for only one section on each serve practice.

I. SET POSITION	**Yes**	**No**	**Yes**	**No**	**Yes**	**No**	**Yes**	**No**
A. Grip 1. Continental grip 2. Fingers spread								
B. Stance 1. Side toward net 2. Weight on rear feet; feet spread								
C. Racquet 1. Pointing to serve area 2. Standing on edge 3. Left hand cradling								
II. BACKSWING (Ball Toss)								
A. Ball Toss 1. Ball thrown to correct height 2. Ball thrown above left foot								
B. Racquet Arm 1. Both arms work smoothly together 2. Racquet raises almost to shoulder level 3. Racquet head drops well behind back (wrist touches shoulder)								
C. Weight Transfer 1. Weight shifts to front foot 2. Balance maintained by front knee bend								
III. FORWARD SWING								
A. Throwing Motion 1. Smooth, continuous motion 2. Elbow leads wrist and racquet forward and up								
B. Contact 1. Highest point above left foot 2. Adequate wrist action 3. Adequate Spin								
C. Follow-Through 1. Racquet head leads through line of shot 2. Racquet finishes on left side of body 3. Right foot comes through to help regain balance								

Tennis Lesson Plan 11

EQUIPMENT:

2 Tennis balls per student
1 Tennis racquet per student
12 Hoops per court available
Tennis rules handout: 1 per student

OBJECTIVES:

1. The student will:
2. Participate in the Flash Drill to improve agility, eye-hand coordination and warm-up the body.
3. Participate in an Aerobic Workout during the fitness section of class to improve strength, agility, flexibility, aerobic and muscular endurance levels.
4. Demonstrate the tennis ground strokes using form demonstrated by the instructor and following the items on the task sheet.
5. Demonstrate the serve on the court using the task sheet and form demonstrated by the instructor.
6. Demonstrate cooperative skills, running and agility and tennis skills while playing Alley Rally using rules explained by the instructor.
7. Demonstrate knowledge of rules and etiquette while playing a tennis match using skills learned throughout the unit.

National Standards Met in this Lesson: **1, 2, 3, 4, 5, 6**

INSTRUCTIONAL ACTIVITIES	TEACHING HINTS
INTRODUCTORY ACTIVITY (2 - 3 MINUTES)	
In the Hoop Place hoops on the ground on different places on the court.	Using Whistle Mixer or squads make groups of 3. Place 2-3 groups of 3 at each baseline. Each student drop hits a ball using a forehand drive and tries to place ball in any hoop. Collect balls after each student hits their two. Student selects own hoop(s) to use as target.
FITNESS DEVELOPMENT (8 - 12 MINUTES)	
Run, Stop, Stretch and Strengthen Exercise Routine **Stretches** Lower leg stretch (with partner, or wall). Balance beam stretch. Sit and reach. Side leg stretch. Groin stretch. Body twist. Ankle hold, or hand down. Squat stretch. Standing hip stretch. **Strengthening** Push-ups Curl-ups Rocking Chair Reverse curl Pelvis Tilter	**See DPESS Chapter 16 for details.** Scattered within boundaries set by cones. Direct students to run throughout area. On signal, student stops and performs a designated stretch/strengthening exercise. Can ask to call out muscles being worked. Music can be used to cue the running and during the silence you can either call out the exercise or cue it on the CD/tape.

INSTRUCTIONAL ACTIVITIES	TEACHING HINTS

LESSON FOCUS (15 - 20 MINUTES)

Rules and Etiquette

See DPESS Chapter 20 for details.
Discuss rules and etiquette of game.
Give handout for homework.

Rally and Play Tennis

Use Whistle Mixer to create groups of 4 per court.
Direct students to Rally the ball to each other practicing all strokes.

Students will demonstrate positive and encouraging attitudes while playing their tennis match.

GAME (5 MINUTES)

Four Player Figure 8 Rally

Assign two players to hit all forehands and the other two all backhands. Right-handed players should be assigned forehands when they are stationed in the deuce court (right side when facing the net) and backhands when in the ad court. Left-handed players are given opposite directions.
Forehands DOWN THE LINE, Backhands CROSSCOURT, Backhands DOWN THE LINE, and Forehands CROSSCOURT.

Direct students to play.
Partners should stand close together. Length of court can be increased gradually as players' skills improve.
Each of the four players is practicing a different shot.
Rotate them through all four positions so that they will try all shots.

Students should attempt to give partners good passes in order for them to return.

EVALUATION/REVIEW AND CHEER

Review important rules of tennis.
What was important to do to make the Four Player Figure 8 Rally successful?

Cheer: 2, 4, 6, 8 Playing tennis is so great!

Tennis Lesson Plan 12

EQUIPMENT:

1 Tennis racquet per student
2 Tennis balls per student
CD/Cassette player
Music CD/tape for Continuity Exercise Routine

OBJECTIVES:

The student will:

1. Participate in Continuity Exercises during the fitness section of class to improve strength, agility, flexibility, aerobic and muscular endurance levels while preparing to play tennis.
2. Demonstrate the ability to play doubles tennis demonstrating knowledge of rules and a positive attitude.

National Standards Met in this Lesson: **1, 2, 3, 4, 5, 6**

INSTRUCTIONAL ACTIVITIES	TEACHING HINTS

INTRODUCTORY ACTIVITY (2 - 3 MINUTES)

Eliminate today to allow more time for Doubles Tennis.

FITNESS DEVELOPMENT (8 - 12 MINUTES)

Continuity Exercises

These exercises are a type of interval training. Create a CD/cassette tape with 30 - 35 seconds of music and 20 seconds of silence. Students jump rope during music. During silence, instruct students to perform an exercise i.e. push-ups, curl-ups, reverse push-ups, side leg lifts, arm circling, crab walks, coffee grinder, etc. When the music resumes, the students will jump rope.

See DPESS Chapter 16 for details.
See lesson 2 this unit for complete details.

LESSON FOCUS AND GAME (20 MINUTES)

Play Tennis Doubles Games

Use "elbow-to-elbow" technique to create partners.
Then, have those partners join with another group to create doubles groups.
Assign groups to courts.

Students should maintain positive attitudes while playing game.

EVALUATION/REVIEW AND CHEER

Discuss how games went. Ask if any rules questions came up during game play that need clarification.
Review rules and etiquette for exam.

Cheer: 3, 2, 1 Tennis is really fun!

Tennis Lesson Plan 13

EQUIPMENT:

1 Tennis racquet per student
2 Tennis balls per student
CD/Cassette player
Music CD/tape for Exercise Routine

OBJECTIVES:

The student will:

1. Participate in the given Exercise Routine during the fitness section of class to improve strength, agility, flexibility, aerobic and muscular endurance levels.
2. Demonstrate the knowledge of rules and etiquette of tennis by completing a written exam during class.
3. Demonstrate mastery of skills taught during the unit completing a skills test during class.

National Standards Met in this Lesson: **2, 3, 4**

INSTRUCTIONAL ACTIVITIES	TEACHING HINTS
INTRODUCTORY ACTIVITY (2 - 3 MINUTES)	
Eliminate today to allow time for exam.	
FITNESS DEVELOPMENT (8 - 12 MINUTES)	
Exercise Routine Intersperse jogging, stretching and strengthening activities. **Stretches** Lower leg stretch (with partner, or wall) Balance beam stretch Sit and reach Side leg stretch Groin stretch Body twist Ankle hold, or hand down Squat stretch Standing hip stretch **Strengthening** Push-ups; Curl-ups; Rocking Chair; Reverse curl; Pelvis Tilter	**See DPESS Chapter 16 for details.** Scattered within boundaries set by cones. Direct students to run throughout the area. On signal, they will stop and perform a designated stretch/strengthening exercise. The student will name the muscle being stretched/strengthened when asked to call it out. Music can be used to cue the running and during the silence you can either call out the exercise or cue it on the CD/tape. Elbow grab stretch.
LESSON FOCUS AND GAME (20 MINUTES)	
Distribute written exam to one half of the class. Distribute skills exam to other half of the class.	Use a management game to divide class in half. When students complete skill exam, have them take written exam. Rotate written exam students to skills exam.

TENNIS WRITTEN EXAM

NAME: ____

True-False - Please mark a true state with a "+" and if the statement is false mark it with an "O."

_______ 1. If you leave the ground with both feet while serving, it is illegal.

_______ 2. Is it legal to step on the base line while serving?

_______ 3. The serving grip is pure eastern grip.

_______ 4. The slide service is less accurate than the flat serve.

_______ 5. The ball should be contacted by the racquet on its downward flight.

_______ 6. In preparing to serve, stand with your right side toward the net.

Multiple Choice - Please put the correct letter in the blank.

_______ 1. In the set position, the feet are:
- a. together, weight is even
- b. comfortable apart, weight on balls of feet
- c. apart. weight is even

_______ 2. In the grip, the racquet is:
- a. perpendicular to ground, palm of hand down
- b. parallel to ground, racquet face standing on edge
- c. parallel, racquet face at a slant

_______ 3. Most of the time your knees should be:
- a. stiff, and bend when ball reaches the racquet
- b. bent and flexible
- c. any way that is comfortable

_______ 4. The tennis swing should be:
- a. in definite steps
- b. smooth, slow and continuous motion
- c. hurried swing, not too loose

_______ 5. In the serve the set position is:
- a. facing net, feet together, weight even on both feet
- b. side toward net, feet shoulder width apart, weight on back foot
- c. body and racquet in a comfortable position

Fill in the blank:

1. In the back swing shift your weight to the (right/left) ___________ foot.
2. In the forward swing the racquet should be at the (highest/ lowest)____________ point.
3. For a slice serve, the ball is on the (right/left)_________ side.
4. When serving on the right side of the court, the ball should land in the opponent's (right/left)_________ court.
5. In the follow through, the racquet ______________________.

Tennis Lesson Plan 14

EQUIPMENT:

1 Tennis racquet per student
2 Tennis balls per student
CD/Cassette player
Music CD/tape for Aerobic Workout

OBJECTIVES:

The student will:

1. Participate in an Aerobic Workout during the fitness section of class to improve strength, agility, flexibility, aerobic and muscular endurance levels while preparing to play tennis.
2. Demonstrate the ability to play tennis by participating in an in-class tournament while demonstrating knowledge of rules and a positive attitude.

National Standards Met in this Lesson: **1, 2, 3, 4, 5, 6**

INSTRUCTIONAL ACTIVITIES	TEACHING HINTS

INTRODUCTORY ACTIVITY (2 - 3 MINUTES)

Eliminate to allow time to play tennis.

FITNESS DEVELOPMENT (8 - 12 MINUTES)

Aerobic Workout

Create and Aerobic Exercise Routine lasting 8 - 10 minutes. The CD/tape you make should be 120 to 150 beats per minute. A pre-recorded Aerobic Dance Exercise CD/tape allowing the last two minutes to be used for a short cool down activity and approximately 5 minutes for abdominal and upper body strengthening, as well as stretching.

A: Hop on the left foot 8 times while pointing and tapping the right foot forward and then to the side (e.g., forward, side, forward, side, forward, side). Repeat the entire phrase while hopping (bouncing) on the right foot 8 times and tapping the left foot forward and to the side as described.
B: Run in place 8 times and clap on each run.
C: 8 jumping jacks using full arm movements.
D: Slide to the right 8 times and clap on the 8th slide. Repeat to the left.

See DPESS Chapter 16 for details.

You don't have to be a dancer to create an enjoyable, high-energy routine. An example of 4 phrases of movement identified as A, B, C, D, that you could combine into a routine is:

The suggested phrases can be first performed in the A, B, C, D format and then combined in any order to feel works well with the movement and the music. A simple way to add variety to the routine you have created is to add different arm movements each time you repeat the phrase. Then the original 4 phrases of movement can be repeated as originally choreographed.

LESSON FOCUS AND GAME (15 - 25 MINUTES)

Round Robin Tennis Tournament

Assign students to tournament court by explaining Round Robin Chart.
Students not interested in tournament play could be assigned a singles/doubles game.

EVALUATION/REVIEW AND CHEER

Review tournament rules.
Establish which team plays, which team for the final tournament day.

Cheer: Yea, the tournament is here!

Tennis Lesson Plan 15

EQUIPMENT:

1 Tennis racquet per student
2 Tennis balls per student
CD/Cassette player
Music CD/tape for Exercise Routine

OBJECTIVES:

The student will:

1. Participate in a given Exercise routine during the fitness section of class to improve strength, agility, flexibility, aerobic and muscular endurance levels while preparing to play tennis.
2. Demonstrate the ability to play tennis by participating in an in-class tournament while demonstrating knowledge of rules and a positive attitude.

National Standards Met in this Lesson: **1, 2, 3, 4, 5, 6**

INSTRUCTIONAL ACTIVITIES	TEACHING HINTS
INTRODUCTORY ACTIVITY AND FITNESS DEVELOPMENT (8 - 12 MINUTES)	
Exercise Routine	**See DPESS Chapter 16 for details.**
Intersperse jogging, stretching and strengthening activities.	Scattered within boundaries set by cones. Direct students to run throughout the area. On signal, they will stop and perform a designated stretch/strengthening exercise.
Stretches Lower leg stretch (with partner, or wall) Balance beam stretch Sit and reach Side leg stretch Groin stretch Body twist Ankle hold, or hand down Squat stretch Standing hip stretch	The student will name the muscle being stretched/strengthened when asked to call it out. Music can be used to cue the running and during the silence you can either call out the exercise or cue it on the CD/tape. Elbow grab stretch.
Strengthening Push-ups Curl-ups Rocking Chair Reverse curl Pelvis Tilter	
LESSON FOCUS AND GAME (15 - 25 MINUTES)	
Round Robin Tennis Tournament	Continue tournament. Assign students to court area using chart.
EVALUATION/REVIEW AND CHEER	
Conclude unit.	
Cheer: Tennis, Yes!	

SERVE: SKILL TEST CHECK LIST

Name: ________________________________

Directions: Perform four serves in a row. Observer look at 2 check points on each serve.

CHECK LIST RATING SCALE:
3 - Outstanding
2 - Average
1 - Below Average

	Record Rating			
I. SET POSITION				
A. Grip 1. Continental Grip 2. Fingers spread				
B. Stance 1. Side toward net 2. Weight on rear feet; feet spread				
C. Racquet 1. Pointing to serve area 2. Standing on edge 3. Left hand cradling				
II. BACKSWING (Ball Toss)				
A. Ball Toss 1. Ball thrown to correct height 2. Ball thrown above left foot				
B. Racquet Arm 1. Both arms work smoothly together 2. Racquet raises almost to shoulder level 3. Racquet head drops well behind back (wrist touches shoulder)				
C. Weight Transfer 1. Weight shifts to front foot 2. Balance maintained by front knee bend				
III. FORWARD SWING				
A. Throwing Motion 1. Smooth, continuous motion 2. Elbow leads wrist and racquet forward and up				
B. Contact 1. Highest point above left foot 2. Adequate wrist action 3. Adequate Spin				
C. Follow-Through 1. Racquet head leads through line of shot 2. Racquet finishes on left side of body 3. Right foot comes through to help regain balance				
Total Points				

FOREHAND AND BACKHAND SKILL: SKILL TEST CHECK LIST

Name: ______________________________

Directions: Observe only one section at a time. Mark rating in column following each practice. Practice 4 forehand drive strokes and 4 backhands before changing roles.

CHECK LIST RATING SCALE:
3 - Outstanding
2 - Average
1 - Below Average

	Record Rating			
I. SET POSITION				
A. Grip 1. Shaking hands (forehand) Palm on top (backhand) 2. Fingers spread				
B. Stance 1. Feet spread; knees bent 2. Weight on balls of feet				
C. Racquet 1. Parallel to ground 2. Standing on edge 3. Left hand, cradling racquet				
II. BACKSWING				
A. Pivot 1. Step promptly toward ball with nearest foot 2. Side turned completely				
B. Racquet 1. Backswing; begun early 2. Racquet head back first, with firm writs (left hand helps backhand)				
C. Run to Ball 1. Move quickly to ball 2. Sets on rear foot				
III. FORWARD SWING				
A. Ready position 1. Racquet head drops below point of contact 2. Racquet nearly parallel to ground, extends toward back fence				
B. Weight Transfer 1. Front foot steps into line of shot 2. All weight on ball of front foot 3. Knees bent; good balance				
C. Point of Contact 1. Ball contacted well in front of body 2. Wrist firm; racquet parallel				
D. Follow-Through 1. Racquet head continues out through line of shot 2. Racquet standing on edge 3. Forehand: wrist eye level; looking over elbow 4. Backhand: wrist above head; racquet nearly vertical to ground 5. Pose				

Observers Signature: ______________________________ Date: __________

Volleyball

This unit has been specifically designed to meet all six components of the NASPE National Standards for Physical Education.

OBJECTIVES:

The student will:

1. Demonstrate teamwork by communicating with classmates to move in same direction during the Loose Caboose.
2. Perform various cardiovascular, strength building and stretching activities as demonstrated in class.
3. Increase his eye hand coordination when throwing and catching a beanbag.
4. Decrease his reaction time and increase quickness by performing various movement activities in the Wave Drill.
5. Demonstrate visual skills and creativity by leading and following movements during the Shadow Partner activity
6. Run smoothly and rhythmically while performing locomotor movements to the beat of the music
7. Dodge classmate quickly without falling or colliding with another student during the Tag Introductory Activity.
8. Demonstrate teamwork by staying connected to teammates during the Capture the Flag Introductory Activity.
9. Demonstrate agility and change of directions while avoiding other students in the Diving Under Freeze Tag game.
10. Perform various fitness activities at different stations, as demonstrated in class to improve her fitness levels.
11. Demonstrate good listening skills by matching movements to the sound of the drum.
12. Demonstrate proper stretching and cardiovascular activities as demonstrated in class.
13. Perform various jump rope activities, and strength building activities as demonstrated in class.
14. Name the changes in body functions that occur when one exercises, e.g. increased heart rate, breathing rate.
15. Perform various jump rope, stretching and strength building activities during the Continuity Exercises.
16. Perform proper arm swing techniques while hitting the ball against the wall as demonstrated in class.
17. Demonstrate proper volleyball approach jumps to the net as demonstrated in class.
18. Execute proper technique when setting the volleyball as demonstrated in class.
19. Perform proper footwork and ball control when setting the volleyball, as demonstrated in class.
20. Improve her eye-hand coordination by hitting and catching a volleyball to herself.
21. Perform the underhand serve as demonstrated in class.
22. Perform the overhand serve using technique demonstrated in class.
23. Perform the forearm pass while using techniques demonstrated in class.
24. Communicate with his teammates calling for the ball as demonstrated in class, e.g. "mine", "yours."
25. Demonstrate eye hand coordination by performing the bump pass for 1 minute as demonstrated in class.
26. Set the ball back and forth with his partner 10 times in a row, using the technique demonstrated in class.
27. Back set to a partner 10 times using the technique demonstrated in class. Execute the spiking approach at the appropriate station using techniques demonstrated in class.
28. Self evaluate her spiking skills while trying to spike the ball into a target at the designated station practice.
29. Practice two-handed blocks and perform two-man blocks during the lesson focus activities.
30. Perform one and two arms forearm passes using skills demonstrated by the instructor.
31. Execute the side roll 5 times while reaching and forearm passing the ball.
32. Perform various volleyball skills correctly during the partner Task Sheet Evaluation activities.
33. Volley the ball in groups of 6 and complete 5 consecutive volleys during the Keep It Up game.
34. Demonstrate an understanding of the Overhand Serve and Forearm Pass by evaluating classmates using Task Sheets.
35. Participate in a game that requires three touches per side before the ball goes over the net using skills demonstrated in class by the instructor.
36. Practice improving communication skills by working with teammates in the game Three-and-Over.
37. Demonstrate his understanding of the game of volleyball by playing a modified game.
38. Demonstrate knowledge and understanding of basic volleyball rules and terminology by scoring a minimum of 75% on a written exam.
39. Demonstrate knowledge and understanding of volleyball skills by playing in the tournament and using techniques demonstrated in class.

Academic Integration Areas:

1. Describe the history of Volleyball in the United States.
2. Explain the physics related to the trajectory of serving, spiking, receiving in Volleyball.
3. Have the students investigate and report on United States Volleyball Olympians.

VOLLEYBALL BLOCK PLAN
3 WEEK UNIT

Week #1	Monday	Tuesday	Wednesday	Thursday	Friday
Introductory Activity	Loose Caboose	Beanbag Toss	Wave Drill	Weave Drill	Formation Rhythmic Running
Fitness	Astronaut Drills	Continuity Exercises	Jump Rope Activities to Music	Four Corners to Music	Circuit Training to Music
Focus	Underhand Serve	Forearm Bump Pass	Overhand Serve	Overhand Set Serves	Forearm Bump Pass
Game	Scooter Cageball Soccer	Wheel Barrow Relay	Tug-of-War	Push-Up Tag	3 Hit Volleyball

Week #2	Monday	Tuesday	Wednesday	Thursday	Friday
Introductory Activity	Beanbag Touch and Go	Seat Roll	Fastest Tag	Addition Tag	Capture the Flag
Fitness	Mini Challenge Course	Parachute Fitness	Continuity Exercises	Squad Leader Exercises	Stations
Focus	Spiking	Setting	Spiking and Dinking	Blocking	Forearm Bump
Game	King & Queen of the Court	Mini Pyramids	Keep it Up or Hula Hoop Targets	Modified Volleyball Game	Dig It

Week #3	Monday	Tuesday	Wednesday	Thursday	Friday
Introductory Activity	Octopus Tag	Following Activity	Diving Under Freeze Tag	Eliminate to allow time for other sections	Eliminate to allow time for other sections
Fitness	Mirror Drills in Place	Fitness Challenge	Walk - Jog - Sprint	Continuity Exercises	Written Volleyball Exam
Focus	Task Sheets	Task Sheets	Volleyball Round Robin Tournament	Volleyball Round Robin Tournament	Continue Tournament after exam
Game	Keep It Afloat	Three- and-Over	Volleyball Round Robin Tournament	Volleyball Round Robin Tournament	Continue Tournament

Volleyball Lesson Plan 1

EQUIPMENT:

1 Volleyball per student
CD/Cassette tape player
1 Scooter per person
Continuity Exercise Music CD/Tape
1 Cageball
Colored pinnies for 1/2 of class

OBJECTIVES:

The student will:

1. Demonstrate agility and cooperation during the Loose Caboose activity as following the rules explained by the instructor.
2. Participate in Astronaut Drills during the fitness section of class to improve agility, flexibility, muscular strength and endurance.
3. Demonstrate the underhand serve during the lesson focus using form demonstrated by the instructor.
4. Participate in the serve and catch activities following the rules and using form demonstrated by the instructor.
5. Demonstrate cooperative skills by playing Scooter Cageball Soccer during the game portion of class.

National Standards Met in this Lesson: **1, 3, 4, 5, 6**

INSTRUCTIONAL ACTIVITIES	TEACHING HINTS
INTRODUCTORY ACTIVITY (2 - 3 MINUTES)	
Loose Caboose One child is designated as the "loose caboose". He tries to hook onto a train. Trains are formed by 3 or 4 children standing in column formation with each child placing their hands on the waist of the child in front of them. The trains, by twisting and turning, try to keep caboose from hooking on to the back. If the caboose hooks on, the front child becomes new caboose.	**See DPESS Chapter 14 for details.** Using Whistle Mixer, create groups of 3 - 4. Select several "its"" and designate them as the "loose caboose".
FITNESS DEVELOPMENT (8-12 MINUTES)	
Astronaut Drills Use intervals of music and silence to signal duration of exercise. Music segments indicate aerobic activity while intervals of silence announce flexibility and strength development activities. Arm Circles; Jump or Hop back & forth, side to side; Crab Alternate Leg Extensions; Skip; Twist; Slide; Lunge; Jumping Jack Variations; Flying Angel Sit-Ups; Hop to Center and Back; Push-Ups; Gallop; Arm Stretch - across body; Trot; Arm Stretch - over head; Power Taped Jumper; Shoulder Rolls; Ankle Circles; Head Circles in frontal plane; Stretch & Touch Toes	**See DPESS Chapter 16 for details.** Circle or scattered formation with space between students. Children should be in constant movement except when stopped to do strength and flexibility activities.

INSTRUCTIONAL ACTIVITIES	TEACHING HINTS

LESSON FOCUS (15-20 MINUTES)

Underhand Serve
Demonstrate:

- Against wall
- Serving to partner over net or posted rope

See DPESS Chapter 19 for details.

Student practices alone.
Use Elbow to elbow technique to create pairs.
Assign pairs to practice area.

Serve and Catch
Start with a ball on each side of the net.
Several balls are served at same time from serving area.
All balls must be caught on the other side of net. Once the ball is caught, the can be served from the opposing serving area. The object is to catch the ball and quickly serve so that the opponent cannot catch the ball.
A point is scored when the ball is served under hand, goes over the net and hits the ground in bounds.

Divide class into even numbers of groups.
Create groups using back-to-back technique.
Direct: Hands on hips - one group
Hands on head - other group
1 scorekeeper is needed for each group.
Assign groups to courts.

The sport of volleyball began in 1895. The sport of volleyball has grown continuously in popularity since its inception. Volleyball has become one of the most popular participant sports worldwide with more than 200 million competitors, a number comparable to the number of soccer participants.

GAME (3-5 MINUTES)

Scooter Cageball Soccer
While sitting on scooter, advance Cageball with feet only to score goals.

See DPESS Chapter 18 for details.
Use a management technique to create teams.
Give pinnies to teams and assign teams to courts.

EVALUATION/REVIEW AND CHEER

Students huddle close together so you can ask review questions.
What were some of the key points to remember about an underhand serve? Answer: Eyes on the ball, dominant foot back, heel of the hand makes contact with the ball, follow through, stand with dominate foot back.
Cheer: We Love Volleyball!

Volleyball Lesson Plan 2

EQUIPMENT:
1 Bean Bag per person
Volleyball courts and nets
1 Volleyball per person
Continuity Exercise Music CD/Tape
CD/Cassette tape player

OBJECTIVES:
The student will:
1. Demonstrate agility and eye-hand coordination in the Bean Bag Toss activity as following the instructions explained by the instructor.
2. Participate in Continuity Exercises during the fitness section of class to improve agility, flexibility, muscular strength, muscular endurance, and aerobic endurance.
3. Demonstrate the forearm bump pass during the lesson focus using form demonstrated by the instructor.
4. Participate in the serving exercises following the rules and using form demonstrated by the instructor.
5. Demonstrate cooperative skills by participating in the Wheelbarrow Relay during the game portion of class.

National Standards Met in this Lesson: **1, 2, 3, 4, 5, 6**

INSTRUCTIONAL ACTIVITIES | **TEACHING HINTS**

INTRODUCTORY ACTIVITY (2 - 3 MINUTES)

Bean Bag Toss
On signal, students pick up a beanbag and throw and catch the bean bag as directed in place and while jogging around the room.

See DPESS Chapter 14 for details.
Scattered Formation
On signal students will return beanbags and scatter themselves on the mat.

FITNESS DEVELOPMENT (8 - 12 MINUTES)

Continuity Exercises
These exercises are a type of interval training.
Create a CD/cassette tape with 30 - 35 seconds of music and 20 seconds of silence. Alternate music and silence.
Students jump rope during music and execute exercises as directed during silence. Sample exercises:
Leg Kicks R/L; Standing Bend & Stretch;
Jumping Jacks; Arm Circles; Arm Thrusts; Stretch Arms Overhead; Sitting Stretch - touch toes;
Push-Ups; Stretch in out-reach; Curl-ups;
Sitting Body Twist; Leg Lunges; Standing stretch and touch toes; Shoulder circles

See DPESS Chapter 16 for details.

LESSON FOCUS (15 - 20 MINUTES)

Forearm bump pass
Demonstrate passing skill
- Stance: shoulder width and square with the ball; hips and knees flexed.
- Arm position.
- When contact is made, bump the ball
- Off of the lower forearms above the wrist.

See DPESS Chapter 19 for details.
Use management technique of: Toe-to-Toe with 3 people:
- 1 places hands on hips =DOER
- 1 places hands on knees =TOSSER/retriever
- 1 kneels on ground = OBSERVER

OBSERVER will observe the doer and give verbal feedback.

Remember that the first contact after a serve is normally the bump, which sets in motion the three-step volleyball offense of bump, set, and spike. You need a flat surface, slightly on an angle to project the ball at the correct trajectory for the setter to receive your pass.

Review serving skills

Repeat practice activity of yesterday.

INSTRUCTIONAL ACTIVITIES	TEACHING HINTS

GAME (5 MINUTES)

Wheelbarrow Relay	**See DPESS Chapter 18 for details.** See Lesson 13, Weight Training Unit for details.

EVALUATION/REVIEW AND CHEER

Students huddle together for review.

Teacher will review by asking students pertinent questions regarding elements of the lesson.

Cheer: 1, 2, 3, 4, forearm passes help us score!

Volleyball Lesson Plan 3

EQUIPMENT:

Partner Tug-of-War rope(s)
Cones
1 Individual jump rope per person
CD/ tape for rope jumping music
Volleyball Courts
1 Volleyball per student
CD/ cassette tape player

OBJECTIVES:

The student will:

1. Demonstrate agility and the ability to follow instructions while participating in the Wave Drill activity while following the instructions given by the leader.
2. Participate in Jump Rope Activities during the fitness section of class to improve agility, flexibility, muscular strength, muscular endurance, and aerobic endurance.
3. Demonstrate the overhand serve during the lesson focus using form demonstrated by the instructor.
4. Participate in the bump pass review activities following the rules and using form demonstrated by the instructor.
5. Demonstrate cooperative skills by participating in the Tug-of-War game during the closing portion of class.

National Standards Met in this Lesson: **1, 2, 3, 4, 5, 6**

INSTRUCTIONAL ACTIVITIES	TEACHING HINTS

INTRODUCTORY ACTIVITY (2 - 3 MINUTES)

Wave Drill

Students are in ready position (knees bent). Students shuffle left, right, backward or forward on whistle or hand signal.

- 1 - whistle = Forward
- 2 - whistles = Backward
- 3 - whistles = Left
- 4 - whistles = Right

See DPESS Chapter 14 for details.

FITNESS DEVELOPMENT (8 - 12 MINUTES)

Rope Jumping Activities

Jump Rope interspersed with the following:
Leg Lunges
Stretch Arms across body
Sit-Ups
Push-Ups
Shoulder Rolls
Ankle Rolls
Stretch Arms overhead
Stretch-touch toes
Sitting-Twist Body

See DPESS Chapter 14 for details.
Scattered Formation
Jump rope to the music. When music stops place rope on the ground and do the instructed activity.

LESSON FOCUS (15 - 20 MINUTES)

Overhand Serves

Demonstrate serve
Review Underhand Serve

See DPESS Chapter 19 for details.
Use Back-to-Back management technique.
Assign students to courts with partner to practice 10 types of serves each.

One of the most important skills in volleyball is this serve. An overhand serve can be very powerful and set the tone of the game. Be award of the biomechanics of serving: Keep your elbow high while serving - during the armswing. Keeping your elbow high increases your chances of getting the ball over the net.

Review Bump Pass

Review drill in Lesson 2.
Repeat drill of Lesson 2 today.

Anticipate the flight of the ball so that you can receive it in a stationary, athletic position with your knees bent, your weight forward on the balls of your feet, and your arms extended forward and down.

INSTRUCTIONAL ACTIVITIES	TEACHING HINTS
GAME (5 MINUTES)	
Tug-of-War • Traditional • Pull rope over head • Pull with backs to opponents • pull with one hand on ground or in air • pull from seated position.	**See DPESS Chapter 18 for details.** Review drill in Lesson 2 Repeat today

Tug-of-War activities are fun, but you must exercise caution and respect for others in this game. You only release the rope when so instructed and using form demonstrated by your instructor to keep all students safe.

EVALUATION/REVIEW AND CHEER

Students huddle close together to answer review questions presented by instructor.
What is one of the most important skills to do well in volleyball?
Of the serves learned so far, which is the most powerful?
What are some of the key elements to bump passing a ball well and with accuracy?
Review some of the safety features to observe when participating in Tug-of-War activities.

Cheer: 2, 4, 6, 8, Teamwork is really great!

Volleyball Lesson Plan 4

EQUIPMENT:

1 Volleyball per student
Cones for markers
CD/Cassette tape player
Music tape for fitness activities

OBJECTIVES:

The student will:

1. Demonstrate agility during the Weave Drill activity while following the directional signals given by the leader.
2. Participate in Four Corners Exercises during the fitness section of class to improve agility, flexibility, muscular strength, muscular endurance, and aerobic endurance.
3. Demonstrate the front overhand pass, over the net set, and serving during the lesson focus using form demonstrated by the instructor.
4. Participate in the serving exercises following the rules and using form demonstrated by the instructor.
5. Demonstrate cooperative skills by participating in Push-Up Tag during the game portion of class.

National Standards Met in this Lesson: **1 , 2, 3, 4, 5, 6**

INSTRUCTIONAL ACTIVITIES	TEACHING HINTS
INTRODUCTORY ACTIVITY (2 - 3 MINUTES)	
Weave Drill The weave drill is similar to the wave drill except that students shuffle in and out of a series of obstacles such as cones. A shuffling step is used rather than a crossover step.	**See DPESS Chapter 14 for details.** Cones are spread out in rows. Each student should stand next to a cone. Everyone is facing the same direction. Wait for signal to go left or right.
FITNESS DEVELOPMENT (8 - 12 MINUTES)	
Four Corners Movement to music. • Skipping Jumping • Hopping Galloping	**See DPESS Chapter 16 for details.** Cones mark a square. Scattered formation around the perimeter of the 4 cones. When music starts they move in a clockwise direction. As they pass a corner they change locomotor movement.
Stretching: Legs • Arms (across body, over head) Roll: Shoulders • Ankles • Wrists Twist Body	**See DPESS Chapter 16 for details.** Teacher or student can direct these activities.
LESSON FOCUS (15- 20 MINUTES)	
3 Station Practice: **1. Front overhand pass** Demonstrate practice drill: Partners stand 8 ft. apart and pass back and forth using the technique.	**See DPESS Chapter 19 for details.** Use Back-to-back technique to make pairs. 1 person puts hands on hips. That person get s1 ball for partners. 2 lines facing partner: x x x x x x x x
2. Over the net set Drill demonstration: Set the ball once to self, then over the net partner.	Partners stand on opposite sides of the net. 2 to 3 partner sets to a court. Variation: 2 people to a side, set to each other and then set over the net. As skills are mastered, groups can be larger.
3. Serving Review Demonstrate drill.	Assign 1/3 of the class to this with partner station.
GAME (5 MINUTES)	
Push-Up Tag "Its" try to tag. Safe position = push-up position and activity. Can only perform 3.	**See DPESS Chapter 14 for details.** Select several "its" to be taggers. Students must stay active throughout game.

EVALUATION/REVIEW AND CHEER

Students huddle close together. Questions: What did you learn today? Name the two types of serves you've practices.
Cheer: Roses are red, violets are blue, P.E. is great, Volleyball Rules.

Volleyball Lesson Plan 5

EQUIPMENT:

1 Individual jump rope per person
1 Volleyball per student
Whistle
Station Cards with Fitness Instructions
Pre-recorded music CD/tape for exercise
CD/Cassette tape player
Drum and beater

OBJECTIVES:

The student will:

1. Demonstrate following a beat and agility during Formation Rhythmic Running activity while following the beat and directional signals given by the leader.
2. Participate in Four Circuit Training to music during the fitness section of class to improve agility, flexibility, muscular strength, muscular endurance, and aerobic endurance.
3. Demonstrate the front overhand pass, over the net set, and serving during the lesson focus using form demonstrated by the instructor.
4. Participate in the serving exercises following the rules and using form demonstrated by the instructor.
5. Demonstrate cooperative skills by participating in Push-Up Tag during the game portion of class.

National Standards Met in this Lesson: **1, 2, 3, 4, 5, 6**

INSTRUCTIONAL ACTIVITIES / TEACHING HINTS

INTRODUCTORY ACTIVITY (2 - 3 MINUTES)

Formation Rhythmic Running

On signal (drum, clap)

- Runners freeze in place. They resume running when the regular beat begins again.
- Runners make a full turn in four running steps, lifting the knees high while turning.
- Runners go backward, changing the direction of the circle.

See DPESS Chapter 14 for details.

Circle Formation: Follow the back of somebody's neck to create a circle.

The tone of the drum controls the quality of the movement, light sound light run, heavy sound heavy run.

When the drum stops students run in scattered formation, when it resumes, they return to circular formation and follow rhythm.

Rhythmic Running is used in many European countries to open the daily lesson (running to the accompaniment of some type of percussion instrument). Much of the running follows a circular path (but can be done in scatter formation). Running should be light, bouncy, and rhythmic in time with the beat. Movement ideas can be combined with the rhythmic running pattern.

FITNESS DEVELOPMENT (8 - 12 MINUTES)

Circuit Training to music

7 Circuits

• Push-Ups • Bend & Stretch • Sit-Ups • Arm Circles • Windmills • Rope Jumping • Sit & Stretch

Record a CD/tape with 60 seconds of music and 5 seconds of silence for rotating to the next station.

See DPESS Chapter 16 for details.

Divide class up into 7 groups.

Assign each group to begin at a given circuit.

Students active while music is playing, when music stops, rotate clockwise to the next station.

LESSON FOCUS (15- 20 MINUTES)

Forearm Bump Pass

Demonstrate drills:

- Pass the ball 2-3 feet off the wall to yourself.
- Partner underhand tosses ball to you. You forearm pass back to your partner. 10 times then switch. Repeat.
- Partner bounces ball to you. You forearm pass back to your partner. 10 times then switch. Repeat.

See DPESS Chapter 19 for details.

Use management game to create groups of two.

Scatter formation throughout Gym.

February 9, 1895, in Holyoke, Massachusetts (USA), William G. Morgan, a YMCA physical education director, created a new game called Mintonette as a pastime to be played preferably indoors and by any number of players. The game took some of its characteristics from tennis and handball. An observer, Alfred Halstead, noticed the volleying nature of the game at its first exhibition match in 1896, played at the International YMCA Training School (now called Springfield College), the game quickly became known as volleyball.

INSTRUCTIONAL ACTIVITIES	TEACHING HINTS
GAME (5 - 7 MINUTES)	
3 Hit Volleyball	**See DPESS Chapter 16 for details.**
6 players per team. Use as many courts as needed. Need to have an even number of teams so everyone is playing.	Use Whistle Mixer to form teams. Use regulation rules, but must have 3 hits per side. Can also allow 2 serves without penalty if desire.

EVALUATION/REVIEW AND CHEER

Review daily activities. Teacher will ask lead up questions for self-discovery. Talk about teamwork.
What is the history of formation running that we did today?
Were there any stations during the Circuit training that you definitely need more work?
What muscles were used in class today?
What is the origin of the name Volleyball?

Cheer: Fun for all, we enjoyed Volleyball!

Volleyball Lesson Plan 6

EQUIPMENT:

1 Volleyball per student
Volleyball courts
1 Beanbag (different colors) per student
Station cards for Fitness activities
20 Cones for markers
Tug-of-War Rope
Mats for Challenge Course
Station cards for Lesson Focus activities

OBJECTIVES:

The student will:

1. Demonstrate agility during Beanbag Touch and Go while following the instructions given by the leader.
2. Participate in a Mini Challenge Course to music during the fitness section of class to improve agility, flexibility, muscular strength, muscular endurance, and aerobic endurance.
3. Demonstrate the approach for spiking, the hit, and tipping of a volleyball during the lesson focus using form demonstrated by the instructor.
4. Demonstrate cooperative and Volleyball skills by participating in King/Queen of the Court during the game portion of class.

National Standards Met in this Lesson: **1, 2, 3, 4, 5, 6**

INSTRUCTIONAL ACTIVITIES	TEACHING HINTS

INTRODUCTORY ACTIVITY (2 - 3 MINUTES)

Beanbag Touch and Go
Spread different colored beanbags throughout the area. On signal, students run to a beanbag, touch it, and resume running. The touch must be made with a designated body part. E.g. "Touch 6 yellow beanbags with your right hand."

See DPESS Chapter 14 for details.
Scattered Formation
To increase the challenge, the color of the beanbag can be specified.
Students can also move to a beanbag, perform a pivot, and resume running.

FITNESS DEVELOPMENT (8 - 12 MINUTES)

Mini Challenge Course (4 courses)
***Course #1**:* Do crouch jumps, pull or scoot movements down a bench; put body through two hoops; and skip to a cone.
***Course #2**:* Weave in out of four wands held upright by cones; Crab Walk to cone; hang from a climbing rope for 5 seconds; gallop to a cone.
***Course #3**:* Do a tumbling activity the length of the mat; agility run through hoops; Frog Jump to cone; slide to cone.
***Course #4**:* Move overt and under six obstacles; Log roll length of mat; while jumping, circle around three cones; run to next cone.

See DPESS Chapter 16 for details.
Whistle Mixer - blow whistle 4 times, groups of 4.
1 person hand on head (course #1)
1 person hand on knees (course #2)
1 person hand on hip s (course #3)
1 person knee on ground (course and #4)
Rotation: Tosser - Retriever - Hitter – Tosser

Create a tape with continuous music the length of the fitness section. Students progress from one station to the next upon completion of the activities at each station.

LESSON FOCUS (15 - 20 MINUTES)

Station Practice
Spiking Station #1: Spike ball against wall using the arm swing form taught in class. Repeat.
Station #2: **Toss and hit.** The tosser tosses ball like a set partner who spikes ball back using the arm swing motion. No foot approach. Switch roles and repeat.
Station #3: Approach and Tip Ball. At the net. Tosser tosses ball up, hitter makes approach and tips the ball into other court. Tosser becomes hitter. Hitter shags ball.

See DPESS Chapter 19 for details.
Toe-to-Toe 1 other person. Pairs combine with another pair to make a group of 4.
Everyone gets a ball.
Assign groups to stations.
Explain rotation.
Two shaggers needed in this activity.

The approach is a critical component of a successful offense in volleyball. Biomechanics dictate the success. A good hitter or spiker will use the approach to achieve a high jump with minimal horizontal motion. During the approach steps, a good hitter will maximize horizontal velocity at touch-down and minimize it at take-off.

INSTRUCTIONAL ACTIVITIES	TEACHING HINTS

GAME (5 - 7 MINUTES)

King/Queen of the Court
3 on 3 game using the spike and tip. Winning team stays on court, other team goes to sideline and new team comes on. Repeat.

See DPESS Chapter 16 for details.
Toe-to-Toe with 3 people. Four groups of 3 to each court. Depending on # of courts, may vary.

EVALUATION/REVIEW AND CHEER

Students huddled close together.

Questions: Which station was the most challenging? Why?
What is important about the approach before the spike?
Was anything difficult about spiking? What?
How was the game?

Cheer: 1, 2, 3, Fit is the way to be!

Volleyball Lesson Plan 7

EQUIPMENT:

1 Volleyball per student
Parachute
CD/ cassette player
Volleyball Courts/Nets
CD/ tape for fitness
Mats for Pyramid Activity

OBJECTIVES:

The student will:

1. Demonstrate agility Seat Roll while following the instructions given by the leader.
2. Participate in a Parachute Fitness to music during the fitness section of class to improve agility, flexibility, muscular strength, muscular endurance, and aerobic endurance.
3. Demonstrate the front and back setting during the lesson focus using form demonstrated by the instructor.
4. Demonstrate cooperative skills by participating in Mini Pyramids during the closing portion of class.

National Standards Met in this Lesson: **1, 2, 3, 4, 5, 6**

INSTRUCTIONAL ACTIVITIES | **TEACHING HINTS**

INTRODUCTORY ACTIVITY (2 - 3 MINUTES)

Seat Roll

Students are on all fours with head up, looking at the instructor. When instructor gives a left or a right hand signal, students respond quickly by rolling that direction on their seat.

See DPESS Chapter 14 for details.
Scattered Formation.
Example for signals could be:
1 whistle = left
2 whistles = right

FITNESS DEVELOPMENT (8 - 12 MINUTES)

Parachute Fitness

1. Jog in a circle with chute held in left hand. Reverse.
2. Standing, raise the chute overhead, lower to waist.
3. Slide to the right; return slide to the left.
4. Sit and perform Abdominal Challenges - 30 sec.
5. Skip.
6. Freeze; face the center, and stretch the chute tightly with bent arms. Hold for 8- 12 seconds. Repeat 5 X.
7. Run in place; hold the chute at waist level.
8. Sit with legs under the chute. Do a seat walk toward the center. Return to the perimeter. Repeat.
9. Place chute on the ground. Jog away from the chute and return on signal. Repeat.
10. On side, perform side leg flex (lift chute with legs).
11. Lie on back with legs under the chute. Shake the chute with the feet.
12. Hop to the center of the chute and return. Repeat.
13. Assume the push-up position with the legs aligned away from the center of the chute. Shake the chute with one arm while the other arm supports the body.
14. Sit with feet under the chute. Stretch by touching the toes with the chute. Relax with other stretches while sitting.
15. Perform parachute stunts like the Dome or Mushroom to end.

See DPESS Chapter 16 for details.
Evenly space students around the parachute.
Use different grips to add variation to the activities.
Encourage students to move together.
Use music to motivate students.

INSTRUCTIONAL ACTIVITIES | **TEACHING HINTS**

LESSON FOCUS (15 - 20 MINUTES)

Setting

Demonstrate drills:

- Stand across from partner and set back and forth.
- Set to self and then to your partner.

See DPESS Chapter 19 for details.

Back-to-Back with someone.

Setter, you must time your push-up with the toss.

Knees bent in ready position, hands always above head.

Back Set

Demonstrate.

- Set once to yourself then back set to your partner.
- Partner, front set back to your partner.

The study of body mechanics has given light to the most efficient form to use in volleyball. The correct body position for setting is with the ball, forehead, and hips in a vertical line.

Set Spike Review at net

Work with the same partner.

GAME (5 - 7 MINUTES)

Mini Pyramids

Partners work together to create pyramids.

See DPESS Chapter 18 for details.

Can combine groups.

EVALUATION/REVIEW AND CHEER

Students huddle close together. Any questions?
What did you learn today?
What did you like best?
Cheer: You bet, we love to set.

Volleyball Lesson Plan 8

EQUIPMENT:

1 Volleyball per student
Volleyball Courts/Nets
Continuity Music CD/Tape
Station instructional cards
1 Jump rope per student
1 Hula Hoop per student
CD/Cassette tape player

OBJECTIVES:

The student will:

1. Demonstrate agility and running during Fastest Tag while following the instructions given by the leader.
2. Participate in a Continuity Exercises to music during the fitness section of class to improve agility, flexibility, muscular strength, muscular endurance, and aerobic endurance.
3. Demonstrate spiking and dinking during the lesson focus using form demonstrated by the instructor.
4. Demonstrate cooperative and volleyball skills by playing Keep it A Float during the closing portion of class.

National Standards Met in this Lesson: **1, 2, 3, 4, 5, 6**

INSTRUCTIONAL ACTIVITIES	TEACHING HINTS
INTRODUCTORY ACTIVITY (2 - 3 MINUTES)	
Fastest Tag	**See DPESS Chapter 14 for details.** See Lesson 8, Badminton unit for instructional details.
FITNESS DEVELOPMENT (8 - 12 MINUTES)	
Continuity Exercises Students alternate jump rope activity with exercises done in two-count fashion. Teacher/ student can lead. Movement examples alternated with rope jumping: Double Crab Kick; Knee Touch Curl-up; Push-Up- Challenges; Bend - touch toes; Rope Jumping: Swing-Step Forward while jumping; Side Flex; Stretch Arms - over head Stretch Arms - across body; Curl - Ups; Rope Jumping: Hot Peppers; Sit and Twist body	**See DPESS Chapter 16 for details.** Scattered Formation Each student gets a jump rope. Recorded intervals of music alternated with silences should be used to signal rope jumping (with music) and performing exercises (without music). Allow each student to adjust the workload to his or her fitness level. This implies resting or walking if the rope jumping is too strenuous.
LESSON FOCUS (15 - 20 MINUTES)	
Station #1: Spiking • Approach without using the ball. Repeat 5 times. • Approach, spike ball out of partner's hand. Partner stands on ladder or jumping box. Repeat 5 - 10 times. Rotate positions.	**See DPESS Chapter 19 for details.** Use management technique to create partners. Assign groups to area in Gym.
Station #2 Toss, **approach, catch:** Person at net tosses up ball as if a set. Partner approaches and catches ball in the air. Repeat 3 times, and then change roles. Repeat.	
S***tation #3*** Spiking: Each group has a tosser, a hitter and two retrievers. The hitter approaches and hits the ball, trying to keep the ball inside the court. Rotate. Repeat until each hits 5 - 10 times.	Combine 2 sets of partners to create groups of 4 when rotate or begin at this station. Assign students to a court.
S***tation #4*** **Dinking:** Same activity as Station 3 but execute a dink shot instead of a spike.	Use the same groups as in Station 4.

INSTRUCTIONAL ACTIVITIES	TEACHING HINTS

GAME (5 - 7 MINUTES)

Keep it Afloat
Set ball to each other and count how many in a certain time period.

See DPESS Chapter 19 for details.
Work in partners.

Hula Hoop Targets
Serve or spike balls into targets. A team scores a point if ball lands in hula-hoop when it touches the ground. Game begins when teacher gives signal.

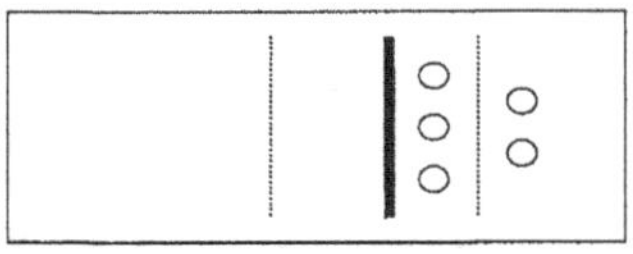

EVALUATION/REVIEW AND CHEER

Huddled around teacher. Any questions? Ask students questions about spiking.
How many steps are in the approach?
What was the hardest part of spiking a ball? The easiest?
When do you Dink rather than Spike a ball?

Cheer: You bet, we love to set!

Volleyball Lesson Plan 9

EQUIPMENT:

1 Volleyball per 4 students
Squad Leader Instructions
CD/ cassette player
4 Cones
Music CD/ tape for fitness
Volleyball courts

OBJECTIVES:

The student will:

1. Demonstrate agility, cooperation, and running during Addition Tag while following the instructions given by the leader.
2. Participate in a Squad Leader Exercises to music during the fitness section of class to improve agility, flexibility, muscular strength, muscular endurance, and aerobic endurance.
3. Demonstrate blocking during the lesson focus using form demonstrated by the instructor.
4. Demonstrate cooperative and volleyball skills by playing a modified volleyball game during the closing portion of class.

National Standards Met in this Lesson: **1, 2, 3, 4, 5, 6**

INSTRUCTIONAL ACTIVITIES | **TEACHING HINTS**

INTRODUCTORY ACTIVITY (2 - 3 MINUTES)

Addition Tag

Two couples are it. "It's "stand with inside hands joined trying to tag with free hands. All tagged join couple. The three then chase until they catch a fourth. Once a fourth person is caught, the four divide and form two couples, adding another set of taggers to the game.

See DPESS Chapter 14 for details.
Scattered Formation. Designate boundaries.
A tag is legal only when the couple or group of three keep their hands joined.

FITNESS DEVELOPMENT (8 - 12 MINUTES)

Squad Leader Exercise

Choose 4 squad leaders. Give each squad leader a card with planned routines on it and a designated area.
Play music for 3 minutes and then stop so squads can rotate clockwise. Squad leaders stay where they are; when music begins, squad leader leads the new group.

See DPESS Chapter 16 for details.
Use Whistle Mixer to make 4 Squads.
Identify Squad Leader
SQUAD #1 Leads Upper Body Exercises
SQUAD #2 Leads Abdominal Exercises
SQUAD #3 Leads Lower Body Exercises
SQUAD #4 Leads Stretching Exercises

LESSON FOCUS (10 - 12 MINUTES)

Blocking

Demonstrate skills and drills:

- Blocking position
- Blocking with person opposite net simulating spiking

Two-person blocks.
Repeat above drills with a setter, a ball and a spiker.

See DPESS Chapter 19 for details.
Use a management technique to create groups of 3.
Assign students to courts and sides of courts.
Everyone should repeat each drill 5 times.

The biomechanics of blocking involves both blocking players jumping so their hands are above the height of the net and the receiving player(s) attempt with their hands to stop the ball from crossing the net in such an angle that the ball is difficult to return.

GAME (5 - 7 MINUTES)

Modified game

Play 4 minutes then rotate courts. 6 players per team.

See DPESS Chapter 16 for details.
When whistle blows, rotate clockwise.

EVALUATION/REVIEW AND CHEER

Students are huddled close to teacher. Ask for questions about the lesson.
Describe blocking.
When should players try to block balls?

Cheer: 3, 5, 7, 9, P.E. is so fine

Volleyball Lesson Plan 10

EQUIPMENT:

8 Jump Ropes
20 Tennis Balls
8 10" Playground Balls
8 Basketballs
8 Hula Hoops
1 Flag belt /Scarf per student
1 Volleyball per student
CD/ tape for Circuit Training
CD/ cassette tape player
Circuit Training Station Signs

OBJECTIVES:

The student will:

1. Demonstrate agility, cooperation, and running during Capture the Flag while following the instructions given by the leader.
2. Participate in Circuit Training activities to music during the fitness section of class to improve agility, flexibility, muscular strength, muscular endurance, and aerobic endurance.
3. Demonstrate the forearm pass during the lesson focus using form demonstrated by the instructor.
4. Demonstrate cooperative and volleyball skills by playing a modified volleyball game Dig It during the closing portion of class.

National Standards Met in this Lesson: **1, 2, 3, 4, 5, 6**

INSTRUCTIONAL ACTIVITIES	TEACHING HINTS

INTRODUCTORY ACTIVITY (2 - 3 MINUTES)

Capture the Flag (Variation of Flag Grab). Single file line. Person at end of the line tucks flag into waistband. At whistle, teams connect with their teammates with hands on shoulders in front of them. Teams run around trying to pull flag out of the other teams' pants without having flag stolen.

See DPESS Chapter 14 for details.
Scattered formation
Use a management game to create teams of equal size (5 - 6)
Identify the boundaries. Make sure that the area is clear/safe to run.

FITNESS DEVELOPMENT (8 - 12 MINUTES)

Circuit Training Stations
#1: Sit-Ups; #2: Juggle 3 tennis balls; #3: Run in place; #4: Dribble basketball / switch hands; #5: Push-Ups; #6: Jump Rope; #7: Balance a Ball; #8: Hula Hoops;
Cool down walking for 30 seconds.
Stretch areas worked in the station fitness activities.

See DPESS Chapter 16 for details.
8 Stations - 2 minutes at each station
Use music to indicate activity time, no music time to rotate counter clockwise to the next station.
Divide class up evenly for stations.
Lay out equipment so that each person will have his or her own.

LESSON FOCUS (10 - 12 MINUTES)

Forearm Passes
Drill #1: Two arm pass;
Drill #2: One arm pass/ bump;
Drill #3: Bump and side roll;
Drill #4: Back rolls. Start with drill #1, one partner tosses or hits the ball to the other who performs the drill 10 times.

See DPESS Chapter 19 for details.
Elbow-to-Elbow with another person
1 person put your hands on your hips.
Person with hands on your hips, goes get 2 balls.

GAME (5 - 7 MINUTES)

Dig It: Regulation volleyball, except there has to be at least one dig before the ball goes over the net.

Toe-to-Toe with 6 people.
Any 1 handed, underhand hit will qualify for a dig.

EVALUATION/REVIEW AND CHEER

Students huddled close together. Review elements of forearm pass and roll.

Cheer: 3, 5, 7, 9, P.E. is so fine!

Volleyball Lesson Plan 11

EQUIPMENT:

1 Volleyball per student
Volleyball Courts/Nets
10 Cones
CD/Cassette player
Music CD/tape for exercise
1Task Sheet, Clipboard, Pencil per 3 people

OBJECTIVES:

The student will:

1. Demonstrate agility, cooperation, and running during Octopus Tag while following the instructions given by the leader.
2. Participate in Mirror Drill in Place activities to music during the fitness section of class to improve agility, flexibility, muscular strength, muscular endurance, and aerobic endurance.
3. Participate in the Skill self-evaluation completing the Task Sheet following the instructions given by the instructor.
4. Demonstrate cooperative and volleyball skills by playing a modified volleyball game Keep it Afloat during the closing portion of class.

National Standards Met in this Lesson: **1, 2, 3, 4, 5, 6**

INSTRUCTIONAL ACTIVITIES	TEACHING HINTS

INTRODUCTORY ACTIVITY (2 - 3 MINUTES)

Octopus Tag (similar to Addition Tag)	**See DPESS Chapter 14 for details.**
Start off with two "its". Each time someone is tagged they join onto one of the ends. Students stay hooked together by either holding hands or interlocking arms. Only person on the end can tag. For tag to be valid, students must remain hooked. Play until all are tagged.	Scattered Formation. Designate boundaries. Work on teamwork. Communicate with each other.

FITNESS DEVELOPMENT (8 – 12 MINUTES)

Mirror Drill in Place	**See DPESS Chapter 14 for details.**
Mirror/Shadow exercises partner executes. 1. Do an aerobic type exercise to music. 2. Do a stretching activity when the music stops. Each partner does 1 and 2 above and then switch roles. REPEAT until signal is given.	Back-to-Back with someone 1 person put your hands on your hips - LEADER FIRST.

LESSON FOCUS (15 - 20 MINUTES)

Task Sheets Skill Evaluation	Toe-to-Toe with 3 people
Develop a task sheet covering all skills taught. List specific areas students are to observe. Rotation: DOER-RETRIEVER-OBSERVER-DOER	DOER = 1 person hands on hips get 3 task sheets/1 pencil/ 1 clipboard RETRIEVER = 1 person hand on knee OBSERVER = 1 person hand on shoulder

GAME (5 - 7 MINUTES)

Keep it Afloat	**See DPESS Chapter 19 for details.**
Each team forms a circle of no more than 6 students. The object of the game is to see which team can make the greater number of volleys in a specified time or which team can keep the ball in the air for the greater number of consecutive volleys without error.	Use management game to create 5 - 6 to a group/team Circle Formation On teachers signal, the game is started with a volley by one of the players.

EVALUATION/REVIEW AND CHEER

Students are huddled close together. Discuss the task sheets
Cheer: 6, 4, 2, teamwork's for me and you.

Volleyball Lesson Plan 12

EQUIPMENT:

Individual mats
1 Volleyball per person
Continuity Exercise CD/Tape
Volleyball Courts/Nets
1 Task Sheet per person, Clipboard, Pencil
CD/Cassette tape player

OBJECTIVES:

The student will:

1. Demonstrate agility, cooperation, and running during Follow the Leader Activity while following the instructions given by the instructor.
2. Participate in Fitness Challenge activities to music during the fitness section of class to improve agility, flexibility, muscular strength, muscular endurance, and aerobic endurance.
3. Participate in the Skill self-evaluation completing the Task Sheet following the instructions given by the instructor.
4. Demonstrate cooperative and volleyball skills by playing a modified volleyball game Keep it Afloat during the closing portion of class.

National Standards Met in this Lesson: **1, 2, 3, 4, 5,6**

INSTRUCTIONAL ACTIVITIES / TEACHING HINTS

INTRODUCTORY ACTIVITY (2 - 3 MINUTES)

Follow the Leader Activity

Leader performs aerobic type activity when the music is playing and a stretching activity when there is no music, then that leader drops to end of line, next person in line is new leader. REPEAT.

EVERYONE IN LINE FOLLOWS THE LEADER AND DOES WHAT THE LEADER IS DOING.

See DPESS Chapter 14 for details.

Toe-to-Toe with 4-6 people. 1 person put your hands on your hips, YOUR THE LEADER FIRST.

Scattered Squad Formation with Leaders

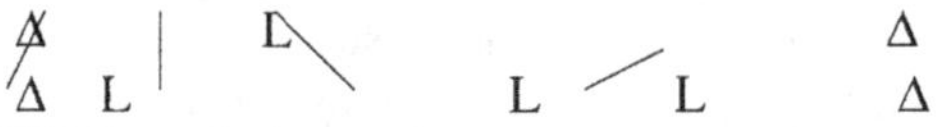

Within a designated area.

The leader can stay in one place or move around designated area.

FITNESS DEVELOPMENT (8 - 12 MINUTES)

Fitness Challenge

Alternate locomotor movements with strength challenges. Repeat the challenges as necessary. Challenge movement suggestions follow:

Flexibility and Trunk Development Challenges

1. Bend in different directions; 2. Stretch down slowly and back up; 3. Combine bending and stretching movements; 4. Sway back and forth; 5. Twist one body part; add body parts; 6. Make your body move in a large circle; 7. In a sitting position, wave your legs at a friend; 8. Make circles with your legs.

Shoulder Girdle Challenges

In a push-up position, do the following challenges:

1. Lift one foot; the other foot; 2. Wave at a friend; wave with the other arm; 3. Scratch your back with one hand; reverse; 4. Walk your feet to your hands; 5. Turn over; shake a leg; crab walk.

Abdominal Development

From a supine position:

1. Lift your head and look at your toes; 2. Lift your knees to your chest; 3. Wave your legs at a friend.

From a sitting position: 1. Slowly lay down with hands on tummy; 2. Lift legs and touch toes.

Scattered formation.

Music can be used, e.g. locomotor movement to music, other movements when there is no music.

Individual mats can be used as a "home" to keep students spaced properly.

Repeat the various trunk challenges as necessary.

Use different qualities of movement such as giant skips, tiny and quick gallops, or slow giant steps during locomotor activities to motivate students.

As students become more fit, repeat the entire sequence.

INSTRUCTIONAL ACTIVITIES	**TEACHING HINTS**
LESSON FOCUS (15 - 20 MINUTES)	
Task Sheet: Overhand Serve, Forearm Pass, Set Explain task sheet. Rotation: Receiver → Setter →Server →Receiver	**See DPESS Chapter 19 for details.** Toe-to-Toe with 2 other people 1 person hands on hips = Receiver 1 person hand on knees = Setter 1 person hand on shoulder = Server Direct Setter and Receiver to bring equipment to group: Clipboard, pencil and 1 task sheet, 2 balls.
GAME (5 - 7 MINUTES)	
Three Hit Volleyball This game emphasizes the basic offensive strategy of volleyball. The game follows regular volleyball rules with the exception that the ball must be hit three times before going over the net.	**See DPESS Chapter 19 for details.** Use as many courts as possible. Combine 2 practice groups to make a team. Encourage the students to count out loud the number of times the ball has been or is being played. The team loses the serve or the point if the ball is not played three times.

Reciprocal Task Sheet: Volleyball Serve, Pass, Set

Server's Name: ______________________

Receiver's Name: ______________________

Setter's Name: ______________________

Directions: This task is performed in groups of three: Server, Receiver, and a Setter

The Server: Serve to the back court

The Receiver: Use a forearm pass to receive the served ball and set it up to the setter.

Rotate roles after the doer hits 2 Forehand Clear Shots and 2 Serves.

The Setter: Set the ball to a pretend hitter and catch the ball.

ROTATION: Receiver → Setter → Server → Receiver

A serves over net to C
C receives ball with forearm pass to B
B catches ball, runs under net and becomes the server
C rotates to position B
Keep rotating positions.

Diagram of starting positions

A = server

Net

B = target with back to net and arms up

C = pass receiver

Volleyball Lesson Plan 13

EQUIPMENT:
8 Cones
Continuity Exercise Music CD/Tape
CD/Cassette tape player
1 Volleyball per student
Volleyball courts and nets

OBJECTIVES:
The student will:
1. Demonstrate cooperation, and running during the Frozen Tag with variation activity while following the instructions given by the instructor.
2. Participate in Walk-Jog-Sprint activities during the fitness section of class to improve agility, flexibility, muscular strength, muscular endurance, and aerobic endurance.
3. Participate in the Round Robin Volleyball Tournament following the instructions given by the instructor.

National Standards Met in this Lesson: **1, 2, 3, 4, 5, 6**

INSTRUCTIONAL ACTIVITIES	TEACHING HINTS

INTRODUCTORY ACTIVITY (2 - 3 MINUTES)

Frozen Tag with variation
Students move in a designated area, when tagged they freeze. They can be unfrozen when someone crawls or dives under and between their legs.

See DPESS Chapter 14 for details.
Scattered formation.
Select 1 - 3 "its".
When player goes out side the area equivalent to being tagged.

FITNESS DEVELOPMENT (8 - 12 MINUTES)

Walk-Jog-Sprint
When the music is playing walk, jog, or sprint. When there is no music, students will follow exercise led by the teacher. Exercises are to increase strength, and flexibility.

See DPESS Chapter 16 for details.
Scattered formation.
Designate the running perimeter.
Faster students may pass on the outside only.

LESSON FOCUS (15 - 20 MINUTES)

Round Robin Volleyball Tournament

Explain Round Robin Chart.

GAME (5 - 7 MINUTES)

Volleyball Tournament continues

EVALUATION/REVIEW AND CHEER

Students are huddled close together.
What were some of the skills that you used today?
Which skill did you use the most?
Explain rotation for tomorrow.

Cheer: 2, 4, 6, 8, Volleyball is really great!

Volleyball Lesson Plan 14

EQUIPMENT:
2 Volleyballs per court
Tournament Chart
Volleyball Courts/Nets (5-6 players per team)

OBJECTIVES:
The student will:
1. Participate in Continuity Exercises during the fitness section of class to improve agility, flexibility, muscular strength, muscular endurance, and aerobic endurance.
2. Participate in the Round Robin Volleyball Tournament following the instructions given by the instructor.

National Standards Met in this Lesson: **1, 2, 3, 4, 5, 6**

INSTRUCTIONAL ACTIVITIES	TEACHING HINTS
INTRODUCTORY ACTIVITY (2 - 3 MINUTES)	
Eliminate today to allow time for tournament.	
FITNESS DEVELOPMENT (8 - 12 MINUTES)	
Continuity Exercises	**See DPESS Chapter 16 for details.** See Lesson 2, this unit for details.
LESSON FOCUS (15 - 20 MINUTES)	
Volleyball Tournament Continued	
GAME (5 - 7 MINUTES)	
Volleyball Tournament Continued	
EVALUATION/REVIEW AND CHEER	
Ask how tournament is going. Are there any questions on rules, or the Round Robin Tournament?	

Cheer: 6, 4, 2, we enjoyed playing you.

Volleyball Lesson Plan 15

EQUIPMENT:

2 Volleyballs per court
1 Volleyball Written Exam per student
Volleyball Courts and nets
Pencils

OBJECTIVES:

The student will:

1. Complete a written exam on Volleyball during the class period.
2. Participate in a personal warm-up during the fitness section of class to prepare for playing in the tournament.
3. Participate in the Round Robin Volleyball Tournament following the instructions given by the instructor.

National Standards Met in this Lesson: **1, 2, 3, 4, 5, 6**

INSTRUCTIONAL ACTIVITIES	TEACHING HINTS
INTRODUCTORY ACTIVITY (2 - 3 MINUTES)	
Eliminate today to allow exam and tournament time	
FITNESS DEVELOPMENT (8 - 12 MINUTES)	
Stretch and Jog upon completion of exam	
LESSON FOCUS (15 - 20 MINUTES)	
WRITTEN EXAM	
GAME (5 - 7 MINUTES)	
Continue Tournament Play	Be sure to direct students to stretch and job before playing Volleyball.

EVALUATION/REVIEW AND CHEER

Teams huddle together. Are there any questions regarding the exam?
Introduce the next unit.
Cheer: 3, 5, 7, 9, P.E. is so fine.

VOLLEYBALL EXAM

MATCHING

Directions: Write the letter of the choice that gives the best definition or best matches the term on your answer sheet.

_____ 1. defense system
_____ 2. save
_____ 3. offensive system
_____ 4. "roof"
_____ 5. off-hand spike
_____ 6. kill
_____ 7. dink
_____ 8. strong side right-hander
_____ 9. strong side left-hander
_____ 10. topspin
_____ 11. W-formation
_____ 12. back set
_____ 13. bump
_____ 14. off-speed hit
_____ 15. free ball
_____ 16. opening up
_____ 17. side out
_____ 18. crosscourt hit
_____ 19. double hit
_____ 20. floater
_____ 21. wrist snap
_____ 22. heal plant
_____ 23. open hand
_____ 24. ace
_____ 25. turn outside hand in

a. 4-2
b. the setter is on the side opposite the hitter's hitting hand
c. offensive drop shot
d. left front position
e. 2-1-3
f. blockers have their hands over the net
g. one-arm desperation play to save a hard-driven ball
h. the setter is on the hitter's strong-arm side
i. no spin
j. a spiked ball that isn't returned
k. ball will float
l. puts topspin on the ball
m. ball will drop
n. right front position
o. transfers forward momentum into upward momentum
p. setter sets the ball over a head to the player behind the setter.
q. an easy return from the opponent
r. a serve that is not returned
s. serve reception
t. turning to face the player who is playing the ball
u. a spike directed diagonally to the longest part of the court.
v. the serve changes hands
w. hand position of the blocker closest to sideline
x. a player plays the ball twice in succession
y. a spike that is hit after the speed of the striking arm is greatly reduced
z. forearm pass
aa. correct hand position for spike and serve

MULTIPLE CHOICE

Directions: Select the **best** answer and mark it on your answer sheet.

26. The main difference in execution between the floater and the topspin serve is
    a. how you stand in relation to the net in the ready position
    b. where you contact the ball and how you follow through
    c. in how you swing your hitting arm
    d. how high you release the ball on the toss
27. The reason for a player being unsuccessful in serving accurately with an overhand serve is
    a. no weight shiftb. poor ball toss c. no backswing d. no arm extension e. All
28. An on-hand spike is
    a. always performed by the right forward
    b. hit on the opposite side of your body as the approaching set
    c. hit without an approach
    d. hit on the same side of your body as the approaching set
29. Once the serve is passed to the setter, the setter should make every effort to play the ball using
    a. an overhead pass or set
    b. an under hand pass
    c. a block
    d. a spike

30. A ball that is served to the opponent and hits the court in bounds without anyone hitting it is called
    a. a kill   b. a perfect serve   c. an ace   d. a spike
31. A ball not spiked by your opponent but returned to you high and easy is called
    a. a block   b. a free ball   c. a cake   d. a base defense
32. When your opponent plays the ball and you are waiting to see what they will do, you should be in
    a. serve reception formation   c. base defensive formation
    b. free ball formation   d. block + 2-1-3 defensive formation
33. When spiking a ball, the ball is contacted with
    a. the heel of an open hand   c. the side of a closed fist
    b. the fingertips   d. the front of a closed fist
34. The most accurate method of playing the ball is
    a. the block   b. the overhead pass   c. the spike   d. the forearm pass
35. The reason the floater serve moves during flight is because
    a. The ball has no spin on it   c. The ball has backspin
    b. The ball has topspin on it   d. The ball is hit with a closed fist
36. When performing a forearm pass, the arms generally
    a. Swing upward with force   c. Remain almost stationary
    b. Make contact at shoulder level   d. Follow through above the shoulders
37. The term used to describe one team's losing the serve is
    a. Hand out   b. Side out   c. Point   d. Rotation
38. When the right back has called for the ball, indicating to his/her teammates that he/she will receive the serve, all of his teammates should
    a. Open up to the right back   c. Get ready for the 2-1-3 formation
    b. Run toward the right back to help out   d. Call the lines for him/her
39. The serve is approaching the left back of the receiving team. The person who has the prime responsibility of calling the ball out over the end line is the (see diagram ⇓ ⇓)

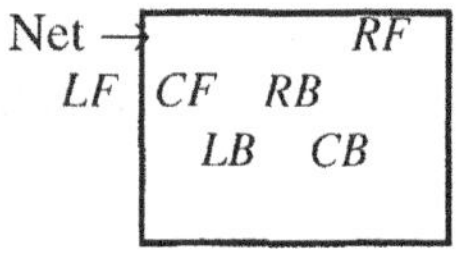

    a. LF   b. LB   c. RB   d. CB
40. The following are all defensive plays, **except for**
    a. A spike   b. A block   c. A dig   d. A save
41. All the following terms are associated with the spike, **except**
    a. Off-hand   b. Cushioning   c. Off-speed   d. Step-close takeoff
42. The primary responsibility of the center back in the 2-1-3 defensive alignments is
    a. To dig the spike   c. To pick up all drinks that come over the block
    b. To block the spike   d. Not to play the ball, if at all possible
43. The purpose of the heel plant in the spike is to
    a. Avoid too much force on the toes
    b. Change forward momentum into upward momentum
    c. Prevent wear and tear on the soles of your sneakers
    d. To help you get greater arm swing

Weight Training

OBJECTIVES:

The student will:

1. Execute given locomotor movements when called out by the instructor during the High Five activity.
2. Demonstrate starting, stopping, dodging, tagging and cooperation during the Tag Game Introductory activity.
3. Participate in parachute aerobic activities and weight training to improve their fitness.
4. Participate in the Weave Drill demonstrating agility and the ability to follow directions during movements.
5. Participate in the PACER running activity to improve their cardiovascular endurance.
6. Participate in Aerobic Workout to improve his cardiovascular endurance and muscle strength and tone.
7. Participate in Continuity Exercises to improve her cardiovascular endurance fitness level.
8. On a self-check test, write six of the nine benefits of weight training covered in the lesson.
9. Identify all of the equipment available for use in the weight room by passing a self-check test.
10. Demonstrate an understanding of acceptable conduct while using the weight room by passing an objective exam with a score of 100%.
11. Demonstrate an understanding of general safety procedures while using the weight room by passing an objective exam with a score of 100%.
12. Complete the Warm-Up/Cool-Down and Overload Principles lessons to the satisfaction of the instructor.
13. Execute an overhand grip using the techniques demonstrated in the videotape in class.
14. Execute an underhand grip using the technique demonstrated on the videotape in class.
15. Demonstrate an understanding of repetition, set and cadence by completing lesson 10 with 100% accuracy.
16. Execute the proper procedure for adding and removing weights from a bar while it is resting on the rack and floor.
17. Demonstrate proficiency in spotting to the satisfaction of the instructor.
18. Demonstrate an understanding of the principle of progression by passing a self-check test with a score of 100%.
19. Perform two sets of ten repetitions of bench press using the maximum amount of weight and proper form.
20. Execute two sets of ten repetitions of lat pull downs using the maximum amount of weight and proper form.
21. Perform two sets of ten repetitions of shoulder press using the maximum amount of weight and proper form.
22. Identify the major muscle groups of the body by passing an objective exam with a score of 90%.
23. Execute two sets of ten repetitions of barbell curls using the maximum amount of weight and proper form.
24. Execute two sets of ten repetitions of Triceps extensions using the maximum amount of weight and proper form.
25. Perform two sets of abdominal crunches while performing the maximum number of repetitions in each of the sets and using proper form.
26. Complete two sets of ten repetitions of leg press using maximum weight and proper form.
27. Perform two sets of ten repetitions of leg extensions using the maximum amount of weight and proper form.
28. Execute two sets of ten repetitions of leg curls using the maximum amount of weight and proper form.
29. Complete 2 sets of heel lifts using her maximum number of repetitions in each of the sets and proper form.
30. List the exercises in the proper sequence beginning with exercises for the larger muscles to the smaller muscles for each major muscle group in the upper body by passing a self-check test with a score of 90%.
31. List the exercises in the proper sequence beginning with exercises for the larger muscles to the smaller muscles for each major muscle group in the lower body by passing a self-check test with a score of 100%.
32. Demonstrate an understanding of the elements in a program designed to increase muscular strength and size by passing a self-check test with a score of 100%.
33. Demonstrate an understanding of the elements in a program designed to increase muscular endurance and tone by passing a self-check test with a score of 100%.
34. By completing a written assignment, develop, write practice, and modify a personal weight-training program demonstrating an understanding of the scientific principles and practical theories covered in this class.
35. Play Crab Cage ball demonstrating cooperative and teamwork skills.
36. Play Butt Tug demonstrating agility, and cooperative skills.
37. Juggle scarves during the Game portion of class using techniques demonstrated in class.
38. Play Long Team Cage ball demonstrating teamwork and using skills demonstrated in class.
39. Demonstrate teamwork and cooperation during the Mass Stand Up Game and Wheelbarrow Relay Games.
40. Demonstrate cooperation and agility during the Spider Tag Game.
41. Demonstrate cooperation and teamwork during the Parachute Team Ball Game.
42. The student will pass a comprehensive written exam covering material from the preceding lessons with a score of 75% or better.
43. The student will demonstrate an understanding of the basic physiological and theoretical concepts of weight training by passing an objective exam with a score of 75%.

Academic Integration Areas:

1. The Task Sheets within this unit cover areas of exercise physiology, anatomy, and weight training rationales.
2. The Self-Check Task sheets offer integration of weight training and cooperative/social skill development for the student.
3. Principles of aerobic training and weight training are covered in the lessons.
4. Anatomy and strength and conditioning principles are integrated into the lessons.
5. Strength and conditioning principles are integrated into the lessons.
6. Overload principles are taught.

WEIGHT TRAINING BLOCK PLAN
3 WEEK UNIT

Week #1	Monday	Tuesday	Wednesday	Thursday	Friday
Introductory Activity	Move and Perform Stretch	Weave Drill	Rooster Hop Drill	Coffee Grinder Square	Flash Drill
Fitness	Aerobic Workout	Continuity Exercises	Running	Rope Jumping to Music	Aerobic Workout
Focus	Introduce Weight Room: Safety, Conduct, Format	Upper Body Lifts	Demonstrate Safe Equipment	Anatomy and Progression	Upper and Lower Body Weight Exercises
Game	Frisbee 21	Juggling Scarves	Frisbee Tennis	Juggling Scarves	Frisbee Around 9

Week #2	Monday	Tuesday	Wednesday	Thursday	Friday
Introductory Activity	Burpee Drill	Eliminate	Move and Stretch	Over, Under and Around	Move and Change Directions
Fitness	PACER Running	Continuity Exercises	PACER Running	Jog, Walk, Jog	Jog, Walk, Jog
Focus	Heel Lift Shoulder Press Program Design Sequencing	Create Individual Weight Training Programs	Individual Weight Training Program	Individual Weight Training Program	Individual Weight Training Program
Game	Team Tug-of-War	Bowling Pin Relay	Crab Cage ball	Butt Tug	Mass Stand Up

Week #3	Monday	Tuesday	Wednesday	Thursday	Friday
Introductory Activity	Fastest Tag	Throwing and Catching Bean Bags on the Move	Aerobic Workout	Running High Fives	Eliminate today
Fitness	Parachute Aerobic Activities	Walk-Jog-Sprint	Individual Weight Training Program	Partner Fitnessgram Testing	Rhythmic Aerobic Exercise
Focus	Individual Weight Training Program	Individual Weight Training Program	Individual Weight Training Program	Partner Fitnessgram Testing	Individual Weight Training Program
Game	Long Team Cage ball	Addition Tag	Wheelbarrow Relay	Spider Tag	Parachute Activities

Weight Training Lesson Plan 1

EQUIPMENT:

Task sheet 1- 4 for each student
1 Frisbee per 2 students
CD/Cassette Player
Rhythmic Aerobic Fitness CD/Tape

National Standards Met in this Lesson: **1, 2, 3, 4, 5, 6**

INSTRUCTIONAL ACTIVITIES	TEACHING HINTS
INTRODUCTORY ACTIVITY (2 - 3 MINUTES)	
Move and Perform a Stretch Move and perform a stretching activity on the sound of the whistle. Move and stretch to the sound of music. Skip, hop, shuffle, jog and walk.	**See DPESS Chapter 14 for details.** Scatter formation Direct starting and stopping locomotor movements to selected stretches using a whistle or a timed music CD/tape.
FITNESS DEVELOPMENT (8 - 12 MINUTES)	
Aerobics Workout Create a music CD/tape or purchase a pre-recorded Aerobic Exercise CD/tape with 120-150 BPM.	**See DPESS Chapter 16 for details.** Scattered formation. See Lesson Plan 7 in Racquetball for details
LESSON FOCUS (15 - 20 MINUTES)	
Introduce Weight Room: 1. Equipment 2. Safety 3. Conduct 4. Lesson formats **Demonstrate Lunges and Bench Step Ups** Explain benefits.	**See DPESS Chapter 20 for details.** Explain safety rules. Explain use of Task sheets. Explain and distribute Lessons 1, 2, 3, & 4. Divide class up into 3 groups. Assign each group to begin on a different lesson. Describe rotation procedures. When a group has completed one lesson and the group has not rotated, assign Lesson 1.
GAME (5 MINUTES)	
Frisbee 21 Game Rules: • Players stand 10 yards apart • Throw disc back and forth. Throws must be catchable. 1 point = 1 hand catch 2 points = 2 hand catch	**See DPESS Chapter 20 for details.** Create partners using "elbow-to-elbow" technique. Have 1 person kneel. The standing partner get a Frisbee from perimeter of area and brings to partner. Player must get 21 points to win and win by 2 points.

TASK SHEET 1: THE BENEFITS OF WEIGHT TRAINING

Name: ____

Objectives:

Upon completion of the lesson you will:

1. Demonstrate an understanding of the benefits of weight training by writing six of the nine benefits described in the lesson.
2. Demonstrate a positive attitude while participating in weight training activities as a means towards achieving a positive attitude toward lifetime fitness.

Instructions:

This lesson consists of a list of nine benefits of weight training. Each of the benefits is followed by a brief description of the benefit. After carefully studying the list, go to the instructor for your self-check test on this lesson. On the self-check test, you will be asked to write six of the nine benefits of weight training. If you are unable to write six benefits, you must retake the test until you are able to do so.

The Benefits Of Weight Training

Through your enthusiastic and dedicated participation in a quality weight-training program you may experience one or more of the following benefits:

1. **Improve strength**: In the course of this class, you may experience measurable gains in muscular strength. Your body will respond to the workload placed upon it (weights) by increasing the strength of the working muscles.
2. **Improved muscular endurance**: You will be able to lift a specific amount of weight more times after participating in weight training activities.
3. **Increased muscle size**: Some gains in the size of the muscle may accompany any gains in strength or endurance.
4. **Decreased body fat**: Excessive calories result in fat storage. Exercise burns calories. You will burn calories FASTER both DURING exercise and AFTER exercise. Calories are burned in the muscles. By increasing the size of your muscles, you are increasing your body's ability to burn calories.
5. **Improved appearance**: By reducing visible body fat and increasing the size or tone of your muscles, you can improve your physical appearance.
6. **Improved self-concept**: By improving your muscular strength, size, or endurance, you may also experience an increase in self-esteem, pride, and confidence. Also, you may experience positive feeling from reducing body fat and weight.
7. **Decreased fatigue**: After participating in a weight-training program, you will experience more energy and less fatigue in performing your everyday activities.
8. **Reduce chance of injury**: By strengthening the muscles and joints in your body, you may decrease both the frequency and degree of any possible injuries.
9. **Increased physical efficiency and productivity**: All of your bodily functions may appear to work better and require less energy. You will have more energy during and at the end of your day for enjoyable experiences.

REVIEW THE LESSON CAREFULLY AND PROCEED TO TAKE THE SELF-CHECK TEST.

SELF-CHECK TEST FOR: THE BENEFITS OF WEIGHT TRAINING

Name: ____

Date: ______________________________ **Period** ______

Directions: Write six of the nine benefits of weight training covered in the previous lesson. When you have finished, get an answer key from the instructor and correct your test. If you miss any answers, go back and review the previous lesson and retake the test. Continue this procedure until you can write six of the nine benefits of weight training.

Write six of the nine benefits of weight training:

1. ____
2. ____
3. ____
4. ____
5. ____
6. ____

(OPTIONAL): Write the other three benefits if you can:

7. ____
8. ____
9. ____

(ANSWER KEY)
SELF-CHECK TEST FOR:

THE BENEFITS OF WEIGHT TRAINING

Write six of the nine benefits of weight training:

1. *Improve strength*
2. *Improve muscular endurance*
3. *Increase muscle size*
4. *Decrease body fat*
5. *Improve appearance*
6. *Improve self-concept*

(optional): write the other three benefits if you can:

7. *Decrease fatigue*
8. *Reduce chance of injury*
9. *Increase physical efficiency and productivity*

TASK SHEET 2: EQUIPMENT IDENTIFICATION

Name: ____

Date: ________________________________ **Period** _______

Objectives:

Upon completion of this lesson you will:

1. Identify all of the equipment available for your use in the weight room.

Instructions:

A display of the various equipment is arranged for you to walk by and identify. Each piece of equipment will have a folded card attached to it. On the outside of the card you will find a number. The name of that particular piece of equipment will be written on the inside of the card. As you walk by the equipment, carefully open the cards to learn the names of the equipment. Mark a check on this sheet next to the number of each piece of equipment that you studied. After you have studied the equipment, ask your instructor for a self-check test.

1. _____ Universal machine
2. _____ barbell
3. _____ barbell rack
4. _____ dumbbell
5. _____ dumbbell rack
6. _____ standard plate
7. _____ standard collar
8. _____ Olympic bar
9. _____ Olympic plate
10. _____ leg extension/ leg curl
11. _____ weight training belt
12. _____ Olympic curl bar
13. _____ Olympic bench
14. _____ squat rack
15. _____ adjustable standard bench
16. _____ adjustable slate board
17. _____ abductor/adductor machine
18. _____ heel lift board
19. _____ lat pull down
20. _____ Olympic collar

SELF-CHECK TEST FOR: EQUIPMENT IDENTIFICATION

Name: ____

Date: ______________________________ **Period** _______

Directions: A display of the various equipment will be arranged for you to walk by and identify. Each piece of equipment will have a number attached to it. You are to identify the equipment by writing the number next to the appropriate piece of equipment listed below. After completing the test, get an answer key from your instructor and correct your own test. If you missed any answer, go back to the display and correctly identify the items missed.

1.	_____	Universal machine	11.	_____	weight training belt
2.	_____	barbell	12.	_____	Olympic curl bar
3.	_____	barbell rack	13.	_____	Olympic bench
4.	_____	dumbbell	14.	_____	squat rack
5.	_____	dumbbell rack	15.	_____	adjustable standard bench
6.	_____	standard plate	16.	_____	adjustable slate board
7.	_____	standard collar	17.	_____	abductor/adductor machine
8.	_____	Olympic bar	18.	_____	heel lift board
9.	_____	Olympic plate	19.	_____	lat pull down
10.	_____	leg extension/leg curl	20.	_____	Olympic collar

TASK SHEET 3: ACCEPTABLE CONDUCT

Name: ____

Date: ______________________________ **Period** _______

Objectives:

Upon completion of this lesson you will:

1. Demonstrate an understanding of acceptable conduct while utilizing the weight room by passing an objective exam with a score of 100%.

Instructions:

This lesson consists of a list of guidelines for acceptable conduct. You will find the behavior or rule listed and followed by the reason for the rule. After carefully studying the lesson, you will take a test covering acceptable conduct. You must pass with a score of 100%. You must understand and adhere to the safety rules if you are to participate in this class. If you score less than 100% on the test, your instructor will have you review the lesson and retake the test.

Acceptable Conduct

While using the weight room, you will display acceptable conduct by:

RULE: Not touching any equipment until directed to do so by your instructor.

REASON: If you are occupied with the equipment, you cannot listen for any important information or directions from your instructor. Also, you may be making noise and keeping others from hearing directions.

RULE: Dressing appropriately for activity.

REASON: You must have freedom of movement. Your clothes cannot inhibit your ability to exercise through the full range of motion. Street clothes are unacceptable.

RULE: Refraining from making excessive noise or engaging in horseplay.

REASON: Noise and horseplay disturb other students and make it difficult to communicate and concentrate. It is unsafe.

RULE: Not eating or drinking in the weight room.

REASON: You can easily choke on food if you eat while exercising. You cannot adequately digest food while you are exercising. You may spill your food or drink in the weight room.

RULE: Not banging or dropping of the weights.

REASON: You can damage the equipment or floor or drop a weight on yourself or a classmate. Banging weights creates annoying noises and disturbs others. You are not exercising properly when you allow the weights to drop quickly.

RULE: Returning all equipment to the proper place.

REASON: Other students may be looking for that piece of equipment. It is not safe to leave weights or equipment on the floor.

RULE: Using a towel when appropriate to keep equipment clean and free from sweat, grease, and dirt.

REASON: It is highly undesirable to sit or lay in someone else's sweat or grease. All forms of dirt can corrode the equipment and keep it from working properly.

* If necessary, review the lesson again prior to taking your test.

SELF-CHECK TEST FOR: WEIGHT ROOM ACCEPTABLE CONDUCT TEST

Name: ____
Date: ________________________________ **Period** _______

Directions: (TRUE/FALSE) Write the entire word TRUE or FALSE in the space provided. Any other symbol or mark will be scored as incorrect.

1. _____ Students should not touch any equipment until directed to do so by the instructor.
2. _____ Students may drop or bang the weights as long as it doesn't bother anybody.
3. _____ Students should return all equipment to the proper place.
4. _____ Students should use a towel to keep equipment clean and free from sweat, grease, and dirt.
5. _____ Students may eat or drink in the weight room as long as they are neat and clean up after themselves.
6. _____ Screaming and yelling in the weight room is acceptable because it helps you to lift more weight.
7. _____ Physical education uniforms are permitted in the weight room since they will not restrict your movement. Street clothes are not permitted for working out.

TASK SHEET 4: GENERAL SAFETY PROCEDURES

Name: ____
Date: ________________________________ **Period** _______

Objectives:

Upon completion of the lesson you will:

1. Demonstrate an understanding of general safety procedures while using the weight room by passing an objective exam with a score of 100%.

Instructions:

This lesson consists of a list of guidelines for general safety procedures. You will find the behavior or rule listed followed by the reason for the rule. After carefully studying the lesson, you will take a test on the general safety procedures and pass with a score of 100%. You must understand and adhere to the rules if you are to safely and successfully participate in this class. If you score less than 100% on the test, your instructor will have you review the lesson and retake the test.

General Safety Procedures

While using the weight room, you will demonstrate an understanding of general safety procedures by:

RULE: Always following the rules of acceptable conduct.
REASON: By doing so, you are contributing to a safe environment for all students.
RULE: Performing only the lifts taught in this class.
REASON: The lifts for this class were carefully analyzed and explained. You might not perform another lift properly or safely. Someone else may see you do it and try to imitate you unsuccessfully.
RULE: Utilizing proper exercise techniques.
REASON: Any deviation may be dangerous to your health and safety or to the health and safety of others. You may not receive the full benefit of the exercise if you change the technique.
RULE: Using spotters on all required lifts and whenever desired.
REASON: Spotters ensure safety and can provide motivation.
RULE: Using weight training belts on all required lifts and whenever desired.
REASON: The belts will help support your back and reduce the chance of injury.
RULE: Inspecting the cables/collars prior to each exercise and notify the instructor if they need repair.
REASON: The weights may fall off the bar and injure you or another student.
RULE: Reporting any broken or damaged equipment to the instructor.
REASON: The instructor may not be aware of it. The instructor can inform other students of the situation. The instructor may be able to fix it.

GENERAL SAFETY PROCEDURES TEST

Name: ____
Date: ______________________________ **Period** _______

Directions: (TRUE/FALSE) Write the entire word TRUE or FALSE in the space provided. Any other symbol or mark will be scored as incorrect.

1. _____ Students are demonstrating safe behavior when following the guidelines for acceptable conduct.
2. _____ Students may perform exercises that were learned from a magazine or book.
3. _____ Students may change an exercise technique as long as it makes it easier for them to lift the weight and they are careful.
4. _____ Students must use spotters on all required lifts.
5. _____ Students must use weight belts on all required lifts.
6. _____ Students may not use spotters whenever they desire because spotters are scarce in the weight room.
7. _____ Students do not need to inspect the collars prior to each exercise because the instructor does it before class.
8. _____ Students should notify the instructor if a collar needs tightening.
9. _____ When students discover broken equipment, they should remain silent because they may be blamed for damaging it.

Weight Training Lesson Plan 2

EQUIPMENT:

Task sheets 5 - 9
3 Juggling Scarves per student
CD/Cassette Player
Continuity Exercise CD/Tape

National Standards Met in this Lesson: **1, 2, 3, 4, 5, 6**

INSTRUCTIONAL ACTIVITIES	TEACHING HINTS
INTRODUCTORY ACTIVITY (2 - 3 MINUTES)	
Weave Drill	**See DPESS Chapter 14 for details.**
Use locomotor movements: carioca, skip, slide, jog, etc.	Scattered formation.
Give directions with whistle signal and arm movements.	Have cones set up that students must "weave" in and around.
FITNESS DEVELOPMENT (8 - 12 MINUTES)	
Continuity Exercises	**See DPESS Chapter 16 for details.**
Jump Rope Sit ups Jump Rope Push-ups Jump Rope Double Crab Kick (20) Side Leg Flex (12 each side) Jump Rope	Scattered formation alternate jumping rope and performing two count exercises. Rope jumping is done to pre-recorded music (40 seconds) and exercise done on silence pre-recorded to 30 seconds.
Reclining Partner Pull-up (10 times each) Jump Rope Curl-ups Jump Rope Reverse Curl-ups Jump Rope Stretch all body parts	**See DPESS Chapter 16 for details.**
LESSON FOCUS (15 - 20 MINUTES)	
Demonstrate Upper Body Equipment, Lifts, and Grips	**See DPESS Chapter 20 for details.** Divide class in half Distribute Lessons 5 and 6 to 1/2 of class. Distribute Lessons 7-9 to the other 1/2 of class. Describe rotation procedures. Task sheets can be completed outside of class.
GAME (5 MINUTES)	
Juggling Scarves: 2-3 scarf cascading	**See DPESS Chapter 18 for details.** Add challenges.

TASK SHEET 5: WARM-UP AND COOL-DOWN

Name: ______________________________

Objectives:

Upon completion of this lesson you will:

1. Understand the importance of the warm-up.
2. Understand the importance of cool-down.

Instructions:

This lesson is presented with a paragraph of information followed by questions pertaining to the paragraph. The answers to the questions are found below the three asterisks (***) that follow each question. By folding a piece of paper and sliding it down the page, you keep the answers covered until you have made a response to the question. After you respond, slide the paper down and compare your answer with the answer given below the asterisks. If your answer is correct, then go to the next question. If your answer is incorrect, then review the preceding paragraph and find out why your answer was wrong. Be sure to write the correct answer on your lesson.

Warm-Up

Prior to any vigorous exercise, including weight training, you should engage in an appropriate warm-up activity. Your body is very much like a car in that it performs much better after a few minutes of warming up prior to driving it in the morning. Much of the wear and tear on a car occurs during the first few minutes of driving after an inadequate warm-up.

Appropriate warm-up activities for weight training consist of performing exercises that are intense enough to cause perspiration and increase body temperature. By increasing the temperature of the body and muscles, you make it easier for the muscles to contract and they are less prone to injury. The warm-up exercises you choose should come from the exercises you are going to perform in your workout. Prior to beginning your workout set, you should perform the exercise with a very light weight that you can lift ten times very easily. This will get your muscles accustomed to performing the movement with a light weight so they are better prepared for the heavier workout weight.

1. Prior to any vigorous physical activity you should engage in an appropriate ________ activity.
   *** warm-up
2. Your body can suffer extra wear and tear and possibly _______ from an inadequate warm-up.
   *** injury
3. An appropriate warm-up activity should be intense enough to cause __________ and increase body temperature.
   *** perspiration
4. Increasing the temperature of the muscles makes it easier for them to __________.
   *** contract
5. Your warm-up set should be performed with a light weight that you can easily lift _______ times.
   *** ten

Cool-Down

You have already learned the importance of an adequate warm-up prior to vigorous exercise. An adequate cool-down after exercise is equally important. It is not good for the human body to exercise hard for a period of time and then to stop abruptly. It needs to be cooled down gradually.

The blood in your body will go to the place that it is needed the most. After eating a meal, a great deal of blood will go to the digestive system to help digest the food. This means that there would be less blood available for the working muscles if you were to engage in physical activity immediately after eating. For this reason, it is recommended that you do not eat for approximately thirty minutes prior to or after exercising. During vigorous exercise, the blood in your body goes to the working muscles to supply them with the necessary oxygen and nutrients and to carry off the waste products produced by exercise. When you stop exercising, the blood is still in the muscles and needs time to circulate back to the heart and brain. If you stop suddenly and sit down, blood may pool in your muscles and prevent an adequate supply of blood from reaching the brain. This may cause you to be become a little light headed or dizzy. By walking or moving around for a few minutes after exercise, your muscles will help to pump the blood out of the muscles and back to the heart. This will also reduce the amount of post-exercise soreness.

1. The cool-down is ______ important as the warm-up.
   a. more   b. less   c. just as
   *** c
2. It is not good for you to exercise hard and then to ______ abruptly.
   *** stop
3. The blood in your body will go to the place that it is ______ the most.
   *** needed
4. It is recommended that you do not eat for approximately ________ minutes prior to or after exercising.
   a. ten   b. thirty   c. five   d. fifteen
   *** thirty
5. During exercise, the blood goes to the working muscles to supply them with the necessary nutrients and ______.
   *** oxygen
6. Sitting down immediately after exercising may cause the blood to _______ in the muscles.
   *** pool
7. Walking or moving around after exercise will help to reduce the amount of _______ in working muscles.
   *** soreness

TASK SHEET 6: THE OVERLOAD PRINCIPLE AND THE PRINCIPLE OF SPECIFICITY

Name: ____

Objectives:

Upon completion of this lesson you will:

1. Identify the overload principle on a written exam.
2. Identify the principle of specificity on a written exam.

Instructions:

This lesson is presented with a paragraph of information followed by questions pertaining to the paragraph. The answers to the questions are found below the three asterisks (***) that follow each question. By folding a piece of paper and sliding it down the page, you keep the answers covered until you have made a response to the question. After respond, slide the paper down and compare our answer with the answer given below the asterisks. If your answer is correct, then go to the next question. If your answer is incorrect, then review the preceding paragraph and find out why your answer was wrong. Be sure to write the correct answer on your lesson.

Overload Principle

In order to improve in any area of physical fitness, you must constantly work your body at levels that it normally doesn't encounter. For example, to improve flexibility you must stretch your muscles beyond the point that they are normally stretched in your everyday activities. To improve your muscular strength or endurance through weight training, you must lift an amount of weight beyond what is normal for you. In order to increase the size and strength of your biceps (upper arm), you would need to curl a barbell or dumbbell of adequate weight. You would not "overload" your muscles or benefit from simply flexing your arm a few times. Moving the weight of your arm is an activity that is encountered everyday.

1. The overload principle states that you must work your body at levels that it (does/doesn't) ________ normally encounter in your everyday activities.
   *** doesn't
2. To improve flexibility you must ________ your muscles beyond the point that they are in your everyday activities.
   *** stretch
3. To improve your muscular __________ or endurance you must lift an amount of weight that is beyond what is normal for you.
   *** strength

Principle of Specificity

The principle of specificity states that you must exercise a particular component of fitness in order to improve that particular component. For example, in order to improve cardiovascular fitness, you would run between fifteen and thirty minutes several times per week. To increase your flexibility, you would do a variety of stretching exercises. Therefore, if it is gains in muscular size, strength, endurance, or tone that you are seeking, you should engage in a quality weight training program.

1. The principle of specificity states that you must __________ a particular component of fitness in order to improve that particular component.
   *** exercise
2. In order to improve flexibility, you would perform ___________ exercises.
   a. running   c. stretching
   b. lifting   d. no
   *** c
3. In order to improve muscular strength, size, endurance, or tone, you would engage in a ______________ program.
   *** weight training

TASK SHEET 7: THE BASIC LIFTING TECHNIQUE

Name: ______________________________ **Date:** ________

Partner's Name: ______________________________ **Period** ________

Student Information: You will be working with a partner in this lesson. In this lesson you will learn how to perform the basic lifting technique. This technique includes both lifting the weight from the floor as well as returning it. The two parts are equally important in weight training. Mastery of the basic lifting technique will greatly reduce your chances of back injury.

Objective: Using a barbell weighing 20 pounds or less, you will perform ten repetitions of the basic lifting technique demonstrating proper form.

Directions:

1. Choose a partner that you would like to work with while completing this lesson.
2. Go to the appropriate viewing station with your partner and view the videotape on the basic lifting technique.
3. Go to the practice area with your partner and decide who will be the doer (lifter) and who will be the observer.
4. The doer will practice performing the basic lifting technique while the observer records and gives feedback.
5. The observer will mark the appropriate response (YES/NO) for each check point and give verbal feedback for each "no" response.
6. The observer should check only one check point at a time.
7. Be sure to switch roles with your partner.
8. You will repeat this lesson until you receive a "yes" response on all of the check points.

BASIC LIFTING TECHNIQUE

LIFTING THE WEIGHT FROM THE FLOOR		Yes	No
1.	Assume a stance with the feet shoulder width apart and the toes slightly pointed out and directly underneath the bar		
2.	Keep the back straight throughout the task.		
3.	Keep the arms straight throughout the task, keeping them shoulder width apart along the outside of legs.		
4.	Bend at the hips and knees until the hands reach the bar.		
5.	Grasp the bar firmly, keeping the back and arms straight		
6.	Keep the head in a vertical position with the eyes looking forward.		
7.	Inhale prior to lifting the bar.		
8.	Stand slowly, extending the hips and legs until the body is in a vertical position.		
9.	Exhale approximately two-thirds of the way up.		
RETURNING THE WEIGHT TO THE FLOOR		**Yes**	**No**
10.	Keep the head in a vertical position with the eyes looking forward.		
11.	Keep the back and arms straight at all times.		
12.	Slowly bend at the hips and knees until the bar touches the floor.		
13.	Repeat for a total of ten repetitions.		

TASK SHEET 8: OVERHAND GRIP

Name: ____

Student Information: In this lesson you will learn how to perform an overhand grip. Use of the proper grip is very important in performing any lift with proper form. You will use the overhand grip in performing the bench press, lat pull down, shoulder press, and Triceps press down.

Objective: You will perform ten repetitions of the overhand grip on a barbell using the proper form.

Directions:
1. Go to any area with an unused barbell. Leaving the barbell on the floor, practice the correct form for an overhand grip.
2. Mark the appropriate response (YES/NO) for each checkpoint for the overhand grip.
3. Repeat this lesson until you have responded "yes" to all of the checkpoints.

OVERHAND GRIP		Yes	No
1.	Assume a position close to the barbell with your toes directly underneath the bar.		
2.	Perform the basic technique for lifting a weight from the floor while keeping the arms shoulder width apart along the outside of the legs. Pause at the grip stage.		
3.	Assume a position with the hands where the thumbs are pointed towards each other.		
4.	Place the palms of the hands on the bar making sure they are an equal distance from the weights on the ends.		
5.	Firmly wrap the fingers around the bar.		
6.	Wrap the thumbs firmly around the opposite side of the bar.		
7.	Complete the basic technique for lifting a weight from the floor while using an overhand grip.		
8.	Perform the basic technique for returning the weight to the floor.		
9.	Repeat for a total of ten repetitions.		

Does your grip look like the one below?

TASK SHEET 9: UNDERHAND GRIP

Name: ____

Student Information: In this lesson you will learn how to perform an underhand grip. Use of the proper grip is very important in performing any lift with proper form. You will use the underhand grip in performing the Biceps curl.

Objective: You will perform ten repetitions of the underhand grip on a barbell using the proper form.

Directions:
1. Go to any area with an unused barbell. Leaving the barbell on the floor, practice the correct form for an underhand grip.
2. Mark the appropriate response (YES/NO) for each checkpoint for the underhand grip.
3. Repeat this lesson until you have responded "yes" to all of the checkpoints.

UNDERHAND GRIP		Yes	No
1.	Assume a position close to the barbell with your toes directly underneath the bar.		
2.	Perform the basic technique for lifting a weight from the floor while keeping the arms shoulder width apart along the outside of the legs. Pause at the grip stage.		
3.	Assume a position with the hands where the thumbs are pointed out away from each other.		
4.	Place the palms of the hands on the bar making sure they are an equal distance from the weights on the ends.		
5.	Firmly wrap the fingers around the bar.		
6.	Wrap the thumbs firmly around the opposite side of the bar.		
7.	Complete the basic technique for lifting a weight from the floor while using an underhand grip.		
8.	Perform the basic technique for returning the weight to the floor.		
9.	Repeat for a total of ten repetitions.		

Does your grip look like the one below?

Weight Training Lesson Plan 3

EQUIPMENT:

PACER running CD/tape
CD/Cassette Player
Written task sheets 10-15
1 Frisbee per 2 students

National Standards Met in this Lesson: **1, 2, 3, 4, 5, 6**

INSTRUCTIONAL ACTIVITIES	TEACHING HINTS

INTRODUCTORY ACTIVITY (2 - 3 MINUTES)

Rooster Hop Drill

Students hop 10 yards on one leg in the following sequence:

1. Left hand touching the right toe, which is on the ground.
2. Right hand touching the left toe on the ground.
3. Right hand
4. Bend the knees, hands on the floor or ground.
5. Legs kick back into an all fours position, head up.

See DPESS Chapter 14 for details.
Scattered formation
Direct students through a variety of movements

FITNESS DEVELOPMENT (8 - 12 MINUTES)

PACER Running

Progressive aerobic cardiovascular endurance run.

See DPESS Chapter 2 for details.
Use a timed CD/tape
Scatter formation

LESSON FOCUS (15 - 20 MINUTES)

Demonstrate Spotting and Adding Weight to Equipment

Scatter formation
Divide class into two groups.
Distribute and explain Task Sheets 7-9 to Group 1 and 14-16 to Group 2.
Explain rotation procedures.

GAME (5 MINUTES)

Frisbee Tennis

The same game as regular tennis, but the player must catch the Frisbee and throw from that spot. The serve starts to the right of the center mark and must go to the opposite backcourt, not into the serve box.

See DPESS Chapter 20 for details.

EVALUATION/REVIEW AND CHEER

Review elements of spotting and Frisbee Tennis.

Cheer: Weight Training, yea!

TASK SHEET 10: REPETITION, SET, AND CADENCE

Name: ____

Objectives:

Upon completion of this lesson you will:

1. Demonstrate the meaning of the term "repetition" as it applies to weight training.
2. Demonstrate the meaning of the term "set" as it applies to weight training.
3. Demonstrate the meaning of the term "cadence" as it applies to weight training

Instructions:

This lesson is presented with a paragraph of information followed by questions pertaining to the paragraph. The answers to the questions are found below the three asterisks (***) that follow each question. By folding a piece of paper and sliding it down the page, you keep the answers covered until you have made a response to the question. After respond, slide the paper down and compare our answer with the answer given below the asterisks. If your answer is correct, then go to the next question. If your answer is incorrect, then review the preceding paragraph and find out why your answer was wrong. Be sure to write the correct answer on your lesson.

Repetition, Set, and Cadence

The term "repetition" refers to repeated practice of a complete skill or act. In weight training a repetition refers to the number of times an exercise is to be performed. If only one complete cycle (from beginning to end) of the exercise was performed, then we say that one repetition was performed. A person who performs eight complete cycles of Biceps curls has performed eight repetitions of the exercise. The term "rep" is used when describing repetitions.
The term "set" refers to a collection or group of similar items. In weight training a set consists of a group of repetitions. A person who performs ten repetitions of bench press is said to have performed one set of ten repetitions. If a second set of ten repetitions is performed, then two sets of ten repetitions were performed.
The term "cadence" refers to rhythm, beat or time. In weight training, cadence refers to the rate or speed at which a repetition is performed. All exercises should be performed in a smooth and controlled fashion. You should never exercise in a speedy or jerky manner as this may increase the change of injury.

1. In weight training a (repetition/set) __________ refers to the number of times an exercise is to be performed.
   ***

   repetition
2. Exercises should be performed in a ________ manner.
   a. speedy
   b. smooth
   c. controlled
   d. jerky
   e. both b and c
   ***

   e
3. A ______ consists of a group of repetitions.
   ***

   set
4. Cadence refers to the (number/rate) _________ at which an exercise is performed.
   ***

   rate
5. A person who performed two groups of ten repetitions of leg curls is said to have completed ______ sets.
   a. two b. ten c. twenty
   ***

   two

TASK SHEET 11: RANGE OF MOTION AND BREATHING

Name: ____

Objectives:

Upon completion of this lesson you will:

1. Identify the term of full range of motion and apply it to your work-outs.
2. State the importance of breathing during exercise.

Instructions:

This lesson is presented with a paragraph of information followed by questions pertaining to the paragraph. The answers to the questions are found below the three asterisks (***) that follow each question. By folding a piece of paper and sliding it down the page, you keep the answers covered until you have made a response to the question. After you respond, slide the paper down and compare your answer with the answer given below the asterisks. If your answer is correct, then go to the next question. If your answer is incorrect, then review the preceding paragraph and find out why your answer was wrong. Be sure to write the correct answer on your lesson.

Range of Motion

In order to achieve maximal benefits from your weight training program, you must perform your exercises through the full range of motion. Range of motion refers to the area covered from the beginning of a movement to the end of a movement. The full range of motion is the greatest amount of movement possible in either direction. For example, in performing a push-up, a person who touches his chest to the ground and then fully extends his arms is considered to have performed the exercise through the full range of motion. However, if a person were to lower his body so his chest was six inches from the ground and only partially extended his arms, then he did not exercise through the full range of motion. When you perform an exercise through the full range of motion you are strengthening your muscles through the full range. If you perform an exercise through less than the full range of motion, then you are limiting your strength development to that particular range.

1. Range of motion refers to the area covered from the ________ of a movement to the ________ of a movement.
   ***
   beginning and end

2. If you perform an exercise through less than the full range of motion, then you are __________ your strength development to that particular range.
   ***
   limiting

3. Full range of motion is the ________ amount of movement possible in either direction.
   ***
   greatest

4. If you perform an exercise through the full range of motion, then you will __________ your muscles through the full range.
   ***
   strengthen

5. In performing a push-up, if you touch your chest to the ground and fully extend your arms, you are exercising through _____________.
   ***
   the full range of motion

Breathing

Your muscles must have an adequate supply of oxygen in order to function properly. This is especially true in the case of exercise and weight training. Breathing is an important part of exercising since you must breathe air into the lungs in order for your body to transport the much-needed oxygen to the working muscles. In addition, your muscles produce waste products from exercising and some of these waste products can be emitted through the air you exhale from your lungs.

In weight training you must be very careful not to hold your breath during a lift. By doing so you may temporarily raise the pressure in your chest cavity, as well as your blood pressure, to abnormal levels. This may cause you to black out and possibly injure yourself.

There are different and sometimes conflicting theories concerning the method of breathing during weight training. For the purposes of this class and for simplicity, you will exhale during the last third of the positive phase of a lift and inhale during the last third of the negative phase.

For example:
<u>Bench Press:</u>
<u>(positive/exhale)</u>: After two-thirds (during the last one-third) of the movement of pushing the bar off of the chest.
<u>(negative/inhale)</u>: After two-thirds (during the last third) of the movement of returning the bar to the chest.

1. Your muscles must have an adequate supply of ____________ in order to function properly during exercise.
   ***
   oxygen

2. Your muscles produce _________________ from exercising.
   a. oxygen
   b. waste products
   c. pressure
   ***
   b

3. You must be very careful not to ________________ your breath during a lift.
   ***
   hold

4. You will ________ during the last third of the positive phase of a lift.
   ***
   exhale

5. You will ___________ during the last third of the negative phase of a lift.
   ***
   inhale

TASK SHEET 12: REST BETWEEN SETS, EXERCISES AND WORKOUTS

Name: ____

Objectives:

Upon completion of this lesson you will:

1. State the importance and time of rest between sets.
2. State the importance and time of rest between exercises.
3. Identify the importance and time of rest between workouts.

Instructions:

This lesson is presented with a paragraph of information followed by questions pertaining to the paragraph. The answers to the questions are found below the three asterisks (***) that follow each question. By folding a piece of paper and sliding it down the page, you keep the answers covered until you have made a response to the question. After you respond, slide the paper down and compare your answer with the answer given below the asterisks. If your answer is correct, then go to the next question. If your answer is incorrect, then review the preceding paragraph and find out why your answer was wrong. Be sure to write the correct answer on your lesson.

Rest Between Sets

Rest plays a vital role in the success of any weight-training program. Your muscles must have sufficient rest in order to perform effectively. You should rest from 1 to 1 1/2 minutes between sets. After this time your muscles have recovered adequately (about 75% recovered) and are ready to perform another set of the same exercise. If you rest less than one minute you may not be working hard enough. Rest of more than 1 1/2 minutes is too much and will also reduce the intensity of your workout.

1. You should rest from ______ to ______ minutes between sets.
   ***
   1 to 1 1/2
2. Rest of more than 1 1/2 minutes will reduce the __________ of your workout.
   ***
   intensity
3. After 1 1/2 minutes your muscles are about _________ recovered and ready to perform another set.
   ***
   75%

Rest Between Exercises

The amount of rest you take between different exercises can also affect the quality of your workout. The time of rest between your last set and the start of a new exercise should be between three and five minutes. After three minutes the energy in your muscles will have been restored to 100%. During this time you may be able to get a drink of water, perform a stretch, work with another person, or take care of some other needs.

1. The time of rest between your last set and the start of a new exercise should be between _________ and _________ minutes.
   ***
   three and five
2. After three minutes the energy in your muscles will have been restored to _________.
   ***
   100%

Rest Between Workouts

The time of rest between workouts is considered by some people to be the most important. During a very hard workout, you break your muscles down. Your body's response to this hard workload placed upon it is to rebuild the muscles to a level even greater than before the workout. Your body will adjust to meet the demands placed upon it. The greater the demands, the greater the adjustments or gains. If there are no demands placed upon the body, then there will be no gains made. This is true with ALL of the components of physical fitness including flexibility and cardiovascular fitness. Therefore, you should rest between one and two days between workouts exercising the same muscle group, you will not be giving your muscles a change to rebuild and you may find that you actually LOSE strength.

1. During a hard weight training workout you ____________ your muscles down.
   ***
   break
2. Your body will adjust to meet the ____________ placed upon it.
   ***
   demands
3. You should rest between _______ and _______ days between workouts exercising the same muscle group.
   ***
   one and two

TASK SHEET 13: ADDING AND REMOVING WEIGHTS FROM A BAR RESTING ON THE FLOOR

Name: ____

Student Information: In this lesson you will learn the proper procedure for adding and removing weights from a bar while it is resting on the floor. The weights must be added properly and secured tightly on the bar with the collars in order to ensure safety.

Objectives: You will perform the proper procedure for adding and removing weights from a bar while it is resting on the floor.

Directions:
1. Go to any area with an unused barbell. Practice the proper procedure for adding and removing weights from the bar while it is resting on the ground.
2. Mark the appropriate response (YES/NO) for each checkpoint for the proper procedure.
3. Check only one checkpoint at a time.
4. Repeat this lesson until you have responded "yes" to all of the checkpoints.

ADDING AND REMOVING WEIGHTS

ADDING WEIGHTS TO THE BAR		Yes	No
1.	Slide one of the heaviest plates on one end of the bar until it makes contact with the inside collar		
2.	Slide a plate of similar weight on the opposite end of the bar until it makes contact with the inside collar.		
3.	Slide the next heaviest plate on one end of the bar until it makes contact with the first plate..		
4.	Slide a plate of similar weight on the opposite end of the bar until it makes contact with the first plate.		
5.	Repeat the procedure for every plate to be added until reaching the desired amount of weight.		
6.	Slide the collars on the bar, pressing all of the weights tightly together against the inside collar.		
7.	Tighten the collar by turning the bolt in the appropriate manner until it stops turning.		
8.	Slide the remaining collar on the opposite end of the bar, pressing all of the weights tightly together against the inside collar.		
REMOVING WEIGHTS FROM THE BAR		**Yes**	**No**
1.	Loosen the collar bolt until able to slide the collar easily off the end of the bar.		
2.	On the opposite collar, loosen the collar bolt until able to slide the collar easily off the end of the bar.		
3.	Remove one plate from one end of the bar.		
4.	Remove one plate from the opposite end of the bar.		
5.	Continue to alternate removing one plate at a time from each end of bar until the desired amount of weight remains.		
6.	Replace and tighten the collars if leaving plates on the bar.		

TASK SHEET 14: ADDING AND REMOVING WEIGHTS FROM A BAR RESTING ON A RACK

Name: ______________________________ **Date:**________

Student Information: In this lesson you will be working with a partner in practicing the proper procedure for adding and removing weights from a bar while it is resting on a rack. The weights must be added and removed simultaneously to ensure safety. Also, be sure to secure the weights tightly with the collars.

Objectives: With the use of a partner, you will perform the proper procedure for adding and removing weights from a bar while it is resting on a rack.

Directions:
1. Go to any rack with an unused barbell. With your partner, practice the proper procedure for adding and removing weights from the bar while it is resting on the rack.
2. Mark the appropriate response (YES/NO) for each checkpoint for the proper procedure.
3. Check only one checkpoint at a time.
4. Repeat this lesson until you have responded "yes" to all of the checkpoints.

ADDING AND REMOVING WEIGHTS

ADDING WEIGHTS TO THE BAR		Yes	No
1.	Simultaneously slide the heaviest plates on the ends of the bar until they make contact with the inside collar		
2.	Simultaneously slide the next heaviest plates on the ends of the bar until they makes contact with the first plate.		
3.	Repeat the procedure for every plate to be added until reaching the desired amount of weight.		
4.	Slide the collars on the bar, pressing all of the weights tightly together against the inside collar.		
5.	Tighten the collar by turning the bolt in the appropriate manner until it stops turning.		
REMOVING WEIGHTS FROM THE BAR		**Yes**	**No**
1.	Loosen the collar bolts until you are able to slide the collars easily off the ends of the bar.		
2.	Simultaneously remove one plate the bar.		
3.	Simultaneously remove one plate at a time from the bar until the desired amount of weight remains.		
4.	Replace and tighten the collars if leaving plates on the bar.		

TASK SHEET 15: SPOTTING

Name: ____

Objective:

Upon completion of this lesson you will:

1. Demonstrate an understanding of the responsibilities involved in spotting another lifter to the satisfaction of the instructor.

Instructions:

This lesson contains the responsibilities and skills required of a competent spotter. Carefully review and follow the guidelines in the following lessons. Good spotting skills are essential to success and safety in the weight room. After reviewing the lesson, ask your instructor to observe you while you spot another student.

Components of Spotting

1. Focus your full attention on the lifter. Do not look around the room or talk to other students while spotting.
2. Listen for any pre-lift instructions from the lifter concerning the number or type of exercises to be performed.
3. Verbally communicate and coordinate actions with any assisting spotters.
4. Assist the lifter in receiving the weight in the proper starting position for the exercise.
5. Verbally encourage the lifter during the exercise.
6. Give any necessary physical assistance to enable the lifter to complete the desired number of repetitions.
7. Assist the lifter in returning the weight to its resting place.

SELF-CHECK TEST FOR: THE COMPONENTS OF SPOTTING

Directions: (TRUE/FALSE) Write the entire word TRUE or FALSE in the space provided. Any other symbol or mark will be scored as incorrect. After taking the test, use the answer key to correct your exam. If you do not score 100%, you must review the lesson and retake the test.

1. _____ The spotter at the lifter's head is the head spotter.
2. _____ The head spotter does not have to listen to anybody, including the lifter.
3. _____ The spotter should give the lifter more than enough assistance than is necessary so the lifter doesn't get tired.
4. _____ The head spotter is the only one who really needs to pay attention. The other spotters may look around the room to see what they would like to do next.
5. _____ The pre-lift instructions given to a spotter by a lifter should include the number of repetitions to be attempted.

ANSWER KEY

1. True
2. False
3. False
4. False
5. True

Weight Training Lesson Plan 4

EQUIPMENT:

Task Sheets 16-20
Individual jump ropes
CD/Cassette Player
CD/Tape for rope jumping
3 Juggling scarves per student
Bases /Bean bag markers

National Standards Met in this Lesson: **1, 2, 3, 4, 5, 6**

INSTRUCTIONAL ACTIVITIES	TEACHING HINTS

INTRODUCTORY ACTIVITY (2 - 3 MINUTES)

Coffee Grinder Square

Identify a locomotor activity to move from one corner to next. Student performs "Coffee Grinder" on alternate arms at each corner.

See DPESS Chapter 14 for details.

Use Whistle Mixer to create 4 groups.
Direct starting corner for each group.
Set up square in area using bean bags or bases.

FITNESS DEVELOPMENT (8 - 12 MINUTES)

Rope Jumping

- **Single jump**
- **Double jump**
- **Hot Peppers**
- **Challenges**

See DPESS Chapter 20 for details.

Scatter formation
Use music CD/tape to motivate movement
Can direct or allow student to alternate activities.

LESSON FOCUS (15 - 20 MINUTES)

Muscle Anatomy Principle of Progression

- Bench Press, Lat Pull down, Shoulder Press

See DPESS Chapter 20 for details.

Explain Task Sheets
Divide class into 2 groups
Assign **Group 1**: Task Sheets 16-17,
Group 2: Task Sheets 18-20
Describe rotation

GAME (5 MINUTES)

Juggling Scarves

2-3 Scarves Cascading

See DPESS Chapter 18 for details.

Add challenges i.e., under leg, behind back.

EVALUATION/REVIEW AND CHEER

Review the Muscle Anatomy Principle of Progressions

CHEER

Cheer: Weight Training, yes!

TASK SHEET 16: MUSCLE GROUPS OF THE BODY

Name: ____

Objective:

Upon completion of this lesson you will:

1. Identify the major muscle groups of the body on a chart.

Instructions:

In this lesson you will study the major muscle groups of the body. It is important for you to know the location of the muscles in your body in order to improve your understanding of how they work and how to exercise them. Study a diagram of the body until you feel that you are ready to be tested on the muscle locations. When you are ready, see your instructor for the exam. You must pass the exam with a score of 80% before you go on to the next lesson. If you do not score 80% on the exam, study the diagram again and retake the test.

TASK SHEET 17: THE PRINCIPLE OF PROGRESSION

Name: ____

Date: ____ **Period** _____________

Objective:
Upon completion of this lesson you will:

1. Demonstrate an understanding of the principle of progression by passing a self-check test with a score of 100%.

Instructions:

This lesson consists of information and guidelines for applying the principle of progression. It is very important that you fully understand and apply the principle of progression if you are to successfully overload your muscles. Study the steps carefully to prepare yourself for the self-check test at the end of the lesson. You must pass the self-check test with a score of 100%. If you do not score 100%, review the lesson and retake the test.

Principle of Progression

STEPS:

1. Decide on the number of sets and repetitions to be performed.
2. Select a reasonable amount of weight that might be lifted to complete the desired amount of repetitions successfully.
3. Perform the exercise with proper form until muscular failure or until unable to maintain correct form.
4. On the following sets, slightly increase the weight used when able to perform one additional repetition above the desired amount. Continue to do so until you are able to perform only the desired number of repetitions.
5. On the following sets, slightly decrease the weight used when unable to perform the desired number of repetitions with proper form. Continue to do so until you are able to perform the desired number of repetitions.

* Carefully review the steps if necessary prior to taking the self-check test.

SELF-CHECK TEST FOR: THE PRINCIPLE OF PROGRESSION

Directions: Fill in the blank with the correct word. After completing the test, get an answer key from the instructor and correct your test. If you miss any questions, review the previous lesson and retake the test. Continue this procedure until you score 100% on this test.

1. You should perform the exercise with proper form until muscular __________ or until unable to maintain correct form.
2. You should slightly __________ the weight used when you can perform one additional repetition above the desired amount while maintaining proper form.
3. You should slightly __________ the weight used when you are unable to perform the desired amount of repetitions with proper form.
4. Kim's goal is to perform ten repetitions of bench press using the maximum amount of weight. She did 12 reps easily on her last set. On her next set Kim should __________ the amount of weight she uses.
5. Jim's goal is to perform ten repetitions of lat pull downs using the maximum amount of weight. On his last set he was only able to perform seven repetitions. On his next set Jim should __________ the amount of weight he uses.

ANSWER KEY

1. Failure
2. Increase
3. Decrease
4. Increase
5. Decrease

TASK SHEET 18: BENCH PRESS

Student's Name: ______________________________ **Date**: __________

Observer's Name: ______________________________ **Period**: __________

Spotter's Name: ______________________________

Student Information: In this lesson you will learn the proper form for performing the bench press. You will be working with two partners in this lesson. One person will act as the lifter (doer), one as the observer (recorder), and the other person will be the spotter. You will rotate until all students have acted in all three roles. All weight training exercises must be performed slowly and with the proper form in order to gain the maximum benefits and to ensure safety. The bench press exercises the pectoral muscles in the chest and the triceps in the upper arm.

Objectives: You will perform one set of ten repetitions of bench press while using your maximum amount of weight and proper form.

Directions:
1. Choose two partners that you would like to work with while completing this lesson.
2. Go to the appropriate viewing station with your partners and view the videotape on performing the bench press.
3. Go to the bench press area with your partners and decide who will act first as the doer, observer, and spotter.
4. The doer will practice performing the bench press while the observer records and gives feedback to the doer. You will repeat this lesson until you have received "yes" responses on all of the checkpoints.
5. The observer will check the appropriate response (YES/NO) for each checkpoint for the bench press. The observer should check only one checkpoint at a time and give verbal feedback to the lifter on each checkpoint marked "no".
6. You will always use at least one spotter when performing the bench press. The spotter's only responsibility is that of spotting the lifter (doer). The observer is <u>not</u> to act as a spotter.

BENCH PRESS		**Yes**	**No**
1.	Select a weight that might be performed for a total of only ten repetitions.		
2.	While on your back, assume a position on the bench with the eyes directly under the bar.		
3.	Spread the feet and legs wide for good balance and support.		
4.	Keep the feet flat on the floor at all times.		
5.	Keep the head, shoulders, and hips on the bench throughout the lift.		
6.	Using an overhand grip, grasp the bar between one and two handgrips out from a shoulder width grip. Make sure the grip is evenly centered on the bar.		
7.	Lift the bar off the rack until the arms are fully extended.		
8.	Position the bar directly over the shoulders.		
9.	Slowly lower the bar to the center of the chest while keeping the elbows out.		
10.	Inhale approximately two-thirds of the way down.		
11.	Touch the bar lightly on the center of the chest.		
12.	While keeping the elbows out, straighten the arms and press the bar back to the starting position above the shoulders.		
13.	Exhale approximately two-thirds of the way up.		
14.	Perform one set of as many repetitions as possible using proper form.		
15.	Apply the principle of progression to find the maximum weight for ten repetitions.		
16.	Perform one set of ten repetitions using maximum weight and proper form.		

TASK SHEET 19: LAT PULLDOWN

Student's Name: ___________________________________ **Date**: _________

Student Information: In this lesson you will learn the proper form for performing the lat pull down. You will be working with two partners in this lesson. One person will act as the lifter (doer), one as the observer/recorder. You will rotate with your partner after completing the lesson. All weight training exercises must be performed slowly and with the proper form in order to gain the maximum benefits and to ensure safety. The lat pull down exercises the latissimus dorsi muscles in the back and the biceps in the upper arm.

Objectives: You will perform one set of ten repetitions of lat pull downs while using your maximum amount of weight and proper form.

Directions:

1. Choose two partners that you would like to work with while completing this lesson.
2. Go to the appropriate viewing station with your partner and view the videotape on performing the lat pull down.
3. Go to the lat pull down machine with your partner and decide who will be the doer and the observer.
4. The doer will practice performing the lat pull down while the observer records and gives feedback. You will repeat this lesson until you have received "yes" responses at all of the checkpoints.
5. The observer will check the appropriate response (YES/NO) for each checkpoint for the lat pull down. The observer should check only one checkpoint at a time and give verbal feedback to the lifter on each checkpoint marked "no."

LAT PULLMAN		Yes	No
1.	Select a weight that might be performed for a total of only ten repetitions.		
2.	Face the machine and assume as wide an overhand grip as possible on the bar.		
3.	Slowly lower the body until the arms are fully extended.		
4.	Allow the body's weight to pull the bar down until reaching a sitting or kneeling position..		
5.	Keep the back perpendicular to the ground.		
6.	Tuck the chin slightly.		
7.	Inhale.		
8.	Smoothly pull the bar down behind the head to the base of the neck.		
9.	Exhale approximately two-thirds of the way down.		
10.	Allow the bar to slowly raise to the starting position.		
11.	Inhale approximately two-thirds of the way up.		
12.	Perform one set of as many repetitions as possible using proper form.		
13.	Apply the principle of progression to find your maximum weight for ten repetitions.		
14.	Perform one set of ten repetitions using your maximum weight and proper form.		

TASK SHEET 20: SHOULDER PRESS

Student's Name: ______________________________ **Date:** ____________________

Observer's Name: ______________________________ **Period** ____________________

Spotter's Name: ______________________ **Spotter's Name:** ______________________

Student Information: In this lesson you will learn the proper form for performing the shoulder press. You will be working with three partners in this lesson. One person will act as the lifter (doer), and one as the observer/recorder. You will rotate with your partner after completing the lesson until all students have had an opportunity to act in each role. All weight training exercises must be performed slowly and with the proper form in order to gain the maximum benefits and to ensure safety. The shoulder press exercises the deltoid muscles in the shoulders and the triceps in the upper arm.

Objectives: You will perform one set of ten repetitions of shoulder press while using your maximum amount of weight and proper form.

Directions:

1. Choose three partners that you would like to work with while completing this lesson.
2. Go to the appropriate viewing station with your partner and view the videotape on performing the shoulder press.
3. The doer will practice performing the shoulder press while the observer records and gives feedback. You will repeat this lesson until you have received "yes" responses at all of the check points.
4. The observer will check the appropriate response (YES/NO) for each check point for the shoulder press. The observer should check only one check point at a time and give verbal feedback to the lifter on each check point marked "no."
5. The two spotters will give the bar to the lifter at the beginning of the lift and take it from the lifter at the end of the lift.
6. You will always use two spotters when performing the shoulder press. The spotters' only responsibility is that of spotting the doer (lifter). The observer is <u>not</u> to act as a spotter.

SHOULDER PRESS		**Yes**	**No**
1.	Select a weight that might be performed for a total of only ten repetitions.		
2.	Stand erect with the feet slightly wider than shoulder width apart.		
3.	Receive the bar from the spotters with the bar resting on the upper chest just below the collarbone.		
4.	Assume an overhand grip at shoulder width.		
5.	Inhale.		
6.	Keep the legs and back straight throughout the lift.		
7.	Extend the arms and press the bar overhead until the arms are straight with the bar directly over the shoulders and hips.		
8.	Exhale approximately two-thirds of the way up.		
9.	Lower the bar slowly to the starting position.		
10.	Inhale approximately two-thirds of the way down.		
11.	Perform one set of as many repetitions as possible using proper form.		
12.	Apply the principle of progression to find your maximum weight for ten repetitions.		
13.	Perform one set of ten repetitions using your maximum weight and proper form.		

Weight Training Lesson Plan 5

EQUIPMENT:
Aerobic Exercise CD/Tape
CD/Cassette Player
Task sheets
1 Frisbee per 2 students
Task Sheets 21- 26

National Standards Met in this Lesson: **1, 2, 3, 4, 5, 6**

INSTRUCTIONAL ACTIVITIES	TEACHING HINTS
INTRODUCTORY ACTIVITY (2 - 3 MINUTES)	
Flash Drill Students stand in a ready position facing the teacher. The teacher exclaims "feet," and students stutter the feet quickly.	**See DPESS Chapter 14 for details.** Scattered formation. See Lesson 3, Tennis Unit for complete details.
FITNESS DEVELOPMENT (8 - 12 MINUTES)	
Aerobic Workout Create a music CD/tape or purchase a pre-recorded Aerobic Exercise CD/tape with 120-150 BPM.	**See DPESS Chapter 16 for details.** Scattered formation. (See Lesson Plan 7, Racquetball Unit for details)
LESSON FOCUS (15 - 20 MINUTES)	
Biceps Curl Task sheet **Triceps Extension Task sheet** **Abdominal Exercise Task sheet** **Leg Press Task sheet** **Leg Extension Task sheet** **Leg Curl Task sheet**	**See DPESS Chapter 20 for details.** Divide class into 5 groups. Assign students exercises to complete of previously learned materials while waiting for equipment. Assign each group to a Task sheet and a station to begin at. Describe rotation.
GAME (5 MINUTES)	
Frisbee Around 9 A target is set up with 9 different throwing positions around it, each 2 feet farther away. The throwing positions can be clockwise or counterclockwise around the target. They can also be in a straight line from the target. Points are awarded based on the throwing position number (for example, number 7 means 7 points for hitting the target). The game can be played indoors or out.	**See DPESS Chapter 20 for details.** Create partners using Elbow-to Elbow technique.

EVALUATION/REVIEW AND CHEER

What muscles did you learn about and work on today?
What do you find more challenging? Aerobics or Weight Training? Why?
2, 4, 6, 8, Weight Training is full of weight!

TASK SHEET 21: BICEPS CURL

Student's Name: ______________________________ **Date**: ________

Student Information: In this lesson you will learn the proper form for performing the biceps curl. You will be working with a partner in this lesson. One person will act as the lifter (doer), and one as the observer/recorder. You will rotate with your partner after completing the lesson. All weight training exercises must be performed slowly and with the proper form in order to gain the maximum benefits and to ensure safety. The biceps curl exercises the biceps in the upper arm.

Objective: You will perform one set of ten repetitions of biceps curls while using your maximum amount of weight and proper form.

Directions:
1. Choose three partners that you would like to work with while completing this lesson.
2. Go to the appropriate viewing station with your partner and view the videotape on performing the biceps curl.
3. Go to any unused barbell with your partner and decide who will be the doer and the observer.
4. The doer will practice performing the biceps curl while the observer records and gives feedback. You will repeat this lesson until you have received "yes" responses at all of the checkpoints.
5. The observer will check the appropriate response (YES/NO) for each checkpoint for the biceps curl. The observer should check only one checkpoint at a time and give verbal feedback to the lifter on each checkpoint marked "no."

BICEPS CURL		**Yes**	**No**
1.	Select a weight that might be performed for a total of only ten repetitions.		
2.	Lift the barbell from the floor using the basic lifting technique with an underhand grip at shoulder width.		
3.	Keep the head in a vertical position throughout the lift.		
4.	Keep the back and legs straight at all times.		
5.	Keep the upper arms perpendicular to the floor throughout the lift.		
6.	Keep the elbows and upper arms in contact with the sides of the body throughout the lift.		
7.	Inhale.		
8.	Flex the arms fully, curling the bar to a position towards the upper chest.		
9.	Exhale approximately two-thirds of the way up.		
10.	Slowly lower the bar until the arms are fully extended		
11.	Inhale approximately two-thirds of the way down.		
12.	Perform one set of as many repetitions as possible using proper form.		
13.	Apply the principle of progression to find your maximum weight for ten repetitions.		
14.	Perform one set of ten repetitions using your maximum weight and proper form.		

TASK SHEET 22: TRICEPS EXTENSION

Student's Name: ______________________________ **Date**: ________

Student Information: In this lesson you will learn the proper form for performing the triceps extension. You will be working with a partner in this lesson. One person will act as the lifter (doer), and one as the observer/recorder. You will rotate with your partner after completing the lesson. All weight training exercises must be performed slowly and with the proper form in order to gain the maximum benefits and to ensure safety. The triceps extension exercises the triceps muscles in the upper arm.

Objective: You will perform one set of ten repetitions of triceps extensions while using your maximum amount of weight and proper form.

Directions:

1. Choose three partners that you would like to work with while completing this lesson.
2. Go to the appropriate viewing station with your partner and view the videotape on performing the triceps extension.
3. Go to any unused barbell with your partner and decide who will be the doer and the observer.
4. The doer will practice performing the triceps extension while the observer records and gives feedback. You will repeat this lesson until you have received "yes" responses at all of the checkpoints.
5. The observer will check the appropriate response (YES/NO) for each checkpoint for the triceps extension. The observer should check only one checkpoint at a time and give verbal feedback to the lifter on each checkpoint marked "no."

TRICEPS EXTENSION		Yes	No
1.	Select a weight that might be performed for a total of only ten repetitions.		
2.	Face the machine and stand erect with the feet shoulder width apart.		
3.	Assume a narrow overhand grip approximately four inches wide.		
4.	Pull the bar to the chest until the elbows and upper arms point straight down..		
5.	Keep the upper arms stable and elbows pointed straight down throughout the exercise.		
6.	Keep the upper arms and elbows in contact with the sides of the body throughout the lift.		
7.	Inhale.		
8.	Keep the back and legs straight.		
9.	Press the bar down until the arms are fully extended.		
10.	Exhale approximately two-thirds of the way down.		
11.	Control the bar slowly back to the starting position.		
12.	Inhale approximately two-thirds of the way up.		
13.	Perform one set of as many repetitions as possible using proper form.		
14.	Apply the principle of progression to find your maximum weight for ten repetitions.		
15.	Perform one set of ten repetitions using your maximum weight and proper form.		

TASK SHEET 23: ABDOMINAL CRUNCH

Student's Name: ___________________________________ **Date**: ________

Student Information: In this lesson you will learn the proper form for performing the abdominal crunch. Stronger abdominal muscles will help support your upper body and take the burden off of your weaker lower back muscles. By strengthening your abdominal muscles you can help reduce your chance of lower back injury.

Objective: While using proper form, you will perform two sets of abdominal crunches, performing the maximum number of repetitions in each of the sets.

Directions:
1. Go to the abdominal exercise area and practice performing the abdominal crunch.
2. Mark the appropriate response (YES/NO) for each checkpoint for the abdominal crunch.
3. Repeat this lesson until you have responded "yes" to all of the checkpoints.
4. After successfully completing this lesson, go to your instructor for your skills test on the lesson.

ABDOMINAL CRUNCH		Yes	No
1.	Assume a supine position (on your back) on the floor with your knees bent and our feet flat on the floor.		
2.	Cross your arms over your chest with your hands touching the opposite shoulders.		
3.	Tuck your chin to your chest..		
4.	Keep you lower back in contact wit the floor at all times.		
5.	Inhale.		
6.	Curl up, lifting only the shoulder blades off of the ground.		
7.	Exhale in the "up" position.		
8.	Return to the starting position.		
9.	Inhale in the "down" position.		
10.	Perform one set of as many repetitions as possible using proper form.		
11.	Perform a second set of as many repetitions as possible using proper form.		

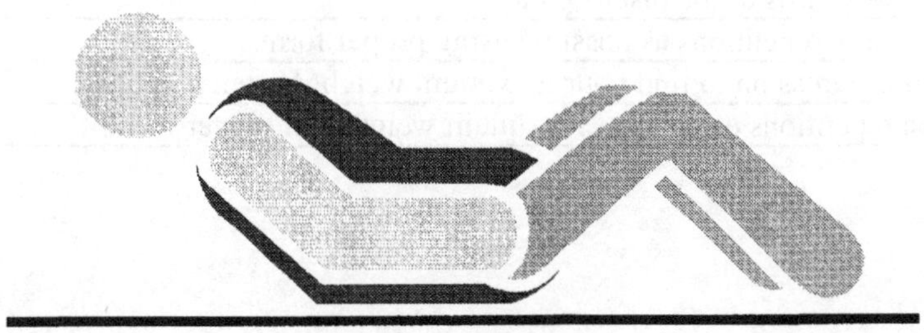

TASK SHEET 24: LEG PRESS

Student's Name: ______________________________________ **Date:** _________

Student Information: In this lesson you will learn the proper form for performing the leg press. You will be working with a partner in this lesson. One person will be the lifter (doer), and one will be the observer/recorder. Change roles with your partner after completing the lesson. Avoid "locking" the knee joints when performing the leg press as this places excessive stress on the joints and may increase your chance of injury.  The leg press exercises the quadriceps muscles.

Objective: You will perform one set of ten repetitions of leg presses while using your maximum amount of weight and proper form.

Directions:
1. Choose a partner that you would like to work with while completing this lesson.
2. Go to the appropriate viewing station with your partner and view the videotape on performing the leg press.
3. Go to the leg press machine with your partner and decide who will be the doer and the observer.
4. The doer will practice performing the leg press while the observer records and gives feedback. You will repeat this lesson until you have received "yes" responses at all of the checkpoints.
5. The observer will check the appropriate response (YES/NO) for each checkpoint for the leg press. The observer should check only one checkpoint at a time and give verbal feedback to the lifter on each checkpoint marked "no."

LEG PRESS		Yes	No
1.	Select a weight that might be performed for a total of only ten repetitions.		
2.	Assume a position in the seat with your back resting against the backrest.		
3.	Place the balls of your feet against the pedals with the toes pointed straight up.		
4.	If possible, adjust the seat to a position where your legs are bent at or slightly less than right angles.		
5.	Grasp the handles if provided, or fold your arms in front of your body.		
6.	Maintain body contact with the bottom and back of the seat throughout the lift.		
7.	Inhale.		
8.	Extend your legs completely and avoid "locking" the knees.		
9.	Exhale when your legs are extended approximately two-thirds of the distance.		
10.	Slowly control the weight back to the starting position.		
11.	Inhale approximately two-thirds of the distance back.		
12.	Perform one set of as many repetitions as possible using proper form.		
13.	Apply the principle of progression to find your maximum weight for ten repetitions.		
14.	Perform one set of ten repetitions using your maximum weight and proper form.		

TASK SHEET 25: LEG EXTENSION

Student's Name: ______________________________ **Date:** ________

Student Information: In this lesson you will learn the proper form for performing the leg extension. You will be working with a partner in this lesson. One person will act as the lifter (doer), and one as the observer/recorder. You will rotate with your partner after completing the lesson. All weight training exercises must be performed slowly and with the proper form in order to gain the maximum benefits and to ensure safety. Avoid "locking" the knee joints when performing the leg extension as this places excessive stress on the joints and may increase your chance of injury.

The leg extension exercises the quadriceps muscles in the front of the upper leg.

Objective: You will perform one set of ten repetitions of leg extensions while using your maximum amount of weight and proper form.

Directions:

1. Choose a partner that you would like to work with while completing this lesson.
2. Go to the appropriate viewing station with your partner and view the videotape on performing the leg extension.
3. Go to the leg extension machine with your partner and decide who will be the doer and the observer.
4. The doer will practice performing the leg extension while the observer records and gives feedback. You will repeat this lesson until you have received "yes" responses at all of the checkpoints.
5. The observer will check the appropriate response (Yes/No) for each checkpoint for the leg extension. The observer should check only one checkpoint at a time and give verbal feedback to the lifter on each check point marked "no."

LEG EXTENSION		**Yes**	**No**
1.	Select a weight that might be performed for a total of only ten repetitions.		
2.	Sit upright on the bench with your legs hanging over the end at right angles.		
3.	Place the top of your feet under the padded rollers.		
4.	Keep the back straight throughout the lift.		
5.	Support your upper body by gripping the sides of the bench.		
6.	Inhale.		
7.	Extend the legs completely and avoid locking the knees.		
8.	Exhale when the legs are approximately two-thirds extended.		
9.	Slowly return the weight to the starting position.		
10.	Inhale when the legs are approximately two-thirds flexed.		
11.	Perform one set of as many repetitions as possible using proper form.		
12.	Apply the principle of progression to find your maximum weight for ten repetitions.		
13.	Perform one set of ten repetitions using your maximum weight and proper form.		

TASK SHEET 26: LEG CURL

Student's Name: ____ **Date**: ________

Student Information: In this lesson you will learn the proper form for performing the leg curl. You will be working with a partner in this lesson. One person will act as the lifter (doer), and one as the observer/recorder. You will rotate with your partner after completing the lesson. All weight training exercises must be performed slowly and with the proper form in order to gain the maximum benefits and to ensure safety. The leg curl exercises the hamstring muscles in the back of the upper leg.

Objectives: You will perform one set of ten repetitions of leg curls while using your maximum amount of weight and proper form.

Directions:

1. Choose a partner that you would like to work with while completing this lesson.
2. Go to the appropriate viewing station with your partner and view the videotape on performing the leg curl.
3. Go to the leg curl machine with your partner and decide who will be the doer and the observer.
4. The doer will practice performing the leg curl while the observer records and gives feedback. You will repeat this lesson until you have received "yes" responses at all of the checkpoints.
5. The observer will check the appropriate response (YES/NO) for each checkpoint for the leg curl. The observer should check only one checkpoint at a time and give verbal feedback to the lifter on each checkpoint marked "no."

LEG CURL		Yes	No
1.	Select a weight that might be performed for a total of only ten repetitions.		
2.	Assume a prone (on your stomach) position on the bench with your knees over the edge		
3.	Place your heels under the padded rollers.		
4.	Keep your chest, hips, and thighs in contact with the bench at all times.		
5.	Grip the sides of the bench for support.		
6.	Inhale.		
7.	Flex your legs, bringing your heels as close to your buttocks as possible.		
8.	Exhale when the legs are approximately two-thirds extended.		
9.	Slowly return the weight to the starting position.		
10.	Inhale when the legs are approximately two-thirds flexed.		
11.	Perform one set of as many repetitions as possible using proper form.		
12.	Apply the principle of progression to find your maximum weight for ten repetitions.		
13.	Perform one set of ten repetitions using your maximum weight and proper form.		

Training the lower body is crucial for balance, speed and coordination and the best exercises for developing the quadriceps and leg biceps are, without a doubt, the leg extension and leg curl.

Weight Training Lesson Plan 6

EQUIPMENT:

Task sheets 27-30
PACER Running CD
CD/Cassette Tape Player
1-2 Long Tug of War ropes

National Standards Met in this Lesson: **1, 2, 3, 4, 5, 6**

INSTRUCTIONAL ACTIVITIES | **TEACHING HINTS**

INTRODUCTORY ACTIVITY (2 - 3 MINUTES)

Burpee-Flip Drill

Call out a number, and students yell the number while performing the movement. The sequence is as follows:

1. Standing position
2. Bend knees, hands on floor
3. Legs back into an all fours position, head up
4. Half flip right to a crab position
5. Half flip right to an all-fours position

This drill can also be done with a left flip or with two flips, one left and one right, and so forth. Challenge students work in unison with a group.

See DPESS Chapter 14 for details.

Scatter formation

Variation: put a push-up in before the flip. Step 4 would be the down motion and Step 5 would be the up motion. Use caution to ensure that students are far enough apart in case one student flips the wrong way.

FITNESS DEVELOPMENT (8 - 12 MINUTES)

PACER Running

See DPESS Chapter 2 for details.

LESSON FOCUS (15 - 20 MINUTES)

Heel Lift Task sheet
Shoulder Press Task sheet
Program Design Task sheet
Sequencing Task sheet

See DPESS Chapter 20 for details.

Demonstrate skills
Describe Program Design/Task sheets and Sequencing
Divide class in half
  Half given Task sheets 27-28
  Half given Task sheets 29-30

GAME (5 MINUTES)

Team Tug-of-War

Small groups and classes can have contests with the large commercially available tug-of-war ropes.

See DPESS Chapter 16 for details.

Divide class into equal groups of 2 or 4 for this game.
Explain safety rules before beginning game.

EVALUATION/ REVIEW/ CHEER

What muscles were worked on in class today?
Explain one muscle used today and the movement/action it performs.
What was the most challenging part of class today?

Cheer: Pacer running keeps me fit!

TASK SHEET 27: HEEL LIFT

Student's Name: ________________________________ **Date**: ________

Partner's Name: ________________________________ **Period**: ________

Student Information: In this lesson you will learn the proper form for performing the heel lift. The heel lift exercises the Gastrocnemius muscle in the lower leg.

Objective: While using proper form, you will perform two sets of heel lifts, performing the maximum number of repetitions in each of the sets.

Directions:
1. Go to the heel lift board and practice performing the heel lift.
2. Mark the appropriate response (YES/NO) for each checkpoint for the heel lift.
3. Repeat this lesson until you have responded "yes" to all of the checkpoints.
4. After successfully completing this lesson, go on to the next Task sheet.

HEEL LIFT		Yes	No
1.	Assume a position with the balls of your feet on the heel lift board and your heels as low as possible.		
2.	Point your toes straightforward.		
3.	Keep your back and legs straight.		
4.	Extend your arms to the wall or a permanent structure for support and balance.		
5.	Raise up on the toes as far as possible.		
6.	Exhale approximately two-thirds of the way up.		
7.	Slowly return to the starting position, fully stretching the calf muscles.		
8.	Inhale approximately two-thirds of the way down.		
9.	Perform one set of as many repetitions as possible using proper form.		
10.	Perform a second set of as many repetitions as possible using proper form.		

TASK SHEET 28: SHOULDER PRESS

Student's Name: ______________________________ **Date**: ________

Observer's Name: ______________________________ **Period** ________

Spotter's Name: ______________________________

Spotter's Name: ______________________________

Student Information: In this lesson you will learn the proper form for performing the shoulder press. You will be working with three partners in this lesson. One person will act as the lifter (doer), and one as the observer/recorder. The other two partners will act as spotters on each end of the bar. You will rotate with your partner after completing the lesson until all students have had an opportunity to act in each role. All weight training exercises must be performed slowly using the proper form in order to gain the maximum benefits and to ensure safety. The shoulder press exercises the deltoid muscles in the shoulders and the triceps in the upper arm.

Objective: You will perform one set of ten repetitions of shoulder press while using your maximum amount of weight and proper form.

Directions:

1. Choose three partners that you would like to work with while completing this lesson.
2. Go to unused barbell with your partners and decide who will be the doer, observer, and two spotters.
3. The doer will practice performing the shoulder press while the observer records and gives feedback. You will repeat this lesson until you have received "yes" responses at all of the checkpoints.
4. The observer will check the appropriate response (YES/NO) for each checkpoint for the shoulder press. The observer should check only one checkpoint at a time and give verbal feedback to the lifter on each checkpoint marked "no."
5. The two spotters will give the bar to the lifter at the beginning of the lift and take if from the lifter at the end of the lift.
6. You will always use two spotters when performing the shoulder press. The spotters' only responsibility is that of spotting the doer (lifter). The observer is <u>not</u> to act as a spotter.
7. After successfully completing this lesson, go on to the next activity.

SHOULDER PRESS		Yes	No
1.	Select your maximum weight that you performed for a total of ten repetitions.		
2.	Stand erect with the feet slightly wider than shoulder width apart.		
3.	Receive the bar from the spotters with the bar resting on the upper chest just below the collarbone.		
4.	Assume an overhand grip at shoulder width.		
5.	Inhale.		
6.	Keep the legs and back straight throughout the lift.		
7.	Extend the arms and press the bar overhead until the arms are straight with the bar directly over the shoulders and hips.		
8.	Exhale approximately two-thirds of the way up.		
9.	Lower the bar slowly to the starting position.		
10.	Inhale approximately two-thirds of the way down.		
11.	Perform one set of ten repetitions using your maximum weight and proper form.		
12.	Perform a second set of ten repetitions using your maximum weight and proper form.		

TASK SHEET 29: PROGRAM DESIGNS

Student's Name: ______________________________ **Date**: ________

Objectives:

Upon completion of this lesson you will:

1. Demonstrate an understanding of the elements in a program designed to increase muscular strength and size by passing a self-check test with a score of 100%.
2. Demonstrate an understanding of the elements in a program designed to increase muscular endurance and tone by passing a self-check test with a score of 100%.

Instructions:

This lesson consists of information describing the elements of two program designs. The first description describes a program designed to increase muscular strength and size. The second description concerns a program designed to increase muscular endurance and tone. You will study the elements of both programs prior to taking the self-check tests. You must score 100% on the test. If you fail to score 100%, review the lesson and retake the test until you are able to do so. The answer key for the self-check test is available from your instructor.

PROGRAM DESIGNS

A PROGRAM DESIGNED TO INCREASE MUSCULAR STRENGTH AND SIZE:

1. Consists of a program emphasizing LOW repetitions and HIGH weights.
2. Your overload is in the amount of weight lifted, not the number of repetitions performed.
3. Generally, any number of repetitions under ten can be considered as LOW.

A PROGRAM DESIGNED TO INCREASE MUSCULAR ENDURANCE AND TONE:

1. Consists of a program emphasizing HIGH repetitions and LOW weights.
2. Your overload is in the number of repetitions performed, not weight lifted.
3. Generally, any number of repetitions over ten can be considered as HIGH.

REVIEW THIS LESSON CAREFULLY, THEN TAKE THE SELF-CHECK TEST ON PROGRAM DESIGNS

SELF-CHECK TEST FOR: PROGRAM DESIGNS

Name: ____

Date: ______________________ **Period:** _______ **Score:** _________

Directions: Fill in the blank with the correct word. After completing the test, get an answer key from the instructor and correct your test. If you miss any questions, review the previous lesson and retake the test. Continue this procedure until you score 100% on this test.

1. A program design consisting of _________ repetitions and _______ weight will improve muscular strength and size.
2. A program design consisting of _________ repetitions and _______ weight will improve muscular endurance and tone.
3. Nancy's program consists of performing fifteen repetitions of each upper body exercise and twenty repetitions of each lower body exercise. Nancy is trying to improve her muscular _________ and _________..
4. Rich's program consists of performing five repetitions of each upper body exercise and eight repetitions of each lower body exercise. Rich is trying to improve his muscular _________ and _________..

ANSWER KEY

1. A program design consisting of LOW repetitions and HIGH weight will improve muscular strength and size.
2. A program design consisting of HIGH repetitions and LOW weight will improve muscular endurance and tone.
3. Nancy's program consists of performing fifteen repetitions of each upper body exercise and twenty repetitions of each lower body exercise. Nancy is trying to improve her muscular ENDURANCE and TONE.
4. Rich's program consists of performing five repetitions of each upper body exercise and eight repetitions of each lower body exercise. Rich is trying to improve his muscular STRENGTH and SIZE .

TASK SHEET 30: SEQUENCING EXERCISES

Student's Name: ________________________________ **Date**: ________

Objectives:
Upon completion of this lesson you will:
1. Understand the concept of sequencing exercises.
2. Understand the advantages of working large muscle groups before working small muscle groups.
3. List exercises in the proper sequence according to the size of the muscle groups for both the upper and lower body.

Instructions:
This lesson is presented with paragraphs of information followed by questions pertaining to the material. The answers to the questions are found below the three asterisks (***) that follow each question. By folding a piece of paper and sliding it down the page, you keep the answers covered until you have made a response to the question. You are not to write on this lesson. Instead, write your answers on the programmed lessons answer sheets. After responding, slide the paper down and compare your answer with the answer given below the asterisks. If your answer is correct, then go on to the next question. If your answer is incorrect, then review the preceding paragraph and find out why your answer was wrong. Be sure to write the correct answer on your answer sheet. After completing the lesson, you must pass a self-check test with a score of 100%. If you do not score 100%, review the lesson and retake the test. The answer key for the self-check test is available from your instructor.

SEQUENCING EXERCISES

In order to achieve the desired results from a weight-training program, you must perform the exercises in the proper sequence or order. There are different methods of sequencing exercises. The order the exercises are performed will be determined by the desired outcome or goals. For this class, you will utilize one of the simplest and yet effective procedures for sequencing exercises. You will exercise the large muscle groups prior to exercising the small muscle groups. For example, you should work your back muscles before working your arm muscles. If you worked your arms before working your back, you would be limiting your very large back muscles to the limit of the weaker and now fatigued arm muscles.

Questions:

1. Sequencing refers to the (order/number) ________ of exercises to be performed.
   ***
   order
2. The method of sequencing exercises is determined by:
   a. the amount of time a person has to work out
   b. the desired outcome or goals of the individual
   c. the workout partner
   ***
   b
3. For the purpose and goals of this class, you will sequence your exercises working your large muscle groups before your ________ muscle groups.
   ***
   small
4. If you exercise the small muscle groups before the large ones, you are ________ the large muscle groups to the limit of the weaker and now fatigued small muscle groups.
   ***
   limiting
5. While working your upper body, you should exercise you back muscles before your _______ muscle.
   a. neck
   b. chest
   c. arm
   ***
   c

(Sequencing, cont.)

Your arms are used in performing the bench press, lat pull down, and shoulder press, as well as every other upper body exercise. The smaller muscles (arms) will be getting worked very hard while you are working the large muscle groups (chest, back, and shoulders). This same principle of sequencing may be applied to the muscle groups of the lower body.

The suggested order of sequencing exercises for your UPPER BODY is as follows:

1. Bench press	and/or	Incline bench press
2. Lat pulldown	and/or	Upright row
3. Shoulder press	and/or	Behind the neck press
4. Biceps curl	and/or	Low pulley curl
5. Triceps extension	and/or	Low pulley triceps extension
6. Abdominal crunch	and/or	Abdominal curl

The suggested order of sequencing exercises for the LOWER BODY is as follows:

1. Leg press
2. Leg extension
3. Leg curl
4. Heel lift

Questions:

6. The bench press should be performed before the _______________.
   a. lat pull down
   b. triceps extension
   c. biceps curl
   d. all of the above
   ***
   d

7. The leg curl should be performed after the _______________.
   a. abdominal crunch
   b. leg extension
   c. heel lift
   ***
   b

8. The lat pull down should be performed before the _______________.
   a. leg press
   b. bench press
   c. shoulder press
   ***
   c

PROCEED TO TAKE THE SELF-CHECK TEST ON SEQUENCING EXERCISES.

SELF-CHECK TEST FOR: THE PRINCIPLE OF SEQUENCING

Name: ____

Date: ______________________ **Period:** _______ **Score:** _______

Directions: List the exercises in the proper sequence beginning with exercises for the larger muscles to the smaller muscles for each of the major muscle groups listed below. Write the number representing the order the exercise should be performed in the space provided. When you have completed the test, check the answer key to correct your test. If you miss any questions, review the previous lesson and retake the test. Continue this procedure until you are able to score 100% on this test.

EXERCISES FOR THE UPPER BODY:

GROUP 1:

_______ barbell
_______ bench press
_______ abdominal crunch
_______ lat pull down
_______ triceps extension
_______ should press

GROUP 2:

_______ behind the neck press
_______ low pulley curl
_______ incline bench press
_______ low pulley triceps extension
_______ upright row
_______ abdominal curl

EXERCISES FOR THE LOWER BODY:

_______ leg curl
_______ heel lift
_______ leg press
_______ leg extension

(ANSWER KEY)

EXERCISES FOR THE UPPER BODY:

GROUP 1:

(4) barbell
(1) bench press
(6) abdominal crunch
(2) lat pull down
(5) triceps extension
(3) should press

GROUP 2:

(3) behind the neck press
(4) low pulley curl
(1) incline bench press
(5) low pulley triceps extension
(2) upright row
(6) abdominal curl

EXERCISES FOR THE LOWER BODY:

(3) leg curl
(4) heel lift
(1) leg press
(2) leg extension

Weight Training Lesson Plan 7

EQUIPMENT:
Continuity Exercise Music CD/Tape
CD/Cassette Tape Player
4 Bowling pins per 5 students

National Standards Met in this Lesson: **1, 2, 3, 4, 5, 6**

INSTRUCTIONAL ACTIVITIES	TEACHING HINTS

INTRODUCTORY ACTIVITY (2 - 3 MINUTES)

Eliminate to allow more time for Lesson Focus.

FITNESS DEVELOPMENT (8 - 12 MINUTES)

Continuity Exercises
These exercises are a type of interval training. Create a CD/cassette tape with 30 - 35 seconds of music and 20 seconds of silence. During the music, the students will jump rope.
During the silence, instruct the students to do an exercise i.e. push-ups; curl ups; reverse push-ups; side leg lifts on each side; coffee grinder, arm circling, crab walks forward and backward, etc.

See DPESS Chapter 16 for details.
Scattered formation
When the music resumes, the students jump rope. During each silence direct a different exercise.

LESSON FOCUS (15 - 20 MINUTES)

Discuss creating own program
- Setting fitness goals
- Weight Training record chart

Divide class in half.
- Half given Task sheet 31 & 32
  Half given Task sheet 33 to create Weight Training Chart. This group will need to make sure their goals match their chart.

Distribute Task sheet 32
- Look at chart.

Direct students to go to stations and evaluate weights to create own chart.

Review sequencing, progression, and safe workouts.

Describe daily procedures.

GAME (5 MINUTES)

Bowling Pin Relay
Four bowling pins per squad are used. They are evenly spaced in front of each squad in a fashion similar to the potato relay. The first person in line lays all of the pins down, and the next person stands them up. Only 1 hand can be used.

See DPESS Chapter 17 for details.
Use Whistle Mixer to create equal groups of 5.
Assign each group to a relay line.

REVIEW/EVALUATION AND CHEER

Review elements of personal goal setting.
Discuss personal progress in goals to date.

Students create cheer.

TASK SHEET 31: FITNESS GOALS

Student's Name: ______________________________ **Date:** ________

Objectives:

Upon completion of this lesson you will:

1. Have read the lesson covering the benefits of weight training.
2. Evaluate personal fitness needs by completing a check list.
3. State your personal fitness goals pertaining to weight training.

Instructions:

This lesson will help you to evaluate your fitness needs, thus, enabling you to state your personal fitness goals. First, go back and review lesson #1 on the benefits of weight training. Then complete this lesson. When stating your goals you may want to refer to the benefits listed. Complete the checklist below.

PERSONAL FITNESS NEEDS & GOALS CHECK LIST

I. Place a check next to the benefits that you would like to gain.

_______ improve strength
_______ improve muscular endurance
_______ increase muscle size
_______ decrease body fat
_______ improve appearance
_______ improve self-concept
_______ decrease fatigue
_______ reduce chance of injury
_______ increase physical efficiency and productivity

II. Place a check next to the general areas that you would like to concentrate on and improve.

_______ strength and size
_______ endurance and tone
_______ upper body
_______ lower body
_______ overall (upper & lower) body development

III. Place a check next to the specific areas that you would like to concentrate on and improve.

Gain strength and size in the:	Firm and tone the:
_______ arms	_______ arms
_______ back	_______ back
_______ shoulders	_______ shoulders
_______ chest	_______ chest
_______ waist	_______ waist
_______ thighs	_______ thighs
_______ hips	_______ hips
_______ calves	_______ calves

IV. Study the items that you have a checked. Review the preceding lessons for any information concerning the attainment of these goals.

TASK SHEET 32: WRITTEN ASSIGNMENT

Student's Name: ______________________________ **Date**: ________

Objective:
Upon completion of this lesson you will:

1. Develop, write, practice, and modify a personal weight-training program demonstrating an understanding of the scientific principles and practical theories covered in this class.

Instructions:
This lesson will help you to learn the steps in developing, writing, and modifying a personal fitness and weight training program.  Write an outline of a daily workout to include cardiovascular endurance, flexibility, strength and muscular endurance. You may want to refer to some of the previous lessons for assistance.

TASK SHEET 33: WEIGHT TRAINING CHART

Objectives:

Upon completion of this lesson you will:
1. Understand the usefulness of a weight-training chart for monitoring your workouts.
2. Use a weight-training chart to record your exercises.

Instructions:
The weight-training chart on the following two pages is an example you can follow to properly sequence exercises and use the principle of progression. Look at the charts. Notice how Kimbie has ordered her exercises beginning with the larger muscles then working the smaller muscles. Also, if you will look at the dates of her workouts and the exercises she performed, you will notice that Kimbie has broken her workouts into upper body days and lower body days. This philosophy is just one of many that is supported in the field of weight training. Basically, any workout that you develop based on the previously explained concepts and principles will be sound. Do you see that Kimbie is constantly striving for improvement as evidenced by her small yet consistent increases in the weight she attempts? Study the chart carefully. You will be required to make a weight-training chart while participating in this class. When you are finished analyzing the chart, go to your instructor and ask for a chart for yourself. Fill in all of the required information at the top of your chart. The "% FAT" and "IDEAL WEIGHT" are optional items. However, you may fill them in if you have access to the information and want to keep a record of it. Keep your chart with you in class. When you have filled one chart completely, keep it in your notebook for your records. Then, get another blank form from your instructor to continue keeping a record of your progress.

*** **WORK HARD AND HAVE FUN!**

NAME Kimbie Casten AGE 17 SEX F HEIGHT 5'2" WEIGHT 110 lbs.

DATE STARTED PROGRAM September 1, 2008 % FAT 22% TARGET % FAT 22% IDEAL WEIGHT 110 lbs.

DATE			9/1	9/2	9/3	9/4	9/5								
EXERCISE	EQUIPMENT	Reps	WT.	WT.	WT.	WT.	QT.	WT.	WT.	WT.	WT.	WT.	WT.	WT.	WT.
WARM-UP:	CYCLE:	1	5 min	5 min	5 min	10 min	10 min								
Incline Bench Press	Olympic Incline Bench	10	45	45	45	50	50								
		8	50	50	50	55	55								
		6	55	55	55	60	60								
		4	60	60	60	65	65								
		4	60	60	60	65	65								
Lat Pull down	Universal	10	30	30	30	30	40								
		10	30	30	30	30	40								
		10	30	30	30	30	40								
Shoulder Press	Olympic	10	45	45	45	45	50								
		10	45	45	45	45	50								
		10	45	45	45	45	50								
Biceps Curls	Olympic	10	20	20	20	20	30								
		10	20	20	20	20	30								
		10	20	20	20	20	30								
Triceps Extension	Universal	10	20	20	20	20	30								
		10	20	20	20	20	30								
		10	20	20	20	20	30								
Abdominal Curls	Slant Board	20	20	20	20	25	25								
		20	20	20	20	25	25								
		20	20	20	20	25	25								

NAME Kimbie Casten AGE 17 SEX F HEIGHT 5'2" WEIGHT 110 lbs.

DATE STARTED PROGRAM September 1, 2008 % FAT 22% TARGET % FAT 22% IDEAL WEIGHT 110 lbs.

DATE			9/1	9/2	9/3	9/4	9/5								
EXERCISE	EQUIPMENT	Reps	WT.	WT.	WT.	WT.	QT.	WT.	WT.	WT.	WT.	WT.	WT.	WT.	WT.
WARM-UP:	CYCLE:														
Leg Press	Universal	10	100	100	100	100	110								
		8	120	120	120	120	130								
		8	120	120	120	120	130								
		8	120	120	120	120	130								
Leg Extension	Universal	10	50	50	50	50	60								
		10	50	50	50	50	60								
		10	50	50	50	50	60								
Leg Curls	Universal	10	30	30	30	30	40								
		10	30	30	30	30	40								
		10	30	30	30	30	40								
Heel Lift	Heel Lift Machine	10	60	60	60	60	70								
		10	60	60	60	60	70								
		10	60	60	60	60	70								

Weight Training Lesson Plan 8

EQUIPMENT:
PACER Running CD/Tape
CD/Cassette Tape Player
Cage ball

National Standards Met in this Lesson: **1, 2, 3, 4, 5, 6**

INSTRUCTIONAL ACTIVITIES	TEACHING HINTS
INTRODUCTORY ACTIVITY (2 - 3 MINUTES)	
Move and Perform a Stretch Move and perform a stretching activity on the sound of the whistle. Move and stretch to the sound of music. Skip, hop, shuffle, jog and walk.	**See DPESS Chapter 14 for details.** Scatter formation Direct starting and stopping locomotor movements to selected stretches using a whistle or a timed music CD/tape.
FITNESS DEVELOPMENT (8 - 12 MINUTES)	
PACER Running Progressive aerobic cardiovascular endurance run.	**See DPESS Chapter 2 for details.** Use a timed CD/tape Scattered formation
LESSON FOCUS (15 - 20 MINUTES)	
Individual Weight Training Programs	
GAME (5 MINUTES)	
Crab Cage ball	**See DPESS Chapter 18 for details.** See Lesson Plan 7, Racquetball Unit for details

Weight Training Lesson Plan 9

EQUIPMENT:
Whistle

National Standards Met in this Lesson: **1, 2, and 3**

INSTRUCTIONAL ACTIVITIES	TEACHING HINTS
INTRODUCTORY ACTIVITY (2 - 3 MINUTES)	
Over, Under, and Around	**See DPESS Chapter 14 for details.** See Lesson Plan 5 from Racquetball Unit for details
FITNESS DEVELOPMENT (8 - 12 MINUTES)	
Jog, Walk, Jog Direct students to jog as far as they can. When tired, they can walk, and resume jogging when able.	**See DPESS Chapter 16 for details.**
LESSON FOCUS (15 - 20 MINUTES)	
Individual Weight Training Program	
GAME (5 MINUTES)	
Butt Tug One line moves to the left 1 step. Bend over, cross the arms between the legs, and grasp the hand of 2 different people from the other team. Now begin tugging. Try forming 2 teams in the described position and have a race while maintaining the handgrips.	**See DPESS Chapter 18 for details.** Divide class into even lines Each line stands back to back with another line.

Weight Training Lesson Plan 10

EQUIPMENT:

Whistle

Individual Weight Training Programs

National Standards Met in this Lesson: **1, 2, 3, 4, 5, 6**

INSTRUCTIONAL ACTIVITIES	TEACHING HINTS
INTRODUCTORY ACTIVITY (2 - 3 MINUTES)	
Move and Change Direction Indicate direction change with whistle.	**See DPESS Chapter 14 for details.** Scattered formation
FITNESS DEVELOPMENT (8 - 12 MINUTES)	
Jog, Walk, Jog Direct students to jog as far as they can. When tired, they can walk, and resume jogging when able.	**See DPESS Chapter 16 for details.**
LESSON FOCUS (15 - 20 MINUTES)	
Individual Weight Training Program	
GAME (5 MINUTES)	
Mass Stand Up Start with 2 people sitting back to back. Lock elbows and try to stand up. Increase the number to 3 people, then 4, and so forth. See how many people can stand up simultaneously.	**See DPESS Chapter 18 for details.** Using Back-to-Back, create partners.

Weight Training Lesson Plan 11

EQUIPMENT:

Parachute

CD/Cassette Tape Player

Music CD/Tape

Cage ball

National Standards Met in this Lesson: **1, 2, 3, 5, 6**

INSTRUCTIONAL ACTIVITIES	TEACHING HINTS
INTRODUCTORY ACTIVITY (2 - 3 MINUTES)	
Fastest Tag: Every player is a tagger. Object is to tag other players without being tagged. Players that get tagged must sit where they are and wait till only one person or 2 or 3 is left. If two people tag each other at the same time both are out.	**See DPESS Chapter 14 for details.** Create boundaries with cones/lines. Establish number left that indicates that game complete.
FITNESS DEVELOPMENT (8 - 12 MINUTES)	
Parachute Rhythmic Aerobic Activities	**See DPESS Chapter 14 for details.** See Lesson Plan 11, Badminton Unit for details
LESSON FOCUS (15 - 20 MINUTES)	
Individual Weight Training Program	
GAME (5 MINUTES)	
Long Team Cage ball The teams move into sitting position in 2 lines facing each other 10 to 15 feet apart. The teacher rolls or throws a cage ball between the 2 lines. The object is for 1 team to kick the ball over the other team. A point is scored against a team when the ball goes over or through a line. The team with the fewer points wins. Again, a point is awarded if a player stands or touches the ball with the hands. More than 1 cage ball can be used simultaneously.	**See DPESS Chapter 18 for details.** Use a management game to create 2 teams.

Weight Training Lesson Plan 12

EQUIPMENT:
1 Bean Bag per 2 students
Whistle

National Standards Met in this Lesson: **1, 2, 3, 4, 5, 6**

INSTRUCTIONAL ACTIVITIES	TEACHING HINTS
INTRODUCTORY ACTIVITY (2 - 3 MINUTES)	
Throwing and Catching Bean Bags on the Run Toss, move, and catch. Cover as much ground as possible between the toss and catch. Move forward, backward, and sideways, using different steps such as running, the carioca, shuffle, and slide.	**See DPESS Chapter 18 for details.** Scattered formation Use Elbow-to-Elbow to create partners. 1 Bean Bag per group Direct running activity and tossing challenges.
FITNESS DEVELOPMENT (8 - 12 MINUTES)	
Walk-Jog-Sprint Direct movements with whistle signals: 1 whistle = walk 2 whistles = jog 3 whistles = sprint Alternate jogging, walking, sprinting	**See DPESS Chapter 16 for details.** Scattered formation Students begin by walking around the area.
LESSON FOCUS (15 - 20 MINUTES)	
Individual Weight Training Program	
GAME (5 MINUTES)	
Addition Tag The "its" must hold hands and can tag only with their outside hands. When they tag someone, that person must hook on. This continues and the tagging line becomes longer and longer. Regardless of the length of the line, only the hand of the line is eligible to tag.	**See DPESS Chapter 14 for details.** Select 2-4 its. Set boundaries.

Weight Training Lesson Plan 13

EQUIPMENT:
Whistle
Music
CD/Cassette Tape Player

National Standards Met in this Lesson: **1, 2, 3, 4, 5, 6**

INSTRUCTIONAL ACTIVITIES	TEACHING HINTS
INTRODUCTORY ACTIVITY (2 - 3 MINUTES)	
Eliminate to allow more time for Individual Program.	
FITNESS DEVELOPMENT (8 - 12 MINUTES)	
Aerobic Workout	**See DPESS Chapter 16 for details.** See Lesson Plan 7, Racquetball Unit for details.
LESSON FOCUS (15 - 20 MINUTES)	
Individual Weight Training Program	
GAME (5 MINUTES)	
Wheelbarrow Relay Use the wheelbarrow position as the means of locomotion. All members of each squad must participate in both the carrying position and the down formation.	**See DPESS Chapter 18 for details.** Create squads of 6 people. Assign squad to a space. Explain rules and boundaries.

Weight Training Lesson Plan 14

EQUIPMENT:
Fitnessgram Testing Cards
Sit and Reach Boxes
Equipment described in manual for test

National Standards Met in this Lesson: **1, 2 , 3, 4, 5, 6**

INSTRUCTIONAL ACTIVITIES | **TEACHING HINTS**

INTRODUCTORY ACTIVITY (2 - 3 MINUTES)

Running High Fives
Students' jog/skip around when whistle is blown students run to a partner and jumps in air and give each other a "high five" and them continue moving until whistle is blown again.

See DPESS Chapter 14 for details.
Scatter formation.
Explain rules.
High 5 at peak of jump.

FITNESS DEVELOPMENT (8 - 12 MINUTES)

Combine with Lesson Focus today.

LESSON FOCUS (15 - 20 MINUTES)

Fitnessgram Testing

See DPESS Chapter 10 for details.
Allow students to select a partner to work with.
- If complete test, work on Weight Training.

GAME (5 MINUTES)

Spider Tag
A pair is "it" and they chase until they tag another pair. The new pair becomes "it."

See DPESS Chapter 14 for details.
Use Back-to-Back to make pairs.
Stand back to back with partner with elbows locked.
- Variation: Each group tagged can join the original "its." Until a selected number are "its" and begin game again.

Weight Training Lesson Plan 15

EQUIPMENT:
CD/Cassette Tape Player
Aerobic Exercise CD/Tape
Parachute
4-6 Rubber balls/Volleyballs

National Standards Met in this Lesson: **1, 2, 3, 4, 5, 6**

INSTRUCTIONAL ACTIVITIES | **TEACHING HINTS**

INTRODUCTORY ACTIVITY (2 - 3 MINUTES)

Eliminate today.

FITNESS DEVELOPMENT (8 - 12 MINUTES)

Aerobic Workout

See DPESS Chapter 16 for details.
See Lesson Plan 7, Racquetball Unit for details.

LESSON FOCUS (15 - 20 MINUTES)

Individual Weight training Program

GAME (5 MINUTES)

Parachute Team Ball
Use two to six balls. Try to bounce the balls off the opponents' side, scoring one point for each ball.

Create teams around taut parachute.
Each team defends half of the chute.

Note:
Written exam could be administered.

MUSCLE IDENTIFICATION EXAM

Name: ____

Date: ____________________ **Period** ___________ **Score:** ___________

Directions: Write the name of the muscle on the blank line pointing to the muscle.

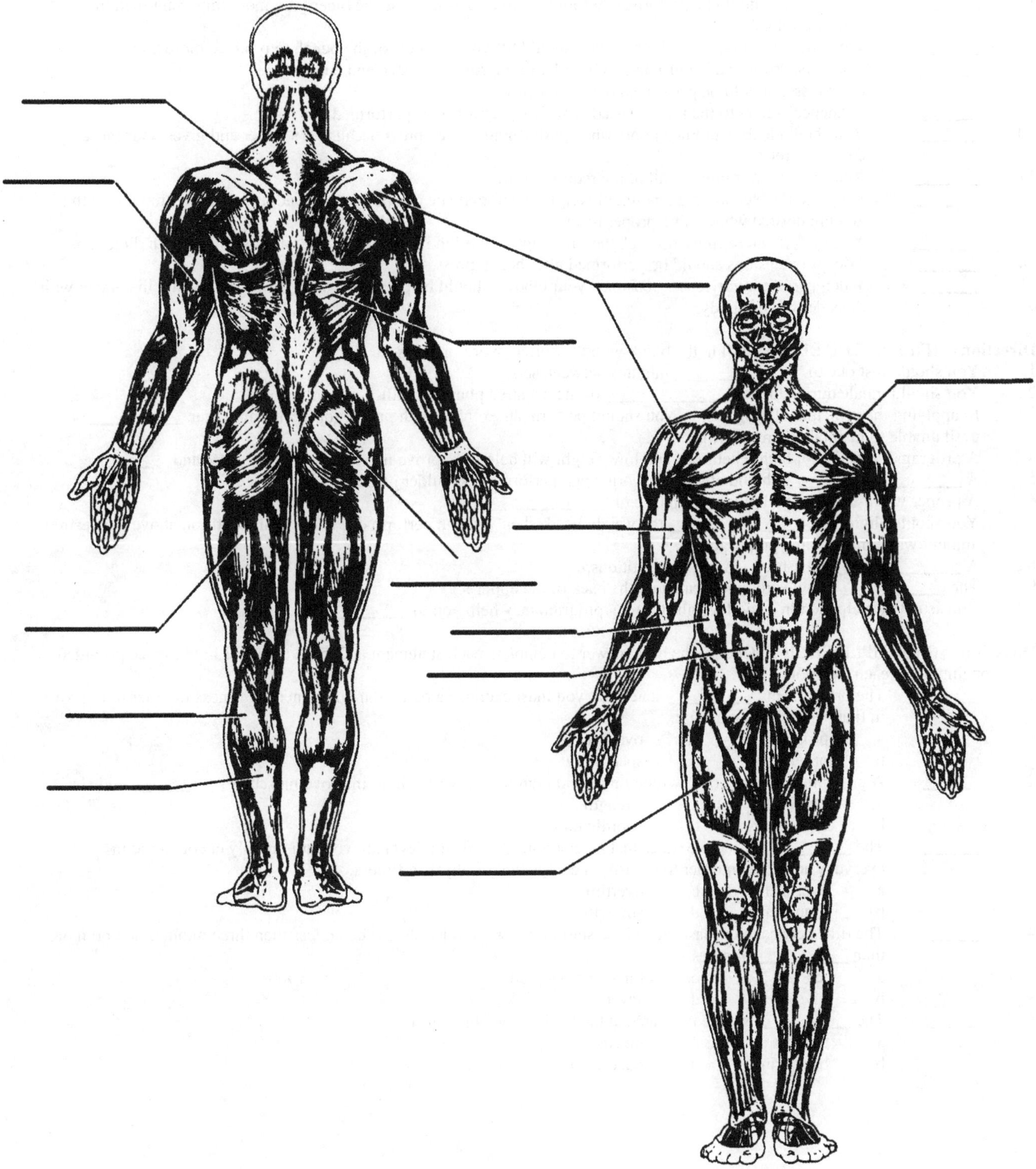

EXAM PAGE 2

Directions: (TRUE/FALSE) Write the entire word TRUE or FALSE in the space provided. Any other symbol or mark will be scored as incorrect.

1. ______ You should not scream or yell in the weight room because it makes it difficult for others to concentrate.
2. ______ Weight training will help to improve your flexibility.
3. ______ The cool-down is not as important as the warm-up and should only be performed if time permits.
4. ______ You should use the proper lifting technique even when lifting a light object from the floor.
5. ______ Barbell curls should be performed before lat pull downs because the biceps are more important then the latissimus dorsi.
6. ______ When performing the bench press, you should lift your hips off of the bench to produce more power.
7. ______ You must "overload" your muscles in order to improve their size and endurance.
8. ______ Leg presses should be performed before leg curls.
9. ______ "Cadence" refers to the rate or speed at which a repetition is performed.
10. ______ You should lock your knee joints when performing the leg press because it's easier and gives your muscles a chance to relax.
11. ______ You must use a spotter on all of the required lifts.
12. ______ Sally should decrease the amount of weight she uses if she can perform one additional repetition above the amount desired while using proper form.
13. ______ You perform an exercise through the full range of motion if you move as far as possible in both directions.
14. ______ Triceps extensions should be performed after bench press.
15. ______ When performing triceps extensions, your elbows should be pointed straight down and remain in contact with the sides of your body.

Directions: (FILL IN THE BLANK) Fill in the blank with the correct word or phrase.

1. You should rest one to ______ minutes between sets.
2. You should inhale during the last ______ of the negative phase of a lift.
3. In applying the principle of progression, you should perform an exercise with proper form until muscular ______ or until unable to maintain correct form.
4. A program consisting of high repetitions and low weight will help to improve muscular ______ and ______.
5. A ______ should always be worn when performing shoulder presses.
6. A proper warm-up can help reduce the chance of ______.
7. You should slightly ______ the weight used when you can perform one additional repetition above the desired amount while maintaining proper form.
8. A ______ consists of a group of repetitions.
9. The ______ muscle group is located on the back of the upper leg.
10. Consistent participation in a good weight-training program may help you to ______ your body fat.

Directions: (MULTIPLE CHOICE) Choose the best answer to complete each statement and write the letter in the space provided at the beginning of each question.

1. ______ The principle of ______ states that you must exercise a particular component of fitness in order to improve in that particular component.
   - a. progression
   - b. order
   - c. overload
   - d. specificity
2. ______ A program consisting of low repetitions and high weight will help to improve muscular ______ and size.
   - a. flexibility
   - b. endurance
   - c. strength
   - d. coordination
3. ______ The ______ principle states that a person must work at a level above that normally encountered in everyday activities in order to improve a component of physical fitness.
   - a. overload
   - b. sequencing
   - c. overtime
   - d. strength
4. ______ The time between your last set and the start of a new exercise should be no less than three minutes and no more than ______ minutes.
   - a. ten
   - b. five
   - c. three and one-half
   - d. seven
5. ______ The ______ muscle is located at the back of the upper arm.
   - a. triceps
   - b. back arms
   - c. biceps
   - d. quadriceps

Flag Football

OBJECTIVES:

This unit has been specifically designed to meet all six components of the NASPE National Standards for Physical Education.

The student will:

1. Run, change directions, pivot, evade other students, and assume poses during Introductory Activities.
2. Demonstrate cooperation and cooperation in the High Five's, Blob Tag, Triangle Tag and Mini Pyramids activities.
3. Participate in continuity Exercises, Parachute Fitness, Partner Racetrack Fitness, Challenge Courses, Circuit and Aerobic Workout activities to improve their fitness.
4. Demonstrate a variety of passes, catches, and stances during the lesson focus portion of class.
5. Demonstrate hand-offs, blocks and punting skills during the lesson focus portion of class.
6. Practice a variety of Flag Football Plays as demonstrated in class, to the satisfaction of the instructor.
7. Practice offensive and defensive plays as demonstrated in class to the satisfaction of the instructor.
8. Participate in a Flag Football Tournament during class.
9. Pass a skill exam scoring 70% or better.
10. Pass a written exam scoring 70% or better.

FLAG FOOTBALL BLOCK PLAN
2 WEEK UNIT

Week #1	Monday	Tuesday	Wednesday	Thursday	Friday
Introductory Activity	Run and Change Direction	Weave Drill	Vanishing Bean Bags	Blob Tag	Run and Assume a Pose
Fitness	Parachute Fitness	Partner Racetrack Fitness	Continuity Exercises	Fitness Scavenger Hunt	Circuit Training
Lesson focus	Passing and Lateral Pass	Passing/ Catching	Stances Centering the Ball	Shoulder & Pass Blocks/ Spinning Drill	Hand-Offs Punting
Game	Triangle plus 1 Tag	Leapfrog	Mad Scramble	Hoops and Plyometrics	Foot Tag

Week #2	Monday	Tuesday	Wednesday	Thursday	Friday
Introductory Activity	Rubber band	Triangle Tag	Move, Stop, Pivot	Mini Pyramids	Mass Stand Up
Fitness	Jump and Jog Fitness	Partner Racetrack	Mini Challenge Course	Aerobic Workout	Random Running
Lesson focus	Rules, Strategies, Plays	Flag Football Skills Test	Flag Football Written Exam	Flag Football Tournament	Flag Football Tournament
Game	Sitting Wrestle	Spider Tag	Flag Football		

Flag Football Lesson Plan 1

EQUIPMENT:

1 Football per Student
40 Small Cones
1 Task Sheet per Student
1 Pencil and clipboard per 3 Students
10 Flags
1 Exercise CD/Tape
1 CD/Cassette Player
1 Large Parachute

OBJECTIVES:

The student will:

1. Run, change directions, pivot, evade other students, and assume poses during the Introductory Activity following the instructions established by the instructor.
2. Demonstrate cooperation and cooperation in Triangle Tag activities during the game portion of class following the instructions established by the instructor..
3. Participate in Parachute to improve fitness using activities demonstrated by the instructor.
4. Demonstrate passing and lateral passing during the lesson focus portion of class using form demonstrated by the instructor.

National Standards Met in this Lesson: **1, 2, 3, 4, 5, 6**

INSTRUCTIONAL ACTIVITIES	TEACHING HINTS

INTRODUCTORY ACTIVITY (2 - 3 MINUTES)

Run and Change Direction
Students run in any direction, changing directions on signal

Scatter formation
Specify type of angle (i.e., right, obtuse, 45-degree.)

FITNESS DEVELOPMENT (8 - 12 MINUTES)

Parachute Fitness
Jog: hold chute in right hand; Change directions, switch hands. Slide, hold chute with both hands.
Skip: hold chute with right hand. Change directions, switch hands. Freeze and shake chute.
Sit with bent legs under chute for curl-ups. Lay on right side, lift left leg up. Reverse. Stand up and shake chute.
Jog and lift chute up and down. Repeat.

See DPESS Chapter 16 for details.
Use music to make fitness fun and exciting.
Use signal to change task
Keep all movements under control

LESSON FOCUS (15 - 20 MINUTES)

Reciprocal Task Sheet: Passing and Lateral Passing Practice: Assign groups to coned areas.
Explain Task Sheets. Demonstrate skills on the task sheets. When complete one, take the second one.

See DPESS Chapter 19 for details.
Use whistle mixer to make groups of 3.
Have equipment and task sheets at assigned stations.
Cones set up 15 feet apart, opposite each other.

Similar to most other forms of football, but with typically six to nine players. Tackling is not permitted.

GAME (5 MINUTES)

Triangle plus 1 Tag
Triangle moves around to avoid getting leader tagged.
Tagger tries to tag leader.

See DPESS Chapter 14 for details.
Use whistle mixer to make groups of 4
Identify leader and tagger.
3 make triangle and hold hands.

EVALUATION/REVIEW AND CHEER

Review elements of passing and lateral skills practiced.

Cheer: 2, 4, 6, 8, Flag Football is Great!

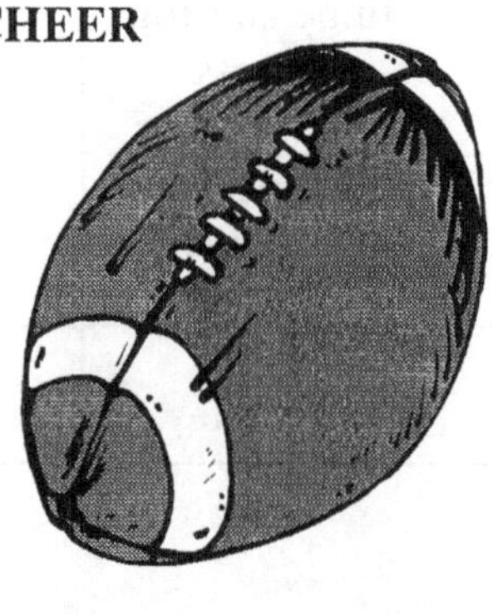

Reciprocal Task Sheet: Flag Football Passing

Doer: ______________________ **"Shagger"**: ____________________

Observer: __________________

Directions: Student will work in groups of three. Place first and last name on lines provided above. One person performs the task while partner shags the ball. Observer checks "yes" or "no" after each performance. Observer will also provide feedback on the performance. Perform task 10 times and rotate positions. Each student will turn in a task sheet.

Objective: The student will perform a flag football pass 10 times using technique demonstrated by the instructor.

Check "Yes" (Y) or "No" (N)

	Y/N	Y/N	Y/N	Y/N	Y/N	Y/N	Y/N	Y/N	Y/N	Y/N
Point shoulder opposite of the throwing arm towards receiver.										
Bring ball up to the throwing shoulder with both hands.										
Throwing hand fingers are placed on laces of the ball.										
Weight on rear leg.										
On throw, step forward with front foot in the direction of the receiver.										
Throwing arm is extended and wrist is flicked upon release.										
Follow through										

Reciprocal Task Sheet: Flag Football Lateral Pass

Doer: ______________________ **"Shagger"**: ____________________

Observer: __________________

Directions: Student will work in groups of three. Place first and last name on lines provided above. One person performs the task while partner shags the ball. Observer checks "yes" or "no" after each performance. Observer will also provide feedback on the performance. Perform task 10 times and rotate positions. Each student will turn in a task sheet.

Objective: The student will perform a lateral pass 10 times using technique demonstrated by the instructor.

Check "Yes" (Y) or "No" (N)

	Y/N	Y/N	Y/N	Y/N	Y/N	Y/N	Y/N	Y/N	Y/N	Y/N
Hold ball in both hands										
Side to target before pass										
Pass ball to partner										
Ball passed sideways or behind										
Ball aimed at chest area										
Follow-through with both hands										
Ball "floats" during pass										
Ball spirals (That's not what you are trying to do in this pass).										

Flag Football Lesson Plan 2

EQUIPMENT:

1 Football per 3 students
5 Jump Ropes
40 Small Cones
1 Task Sheet per Student
1 Pencil and Clipboard per 3 students
Music exercise CD/tape & CD/cassette player

OBJECTIVES:

The student will:

1. Participate in the Weave Drill demonstrating agility, speed, and coordination during the Introductory Activity following the instructions established by the instructor.
2. Demonstrate cooperation and focus during Partner Racetrack Fitness activities during the fitness portion of class following the instructions established by the instructor..
3. Complete the Catching Task Sheet using activities demonstrated by the instructor and following instructions established by the instructor.
4. Participate in Leap Frog demonstrating agility and cooperative skills during the game portion of class using form demonstrated by the instructor.

National Standards Met in this Lesson: **1, 2, 3, 4, 5, 6**

INSTRUCTIONAL ACTIVITIES	TEACHING HINTS

INTRODUCTORY ACTIVITY (2 - 3 MINUTES)

Weave Drill
Students are in ready position. They will shuffle left, right, forward, backward, over, and around obstacles on signal by the teacher's hand motion.

See DPESS Chapter 14 for details.
Scattered formation in front of teacher. Mark area with cones.

FITNESS DEVELOPMENT (8 - 12 MINUTES)

Partner Racetrack Fitness
Set up 10 stations in a circle track formation. Students have Task Card with exercise to perform. 2 students perform task while other 2 partners run around the track.

See DPESS Chapter 16 for details.
Use Whistle Mixer to create groups of 4. Use toe-to-toe to make partners in the group. Use music for motivation.

Endurance is developed when someone regularly engages in aerobic activity (aerobic means "with air"). During aerobic exercise, the heart beats faster and a person breathes harder. When done regularly and for continuous periods of time, aerobic activity strengthens the heart and improves the body's ability to deliver oxygen to all its cells.

LESSON FOCUS (15 - 20 MINUTES)

Task Sheet: Catching
Demonstrate skills on Task Sheet.
Partners stand 10' apart and across from each other.
Observer on side of doer.

See DPESS Chapter 19 for details.
Use Whistle Mixer to make groups of 3.
Have equipment and Task Sheets at assigned areas with cones marking 10'

Wide Receiver is an offensive player who lines up on or near the line of scrimmage, but split to the outside. His primary job is to catch passes from the quarterback.

Passing: Review Passing Skills from day before.

GAME (5 MINUTES)

Leap Frog
Rotate positions

See DPESS Chapter 18 for details.
Use Whistle Mixer to make groups of 2 - 3.

EVALUATION/REVIEW AND CHEER

Review elements and difficulties of skills practiced.

Cheer: 1, 2, 3 catch the ball thrown to me!!!!!

Reciprocal Task Sheet: Catching

Doer: ______________________ **"Shagger"**: ______________________

Observer: ______________________

Directions: Student will work in groups of three. Place first and last name on lines provided above. One person performs the task while partner throws the ball to the catcher. Observer checks "yes" or "no" after each performance while providing feedback. Perform task 10 times then rotate positions. Each student will turn in a task sheet.

Objective: The student will catch the football 10 times using form demonstrated by the instructor.

Check "Yes" (Y) or "No" (N)

	Y/N	Y/N	Y/N	Y/N	Y/N	Y/N	Y/N	Y/N	Y/N	Y/N
Begin in stationary position facing the thrower.										
Feet shoulder width apart.										
Hands held at chest anticipating the throw.										
Catch ball with fingers spread apart and										
Absorb force when ball comes into hands.										
Bring ball into chest upon catch										

Flag Football Lesson Plan 3

EQUIPMENT:

2 Small cones per 2 students
1 Task Sheet per Student
1 Pencil and Clipboard per 3 Students
Continuity Exercise CD/Tape & Player
1 Football per 3 Students
1 Jump rope per Student

OBJECTIVES:

The student will:

1. Participate in the Vanishing Bean Bags demonstrating agility, speed, and coordination during the Introductory Activity following the instructions established by the instructor.
2. Participate in Continuity Exercises during the fitness portion of class following the instructions established by the instructor..
3. Demonstrate stances and complete the Centering the Ball Task Sheet using activities demonstrated by the instructor and following instructions established by the instructor.
4. Participate in Mad Scramble demonstrating agility and cooperative skills during the game portion of class using form demonstrated by the instructor.

National Standards Met in this Lesson: **1, 2, 3, 4, 5, 6**

INSTRUCTIONAL ACTIVITIES	TEACHING HINTS

INTRODUCTORY ACTIVITY (2 - 3 MINUTES)

Vanishing Bean Bags
Take away bean bags after each episode

See DPESS Chapter 14 for details.
Scatter formation

FITNESS DEVELOPMENT (8 - 12 MINUTES)

Continuity Exercises
Students jump rope during music. During music pause, students perform exercises i.e. push-ups, crab walk, curl-ups, arm circles, stretches, etc.

See DPESS Chapter 16 for details.
Scatter formation
Use music to make fitness fun.

Continuity Exercises are a form of interval training. Interval training helps prevent the injuries associated with repetitive endurance exercise. Interval training allows you to increase your training intensity without overtraining or burn-out. In this way, adding intervals to your workout routine is a good way to cross train.

LESSON FOCUS (15 - 20 MINUTES)

Stances: Demonstrate the following stances.
2-point stance; 3-point stance; 4-point stance

See DPESS Chapter 19 for details.
Have students demonstrate when you call out 2, 3 or 4
Use whistle mixer to make groups of 3 for Task Sheet.

Centering the Ball Task Sheet
Model task sheet activities

Have equipment and task sheets in designated areas.

Linemen usually get down in a stance where they have at least one hand on the ground when the ball is snapped.

GAME (5 MINUTES)

Mad Scramble
Student tries to pull the flags on others while protecting their own flag from being pulled off.

Scatter formation
Use Whistle Mixer to me groups of 7 with assigned color flags.

EVALUATION/REVIEW AND CHEER

Review types of Stances and elements of Centering the Ball.
What is the position linemen use?
What muscles were used in class today?

Cheer: 5, 3,1, Flag Football is Really Fun!!

Reciprocal Task Sheet: Centering the Ball

Doer: ______________________ **"Shagger"**: ______________________

Observer: ______________________

Directions: Work in groups of three. Place your first and last name on lines provided. One person performs the task while the other acts as a quarterback; the third person is the observer. The observer will check "yes" or "no" in the appropriate box after the task is performed while providing feedback to the doer. Rotate roles after 10 attempts. Each student will turn in a task sheet.

Objective: The student will demonstrate the 2, 3, 4-Point Stance using technique demonstrated by the instructor.

Check "Yes" (Y) or "No" (N)

	Y/N	Y/N	Y/N	Y/N	Y/N	Y/N	Y/N	Y/N	Y/N	Y/N
Position yourself so that you reach for the ball.										
Bend over and grasp the ball over the laces.										
Left hand on top of ball with fingers parallel to the seams.										
Ball tilts slightly upwards.										
Head between the legs.										
Eyes on the receiver.										
Throw ball between legs.										
Both arms pull backward and upward.										
Ball spirals in air on its way to the quarterback.										

Flag Football Lesson Plan 4

EQUIPMENT:

30 Small cones
20 Scavenger Hunt Direction cards
1 Task sheet per student
1 Pencil and clipboard per 3 students

1 Hoop per student
1 Exercise CD/tape
1 CD/Cassette player
30 Footballs

OBJECTIVES:

The student will:

1. Participate in the Blob Tag demonstrating agility, speed, coordination and cooperation during the Introductory Activity following the instructions established by the instructor.
2. Participate in Fitness Scavenger Hunt during the fitness portion of class following the instructions established by the instructor..
3. Demonstrate Shoulder and Pass Blocks and complete the Spinning Drill Task Sheet using activities demonstrated by the instructor and following instructions established by the instructor.
4. Participate in Hoops and Plyometrics demonstrating agility and cooperative skills during the game portion of class using form demonstrated by the instructor.

National Standards Met in this Lesson: 1, 2, 3, 4, 5, 6

INSTRUCTIONAL ACTIVITIES	TEACHING HINTS
INTRODUCTORY ACTIVITY (2 - 3 MINUTES)	
Blob Tag	**See DPESS Chapter 14 for details.**
Last person in the chain tags.	Scatter formation
	Select first taggers
FITNESS DEVELOPMENT (8 - 12 MINUTES)	
Fitness Scavenger Hunt	**See DPESS Chapter 16 for details.**
Set up 10 stations. Each group has cards giving hints to each station where exercise directions are given.	Scatter formation
	Use whistle mixer to create groups of 4
LESSON FOCUS (15 - 20 MINUTES)	
Shoulder and Pass Blocks and Spinning Drill Task Sheet, next page of LP book.	**See DPESS Chapter 19 for details.**
	Use whistle mixer to make groups of 3. Have equipment and task sheets at designated areas.

Blocking is engaging an opponent in an effort to keep him from getting to a specific part of the field or player.

GAME (5 MINUTES)	
Hoops and Plyometrics	**See DPESS Chapter 14 for details.**
On signal, the students are challenged to move in and out of hoops using a specific movement. Resume jogging on signal with hoop being rolled or held.	Scatter formation. Students' locomote until directions given.
	Music can be used to cue. Create a tape with 20 seconds of music and 20 seconds of no music. During the music students perform your first locomotor direction, during the silence, they perform your directed Plyometrics activity.

EVALUATION/REVIEW AND CHEER

Discuss skills worked on in the lesson: Passing, Catching, Centering, Stances, Blocks
What muscles were used in class today?
Was there any one Fitness Scavenger Hunt instruction that was really challenging?

Cheer: Flag Football is the Game to Play!!

Reciprocal Task Sheet: Shoulder and Pass Blocks; Spinning

Doer: ______________________ **Defensive Player/Blocker**: ______________________

Observer: ______________________

Directions: You will work in groups of three. Place first and last name on lines provided above. One person performs the task while the other acts as a defensive player or blocker. The third person will be the observer and check "yes" or "no" after each performance while providing feedback to the doer. Perform the task ten times and rotate positions. Each student will turn in a task sheet.

Objective:
1. The student will execute the shoulder and block pass 10 times using technique demonstrated by the instructor.
2. The student will demonstrate the proper spinning technique ten times using technique demonstrated by the teacher.

Check "Yes" (Y) or "No" (N)

	Y/N	Y/N	Y/N	Y/N	Y/N	Y/N	Y/N	Y/N	Y/N	Y/N
Shoulder Block										
Begin in a 3- or 4-point stance.										
Move forward making shoulder contact with defensive player at chest level.										
Head between opponent and the ball carrier.										
Elbows are out.										
Hands held near the chest.										
Pass Block										
Begin in a 2-, 3- or 4-point stance.										
Move backward slightly with your rear foot as the opponent charges.										
Stay between the quarterback and the rusher.										
Spinning										
Jog towards defensive player.										
As defensive player approaches, turn 360 degrees (full circle) in a spinning motion.										
Fast Footwork										
Defensive player stays square in front of the ball carrier.										

Flag Football Lesson Plan 5

EQUIPMENT:

1 Task Sheet per student
1 Football per 3 students
40 Small cones
1 Pencil and clipboard per 3 students
1 Exercise CD/tape
1 CD/Tape player

OBJECTIVES:

The student will:

1. Participate in the Run and Assume Pose demonstrating agility, speed, coordination and cooperation during the Introductory Activity following the instructions established by the instructor.
2. Participate in Circuit Training during the fitness portion of class following the instructions established by the instructor..
3. Demonstrate Hand-offs and Punting completing the Task Sheet using activities demonstrated by the instructor and following instructions established by the instructor.
4. Participate in Foot Tag demonstrating agility and cooperative skills during the game portion of class using form demonstrated by the instructor.

National Standards Met in this Lesson: **1, 2, 3, 4, 5, 6**

INSTRUCTIONAL ACTIVITIES | **TEACHING HINTS**

INTRODUCTORY ACTIVITY (2 - 3 MINUTES)

Run and Assume Pose

See DPESS Chapter 14 for details.
Scatter formation

FITNESS DEVELOPMENT (8 - 12 MINUTES)

Circuit Training: Rotate stations at music intervals
Jogging; Sit-ups; Jumping jacks; Push-ups; Hop in place; Stretch; Reverse push-ups; Jump rope; Arm circles

See DPESS Chapter 16 for details.
Use whistle mixer to create groups of 4. Continuity CD/tape to signal time at each station.

Positive exercise habits formed now can carry over into adulthood and help reduce morbidity and mortality from Type II diabetes, cardiovascular disease (CVD) and other chronic ailments.

LESSON FOCUS (15 - 20 MINUTES)

Hand-Off and Punting Task Sheet
Explain task sheets and demonstrate as written.
Have each group go to designated areas

See DPESS Chapter 19 for details.
Use whistle mixer to make groups of 4. Have Equipment and task sheets at designated areas.

A punt usually occurs on fourth down and is designed to drive the other team back as far as possible before they take possession of the ball.

GAME (5 MINUTES)

Foot Tag
Students face a partner with hands on shoulders. On signal, students try to touch each other's toes.

See DPESS Chapter 14 for details.
Use toe-to-toe to create groups of 2. Use whistle for signal. Do not stomp toes.

EVALUATION/REVIEW AND CHEER

Review elements of the Hand-Off and Punting Skills
Why is it important to develop positive exercise habits now?

Cheer: We love football!

Reciprocal Task Sheet: Hand-Off Pass

Doer: ___________________________ **Center**: ______________________

Receiver: ________________________ **Observer**: _____________________

Directions: You will work in groups of four. Place first and last name on task sheet. One person performs the task, one is the center and the other a receiver. The fourth person is the observer who marks "yes" or "no" in the box after each attempt while providing feedback. Perform the task ten times and rotate positions. Each student will turn in a task sheet.

Rotation: **Passer =>** **Center=>** **Receiver=>** **Observer=>**

Objective: The student will execute the proper hand-off pass 10 times as demonstrated by the instructor.

Check "Yes" (Y) or "No" (N)

	Y/N	Y/N	Y/N	Y/N	Y/N	Y/N	Y/N	Y/N	Y/N	Y/N
Ball is held with both hands.										
When receiver is 6 feet away, switch ball to hand nearest to receiver.										
Elbow bent and partially away from the body.										
Receiver approaches quarterback with the near arm bent and in front of the chest.										
Other arm is about waist high, with the palm up.										
As ball is exchanged, receiver clamps down on the ball to secure it.										

Reciprocal Task Sheet: Punting

Doer: ___________________________ **Center**: ______________________

Receiver: ________________________ **Observer**: _____________________

Directions: Students will remain in groups of four. Place first and last name on lines provided above. One person performs the task, a second person acts as center and the third person shags the ball. The fourth person is the observer who marks "yes" or "no" after each attempt while providing feedback. Perform the task 10 times and rotate positions. Each student will turn in a task sheet.

Rotation: **Punter =>** **Center =>** **Shagger =>** **Observer=>**

Objective: The student will execute a punt 10 times using technique as demonstrated by the instructor.

Check "Yes" (Y) or "No" (N)

	Y/N	Y/N	Y/N	Y/N	Y/N	Y/N	Y/N	Y/N	Y/N	Y/N
Begin in a standing position with arms extended to receive the ball.										
Kicking foot is placed slightly forward.										
Center passes ball to you.										
After receiving the ball, take two steps forward beginning with your dominant foot										
Ball is slightly turned in and held waist high.										
Kicking leg is swung forward, as impact knee is straightened to provide maximum force on kick.										
Toes are pointed.										
The long axis of the ball makes contact on instep.										
Ball is dropped rather than tossed into the air.										

Flag Football Lesson Plan 6

EQUIPMENT:

Flag football rules and strategy handouts
3 Individual jump ropes per station
Continuity Music CD/Tape & Player
1 cone per station

OBJECTIVES:

The student will:

1. Participate in Rubber Band demonstrating agility, speed, coordination and cooperation during the Introductory Activity following the instructions established by the instructor.
2. Participate in Jump and Jog Fitness following the instructions established by the instructor..
3. Participate in class discussions following the reading of the Rules, Strategy and Plays handout following instructions established by the instructor.
4. Participate in Sitting Wrestle demonstrating agility and cooperative skills during the game portion of class using form demonstrated by the instructor.

National Standards Met in this Lesson: **1, 2, 3, 4, 5, 6**

INSTRUCTIONAL ACTIVITIES / TEACHING HINTS

INTRODUCTORY ACTIVITY (2 - 3 MINUTES)

Rubber Band

Students move away from instructor performing a locomotor movement (jump, hop, slide, etc.). On signal, students run back to instructor

See DPESS Chapter 14 for details.

Scatter formation. Use whistle for signals

FITNESS DEVELOPMENT (8 - 12 MINUTES)

Jump and Jog Fitness

One partner jumps rope at the cone, other jogs around the circle. Change roles.

Variations in moving around circle:

- Slide
- Carioca
- Power Skip

See DPESS Chapter 16 for details.

Use continuity music CD/tape to signal activity change.
Set up 5 – 6 cones in a circle in gym
3 Jump ropes at each cone

LESSON FOCUS (15 - 20 MINUTES)

Flag Football Rules, Strategies and Plays

Prepare handouts for home studying.

See DPESS Chapter 19 for details.

Explain rules, positions, plays and game strategies.

GAME (5 MINUTES)

Sitting Wrestle

Sit on floor facing partner. Bend legs, feet flat on floor, toes touching, and hands grasped.

Use toe-to-toe to create groups of 2.
Try to pull partner's buttocks off floor.

EVALUATION/REVIEW AND CHEER

Review rules of Flag Football.
What muscles were used in class today?
What was the most challenging about Sitting Wrestle?

Cheer: 1, 2, 3 Football Helps Me!

Flag Football Lesson Plan 7

EQUIPMENT:

20 Footballs
1 Individual Jump rope per 2 students
1 Task sheet per student for skills test
1 Pencil and clipboard per 3 students
1 Exercise CD/music & 1 CD/ Music player
Fitness station cards you create

OBJECTIVES:

The student will:

1. Participate in Triangle Tag demonstrating agility, speed, coordination and cooperation during the Introductory Activity following the instructions established by the instructor.
2. Participate in Partner Racetrack Fitness following the instructions established by the instructor.
3. Participate in class completing the Flag Football Skills Test following instructions established by the instructor.
4. Participate in Spider Tag demonstrating agility and cooperative skills during the game portion of class using form demonstrated by the instructor.

National Standards Met in this Lesson: **1, 2, 3, 4, 5, 6**

INSTRUCTIONAL ACTIVITIES	TEACHING HINTS
INTRODUCTORY ACTIVITY (2 - 3 MINUTES)	
Triangle Tag Form a triangle by holding hands. One person puts flag in pocket. Person with flag is leader. Group tries to keep leader from getting flags pulled. When flag pulled, leader becomes tagger and tagger becomes leader.	**See DPESS Chapter 14 for details.** Use whistle mixer, make groups of 3 Choose 3 people to be the taggers
FITNESS DEVELOPMENT (8 - 12 MINUTES)	
Partner Racetrack Fitness 10 stations in circular track formation. Each station has task card with exercise to perform. 2 students perform task while other 2 run around track.	**See DPESS Chapter 16 for details.** Use whistle mixer, create groups of 4. Use toe-to-toe to make partners. Use music for motivation.
LESSON FOCUS (15 - 20 MINUTES)	
Flag Football Skills Test	Assign students to groups and testing areas.
Explain reciprocal task sheet for self-testing.	Distribute clipboards, pencils and task sheets.
GAME (5 MINUTES)	
Spider Tag Students work in partners. One pair of students are "it", and chases other pairs. When tagged, they become "it".	**See DPESS Chapter 14 for details.** Scatter formation in pairs Back-to-back, elbows locked.

EVALUATION/REVIEW AND CHEER

Review rules of Flag Football for Written Exam.
What muscles were used in class today?

Cheer: Let's Play Football!!

Reciprocal Task Sheet: Flag Football Skills Test

Doer: ____________________________ **Catcher/Defender**: ________________________

Observer: ________________________

Directions: Work with 2 other students. Place all names on your task sheet. One person is the "doer", one-person catches, throws, defends, while the third person is the observer. Observer checks "yes" or "no" and provides feedback and completes task sheet. Rotate positions upon completion of task sheet. Each person turns in a task sheet.

Check "Yes" (Y) or "No" (N)

	Y/N	Y/N	Y/N	Y/N	Y/N	Y/N	Y/N	Y/N	Y/N	Y/N
Passing										
Pass ball 10 yards										
Catching										
Catch ball 5 times in a row from a 10 yard pass										
Centering Ball										
Center ball and "hike" 5 times.										
Blocks										
Perform shoulder block on partner										
Perform pass block with partner										
Hand Off										
Hand off to the right										
Hand off to the left										
Punting										
Punt ball 5 times										

Flag Football Lesson Plan 8

EQUIPMENT:

1 Exam per student
1 Pencil per student
1 Flag set per student
2 tumbling mats per 4 students
3 benches; high jump bar; jumping box/ 4 students
1 Football per game

OBJECTIVES:

The student will:

1. Participate in Move, Stop and Pivot demonstrating agility, speed, coordination and cooperation during the Introductory Activity following the instructions established by the instructor.
2. Participate in the Mini-Challenge Course cooperating with classmates and following the instructions established by the instructor..
3. Complete the written exam administrated in class following instructions established by the instructor.
4. Participate in a game of Flag Football demonstrating agility, cooperative skills, and football skills learned in this unit demonstrating form presented by the instructor.

National Standards Met in this Lesson: **1, 2, 3, 4, 5, 6**

INSTRUCTIONAL ACTIVITIES	TEACHING HINTS

INTRODUCTORY ACTIVITY (2 - 3 MINUTES)

Move, Stop and Pivot
Students use locomotor movement; on signal they stop then pivot and resume movement.

See DPESS Chapter 14 for details.
Scatter formation
Teacher directs movements

FITNESS DEVELOPMENT (8 - 12 MINUTES)

Mini-Challenge Course
Start lying face down; Run around 2 chairs; Run; Hurdle over 3 benches; High jump over bar; Crab walk length of mat feet first; Agility run around 3 chairs; Forward roll length of mat; Vault 36 over a jumping box.

See DPESS Chapter 16 for details.
Set up course with space between stations

In addition to the health benefits of regular exercise, youth who are physically fit sleep better and are better able to handle the physical and emotional challenges that a typical day presents - running to catch a bus, bending down to tie a shoe, listening in class, or studying for a test.

LESSON FOCUS (15 MINUTES)

Written Exam

Every student will take the written exam.

GAME (10 MINUTES)

Flag Football

Use management game to divide the class into teams.

EVALUATION/REVIEW AND CHEER

Review game play and questions from written exam.
What muscles were used during today's class?

Cheer: 1, 4, 6, 8 The Game Was Great!!

Flag Football Lesson Plan 9

EQUIPMENT:

1 Football per game
1 Flag set per student
Fitness CD/tape
CD/Cassette player

OBJECTIVES:

The student will:

1. Participate in Mini Pyramids demonstrating agility, speed, coordination and cooperation during the Introductory Activity following the instructions established by the instructor.
2. Participate in the Aerobic Workout during the fitness portion of class and following the instructions established by the instructor..
3. Participate in the Flag Football Tournament demonstrating agility, cooperative skills, and knowledge of rules and football skills learned in this unit demonstrating form presented by the instructor.

National Standards Met in this Lesson: 1, 2, 3, 4, 5, 6

	TEACHING HINTS
INTRODUCTORY ACTIVITY (2 - 3 MINUTES)	
Mini Pyramids	**See DPESS Chapter 18 for details.**
Perform locomotor movement. On signal students find a partner and build pyramid or partner stand.	Scatter formation. Find new partner each time Stand on proper points of support
FITNESS DEVELOPMENT (8 - 12 MINUTES)	
Aerobic Workout	**See DPESS Chapter 16 for details.**
See Racquetball, Lesson 7 for complete details.	Scatter formation Use CD/tape to direct exercise
LESSON FOCUS AND GAME (20 MINUTES)	
Flag Football Tournament	Create teams using management game
EVALUATION/REVIEW AND CHEER	
Discuss tournament play and review any rules necessary.	
Cheer: 3, 2, 1 Football is fun!	

Flag Football Lesson Plan 10

EQUIPMENT:

2 Footballs
1 Flag set per student

OBJECTIVES:

The student will:

1. Participate in the Mass Stand Up Introductory Activity demonstrating agility, speed, coordination and cooperation following the instructions established by the instructor.
2. Participate in Random Running during the fitness portion of class following the instructions by the instructor..
3. Participate in the Flag Football Tournament demonstrating agility, cooperative skills, knowledge of rules and football skills learned in this unit demonstrating form presented by the instructor.

National Standards Met in this Lesson: 1, 2, 3, 4, 5, 6

INSTRUCTIONAL ACTIVITIES	TEACHING HINTS
INTRODUCTORY ACTIVITY (2 - 3 MINUTES)	
Mass Stand Up	**See DPESS Chapter 18 for details.**
Students sitting back to back. Lock elbows and try to stand up.	Scatter formation
FITNESS DEVELOPMENT (8 - 12 MINUTES)	
Random Running	**See DPESS Chapter 16 for details.**
Students run around at own pace. On signal, students will perform assigned exercise	Continuous movement Motivate students with music
LESSON FOCUS AND GAME (20 MINUTES)	
Flag Football Tournament	Continue with teams from yesterday.
EVALUATION/REVIEW AND CHEER	
Discuss tournament play and introduce next unit. What muscles were challenged in class today? What was the most challenging about today's games?	**Cheer: Teamwork wins games!**

Orienteering

OBJECTIVES:

The student will:

1. Move and set up or knock down cones as demonstrated by the instructor.
2. Demonstrate balance and coordination in the Triangle Plus One Tag while following the safety rules as explained by the instructor.
3. Demonstrate agility and coordination in the Weave Drill One Tag while following the safety rules as explained by the instructor.
4. Participate in the Partner Fitness Racetrack to improve his/her personal fitness.
5. Participate in parachute fitness as demonstrated by the instructor.
6. Participate in the fitness obstacle courses using a task sheet as explained by the instructor.
7. Study the use and operation of a compass.
8. Read class safety rules and obtain signature to demonstrate understanding as discussed by the instructor.
9. Complete task sheets covering orienteering activities.
10. Complete a mini-orienteering course as explained by the instructor.
11. Participate in the Orienteering Course Challenge in squads demonstrating the rules and skills learned during the unit.
12. Pass a knowledge test covering the elements of orienteering with a score of 70% or better.

ORIENTEERING BLOCK PLAN
2 WEEK UNIT

Week #1	Monday	Tuesday	Wednesday	Thursday	Friday
Introductory Activity	Combination Movements	Cone up, Cone down	Blob Tag	Follow the Leader	Hoops on the Ground
Fitness	Parachute Fitness Activity	Partner Racetrack Fitness	Circuit Training	Continuity Exercises	Partner Racetrack Fitness
Lesson Focus	Class Rules & Orienteering	Compassing Introductory Activity	Compassing and Bearings	Bearings and Landmarks	Numbers and Numerals
Game	Hula Hoop Pass	Stream Crossing	Boardwalk	Faith Fall and Trust Dive	Snowball Tag Relay

Week #2	Monday	Tuesday	Wednesday	Thursday	Friday
Introductory Activity	Triangle Plus 1 Tag	Weave Drill	Square Drill	Back-to-Back	Push-up Tag
Fitness	Challenge Course	Partner Racetrack Fitness	Challenge Course	Circuit Training	Walk-Jog-Sprint
Lesson Focus	Mt. Robson I	Quiz	Orienteering Course	Orienteering Challenge	Point-to-Point Orienteering
Game	Knots	Bowling Pin Relay	Snowball Tag Relay	Grass in the Wind	Hula Hoop Pass

Orienteering Lesson Plan 1

EQUIPMENT:

Whistle
Class safety rules handout
7 hula-hoops
2 parachutes
CD/Tape player
Pre-recorded continuity CD/tape

OBJECTIVES:

The student will:

1. Participate in parachute fitness activities demonstrating focus and maximum participation to improve their fitness levels.
2. Demonstrate proper pacing technique as demonstrated by the instructor.
3. Participate in the Reciprocal Task Sheet 1, Pacing Your Steps, following the instructions.
4. Participate in Hula Hoop Pass as directed by the instructor.

National Standards Met in this Lesson: **1, 2, 3, 4, 5, 6**

INSTRUCTIONAL ACTIVITIES	TEACHING HINTS

INTRODUCTORY ACTIVITY (2 - 3 MINUTES)

Combination Movements (Similar to Move and Change the Type of Locomotion) Examples: Hop and turn around; Skip and freeze; Jump turn 180 degrees; Hop and make a pose; Create own moves; Jump, roll, jump up	**See DPESS Chapter 14 for details.** Scattered formation. Direct students to skip. Students will move in space until signal is given to change movements.

FITNESS DEVELOPMENT (8 - 12 MINUTES)

Parachute Fitness Activities Use fitness music CD/tape with 45 sec. for locomotor movements followed by a 20 second music silence for strengthening and stretching.	**See DPESS Chapter 16 for details.** Around parachute.

A parachute is usually a soft fabric device used to slow the motion of an object through an atmosphere. We use it in fitness activities to provide resistance and fun.

LESSON FOCUS (15 - 20 MINUTES)

Class Safety Rules Handout **Introduction to Orienteering** History; standard course; types of courses; describe the differences between feet and meters; pacing activity	**See DPESS Chapter 21 for details.** Scattered formation Pacing activity: students walk the area and find a landmark to pace their steps

Orienteering is a walking and running sport involving navigation with a map and compass.

GAME (5 MINUTES)

Hula Hoop Pass Students will pass the hoop around the circle until it returns to the start without breaking hands.	**See DPESS Chapter 18 for details.** Circle formation. Joined hands. Approximately 5 people per circle. Use Whistle Mixer to create groups.

Early materials used to make hoops include grapevines and stiff grasses.

EVALUATION/REVIEW AND CHEER

Review safety rules, pacing, and types of orienteering courses.

Cheer: Orienteering helps me chart my course!

RECIPROCAL TASK SHEET 1: PACING YOUR STEPS

Doer:_______________________________ **Observer:**____________________

Timer:_______________________________

Directions: Work in groups of three. Doer: Find a landmark in the area and pace your steps to that point. Observer: Watch the posture of doer and give feedback. Timer: Write down the time it takes the doer to get to the landmark. Rotate roles.

List the Landmark:______________________________________

Steps needed to reach landmark:__________ Time to travel to landmark:________

Posture evaluation	Yes	No
Head up facing forward		
Shoulders straight (back as sometimes stated)		
Back upright and in good alignment		
Knees extended to 70 degrees on each stride		
Foot strikes ground in heel toe motion		
Medium size steps used to get to landmark		

High five your partner on completion of the task.

Orienteering Lesson Plan 2

EQUIPMENT:

CD/Tape player

25 cones; 25 carpet squares; 6 padded mats

Pre-recorded continuity CD/tape

36 task sheets; 36 clipboards w/pencils

OBJECTIVES:

The student will:

1. Demonstrate proper use of a compass as demonstrated by the instructor.
2. Participate and demonstrate group cooperation during Stream Crossing as demonstrated by the instructor.

National Standards Met in this Lesson: **1, 2, 3, 4, 5, 6**

INSTRUCTIONAL ACTIVITIES	ORGANIZATION TEACHING HINTS
INTRODUCTORY ACTIVITY (2 - 3 MINUTES)	
Cone up, Cone down On signal, students will move in the space provided and place the cones into their opposite positions.	Place cones, half upright and half on their sides. 2 teams of students designated "up" or "down" teams.
FITNESS (8 - 12 MINUTES)	
Partner Racetrack Fitness	**See DPESS Chapter 16 for details.**
LESSON FOCUS (15 - 20 MINUTES)	
Introduction to the Compass	**See DPESS Chapter 21 for details.** Students will follow the directions on the Task Sheet.
The compass consists of a magnetized pointer free to align itself accurately with Earth's magnetic field	
GAME (5 MINUTES)	
Stream Crossing The first team to move all members across the stream is the winner.	**See DPESS Chapter 21 for details.** Students will have to cooperate with each other in order to get their entire team across.
This activity helps increase cooperative team strategy.	
EVALUATION/REVIEW	
Review elements of reading the compass and cooperative skills developed in this lesson.	

TASK SHEET 2: COMPASSING INTRODUCTION

Name:____________________________ **Date:**______________________

Directions: You will complete this task sheet working on your own. Pick up a compass from your teacher. Read and answer the questions below. Upon completion, turn your compass and this task sheet into your teacher.

1. Place the safety cord on the compass around your wrist. Place the compass in the palm of your hand looking at the dial. Which direction is the needle pointing?

2. Turn the dial on the compass so the arrow lines up when the needle is pointing North. Which direction are you facing now? (Be sure you use the "direction-of-travel arrow)

   Turn yourself around 180 degrees. Which direction is the needle facing now?

3. Once you have established which direction is north, write down the buildings that are to the East.

4. Write down the buildings that are to the West.

5. Look around. Identify an object and write it down.________________ Identify the direction to which you are facing:__________________
   List which direction that object is in relation to you:________________

Return the compass and this paper to your instructor.

Orienteering Lesson Plan 3

EQUIPMENT:

CD/Tape player
1 buddy board per two students
1 compass per student
8 hula-hoops
1 Task Sheet per person

Pre-recorded continuity CD/tape
8 padded mats
1 task sheet per person
1 clipboard w/ pencil per person
8 jump ropes

OBJECTIVES:

The student will:

1. Demonstrate group cooperation in Blob Tag as directed by the instructor.
2. Participate in Circuit Training activities to improve fitness using form demonstrated by the instructor.
3. Demonstrate knowledge of bearings and arrive at the proper destination as demonstrated by the instructor.
4. Play Boardwalk following the instructions and demonstrating a cooperative spirit.

National Standards Met in this Lesson: **1, 2, 3, 4, 5, 6**

INSTRUCTIONAL ACTIVITIES | **ORGANIZATION TEACHING HINTS**

INTRODUCTORY ACTIVITY (2 - 3 MINUTES)

Blob Tag

See DPESS Chapter 14 for details.
Scattered formation

FITNESS DEVELOPMENT (8 - 12 MINUTES)

Circuit Training
Students will execute fitness drills at different stations moving to continuity exercise CD/tape.
Stations include:
Curl-ups on mats
Individual jump roping
Hula Hooping
Stations with other strength and flexibility activities
Mountain climber activities
Jumping Jacks
Push-ups

See DPESS Chapter 16 for details.
When the music ends, students rotate to next station and perform exercise listed.

This activity will increase cardiorespiratory and cardiovascular strength.

LESSON FOCUS (15 - 20 MINUTES)

Compassing and Bearings Task Sheet

See DPESS Chapter 21 for details.
Task Sheet provided that gives directions and degrees to follow.

The traditional form (sometimes referred to as "Foot Orienteering" or "Foot-O") involves cross-country running.

GAME (5 MINUTES)

Boardwalk
Students will use buddy walkers and work together in walking from a beginning point to a finish point.

See DPESS Chapter 21 for details.

Maintaining excellent balance will increase your success in this activity.

EVALUATION/REVIEW

Review activities on Task Sheet.

TASK SHEET 3: COMPASSING AND BEARINGS

Name:__________________________________**Date:**_________________________

Directions: You will complete this task sheet working on your own. Pick up a compass from your teacher.

1. Complete the Compass Check List Below.
2. Complete the Bearings Section Below.

Compass Check List: For each item listed in the Record Bearing Section Below, answer these questions:

	Yes	**No**
Is the compass lying flat on a surface?		
Is the magnetic needle lined up with the North index line?		
Select a target and line up the direction-of-travel arrow with the object you have selected.		
Record the bearing that is lined up with the Index line and the direction-of-travel line.		

Bearings Section

Object	**Bearings**	**Object**	**Bearings**
Gym		Swimming Pool	
School Library		Tennis Courts	
Garden		Cafeteria	
Parking Lot		Write in:	

Congratulations on completing this task sheet. Turn this task sheet and your equipment in to your instructor.

Orienteering Lesson Plan 4

EQUIPMENT:

CD/Tape player
1 compass per student
1 clipboard w/pencil per person
4 jumping boxes or elevated platforms
Pre-recorded continuity CD/tape
1 task sheet per person

OBJECTIVES:

The student will:

1. Participate in Continuity Exercises for fitness using form demonstrated by the instructor.
2. Demonstrate landmark recognition as demonstrated by the instructor and following the task sheet activities.
3. Demonstrate imaginative locomotor skills during Follow the Leader during the Introductory Activity.

National Standards Met in this Lesson: **1, 2, 3, 4, 5, 6**

INSTRUCTIONAL ACTIVITIES / **TEACHING HINTS**

INTRODUCTORY ACTIVITY (2 - 3 MINUTES)

Follow the Leader
Students will alternate leading in a single file line performing an imaginative locomotor skill.

See DPESS Chapter 14 for details.
Single file line
Alternate leaders

FITNESS DEVELOPMENT (8 - 12 MINUTES)

Continuity Exercises
When the music changes the instructor will demonstrate a new skill for the class to perform.

See DPESS Chapter 16 for details.
The CD/tape should have 30 seconds of music followed by a 20 second blank repeat the pattern for 8 minutes.

This activity will increase cardiorespiratory and cardiovascular strength.

LESSON FOCUS (15 - 20 MINUTES)

Bearings and Landmarks

See DPESS Chapter 21 for details.
See Task Sheet listing bearings and topographical items.
Make groups of 3 students for task sheet completion.

The English name derives from the Swedish word "orienteering".

GAME (5 MINUTES)

Faith Fall and Trust Dive

See DPESS Chapter 21 for details.
Stress safety and trust during this activity.

The students catching must maintain strong core stance and protect their trusting partner.

EVALUATION/REVIEW

Review what was needed to help "Faith and Fall" be successful.
Discuss elements covered on Bearings and Landmarks Task Sheet.

TASK SHEET 4: BEARINGS AND LANDMARKS

Doer:________________________________ **Observer:**______________________

Timer:________________________________

Directions: Work in groups of three. Doer: Find a landmark in the area and pace your steps to that point. Observer: Read the map and guide the doer to the landmark. Timer: Write down the time it takes the doer to get to the landmark. There are six landmarks on this map, so everyone should perform each skill twice. Rotate roles.

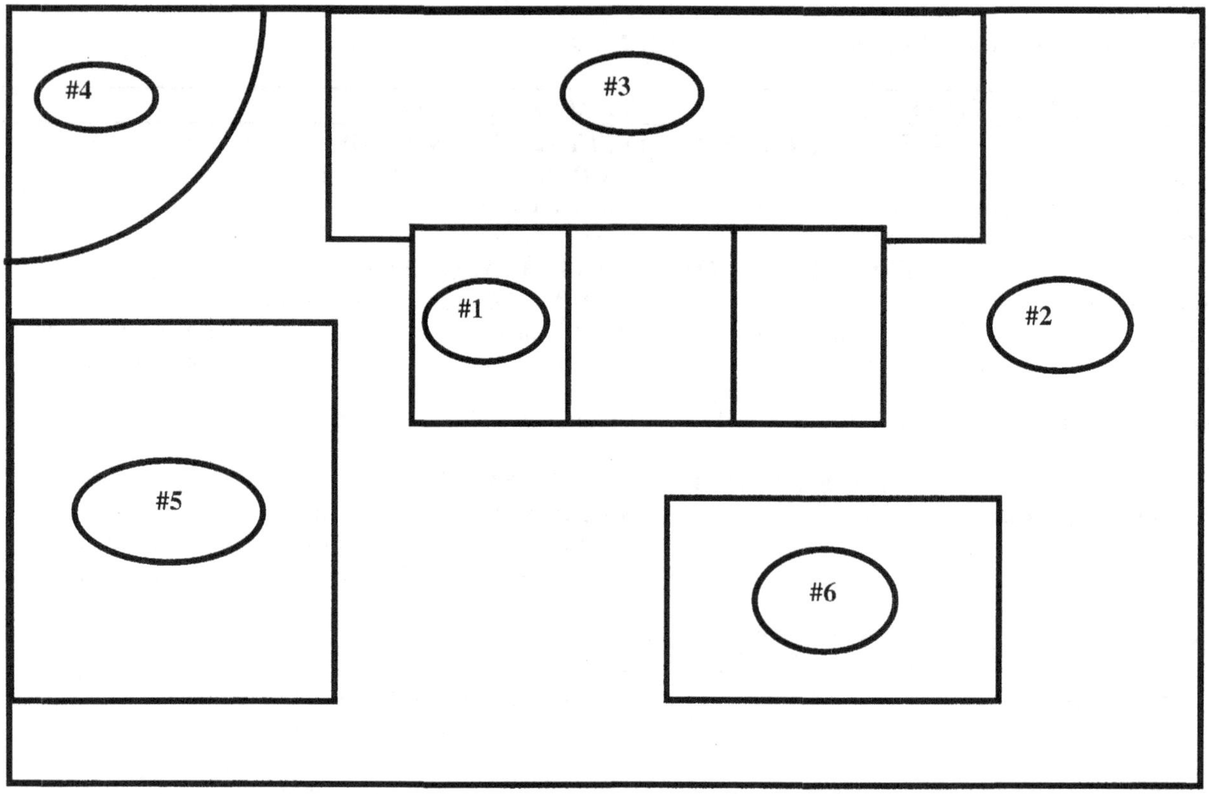

Bearings for Check points / Time and Paces (ex: 120°/2:35/215)	
#1	#4
#2	#5
#3	#6

Orienteering Lesson Plan 5

EQUIPMENT:

CD/Tape player
1 compass per person
1 clipboard w/pencil per person
Pre-recorded continuity CD/tape
1 task sheet per person
8 hula-hoops

OBJECTIVES:

The student will:

1. Participate in Hoops on the Ground demonstrating safety and agility skills taught in class.
2. Demonstrate bearing recognition using their compass as demonstrated by the instructor.
3. Complete the task sheet on Numbers and Numerals as directed by the instructor.
4. Play Snowball Tag Rally demonstrating cooperative skills, agility, and following the safety instructions presented by the instructor.

National Standards Met in this Lesson: **1, 2, 3, 4, 5, 6**

INSTRUCTIONAL ACTIVITIES	ORGANIZATION TEACHING HINTS

INTRODUCTORY ACTIVITY (2 - 3 MINUTES)

Hoops on the Ground
Students will perform an instructor selected locomotor movement run around a group of hula-hoops on the floor.

See DPESS Chapter 14 for details.
Scattered formation
When the teacher blows the whistle a given number of times that number of students that should go into a hoop.

FITNESS DEVELOPMENT (8 - 12 MINUTES)

Partner Racetrack Fitness
Modify activities with a variety of options such as arm curls, fist pull apart, back builder, etc.

See DPESS Chapter 16 for details.
Allow students to work in groups to encourage fun with fitness.

LESSON FOCUS (15 - 20 MINUTES)

Numbers and Numerals
Students will use their compasses and stand on a number on the floor. They will then find the bearings for the corresponding numeral on the walls around them.

See DPESS Chapter 21 for details.

Orienteering originated in Scandinavia, as a military survival exercise in the late 19th century.

GAME (5 MINUTES)

More than one person will be "it" to begin the game and the team with the most people at the end wins.

Snowball Tag Relay
Modify the game with the introduction of two separate teams. The team that catches the most people, or has more people in their line at the end, wins the relays.

See DPESS Chapter 18 for details.

EVALUATION/REVIEW

How does Partner Racetrack Fitness help you?
Review elements of compass reading that students may still need to work on.
How did the sport of Orienteering come to be?

TASK SHEET 5: NUMBERS AND NUMERALS

Name:__________________________________ **Date:**_________________________

Directions: You will complete this task sheet working on your own. Pick up a compass from your teacher. Look for a number on the ground. Then look for the corresponding Roman numeral on the wall. Write down the bearing for each number.

NUMBERS AND NUMERALS

NUMBER&NUMERAL	BEARING	NUMBER&NUMERAL	BEARING
1/ I		**6/ VI**	
2/ II		**7/ VII**	
3/ III		**8/ VIII**	
4/ IV		**9/ IX**	
5/ V		**10/ X**	

Orienteering Lesson Plan 6

EQUIPMENT:

12 jump ropes
CD/Tape player
36 compasses
8 hula-hoops
6 jumping blocks
Pre-recorded continuity CD/tape
36 task sheets; 36 clipboards w/pencils

OBJECTIVES:

The student will:

1. Improve target heart rate during the lesson focus as directed by the instructor.
2. Complete the Challenge Course at their own pace as demonstrated by the instructor.

National Standards Met in this Lesson: **1, 2, 3, 4, 5, 6**

INSTRUCTIONAL ACTIVITIES	ORGANIZATION TEACHING HINTS

INTRODUCTORY ACTIVITY (2 – 3 MINUTES)

Triangle Plus One Tag
Students must cooperate with peers to accomplish task.

See DPESS Chapter 14 for details.

FITNESS DEVELOPMENT (8 – 12 MINUTES)

Challenge Course
Jump over blocks, hop through hops, rope jump, jog, run around cones, etc.

See DPESS Chapter 16 for details.

This activity will challenge each student's ability to adapt to new challenges in a short period of time.

LESSON FOCUS (15 – 20 MINUTES)

Students are in squads to receive the orienteering assignment. Briefly explain the task sheet and have the students move onto the track.

The competitive Orienteering sport form began in Norway in 1897.

Hiking the Mountains Task Sheet #6
This activity is for pacing as well as improving target heart rate during the activity.

See DPESS Chapter 21 for details.
Students walk the track at their pace. Concentrate on personal stride and answering questions on the sheet.

GAME (5 MINUTES)

"Knots" (Entanglement)
Group leader moves the hands of his/her squad until everyone has someone else's hands and are in "knots."

See DPESS Chapter 18 for details.
Students proceed to work cooperatively with peers to "untangle" themselves.

Knot – a fastening or securing of linear material such as rope, by tying or interweaving

EVALUATION/REVIEW AND CHEER

Review elements included in Task Sheet.
What muscles were used in today's Challenge Course?
When and where did the competitive sport of Orienteering begin?
What forms are you creating in the game Entanglement?

Cheer: Fitness and hiking are really fun!

TASK SHEET 6: HOW MANY STEPS TO HIKE THE MOUNTAINS?

Name:____________________________________ **Date:**__________________________

Description: The mountains surrounding Los Angeles extend approximately 30 miles. One of the largest peaks is Mount Wilson. Your task is to find out how many steps it takes to reach Mount Wilson.

1. How many steps will it take?
   Walk one lap around a ¼ mile track. Count every right footstep and keep track of the amount of time it takes to complete the lap. Record your results. Repeat three times. Calculate the average.
   ½ steps:_______________ Time:__________
   ½ steps:_______________ Time:__________
   ½ steps:_______________ Time:__________
   Average:_______________ Average:_______________
2. How many half steps per ¼ mile? ____________
3. How many half steps per mile? _____________
4. How many full steps per mile? ______________
5. How many steps for the entire mountain range? ____________
6. It would take me _________ steps to hike the mountains around Los Angeles.

Orienteering Lesson Plan 7

EQUIPMENT:

4 Bowling Pins per 5 – 6 students
Continuity CD/tape
1 jump rope per 6 students
CD/Tape player
1 mat per 2 students for fitness activities

OBJECTIVES:

The student will:

1. Work cooperatively with their group to make a challenging fitness routine utilizing strength, agility, flexibility and endurance activities demonstrated by the instructor in class.
2. Pass the written quiz with a 70% or higher as directed by the instructor.
3. Participate in Bowling Pin Relay during the game activity as demonstrated by the instructor.

National Standards Met in this Lesson: **1, 2, 3, 4, 5, 6**

INSTRUCTIONAL ACTIVITIES	TEACHING HINTS

INTRODUCTORY ACTIVITY (2 - 3 MINUTES)

Weave Drill
Students shuffle at the signal of the instructor.

See DPESS Chapter 14 for details.
Scattered formation.

FITNESS DEVELOPMENT (8 - 12 MINUTES)

Modify activities with new options: push-ups, jump rope, stretching, sit-ups, back bends, jumping jacks
Work in groups to encourage each other in having fun with fitness.

Partner Racetrack Fitness

See DPESS Chapter 16 for details.
Students participate at their own fitness level.

LESSON FOCUS (15 - 20 MINUTES)

Written Quiz

GAME (5 MINUTES)

Bowling Pin Relay

See DPESS Chapter 18 for details.

This activity works on hand-eye coordination.

EVALUATION/REVIEW AND CHEER

What fitness activities did you perform today that provided the most challenge?

Were there any difficult areas on the quiz that you would like to discuss now?

Cheer: Orienteering… Can't wait!

Orienteering Lesson Plan 8

EQUIPMENT:

CD/Tape player & CD/tape for fitness
Hula-hoops for challenge course
6 jumping blocks
18 cones
12 jump ropes
Cones and signs for Challenge Course

OBJECTIVES:

The student will:

1. Participate in the Square Drill during the Introductory Activity portion of class following instructions established by the instructor.
2. Participate in the fitness Challenge Course using form demonstrated by the instructor at each station.
3. Complete the orienteering course as directed by the instructor.
4. Participate in the Snowball Tag relay during the game activity as demonstrated by the instructor.

National Standards Met in this Lesson: **1, 2, 3, 4, 5, 6**

INSTRUCTIONAL ACTIVITIES	TEACHING HINTS

INTRODUCTORY ACTIVITY (2 - 3 MINUTES)

Square Drill	**See DPESS Chapter 14 for details.** Students need to be aware of peers while moving around the perimeter.

This activity involves more fast-twitch muscle fibers than slow-twitch muscle fibers.

FITNESS DEVELOPMENT (8 - 12 MINUTES)

Challenge Course	**See DPESS Chapter 16 for details.**

This activity may help improve body composition if practiced daily.

LESSON FOCUS (15 - 20 MINUTES)

Orienteering Course Students will incorporate the compassing and mapping skills learned in the previous lessons.	**See DPESS Chapter 21 for details.** Squad formation. Students will work in groups of 5 – 9 and record start and finish times.

An orienteering course is marked in purple or red on a map using a triangle to indicate the start and a double circle to indicate the finish.

There are also bike, ski, and trail orienteering courses.

GAME (5 MINUTES)

Snowball Tag Relay	**DPESS page 406.**

This activity works on hand-eye coordination, agility and cooperation among people.

EVALUATION/REVIEW AND CHEER

What muscles were used in today's lesson?
Were there any activities in the Challenge Course that were particularly challenging?
Discuss any elements on the Orienteering Course that you felt were difficult.

Cheer; Tag games are fun!

ORIENTEERING COURSE

Directions: Work with 3 – 5 other people. Record your start and finish times. List group members.

1. ____

2. ____

3. ____

4. ____

5. ____

Start time:________ **Finish time:** ________

From the Gym, go SW until you reach a building. Write the name of the building:________________. Retrace your steps back to the starting point. Enter the Gym and walk to the center of the basketball court. Name three other sports played in the Gym:______________, ______________, ______________.
Exit the building. Head E 25 steps. Go N 25 steps. Write the name(s) of the edifices you have passed:______________________________________. Count the steps it takes you to go to the school library. What direction did you walk to get there?____
List any types of technology that you see inside the library:_____________________. List the names of the people you see in the library:______________________. Count the steps it takes you to go to the cafeteria:__________. What direction(s) did you walk to get there?__________
Return to the Gym in the most straightforward path. Count your steps to get there. Record the directions you walked:_____________________. How many steps did you walk to get there?_______________.

Congratulations! You finished the Orienteering Course!!!

Orienteering Lesson Plan 9

EQUIPMENT:

12 jump ropes for Circuit Training stations
Circuit training CD/tape
1 task sheet per person w/clipboards and pencils
CD/Tape player
12 mats for Circuit Training activity stations
Cones and signs for Circuit training.

OBJECTIVES:

The student will:

1. Participate in Circuit Training activities using form demonstrated by the instructor.
2. Demonstrate pacing and compassing skills during the orienteering challenge course as demonstrated by the instructor.

National Standards Met in this Lesson: **1, 2, 3, 4, 5, 6**

INSTRUCTIONAL ACTIVITIES	TEACHING HINTS

INTRODUCTORY ACTIVITY (2 - 3 MINUTES)

Back-to-Back	**See DPESS Chapter 7 for details.** Scattered formation.
Students jog around in the space provided. When the music stops, the student partners with another back-to-back as soon as possible.	

FITNESS DEVELOPMENT (8 - 12 MINUTES)

Circuit Training	**See DPESS Chapter 16 for details.**

This activity may help improve body composition with daily use.

LESSON FOCUS (15 - 20 MINUTES)

Challenge Course You need to create a challenge course appropriate to your school and teaching facility. Give the students directions requiring them to use the compass and count their steps.	**See DPESS Chapter 21 for details.** Groups of 3 – 7 work together. Leave rewards at specific points to make the challenge really fun and memorable for the students.

The basic skills involved include reading a topographical map, a compass, and pacing various distances.

GAME (5 MINUTES)

Grass in the Wind (Similar to Human Circle Pass) Students cooperate in their squads to perform "grass in the wind" (human circle pass.)	**DPESS page 505.** The student in the middle learns trust for his/her squad. Rotate.

EVALUATION/REVIEW AND CHEER

Explain the value of Circuit Training.
Discuss elements of the Challenge Course that proved to be difficult.

Cheer: Orienteering is a challenge!

Orienteering Lesson Plan 10

EQUIPMENT:
Whistle
1 compass per student
1 hula-hoop per 5 students

OBJECTIVES:
The student will:
1. Demonstrate push-up form during the introductory activity as demonstrated by the instructor.
2. Participate in Walk-Jog- Sprint to improve fitness levels.
3. Demonstrate point-to-point orienteering cognition as demonstrated by the instructor.
4. Participate in Hula Hoop Pass during the game demonstrating cooperative skills and creativity.

National Standards Met in this Lesson: **1, 2, 3, 4, 5, 6**

INSTRUCTIONAL ACTIVITIES | **TEACHING HINTS**

INTRODUCTORY ACTIVITY (2 - 3 MINUTES)

Push Up Tag
To avoid being tagged student assumes a push-up position.

See DPESS Chapter 14 for details.
Scattered formation.
Rules the same as any other tag game.

This activity improves muscular strength in the biceps brachii and triceps brachii.

FITNESS DEVELOPMENT (8 - 12 MINUTES)

Walk-Jog-Sprint
When teacher blows the whistle, one = walk; two = jog; and three whistles= sprint.

See DPESS Chapter 16 for details.
Scatter formation within boundaries.

This activity may help improve cardiovascular strength.

LESSON FOCUS (15 - 20 MINUTES)

Point to Point Orienteering

See DPESS Chapter 21 for details.

The first large scale orienteering meet was organized in 1918.

GAME (5 MINUTES)

Hula Hoop Pass
Students will try to pass the hoop around without breaking the chain.

See DPESS Chapter 18 for details.
Circle formation
See lesson #1 for more details.

In 1957 the hula hoop was reinvented by Richard Knerr and Arthur "Spud" Medlin,

EVALUATION/REVIEW

Discuss elements of the Point-to-Point Orienteering that may have been difficult.
Discuss what is necessary to make the Hula Hoop Pass game successful.
What muscles were used today:
When was the first orienteering meet held?
Cheer: Orienteering, yes!

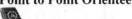

Rhythmic Gymnastics

This unit has been specifically designed to meet all six components of the NASPE National Standards for Physical Education.

OBJECTIVES:

The student will:

1. Participate in Blob tag, Fugitive Tag, Push-Up Tag, Vanishing Beanbags and Flag Grab demonstrating agility, quick changes in direction and sportsmanship.
2. Participate in Parachute Fitness Activities to improve arm strength and overall fitness.
3. Participate in Circuit Training, Continuity Exercises, Fitness Scavenger and Aerobic workout to improve fitness.
4. Perform Rhythmic Gymnastics Ball, Rope, Hoop and Ribbon skills using form demonstrated in class.
5. Create and perform alone or with a partner a routine demonstrating skills learned in class to the music provided by the instructor.

RHYTHMIC GYMNASTICS BLOCK PLAN
2 WEEK UNIT

Week #1	Monday	Tuesday	Wednesday	Thursday	Friday
Introductory Activity	Blob tag	Whistle March	Vanishing Beanbags	Parachute Locomotor Activity	New Leader Activity
Fitness	Continuity Exercises	Parachute Fitness Activities	Fitness Scavenger Hunt	Fitness Scavenger Hunt	Circuit Training with Jog
Lesson Focus	Ball	Ball Routine	Ribbon	Ribbon Exchanges	Hoop
Game	Frisbee Catch	Push-Up Tag	Hula Hoop Pass	Pentabridge Hustle	Musical Hoops

Week #2	Monday	Tuesday	Wednesday	Thursday	Friday
Introductory Activity	Mirror Drill	New Leader Activity with Music	Frozen Tag	Formation Rhythmic Running	Juggling Scarves
Fitness	Aerobic Workout	Walk, Jog, Sprint	Fitness Challenge Course	Circuit Training with Jog	Aerobic workout
Lesson Focus	Rope	Rope Routine	Review All Apparatus	Develop Routine	Perform Routine
Game	Frisbee 21	Fugitive Tag	Flag Grab and Chase		

Rhythmic Gymnastics Lesson Plan 1

EQUIPMENT:

Continuity Music CD/Tape for Fitness Music player
Frisbee per 2 students
1 volleyball/rubber ball/ team handball/ Rhythmic Gymnastics Ball per student
1 individual jump rope per student

OBJECTIVES:

The student will:
1. Participate in Blob tag demonstrating agility, quick changes in direction and sportsmanship.
2. Demonstrating rolling, bouncing, tossing and catching, and swinging a ball as demonstrated by the instructor.
3. Participate in Continuity Exercises to improve fitness.
4. Participate in Frisbee Catch playing cooperatively with their partner and using form demonstrated by the instructor.

Standards Met in this Lesson: **1, 2, 3, 4, 5, 6**

INSTRUCTIONAL ACTIVITIES	TEACHING HINTS
INTRODUCTORY ACTIVITY (2 - 3 MINUTES)	
Blob tag	See DPESS Chapter 14 for details.
Select 2 – 3 it's	Change it's 1 or 2 times during activity
FITNESS DEVELOPMENT (8 - 12 MINUTES)	
Continuity Exercises	See DPESS Chapter 16 for details.
These exercises are a type of interval training. Create a CD/cassette tape with 30 - 35 seconds of music and 20 seconds of silence. During music the students jump rope. During pause, lead floor exercises.	When the silence begins, instruct the students to do an exercise i.e. push-ups; curl ups; reverse push-ups; etc. When the music resumes, the students jump rope. During each silence direct a difference exercise.
Stretching	See DPESS Chapter 16 for details.
During the last silence, conduct stretching exercises to stretch the areas worked i.e. calves; quadriceps; etc.	Slower and lower volume music should be added to this portion of the CD/tape for enjoyable stretching.
Bear Hug	See DPESS Chapter 16 for details.
Lunge Forward: Achilles and calf stretch	Attempt to place the rear foot flat on the floor. Hands on front thigh for support. Back flat and on upward diagonal.
Lunge forward and extend rear leg straight back.	
Hamstring Stretch-Reverse Lunge: From the lunge position, shift lunge and weight to rear leg, extend front leg. Keep heel on ground, toe flexed, pointing to sky.	Hold stretch for 30 seconds. Change legs. Hands on front thigh for support, back flat but on upward diagonal.
Standing Hip Bend (Both sides)	See DPESS Chapter 16 for details.
Hold the position for 20 - 20 seconds.	
Elbow Puller and Pusher (Both sides)	See DPESS Chapter 16 for details.
LESSON FOCUS (15 - 20 MINUTES)	

Rhythmic gymnastics is a sport in which single competitors or pairs, trios, or even more manipulate one or two apparatuses including a ball, clubs, hoop, ribbon or rope.

Rhythmic Gymnastics Ball Activities	See DPESS Chapter 19 for details.
Rolling: In a sitting position: Roll ball under the legs, around the back; around the body; down the legs; down the arms; down the legs, lift legs and toss the ball off the toes into the air and catch.	In handling the ball, the fingers should be closed slightly bent, with the ball resting in the palm. In wing, the ball can roll from the fingertips
Bouncing: Combine basketball-dribbling drills with graceful body movements; execute locomotor dance-type movements while bouncing.	Locomotor suggestions: Chase, slides, run and leap, skip, walk on toes, etc.
Toss and catch the ball while on sitting/kneeling on floor, walking, skipping, galloping, leaping, and running.	Use one hand only while tossing and catching the ball. Try each hand. Perform body waves with the ball.

INSTRUCTIONAL ACTIVITIES	TEACHING HINTS
Swinging: Swing ball in front of body from side to side. Circle ball around body, neck, legs and around palm. Let ball rest on palm of hand as you turn around.	The ball must rest lightly in the palm while the movements are performed. No gripping of ball with fingers is permitted.

GAME (5 MINUTES)

Frisbee Catch Partners can keep score or just free throwing and catching. 1 hand catch = 2 points 2 hand catch = 1 point Keep score to 20 points and then start over.	**See DPESS Chapter 20 for details.** Demonstrate throwing and catching a Frisbee. Use back to back with a new person to create partners. One person puts a hand on their head. The person with his hand on his head is to go and get a Frisbee for the pair and return to the partner.

EVALUATION/REVIEW AND CHEER

Were there any fitness activities you did today that were particularly difficult and need more work?
What muscles were used in class today?
Which of the Rhythmic Gymnastics ball activities that you did today were the best? Were any of them hard to do?

Cheer: Frisbee, yea!

Rhythmic Gymnastics Lesson Plan 2

EQUIPMENT:

Music for Whistle March
Parachute
1 ball per student
CD/Tape player
Music for Fitness

OBJECTIVES:

The student will:
1. Participate in Whistle March demonstrating rhythm, agility, quick changes in direction and sportsmanship.
2. Demonstrating ball skills and a routine demonstrated by the instructor.
3. Participate in Parachute Fitness activities to improve strength, endurance, coordination and aerobic capacities.
4. Participate in Push-up Tag playing cooperatively with their partner and using form demonstrated by the instructor.

Standards Met in this Lesson: **1, 2, 3, 4, 5, 6**

INSTRUCTIONAL ACTIVITIES	TEACHING HINTS
INTRODUCTORY ACTIVITY (2 - 3 MINUTES)	
Whistle March: Clap dominant beat. Clap and march in place to beat. March around room in time to music played while moving around room. When blow whistle a given number, students make groups that size by linking elbows. Blow whistle once to signal solo marching.	Direct students to create new groups each time. Students without group go to center to find others. **Play music tape with dominant beat.**
FITNESS DEVELOPMENT (8 - 12 MINUTES)	
Parachute Fitness Activities	**See DPESS Chapter 16 for details.** See Golf, Lesson Plan 2 for complete details.
LESSON FOCUS (15 - 20 MINUTES)	

Rhythmic gymnastics became an Olympic Sport in the 1984 Olympics held in Los Angeles. At this point only females compete in the sport, but it is done in schools by both men and women.

Review ball activities taught in Lesson 1	All students have their own ball to practice skills.

INSTRUCTIONAL ACTIVITIES	TEACHING HINTS
Balancing movements plus ball skills Balance on 1 foot with 1 arm extended out while tossing ball with other hand. Hold a balance while kneeling on the floor and circle or swing ball, etc.	Direct various balances combined with circling, tossing, swinging ball movements practiced in Lesson 1.
Ball Routine: Bounce the ball in place while extending opposite arm out horizontally; Bounce the ball while moving forward slowly walking or sliding using an arm movement; Run forward while making swing tosses from side to side; Bounce the ball while making a full turn; Run low to the ground in a figure-eight pattern; Toss the ball up and catch it with one hand; repeat on other side; Finish with a toss and catch the ball blindly behind the back.	You can draw the floor pattern on a poster board for students to follow or you can allow them to draw a floor pattern. First practice routine without any music, and then add music.

GAME (5 MINUTES)

Push-Up Tag Select several it's. Rotate roles frequently.	**See DPESS Chapter 14 for details.** Perform push-ups or push-up position to be "safe".

EVALUATION/REVIEW AND CHEER

Were you able to perform the routine? What areas caused difficulty?
Which fitness activities were particularly challenging?
What muscles did you use in class today?
What is the history of Rhythmic Gymnastics in the United States?

Cheer: Rhythmic Gymnastics rocks and rolls!

Rhythmic Gymnastics Lesson Plan 3

EQUIPMENT:

1 beanbag per student
Cones for station markers
1 Hula hoop per student
Fitness Scavenger Hunt cards
1 Rhythmic Gymnastics Ribbon per student

OBJECTIVES:

The student will:

1. Participate in Vanishing Bean Bags demonstrating agility, quick changes in direction and cooperative skills.
2. Demonstrating ribbon swinging, circling, figure-eights, zigzags and spiraling skills using form demonstrated by the instructor.
3. Participate in a Fitness Scavenger Hunt to improve strength, endurance, coordination and aerobic capacities.
4. Participate in Hula Hoop Pass demonstrating creative and cooperative skills with their group mates and following the rules established by the instructor.

Standards Met in this Lesson: **1, 2, 3, 4, 5, 6**

INSTRUCTIONAL ACTIVITIES	TEACHING HINTS
INTRODUCTORY ACTIVITY (2 - 3 MINUTES)	
Vanishing Bean Bags	**See DPESS Chapter 14 for details.** Spread beanbags out in area. Begin with 1 bag/student. Have students begin by moving around the area until you give a signal.
FITNESS DEVELOPMENT (8 - 12 MINUTES)	
Fitness Scavenger Hunt Each group is given a card indicating where to go. Once at the station another card will be there indicating the exercise/activity to perform and how.	**See DPESS Chapter 16 for details.** Scatter formation Use whistle mixer to create groups of four 10 stations
LESSON FOCUS (15 - 20 MINUTES)	

The ribbon is one of five individual events performed in the Olympics. The other events are: rope, ball, hoop, and clubs. It is a humbling event because the performer can become tangled in the ribbon.

Swinging the Ribbon: The entire body should coordinate with these large, swinging motions:	Spread students out so ribbons won't tie up with other students' ribbon.
Swing the ribbon forward and backward in the sagittal plane on the side of the body.	Step forward and backward as the ribbon is swung. Follow-through very high with the working arm.
Swing the ribbon across and in front of the body in the frontal plane. Swing the ribbon overhead from side to side; Swing the ribbon upward and catch the end of it. While holding both ends of the ribbon, swing it upward, around, and over the body. Jump through it.	This can be done while still or while sliding to the side. Overhead swings coordinate well with a balance movement.
Circling movements: Large circles are made in front, on the side and around the body. Use the whole arm to create the circular movements; smaller circles involve the wrist. Circles are made in different planes: frontal, sagittal, and horizontal.	Body can circle in place or through space. Student can run and leap through the large circles being made with the ribbon. Circle the ribbon at different levels.
Circle the ribbon horizontally, vertically, or diagonally. Circle the ribbon in front of the body, around the body, and overhead and behind the body.	Small movements on the toes coordinate with this action. Coordinate body movements with the ribbon movements.
Run while circling the ribbon overhead; leap as the ribbon is circled downward and under the legs.	Add dance steps and turns while circling the ribbon.
Figure-Eight Movements. Figure eights are made in the three planes. The two halves of the figure eight should be the same size and on the same plane level. The figure can be made with long arm movements or with movements of the lower arm or wrist. Practice both types	While performing a figure eight, hop through the loop when the ribbon passes the side of the body.

INSTRUCTIONAL ACTIVITIES	TEACHING HINTS
Zigzag Movements: Zigzag movements are made in the air or on the floor. These are done with continuous up-and-down hand movements, using primarily wrist action.	Execute the zigzag in the air in front, around, and behind the body.
Run backward while zigzagging the ribbon in front of the body. Run forward while zigzagging ribbon behind the body at different levels.	Perform zigzagging of ribbon at different levels in front, side, and back of body..
Spiraling movements: The circles making up the spiraling action can be the same size or of an increasing or decreasing progression.	Spirals can be made from left to right or the reverse. Execute spirals around, in front of, on the side the body while performing locomotor dance steps.
Perform forward and backward rolls while spiraling.	

INSTRUCTIONAL ACTIVITIES	TEACHING HINTS

GAME (5 MINUTES)

Hula Hoop Pass	**See DPESS Chapter 18 for details.**
Place a hula-hoop over the clasped hands of two members of each squad. On signal - pass the hoop around the circle without releasing handgrips.	Scattered - in groups. Approximately 5 per group. Members of each group hold hands.

Students will work together in a positive, cooperative manner to complete the task before other teams.

EVALUATION/REVIEW AND CHEER

What was challenging about today's Scavenger Fitness Hunt?
What muscles did you use today?
Was there any difficulty with any particular ribbon movement?
How many individual competitive events are used in the Olympics? Can you name the five events?
What was needed to make the Hula Hoop Pass successful?

Cheer: Ribbon rocks!

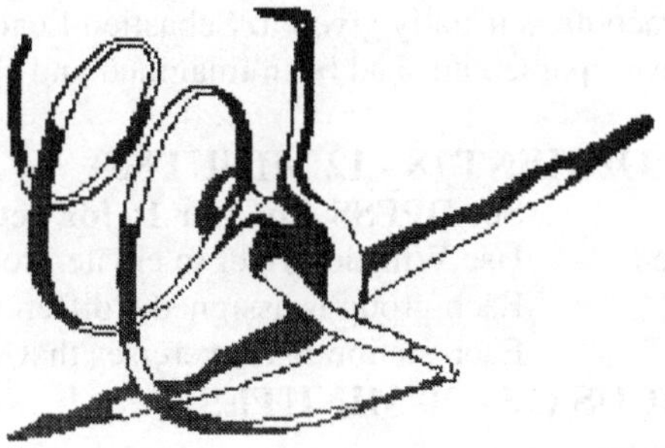

Rhythmic Gymnastics Lesson Plan 4

EQUIPMENT:

1 Parachute
Fitness Scavenger Hunt cards
Cassette/CD player
1 Rhythmic Gymnastics Ribbon per student
Music for ribbon activities

OBJECTIVES:

The student will:

1. Participate in the Parachute Locomotor Routine demonstrating agility, quick changes in direction, rhythmic awareness and cooperative skills.
2. Participate in a Fitness Scavenger Hunt to improve strength, endurance, coordination and aerobic capacities.
3. Demonstrate ribbon swinging, circling, figure-eights, zigzags and spiraling skills using form demonstrated by the instructor.
4. Demonstrate ribbon exchange to a partner using skills demonstrated by the instructor.
5. Participate in Pentabridge demonstrating agility, cooperative skills and following the rules established by the instructor.

Standards Met in this Lesson: **1, 2, 3, 4, 5, 6**

INSTRUCTIONAL ACTIVITIES	TEACHING HINTS

INTRODUCTORY ACTIVITY (2 - 3 MINUTES)

Parachute Locomotor Routine: Use popular music
16 runs CW; 16 runs CCW; 8 jumps in place;
16 skips forward; 8 count lift overhead; 8 count lower to toes; 4 count lift; 4 count lower to toes; Repeat all
Face chute and hold with 2 hands: Slide CW; Slide CCW

See DPESS Chapter 16 for details.
Whistle to change action
"Tighten 'chute!"
Hold 'chute overhead on CW run.
Whistle to signal direction change.

Credit for the invention of the first practical parachute is usually given to Sebastien Lenormand who demonstrated the parachute principle in 1783. However, parachutes had been imagined and sketched by Leonardo Da Vinci (1452-1519) centuries earlier.

FITNESS DEVELOPMENT (8 - 12 MINUTES)

Fitness Scavenger Hunt
Each group is given a list directing them to designated areas to find directions for exercise/activity at that location.

See DPESS Chapter 16 for details.
Use Whistle Mixer to create groups of 3.
Each group is assigned a different starting point.
Each station lists exercises that work the entire body.

LESSON FOCUS (15 - 20 MINUTES)

Review Ribbon Swinging, Circling, Spiraling, Figure 8, and Zig Zag movements from yesterday's lesson.

Throwing and Catching: These skills are usually combined with swinging, circling, or figure-8 movements.

The ribbon is tossed with one hand and is caught with the same hand or with the other hand. Throwing and catching is a difficult maneuver.

Exchanges: During group routines, the ribbon is handed or tossed to a partner. The wand is usually exchanged although both ribbon and wand can be handed off.

Practice with a partner.
Create partners using Elbow-to-Elbow technique.

Students create a routine using movements learned
Direct students to create a 30 second to 1 minute routine.

Allow students a given amount of time to create routine. Play music for the routine. Have several groups "show" their created routines at once.

GAME (5 MINUTES)

Pentabridge Hustle

See DPESS Chapter 14 for details.
See Golf Lesson Plan 5 for complete details.

EVALUATION/REVIEW AND CHEER

Were any parts of the Fitness Scavenger Hunt particularly difficult?
Review positive elements of the routines created during the class period.
Who is credited with developing a parachute?
Cheer: Ribbon Figures 8, yes!

Rhythmic Gymnastics Lesson Plan 5

EQUIPMENT:

Music for Introductory activity, Fitness and Game
1 hoop per student
Music player
Circuit Training cones and signs

OBJECTIVES:

The student will:

1. Participate in the New Leader activity demonstrating creativity, changes in direction, rhythmic awareness and cooperative skills.
2. Participate in Circuit Training Fitness to improve strength, endurance, coordination and aerobic capacities.
3. Demonstrate hoop swinging, spinning, circling, skills using form demonstrated by the instructor.
4. Participate in Musical Hoops demonstrating rhythm, agility, cooperative skills and following the rules established by the instructor.

Standards Met in this Lesson: **1, 2, 3, 4, 5, 6**

INSTRUCTIONAL ACTIVITIES	TEACHING HINTS
INTRODUCTORY ACTIVITY (2 - 3 MINUTES)	
New Leader Activity moving to music Leader begins moving to beat/style of music. Others follow until you signal for a leader change.	**See DPESS Chapter 14 for details.** Use management game to create groups of 3 – 5 Use management technique to identify first leader
FITNESS DEVELOPMENT (8 - 12 MINUTES)	
Circuit Training Fitness with Jog Explain each station	**See DPESS Chapter 16 for details.** Using Whistle Mixer, create groups to go to Stations
LESSON FOCUS (15 - 20 MINUTES)	
Hoop: Swing the hoop- across the body; around the body with same hand, then a hand change; overhead same hand, then change hands; swing down and up on side of body; in figure-eight pattern in front of the body.	The swinging movement should be very large. Good alignment between body and the hoop is important. Hoops can be swung in frontal, sagittal, or horizontal plane. Add locomotor movements i.e. slide, chase, etc.
Spin the hoop: Spin in front of the body; Spin on the floor; Spin and kick one leg over the hoop; Reverse; Add a full turn after the kick over; Reverse.	One or both hands can be used when spinning the hoop. Locomotor movements can be performed around the spinning hoop.
Circling Movements: Hoops can be circled on the hand, wrist, arm, leg, or body. Changes from one hand to the other can be performed. Circle the hoop while swaying or sliding from side to side. Hold onto both sides of the hoop circle it in front of the body.	Extend the arm in front of the body, to the side or overhead. Circle the hoop on the hand between the thumb and first finger. Add locomotor movements such as: gallop, slide, skip, run, leaps while circling the hoop in all planes.

The hula hoop is an ancient invention - no modern company and no single inventor can claim that they invented the first hula hoop. The Greeks used Hooping as a form of exercise. Older hoops have been made from metal, bamboo, wood, grasses, and even vines. However, modern companies "re-invented" their own versions of the hula hoop using unusual materials, for example; plastic hula hoops with added bits of glitter and noise makers, and hoops that are collapsible.

INSTRUCTIONAL ACTIVITIES	TEACHING HINTS
GAME (5 MINUTES)	
Musical Hoops Hoops, one fewer than the number of students, placed on the floor. Players are given a locomotor movement to do around the hoops while the music is played.	Scattered formation. When the music stops, the students step inside and empty hoop. One student per hoop. Repeat with another locomotor movement. Examples are: slide, gallop, run, skip, leap, and carioca.

EVALUATION/REVIEW AND CHEER

Were any hoop activities particularly difficult? Which activity did you enjoy the most?
Did Mattel invent the hula-hoop? If not, what is the history of the hula hoop?

Cheer: Hoops rock and roll!

Rhythmic Gymnastics Lesson Plan 6

EQUIPMENT:

1 woven rope per student
Aerobic Exercise tape/CD
Tape or CD player

OBJECTIVES:

The student will:

1. Participate in the Mirror Drill activity demonstrating creativity, changes in direction, rhythmic awareness and cooperative skills.
2. Participate in an Aerobic Workout to Music to improve strength, endurance, coordination and aerobic capacities.
3. Demonstrate rope swinging, circling, figure-eights, and Schottische step skills using form demonstrated by the instructor.
4. Participate in Frisbee 21 demonstrating throwing and catching skills, cooperative skills and following the rules established by the instructor.

Standards Met in this Lesson: **1, 2, 3, 4, 5, 6**

INSTRUCTIONAL ACTIVITIES	TEACHING HINTS

INTRODUCTORY ACTIVITY (2 - 3 MINUTES)

Mirror Drill in Place

See DPESS Chapter 14 for details.
Use a management game to make pairs. Identify first leader/follower. Signal time for leader and follower to change roles after approximately 30-40 seconds.

FITNESS DEVELOPMENT (8 - 12 MINUTES)

Aerobic Workout to Music

Create a music CD/tape 120-150 beats per minute or use Aerobic Exercise CD/Tape.

Standing Hip Bend	40 seconds
Trunk Twist	30 seconds
Slides each direction	30 seconds
Skip around cones	30 seconds
Jumping Jacks	30 seconds
Triceps Push-Ups	30 seconds
Curl-Ups	30 seconds
Knee Touch Curl-Ups	30 seconds
Push-Ups	30 seconds
Gallop around cones	30 seconds
Jump Rope	1 minutes
Lower Leg Stretch	30 seconds
Balance Beam Stretch	30 seconds
Rocking Chair	30 seconds
Carioca around cones	1 minutes
Jog in place	
Calf Stretch	

See DPESS Chapter 16 for details.

Scatter formation within a coned area on the athletic field.

See DPESS Chapter 16 for details.

Aerobic exercise is defined as any repetitive physical activity that is done long and hard enough, to enhance circulatory and respiratory efficiency. Aerobic means 'with oxygen' and it requires the lungs and heart to meet the body's increased oxygen demand.

LESSON FOCUS (15 - 20 MINUTES)

Rope: Circle the rope on each side of the body while holding both ends of the rope.

Rope size is determined by standing on the center of the rope with both feet and extending the rope ends to the hands held at the "armpit" level. There should not be handles on the ends of the rope.

Make **figure 8 swings**: Holding both ends of the rope, or, holding the center of the rope and swinging the ends.

Allow students plenty of time to practice these skills.

INSTRUCTIONAL ACTIVITIES	TEACHING HINTS
Pendulum swing rope in front of body and jump it.	Hold one hand near midline of body, the other parallel and approximately 12" in front of body.
Run or skip over rope turned forward and backward.	Direct students to be safe and watch out for others.
Schottische step over a turning rope.	Spread students out for safety.
Jump over a backward turning rope, and then **toss** the rope into the air. Catch both ends of rope.	
Holding the ends and center of the rope, kneel and horizontally circle the rope close to the floor.	Variation: Stand and circle the rope horizontally overhead.
Perform a body wrap with the rope.	Hold one end on the hip, wrap the rope around the body with the other hand.

Rope routines typically are performed individually, but a group routine can be created including rope exchange movements.

GAME (5 MINUTES)

"Frisbee 21"
Game Rules:
- Players stand 10 yards apart
- Throw disc back and forth. Throws must be catchable.
- 1 point = 1 hand catch
- 2 points = 2 hand catch

See DPESS Chapter 20 for details.
Create partners using "elbow-to-elbow" technique.
Have 1 person kneel. The standing partner gets a Frisbee from perimeter of area and brings to partner.

Player must get 21 points to win and win by 2 points.

EVALUATION/REVIEW AND CHEER

Explain all the parts of the body and muscles that were used in today's Aerobic Workout Routine.
Were there any rope activities that were really challenging yet fun? Which ones?
What was challenging about Frisbee 21?

Cheer: Fun, Fun, Frisbee 21!

Rhythmic Gymnastics Lesson Plan 7

EQUIPMENT:

Music for Introductory Activity
1 rhythmic rope per student
Music player
1 Flag belt per person

OBJECTIVES:

The student will:

1. Participate in the New Leader activity demonstrating creativity, changes in direction, rhythmic awareness and cooperative skills.
2. Participate in Walk-Jog-Sprint to improve strength, endurance, coordination and aerobic capacities.
3. Demonstrate rope swinging, circling, figure-eights, and Schottische step skills using form demonstrated by the instructor.
4. Participate in Fugitive Tag demonstrating cooperative skills and following the rules established by the instructor.

Standards Met in this Lesson: **1, 2, 3, 4, 5, 6**

INSTRUCTIONAL ACTIVITIES	TEACHING HINTS
INTRODUCTORY ACTIVITY (2 - 3 MINUTES)	
New Leader Play music and leader must create movements to music.	**See DPESS Chapter 14 for details.** Create pairs by playing "Back to Back."
FITNESS DEVELOPMENT (8 - 12 MINUTES)	
Walk-Jog-Sprint 1 Whistle = Sprint 2 Whistle = Walk 3 Whistle = Jog	**See DPESS Chapter 16 for details.** Scatter formation within boundaries. Teacher directs length of time for each activity by monitoring class. Progressively increase the time of each activity.
Stretch: Achilles Tendon; Lower Leg; Balance Beam; Bear Hug; Leg Pick-Up; Side Leg; Hurdler's; Groin Stretch; Sitting Toe Touch; Body Twist	**See DPESS Chapter 16 for details.** Scattered formation
Strength: Crab Walk; Push-ups; Reclining Partner Pull-ups; Curl-ups; Reverse curls; Curl-ups with twist	**See DPESS Chapter 16 for details.**
LESSON FOCUS (15 - 20 MINUTES)	
Review rope skills taught yesterday. Single and double **jump forward and backward**	Spread students out for safety.
While holding both ends of the rope in one hand, **circle the rope sagittally backward** at the side of the body and run forward.	Variation: Toss the rope and catch it while running.
Perform a locomotor dance step and simultaneously toss and catch the rope.	Chase, run and leap, waltz step, slide, triplet, etc. are examples of locomotor steps to use.
Hold both ends of the rope and swing it around the body like a cape.	Variation: Turn the body around simultaneously.
Perform leaps while circling the rope sagittally at one side of the body.	Leaps can be forward or sideward. Rope can circle in front of body as well as on side.
Hold the rope around the foot and make shapes with the body and foot-rope connection. Utilize different balancing movements while stretching the rope.	These involve held body positions, with the rope underneath the foot or hooked around a foot.
Allow students to explore and combine activities previously taught.	Suggest movements that could be combined while students are exploring.

Gymnastics, rhythmic and artistic combined, started in Europe during the eighteenth century as one sport and over time gradually developed into two different yet similar sports. Artistic gymnastics includes floor exercise, balance beam, uneven bars, high bars, side horse, horse vaulting and acrobatic movements. Rhythmic gymnastics combines dance movements on the floor to music with ropes, hoops, ribbons, and clubs.

INSTRUCTIONAL ACTIVITIES	TEACHING HINTS

GAME (5 MINUTES)

Fugitive Tag	**See DPESS Chapter 14 for details.**
Identify leader in group. They are first fugitive. Rotate.	Use Back-to-Back to create partners. Both wear belts.

EVALUATION/REVIEW AND CHEER

Were any rope activities particularly challenging? Which one do you enjoy most and why?
What muscles were used in class today?
Describe the history of rhythmic gymnastics.
What is the difference between artistic and rhythmic gymnastics?

Cheer: Rhythmic rope is great!

Rhythmic Gymnastics Lesson Plan 8

EQUIPMENT:

Challenge Course instructions and cones
Balance beam for Challenge Course
Ropes, balls, ribbons, hoops: 1 per student
Ladder for fitness course
Music for fitness
Music player

OBJECTIVES:

The student will:

1. Participate in the Frozen Tag activity demonstrating balance, creativity, changes in direction, and cooperative skills.
2. Participate in Fitness Challenge to improve strength, endurance, coordination and aerobic capacities.
3. Demonstrate rope, ribbon, ball, and hoop swinging, circling, figure-eights, and Schottische step skills using form demonstrated by the instructor.
4. Participate in Flag Grab and Chase demonstrating cooperative skills and following the rules established by the instructor.

Standards Met in this Lesson: **1, 2, 3, 4, 5, 6**

INSTRUCTIONAL ACTIVITIES	TEACHING HINTS

INTRODUCTORY ACTIVITY (2 - 3 MINUTES)

Frozen Tag	**See DPESS Chapter 14 for details.**
Select 2 it's	Scatter formation.

FITNESS DEVELOPMENT (8 - 12 MINUTES)

Fitness Challenge Course

Design a course using the following components:

- Agility run through hoops
- Log rolls
- Run and weave through a coned course
- Leap over a taut rope
- Cross a horizontal ladder (or hang for 5-10 seconds)
- Power jump onto and off of three jumping boxes
- Walk the length of a balance beam
- Run high knees for 50 yards
- Curl-ups
- Crab Walks from one cone to another
- Stretching exercises

See DPESS Chapter 16 for details.

Divide class into groups of 4 - 5. Assign each group a starting point on the Challenge Course. Use music to motivate.

Course should be created to exercise all parts of the body
Allow students to run the Challenge Course 3 times
Allow students to develop new challenges for the course
Music can be used for fun and to motivate students
Students will travel the course at their own pace. Have a passing lane to the right.

INSTRUCTIONAL ACTIVITIES	TEACHING HINTS

LESSON FOCUS (15 - 20 MINUTES)

Review rope, ball, ribbon, hoop skills previously taught	Guide students through review of each apparatus.

Rhythmic gymnastics started as an independent competitive sport in the early 1950's by the Russians. Then in 1963 the first rhythmic gymnastics world championship was held in Europe. Even though rhythmic gymnastics has its own world championships it did not become an Olympic medal sport until 1984 at the Olympics held in Los Angeles. This is partly why rhythmic gymnastics is such a little known and hardly recognized sport in the U.S.

GAME (5 MINUTES)

Flag Grab and Chase One team wears flags positioned in the back of the belt. On signal, the chase team captures as many flags as possible within a designated amount of time. The captured flags are counted. The teams switch positions and the team that captures the most flags wins.	**See DPESS Chapter 16 for details.** Scatter formation inside large boundary area. Split class into using a management game such as back-to-back; toe-to-toe; or elbow-to-elbow to make two groups by then directing one in the group to put hand on hips. Then separate the two groups into teams. Direct one team to pick up belts with flags attached.

EVALUATION/REVIEW AND CHEER

Identify which apparatus you enjoy most and explain why. What was challenging in the Challenge Course?

Students create cheer today.

Rhythmic Gymnastics Lesson Plan 9

EQUIPMENT:

Circuit training station signs and cones	Ribbons, balls, hoops, ropes for whole class
Music for Rhythmic Gymnastics routines	Music player

OBJECTIVES:

The student will:

1. Participate in the Formation Rhythmic Running demonstrating balance, creativity, rhythmic awareness and changes in direction, and cooperative skills.
2. Participate in Circuit Training Fitness Jog to improve strength, endurance, coordination and aerobic capacities.
3. Demonstrate rope, ribbon, ball, and hoop swinging, circling, figure-eights, and Schottische step skills using form demonstrated by the instructor and create a routine using the apparatus of her choice.

Standards Met in this Lesson: **1, 2, 3, 4, 5, 6**

INSTRUCTIONAL ACTIVITIES	TEACHING HINTS

INTRODUCTORY ACTIVITY (2 - 3 MINUTES)

Formation Rhythmic Running Run 3 times Run in a small circle 4 times Jump in place 8 times Run 8 times and clap on counts 1, 4, 5, 7, and 8 Repeat above	**See DPESS Chapter 14 for details.** Give instructions to "fall in" to a circle or lines. Play drum or tambourine to set rhythm. Increase tempo when you repeat.

FITNESS DEVELOPMENT (8 - 12 MINUTES)

Circuit Training Fitness with Jog Explain each station	**See DPESS Chapter 16 for details.** Using Whistle Mixer, create groups to go to Stations

LESSON FOCUS AND GAME COMBINED (20 MINUTES)

Students create a routine using apparatus of their choice. Routine can be done in 2's or solo.	Play music that can be used for the routine.

INSTRUCTIONAL ACTIVITIES | **TEACHING HINTS**

Group Rhythmic Gymnastics consists of four to five gymnasts doing a routine at the same time with each other. They may all use the same apparatus or they could have different apparatus at the same time. The main idea is to have all the gymnasts doing the movements at the same time. They also have to exchange apparatus with each other and meet other requirements. Of course they must have the same good quality of movement to music, grace, flexibly and difficulty as are required in individual rhythmic gymnastics routines.

EVALUATION/REVIEW AND CHEER

Discuss creative presentations due the next day.
Students create cheer.

Rhythmic Gymnastics Lesson Plan 10

EQUIPMENT:

3 Juggling Scarves per student
CD/tape for Aerobic workout
Music for routines
Music player
Ropes, hoops, ribbons, balls: 1 per student

OBJECTIVES:

The student will:

1. Participate in Juggling Scarves activities demonstrating eye hand coordination and the techniques of column and cascading juggling demonstrated by the instructor.
2. Participate in an Aerobic Workout to improve strength, endurance, agility coordination and aerobic capacities.
3. Demonstrate a self-created routine using the apparatus of her choice.

Standards Met in this Lesson: **1, 2, 3, 4, 5, 6**

INSTRUCTIONAL ACTIVITIES | **TEACHING HINTS**

INTRODUCTORY ACTIVITY (2 - 3 MINUTES)

Juggling Scarves
Column juggling; Cascading

See DPESS Chapter 18 for details.
Scattered formation; 3 scarves per student

FITNESS DEVELOPMENT (8 - 12 MINUTES)

Aerobic Workout

See DPESS Chapter 16 for details.
See Lesson 7, Racquetball Unit for details

LESSON FOCUS AND GAME COMBINED (20 MINUTES)

Several groups perform routines for class simultaneously.
Play appropriate music for the routines.

Do not have anyone perform alone as it can cause embarrassment. Set etiquette/ behavior rules before presentations begin. Clap for all students.

EVALUATION/REVIEW AND CHEER

Make a general comment praising student creativity.
Cheer: Rhythmic Gymnastics, yeh!

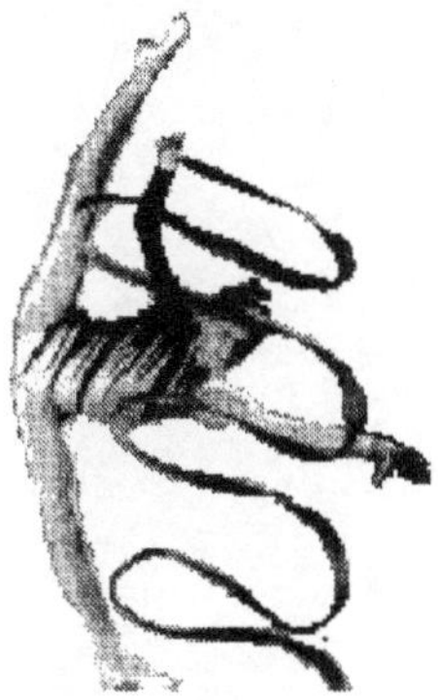

Rhythms and Dance

This unit has been specifically designed to meet all six components of the NASPE National Standards for Physical Education.

OBJECTIVES:

The student will:

1. Identify rhythm and move to the beat played on the drum by the instructor.
2. Demonstrate rhythmical awareness while participating in Whistle March to music.
3. Demonstrate respect for classmates while participating in Standing and Running High Five's.
4. Participate in the Parachute Rhythmic Aerobic Activity, Fitness Scavenger Hunt, Challenge Course, and Aerobic workout to improve fitness.
5. Perform Cotton Eyed Joe, Sweetheart Schottische, 8-Count Polka, Swing, Foxtrot and Waltz demonstrating rhythmical awareness and using form demonstrated in class by the instructor.
6. Demonstrate eye-hand coordination, cooperative skills, and agility while participating in the Wand and Tag activities presented by the instructor.
7. Demonstrate teamwork and cooperative skills while participating in Relay races, Long Rope Routines, Tag and Cageball Games.

RHYTHMS AND DANCE BLOCK PLAN
2 WEEK UNIT

Week #1	Monday	Tuesday	Wednesday	Thursday	Friday
Introductory Activities	Rhythm Identification	Whistle March	Balance Tag	Whistle March Schottische	Hoops and Plyometrics
Fitness	Parachute Rhythmic Aerobic Activity	Fitness Scavenger Hunt	Aerobic workout	Continuity Exercises	Circuit Training Fitness with Jog
Lesson Focus	California Strut Cotton Eyed Joe Line Sweetheart Schottische	Cotton Eyed Joe Partners Sweetheart Schottische	8-Count Polka	East Coast Swing and Turns	California Strut, Cotton Eyed Joe, Sweetheart Schottische, 8-Count Polka, Swing
Game	Wands: Reaction Time & Broomstick Balance	Blob tag	Long Team Cageball	Long Jump Rope Routines	Scooter Cageball Soccer

Week #2	Monday	Tuesday	Wednesday	Thursday	Friday
Introductory Activities	New Leader Activity to Music	Standing High Five's	Mirror Drill in Place to Music	Running High Five's	Whistle March to Music
Fitness	12 Ways of fitness	Aerobic workout	Fitness Cookie Jar Exchange	Challenge Course	Long Jump Rope Fitness Routine
Lesson Focus	Cha-Cha, Swing & Pretzel Steps	Waltz Swing	Waltz Cha Cha	Waltz Foxtrot	Review all Dances
Game	Spider Tag	Clothespin Tag	Loose Caboose	Pass and Squat Relays	

Rhythms and Dance Lesson Plan 1

EQUIPMENT:
Drum and beater | 1 Wand per student
CD/ music | Parachute
CD/ music for Fitness, Cotton Eyed Joe, Sweetheart Schottische
CD/ Music player

OBJECTIVES:
The student will:
1. Participate in Rhythm Identification activities following the instructions described by the instructor.
2. Demonstrate agility and cooperation during Parachute Rhythmic Aerobic Activity.
3. Participate in the dances as led by the instructor: California Strut, Cotton Eyed Joe, and Sweetheart Schottische.
4. Participate in the Wand activities presented by the instructor during the closing portion of class.

National Standards Met in this Lesson: 1, 2, 3, 4, 5, 6

INSTRUCTIONAL ACTIVITIES	TEACHING HINTS
INTRODUCTORY ACTIVITY (2 - 3 MINUTES)	
Rhythm Identification	Students sit or lay on ground with eyes closed.
Play simple rhythmical patterns on drum. Students pat the rhythm on their thighs. Change rhythm and tempo.	Repeat with student's eyes open.
Play simple music and have students tap beat on thighs with eyes closed and then open.	Demonstrate sitting and leaning back on hands enabling tapping toes lightly on ground to beat.
Play music. Students clap the beat. Then, march in place to beat while clapping, then walk around and clap.	Students stand and move around room.
Students march to beat of music and High Five students.	Use several pieces of music with easily identifiable beats.
FITNESS DEVELOPMENT (8 - 12 MINUTES)	
Parachute Rhythmic Aerobic Activity	**See DPESS Chapter 16 for details.**
Direct a variety of locomotor movements holding the chute with one hand or both. Activities include: sliding; skipping; galloping; jogging; etc. Then add stretching and strengthening exercises while standing, seated, or lying down on side, back, or stomach.	Use a lively piece of music with a bold beat.
LESSON FOCUS (15 - 20 MINUTES)	
California Strut	Weikart, P., **Rhythmically Moving, 4.** *
Cotton Eyed Joe as a line dance	Music and instructions for <u>all dances</u> available from:
First, students tap beat on thigh by listening to music. Demonstrate dance using Whole-Part-Whole teaching method.	*Wagon Wheel Books and Records; 16812 Pembrook Lane; Huntington Beach, CA 92649; (714) 846-8169* * *http://www.wagonwheelrecords.net*

"Cotton Eye Joe" is also a popular couples or line dance that can be seen and danced at country western dance venues. The precise origins of this song are unclear, although it predates the American Civil War.

Sweetheart Schottische line dance or couples dance	Use Elbow-to-Elbow to make couples.
Have students move forward to new partner every other schottische pattern.	Couples follow the back of another couple's neck while walking to create a circle and "fall-in".
GAME (5 MINUTES)	
Wands: Reaction Time	**See DPESS Chapter 18 for details.**
Broomstick Balance	**See DPESS Chapter 18 for details.**
	Use same partners students ended with during dance.

EVALUATION/REVIEW AND CHEER
Were there any dance steps you learned today that you need to practice more?

Cheer: Hear the beat

Rhythms and Dance Lesson Plan 2

EQUIPMENT:

CD/ music
Music for Whistle March, Cotton Eyed Joe, Sweetheart Schottische
Fitness Scavenger Hunt instruction cards
CD/ music player

OBJECTIVES:

The student will:

1. Participate in Whistle March activities demonstrating rhythmic awareness and following the instructions described by the instructor.
2. Participate in the Fitness Scavenger Hunt to improve strength, endurance, flexibility and cardiovascular endurance.
3. Participate in the dances as led by the instructor: Cotton Eyed Joe, and Sweetheart Schottische.
4. Play Blob Tag during the closing portion of class demonstrating cooperative skills and agility.

National Standards Met in this Lesson: 1, 2, 3, 4, 5, 6

INSTRUCTIONAL ACTIVITIES	TEACHING HINTS
INTRODUCTORY ACTIVITY (2 - 3 MINUTES)	
Whistle March: Clap dominant beat. Clap and march in place to beat. March in time to music played while moving around room. When blow whistle a given number, students make groups that size by linking elbows. Blow whistle once to signal solo marching.	Direct students to create new groups each time. Students without group go to center to find others. Play music with a dominant beat.
FITNESS DEVELOPMENT (8 - 12 MINUTES)	
Fitness Scavenger Hunt Each group is given a card indicating where to go. Once at the station another card will be there indicating the exercise/activity to perform and how.	**See DPESS Chapter 16 for details.** Scatter formation Use whistle mixer to create groups of four 10 stations
LESSON FOCUS (15 - 20 MINUTES)	
Review Cotton Eyed Joe and Sweetheart Schottische. Teach both dances as a line dance and then a couples dance following each review in a double circle. Partners face counter clockwise (CCW).	Scattered formation. Use Elbow-to-elbow to create partners following the teaching of the dances as a line dance. Once have partner, they follow the back of the necks of another couple and "fall-in" to make a circle.

Line dancing in one form or another has been around since recorded time.

GAME (5 MINUTES)	
Blob tag Select 2 it's. Only the person at the end of the line tags.	**See DPESS Chapter 14 for details.**

EVALUATION/REVIEW AND CHEER

Were any of the Fitness Scavenger Hunt activities especially challenging today?
Which dance steps are used in both 8-Count Polka and Cotton-Eyed Joe?
What is the main dance step in Sweetheart Schottische?

Cheer: Country Western Dance, yea!

Rhythms and Dance Lesson Plan 3

EQUIPMENT:

Music for Aerobic Exercises
Music for 8-Count Polka
Music/ CD player
Cage Ball

OBJECTIVES:

The student will:

1. Participate in Balance Tag activities demonstrating creativity, balance and following the instructions described by the instructor.
2. Participate in an Aerobic Workout to improve strength, endurance, flexibility and cardiovascular endurance.
3. Participate in the 8-Count Polka dance demonstrating rhythm and using form demonstrated by the instructor.
4. Play Long Team Cage Ball during the closing portion of class demonstrating cooperative skills and agility.

National Standards Met in this Lesson: **1, 2, 3, 4, 5, 6**

INSTRUCTIONAL ACTIVITIES / **TEACHING HINTS**

INTRODUCTORY ACTIVITY (2 - 3 MINUTES)

Balance Tag
Select 2 – 3 It's

See DPESS Chapter 14 for details.
Designate how many seconds one must balance if tagged

FITNESS DEVELOPMENT (8 - 12 MINUTES)

Aerobic Workout

- Walk in place with knees high to the beat.
- Jump in place 8 x hitting the sides of thighs hands and with straight arms.
- Walk in place on toes performing 16 steps moving arms down and up on the sides/front of body
- Run in place 8 x while lifting feet high in the rear.
- Run in place 8 x while lifting knees high in front.
- 8 jumping jacks full arm movements
- 8 jumping jacks moving arms down and only half way up (to the shoulder level).
- Mountain Climber 8 x alternating feet
- Pony: "Hop, step, step." Repeat on the other side.
- Heel, toe, slide, and slide 4 x each direction
- Hop on one foot and lift up the opposite knee. Reverse.
- Hop on one foot, and swing kick the opposite foot forward. Reverse.
- Charleston Bounce Step: Step R, kick the L foot forward, step back on the L foot, and touch the R toe back. Repeat 8 x. Reverse.
- Can-Can Kick: Hop, kick opposite leg high.
- Perform full body stretches
- Strengthening exercises

Casten, Jordan, AEROBICS TODAY, 2ND ED., WADSWORTH PUBLISHERS, 2002.

Use music appropriate for Aerobic Exercise, 120 – 170 beats per minute.

See DPESS Chapter 16 for details.

See DPESS Chapter 16 for details.

Mountain Climber: Jump and land forward and backward a distance of about one foot. Alternate feet. Arms swing in opposition to leg movements.

Heel, toe, slide, and slide: Hop on the left foot while tapping the right heel to the right side. While hopping again on the left foot, swing the right foot to the front and touch the toe on the floor. Perform 2 slides to the right. Repeat the entire phrase by hopping on the right foot and sliding to the left.

LESSON FOCUS (15 - 20 MINUTES)

Introduce 8-Count Polka without partners.

Instructions on record/tape/CD.
Scattered formation.

INSTRUCTIONAL ACTIVITIES	TEACHING HINTS
Practice with partners and in a double circle CCW	Scattered formation with partner Use management games in Lesson 2 to make circle with partners.

8-Count Polka is another popular couples or line dance that can be seen and danced at country western dance venues. Variations of the dance include 10-Count Polka and 16-Count Polka.

GAME (5 MINUTES)

Long Team Cage Ball Create two teams using management game.	**See DPESS Chapter 18 for details.** Use Back-to-Back to make pairs. Identify each person by placing a hand on a different body part. People with hand on "head" go to one side to become a team. Other person goes to other side to become the other team.

EVALUATION/REVIEW AND CHEER

What steps in 8-Count Polka and Swing are similar? Were there any steps used in Aerobics that were challenging? Tomorrow, we will review all the dances you have learned so far.

Cheer: Dance, yea!

Rhythms and Dance Lesson Plan 4

EQUIPMENT:

Continuity music CD/ music
Schottische music CD/ music
Swing Music
CD/tape for Continuity Exercises
CD/ music Player
1 jump rope per student
1 long jump rope per 5 students

OBJECTIVES:

The student will:

1. Participate in Whistle March Schottische demonstrating rhythm, the schottische step and following the instructions described by the instructor.
2. Participate in Continuity Exercises to improve strength, endurance, flexibility and cardiovascular endurance.
3. Participate in the East Coast Swing lesson demonstrating rhythm and using form demonstrated by the instructor.
4. Play Long Rope Routines during the closing portion of class demonstrating rhythm, cooperative skills and agility while following the instructions of the game.

National Standards Met in this Lesson: **1, 2, 3, 4, 5, 6**

INSTRUCTIONAL ACTIVITIES	TEACHING HINTS

INTRODUCTORY ACTIVITY (2 - 3 MINUTES)

Whistle March Schottische	Just like Whistle March except use Schottische music
Identify beat by saying steps out loud first.	Sound whistle to make group sizes. Change frequently.

FITNESS DEVELOPMENT (8 - 12 MINUTES)

Continuity Exercises	**See DPESS Chapter 16 for details.**
Use a variety of floor strengthening exercises.	Jump on music, floor work on 20 sec. pause in music.

Continuity Exercises use the theory of interval training to improve fitness levels. During these exercises you will use muscles in your entire body as well as improve your cardiovascular aerobic fitness level.

LESSON FOCUS (15 - 20 MINUTES)

Teach East Coast Swing basic steps without partners	Scattered formation.
Use whole-part-whole teaching method.	Music tape/CD has instructions listed. *
East Coast Swing with Partners	Use management, Lesson 2 to make partners. Scattered formation.
Introduce turns for each partner in Swing Practice	Demonstrate with a student partner. Demonstrate both leader (male) and follower (female) parts.

East Coast Swing is a ballroom dance adaptation derived from various street swing dancing patterns and styles (especially Lindy Hop) developed at the height of the Swing Era in the 1940's.

GAME (5 MINUTES)

Long Rope Routines	
1 whistle = rope up and over	Use Whistle Mixer to create groups of 4 – 5
2 whistles = run to end of line	Stretch long rope out on L side of students
Practice trotting and responding to whistles	Add music for fun and interest

EVALUATION/REVIEW AND CHEER

What areas of fitness did you work on improving today?
Which dance learned so far is your favorite? Why.
Was there any part of learning the Swing with turns that presented difficulty?
What is the history of the East Coast Swing?
Cheer: 2, 4, 8, Swing is great!

Rhythms and Dance Lesson Plan 5

EQUIPMENT:

Music for Cotton Eyed Joe, Sweetheart Schottische, 8 Count Polka, Swing
Music/ CD player
Cageball
1 hoop per student
1 scooter per student

OBJECTIVES:

The student will:

1. Participate in Hoops and Plyometrics activities demonstrating strength, agility, cooperative skills, and following the instructions described by the instructor.
2. Participate in Circuit Training activities to improve strength, endurance, flexibility and cardiovascular endurance.
3. Participate in the Swing, Cotton Eyed Joe, Sweetheart Schottische, and 8-Count Polka demonstrating rhythm, motor memory and using form demonstrated by the instructor.
4. Play Scooter Cageball Soccer during the closing portion of class demonstrating cooperative skills, eye foot coordination and agility while following the instructions of the game.

National Standards Met in this Lesson: **1, 2, 3, 5, 6**

INSTRUCTIONAL ACTIVITIES	TEACHING HINTS
INTRODUCTORY ACTIVITY (2 - 3 MINUTES)	
Hoops and plyometrics	**See DPESS Chapter 14 for details.**
Sound whistle to signal movement challenges	
FITNESS DEVELOPMENT (8 - 12 MINUTES)	
Circuit Training Fitness with Jog	**See DPESS Chapter 16 for details.**
Explain each station	Using Whistle Mixer, create groups to go to Stations

Circuit training is a type of interval training whereby strength exercises are alternated with endurance/aerobic exercises at different stations, combining the benefits of both a cardiovascular and strength training workout.

INSTRUCTIONAL ACTIVITIES	TEACHING HINTS
LESSON FOCUS (15 - 20 MINUTES)	
Review Swing with turns; Cotton Eyed Joe, Sweetheart Schottische, and 8-Count Polka	Change partners frequently using management games.

Long ago in American history, these dances were performed in barns at community parties.

INSTRUCTIONAL ACTIVITIES	TEACHING HINTS
GAME (5 MINUTES)	
Scooter Cageball Soccer	**See DPESS Chapter 18 for details.**
Must remain on scooter to earn goal point	Using management games, create two teams

EVALUATION/REVIEW AND CHEER

Was there one station on the Circuit Training that was particularly challenging? Why?
What muscles did you use during Circuit Training Fitness?
Which dance is your favorite and why?

Use name of the favorite dance for today's cheer.

Rhythms and Dance Lesson Plan 6

EQUIPMENT:

Music for Leader Activity
Music for Cha Cha
Music / CD player

OBJECTIVES:

The student will:

1. Participate in New Leader Activities demonstrating rhythm, agility, cooperative skills, and following the instructions described by the instructor.
2. Participate in 12 Ways of Fitness activities to improve strength, endurance, flexibility and cardiovascular endurance.
3. Demonstrate Cha Cha and Swing Dance steps demonstrating rhythm, motor memory and using form demonstrated by the instructor.
4. Play Spider Tag during the closing portion of class demonstrating cooperative skills and agility while following the instructions of the game.

National Standards Met in this Lesson: **1, 2, 3, 4, 5, 6**

INSTRUCTIONAL ACTIVITIES	TEACHING HINTS

INTRODUCTORY ACTIVITY (2 - 3 MINUTES)

New Leader Activity moving to music Leader begins moving to beat/style of music. Others follow until you signal for a leader change.	**See DPESS Chapter 14 for details.** Use management game to create groups of 3 – 5 Use management technique to identify first leader

FITNESS DEVELOPMENT (8 - 12 MINUTES)

12 Ways of Fitness	**See DPESS Chapter 16 for details.** Select 12 leaders

LESSON FOCUS (15 - 20 MINUTES)

Demonstrate Cha-Cha basic steps Explain history. Show video clip of Cha-Cha.	**See DPESS Chapter 20 for details.** Wright, J., "**Social Dance**", Human Kinetics Publishers.

The cha-cha-cha is a Latin American dance of Cuban origin. The music for the ballroom Cha-cha-cha is energetic and with a steady beat. The "Latin" cha-cha-cha is slower, more sensual and may involve complicated rhythms. The phrase to the Cha Cha is: one-two-cha cha cha.

Review Swing and add the Pretzel step	Use management game to create partners. Change often.

GAME (5 MINUTES)

Spider Tag Select it's and change them frequently	**See DPESS Chapter 14 for details.** Use Back-to-Back to create pairs

EVALUATION/REVIEW AND CHEER

Review history of Cha-cha and basic steps taught.
What was the most difficult aspect of Spider Tag?

Cheer: Cha, cha, cha, yea!

Rhythms and Dance Lesson Plan 7

EQUIPMENT:

Music for Waltz and Swing
3 clothes pins
Music / CD player
Music for Aerobic Exercises

OBJECTIVES:

The student will:

1. Participate in Standing High Fives demonstrating agility, cooperative skills, and following the instructions described by the instructor.
2. Participate in an Aerobic workout to improve strength, endurance, flexibility and cardiovascular endurance.
3. Demonstrate Waltz and Swing dance steps demonstrating rhythm, motor memory and using form demonstrated by the instructor.
4. Play Clothespin Tag during the closing portion of class demonstrating cooperative skills and agility while following the instructions of the game.

National Standards Met in this Lesson: **1, 2, 3, 4, 5, 6**

INSTRUCTIONAL ACTIVITIES	TEACHING HINTS

INTRODUCTORY ACTIVITY (2 - 3 MINUTES)

Standing High Fives	**See DPESS Chapter 14 for details.** Use Toe-to-Toe to create partners about the same height

FITNESS DEVELOPMENT (8 - 12 MINUTES)

Aerobic Workout	See Lesson 3 for details Scattered formation

LESSON FOCUS (15 - 20 MINUTES)

Demonstrate Waltz basic steps	**See DPESS Chapter 20 for details.**
Explain history. Show video clip of Waltz.	Wright, J., "**Social Dance**", Human Kinetics Publishers.
Teach in scattered formation, then as couples.	Use management game to create partners
Practice Swing	Use management game to change partners

The Waltz originated from the peasants of Bavaria, Tyrol, and Styria who began dancing a dance called Walzer, a dance for couples, around 1750. The waltz became fashionable in Vienna around the 1780s. There are various types of Waltz including a Country Western Waltz. All use ¾ time.

GAME (5 MINUTES)

Clothespin Tag	**See DPESS Chapter 14 for details.**
Select 2 – 3 it's to begin. Change often.	

EVALUATION/REVIEW AND CHEER

What were the most challenging activities during the Aerobic Workout?
What was the hardest activity worked on today and why?
Which dance taught so far is the favorite and why?

Cheer: We Love to Swing!

Rhythms and Dance Lesson Plan 8

EQUIPMENT:

Music for Mirror Drill
Music for Waltz and Cha Cha
Cones to mark Fitness area
CD/ music player
Fitness Cookie Jar & instructions

OBJECTIVES:

The student will:

1. Participate in Mirror Drills to music demonstrating rhythmic awareness, cooperative skills, and following the instructions described by the instructor.
2. Participate in the Fitness Cookie Jar Exchange activities to improve strength, endurance, flexibility and cardiovascular endurance.
3. Demonstrate Waltz and Cha Cha dance steps demonstrating rhythm, motor memory and using form demonstrated by the instructor.
4. Play Loose Caboose during the closing portion of class demonstrating cooperative skills and agility while following the instructions of the game.

National Standards Met in this Lesson: **1, 2, 3, 4, 5, 6**

INSTRUCTIONAL ACTIVITIES	TEACHING HINTS
INTRODUCTORY ACTIVITY (2 - 3 MINUTES)	
Mirror Drill in Place to Music	**See DPESS Chapter 14 for details.**
Leader makes movements motivated by the style music	Use Back-to-Back to create partners
FITNESS DEVELOPMENT (8 - 12 MINUTES)	
Fitness Cookie Jar Exchange	**See DPESS Chapter 16 for details.**
Play music for motivation and fun	Place Cookie Jar in center of Gym/space
LESSON FOCUS (15 - 20 MINUTES)	
Review Waltz steps in square and balance pattern	Scattered formation
Practice with a partner	Use management game to create partners
Review Cha-Cha and practice	Change partners with management game
Teach the Cha-Cha chase step	Change partners with management game
GAME (5 MINUTES)	
Loose Caboose	**See DPESS Chapter 14 for details.**
Select 2 it's	Use Toe-to-toe to make pairs of students.

EVALUATION/REVIEW AND CHEER

Were there any exercises in the Fitness Cookie Jar that were particularly difficult? Why?
Do you like the chase step? Why?

Cheer: Waltz rules!

Rhythms and Dance Lesson Plan 9

EQUIPMENT:

Cones for station markers
Challenge Course signs
Hoops, ropes, jumping boxes for Challenge activities
Music for Challenge course, Waltz, Foxtrot
CD/ music player
1 Basketball per relay squad

OBJECTIVES:

The student will:

1. Participate in Running High-Fives demonstrating cooperative skills, and following the instructions described by the instructor.
2. Participate in the Challenge Course activities to improve strength, endurance, flexibility and cardiovascular endurance.
3. Demonstrate Waltz and Foxtrot dance steps demonstrating rhythm, motor memory and using form demonstrated by the instructor.
4. Participate in Pass and Squat Relays during the closing portion of class demonstrating cooperative skills and agility while following the instructions of the game.

National Standards Met in this Lesson: **1, 2, 3, 4, 5, 6**

INSTRUCTIONAL ACTIVITIES	TEACHING HINTS

INTRODUCTORY ACTIVITY (2 - 3 MINUTES)

Running High-Fives Create interval music CD/tape: 15 sec. on, 15 sec. off	**See DPESS Chapter 14 for details.** Alternate with high and low five's

FITNESS DEVELOPMENT (8 - 12 MINUTES)

Challenge Course Have cones at each station with instructions Use music for fitness fun	**See DPESS Chapter 16 for details.** Using Whistle Mixer create equal groups for the stations you have created.

LESSON FOCUS (15 - 20 MINUTES)

Teach Waltz turns and practice Waltz patterns **Box pattern 4 x, balance 4x, box 4 x, 6 count turn, repeat**	**See DPESS Chapter 20 for details.**
Teach Foxtrot basic step without partners **Teach Foxtrot with partners**	Wright, J., **"Social Dance"**, Human Kinetics Publishers. Use management game to create partners

The Foxtrot is a ballroom dance which takes its name from the vaudeville actor Harry Fox. The basic Foxtrot rhythm is slow-slow-quick-quick. The dance was premiered in a stage production in 1914. From the late teens through the 1940's, the foxtrot was the most popular fast dance and the majority of records made during these years were foxtrots.

GAME (5 MINUTES)

Pass and Squat Relays Direct relay and repeat challenge	**See DPESS Chapter 18 for details.** Using Whistle Mixer, create 5 – 7 equal teams

EVALUATION/REVIEW AND CHEER

What is the history of the dance Foxtrot?
What was the most challenging activity on the Challenge Course?
What are the similarities between the Waltz and Foxtrot? Who is the Foxtrot named after?

Cheer: Foxtrot is hot!

Rhythms and Dance Lesson Plan 10

EQUIPMENT:

1 long jump rope per 3 students CD/ music player

Music for: Whistle March, Long Rope Fitness, Foxtrot, Cotton Eyed Joe, 8 Count Polka, Sweetheart Schottische, Swing, and Waltz

OBJECTIVES:

The student will:

1. Participate in Whistle March demonstrating cooperative skills, and following the instructions described by the instructor.
2. Participate in the Long Jump Rope Fitness Routine activities to improve strength, endurance, flexibility and cardiovascular endurance.
3. Demonstrate Cotton Eyed Joe, 8-Count Polka, Sweetheart Schottische, Swing, Waltz and Foxtrot dances demonstrating rhythm, motor memory and using form demonstrated by the instructor.

National Standards Met in this Lesson: **1, 2, 3, 4, 5, 6**

INSTRUCTIONAL ACTIVITIES	TEACHING HINTS
INTRODUCTORY ACTIVITY (2 - 3 MINUTES)	
Whistle March Sound whistle to make group sizes and return to 1 sound	See Lesson 2 for details
FITNESS DEVELOPMENT (8 - 12 MINUTES)	
Long Jump Rope Fitness Routine	**See DPESS Chapter 16 for details.** Use Whistle Mixer to make groups of 3
LESSON FOCUS AND GAME (20 MINUTES)	
Foxtrot patterns: Box 4x, progressive 4x, hesitation L turn; repeat with hesitation turn to R.	**See DPESS Chapter 20 for details.**
Review and practice all dances taught during the unit: Cotton Eyed Joe, 8-Count Polka, Sweetheart Schottische, Swing, Waltz, Foxtrot	Use management games to continually change partners.
Other dances that can be taught in unit: Miserlou, Mayim, Mayim, Polka, popular line dances.	**See DPESS Chapter 16 for details.**

EVALUATION/REVIEW AND CHEER

What muscles were used in fitness today?

Recite the history of one of the dances performed today.

Out of all the dances learned which were the hardest? Why? Which were the most fun? Why?

Cheer: 2,4,6,8, Dancing is really great!

Softball

This unit has been specifically designed to meet all six components of the NASPE National Standards for Physical Education.

OBJECTIVES:

The student will:

1. Participate in PACER Running, Rhythmic Parachute Exercises, Jog, Walk, Jog and Continuity Exercises using form demonstrated by the instructor to improve fitness.
2. Participate in the Rooster Hop Drill, Flash Drill, Coffee Grinder Square, Move and Perform a Stretch, and Over, Under and Around to improve agility and demonstrate cooperation with peers.
3. Play Frisbee Softball, Two Pitch Softball, Frisbee Around Nine, and Home Run demonstrating sportsmanship and cooperation.
4. Play Softball following regulation rules and demonstrating skills demonstrated by the instructor during the unit.

SOFTBALL BLOCK PLAN
1 WEEK UNIT

Week #1	Monday	Tuesday	Wednesday	Thursday	Friday
Introductory Activity	Rooster Hop Drill	Mirror Drill in Place	Flash Drill	Coffee Grinder Square	Pacman
Fitness	PACER Run	Rhythmic Aerobic Activities	Aerobic Workout	Continuity Exercises	Nine Station Course
Lesson Focus	Catching Throwing Rules	Throwing Running and Throwing	Batting Throwing Catching	Catching Base Running	Bunting
Game	Frisbee Around Nine	Pepper	Frisbee Softball	Two Pitch Softball	In a Pickle

Week #2	Monday	Tuesday	Wednesday	Thursday	Friday
Introductory Activity	Builders/ Destroyers	Move, Stop, Pivot	Frozen Tag with Variation	Move and Perform Stretch	Over, Under, and Around
Fitness	Scavenger Hunt Fitness	Partner Resistance Exercises	Continuity Exercises	Jog, Walk, Jog	Parachute Rhythmic Exercises
Lesson Focus	Infield Short Play	Easy Does It Grounders	Swing It	Play Softball	Play Softball
Game	Wands	Addition Tag	Team Tug-of-War	Home Run	

Softball Lesson Plan 1

EQUIPMENT:

1 softball per 2 students
Cones to mark throwing and catching area
CD/ tape for PACER
1 glove per 2 students
CD/ tape player
Softball rules handout you create

OBJECTIVES:

The student will:

1. Participate in the Rooster Hop Drill demonstrating hopping skills, quickness, agility, and following the instructions described by the instructor.
2. Participate in PACER running to improve aerobic endurance during the Fitness section of class.
3. Demonstrate throwing and catching skills as demonstrated by the instructor.
4. Participate in Frisbee Around Nine with a partner as presented by the instructor during the closing portion of class.

National Standards Met in this Lesson: **1, 2, 3, 4, 5, 6**

INSTRUCTIONAL ACTIVITIES	TEACHING HINTS

INTRODUCTORY ACTIVITY (2 - 3 MINUTES)

Rooster Hop Drill

Students hop 10 yards on one leg in the following sequence:

1. Left hand touching the right toe, which is on the ground.
2. Right hand touching the left toe on the ground.
3. Right hand
4. Bend the knees, hands on the floor or ground.
5. Legs kick back into an all fours position, head up.

See DPESS Chapter 14 for details.
Scattered formation
Direct students through a variety of movements

FITNESS DEVELOPMENT (8 - 12 MINUTES)

PACER Running

Progressive aerobic cardiovascular endurance runs.

See DPESS Chapter 2 for details.
Use a timed CD/tape
Scatter formation

PACER running is part of the Fitnessgram aerobic fitness testing. Practicing the PACER run will help you progressively improve your cardiovascular endurance.

LESSON FOCUS (15 - 20 MINUTES)

Catching skills: Demonstrate catching skills

See DPESS Chapter 19 for details.

Ground Balls: Demonstrate drill

Students roll softball to partner 10 x with and without a glove. Increase distance between partners.

Use Elbow-to-Elbow to create partners.

Throwing: Demonstrate throwing from standing and running.

Students 10 – 20' apart to throw and catch from standing

Scattered formation where student can view demonstration.
Use a glove in this drill.

Teach rules of Softball

Give handout and read in class.

Softball originated in Chicago on Thanksgiving Day, 1887. A group of about twenty young men had gathered in a Gym to hear the outcome of the Harvard-Yale football game. After Yale's victory was announced and bets were paid, a man picked up a boxing glove and threw it at someone, who hit it with a pole. George Hancock, usually considered the inventor of softball, shouted, "Let's play ball!" He tied the boxing glove so that it resembled a ball, chalked out a diamond on the floor and broke off a broom handle to serve as a bat.

INSTRUCTIONAL ACTIVITIES | **TEACHING HINTS**

GAME (5 MINUTES)

Frisbee Around Nine
A target is set up with 9 different throwing positions around it, each 2 feet farther away. The throwing positions can be clockwise or counterclockwise around the target. They can also be in a straight line from the target. Points are awarded based on the throwing position number (for example, number 7 means 7 points for hitting the target). The game can be played indoors or out.

See DPESS Chapter 20 for details.
Create partners using Elbow-to Elbow technique.

EVALUATION/REVIEW AND CHEER

What is the reason for doing PACER running?
Name the two drills used in the lesson focus?
Where should you be looking during softball?
How and when did softball originate?
Is there any similarity between Frisbee Around 9 and Softball?

Cheer: 2, 4,6,8, P.E. is really great

Softball Lesson Plan 2

EQUIPMENT:

1 Incredi-ball per student
Cones to mark throwing and catching area
CD/ music for Rhythmic Aerobic Activity
1 glove per 2 students
CD/ music player

OBJECTIVES:

The student will:

1. Participate in the Mirror Drill Introductory Activity following the movements of a partner.
2. Participate in Rhythmic Aerobic Activity as led by the instructor to improve cardiovascular respiratory and muscular endurance.
3. Demonstrate proper throwing technique using form demonstrated by the instructor.
4. Demonstrate the basics of bat control by putting the bat on the ground after hitting the ball during Pepper.

National Standards Met in this Lesson: **1, 2, 3, 4, 5, 6**

INSTRUCTIONAL ACTIVITIES | **TEACHING HINTS**

INTRODUCTORY ACTIVITY (2 - 3 MINUTES)

Mirror Drill in Place
Demonstrate proficient movement skills in aquatic, rhythms/dance, and individual and dual activities.
Using quick movements of head, arms, legs or body

See DPESS Chapter 14 for details.
Use toe-to-toe to make partners
Identify leader and follower

FITNESS DEVELOPMENT (8 - 12 MINUTES)

Rhythmic Aerobic Activity
Create a CD/ music or purchase a pre-recorded Aerobic Exercise CD with 120-150 BPM

See DPESS Chapter 16 for details.
Scattered formation
Students follow lead of instructor

Rhythmic Aerobic Activities improve the cardiovascular respiratory system while providing exercise for the entire body. They also allow people to enjoy exercising as a group to music. This is popular in health clubs.

LESSON FOCUS (15 - 20 MINUTES)

Throwing Skills

See DPESS Chapter 19 for details.

INSTRUCTIONAL ACTIVITIES	TEACHING HINTS
Break down throw into 4 steps 1. Point to target with glove hand 2. Bring throwing arm back to a 90 degree angle at the elbow 3. Step with foot opposite of throwing arm 4. Arm swing, release ball	Practice without a ball until the students perform the proper mechanics. Add the ball to the practice.
Run and Throw Drill: Demonstrate drill. On signal students will run and throw to another student who is directly across from the thrower at twenty feet. Repeat. Each student throws 10 x	Use same partners Can vary distances as needed.
GAME (5 MINUTES)	
Pepper At least 10 yards apart from batter and fielders Always use safety precautions when students are near a bat	**See DPESS Chapter 19 for details.** Whistle mixer to make groups of 4-6

EVALUATION/REVIEW AND CHEER

What is the value of Rhythmic Aerobic Activity?
Review proper throwing techniques and an improper throwing technique.
At what angle should the arm be while throwing?

Cheer: 3-6-9, I shine!

Softball Lesson Plan 3

EQUIPMENT:

Aerobics Workouts music CD/tape

1 bat per 6 – 8 students

30 Wiffle balls

2 Frisbee's

CD/music player

1 glove per 6 – 8 students

6 batting tee's

OBJECTIVES:

The student will:

1. Participate in the Flash Drill Introductory Activity following the movements of a partner.
2. Participate in Aerobics Workout as led by the instructor to improve cardiovascular respiratory and muscular endurance.
3. Demonstrate proper batting from a tee, throwing, catching, and running techniques using form demonstrated by the instructor.
4. Participate in Frisbee Softball during the game portions of class demonstrating throwing and catching skills and following the rules established by the instructor.

National Standards Met in this Lesson: **1, 2, 3, 4, 5, 6**

INSTRUCTIONAL ACTIVITIES	TEACHING HINTS
INTRODUCTORY ACTIVITY (2 - 3 MINUTES)	
Flash Drill	**See DPESS Chapter 14 for details.**
Students stand in a ready position facing the teacher. The teacher exclaims "feet," and students stutter the feet quickly. Teacher moves arms and students move in that direction.	Scattered formation. See Lesson 3, Tennis Unit for complete details.
FITNESS DEVELOPMENT (8 - 12 MINUTES)	
Aerobics Workout	**See DPESS Chapter 16 for details.**
Create a music CD/tape or purchase a pre-recorded Aerobic Exercise CD with 120-150 BPM.	Scattered formation. See Lesson Plan 7, Racquetball Unit for details.
LESSON FOCUS (15 - 20 MINUTES)	
Batting Skills: Demonstrate batting skills	**See DPESS Chapter 19 for details.**
4 Stations: 1) From a tee; 2) Soft toss; 3) Throwing and Catching Review; 4) Run, Throw and Catch	Use Toe-to-Toe to create partners. Combine 3 - 4 sets of partners to create groups for stations.
Hitting from a Tee. Demonstrate skill.	Scattered formation where student can view demonstration.
Partners rotate hitting wiffle balls off a tee and into a fence. Each student will hit 5 balls then change rolls.	One student will place a wiffle ball on a tee and the other will hit the ball into a fence. Hitter retrieves balls.
Demonstrate the **Soft Toss Drill**: Partners will rotate tossing and hitting wiffle balls into a fence. One person tosses a wiffle ball at waist level and the partner hits it into a fence.	Each student will hit 5 balls and then change roles. Hitter retrieves balls.
Review Run, Throw, Catch drill from yesterday and Throwing and Catching drill from yesterday.	Assign groups to stations. Signal rotation at equal intervals.

The first women's softball team was formed in 1895 at Chicago's West Division High School. They did not obtain a coach for competitive play until 1899 and it was difficult to create interest among fans.

GAME (5 MINUTES)

Frisbee Softball **See DPESS Chapter 20 for details.**

Use Whistle Mixer to create teams.

EVALUATION/REVIEW AND CHEER

Name the drills used in the lesson focus today?

Name the 3 key points for hitting off of the tee?

When and where did women's softball begin?

Cheer: 2,4,6,8, Softball is Really Great!

Softball Lesson Plan 4

EQUIPMENT:

Music/ CD for Continuity Exercises
1 glove per 2 students
CD/ Music player
1 – 2 sets of bases

OBJECTIVES:

The student will:

1. Participate in Coffee Grinder Square demonstrating strength and agility while following the instructions established by the instructor.
2. Participate in Continuity Exercises to improve overall body strength, aerobic endurance, and flexibility during the Fitness portion of class.
3. Demonstrate the proper basic mechanics of throwing a fly ball, catching a fly ball, base running, and catching ground balls as demonstrated by the instructor.
4. Play Two Pitch Softball demonstrating pitching, ball control and cooperative skills during the game portion of class.

National Standards Met in this Lesson: **1, 2, 3, 4, 5, 6**

INSTRUCTIONAL ACTIVITIES	TEACHING HINTS
INTRODUCTORY ACTIVITY (2 - 3 MINUTES)	
Coffee Grinder Square Identify a locomotor activity to move from one corner to next. Student performs "Coffee Grinder" on alternate arms at each corner.	**See DPESS Chapter 14 for details.** Use Whistle Mixer to create 4 groups. Direct starting corner for each group. Set up square in area using beanbags or bases.
FITNESS DEVELOPMENT (8 - 12 MINUTES)	
Continuity Exercises These exercises are a type of interval training. Create a CD/cassette tape with 30 - 35 seconds of music and 20 seconds of silence. During the music, the students will jump rope. During the silence, instruct the students to do an exercise i.e. push-ups; curl ups; reverse push-ups; side leg lifts on each side; coffee grinder, arm circling, crab walks forward and backward, etc.	**See DPESS Chapter 16 for details.** Scattered formation When the music resumes, the students jump rope. During each silence direct a different exercise.
LESSON FOCUS (15 - 20 MINUTES)	
Three Fly Drill: On signal one partner throws a fly ball directly to the other. The 2nd fly ball should be thrown so the student drop-steps and runs backward without back peddling. The 3rd fly ball should be thrown so the partner has to sprint forward to catch the ball. Switch roles after 5 tries.	**See DPESS Chapter 19 for details.** Demonstrate three fly drill. Use Back-to-Back to create partners.
Get Up and Catch 2 students work together. One says, "go" and throws a fly ball while the other lies on stomach on the grass and gets up, locates and catches the fly ball. Repeat 3 x. Rotate.	**Demonstrate drill.** Be sure you have enough space between groups so students won't run into each other.
Ground ball drills: 2 students work together. First partner throws 3 easy ground balls to the other. One to the left, one directly at student and one to the right. Perform the drills 3 times each. Rotate.	**Demonstrate the drills** Increase difficulty with speed of throws, proximity and distance when appropriate.
Base Running Drills: Students run the bases in order Teach sound base running technique.	Use 3 or 4 areas set up with bases. Students will get tired, so let them run at their own pace.

INSTRUCTIONAL ACTIVITIES	TEACHING HINTS

The United States won its first Gold Medal in softball in 1996. Dr. Dorothy ("Dot") Richardson was the shortstop on the gold medal softball team. She was a key part of the United States national team that won the gold medal during the sport's Olympic debut in 1996. After her win at the Olympics, she continued with her career as an orthopedic surgeon. She won gold again in Sydney in the 2000 Olympics. Dr. Richardson is a great softball player and a great physician.

GAME (5 MINUTES)

Two Pitch Softball	**See DPESS Chapter 19 for details.**
Every team member pitches at least once.	Use Whistle Mixer to create teams.

EVALUATION/REVIEW AND CHEER

Name the two time Olympic softball shortstop.
What is the main difference between catching ground balls and fly balls?
Cheer: Softball's here, yea!

Softball Lesson Plan 5

EQUIPMENT:

3 wiffle balls per group
1 jump rope per 4 students
3 Hula Hoops per 4 students
2 bases/ poly spots per 3 students
1 Incredi-ball per 2 students
1 glove per 2 students

OBJECTIVES:

The student will:

1. Participate in the Introductory Activity, Pacman, demonstrating cooperation while following the instructions established by the instructor.
2. Participate in the Nine Station Fitness Course to improve overall body strength, aerobic endurance, and flexibility during the Fitness portion of class.
3. Demonstrate the proper basic mechanics of bunting a softball as demonstrated by the instructor.
4. Play the game of In-a-Pickle demonstrating ball control and cooperative skills.

National Standards Met in this Lesson: **1, 2, 3, 4, 5, 6**

INSTRUCTIONAL ACTIVITIES	TEACHING HINTS

INTRODUCTORY ACTIVITY (2 - 3 MINUTES)

Pacman	**See DPESS Chapter 14 for details.**
Use lines on the gym floor	About 5 students are given the Pacman designation.
Change locomotor movements for each game played	Pacman's are the taggers.

INSTRUCTIONAL ACTIVITIES | **TEACHING HINTS**

Pac-Man is a Japanese arcade game developed in 1980. It became very popular very quickly and still is enjoyed today.

FITNESS DEVELOPMENT (8 - 12 MINUTES)

Nine Station Course

Station 1:Jump Ropes
Station 2: Push-ups
Station 3: Agility Run
Station 4: Arm Circles
Station 5: Rowing
Station 6: Crab Walk
Station 7: Treadmill
Station 8: Windmill
Staion 9: Hula-Hoops

See DPESS Chapter 16 for details.

Organize stations that each station uses a different muscle group
Emphasize proper form

LESSON FOCUS (15 - 20 MINUTES)

Bunting

Toes and chest point to the pitcher
Bat is about eye level over the plate
Bat should be in front of home plate
Knees bent
Grip: fingers hide behind bat. One hand on knob of the bat, other hand below barrel of the bat

Groups: a tosser, a bunter, shagger, observer

See DPESS Chapter 19 for details.

Demonstrate bunting
Scattered formation

Use whistle mixer to make groups of 4
Distribute and explain the bunting task sheet

Bunting is defined as: Using the bat to just block the ball without following through.

GAME (5 MINUTES)

In-a-Pickle

Using Incredi-balls and gloves, a student tries to avoid a tag from the other students playing the bases. Stay between two bases. Example: between second and third base.

See DPESS Chapter 19 for details.

Set out two markers to indicate two bases per group.
Use Whistle Mixer to create groups of 3.
Identify a runner and two fielders.
The runner tries to get to the next base without being tagged by the fielder. Rotate positions.

EVALUATION/REVIEW AND CHEER

Of the stations used in Fitness today, which one worked on aerobic endurance?
Describe bunting.
What are two keys points to being a successful bunter?
Are knees bent or straight?
Cheer: Super bunters!!

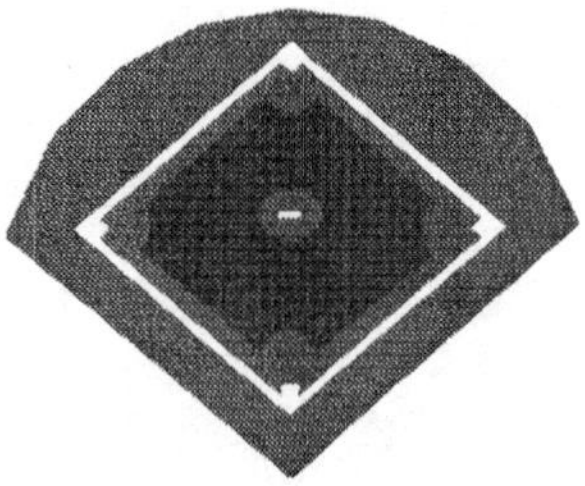

Task Sheet: Bunting

Directions:

1. Work in groups of four people: a batter, shagger, pitcher, a recorder.
2. Record the name of each group member on the chart below.
3. Use bunting form taught in class.
4. Place 3 hula hoops in front of the batter.
5. Pitcher stands behind the center hoop.
6. Mark the areas the ball is bunted into with an "X". Keep score.

Pitcher

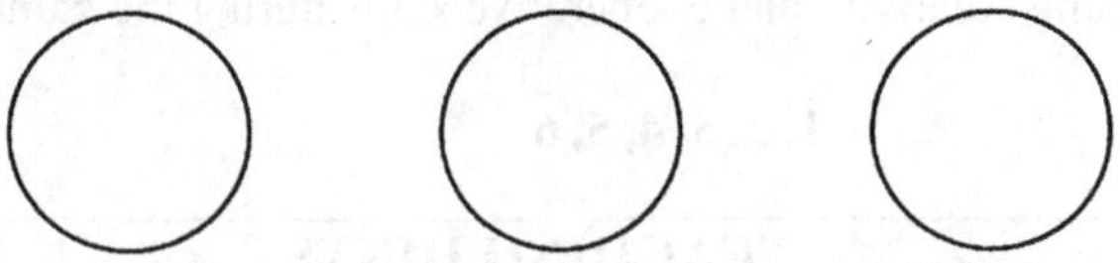

3 points 2 points 1 Point

Batter

1. Names	**2. Points**
3.	4.
5.	6.
7.	8.
9.	10.

USE "X" MARKS TO KEEP SCORE

Softball Lesson Plan 6

EQUIPMENT:

Incredi-balls
4 Bases per field
1 bat for each instructor/ leader
Scavenger station cards
35 Cones
1 Magic Wand per student
1 glove per two students

OBJECTIVES:

The student will:

1. Participate in Builders/Destroyers demonstrating agility, quickness, and cooperative skills during the Introductory Activity.
2. Participate in the Fitness Scavenger Hunt for the Fitness Activity to increase strength, flexibility, and cardiovascular respiratory endurance.
3. Demonstrate the proper way to address a ball for short play in the game of softball as demonstrated by the instructor.
4. Participate in Wand activities demonstrating creativity and cooperative skills during the game portion of class.

National Standards Met in this Lesson: **1, 2, 3, 4, 5, 6**

INSTRUCTIONAL ACTIVITIES	TEACHING HINTS
INTRODUCTORY ACTIVITY (2 - 3 MINUTES)	
Builders/Destroyers	**See DPESS Chapter 14 for details.**
Use about 30 cones on the gym floor in scatter formation with half of the cones tipped over. Half of the students are builders that are setting up the cones and the other half are destroyers that are tipping over the cones.	Start in scatter formation Keep track of how many cones are set up to challenge the students to get more the next time. Switch groups.
FITNESS DEVELOPMENT (8 - 12 MINUTES)	
Fitness Scavenger Hunt	**See DPESS Chapter 16 for details.**
Exercises listed on scavenger cards at stations	Use whistle mixer to create groups of 3. Assign each group to a starting point.
LESSON FOCUS (15 - 20 MINUTES)	
Infield Short Plays	**See DPESS Chapter 19 for details.**
Underhand toss to first base Toss and follow Underhand toss to second base Toss and follow Underhand toss to third base Toss and follow Have students split up by positions. Hit a grounder to each position. The student will toss and follow the ball to the base they are throwing to. That student replaces the student on the base and the student that was on the base goes to the line to get a grounder.	Use scatter formation to demonstrate Whistle mixer to set up in positions on the bases and in the field. Use the infield only
GAME (5 MINUTES)	
Wands	**See DPESS Chapter 14 for details.**
Wand Kicker Over Partner Exchange Partner creative exploration	Use scatter formation Use back-to-back to create pairs.

EVALUATION/REVIEW AND CHEER

What was challenging about Builders/ Destroyers today?
What muscles were used in class today?
When tossing the ball underhand to the bases, was one base easier/harder then another base? Why? How?
Cheer: Tossers are great!

Softball Lesson Plan 7

EQUIPMENT:

A lot of Tennis balls
Music/ CD for Fitness
Helmets
1 bat for each leader/field
Music Player

OBJECTIVES:

The student will:

1. Perform footwork inside the teaching area to increase reflexes as an individual when given a command by the instructor.
2. Participate in Partner Resistance Exercises in the Fitness lesson to help improve flexibility.
3. Learn fielding techniques for a grounder and the ready position as demonstrated by the instructor from all softball positions
4. Demonstrate cooperation and teamwork while participating in Addition Tag

National Standards Met in this Lesson: **1, 2, 3, 4, 5, 6**

INSTRUCTIONAL ACTIVITIES	TEACHING HINTS
INTRODUCTORY ACTIVITY (2 - 3 MINUTES)	
Move, Stop, Pivot Teacher blows whistle Once=jog Twice=stop and pivot Three times=Tap feet in place	**See DPESS Chapter 14 for details.** Scatter formation
FITNESS DEVELOPMENT (8 - 12 MINUTES)	
Partner Resistance Exercises Arm curl-ups Forearm Flex First Pull-Apart Butterfly Back Builder **Seated Stretch and Pull** **Scissors** **Bear Trap**	**See DPESS Chapter 16 for details.** Use elbow-to-elbow with someone to make pairs Scatter formation, standing next to partner Use music to motivate fitness session
LESSON FOCUS (15 - 20 MINUTES)	
Easy Does it Grounders Designate 10 positions on the field. Designate base runners. Begin with bases loaded.	Use whistle mixer to separate groups and assign positions
Leader hits grounders using tennis balls to all positions on the field. Repeat rotating positions often. Create double plays	Use Tennis balls. Tennis balls add fun to fielding grounders. The students may not be worried about getting hit by a tennis ball. If helmets are available, please use them

In softball and baseball, a double play for a team or a fielder is when two outs are made during the same continuous playing action. In baseball slang, making a double play is referred to as "turning two", or as Ernie Harwell has coined it, "two for the price of one".

GAME (5 MINUTES)	
Addition Tag	**See DPESS Chapter 14 for details.** Select several "its". Play the game 2-3 times

EVALUATION/REVIEW AND CHEER

How many outs are made in a double play?
Cheer: 3-2-1 Softball is fun!

Softball Lesson Plan 8

EQUIPMENT:

Wiffle balls
CD / Music Player
Tennis racquet
3 bats
Music for Continuity Exercises
1 jump rope per person 2 Tee's
Tug-of-War Rope

OBJECTIVES:

The student will:

1. Demonstrate agility and cooperation during Frozen Tag during the Introductory Activity.
2. Perform Continuity Exercises to improve endurance, flexibility and strength during the Fitness portion of class.
3. Participate in stations to improve his/her swings for the game of softball as demonstrated by the instructor.
4. Play Team Tug-of-War in two teams demonstrating cooperative and strength skills.

National Standards Met in this Lesson: **1, 2, 3, 4, 5, 6**

INSTRUCTIONAL ACTIVITIES	TEACHING HINTS
INTRODUCTORY ACTIVITY (2 - 3 MINUTES)	
Frozen Tag with Variation Students move in a designated area, when tagged they freeze. They can be unfrozen when someone crawls or dives under / between their legs.	**See DPESS Chapter 14 for details.** Scattered formation Select 1-3 Its
FITNESS DEVELOPMENT (8 - 12 MINUTES)	
Continuity Exercises Music is the signal. Music plays – Jump rope Music stops – push ups Sit ups Leg extension Crab walk	**See DPESS Chapter 16 for details.** Scattered formation On the crab walk cue, crab walk to a different jump rope other than their rope they just had
LESSON FOCUS (15 - 20 MINUTES)	
Swing it!	
Station 1: Drop ball Student drops a ball from behind the batter and batter has to hit the ball before it hits the ground	Goal is to hit the ball on the ground and not in the air.
Station 2: Pepper Use the game of pepper for bat control	
Station 3: Tee Place 1 tee in the inside corner, 1 tee on the outside corner. One person will call out inside or outside for the batter to hit.	
Station 4: Racquet Swinging Use a tennis racquet to hit wiffle balls. The face of the racquet should hit the ball.	Always use safety precautions when a bat is in play.
GAME (5 MINUTES)	
Team Tug- of -War Use teams of two. If there are a lot of students, make teams of 3 and do tournament style	**See DPESS Chapter 18 for details.** Different positions, Pick up and pull
EVALUATION/REVIEW AND CHEER	
Does your swing or the bat position change when hitting an inside and outside pitch? Which pitch is easier to hit, inside or outside? **Cheer: I am a homerun hitter!**	

Softball Lesson Plan 9

EQUIPMENT:

Bases for as many fields as you have

Several bats and balls

OBJECTIVES:

The student will:

1. Participate in Move and Perform a Stretch demonstrating stretching and locomotor skills during the Introductory Activity.
2. Perform Jog, Walk, Jog to improve endurance, flexibility and strength during the Fitness portion of class.
3. Play softball following given rules and demonstrating hitting, catching, batting and cooperative skills demonstrated in class during the unit.
4. Play Home Run demonstrating swinging, jogging, and skills during the game portion of class.

National Standards Met in this Lesson: **1, 2, 3, 4, 5, 6**

INSTRUCTIONAL ACTIVITIES	TEACHING HINTS
INTRODUCTORY ACTIVITY (2 - 3 MINUTES)	
Move and Perform a Stretch Move and perform a stretching activity on the sound of the whistle. Move and stretch to the sound of music. Skip, hop, shuffle, jog and walk.	**See DPESS Chapter 14 for details.** Scatter formation Direct starting and stopping locomotor movements to selected stretches using a whistle or a timed music CD/tape.
FITNESS DEVELOPMENT (8 - 12 MINUTES)	
Jog, Walk, Jog Direct students to jog as far as they can. When tired, they can walk, and resume jogging when able.	**See DPESS Chapter 16 for details.**
LESSON FOCUS (15 - 20 MINUTES)	
Play Softball	Use Whistle Mixer to create teams. Assign teams to field to play.
GAME (5 MINUTES)	
Home Run: This is a fun drill that allows the students to do a fake homerun swing and jog the bases slowly like they have hit a homerun. Each student should do this 3 times to cool down from 4 x 4 drill.	**See DPESS Chapter 19 for details.** Use Whistle Mixer to make appropriate groups for the base running set up.

EVALUATION/REVIEW AND CHEER

What did you work on during fitness today?

Are there any rules of softball you need to review?

Cheer: 3, 2, 1, Softball's really fun!

Softball Lesson Plan 10

EQUIPMENT:
Bases for as many fields as you have
Parachute
Music player
Several bats and balls
Music for fitness

OBJECTIVES:
The student will:
1. Participate in Over, Under, and Around #1 agility and cooperative skills during the Introductory Activity.
2. Participate in Parachute Rhythmic Aerobic Activities to improve aerobic endurance, flexibility and strength and during the Fitness portion of class.
3. Play softball following given rules and demonstrating hitting, catching, batting and cooperative skills demonstrated in class during the unit.

National Standards Met in this Lesson: **1, 2, 3, 4, 5, 6**

INSTRUCTIONAL ACTIVITIES	TEACHING HINTS
INTRODUCTORY ACTIVITY (2 - 3 MINUTES)	
Over, Under, and Around #1	**See DPESS Chapter 14 for details.** See Lesson Plan 5 from Racquetball Unit for details Use Back-to-back to create partners
FITNESS DEVELOPMENT (8 - 12 MINUTES)	
Parachute Rhythmic Aerobic Activities	**See DPESS Chapter 16 for details.** See Lesson Plan 11, Badminton Unit for details
LESSON FOCUSAND GAME (20 MINUTES)	
Play softball games	Use teams from yesterday or play Whistle Mixer to create new teams.

If a ball is pitched with spin on it, the air pressure on one side of the ball is greater than it is on the other, hence making the ball curve.

EVALUATION/REVIEW AND CHEER
Were there any skills in Softball that you still need to improve?
Cheer: Softball, softball, yea, softball!

Softball Lesson Plan 10 – Alternate Plan

EQUIPMENT:

1 Hula Hoop per person
Parachute
Bases
Music player
Bats
Incredi-balls
Gloves
Helmets
Music for fitness

OBJECTIVES:

The student will:

1. Participate in Musical Hoops during the Introductory Activity demonstrating locomotor and cooperative skills.
2. Participate in Parachute Rhythmic Aerobic Activities to improve strengthen, flexibility and rhythm during the Fitness section of class.
3. Participate in the softball World Series demonstrating softball skills, teamwork, cooperative skills demonstrated during the Softball Unit by the instructor.

National Standards Met in this Lesson: **1, 2, 3, 4, 5, 6**

INSTRUCTIONAL ACTIVITIES | **TEACHING HINTS**

INTRODUCTORY ACTIVITY (2 - 3 MINUTES)

Musical Hoops
Similar to musical chairs. Remove hoops as game is played. One or two feet are placed in the hoop to reserve the spot. The eliminated students return to the outside of the teaching area and perform a stretch until the music is played again. When the music resumes, student eliminated return to the game

See DPESS Chapter 14 for details.
Scatter formation

FITNESS DEVELOPMENT (8 - 12 MINUTES)

Parachute Rhythmic Aerobic Activities

Skip both directions
Slide both directions
Run both directions
Jump to center
Hop backward
Lift parachute over head

See DPESS Chapter 16 for details.
Direct loco motor movements while holding parachute.

Use music to motivate

LESSON FOCUS AND GAME COMBINED (20 - 25 MINUTES)

Softball World Series
Tournament Bracket Play
Make 4 teams of 10

Break class into teams with at least 10 on each team. If there needs to be more players on the team due to a large class size, there can be an outfielder added in the "rover" position. Stress teamwork, communication, and positive attitudes.

Always use safety precautions when using hard softball equipment

Four Teams – Allow students to chose team names
A VS B
C VS D
Winners play winners on next day
Other teams play each other on next day

EVALUATION/REVIEW

What is the most challenging aspect of softball?
Would you play softball again on your own time?
Cheer: Champions!

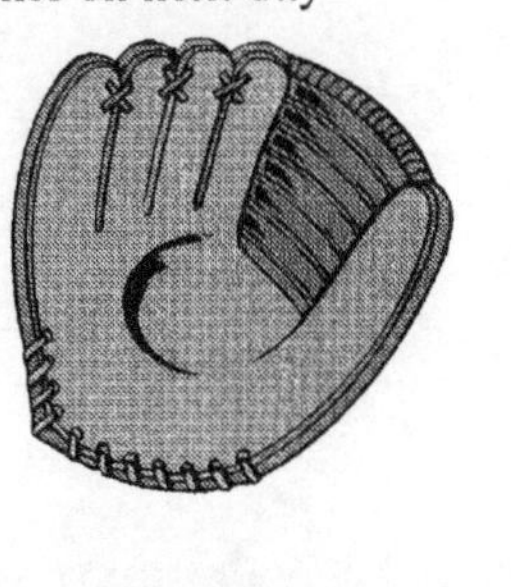

Team Handball

This unit has been specifically designed to meet all six components of the NASPE National Standards for Physical Education.

OBJECTIVES:

The student will:

1. Participate in Medic Tag demonstrating knowledge of rules and good sportsmanship.
2. Demonstrate agility in Bean Bag Touch and Go.
3. Demonstrate awareness and respect for classmates during the High Fives game.
4. Participate in Circuit training, Four Corners, Astronaut Drills and Aerobics Workouts to improve overall fitness.
5. Demonstrate dribbling skills using the team handball.
6. Demonstrate the following passes: chest, bounce, overhead, one-handed shoulder/baseball, side arm, hand-off, roller, hook, jump, and the behind-the-back pass.
7. Demonstrate goal shooting using the following passes: chest, bounce, overhead, one-handed shoulder/baseball, side arm, hand-off, roller, hook, jump, and the behind-the-back pass.
8. Demonstrate goal shooting using the following techniques: Jump shot, dive shot, lob shot, penalty shot, and behind-the-back.
9. Participate in the following games demonstrating cooperation with classmates and good sportsmanship: Frisbee 21, Over and Under Ball Relay, Octopus, Chain tag, and Over the Wall.
10. Perform the No Bounce, No Steps, and No Contact game technique demonstrated by the instructor.
11. Demonstrate passing, shooting skills when playing Sideline Team Handball.
12. Demonstrate good sportsmanship in all games.
13. Demonstrate knowledge of the rules of Team Handball while playing the game.
14. Pass a skills test demonstrating skills taught during the unit and to the satisfaction of the instructor.
15. Pass a written exam with a score of 70% or better.

Academic Integration Areas

1. Describe the history of Team Handball in the United States.
2. Student report: Olympians in Team Handball from the United States.
3. Integrate the physics of Team Handball into each skill lesson.

TEAM HANDBALL BLOCK PLAN
2 WEEK UNIT

Week #1	Monday	Tuesday	Wednesday	Thursday	Friday
Introductory Activity	Medic Tag	Back to Back Takedown	Fetch Relay	Beanbag Touch and Go	Flash Drill
Fitness	Circuit Training	Continuity Exercises	Four Corners Fitness	Aerobics Workout	Astronaut Drills
Lesson Focus	Passing Skills	Passing Skills and Goal Shooting	Goal Shooting and Dribbling	Task Sheet Skill Review	Three Bounces, Three Steps, and No Contact
Game	Frisbee 21	Over and Under Ball Relay	No bounce, No Step and No Contact	Balance Tag	Octopus

Week #2	Monday	Tuesday	Wednesday	Thursday	Friday
Introductory Activity	Addition Tag	Mirror Drill in Place	Running High Fives	Mass Stand-Up	Wave Drill
Fitness	Astronaut Drills	Parachute Fitness Activities	Fitness Scavenger Hunt	Partner Racetrack Fitness	Fitness Cookie Jar Exchange
Lesson Focus	Rules of the Game	Skill and Written Test	Team Handball Tournament	Team Handball Tournament	Team Handball Tournament
Game	Sideline Team Handball	Sideline Team Handball			

Team Handball Lesson Plan 1

EQUIPMENT:

Circuit training signs for each station
1 team handball per 2 students
1 Frisbee per 2 students
CD/Cassette player
Fitness CD/tape for circuit training

OBJECTIVES:

The student will:

1. Participate in Medic Tag activities following the instructions described by the instructor.
2. Participate in Circuit Training to improve their strength, endurance, and flexibility during the Fitness section of class.
3. Demonstrate passing and cooperative skills using form demonstrated by the instructor.
4. Participate in Frisbee 21 game presented by the instructor during the closing portion of class.

National Standards Met in this Lesson: **1, 2, 3, 4, 5, 6**

INSTRUCTIONAL ACTIVITIES	TEACHING HINTS

INTRODUCTORY ACTIVITY (2 - 3 MINUTES)

Medic Tag	**See DPESS Chapter 14 for details.** Different types of rehabilitation can be used. The easiest is to touch a body part or run a full circle around the person.

FITNESS DEVELOPMENT (8 - 12 MINUTES)

Circuit Training	**See DPESS Chapter 16 for details.** See Golf Unit, Lesson Plan 10 for details.

Circuit Training keeps the heart rate up during strength training by having you move quickly from one station to another. Therefore, you gain an aerobic workout while strengthening body parts. Move from an upper body exercise to lower body exercise. The heart rate remains high while individual muscle groups rest and recover. Typically you try to do three sets of each exercise.

LESSON FOCUS (15 - 20 MINUTES)

Passing skills: Demonstrate the following skills: chest, bounce, overhead, one-handed shoulder/baseball, side arm, hand-off and roller pass.	**See DPESS Chapter 19 for details.** Students work in pairs practicing each skill.

Team handball grew out of three sports that were developed, independently, in three different European countries. The three games were based on soccer, but essentially replaced the foot with the hand, so that the ball could be advanced by hitting or throwing, rather than by kicking.

GAME (5 MINUTES)

Frisbee 21	**See DPESS Chapter 19 for details.** Use a management game to create pairs of students.

EVALUATION/REVIEW AND CHEER

What was the origin of Team Handball?
What muscles did you use in Circuit Training today?
What is the value of Circuit Training?
Discuss each pass taught and any problems students may have encountered in the learning process.

Cheer: 2, 4, 6, 8, Team Handball is G-R-E-A-T!

Team Handball Lesson Plan 2

EQUIPMENT:

1 rubber ball per 5 – 7 students for relay
5 Cones for station markers
Station signs
CD/ tape for Continuity Exercises
CD/ tape player

OBJECTIVES:

The student will:

1. Participate in Back to Back Takedown activities following the instructions described by the instructor.
2. Participate in Continuity Exercises to improve their aerobic endurance, strength, muscular endurance, and flexibility during the Fitness section of class.
3. Demonstrate passing, shooting, and cooperative skills using form demonstrated by the instructor.
4. Participate in the Over and Under Ball Relay game presented by the instructor during the closing portion of class.

National Standards Met in this Lesson: 1, 2, 3, 4, 5, 6

INSTRUCTIONAL ACTIVITIES	TEACHING HINTS

INTRODUCTORY ACTIVITY (2 - 3 MINUTES)

Back to Back Takedown

See DPESS Chapter 18 for details.
Use Back to Back game to create pairs.

FITNESS DEVELOPMENT (8 - 12 MINUTES)

Continuity Exercises
Direct the exercises students should complete during the silence on the CD/tape: i.e. push-ups, side leg lifts, etc.

See DPESS Chapter 16 for details.
Create music CD/tape to guide the continuity exercises.

Continuity exercises alternate jump roping with strengthening and flexibility exercises to give you an aerobic workout plus strengthening and flexibility work.

LESSON FOCUS (15 - 20 MINUTES)

Review passing skills taught yesterday.
Teach: Hook pass, jump pass, behind-the-back pass
Demonstrate use of all passes for goal shooting.
Practice all skills in stations:
Station 1: chest, bounce, overhead, one-handed shoulder/baseball;
Station 2: side arm, hand-off and roller pass;
Station 3: Hook pass, jump pass, behind-the-back pass;
Stations 4 & 5: Goal shooting using passes learned.

See DPESS Chapter 19 for details.

By 1925, team handball had become fairly popular in many European countries. The International Amateur Handball Federation (IAHF) was established in 1928; handball was a demonstration sport at the Olympics in 1928 and again in 1932.

GAME (5 MINUTES)

Over and Under Ball Relay

See DPESS Chapter 18 for details.
Use management game to make groups of 5 –7 for relay.

EVALUATION/REVIEW AND CHEER

When and where did the popularity of Team Handball begin?
When did it appear in the Olympics?
Discuss the challenges of each pass and style of goal shooting.

Cheer: Goal shooting, that's for me!

Team Handball Lesson Plan 3

EQUIPMENT:

2 foam balls per student for goal shooting
4 cones
Fitness station signs
Goals
CD/Cassette tape player
Fitness tape/CD

OBJECTIVES:

The student will:

1. Participate in the Fetch Relay demonstrating cooperative skills, speed, and agility and following the instructions described by the instructor.
2. Participate in Four Corners Fitness to improve aerobic endurance, strength, muscular endurance, and flexibility during the Fitness section of class.
3. Demonstrate goal shooting and cooperative skills using form demonstrated by the instructor.
4. Participate in Entanglement demonstrating creativity and cooperative skills following the instructions set by the instructor during the closing portion of class.

National Standards Met in this Lesson: **1, 2, 3, 4, 5, 6**

INSTRUCTIONAL ACTIVITIES	TEACHING HINTS
INTRODUCTORY ACTIVITY (2 - 3 MINUTES)	
Fetch Relay	**See DPESS Chapter 17 for details.** Three students are designated as "taggers."
FITNESS DEVELOPMENT (8 - 12 MINUTES)	
Four Corners Fitness Post signs on cones to direct activities at each station.	**See DPESS Chapter 16 for details.** Using whistle mixer, divide class into groups of 4. Use music CD/tape with short silences to indicate rotation.
LESSON FOCUS (15 - 20 MINUTES)	
Demonstrate and practice Goal Shooting Skills: jump shot, dive shot, lob shot, penalty shot, behind the back shot.	**See DPESS Chapter 19 for details.**
No Bounce, No Steps, and No Contact Game Use passing skills practiced in previous lessons.	Scattered formation. Use 3 – 5 balls in the playing area.

Team Handball played outdoors by teams of eleven players, became an Olympic sport at the 1936 Munich Games. The United States finished sixth and last in the competition.

INSTRUCTIONAL ACTIVITIES	TEACHING HINTS
GAME (5 MINUTES)	
Entanglement	**See DPESS Chapter 18 for details.** Players may not hold both hands of the same player.

EVALUATION/REVIEW AND CHEER

How many players are on a Team Handball team?
What other sport is similar to this game?
When did Team Handball become an Olympic Sport?
Discuss the Goal Shooting skills taught.
Ask what was challenging about the No Bounce, No Steps, No Contact Game

Cheer: 1, 2, 3 teamwork is great!!

Team Handball Lesson Plan 4

EQUIPMENT:

1 team handball ball per student
1 beanbag per student
Cassette Tape/CD for fitness
1 Task Sheet per person
One clipboard and pencil per 3 students
CD/Cassette player

OBJECTIVES:

The student will:

1. Participate in the Beanbag Touch and Go demonstrating cooperative skills, speed, and agility and following the instructions described by the instructor.
2. Participate in Rhythmic Aerobic Exercises to improve aerobic endurance, strength, muscular endurance, and flexibility during the Fitness section of class.
3. Demonstrate throwing, catching, goal shooting and cooperative skills following the Task Sheet and using form demonstrated by the instructor.
4. Participate in Balance Tag demonstrating balancing skills, creativity, agility, and cooperative skills following the instructions set by the instructor during the closing portion of class.

National Standards Met in this Lesson: **1, 2, 3, 4, 5, 6**

INSTRUCTIONAL ACTIVITIES	TEACHING HINTS

INTRODUCTORY ACTIVITY (2 - 3 MINUTES)

Beanbag Touch & Go
On signal, students move and touch as many beanbags as possible.

See DPESS Chapter 14 for details.
Scattered formation.
Spread beanbags throughout the area.
Direct various locomotor movements.

FITNESS DEVELOPMENT (8 - 12 MINUTES)

Rhythmic Aerobic Exercise
Model the exercises to music.

See DPESS Chapter 16 for details.
Use a tape or CD for the exercises.

Rhythm is a part of all movements. Combing rhythmic activities with strength, agility, balance and endurance enhances not only your fitness conditioning, but all of your other activities in life.

LESSON FOCUS (15 - 20 MINUTES)

Task Sheet practice reviewing skills

See DPESS Chapter 19 for details.
Demonstrate skills and activities on task sheet.
Use whistle mixer to make groups of 3 for task sheet.

Team handball is very popular in other parts of the world, but was little known in North America until it appeared in the Olympics.

GAME (5 MINUTES)

Balance Tag

See DPESS Chapter 14 for details.
Select several "its"

EVALUATION/REVIEW AND CHEER

Why are Rhythmic Aerobic Exercises valuable to you?
What muscles did you work today during the Fitness portion of class?
When did Team Handball gain popularity in the United States?
Review elements of skills practiced on Task Sheet.

Cheer: 1, 2, 3 we love P.E.!!

RECIPROCAL TASK SHEET: PASSING AND GOAL SHOOTING

Doer's Name: ______________________________

Observer's Name: ______________________________

Shagger's Name: ______________________________

Directions: Work with a partner. Record the dates and check the appropriate response for each checkpoint for each skill listed. Have your partner check you a minimum of 4 times per skill. See your instructor for additional task sheets. Partner (observer) - try to observe no more than two checkpoints at one time. Shagger: retrieve the ball and return to doer. On Penalty Shot, you become the "goalie". Rotate positions after each person completes one type of shot.

	DATES							
(Record date of practice)								
OVERHEAD PASS TEAM HANDBALL TO TARGET 10 FEET AWAY	**Yes**	**No**	**Yes**	**No**	**Yes**	**No**	**Yes**	**No**
1 Eyes on target								
2 Steps into pass								
3 Hits target area								
4 Short of target								
OVERHEAD PASS TEAM HANDBALL TO TARGET 15 FEET AWAY								
1 Eyes on target								
2 Steps into pass								
3 Hits target area								
4 Short of target								
JUMP PASS TEAM HANDBALL TO TARGET 5 FEET AWAY								
1 Eyes on target								
2 Jumps and then passes								
3 Hits target area								
4 Short of target								
JUMP PASS TEAM HANDBALL TO TARGET 10 FEET AWAY								
1 Eyes on target								
2 Jumps and then passes								
3 Hits target area								
4 Short of target								
PENALTY SHOOTING								
1. Stand 7 meters from goal with "goalie" 3 meters ahead of you, between you and the goal								
2. Keeps foot stationary until ball thrown								
3. Releases ball in 3 seconds or less								
4. Uses side-arm throw								
5. Uses shoulder throw								

Team Handball Lesson Plan 5

EQUIPMENT:

1 Double disk Frisbee / 3 – 4 students
Goals
4 –5 Team Handballs
Music and music player for Astronaut Drills (optional)

OBJECTIVES:

The student will:

1. Participate in the Flash Drill demonstrating the ability to following movements, speed, and agility and following the instructions demonstrated by the instructor.
2. Participate in Astronaut Drills to improve aerobic endurance, strength, muscular endurance, and flexibility during the Fitness section of class.
3. Demonstrate throwing, catching and cooperative skills and using form demonstrated by the instructor.
4. Participate in Double Disc Frisbees demonstrating catching skills, eye hand coordination, creativity, agility, and cooperative skills following the instructions set by the instructor during the closing portion of class.

National Standards Met in this Lesson: **1, 2, 3, 4, 5, 6**

INSTRUCTIONAL ACTIVITIES	TEACHING HINTS

INTRODUCTORY ACTIVITY (2 – 3 MINUTES)

Flash Drill
Teacher/leader directs movements

See DPESS Chapter 14 for details.
Scattered formation

FITNESS DEVELOPMENT (8 – 12 MINUTES)

Astronaut Drills: Direct locomotor, stretching, strengthening, and aerobic exercises.

See DPESS Chapter 16 for details.

These fitness activities work on your core muscles, legs including the hamstrings and quadriceps, your arms including the biceps and triceps muscles and the postural muscles of your back.

LESSON FOCUS (15 – 20 MINUTES)

Three Bounces, Three Steps, and No Contact
Behind-the-back, chess pass, and
Catching skills reinforced.
Students pass the ball rather than dribble. Five balls being tossed at the same time.

See DPESS Chapter 19 for details.
Scattered formation.
Students will practice all the passing techniques.

GAME (5 MINUTES)

Double Disc Frisbees

See DPESS Chapter 20 for details.
Create groups of 3 – 4 students using Whistle Mixer.

A baker named William Russel Frisbie, of Warren, Connecticut, came up with a clever marketing idea back in the 1870s. He put the family name in relief on the bottom of the tin pans in which his company's homemade pies were sold. Then, sometime in the 1940s, Yale students began sailing the pie tins through the air and catching them. It is at Yale University that the game was created.

EVALUATION/REVIEW AND CHEER

What muscles and body parts were used during today's fitness activities?
Discuss the day's team handball activities.
What are the origins of today's Frisbee games?

Cheer: 1, 2, 3 teamwork is great!!

Team Handball Lesson Plan 6

EQUIPMENT:

Music CD/tape for fitness
Goals
Rules Handout
Music player
3 – 5 Team Handballs
Goals for Team Handball

OBJECTIVES:

The student will:

1. Participate in the Addition Tag demonstrating cooperative skills, speed, agility and following the instructions demonstrated by the instructor.
2. Participate in Astronaut Drills to improve aerobic endurance, strength, muscular endurance, and flexibility during the Fitness section of class.
3. Read the rules of handball and then when asked, recite several rules as requested by the instructor.
4. Demonstrate throwing, catching and cooperative skills during the game of Sideline Team Handball using form demonstrated by the instructor.

National Standards Met in this Lesson: **1, 2, 3, 4, 5, 6**

INSTRUCTIONAL ACTIVITIES	TEACHING HINTS

INTRODUCTORY ACTIVITY (2 – 3 MINUTES)

Addition Tag	**See DPESS Chapter 14 for details.** Rotate "its" several times Stop each round when a line has about 10 people.

Direct students to call out the number they have made with each additional player.
Then, on the next round of play, you can ask them to quickly add a number you identify to their group size and call out that number.

FITNESS DEVELOPMENT (8 – 12 MINUTES)

Astronaut Drills Timed music CDs/tapes for the Astronaut Drills adds fun and motivation.	**See DPESS Chapter 16 for details.**

LESSON FOCUS (15 – 20 MINUTES)

Teach the Rules of Team Handball	**See DPESS Chapter 19 for details.** Instructor creates written handout for studying rules

GAME (5 MINUTES)

Sideline Team Handball Create 2 – 3 games depending on class size	**See DPESS Chapter 19 for details.** Place opposite team members on each sideline

EVALUATION/REVIEW AND CHEER

Was there any particular numbers that were difficult to add during Addition Tag?
What muscles were used during the Astronaut Drills today?
Ask students to recite several of the rules of handball.
Review outcome of the Sideline Team Handball Game

Cheer: Team Handball, yea!

Team Handball Lesson Plan 7

EQUIPMENT:

1 Written exam per student
1 Skill checklist and pencil per student
Music for Parachute fitness
Goals
4 – 5 Team Handballs
Parachute
Music player

OBJECTIVES:

The student will:

1. Participate in the Mirror Drill in Place demonstrating cooperative skills and following the instructions demonstrated by the instructor.
2. Participate in Parachute Fitness Activities to improve aerobic endurance, strength, muscular endurance, and flexibility during the Fitness section of class.
3. Complete a skill and written exam on rules and skills taught during the unit passing with a score considered acceptable to the instructor.
4. Demonstrate throwing, catching and cooperative skills during the game of Sideline Team Handball using form demonstrated by the instructor.

National Standards Met in this Lesson: **1, 2, 3, 4, 5, 6**

INSTRUCTIONAL ACTIVITIES	TEACHING HINTS

INTRODUCTORY ACTIVITY (2 - 3 MINUTES)

Mirror Drill in Place
Identify first leader and follower. Rotate.

See DPESS Chapter 14 for details.
Use back-to-back to make partners

FITNESS DEVELOPMENT (8 - 12 MINUTES)

Parachute Fitness Activities
Direct locomotor movements around parachute: slide, gallop, trot, skip, etc.

See DPESS Chapter 16 for details.
Direct stretching and strengthening activities between locomotor activities: Curl-up, Toe Toucher, Sitting Leg Lifts, Sitting Pulls, Isometric exercises, etc.
Create music with 30 seconds of music and 30 seconds of silence for the identified activities between the locomotor activities. Time the music to be the length of the fitness section of class.

LESSON FOCUS (15 - 20 MINUTES)

Skill and Written Test on rules and skill techniques
Cognitive and motor skills assessment.

Divide class in half. Half of class skill tests/ other half written tests. Switch.

GAME (5 MINUTES)

Sideline Team Handball

See DPESS Chapter 19 for details.
Create different teams than used the day before.

EVALUATION/REVIEW AND CHEER

What muscles were used during class today?
Review elements of exams that caused difficulty.
What do you need to work on to make the game of Sideline Team Handball better?

Students create cheer

Team Handball Lesson Plan 8

EQUIPMENT:

Interval music tape/CD
Team Handballs for Game
CD/ cassette tape player
Laminated scavenger hunt cards

OBJECTIVES:

The student will:

1. Participate in Running High Fives demonstrating cooperative skills, running and jumping skills and following the instructions demonstrated by the instructor.
2. Participate in a Fitness Scavenger Hunt to improve aerobic endurance, strength, muscular endurance, and flexibility during the Fitness section of class.
3. Play Team Handball demonstrating knowledge of the rules of the game, good sportsmanship and skills taught during the unit.

National Standards Met in this Lesson: **1, 2, 3, 4, 5, 6**

INSTRUCTIONAL ACTIVITIES	TEACHING HINTS
INTRODUCTORY ACTIVITY (2 - 3 MINUTES)	
Running High Fives	**See DPESS Chapter 14 for details.** Create interval music CD/tape
FITNESS DEVELOPMENT (8 - 12 MINUTES)	
Fitness Scavenger Hunt	**See DPESS Chapter 16 for details.** Create small groups using Whistle Mixer
LESSON FOCUS AND GAME COMBINED (15 - 20 MINUTES)	
Play Team Handball	Create Round Robin Tournament Set-Up

EVALUATION/REVIEW AND CHEER

Review rules of Team Handball and skills that you observed need to be worked on.

Cheer: Team Handball Teams Rule!

Team Handball Lesson Plan 9

EQUIPMENT:

Cones for station signs
Station signs for Partner Racetrack Fitness Instructions
Music and Player for Fitness
Goals
Team Handballs for Tournament

OBJECTIVES:

The student will:

1. Participate in Mass Stand Up demonstrating cooperative and balancing skills while following the instructions established by the instructor.
2. Participate in a Partner Racetrack Fitness to improve aerobic endurance, strength, muscular endurance, and flexibility during the Fitness section of class.
3. Play Team Handball demonstrating knowledge of the rules of the game, good sportsmanship and skills taught during the unit.

National Standards Met in this Lesson: **1, 2, 3, 4, 5, 6**

INSTRUCTIONAL ACTIVITIES	TEACHING HINTS
INTRODUCTORY ACTIVITY (2 - 3 MINUTES)	
Mass Stand Up	**See DPESS Chapter 18 for details.** Create pairs using back-to-back technique
FITNESS DEVELOPMENT (8 - 12 MINUTES)	
Partner Racetrack Fitness	**See DPESS Chapter 16 for details.** Create new pairs using elbow-to-elbow technique
LESSON FOCUS AND GAME COMBINED FOR TOURNAMENT (15 - 20 MINUTES)	
Play Team Handball Review rules of Team Handball and skills that you observed need to be worked on.	Continue Round Robin Tournament
EVALUATION/REVIEW AND CHEER	
Cheer: Team Handball, yes!	

Team Handball Lesson Plan 10

EQUIPMENT:

Cones for marking Wave Drill
Fitness Cookie Jar and instruction cards
Goals
Music for fitness
Team Handballs for Tournament
Music player

OBJECTIVES:

The student will:

1. Participate in the Wave Drill while following the directions demonstrated by the instructor.
2. Participate in the Fitness Cookie Jar Exchange to improve fitness during the Fitness section of class.
3. Play Team Handball demonstrating knowledge of the rules of the game, good sportsmanship and skills taught during the unit.

National Standards Met in this Lesson: **1, 2, 3, 4, 5, 6**

INSTRUCTIONAL ACTIVITIES	TEACHING HINTS
INTRODUCTORY ACTIVITY (2 - 3 MINUTES)	
Wave Drill	**See DPESS Chapter 14 for details.**
FITNESS DEVELOPMENT (8 - 12 MINUTES)	
Fitness Cookie Jar Exchange	**See DPESS Chapter 16 for details.** Students can work in pairs or alone
LESSON FOCUS AND GAME COMBINED (20 MINUTES)	
Play Team Handball	Continue Round Robin Tournament
EVALUATION/REVIEW AND CHEER	
Discuss results of tournament and make all students feel comfortable with the outcome. **Cheer: Everybody is a winner!**	

Track And Field

This unit has been specifically designed to meet all six components of the NASPE National Standards for Physical Education.

OBJECTIVES:

The student will:
1. Participate in Spider tag demonstrating agility and sportsmanship.
2. Demonstrate proper tagging skills demonstrating safety rules explained by the instructor.
3. Participate in the Four Corners Fitness Activities to improve her overall fitness levels.
4. Demonstrate changing from walking, to sprinting quickly when given a signal by the instructor.
5. Demonstrate the ability to perform locomotor movements and change directions on command.
6. Rapidly change movements and count the number of repetitions performed during the Magic Number Challenge.
7. Participate in Continuity Exercise Activities to increase cardiovascular endurance, strength, and flexibility.
8. Participate in Circuit Training activities to improve fitness.
9. Participate in Sprinting, Running Long Jump, High Jump, Hurdling, Shot Put, Discus, Relays and Long Distance running events using form demonstrated in class.
10. Demonstrate starting, stopping, running skills in Bean Bag Touch and Go.
11. Play "Frisbee 21" with a partner demonstrating one and two hand catching and throwing accuracy.
12. Demonstrate good sportsmanship and cooperation during partner and team Tug-of-War activities.

TRACK AND FIELD BLOCK PLAN
2 WEEK UNIT

Week #1	Monday	Tuesday	Wednesday	Thursday	Friday
Introductory Activity	Spider Tag	Move and Change Directions	Leaping Lena with a Forward Roll	Coffee Grinder Square	Burpee Flip Drill
Fitness	Walk, Jog, Sprint	Circuit Training	Fitness Scavenger Hunt	Rope Jumping Partner Resistance Exercises	Parachute Fitness
Lesson Focus	Videotape Introduction Starts	Running Long Jump	Relays Long Jump 50 meter run	Shot Put Review other skills	High Jump Review other skills
Game	Team Tug-of-War	Triangle Plus One Tag	Frisbee 21	Mini Pyramids	Hula Hoop Pass

Week #2	Monday	Tuesday	Wednesday	Thursday	Friday
Introductory Activity	Gauntlet Run	Running High 5's	Partner Tug-of-War	Pentabridge Hustle	
Fitness	Fitness Scavenger Hunt	Continuity Exercises	Circuit Training	Four Corners & Stretching Exercises	Parachute Fitness
Lesson Focus	Discus Long Distance Running	Hurdling 7 Station Activities	Continue 7 Station Activities	Review all events for Track Meet	Class Track Meet
Game	Beanbag Touch and Go		Frisbee Catch		

Track and Field Lesson Plan 1

EQUIPMENT:

Video/DVD on Track and Field
Team Tug of War Rope
Starting blocks, as many as possible

OBJECTIVES:

The student will:

1. Participate in Spider tag demonstrating cooperative skills and agility and following the instructions described by the instructor.
2. Participate in Walk, Jog, Sprint and Strength Exercises to improve strength, endurance, and flexibility during the Fitness section of class.
3. Demonstrate race starting with and without blocks using form viewed in the video demonstration.
4. Demonstrate high knee running using form viewed in the video demonstration.
5. Participate in Team Tug-of-War presented by the instructor during the closing portion of class.

National Standards Met in this Lesson: **1, 2, 3, 4, 5, 6**

INSTRUCTIONAL ACTIVITIES	TEACHING HINTS

INTRODUCTORY ACTIVITY (2 - 3 MINUTES)

Spider tag	**See DPESS Chapter 14 for details.** Use toe-to-toe to make groups of 2. Select one pair to be it.

FITNESS DEVELOPMENT (8 - 12 MINUTES)

Walk, Jog, Sprint 1st whistle = WALK; 2nd whistle = JOG; 3rd whistle = SPRINT	**See DPESS Chapter 16 for details.** Explain directions for this activity. Keep continuous movements going for good aerobic exercising.
Strength Exercises: Push-ups, curl-ups, reverse push-ups, coffee grinder, etc.	**See DPESS Chapter 16 for details.**

LESSON FOCUS (15 - 20 MINUTES)

Introduce all Track and Field events with a video	**See DPESS Chapter 19 for details.**
Demonstrate starts with and without blocks	Scattered formation around demonstrator
Demonstrate techniques for crossing finish line	
High knee running	Practice various distances running with high knees
Practice starts and finishes in a 50 yard/meter race	

The ancient Olympic Games began in the year 776 BC. Thos Olympic Games consisted of only the stadium race, a foot race 600 feet long. The stadium race was the only athletic event of the games for the first 13 Olympic festivals.

GAME (5 MINUTES)

Team Tug-of-War 2 teams; each team on half of the rope. On signal, teams pull rope. First team to pull others over the line wins.	**See DPESS Chapter 18 for details.** Use a "back-to-back" to create two groups.

Tug-of-War is actually a competitive team sport in England, Scotland, Sweden and many other countries with a sea-faring tradition. It originated in the early days of sailing when teams of men were required to tug on lines to adjust sails while ships were underway or even in combat.

EVALUATION/REVIEW AND CHEER

What are the important points to remember when using starting blocks in a race?
What are some tricks you learned today about crossing the finish line?
What is the history of track racing in the Olympics?
Describe how the game of Tug-of-War began?
Cheer: 1, 2, 3, I Love P.E.!

Track and Field Lesson Plan 2

EQUIPMENT:

Music for Circuit Training
Station cones and instructional signs for fitness
Cones to mark 50 yard/meter start and finish lines
Music player
Rake for Long jump

OBJECTIVES:

The student will:

1. Participate in Move and Change Direction demonstrating cooperative skills and agility and following the instructions described by the instructor.
2. Participate in Circuit Training to improve strength, endurance, and flexibility during the Fitness section of class.
3. Demonstrate running long jump using form demonstrated by the instructor.
4. Participate in Triangle Plus One Tag demonstrating running and cooperative skills during the closing portion of class.

National Standards Met in this Lesson: **1, 2, 3, 4, 5, 6**

INSTRUCTIONAL ACTIVITIES	TEACHING HINTS
INTRODUCTORY ACTIVITY (2 - 3 MINUTES)	
Move and Change Direction Students will jog towards each other and give high fives to the other group. Then, skip the other direction, and return giving high fives as the students meet the other group again.	**See DPESS Chapter 14 for details.** Divide the student into two groups using Toe- to-Toe and then separating into two halves.
FITNESS DEVELOPMENT (8 - 12 MINUTES)	
Circuit Training When the music starts, each group will perform the exercise described on each labeled cone. When the music stops, students walk counter-clockwise to the next station performing arm circles.	**See DPESS Chapter 16 for details.** Using Whistle Mixer, make groups of 5 - 6 to begin at each station.
Exercises listed at **stations**: Push-ups, knee-lifts, jumping jacks, trunk twisters, sit-ups, arm extensions, single crab kicks, arms up and down, jog in place, triceps push- ups.	Place instructions for each station on cones set-up to identify location of station. Use illustrations to assist in understanding of the activities.

INSTRUCTIONAL ACTIVITIES	TEACHING HINTS
LESSON FOCUS (15 - 20 MINUTES)	
Running Long Jump: Demonstrate taking off board and deciding on distance to run.	**See DPESS Chapter 19 for details.**
Stations: 1) Running Long Jump **2) 50 yard/ meter run**	Use Toe-to-Toe to make partners; separate class into 2 them to a particular stations, repeat.

GAME (5 MINUTES)	
Triangle Plus 1 Tag Person outside triangle tries to tag leader. Leader and tagger change places when tagged.	**See DPESS Chapter 14 for details.** Create groups of 4 using management game. 3 make triangle formation holding hands. Select leader in group.
EVALUATION/REVIEW AND CHEER	
How did you feel after running a sprinting event? What is fun about running long jump? Who can tell us how one decides where to begin the run for the Running Long Jump Event? **Cheer: P.E., P.E., yea, P.E.!**	

Track and Field Lesson Plan 3

EQUIPMENT:

Fitness Scavenger Hunt instructional cards
Batons
Cones to mark finish line
VCR/DVD player
Video/ DVD on Relay Races
Rake for Long Jump
1 Frisbee per 2 students

OBJECTIVES:

The student will:

1. Participate in Leaping Lena with a Forward Roll demonstrating agility and following the instructions described by the instructor.
2. Participate in a Fitness Scavenger Hunt to improve strength, endurance, and flexibility during the Fitness section of class.
3. Demonstrate relay racing and baton hand-offs using form demonstrated by the video.
4. Practice running long jump activities using form demonstrated in class and on the video.
5. Participate in Frisbee 21 demonstrating eye-hand coordination, throwing, catching and cooperative skills during the closing portion of class.

National Standards Met in this Lesson: **1, 2, 3, 4, 5, 6**

INSTRUCTIONAL ACTIVITIES	TEACHING HINTS
INTRODUCTORY ACTIVITY (2 - 3 MINUTES)	
Leaping Lena with a Forward Roll Practice forward rolls before beginning this drill.	**See DPESS Chapter 14 for details.** Scattered formation.
FITNESS DEVELOPMENT (8 - 12 MINUTES)	
Fitness Scavenger Hunt Exercises listed on scavenger cards at stations.	**See DPESS Chapter 16 for details.** Use whistle mixer to create groups of 3. Assign each group to a starting point.
LESSON FOCUS (15 - 20 MINUTES)	
Introduce Relay Races with a videotape **Relays:** Demonstrate baton hand-offs	**See DPESS Chapter 19 for details.** Using batons or paper towel cardboard interior rolls have students work in pairs practicing the hand-off.

INSTRUCTIONAL ACTIVITIES	TEACHING HINTS
3 Stations: Relay practice; Running Long Jump; 50 yard/ meter run. Assign students to station.	Use Whistle Mixer to create groups of 3. Then identify each person in the group differently i.e. hand on head, hand on stomach, hand on knees. Like positions join.

Track and field athletics in the United States began in the 1860s. The Intercollegiate Association of Amateur Athletes of America, held the first collegiate races in 1873, and in 1888 the Amateur Athletic Union (which governed the sport for nearly a century) held its first championships.

GAME (5 MINUTES)

Frisbee 21	**See DPESS Chapter 20 for details.**
Game Rules: Throw disk back and forth; 1 point = 1 hand catch; 2 points = 2 hand catch	Use Elbow-to-Elbow to create partners. Identify student to bring Frisbee to partner.

In the 1950's in California, a flying-saucer enthusiast named Walter Frederick Morrison designed a saucer-like disk for playing catch. It was produced by a company named Wham-O. When Mr. Morrison saw the Yale students playing with the Frisbie Pie Plates, he decided to name the game Frisbee.

EVALUATION/REVIEW AND CHEER

What muscles were used in Fitness today?
Ask if any fitness challenges were difficult and why?
Explain the cues used when passing a baton to a teammate in a relay race.
Describe the beginning of Track and Field in the United States
Describe the history of the game of Frisbee.

Cheer: Relays, OK!

Track and Field Lesson Plan 4

EQUIPMENT:

Cones to mark square for Coffee Grinder Square	1 individual rope per person
Tape/CD for rope jumping	Tape/CD player
Shot Put	Rake for Long Jump
Batons	Tennis Balls to use as shots

OBJECTIVES:

The student will:

1. Participate in Coffee Grinder Square demonstrating agility and following the instructions described by the instructor.
2. Participate in Rope Jumping and Partner Resistance Exercises to improve strength and aerobic endurance during the Fitness section of class.
3. Demonstrate shot put throwing, running long jump, 50 meter running, and relay racing using form demonstrated by the video/ instructor.
4. Participate in Mini Pyramids demonstrating cooperative skills during the closing portion of class.

National Standards Met in this Lesson: **1, 2, 3, 4, 5, 6**

INSTRUCTIONAL ACTIVITIES	TEACHING HINTS
INTRODUCTORY ACTIVITY (2 - 3 MINUTES)	
Coffee Grinder Square	**See DPESS Chapter 14 for details.**
Demonstrate Coffee Grinder activity.	Have cones set up to delineate square for activity.
FITNESS DEVELOPMENT (8 - 12 MINUTES)	
Rope Jumping	**See DPESS Chapter 14 for details.**
	Use music to make rope jumping more enjoyable.
Partner Resistance Exercises	**See DPESS Chapter 16 for details.**
Demonstrate the exercises focusing on the upper body listed in this section of the textbook.	Use Back-to-Back to create partners. Best to find partner of equal height (and girth).
LESSON FOCUS (15 - 20 MINUTES)	
Shot Put: Demonstrate shot put throw.	**See DPESS Chapter 19 for details.**
All students practice by using a tennis ball.	Create safe throwing situation.
4 Stations: Shot Put; Running Long Jump; 50 yard/meter run; Relay racing. Rotate.	Teacher supervises Shot Put station since newest activity Use management game to create groups for stations

The first NCAA national championships were held for men in 1921, and women's track and field became part of the Olympic Games in 1928.

GAME (5 MINUTES)	
Mini Pyramids	**See DPESS Chapter 18 for details.**
On signal student finds group and builds a group stunt/ pyramid. On next signal, pyramids safely dismantled and students move around again until signal.	Use Whistle Mixer to make groups of 3 - 5.

EVALUATION/REVIEW AND CHEER

Were any of the partner resistance exercises particularly difficult? Which ones and why?
Which Track and Field event is your favorite and why?
In what year did Women's Track and Field join the Olympics?

Cheer: 2,4,6,8 Track and Field is really great!

Track and Field Lesson Plan 5

EQUIPMENT:

High Jump videotape	VCR/DVD Player
Station markers and instructions	High jump equipment
Shot Put	Rake
Batons	Parachute
1 hula hoop per 5 students for game(s)	

OBJECTIVES:

The student will:

1. Participate in the Burpee-Flip-Drill demonstrating agility and following the instructions described by the instructor.
2. Participate in Parachute Fitness Activities to improve strength, aerobic endurance and flexibility during the Fitness section of class.
3. Demonstrate high jumping, shot putting, running long jump, 50 yard run, and relay racing using form demonstrated by the video/ instructor.
4. Participate in Hula Hoop Pass demonstrating creativity, agility, and cooperative skills during the closing portion of class.

National Standards Met in this Lesson: **1, 2, 3, 4, 5, 6**

INSTRUCTIONAL ACTIVITIES	TEACHING HINTS
INTRODUCTORY ACTIVITY (2 - 3 MINUTES)	
Burpee-Flip-Drill	**See DPESS Chapter 14 for details.**
FITNESS DEVELOPMENT (8 - 12 MINUTES)	
Parachute Fitness Activities	**See DPESS Chapter 16 for details.**
Toe Touches Explain isometrics. Lift chute taut to chin. Bend forward and touch grip to toes. Hold taut to chin.	Hold parachute sitting while in extended leg position around the parachute. 16 repetitions.
Curl Ups: Curl-up, bend knees, lie back, extend legs. Repeat 16 times.	Hold Parachute sitting position in a circle. Curl up, bent knees. Extended legs under chute and lie on back.
Dorsal Lifts	Lying prone head toward chute arms straight chest taut. Lift arms and chest, lower, repeat 8 times.
Sitting leg lift: Sit - legs under chute, on signal lift a leg off ground for 6 to 10 seconds. Try to keep leg straight. Alternate legs.	When Blow whistle: Freeze. Try variation: Side leg lefts. Lie on side. Lift top leg and lower.
Run while holding L hand on parachute. Reverse	Stress safety.
Skip while holding L hand on parachute. Reverse	Move around carefully.
Slide while holding both hands on parachute. Reverse directions.	Review good technique for each locomotor movement.
Trot while holding L hand on parachute. Reverse	
LESSON FOCUS (15 - 20 MINUTES)	
High Jump Introduction with a videotape	**See DPESS Chapter 19 for details.**
Demonstrate high jump take-offs and landings Use a student to demonstrate if you are unable to.	Supervise the High Jump station since that is the newest skill introduced.
5 Stations: High jump; Shot Put; Running Long Jump; 50 yard/meter run; Relay racing. Rotate.	Use management game to create the five groups for the stations. Assign groups to stations.

The high jump predated the Olympics in ancient Greece. The first recorded high jump event took place in Scotland in the 19th century, with heights of up to (1.68 m) reported.

GAME (5 MINUTES)	
Hula Hoop Pass	**See DPESS Chapter 18 for details.**
Place a hula-hoop over the clasped hands of two members of each squad. On signal - pass the hoop around the circle without releasing handgrips.	Scattered - in groups. Approximately 5 per group. Members of each group hold hands.

EVALUATION/REVIEW AND CHEER

What are the important elements to remember in high jumping? Which style worked best for you and why?
What is the history of the high jump event?
What did you need to do to make the Hula Hoop pass successful? **Cheer: P.E.,… The Best!**

Track and Field Lesson Plan 6

EQUIPMENT:

Challenge items for Gauntlet Run: 5 Hoops, 10 Cones to jump over and run around, 4 Long Jump Ropes to leap across, as if a waterbed/ 20 students.

Long Distance Race videotape/DVD
High Jump standards, pole, landing mat
VCR/ DVD Player
1 Beanbag per student
Shot Put(s)   Rake for Running Long Jump pit
Discus(s)
Fitness Scavenger Hunt instructional cards

OBJECTIVES:

The student will:

1. Participate in the Gauntlet Run demonstrating speed, agility and following the instructions described by the instructor.
2. Participate in the Fitness Scavenger Hunt to improve strength, aerobic endurance and flexibility during the Fitness section of class.
3. Demonstrate high jumping, shot putting, discus throwing, running long jump and distance running using form demonstrated by the video/DVD or instructor.
4. Participate in Bean Bag Touch and Go demonstrating agility, speed, and cooperative skills during the closing portion of class.

National Standards Met in this Lesson: **1, 2, 3, 4, 5, 6**

INSTRUCTIONAL ACTIVITIES	TEACHING HINTS
INTRODUCTORY ACTIVITY (2 - 3 MINUTES)	
Gauntlet Run	**See DPESS Chapter 14 for details.**
FITNESS DEVELOPMENT (8 - 12 MINUTES)	
Fitness Scavenger Hunt Exercises listed on scavenger cards at stations.	**See DPESS Chapter 16 for details.** Use whistle mixer to create groups of 3. Assign each group to a starting point.
LESSON FOCUS (15 - 20 MINUTES)	
Introduce Long Distance races with a videotape/DVD **Introduce Discus Throw with a videotape/DVD** **5 Stations: Discus Throw; Shot Put; Relays; Running Long Jump; High Jump. Rotate.**	**See DPESS Chapter 19 for details.** Use management game to divide students into 5 groups Assign groups to stations. Stay with Discus Throw, since that is the newest activity.

High-jump shoes are different from most other track shoes in that there are an additional one to four holes in the heel of the takeoff shoe, where the user can insert spikes for increased traction. As in the pole vault, heel strike in the high jump is important for lift-off as it allows the user efficiently to transfer energy. In addition, heel spikes aid greatly when the jumper makes the last four to five steps of his/her approach.

GAME (5 MINUTES)

Beanbag Touch and Go Indicate how many beanbags must be touched and the locomotor activity to perform.	**See DPESS Chapter 14 for details.** Scattered formation with beanbags scattered on floor.

EVALUATION/REVIEW AND CHEER

What muscles were used in class today?
Describe something about each track and field event you have learned so far.
Describe the use of special shoes by high jump competitors.
Introduce upcoming class Track meet

Cheer: We Run For Fun!

Track and Field Lesson Plan 7

EQUIPMENT:

Hurdles
Shot Put
High Jump equipment
Music tape/CD for Continuity Exercises
Batons
Discus
Cones and signs to mark stations
Music Player

OBJECTIVES:

The student will:

1. Participate in Running High Five's demonstrating speed, jumping skills, agility and following the instructions described by the instructor.
2. Participate in Continuity Exercises to improve strength, aerobic endurance and flexibility during the Fitness section of class.
3. Demonstrate hurdling, high jumping, shot putting, discus throwing, running long jump, relay racing and distance running using form demonstrated by the video/DVD or instructor.

National Standards Met in this Lesson: **1, 2, 3, 4, 5, 6**

INSTRUCTIONAL ACTIVITIES | **TEACHING HINTS**

INTRODUCTORY ACTIVITY (2 - 3 MINUTES)

Running High Five's
Direct the locomotor movement to be performed.

See DPESS Chapter 14 for details.
Scattered formation.

FITNESS DEVELOPMENT (8 - 12 MINUTES)

Continuity Exercises
Play CD/tape to direct activities. Have exercises to use during music silence well in mind.

See DPESS Chapter 15 for details.
See Golf, Lesson 1 for complete details.

LESSON FOCUS AND GAME (20 MINUTES)

Demonstrate hurdling techniques
7 Stations: Hurdles; High jump; Shot Put; Running Long Jump; 50 yard/meter run; Relay racing; Discus Throw; Rotate.

See DPESS Chapter 19 for details.
Stay with Hurdles, since that is the newest activity.
Use management game to divide students into 7 stations.
Rotate allowing equal time at each station today.
Tomorrow complete rotation.

The first recorded hurdles events took place at Eton College in Great Britain at about 1837. In early hurdling races athletes didn't jump the hurdles in stride but rather broke their stride to jump over each hurdle. The 120 yard hurdles was an official event in the Cambridge-Oxford track and field meet in 1864.

EVALUATION/REVIEW AND CHEER

Were there any fitness activities that were particularly challenging today and why?
What are the important points to remember when hurdling?
Describe the difference between the early hurdling events techniques and today's hurdling techniques.

Cheer: Hurdling, We Like It!

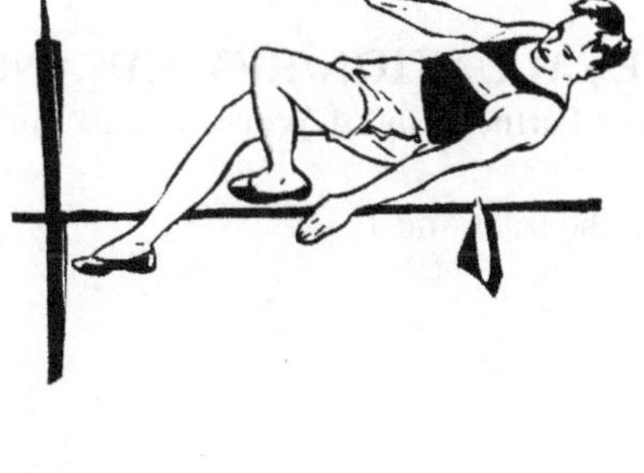

Track and Field Lesson Plan 8

EQUIPMENT:

Cones
Music CD/tape for fitness
Hurdles
Shot Put
Cones to mark start and finish lines
Discus
Circuit Training Signs
Music Player
High Jump equipment
Rake
Batons/ cardboard rolls
1 Frisbee per 2 students

OBJECTIVES:

The student will:

1. Participate in Partner Tug of War activities demonstrating strength, cooperative skills and following the instructions described by the instructor.
2. Participate in Circuit Training to improve strength, aerobic endurance and flexibility during the Fitness section of class.
3. Demonstrate hurdling, high jumping, shot putting, discus throwing, running long jump, relay racing and distance running using form demonstrated by the video/DVD or instructor.
4. Participate in Frisbee Catch games demonstrating throwing, catching and cooperative skills following the instructions of the game.

National Standards Met in this Lesson: **1, 2, 3, 4, 5, 6**

INSTRUCTIONAL ACTIVITIES	TEACHING HINTS
INTRODUCTORY ACTIVITY (2 - 3 MINUTES)	
Partner Tug of War Activities	**See DPESS Chapter 18 for details.**
Partner pulls: Side to side; Facing; Crab position hooked on foot; Back to back	Use elbow-to-elbow to make pairs.
FITNESS DEVELOPMENT (8 - 12 MINUTES)	
Circuit Training	**See DPESS Chapter 16 for details.** See Golf, Lesson 10 for complete details
LESSON FOCUS (15 - 20 MINUTES)	
Continue rotations where left off yesterday. **7 Stations: Hurdles; High jump; Shot Put; Running Long Jump; 50 yard/meter run; Relay racing; Discus Throw; Rotate.**	Review rotation with students from yesterday. Stay with Hurdles, since that is the newest activity. Use management game to divide students into 7 stations. Rotate allowing equal time at each station today.
GAME (5 MINUTES)	
Frisbee Catch	**See DPESS Chapter 20 for details.**
Partners can keep score or just free throwing and catching. 1 hand catch = 2 points 2 hand catch = 1 point Keep score to 20 points and then start over.	Demonstrate throwing and catching a Frisbee. Use back to back with a new person to create partners. One person puts a hand on their head. The person with his hand on his head is to go and get a Frisbee for the pair and return to the partner.

In 1968, high school students created the game of Ultimate Frisbee that is a cross between football, soccer and basketball. Ten years later, a form of Frisbee golf was introduced, complete with professional playing courses and associations.

EVALUATION/REVIEW AND CHEER

What behaviors are necessary to make Partner Tug of War safe and fun?
How did Ultimate Frisbee begin?
What do you need to work on before the track meet?

Cheer: Track, it's for me!

Track and Field Lesson Plan 9

EQUIPMENT:

Cones for Four Corners fitness	Signs for cones
Hurdles	Rake
High Jump Equipment	Shot
Discus	Music CD/Tape for fitness
Music CD/ cassette player	

OBJECTIVES:

The student will:

1. Participate in Pentabridge Hustle demonstrating agility, cooperative skills and following the instructions described by the instructor.
2. Participate in Four Corners Activities to improve strength, aerobic endurance and flexibility during the Fitness section of class.
3. Demonstrate hurdling, high jumping, shot putting, discus throwing, running long jump, relay racing and distance running using form demonstrated by the video/DVD or instructor.

National Standards Met in this Lesson: **1, 2, 3, 4, 5, 6**

INSTRUCTIONAL ACTIVITIES	TEACHING HINTS
INTRODUCTORY ACTIVITY (2 - 3 MINUTES)	
Pentabridge Hustle	**See DPESS Chapter 14 for details.**
Demonstrate bridges and locomotor activities to be used	Use Whistle Mixer to create groups of 5.
FITNESS DEVELOPMENT (8 - 12 MINUTES)	
Stretching	**See DPESS Chapter 16 for details.**
Lower Leg Stretch	Place arms on wall or fence for support.
Achilles Tendon Stretch	
Balance Beam Stretch	
Side Leg Stretch	
Groin Stretch	
Cross-Legged Stretch	
Body Twist	
Standing Hip Bend	
Elbow Grab Stretch	
Aerobic Activity	**See DPESS Chapter 16 for details.**
Four Corners	Set up 4 cones creating a square. Each cone should list two locomotor activities.
Skipping	
Jogging	
Sliding	Student executes the movement on the cone until she gets to next cone.
Running backwards	
Jumping	
Leaping	Music CD/tape directs length of aerobic exercising.
Hopping	
Galloping	
Stretch Activities	**See DPESS Chapter 16 for details.**
Partner Resistance Exercises	
LESSON FOCUS AND GAME (20 MINUTES)	
Review events in tomorrows class Track Meet.	**See DPESS Chapter 19 for details.**
Practice events for tomorrows class Track Meet.	Allow students to pick their event(s) in which to participate during the meet.

EVALUATION/REVIEW AND CHEER

What muscles were used in class today?

Are there any events you need clarified before the meet?

Cheer: I'm Ready to Run!

Track and Field Lesson Plan 10

EQUIPMENT:

Parachute
Music CD/ cassette player
High Jump Equipment
Rake
Batons
Discus
Music for fitness
Magic Number Cards
3 Measuring tapes for field events
Clip boards, pencils and score sheets
Shot put
Hurdles

OBJECTIVES:

The student will:

1. Participate in Magic Number Challenge demonstrating memory and movement skills and following the instructions described by the instructor.
2. Participate in Parachute Fitness Activities to improve strength, aerobic endurance and flexibility during the Fitness section of class.
3. Participate in a class Track Meet demonstrating running, relay racing, hurdling, high jumping, shot putting, discus throwing, running long jump, relay racing and distance running using form demonstrated by the video/DVD or instructor.

National Standards Met in this Lesson: **1, 2, 3, 4, 5, 6**

INSTRUCTIONAL ACTIVITIES	TEACHING HINTS
INTRODUCTORY ACTIVITY (2 - 3 MINUTES)	
Magic Number Challenge Hold up a card with 3 numbers on it (i.e. 8, 10, 5). The students must then perform 3 selected movements the specified number of times.	**See DPESS Chapter 14 for details.** Scattered formation Students put together a series of movements based on the magic numbers given. Suggest movements or ask for student suggestions.
FITNESS DEVELOPMENT (8 MINUTES)	
Parachute Fitness Activities	**See DPESS Chapter 16 for details.** See Lesson 4, Golf Unit for details.
LESSON FOCUS AND GAME (20 MINUTES)	
Class Track Meet Allow students to select the events in which to race.	Locate assistants to help with each event. Hold several events simultaneously.

High school track and field meets date back to the late 1800's in some parts of the country to the early 1900's in the West.

EVALUATION/REVIEW AND CHEER

When did high school track and field meets begin?
Discuss results of track meet.
Introduce next unit of study.

Cheer: 2, 4, 6, 8, Track's Great!

Name:______________________________________ **Class period:**__________

TRACK AND FIELD QUIZ

1. What are the most important techniques for efficient running?
   a. Speed
   b. Long strides
   c. Arm control
   d. a & b
   e. b & c

2. Where is the shot-put placed before the throw?
   a. In the hand, at the neck?
   b. Under the arm?
   c. At waist level?
   d. Anywhere will work

3. When handing off a baton in a relay race, the runner is responsible for telling the receiver when to begin running and place their hand out for receipt of the baton.
   a. True/ False

4. In the Running Long Jump, the jump is measured:
   a. From their hands when landing hands are put down behind the feet
   b. When the runner lands and put hands down in front of their feet it is still measure from the hands
   c. From where ever the runner requests

5. It is important to have a count or a rhythm and take-off on the correct foot when hurdling.
   a. True/ False

6. How many people participate in the 400-meter relay?
   a. 2
   b. 3
   c. 4
   d. 5

7. In a track meet, how many chances does one have in Shot Put?
   a. 1
   b. 2
   c. 3

8. Name the types of jumps/ landings you learned in class for High Jump:

9. In a track meet, how many chances does one have in Discus?
   a. 1
   b. 2
   c. 3

10. Describe the long distance events you learned about in class.

Yoga

This unit has been specifically designed to meet all six components of the NASPE National Standards for Physical Education.

OBJECTIVES:

The student will:

1. Perform locomotor movements on command during the Introductory Activities.
2. Demonstrate balancing in a variety of positions during Move and Assume Pose Introductory Activity.
3. Demonstrate respect for classmates while participating in Standing High Fives.
4. Demonstrate body control while executing 1/2, 1/4, 3/4, and full turns Standing High Fives.
5. Participate in Bean Bag Introductory Activity demonstrating eye-hand coordination and ability to make quick movement changes.
6. Participate in Weave Drill demonstrating agility and the ability to follow directions during movement.
7. Participate in Balance Tag demonstrating good sportsmanship.
8. Participate in Aerobic Exercises during Fitness Development to improve overall fitness.
9. Participate in Continuity Exercises and 12 Ways to Fitness to improve cardiovascular endurance.
10. Execute seven exercises associated with a Yoga Specific Warm-up as demonstrated.
11. Execute nine stretching exercises associated with a Yoga Specific Flexibility Routine as demonstrated.
12. Participate in Aerobic Exercise/ Workout during Fitness Development to cardiovascular and muscle endurance.
13. Demonstrate an understanding of team member interdependence during Partner Racetrack Fitness, 12 Ways Fitness, Mirror Drill, and Yoga Follow-the-Leader.
14. Participate in Racetrack Fitness to improve fitness.
15. Demonstrate respect for classmates while participating in Mirror Drill, 12 Ways to Fitness, and Yoga Follow-the-Leader.
16. Demonstrate an understanding for the importance of alignment and head position in yoga practice.
17. On a self-check test, write five of seven benefits of yoga covered on Task Sheet #1.
18. Execute four Yoga Rest poses as demonstrated to develop repertoire of relaxation techniques.
19. Perform five Yoga Breathing exercises as demonstrated to develop concentration strategies.
20. Practice and observe known and new yoga poses with partner by completing Reciprocal Task Sheet #2.
21. Recognize and perform 10 different yoga postures from drawings by completing Self Check Task Sheet #3.
22. Identify in writing with correct spelling both the English and Sanskrit names for 10 different yoga postures.
23. Practice 10 self-taught yoga postures with the assistance of peer leaders by participating in Yoga Follow-the-Leader.
24. Demonstrate an understanding of some of the opposite forces and actions involved in yoga practice.
25. Perform and demonstrate understanding of multiple poses that comprise Sun Salutation.
26. Play "Frisbee 21" with a partner demonstrating cooperation and 1- and 2- hand catching/throwing accuracy.
27. Improve eye-hand coordination by 1- and 2- hand catching/throwing during Frisbee 21 Game.
28. Demonstrate teamwork skills while executing different locomotors connected to classmates in Loose Caboose.
29. Work cooperatively in large group during parachute activities demonstrating the ability to follow instructions.
30. Participate in Juggling Scarves Game demonstrating eye-hand coordination and ability to make quick movement changes.
31. Participate in Mass Stand-Up Game demonstrating teamwork and concentration skills.
32. Demonstrate cooperation and ability to stand on proper points of support during Mini Pyramids.

YOGA BLOCK PLAN
2 WEEK UNIT

Week #1	Monday	Tuesday	Wednesday	Thursday	Friday
Introductory Activity	Move and Assume Pose	Standing High Fives	Throwing & Catching Bean Bags on the Move	Weave Drill	Mini Pyramids
Fitness	Aerobic Exercises/ Workout	Continuity Exercises	Parachute Rhythmic Aerobic Activity	Aerobic Exercises/ Workout	Partner Racetrack Fitness
Lesson Focus	Introduction to Yoga	Yoga Warm-Up	Yoga Flexibility Routine	Rest Poses & Yoga Breathing	Yoga Partners
Game	Frisbee 21	Loose Caboose	Juggling Scarves	Mass Stand Up	Balance Tag

Week #2	Monday	Tuesday	Wednesday	Thursday	Friday
Introductory Activity	Standing High Fives	Mirror Drill	Move and Assume Pose	Throwing & Catching Bean Bags on the Move	
Fitness	Continuity Exercises	12 Ways to Fitness	Aerobic Exercises/ Workout	Partner Racetrack Fitness	
Lesson Focus	Yoga Posture ID	Yoga Follow-the-Leader	Opposite Forces in Yoga	Intro Sun Salutation	
Game	Loose Caboose	Frisbee 21	Juggling Scarves	Mass Stand Up	

Yoga Lesson Plan 1

EQUIPMENT:

Task sheet #1 (pencils/ pens & clipboards as needed)
1 Frisbee per 2 students
1 non-skid ¼"- foam yoga mat and/or, 1 1"- padded tumbling mat per student
CD/cassette player
Aerobic CD/tape with 120-150 BPM

OBJECTIVES:

The student will:

1. Demonstrate the ability to perform a variety of locomotor movements on command.
2. Demonstrate balancing in a variety of positions during the Move and Assume Pose Introductory Activity.
3. Participate in Aerobic Exercises during Fitness Development to improve overall fitness.
4. Demonstrate an understanding for the importance of alignment and head position in yoga practice.
5. On a self-check test, write five of seven benefits of yoga covered on Task Sheet # 1.
6. Play "Frisbee 21" with a partner demonstrating 1- and 2- hand catching/throwing accuracy.
7. Improve eye-hand coordination by 1- and 2- hand catching/throwing during Frisbee 21 Game.
8. Work cooperatively with partner during Frisbee 21 Game.

National Standards Met in this Lesson: **1, 2, 3, 4, 5, 6**

INSTRUCTIONAL ACTIVITIES	TEACHING HINTS
INTRODUCTORY ACTIVITY (2 - 3 MINUTES)	
Move and Assume Pose	**See DPESS Chapter 16 for details.**
Direct a variety of locomotor movements. Freeze on signal and assume balancing poses on body parts	Scattered formation.
FITNESS DEVELOPMENT (8 - 12 MINUTES)	
Aerobic Exercises/Workout	**See DPESS Chapter 16 for details.** Scattered Formation
Sample 8 Count Aerobic Exercise Phrases of Movement	
Jump in place 8 times.	Hit the sides of thighs with straight arms.
Walk in place 16 times.	On toes, perform 16 steps moving arms down and up on the sides or in front of the body.
Run in place 8 times.	Lift feet high in the rear.
Run in place 8 times.	Lift knees high in the front.
Perform 8 jumping jacks.	Arms move down and up with leg movements.
Perform 8 jumping jacks.	Arms move down and up to shoulder level.
Mountain Climber	Jump and land with feet separated forward and backward. Alternate which foot lands in front and in back on each jump. Arms swing high in opposition to legs.
Run in place 8 times.	Lift feet high in the rear.
Run in place 8 times.	Lift knees high in the front.
Perform 4 slides to the right.	Repeat to the left. Repeat whole phrase.
Hop on one foot and lift up the opposite knee.	Reverse
Hop and swing kick the opposite foot forward.	Alternate.
Charleston Bounce Step	Step L, kick R foot forward, step back, and touch L toe back. Repeat 8 times. Reverse.
Schottische (Run R, L, R, Hop L. Alternate 4X.)	Run 3 times in place or while traveling then hop (clap simultaneously).
Grapevine	Step to R, cross L foot over R, step to R on the R foot, cross L behind the R, and step on R while traveling to R. Repeat phrase 4 times moving to R.
Grapevine Schottische	Step to R on R, cross L behind R, step on R-to-R and hop on R. Reverse. Repeat 4 times.
Walk in place.	To cool down.

INSTRUCTIONAL ACTIVITIES	TEACHING HINTS
LESSON FOCUS (15 - 20 MINUTES)	
Introduce Yoga	
• Reasons to Practice	Explain Benefits.
• Safety	Demonstrate and explain importance of alignment and head position.
• Equipment	A non-skid ¼" foam mat is recommended alone but if students require additional padding, a 1"- padded tumbling mat may be used underneath foam.
• Assign Task Sheet	Distribute and explain Task Sheet #1

The practice of yoga is considered more than a system of physical exercise for health. Yoga is an ancient path to spiritual growth, and originates out of India where Hinduism is practiced.

INSTRUCTIONAL ACTIVITIES	TEACHING HINTS
GAME (5 MINUTES)	
Frisbee 21	**See DPESS Chapter 20 for details.**
Game Rules:	Create partners using elbow-to-elbow technique.
• Players stand 10 yards apart	Have 1 person kneel. The standing partner gets a Frisbee from perimeter of area and rejoins partner.
• Throw disc back & forth. Throws must be catchable.	
• 1 hand catch = 1 point	Player must get 21 points to win & win by 2 points.
• 2 hand catch = 2 points	
EVALUATION/REVIEW AND CHEER	
Self-Evaluation and Review	**Task Sheet #1/ Self Check Test**
Cheer: Yoga is new; Yoga is for me and You!	

TASK SHEET #1: THE BENEFITS OF YOGA

NAME: ____ **DATE:** ________________________________

Objectives: Upon Completion of this lesson, you will:
1. Demonstrate an understanding of the benefits of yoga practice by writing five of seven benefits described.
2. Demonstrate a positive attitude while practicing yoga as a means toward achieving a lifelong commitment to regular physical activity.

Instructions: This lesson consists of seven benefits of yoga practice. Each benefit is followed by a brief description of the benefit. After carefully studying the list, see your instructor for your self-check test. On the self-check test, you will be asked to write five of seven benefits of yoga. If you are unable to write five benefits you must retake the test until you are able to do so.

The Benefits of Yoga

Through enthusiastic and dedicated participation in the quality practice of Yoga, you may experience one or more of the following benefits:

1. **Improved Muscle Strength**: In the course of this unit, you may experience measurable gains in muscle strength and endurance.
2. **Improved Muscle Flexibility**: In the course of this unit, you may experience measurable gains in muscle flexibility.
3. **Improved Posture**: Improved muscle strength and flexibility positively affect posture, as does an understanding of the proper alignment employed in yoga practice. By practicing yoga, you can improve your posture.
4. **Improved Relaxation and Concentration**: By focusing the attention on deep and deliberate breathing as employed in yoga practice, you may experience an improved ability to relax and/or concentrate when desired.
5. **Decreased Fatigue**: After participating in a yoga program, as with any quality exercise program, you will experience more energy and less fatigue in performing your daily activities.
6. **Reduced Chance for Injury**: By improved your muscle strength and flexibility, you may lesson the frequency and severity of possible injury.
7. **Improved Self-Concept**: By improving muscle strength, flexibility and posture, you may also experience an increase in self-esteem, pride and confidence. You may also experience positive feelings by mastering various yoga postures.

SELF-CHECK TEST: BENEFITS OF YOGA

NAME: ____ DATE: ________________________________

Directions: Write five of seven benefits of yoga covered on Task Sheet #1. When you have finished get an answer sheet from your instructor and correct your test. If you miss any answers go back and review the Task Sheet and retake the test. Repeat this procedure until you are able to write five of seven benefits of yoga.

-Write five of seven benefits of yoga.

1. ____
2. ____
3. ____
4. ____
5. ____

-Write the other two benefits if you can. (OPTIONAL):

6. ____
7. ____

ANSWER KEY: THE BENEFITS OF YOGA SELF-CHECK TEST

-Answers may appear in any order, but may not repeat:

1. Improved Muscle Strength
2. Improved Muscle Flexibility
3. Improved Posture
4. Improved Relaxation and Concentration
5. Decreased Fatigue
6. Reduced Chance for Injury
7. Improved Self-Concept

Yoga Lesson Plan 2

EQUIPMENT:

CD/cassette player

Pre-recorded music for Continuity Exercises.

1 jump rope per student (have various lengths available to accommodate different heights).

1 non-skid ¼"- foam yoga mat and/or, 1 1"- padded tumbling mat per student

Recommended Reference book: *The American Yoga Associations New Yoga Challenge* (**AYANYC**)

OBJECTIVES:

The student will:

1. Demonstrate respect for classmates while participating in Standing High Fives.
2. Demonstrate body control while executing 1/2, 1/4, 3/4, and full turns Standing High Fives.
3. Participate in Continuity Exercises to improve cardiovascular endurance.
4. Execute seven exercises associated with a Yoga Specific Warm-up as demonstrated.
5. Demonstrate teamwork skills while executing different locomotors connected to classmates in Loose Caboose.

National Standards Met in this Lesson: 1, 2, 3, 4, 5, 6

INSTRUCTIONAL ACTIVITIES	TEACHING HINTS

INTRODUCTORY ACTIVITY (2 - 3 MINUTES)

Standing High Fives	**See DPESS Chapter 14 for details.** Use Toe-to-Toe to create partners of similar heights.

FITNESS DEVELOPMENT (8 - 12 MINUTES)

Continuity Exercises Direct students in exercise performance during silence.	**See DPESS Chapter 16 for details.** Scattered Formation Alternate jumping rope and 2-count exercises. Rope jumping is done to pre-recorded music 30 - 40 seconds Exercises done on pre-recorded intervals of 30 seconds of silence

LESSON FOCUS (15 - 20 MINUTES)

Yoga Specific Warm-Up • Shoulder Roll • Neck Stretch • Arm Roll • Full Bend • Full Bend Variation • Hip Rotation • Standing Knee Squeeze	**AYANYC page 15-19** Scattered Formation

Yoga is considered to be a practice of connected mind and body exercises. Most people the western cultures separate yoga from its spiritual goal, seeing yoga strictly as an exercise/fitness regimen, or an overall program of keeping physical and emotional wellbeing.

GAME (5 MINUTES)

Loose Caboose Select 2 "its". Direct students to use different locomotors.	**See DPESS Chapter 14 for details.** Use Whistle Mixer to make groups of 3.

EVALUATION/REVIEW AND CHEER

Were there any similarities between the Yoga Specific Warm-Up and other exercise you've done before? What were they?

What warm-up exercises were new to you? Which ones were most challenging?

Cheer: Get on board loose Caboose... stay on track with PE!

"YOGA PARTNERS" RECIPROCAL TASK SHEET #2

Directions: Work with a partner. Begin in *Mountain Pose,* then perform the partner stretch, holding the pictured stretch position for 12 seconds (count: "one one-thousand, two one-thousand," etc.) Next one person will be the "doer" while the other person is the "observer." The observer reads information/ instructions from the table, offers verbal feedback and places a check in the "yes" or "no" column recording the performance of their partner. Each person has his/her own Task Sheet. Place both of your names on each Task Sheet. Be sure to complete all the tasks on each sheet. Alternate observer and doer as appropriate.

NAME: (*Doer*) ____________________________ **NAME:** (*Observer*) ______________________________

PREPARE, STRETCH & POSE								
Always begin and end in *MOUNTAIN POSE* inhaling through the nose deeply and exhaling through the nose at least one time.	Mountain 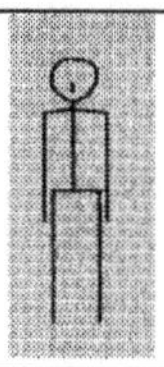 Pose → Inhale → 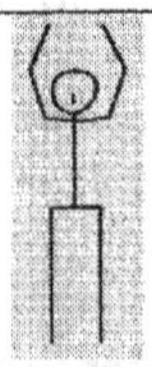 → Exhale → 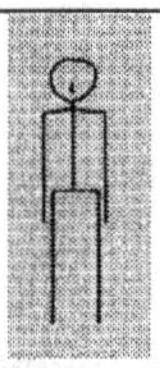							
	DATES							
(Record date of practice)								
1. PARTNER STRETCH	**Yes**	**No**	**Yes**	**No**	**Yes**	**No**	**Yes**	**No**
Standing Forward Bend: hold for 12 seconds. 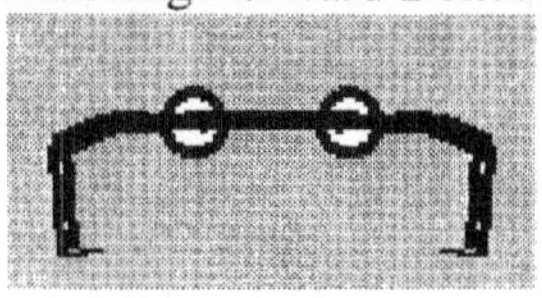 Flat backs, Knees straight.								
2. MOUNTAIN POSE								
DOWNWARD FACING DOG 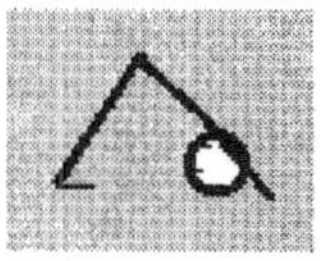 ***3. Your partners body should resemble an up-side down "V."***								
4. Knees straight, but not locked. Heels on floor.								
5. Ears near elbows.								
6. Head below arms, eyes to feet.								
7. MOUNTAIN POSE								
8. PARTNER STRETCH Pre-warrior: hold for 12 seconds, right and left.  Knees over ankles not past toes.								
9. MOUNTAIN POSE								

10. WARRIOR II (Right side, then left side) 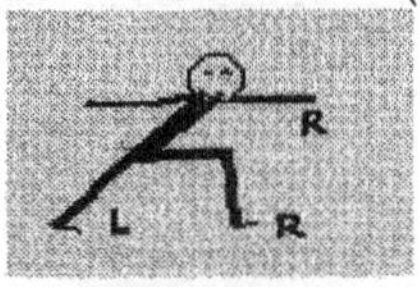 ***11. Right knee at 90° angle.*** ***12. Right knee over ankle; not past toes.*** ***13. Shoulders down & relaxed.*** ***14. Arms extended to fingertips.*** ***15. Left leg long, but not hyper-extended.***								
16. MOUNTAIN POSE								

***Yoga "stick figures" produced for use by teachers by Bridget Luthien available @ <http://www.luthien.co.uk/yoga/bend_forward.html>

Yoga Lesson Plan 3

EQUIPMENT:

CD/cassette player
1 bean bag per 2 students
3 juggling scarves per student
1 non-skid ¼"- foam yoga mat and/or, 1 1"- padded tumbling mat per student
CD/ cassette for Parachute Activity
Parachute
Recommended Instructor Aid: The American Yoga Associations New Yoga Challenge (**AYANYC**)

OBJECTIVES:

The student will:

1. Participate in Bean Bag Introductory Activity demonstrating eye-hand coordination and ability to make quick movement changes.
2. Work cooperatively in large group during parachute activity.
3. Execute nine stretching exercises associated with a Yoga Specific Flexibility Routine as demonstrated.
4. Participate in Juggling Scarves Game demonstrating eye-hand coordination and ability to make quick movement changes.

National Standards Met in this Lesson: **1, 2, 3,4, 5, 6**

INSTRUCTIONAL ACTIVITIES	TEACHING HINTS
INTRODUCTORY ACTIVITY (2 - 3 MINUTES)	
Throwing & Catching Bean Bags on the Move	**See DPESS Chapter 18 for details.**
Toss, move, and catch.	Scattered Formation
Direct students to move forward, backward and sideways using carioca, shuffle and slide.	Use Elbow-to-Elbow to create partners.
FITNESS DEVELOPMENT (8 - 12 MINUTES)	
Parachute Rhythmic Aerobic Activity	**See DPESS Chapter 16 for details.**
Skip both directions. Slide both directions. Run both directions.	Direct students to take hold of parachute loops with 1 or 2 hands depending on class size.
Jump to center. Hop backward. Lift parachute overhead. Lower parachute to toes.	Direct locomotor movements and other parachute activities. Use music to motivate.
Run CW with parachute overhead. Make a dome.	Alternate locomotor movements and other parachute activities with seated strength and stretching exercises.
LESSON FOCUS (15 - 20 MINUTES)	
Yoga Specific Stretches/ Flexibility Routine	**AYANYC page 80-85**
• Standing Sun Pose • Alternate Triangle • Side Triangle • Twisting Triangle • Cobra • Downward Facing Dog • Child's (Baby) Pose • Camel Pose • Pigeon Pose	Scattered Formation

Historians have traced the beginnings of Yoga to Stone Age Shamanism. Originally, it is believed it was used by Shamans to heal the community. Now it is practiced individually, for self-improvement.

GAME (5 MINUTES)

Juggling Scarves — **See DPESS Chapter 16 for details.**

EVALUATION/REVIEW AND CHEER

Were there any similarities between the Yoga Specific stretches and the stretches performed during the parachute activity? Which did you prefer, why?

Cheer: Scarves are cool, Cool-Down!

SELF-CHECK TASK SHEET #3 FOR: YOGA POSTURE IDENTIFICATION

NAME: ______________________________ **DATE:** ______________________

Objectives:
Upon Completion of this lesson, you will:
1. Recognize and perform 8 different yoga postures from drawings.
2. Identify in writing with correct spelling both the English and Sanskrit names for 10 different yoga postures.

Instructions:
There are 8 stations set-up around the teaching area, each with drawings of a single yoga posture identified by name in both English and Sanskrit. When the music begins, go to any station, examine the drawing, practice the posture yourself at least 2 times, then in the space provided below write down both the English and Sanskrit names for each posture. Pay careful attention to spelling. You need *not* begin at Station #1, but be sure that you write the correct names next to the drawing that matches your current station. Two students may work at each station, when the music stops, both students should move to the next station in a clockwise direction. If you complete the task(s) prior to the music stopping, practice the posture again and double check your spelling of posture names.

				POSTURE NAMES:	
STATION #1	***STATION #2***	**Yes**	**No**	***ENGLISH***	***SANSKRIT***
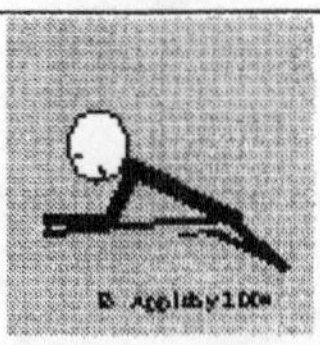		___ ___	___ ___	*#1*__________ *#2*__________	*#1*__________ *#2*__________
Did you practice each posture at least 2 times?					
STATION #3	***STATION #4***	**Yes**	**No**		
		___ ___	___ ___	*#3*__________ *#4*__________	*#3*__________ *#4*__________
Did you practice this posture at least 2 times?					
STATION #5	***STATION #6***	**Yes**	**No**		
	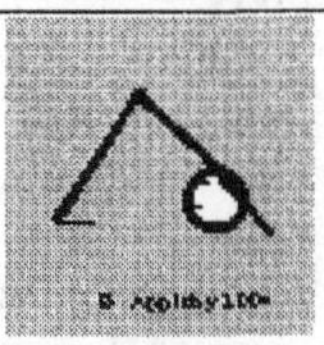	___ ___	___ ___	*#5*__________ *#6*__________	*#5*__________ *#6*__________
Did you practice this posture at least 2 times?					
STATION #7	***STATION #8***	**Yes**	**No**		
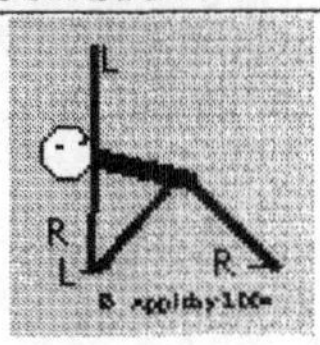	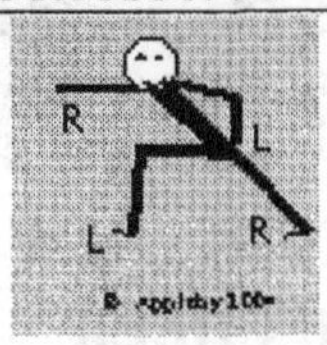	___ ___	___ ___	*#7*__________ *#8*__________	*#7*__________ *#8*__________
Did you practice this posture at least 2 times?					

Yoga Lesson Plan 4

EQUIPMENT:
CD/cassette/ music player
Music/ CD for Lesson Focus meditation/ relaxation
Aerobic CD/tape with 120-150 BPM
Cones for Weave Drill
1 non-skid ¼"- foam yoga mat and/or, 1 1"- padded tumbling mat per student
Recommended Instructor Reference: *The American Yoga Associations New Yoga Challenge* (**AYANYC**)

OBJECTIVES:
The student will:
1. Participate in Weave Drill demonstrating agility and the ability to follow directions during movement.
2. Participate in Aerobic Exercise/ Workout during Fitness Development to cardiovascular and muscle endurance.
3. Execute four Yoga Rest poses as demonstrated.
4. Perform five Yoga Breathing exercises as demonstrated.
5. Participate in Mass Stand Up Game challenging teamwork and concentration skills.

National Standards Met in this Lesson: **1, 2, 3, 4, 5, 6**

INSTRUCTIONAL ACTIVITIES	TEACHING HINTS

INTRODUCTORY ACTIVITY (2 - 3 MINUTES)

Weave Drill
Use locomotor movement slide, skip, gallop, etc. while negotiating cones.

See DPESS Chapter 14 for details.
Scattered Formation
Use whistle signals to add arm movements.

FITNESS DEVELOPMENT (8 - 12 MINUTES)

Exercises/Workout

See DPESS Chapter 16 for details.
Scattered Formation

LESSON FOCUS (15 - 20 MINUTES)

Yoga Rest Poses
- Standing Rest
- Mountain Pose
- Baby Pose
- Corpse Pose

AYANYC pages 80-85
Scattered Formation
Demonstrate each pose and direct students accordingly.
Use music to set tone.

Yoga Breathing
- Complete Breath
- Alternate Nostril Breath
- Cooling Breath
- Soft Bellows Breath
- Rising Breath

AYANYC pages 22-26
Scattered Formation
Demonstrate each breath and direct students accordingly.
Emphasize focus on deep and deliberate breathing.
Use music to set tone.

Yoga was introduced in the West during the early 19th century. It was first studied as part of Eastern Philosophy and began as a movement for health and vegetarianism around the 1930's. Interest in it grew slowly initially.

GAME (5 MINUTES)

Mass Stand Up
Start with partners, lock elbows
And attempt to stand as one.
Increase number of people to 3, 4,
And so on.

See DPESS Chapter 18 for details.
Use Back-to-Back to create partners,
Whistle Mixer for larger groups.

EVALUATION/REVIEW AND CHEER
Can how you breathe affect your ability to relax?
Can how you breathe affect your ability to concentrate?

Cheer: Deep Breathing is Good for Mind and Body!

Yoga Lesson Plan 5

EQUIPMENT:
Task Sheet #2 (pencils/ pens & clipboards as needed)
1 non-skid ¼"- foam yoga mat and/or, 1 1"- padded tumbling mat per student
Recommended Instructor Aid: The American Yoga Associations New Yoga Challenge (**AYANYC**)
10 cones and task cards for Partner Racetrack Fitness

OBJECTIVES:
The student will:
1. Demonstrate cooperation and ability to stand on proper points of support during Mini Pyramids.
2. Participate in Racetrack Fitness to improve fitness.
3. Practice and observe known and new yoga poses with partner by completing Reciprocal Task Sheet #2.
4. Participate in Balance Tag demonstrating balancing skills, agility, and good sportsmanship.

National Standards Met in this Lesson: 1, 2, 3, 4, 5, 6

INSTRUCTIONAL ACTIVITIES	TEACHING HINTS

INTRODUCTORY ACTIVITY (2 - 3 MINUTES)

Mini Pyramids	**See DPESS Chapter 18 for details.**
Perform locomotor movement.	Scattered Formation
On whistle signal students form groups of 3 to build pyramid.	Use Whistle Mixer to form groups of 3. Caution students to select group members of similar size and to use proper points of support.

FITNESS DEVELOPMENT (8 - 12 MINUTES)

Partner Racetrack Fitness	**See DPESS Chapter 16 for details.**
10 stations with unique task cards in circular track formation. 2 students perform task while other 2 run around track.	Use Whistle Mixer to form groups of 4. Use Toe-to-Toe for partners.

LESSON FOCUS (15 - 20 MINUTES)

Reciprocal Task Sheet #2: Yoga Partners	
Review yoga poses; demonstrate new skills.	Use Toe-to-Toe for partners. Distribute and explain Task Sheet #2 Assist *Observer* in correcting *Doer*.

Some of the Yoga vocabulary includes: Asanas or proper exercise; Pranayama or proper breathing; Dhyana or positive thinking and Meditation.

GAME (5 MINUTES)

Balance Tag	**See DPESS Chapter 14 for details.** Select several "its." Stipulate 1-2 balance positions.

EVALUATION/REVIEW AND CHEER
How did working with a partner improve your yoga Practice?
State one Yoga vocabulary word and it's meaning.

Cheer: Yoga is more fun with a partner!

Yoga Lesson Plan 6

EQUIPMENT:

Task sheet #3 (pencils/ pens & clipboards as needed)
CD/cassette/ music player — Pre-recorded music for Continuity Exercises.
CD appropriate to yoga practice.
1 jump rope per student (have various lengths available to accommodate different heights).
1 non-skid ¼"- foam yoga mat and/or, 1 1"- padded tumbling mat per student
10 Cones and yoga posture signs for Fitness Development
Recommended Instructor Reference: *The American Yoga Associations New Yoga Challenge* (**AYANYC**)

OBJECTIVES:

The student will:

1. Demonstrate respect for classmates while participating in Standing High Fives.
2. Demonstrate body control while executing 1/2, 1/4, 3/4, and full turns Standing High Fives.
3. Participate in Continuity Exercises to improve cardiovascular endurance.
4. Recognize and perform 10 different yoga postures from drawings by completing Self Check Task Sheet #3.
5. Identify in writing with correct spelling both the English and Sanskrit names for 10 different yoga postures
6. Demonstrate teamwork skills while executing different locomotors connected to classmates in Loose Caboose.

National Standards Met in this Lesson: **1, 2, 3, 4, 5, 6**

INSTRUCTIONAL ACTIVITIES	TEACHING HINTS
INTRODUCTORY ACTIVITY (2 - 3 MINUTES)	
Standing High Fives	**See DPESS Chapter 14 for details.** Use Toe-to-Toe to create partners of similar heights.
FITNESS DEVELOPMENT (8 - 12 MINUTES)	
Continuity Exercises Direct students in exercise performance during silence.	**See DPESS Chapter 16 for details.** Scattered Formation Alternate jumping rope & 2-count exercises. Rope jumping is done to pre-recorded music (40 sec.) Exercises done on pre-recorded intervals of silence (30 sec.)
LESSON FOCUS (15 - 20 MINUTES)	
Self-Check Task Sheet #3: Yoga Posture ID	**AYANYC** Stations Stop and start music for station rotation.

People practice Yoga for many reasons. Some of the reasons stated are: Yoga relaxes the body and the mind. Even in the midst of stressful environments, Yoga helps control breathing and clears the mind of cluttered thoughts, leaving only deep physical and mental renewal.

GAME (5 MINUTES)	
Loose Caboose Select 2 "its". Direct students to use different locomotors.	**See DPESS Chapter 16 for details.** Use Whistle Mixer to make groups of 3.

EVALUATION/REVIEW AND CHEER

Review 10 self-taught postures.
Discuss origins and use of Sanskrit.
What are some of the reasons people practice Yoga?

Cheer: I can learn by looking!

Yoga Lesson Plan 7

EQUIPMENT:
CD/cassette player
A variety of music including that appropriate to yoga practice.
1 non-skid ¼"- foam yoga mat and/or, 1 1"- padded tumbling mat per student
10 Cones and yoga posture signs from Lesson 6 1 Frisbee per 2 students
Recommended Instructor Reference: *The American Yoga Associations New Yoga Challenge* (**AYANYC**)

OBJECTIVES:
The student will:
1. Demonstrate respect for classmates while participating in Mirror Drill, 12 Ways to Fitness, and Yoga Follow-the-Leader.
2. Participate in 12 Ways to Fitness to improve cardiovascular endurance.
3. Practice 10 self-taught yoga postures with the assistance of peer leaders by participating in Yoga Follow-the-Leader.

National Standards Met in this Lesson: 1, 2, 3, 4, 5, 6

INSTRUCTIONAL ACTIVITIES	TEACHING HINTS

INTRODUCTORY ACTIVITY (2 - 3 MINUTES)

Mirror Drill in Place to Music	**See DPESS Chapter 14 for details.**
Leader makes movements motivated by style of music.	Use Back-to-Back to create partners.
	Use Hand-on-Head to select leader, signal switch with whistle

FITNESS DEVELOPMENT (8 - 12 MINUTES)

12 Ways to Fitness	**See DPESS Chapter 16 for details.**
	Switch leaders again as above.

LESSON FOCUS (15 - 20 MINUTES)

Yoga Follow-the-Leader	**AYANYC**
Students travel from station to station and practice each of 10 postures lead by different peer-leaders.	Use Whistle Mixer to make groups of 4-5. Stop and start music for station rotation and leader switch.

It is believed that for people who are either overweight or underweight, Yoga Exercises can help achieve the desired weight. The principles of balance and moderation in physical activity and diet under Yoga can also lead to a healthier lifestyle and therefore, better control of weight management.

GAME (5 MINUTES)

Frisbee 21	**See DPESS Chapter 16 for details.**

EVALUATION/REVIEW AND CHEER
Are you a better leader or a better follower?
Why are both important?
Why is it believed that Yoga can help people moderate their weight?

Cheer: Mirroring makes me a better Mover!

Yoga Lesson Plan 8

EQUIPMENT:

CD/music/ cassette player
Aerobic music/ CD/tape with 120-150 BPM.
1 non-skid ¼"- foam yoga mat and/or, 1 1"- padded tumbling mat per student
Task sheet #4 (pencils/ pens & clipboards as needed)
3 juggling scarves per student
Recommended Instructor Reference: *The American Yoga Associations New Yoga Challenge* **(AYANYC)**

OBJECTIVES:

The student will:

1. Demonstrate the ability to perform a variety of locomotor movements on command.
2. Demonstrate balancing in a variety of positions during Move & Assume Pose Introductory Activity.
3. Participate in Aerobic Exercises during Fitness Development to improve overall fitness.
4. Demonstrate an understanding of some of the opposite forces and actions involved in yoga practice.
5. Participate in Juggling Scarves Game demonstrating eye-hand coordination and ability to make quick movement changes.

National Standards Met in this Lesson: **1, 2, 3, 4, 5, 6**

INSTRUCTIONAL ACTIVITIES	TEACHING HINTS
INTRODUCTORY ACTIVITY (2 - 3 MINUTES)	
Move and Assume Pose Students will move doing a variety of locomotor movements. Freeze on signal and assume balancing poses on body parts	**See DPESS Chapter 14 for details.** Scattered Formation.
FITNESS DEVELOPMENT (8 - 12 MINUTES)	
Aerobic Exercises/ Workout	**See DPESS Chapter 16 for details.** Scattered Formation
LESSON FOCUS (15 - 20 MINUTES)	
Guided Discovery Task Sheet #4: Opposite Forces in Yoga	**AYANYC**

Some believe that Yoga improves your resistance to disease. The postures and movements in Yoga massage the internal organs, enhancing blood circulation and functionality, thus, lessening the risk of illness.

INSTRUCTIONAL ACTIVITIES	TEACHING HINTS
GAME (5 MINUTES)	
Juggling Scarves	**See DPESS Chapter 18 for details.** Add challenges listed.

EVALUATION/REVIEW AND CHEER

Guided Discovery Task Sheet Review
Cheer: Yoga is for you and me!

GUIDED DISCOVERY TASK SHEET #4: YOGA OPPOSITES

Objective:
Upon completion of this lesson you will:
1. Demonstrate an understanding of some of the opposite forces and actions involved in yoga practice.

Student Information:
Yoga is ancient practice that is an effective form of exercise because it strives to create and maintain *balance* between *opposite* or *opposing* forces or actions. For this reason, almost every yoga posture (asana) involves at least one pair of opposite actions or movements. These opposite actions may involve the same body part or muscle group at the same time or they may involve different body parts at the same time. For your yoga practice to be effective, it is important that you develop an understanding of these forces and actions.

Instructions:
In this lesson you will be given a short list of opposing paired forces or actions. As you perform the pictured postures try to discover as many of these pairs as possible. In the space provided, check-off your discoveries and write down the body part or parts that correspond to each force or action. Perform each posture as many times as you need to help your discovery process. Take your time and pay attention to the forces and actions in your body.

Flexed (bent) / **Extended** (straight)
Contracted / Relaxed
Stretched/ Shortened

POSTURE	FORCE/ ACTION	√	BODY PART(S)
SITTING TWIST	Flexed		
	Extended		
	Contracted		
	Relaxed		
	Stretched		
	Shortened		

POSTURE	FORCE/ ACTION	√	BODY PART(S)
DOWNWARD FACING DOG	Flexed		
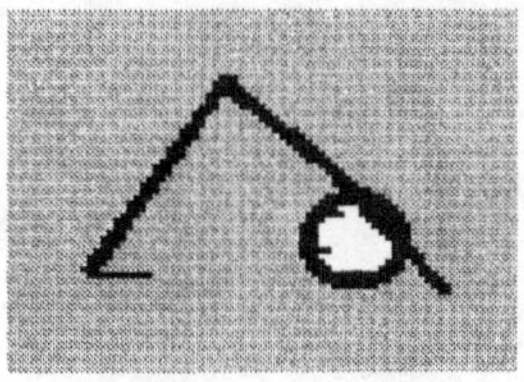	Extended		
	Contracted		
	Relaxed		
	Stretched		
	Shortened		

POSTURE	FORCE/ ACTION	√	BODY PART(S)
WARRIOR II	Flexed		
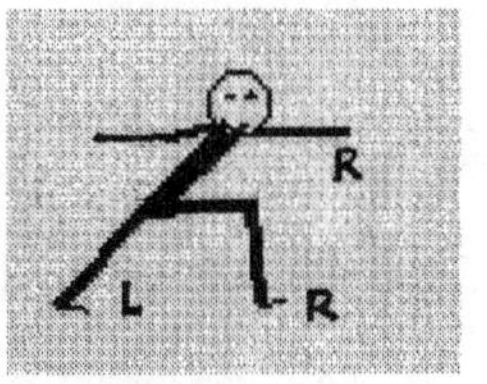	Extended		
	Contracted		
	Relaxed		
	Stretched		
	Shortened		

Yoga Lesson Plan 9

EQUIPMENT:

10 cones and task cards for Partner Racetrack Fitness
1 non-skid ¼"- foam yoga mat and/or, 1 1"- padded tumbling mat per student
1 bean bag per 2 students
Recommended Instructor Aid: The American Yoga Associations New Yoga Challenge (**AYANYC**)

OBJECTIVES:

The student will:

1. Demonstrate the ability to perform a variety of locomotor movements on command.
2. Participate in Bean Bag Introductory Activity demonstrating eye-hand coordination and ability to make quick movement changes.
3. Practice performing Sun Salutation as demonstrated by instructor at least 5 times.
4. Participate in Mass Stand Up Game challenging teamwork and concentration skills

National Standards Met in this Lesson: **1, 4, 5, 6**

INSTRUCTIONAL ACTIVITIES	TEACHING HINTS
INTRODUCTORY ACTIVITY (2 - 3 MINUTES)	
Throwing & Catching Bean Bags on the Move	**See DPESS Chapter 18 for details.**
Toss, move, and catch.	Scattered Formation
Direct students to move forward, backward and sideways using carioca, shuffle and slide.	Use Elbow-to-Elbow to create partners.
FITNESS DEVELOPMENT (8 - 12 MINUTES)	
Partner Racetrack Fitness	**See DPESS Chapter 16 for details.**
10 stations with unique task cards in circular track formation. 2 students perform task while other 2 run around track.	Use Whistle Mixer to form groups of 4. Use Toe-to-Toe for partners
LESSON FOCUS (15 - 20 MINUTES)	
Introduction to Sun Salutation	**AYANYC pages 46-49** Demonstrate as individual poses.

The Sun Salutation or Surya Namaskar is a Yoga Pose that will limber up the whole body in preparation for the Yoga Asanas. It is a graceful sequence of twelve Yoga positions performed as one continuous exercise.

INSTRUCTIONAL ACTIVITIES	TEACHING HINTS
GAME (5 MINUTES)	
Mass Stand Up	**See DPESS Chapter 18 for details.**
Start with partners, lock elbows And attempt to stand as one. Increase number of people to 3, 4, And so on.	Use Back-to-Back to create partners, Whistle Mixer for larger groups.

EVALUATION/REVIEW AND CHEER

Do you recognize all the poses of Sun Salutation?
Can you name them?
What is the purpose of the Sun Salutation?

Cheer: Good Day Sunshine!

Yoga Lesson Plan 10

EQUIPMENT:
Music/ CD/cassette player
A variety of music including that appropriate to yoga practice.
Cones for Weave Drill
1 non-skid ¼"- foam yoga mat and/or, 1 1"- padded tumbling mat per student
Recommended Instructor Reference: *The American Yoga Associations New Yoga Challenge* (**AYANYC**)

OBJECTIVES:
The student will:
1. Participate in Weave Drill demonstrating agility and the ability to follow directions during movement.
2. Participate in 12 Ways to Fitness to improve cardiovascular endurance.
3. Participate in Balance Tag demonstrating good sportsmanship.
4. Practice performing Sun Salutation as demonstrated by instructor in sequence at least 5 times.

National Standards Met in this Lesson: **1, 2, 3, 4, 5, 6**

INSTRUCTIONAL ACTIVITIES	TEACHING HINTS
INTRODUCTORY ACTIVITY (2 - 3 MINUTES)	
Weave Drill Use locomotor movement slide, skip, gallop, etc. while negotiating cones.	**See DPESS Chapter 14 for details.** Scattered Formation Use whistle signals to add arm movements.
FITNESS DEVELOPMENT (8 - 12 MINUTES)	
12 Ways to Fitness	**See DPESS Chapter 16 for details.** Switch leaders again as above.
LESSON FOCUS (15 - 20 MINUTES)	
Sun Salutation	**AYANYC pages 46-49** Now demonstrate poses in sequence only without stopping. Use music to set tone.

Yoga has five Yamas or beliefs and attitudes you practice towards others and the world around you. They cover: non-violence; truthfulness; non-stealing/ honesty; non-lust; and non-possessiveness.

INSTRUCTIONAL ACTIVITIES	TEACHING HINTS
GAME (5 MINUTES)	
Balance Tag	**See DPESS Chapter 14 for details.** Select several "its." Stipulate 1-2 balance positions.

EVALUATION/REVIEW AND CHEER

What does performing poses in sequence remind you of?
Can you remember any of the Sanskrit names for the poses in Sun Salutation?
Describe the five Yamas.

Cheer: The Sun Shines Everyday in PE!

Archery

This unit has been specifically designed to meet all six components of the NASPE National Standards for Physical Education.

OBJECTIVES:

The student will:

1. Eagle demonstrate agility, leg strength, and listening skills participating in the Introductory activities of Seated Rolls, Quarter, Wave Drill, Lateral Shuffle, and the Rooster Hop Drill while following the instructor's directions.
2. Increase her aerobic fitness, strength, and endurance by participating in Continuity Exercises, Four Corners, Astronaut Drill, and Circuit Training using form demonstrated by the instructor.
3. Demonstrate bracing the bow using form demonstrated by the instructor.
4. Demonstrate Nocking the Arrow, Extend and Draw, and Anchor Hold using form demonstrated by the instructor.
5. Describe the methods of aiming at the target when asked by the instructor.
6. Demonstrate Nocking the Arrow, Extend and Draw, Anchor Hold, and Release and Afterhold in a continuous manner using form demonstrated by the instructor.
7. Participate in Partner Bean Bag Challenges, Hoop Challenges demonstrating throwing and catching skills, eye-hand coordination and cooperation following the rules set by the instructor.
8. Participate in Potato Relays, Addition Tag, and Team Paper, Scissors, and Rock games demonstrating cooperation and running speed following the rules of the games.

ARCHERY BLOCK PLAN
1 WEEK UNIT

Week #1	Monday	Tuesday	Wednesday	Thursday	Friday
Introductory Activity	Seat rolls alternated with jogging in place	Quarter Eagle	Wave Drill	Lateral Shuffle	Rooster Hop Drill
Fitness	Continuity Exercises	Four Corners	Astronaut Drills	Continuity Exercises	Circuit Training
Lesson Focus	Brace Bow Stance Nock Arrow Extend and Draw Anchor Hold Release and Afterhold	Safety rules Review Skills Shoot 1 arrow Review skills Shoot 6 arrows at target	Review aiming Shoot for points	Shoot for points	Shoot for points Team Shoot for points
Game	Partner Bean Bag Challenges	Hoop Challenges	Potato Relays	Addition Tag	Team Paper, Scissors, and Rock

Archery Lesson Plan 1

EQUIPMENT:
Continuity Music CD/Tape
1 Bean Bag per two students
6 arrows per person
Cones to mark teaching areas

Music player
1 Bow per person
1 Target per 2 students, if possible

OBJECTIVES:
The student will:
1. Participate in Seat rolls alternated with jogging in place demonstrating quickness, agility, and following the instructions described by the instructor.
2. Participate in Continuity Exercises to improve strength, endurance, and flexibility during the Fitness section of class.
3. Demonstrate bracing the bow, stance, anchor hold, drawing, nocking the arrow, aiming, releasing and after hold as demonstrated by the instructor.
4. Participate in Partner Bean Bag Challenges with a partner as presented by the instructor during the closing portion of class.

National Standards Met in this Lesson: **1, 2, 3, 4, 5, 6**

INSTRUCTIONAL ACTIVITIES	TEACHING HINTS
INTRODUCTORY ACTIVITY (2 - 3 MINUTES)	
Seat rolls alternated with jogging in place	**See DPESS Chapter 14 for details.**
	Teacher directs movement activities
	Be sure students have safe distance between them
FITNESS DEVELOPMENT (8 - 12 MINUTES)	
Continuity Exercises	**See DPESS Chapter 16 for details.**
• Curl-ups	Student jumps rope during music. When music stops,
• Push-ups	teacher directs strengthening, stretching exercises
• Reverse push-ups	
• Coffee grinder	
• Side leg lifts	
• Stretches	
LESSON FOCUS (15 - 20 MINUTES)	
Brace Bow	**See DPESS Chapter 19 for details.**
Stance	Step Through Method demonstrated by teacher
Extend and Draw	
Anchor Hold	Each skill demonstrated one at a time by teacher, student
Nock Arrow	practices
Aiming	
Release and After hold	Allow student to shoot one arrow on command. Retrieve on command.
	Safety rules must be emphasized and followed.

Archery appears to have been invented in Africa as early as 50,000 BC.
Investigators discovered the first stone arrowheads in Africa. They believe the bow and arrow were invented there maybe in conjunction with the invention of the spear thrower. A short bow would be a better hunting weapon to stalk animals in wooded areas, rather than carrying around long spears.

GAME (5 MINUTES)	
Partner Bean Bag Challenges with partner	**See DPESS Chapter 18 for details.**
• Catch with hands	Bean bags spread around perimeter
• Catch on top of hand, palm face down	Student put in groups of 2 using Toe-to-Toe
• Catch on top of foot	1 person picks up bean bag on command
• Toss under leg	Offer partner tossing and catching challenges.
• Toss behind back	

EVALUATION/REVIEW AND CHEER

INSTRUCTIONAL ACTIVITIES	TEACHING HINTS
What was the most challenging part of Fitness?	
Where and when is it believed that the bow and arrow were developed?	
Review procedures for Bracing Bow	
Ask student to explain aiming techniques	
What were the most challenging Bean Bag challenges?	

Cheer: Archery is fun!

Archery Lesson Plan 2

EQUIPMENT:

1 bow per person
Cones to mark teaching area
1 hoop per person
6 arrows per person
Four Corners Signs
6 individual jump ropes for Four Corners

OBJECTIVES:

The student will:

1. Participate in Quarter Eagle demonstrating quickness, agility, and following the instructions described by the instructor.
2. Participate in Four Corners to improve strength, endurance, and flexibility during the Fitness section of class.
3. Demonstrate bracing the bow, stance, anchor hold, drawing, nocking the arrow, aiming, releasing and after hold as demonstrated by the instructor.
4. Follow the safety rules established by the instructor.
5. Participate in Hoop Challenges with a partner as presented by the instructor during the closing portion of class.

National Standards Met in this Lesson: 1, 2, 3, 4, 5, 6

INSTRUCTIONAL ACTIVITIES	TEACHING HINTS
INTRODUCTORY ACTIVITY (2 - 3 MINUTES)	
Quarter Eagle	**See DPESS Chapter 14 for details.** Students in scatter formation Teacher indicates directions for activity
FITNESS DEVELOPMENT (8 - 12 MINUTES)	
Four Corners • Jump rope at one cone • Signs indicating exercises at the other 3 cones: Curl-ups, Sit-ups, Push-ups, Jumping Jacks, Reverse Push-ups	**See DPESS Chapter 16 for details.** Use Whistle Mixer to divide class into 4 groups Assign one group per corner cone Alternate locomotor movement to travel to each corner: running, leaping, sliding, galloping

Four Corners fitness, as most fitness lessons we do, use all of your muscles in the body including the abdominals, biceps, triceps, quadriceps, hamstrings, postural/ core muscles, gastrocnemius, flexors in your feet, the Achilles tendon and others.

INSTRUCTIONAL ACTIVITIES	TEACHING HINTS
LESSON FOCUS (15 - 20 MINUTES)	
Safety rules **Review Skills** **Shoot 1 arrow** **Review skills** **Shoot 6 arrows at target**	**See DPESS Chapter 19 for details.** Practice safety instructions without arrows After shooting 1 arrow, retrieve the arrow and review skills observed needing improvement Direct students to shoot 6 arrows and wait for retrieval signal Repeat

Archery played significant roles in winning early European wars. Even though the bow and arrow is an ancient weapon, archery held military significance in many countries until recent times. Even in the Second World War, a group of American archers were used in several specialized actions in Asia. Even though the use of the bow in the military has declined, it is still pursued as a sport in many countries worldwide.

INSTRUCTIONAL ACTIVITIES	**TEACHING HINTS**

GAME (5 MINUTES)

Hoop Challenges
- Spin hoop on end
- Jump over spinning hoop
- Roll hoop and go through rolling hoop
- Circle hoop on: hand, leg, neck
- Jump through as if rope jumping
- Boomerang hoop
- Toss hoop in air and catch
- Toss hoop in air, let it bounce, then catch
- In partners, roll hoop to partner using simultaneous rolls
- Toss and catch hoop with partner

See DPESS Chapter 18 for details.
One hoop per person gotten from perimeter of room

Use Back-to-back to make partners

EVALUATION/REVIEW AND CHEER

Name some of the muscles used in fitness today?
How many arrows hit the target today?
What do you need to work on to improve in archery?
Explain a little history of archery to the class and the significance of the sport.

Cheer: Archery and hoops…. Fun!

Archery Lesson Plan 3

EQUIPMENT:

Cones to mark teaching area
1 bow per person
Targets
1 cone/spot per person for Wave Drill
6 arrows per person
Bean bags for Potato Relays

OBJECTIVES:

The student will:
1. Participate in the Wave Drill demonstrating quickness, agility, and following the instructions described by the instructor.
2. Participate in Astronaut Drills to improve strength, endurance, and flexibility during the Fitness section of class.
3. Demonstrate bracing the bow, stance, anchor hold, drawing, nocking the arrow, aiming, releasing and after hold as demonstrated by the instructor.
4. Participate in the Archery Relay demonstrating knowledge of safety rules, cooperation, and following the rules established by the instructor.
5. Participate in Potato Relays with a team as presented by the instructor during the closing portion of class.

National Standards Met in this Lesson: **1, 2, 3, 4, 5, 6**

INSTRUCTIONAL ACTIVITIES	**TEACHING HINTS**

INTRODUCTORY ACTIVITY (2 - 3 MINUTES)

Wave Drill

See DPESS Chapter 14 for details.
Teacher directs the movements
Scatter formation

INSTRUCTIONAL ACTIVITIES	TEACHING HINTS

FITNESS DEVELOPMENT (8 - 12 MINUTES)

Astronaut Drills

- Create a pattern of various locomotor movements such as hopping, running, jumping, leaping, skipping, and running on the toes.
- Perform exercises, such as arm circles, body twists, and trunk and upper-body stretches, while moving around the area.

See DPESS Chapter 16 for details.
Scatter formation

Astronaut Drills, as other fitness activities, provide a full body workout using all of the muscles in the body.

LESSON FOCUS (15 - 20 MINUTES)

Review aiming
Shoot for points
Archery Relay

See DPESS Chapter 19 for details.
Spread out in a line double arms distance apart.
Each team has one target; each person has one arrow. The first person in line shoots and goes to end of line. All team members shoot one arrow and then the team score is tallied. The team with the highest score is the winner.

Archery was made part of the Olympics in 1900, in Paris, France. 1904 was the first year women competed.

GAME (5 MINUTES)

Potato Relays
Direct student to pick up bean bag, run to other hoop and drop bean bag. Run to end of line. Continue until all bean bags are in starting hoop.

See DPESS Chapter 18 for details.
Using Whistle Mixer, create teams
Make teams of 5
Place empty hoops 15' from each lined up team
Place 5 bean bags in each hoop in front of each team

EVALUATION/REVIEW AND CHEER

What muscles were used in class today?
What is challenging about aiming for the target in archery?
What is enjoyable about archery?
In what year was Archery made an Olympic sport?
Did men and women complete in the Olympics during the same years?

Cheer: 2, 4, 6, 8, Archery is great!

Archery Lesson Plan 4

EQUIPMENT:

1 individual jump rope per person
Cones to mark teaching area
6 arrows per person
Tic-tac-toe covers for targets
Continuity exercise music CD/tape
1 bow per person
Targets

OBJECTIVES:

The student will:

1. Participate in the Lateral Shuffle demonstrating quickness, agility, and following the instructions described by the instructor.
2. Participate in Continuity Exercises to improve aerobic endurance, strength, endurance, and flexibility during the Fitness section of class.
3. Demonstrate bracing the bow, stance, anchor hold, drawing, nocking the arrow, aiming, releasing and after hold as demonstrated by the instructor.
4. Participate in the Archery Tic-Tac-Toe game demonstrating knowledge of safety rules, cooperation, and following the rules established by the instructor.
5. Participate in Addition Tag as presented by the instructor during the closing portion of class.

National Standards Met in this Lesson: **1, 2, 3, 4, 5, 6**

INSTRUCTIONAL ACTIVITIES	TEACHING HINTS

INTRODUCTORY ACTIVITY (2 - 3 MINUTES)

Lateral Shuffle	**See DPESS Chapter 14 for details.** Scatter formation Teacher directs the direction of shuffling

FITNESS DEVELOPMENT (8 - 12 MINUTES)

Continuity Exercises • Curl-ups • Push-ups • Reverse push-ups • Coffee grinder • Side leg lifts • Stretches	**See DPESS Chapter 16 for details.** Scatter formation Ropes around perimeter of teaching area Direct each student to pick up rope and begin jumping Jump when music playing Direct the exercises when music stops

Continuity Exercises use the theory of Interval Training to enhance fitness levels in participants. Interval training alternates aerobic work with strength, muscular endurance and flexibility exercises to provide a good workout.

LESSON FOCUS (15 - 20 MINUTES)

Archery Aiming Review **Tic-Tac-Toe Archery game**	**See DPESS Chapter 19 for details.** Allow student to practice shooting a 2 rounds of 6 arrows. Retrieve arrows. Place tic-tac-toe covers on each target Each student shoots 1 arrow, at Tic-tac-toe target. First team to get Tic-tac-toe wins

Archery had been dropped from the Olympics for numerous years; it returned in 1972 in Munich, and now is in both the summer (Men's Individual, Women's Individual, Men's Team and Women's Team) and winter Olympics (the Biathlon).

INSTRUCTIONAL ACTIVITIES	TEACHING HINTS
GAME (5 MINUTES)	
Addition Tag	**See DPESS Chapter 18 for details.** Pick several its to begin the game Explain rules Repeat with new Its when lines are pretty long

Direct students to call out the number they have made with each additional player. Then, on the next round of play, you can ask them to quickly add a number you identify to their group size and call out that number.

EVALUATION/REVIEW AND CHEER

Explain the theories and values associated with Continuity Exercises.
What muscles were worked during Continuity Exercises?
What types of fitness were being developed during the Continuity Exercises?
Describe the Olympic history of Archery.
What was the most challenging aspect of the Tic-Tac-Toe Archery Game?

Cheer: Tic-Tac-Toe, yeah!

Archery Lesson Plan 5

EQUIPMENT:

1 bow per person
1 target per 2 - 4 people
Attach signs to cones.
6 – 7 Jump Ropes per 30 students
6 arrows per person
Cones to mark teaching area and 8 for Circuit Training.
Circuit Training Signs

OBJECTIVES:

The student will:

1. Participate in the Rooster Hop Drill demonstrating hopping skills, quickness, agility, and following the instructions described by the instructor.
2. Participate in Circuit Training to improve aerobic endurance, strength, endurance, and flexibility during the Fitness section of class.
3. Demonstrate bracing the bow, stance, anchor hold, drawing, nocking the arrow, aiming, releasing and after hold as demonstrated by the instructor.
4. Participate in the Team Archery game demonstrating knowledge of safety rules, cooperation, and following the rules established by the instructor.
5. Participate in Team Paper Scissors Rock as presented by the instructor during the closing portion of class.

National Standards Met in this Lesson: **1, 2, 3, 4, 5, 6**

INSTRUCTIONAL ACTIVITIES	TEACHING HINTS
INTRODUCTORY ACTIVITY (2 - 3 MINUTES)	
Rooster Hop Drill Hop 10 yards on one leg with: (1) left hand touching the right toe, which is on the ground; (2) right hand touching left toe on the ground; (3) right hand touching the right toe on the ground; (4) left hand touching the left toe on the ground	**See DPESS Chapter 14 for details.** Call out the variations for students to complete Ask for another suggestion from students

INSTRUCTIONAL ACTIVITIES	TEACHING HINTS

FITNESS DEVELOPMENT (8 - 12 MINUTES)

Circuit Training
Station 1: Jump Rope
Station 2: Curl-ups
Station 3: Run in place
Station 4: Push-ups
Station 5: Reverse push-ups
Station 6: Treadmills
Station 7: Jumping Jacks
Station 8: Side leg lifts

See DPESS Chapter 16 for details.
Use Whistle Mixer to create 6 even groups
Create a music CD/tape with 40 seconds for each station
and 5 seconds to rotate to next station.
Run to each new station
Make signs for each circuit training station
Allow enough time for students to go through circuit at
least 2 times.

LESSON FOCUS (15 - 20 MINUTES)

Archery skill review warm-up

See DPESS Chapter 19 for details.
4 students or less per target
Allow each student to shoot 6 arrows

Team Maximum Point Game
Each team tries to accumulate the most points
On 3 rounds of shooting.

Teacher says go
Each person in team shoots 6 arrows
Count points using points in textbook
Team remembers points
Shoot two more rounds
Team with most points is team winner

An Archery target has ten concentric circles. The score of each arrow depends upon where it lands on the target. Ten is the highest score and that is earned when the arrow lands in the center circle or the bulls eye.

GAME (5 MINUTES)

Team Paper, Scissors, and Rock
Two teams huddle on their half of the field. Each team decides which of the three choices (paper, scissors, or rock) they will reveal when the game begins. The teams come out to mid field line and face each other with one foot on the line. The teacher counts: "one, two, three, show." The teams reveal their group decision on the word "show" with the appropriate hand signal and the winning team chases the losing team and tries to tag them before they reach a safe zone. If tagged, they must switch teams.

See DPESS Chapter 18 for details.
Use Toe to Toe technique; then split class into 2 teams
Set boundaries with cones. Safe zone is about 10-20 yards from the starting line.
The teacher counts: "one, two, three, show."

EVALUATION/REVIEW AND CHEER

What muscle groups were worked during fitness today?
What is the score when your arrow lands in the center circle?
What have you enjoyed the most about this Archery Unit?

Cheer: 2,4,6,8 Archery is great!

Bowling

OBJECTIVES:

The student will:

1. Participate in the Rubber Band Introductory Activity demonstrating agility, locomotor movements and the ability to follow instructions given by the instructor.
2. Demonstrate agility and follow the movements and instructions of the leader during the Introductory Activities: Wave Drill and Square Drill.
3. Demonstrate fitness activities including sit-ups, push-ups, crab-kicks, etc. during the 12 Ways of Fitness.
4. Participate in Continuity Exercises demonstrating basic jump roping skills, strength, agility, rhythm and flexibility while following the directions given by the instructor.
5. Follow the directions while participating in Circuit Training Fitness activities as directed by the instructor.
6. Demonstrate the grip, stance, approach and delivery of the bowling ball as demonstrated by the instructor.
7. Demonstrate the 4-Step Approach and Delivery of the bowling ball using the form modeled by the instructor.
8. Practice directed bowling skills directed by the instructor on the indoor carpet using form demonstrated by the instructor.
9. Illustrate proper etiquette and scoring skills by completing a scoring worksheet and participating in etiquette discussions.
10. Demonstrate proper etiquette while on the field trip to the Bowling Center.
11. Participate in the Bowling Pin Relay demonstrating agility, and teamwork while following the rules of the game.
12. Participate in the Over and Under Ball Relay using form demonstrated and following the rules established by the instructor.
13. Participate in the Fetch Relay demonstrating agility, and teamwork while following the rules of the game.
14. Participate in the game of Addition Tag and True or False Partner Tag demonstrating teamwork and cooperation while following the rules of the game.
15. Play a game of Red Pin Bowling using form and rules demonstrated by the instructor.
16. Play a game of Bowling at the Bowling Center using appropriate game rules, etiquette, courtesy, and appropriate behavior for a field trip as established by the instructor.

BOWLING BLOCK PLAN
1 WEEK UNIT

Week #1	Monday	Tuesday	Wednesday	Thursday	Friday
Introductory Activity	Rubber Band	Wave Drill	Square Drill	All Fours Circle	Trip to Bowling Center for Bowling
Fitness	The 12 Ways of Fitness	Continuity Exercises	Circuit Training Fitness with a Jog	Continuity Exercises	
Lesson Focus	Grip, Stance, Approach, 1-Step Delivery of Ball	Aim 4 - Step Approach and Delivery of ball	Rules Etiquette Scoring Practice Bowling	Practice Bowling and Scoring Play Red Pin	
Game	Bowling Pin Relay	Over and Under Ball Relay	True or False Partner Tag	Addition Tag	

Bowling Lesson Plan 1

EQUIPMENT:

Fitness Station signs
Carpet for bowling lane
1-Bowling ball per station. No more than 4 - 5 per station
Bowling demonstration instructional CD/tape
Bowling pins: 4 per group of 4 – 5 students

OBJECTIVES:

The student will:

1. Participate in Rubber Band demonstrating agility, and following the instructions described by the instructor.
2. Participate in 12 Ways of Fitness to improve strength, endurance, and flexibility during the Fitness section of class.
3. Demonstrate grip, stance, and delivery of the bowling ball as demonstrated by the instructor and the videotape.
4. Participate in Bowling Pin Relay as presented by the instructor during the closing portion of class.

National Standards Met in this Lesson: **1, 2, 3, 4, 5, 6**

INSTRUCTIONAL ACTIVITIES — **TEACHING HINTS**

INTRODUCTORY ACTIVITY (2 - 3 MINUTES)

Rubber Band

See DPESS Chapter 14 for details.

FITNESS DEVELOPMENT (8 - 12 MINUTES)

The 12 Ways of Fitness

See DPESS Chapter 16 for details.
Create groups of 12 students.
Have station descriptions printed for each station

LESSON FOCUS (15 - 20 MINUTES)

Play an instructional videotape/ DVD of Bowling.
Demonstrate the grip and stance.
Demonstrate a one-step plus delivery of ball.

See DPESS Chapter 20 for details.
Students practice following each demonstration
Using Whistle Mixer, divide students into appropriate sized groups.
Divide students so half are at one end of the carpet facing the rest of their group.
Students practice and rotate roles: Bowler, retriever/bowler, people on the sides of the gutters to retrieve balls.

Bowling has been traced to the ancient Egyptians when it was a children's game. The game is over 5,000 years old. The first written mention of a bowling-like sport was traced to 1366 in England. King Edward III outlawed the game in order to keep his troops focused on their archery practice. The game was played during the reign of King Henry VIII.

GAME (5 MINUTES)

Bowling Pin Relay

See DPESS Chapter 20 for details.

EVALUATION/REVIEW AND CHEER

What muscles were used in Fitness today?
Discuss fitness challenge stations and ask what needs to be worked on in the future.
Review techniques of grip, stance, and delivery by asking questions such as: Describe the one-step delivery of the bowling ball. Show me the proper grip and stance of a bowling ball.
Describe the early history of bowling.

Cheer: 2, 4, 6, 8 Bowling makes me feel great!

Bowling Lesson Plan 2

EQUIPMENT:

Perimeter cones
Continuity Music CD/Tape
One Bowling ball per carpet
Rubber ball per group of 6 – 10 students for relay game
Obstacle boundary cone for students to shuffle over
One individual jump rope per person
Bowling pins per carpet

OBJECTIVES:

The student will:

1. Participate in Wave Drill demonstrating quick responses and following the movements demonstrated by the instructor.
2. Participate in Continuity Exercises to improve strength, endurance, and flexibility during the Fitness section of class.
3. Demonstrate grip, stance, 4- Step Approach and delivery of the bowling ball as demonstrated by the instructor.
4. Participate in Over and Under Ball Relay as presented by the instructor during the closing portion of class.

National Standards Met in this Lesson: **1, 2, 3, 4, 5, 6**

INSTRUCTIONAL ACTIVITIES	TEACHING HINTS
INTRODUCTORY ACTIVITY (2 - 3 MINUTES)	
Wave Drill	**See DPESS Chapter 14 for details.** Give hand signals for the direction students will shuffle
FITNESS DEVELOPMENT (8 - 12 MINUTES)	
Continuity Exercises Include during music silence: curl-ups, reverse push-ups, coffee grinder, stretches, leg-lifts, etc.	**See DPESS Chapter 16 for details.** Set jump ropes around perimeter of teaching area. One rope per student. Directions: When music is on, student jumps rope; when there is a sound silence, follow the instructor through a variety of strength, agility, and stretching activities.
LESSON FOCUS (15 - 20 MINUTES)	
Demonstrate: • **Aiming the ball** • **4 - Step Approach and Delivery of bowling ball**	**See DPESS Chapter 20 for details.** Student practices Aiming Student practices the 4 Step Approach without a ball Student practices the 4 Step Approach and delivery of the bowling ball on the carpeted alley.

Variations of bowling have come from Europe including Italian bocce ball, and Britain's lawn bowling. The earliest mention of American bowling comes in the form of a quote from Rip Van Winkle when old Rip wakes up to the sounds of "ninepins". The origin of the tenpin game that we play today is still unknown, but it was prevalent in New York, Ohio, and Illinois by the late 1800's.

INSTRUCTIONAL ACTIVITIES	TEACHING HINTS
GAME (5 MINUTES)	
Over and Under Ball Relay	**See DPESS Chapter 17 for details.** Create teams using Whistle Mixer Place teams on spots 10 – 15' apart Ball begins at the front of the line Pass ball overhead and under legs Last person runs to front

EVALUATION/REVIEW AND CHEER

What was the most challenging part of the fitness today?
Tell me the cues I explained about aiming a ball.
Show me the 4-step approach and delivery of the ball.
Where should the thumb be facing when the ball is released?

Cheer: Bowling makes me feel great!

Bowling Lesson Plan 3

EQUIPMENT:

4 perimeter cones
Music CD/tape
Rules handout
Bowling carpets, 10 pins and 2 balls for each station
Cones to put Circuit Training Signs onto
Boom box
Scoring forms

OBJECTIVES:

The student will:

1. Participate in Square Drill demonstrating quick responses and following the movements demonstrated by the instructor.
2. Participate in Circuit Training Fitness with a Jog to improve aerobic endurance, strength, muscular endurance, and flexibility during the Fitness section of class.
3. Demonstrate grip, stance, 4- Step Approach and delivery of the bowling ball as demonstrated by the instructor.
4. Recite rules and etiquette of bowling when asked by the instructor.
5. Participate in True or False Partner Tag demonstrating cooperative and sportsmanship skills while following the rules during the closing portion of class.

National Standards Met in this Lesson: **1, 2, 3, 4, 5, 6**

INSTRUCTIONAL ACTIVITIES / **TEACHING HINTS**

INTRODUCTORY ACTIVITY (2 - 3 MINUTES)

Square Drill

See DPESS Chapter 14 for details.
Mark square off with cones
Students spread out in center and watch for teacher to indicate direction to shuffle around the square

FITNESS DEVELOPMENT (8 - 12 MINUTES)

Circuit Training Fitness with a Jog

See DPESS Chapter 16 for details.
Create music CD/tape to direct the changing of fitness activities. CD/Tape should have 30 seconds of music and 10 seconds of silence.
Direct changing stations during the silence. Students can also jog around the area before progressing to the next station.

LESSON FOCUS (15 - 20 MINUTES)

Explain Rules of the game
Etiquette to use at a bowling center
Scoring: Manual and electronic
Practice Bowling on carpets

See DPESS Chapter 20 for details.
Create Rules of the game Handout. While some students bowl, go over the Handout with the others. Reverse activities.
Go over scoring a small group of the class while others practice bowling skills. Reverse the activities.
Obtain copies of score sheets from a Bowling Center for students to practice on while playing.

The first standardization of the rules of the game was established on September 9, 1895. Pin boys were used to re-set pins before automatic machines were brought in during the 1950's.

GAME (5 MINUTES)

True or False Partner Tag

See DPESS Chapter 14 for details.

EVALUATION/REVIEW AND CHEER

What part of fitness was the most challenging today?
Can you explain how a strike is scored?
How many times can a person roll the ball when it is her turn?
How is a strike marked on the score sheet?

Cheer: Strikes and spares win the game, yeh!

Bowling Lesson Plan 4

EQUIPMENT:

Music /CD for Continuity Exercises
1 set of Bowling Pins per group of 4 students
Music Player
1 red pin per group

OBJECTIVES:

The student will:

1. Participate in All Fours Circle demonstrating quick responses and following the instructions explained by the instructor.
2. Participate in Continuity Exercises to improve aerobic endurance, strength, muscular endurance, and flexibility during the Fitness section of class.
3. Demonstrate grip, stance, 4- Step Approach and delivery of the bowling ball as demonstrated by the instructor.
4. Recite scoring procedures and rules when asked by the instructor.
5. Participate in Addition Tag demonstrating cooperative and sportsmanship skills while following the rules during the closing portion of class.

National Standards Met in this Lesson: **1, 2, 3, 4, 5, 6**

INSTRUCTIONAL ACTIVITIES	TEACHING HINTS
INTRODUCTORY ACTIVITY (2 - 3 MINUTES)	
All Fours Circle	**See DPESS Chapter 14 for details.**
FITNESS DEVELOPMENT (8 - 12 MINUTES)	
Continuity Exercises	**See DPESS Chapter 16 for details.** Set jump ropes around perimeter of teaching area. One rope per student.
During music silence, direct: curl-ups, reverse push-ups, coffee grinder, stretches, leg-lifts, etc.	Directions: When music is on, student jumps rope; when there is a silence, then follow the instructor through a variety of strength, agility, and stretching activities.
LESSON FOCUS (15 - 20 MINUTES)	
Practice Bowling and Scoring (review)	**See DPESS Chapter 20 for details.**
Play Red Pin	Using Whistle Mixer, divide students into appropriate groups based on your equipment

Bowling gained popularity in the United States when the first "Championship Bowling" aired on NBC in the 1950's.

INSTRUCTIONAL ACTIVITIES	TEACHING HINTS
GAME (5 MINUTES)	
Addition Tag	**See DPESS Chapter 14 for details.** Select 2 – 3 its for the game. Change after one group has a long line of students

EVALUATION/REVIEW AND CHEER

What was the most challenging activity during fitness?
What body parts were used today during fitness?
How has your bowling improved?
Are you ready to go to the bowling center tomorrow?
When did bowling become popular in the United States?

Cheer: Bowling… can't wait!

Bowling Lesson Plan 5

EQUIPMENT:

Transportation
Clean socks
Emergency phone numbers
Money for Bowling Center fees
Permission slips

OBJECTIVES:

The student will:

1. Participate in a field trip to a bowling center.
2. Demonstrate knowledge of rules and etiquette while bowling.
3. Demonstrate grip, stance, 4- Step Approach and delivery of the bowling ball as demonstrated by the instructor.

National Standards Met in this Lesson: **1, 2, 3, 4, 5, 6**

INSTRUCTIONAL ACTIVITIES	TEACHING HINTS
Field Trip to a Bowling Center	Remind student on the bus of proper behavior. Divide groups up for Bowling Center lanes before you arrive. Demonstrate electronic scoring. Supervise all students playing at the Center

Game shows such as "Make that Spare", "Bowling for Dollars", and "Celebrity Bowling" were aired on television making the sport more popular. Bowling is enjoyed by people of all ages because it is a sport of the people. It has come from its early forms to evolve into a truly enjoyable American past time.

Have students thank the Bowling Center

EVALUATION/REVIEW AND CHEER

What was the most fun today?
What skills did you discover you need to work on?
Will you bowl on your own now that you've come to a center?

Cheer: Bowling's GREAT!

Bowling Quiz

Name: ____

Class Period: ____

(Use T or F for True or False):

1. It is okay to bowl at the same time as the person in the lane next to you.
   Answer: F

2. Your bonus points for a strike are the sum of your next two rolls of the ball.
   Answer: T

3. When you release the bowling ball, you should be stepping forward on the foot on the *opposite* side of your body from the side where you are releasing the ball.
   Answer: T

4. You do not need to bring socks with you when you go bowling.
   Answer: F

5. If your bowling ball gets stuck in the gutter half way down the lane, it is okay to go and retrieve it as long as you are very careful.
   Answer: F

6. When you release the bowling ball, your palm should be facing up.
   Answer: T

7. Your bonus points for a spare are equal to the last roll of the ball in your *previous* frame.
   Answer: F

8. In one frame of bowling, if you roll a gutter ball and then knock down all of the pins with your second roll of the ball, you will receive a spare.
   Answer: T

9. It's okay to release the ball so that it bounces a little because that will knock down more pins.
   Answer: F

10. Keep your lane neat and tidy while you bowl and throw away any trash before you leave.
    Answer: T

11. When you're finished bowling, just leave your bowling shoes under a chair in your lane.
    Answer: F

12. The highest possible score in a game of bowling is 100 points because there are 10 frames per game and a maximum of 10 points per frame.
    Answer: F

13. Bend your knees as you release the ball when you're bowling.
    Answer: T

14. In frame 10 of a game, you might have to roll the ball three times.
    Answer: T

15. You should always thank the employees at the bowling alley before you leave so that they will be happy to have our class return to bowl.
    Answer: T

Frisbee Golf

This unit has been specifically designed to meet all six components of the NASPE National Standards for Physical Education.

OBJECTIVES:

The student will:

1. Participate in Vanishing Beanbags and Blob Tag in a cooperative manner.
2. Form a variety of pyramids and demonstrate the proper points of support while performing them.
3. Participate in Four Corners activities to improve fitness.
4. Participate in Hexagon Hustle to improve fitness.
5. Participate in Aerobic Workouts to improve overall fitness.
6. Demonstrate the proper grip of a Frisbee.
7. Demonstrate the difference between: Walk-Jog-Sprint in the fitness activity.
8. Cooperatively work with teammates during the Frisbee activities.
9. Execute Frisbee throwing using form demonstrated by the instructor.
10. Pass the Frisbee into a hoop with the right and left hand.
11. Trap a Frisbee with both hands after it has been tossed from 10 feet.
12. Participate in Potato Relays.
13. Demonstrate respect of a partner while Wand Wrestling.
14. Demonstrate rules of safety while participating in Team Tug-of-War.
15. Play group tag demonstrating sportsmanship.

FRISBEE GOLF BLOCK PLAN
1 WEEK UNIT

Week #1	Monday	Tuesday	Wednesday	Thursday	Friday
Introductory Activity	Vanishing Bean Bags	Move & Assume Pose	Blob Tag	Burpee Flip Drill	Mini Pyramid
Fitness	Aerobic Workouts	Hexagon Hustle	Walk-Jog-Sprint	Fitness Scavenger Hunt	Four Corners
Lesson Focus	Frisbee Passing and Catching	Roller Toss Frisbee Keep Away	Tee Off to Target Putting	Throwing Accuracy Rules of Frisbee Golf	Frisbee Golf
Game	Potato Relays	Wand Wrestling	Team Tug of War	Frisbee 21	

Frisbee Golf Lesson Plan 1

EQUIPMENT:
1 Bean bag per student
25 hula hoops

Aerobic Music & music player
1 Frisbee per student

OBJECTIVES:
The student will:
1. Participate in Vanishing Beanbags demonstrating agility, and following the instructions described by the instructor.
2. Participate in an Aerobic Workout to improve aerobic capacity, strength, endurance, and flexibility during the Fitness section of class.
3. Demonstrate throwing and catching a Frisbee as demonstrated by the instructor.
4. Participate in Potato Relays as presented by the instructor during the closing portion of class.

National Standards Met in this Lesson:　　　　　**1, 2, 3, 4, 5, 6**

INSTRUCTIONAL ACTIVITIES	TEACHING HINTS
INTRODUCTORY ACTIVITY (2 – 3 MINUTES)	
Vanishing Beanbags	**See DPESS Chapter 14 for details.**
FITNESS DEVELOPMENT (8 – 12 MINUTES)	
Aerobic Workouts	**See DPESS Chapter 16 for details.**
Jump in place 8 x; Walk in place 16 x; Run in place 8 x; Perform 8 jumping jacks; 8 Mountain climbers; Jump Twist 8 x. Perform 4 slides each side; Hit side of thighs with straight arms; Run while lifting feet high in the rear; Lift knees high in front while running and clapping 8 x; Repeat whole phrase; Hop swing alternate legs 8 x; Charleston bounce step (Step L, kick R foot forward, step back R and touch L toe back. Repeat 8 times). Reverse; Schottische 8 x; Grapevine both directions 4 x; Walk in place 8 x; Leg and upper body stretches; Run 3 x in place then hop and clap. Alternate 4 x; Swing arms overhead while jump-twisting to cool down.	**Casten, Aerobics Today** Use music appropriate for Aerobic Exercise

Aerobic workouts are an effective way to control your weight, exercise your heart, strengthen your muscles and just make you feel healthier. After such a workout, people have a sense of well being. Aerobic workouts are any exercise that helps your body use oxygen more efficiently. This is done by increasing your heart rate and breathing more heavily than usual for an extended period of time.

LESSON FOCUS (15 – 20 MINUTES)	
Frisbee Hoops Toss	**See DPESS Chapter 20 for details.**
Demonstrate passing a Frisbee with each hand using sidearm, backhand and across the chest throws.	Direct each student to stand next to a Frisbee.
Teach how to aim a Frisbee using different throws.	Create groups of 2 using Back-to-Back for passing practice and the "Tossing into Hoops" activity.
Frisbee Catch	**See DPESS Chapter 20 for details.**
Demonstrate passing and catching methods and styles.	Students pass and catch at graduated distances: 5' – 10 '
Frisbee Throwing and Catching Guided Discovery Task Sheet	Distribute the Frisbee Throwing and Catching Guided Discovery Task Sheet one per two students. Allow students to practice the activities listed on the task sheet. Do no distribute the answers on the same sheet. Review answers upon completion or post an answer sheet, or put answers on the back of the sheet.

Disc golf, now called Frisbee Golf, in one form or another has been with us since the beginning of time. The early cavemen in their search for weapons to slay food probably found rocks before clubs to throw at animals. If they could kill something from a safe distance it would be much safer than a club using a sharp stick that they carried.

INSTRUCTIONAL ACTIVITIES	**TEACHING HINTS**
GAME (5 MINUTES)	
Potato Relays	**See DPESS Chapter 18 for details.**
Use hoops and bean bags for the relay	Use Whistle Mixer/ Squads for create teams
EVALUATION/REVIEW AND CHEER	
Discuss the successes and difficulties with passing and catching the Frisbee.	
Cheer: 2, 4, 6, 8, Playing Frisbee is really great!	

Frisbee Throwing and Catching Guided Discovery Task Sheet

Objective: The student will discover how to pass and catch a Frisbee, guided by the task sheet questions during the lesson focus portion of the class.

Organization: Student will go toe-to-toe to get into pairs.

Equipment: Frisbees, Cones, and Whistle

Discovery Questions:

1. With your partner, demonstrate how you can get a Frisbee back and forth to each other. Try several different ways. Which is the best way?

   ____

   Answer: Passing the Frisbee with one hand, thumb up, index finger at the edge of the Frisbee and the other fingers under the Frisbee.

2. When catching a Frisbee above the waist, what is the best way to catch the Frisbee? Try the different ways.

   ____

   Answer: Catching the Frisbee with one hand thumb down.

3. When catching the Frisbee below the waist, what is the correct way to catch the Frisbee? Try several ways.

   ____

   Answer: Catching the Frisbee with one hand thumb up.

4. What changes can you make to get the Frisbee as accurately as possible to your partner? Try different angles and different grips on the Frisbee.

   ____

   Answer: Passing the Frisbee with your thumb on top, your index finger on the edge of the Frisbee, the rest of the fingers at the bottom, bending your elbow, and releasing towards your partner.

5. How can you pass and catch the Frisbee using another part of your body and your hand? Try different body parts.

   ____

   Answer: When passing, throw the Frisbee from under your leg; to catch it, lift your leg up and catch the Frisbee from under your leg.

Frisbee Golf Lesson Plan 2

EQUIPMENT:
1 Hula hoop per student for targets
8 Cones
1 Wand per 2 students
1 Frisbee per student
CD/ Music for Fitness
CD/ Music player

OBJECTIVES:
The student will:
1. Participate in Move and Quickly Stop Assuming Pose demonstrating agility, and following the instructions described by the instructor.
2. Participate in Hexagon Hustle to improve aerobic capacity, strength, endurance, and flexibility during the Fitness section of class.
3. Demonstrate throwing and catching a Frisbee as demonstrated by the instructor.
4. Participate in Wand Wrestling as presented by the instructor during the closing portion of class.

National Standards Met in this Lesson: **1, 2, 3, 4, 5, 6**

INSTRUCTIONAL ACTIVITIES	TEACHING HINTS

INTRODUCTORY ACTIVITY (2 – 3 MINUTES)

Move and Quickly Stop Assuming Pose
Students perform locomotor movements. Freeze on signal and assume various balancing poses on various body parts.

See DPESS Chapter 14 for details.
Scattered formation.

In biomechanics, balance is an ability to maintain the center of gravity of a body within the base of support with minimal postural swaying. Practicing balancing will help you throughout your life.

FITNESS DEVELOPMENT (8 – 12 MINUTES)

Hexagon Hustle (a form of Circuit Training)
Use music for activity as students hustle around perimeter cones. During music silences perform flexibility, stretching, and strengthening activities.

See DPESS Chapter 16 for details.
Make a hexagon with 6 cones. Assign groups to begin at each cone. Place sign with directions on both sides of cone. The signs identify the hustle activity.

LESSON FOCUS (15 – 20 MINUTES)

Roller Toss: Stance; Arm movement; Aiming.
Demonstrate rolling Frisbee on ground to target.
Demonstrate proper posture.
Demonstrate swing technique.

See DPESS Chapter 20 for details.
Use back to back to get students into groups of two.
Create an imaginary line from the position to the target.
Students practice rolling the Frisbee 10 times each, then change roles. Repeat.

Frisbee Keep Away
Students toss Frisbee to each other trying to keep it away from the player standing in the middle.

Use Whistle Mixer to create groups of 3.
Change places when center player catches the Frisbee.

GAME (5 MINUTES)

Wand Wrestling

See DPESS Chapter 16 for details.
Create pairs using Back-to-Back

EVALUATION/REVIEW AND CHEER
Why is it important to practice balancing skills?
Were there any fitness activities done today that you found particularly difficult and why were they difficult?
Discuss elements of Frisbee rolling, passing, catching that may have caused difficulties.
Discuss the challenges of Wand Wrestling.

Cheer: We love to play Frisbee!!!

Frisbee Golf Lesson Plan 3

EQUIPMENT:

1 Beanbag per student
1 Hula hoop per student
8 Cones, 6 hoops, 6 flags, 4 long ropes
40 Frisbees

OBJECTIVES:

The student will:

1. Participate in Blob Tag demonstrating cooperative skills, agility, and following the instructions described by the instructor.
2. Participate in Walk, Jog, Sprint to improve aerobic capacity, strength, endurance, and flexibility during the Fitness section of class.
3. Demonstrate throwing and catching a Frisbee as demonstrated by the instructor.
4. Participate in Team Tug of War demonstrating cooperative skills and following the rules presented by the instructor during the closing portion of class.

National Standards Met in this Lesson: **1, 2, 3, 4, 5, 6**

INSTRUCTIONAL ACTIVITIES	TEACHING HINTS
INTRODUCTORY ACTIVITY (2 – 3 MINUTES)	
Blob Tag When tagged hold hands. Only those at end of chain are eligible to tag.	**See DPESS Chapter 14 for details.** Select 2 or 3 "its".
FITNESS DEVELOPMENT (8 – 12 MINUTES)	
Walk, Jog, Sprint 1st whistle = WALK; 2nd whistle = JOG; 3rd whistle = SPRINT	**See DPESS Chapter 16 for details.**
Strength Exercises: Push-ups, curl-ups, reverse push-ups, coffee grinder, etc.	**See DPESS Chapter 16 for details.**
LESSON FOCUS (15 – 20 MINUTES)	
Tee Off Target Left and right hand throw; Full swing review; Aiming technique.	**See DPESS Chapter 20 for details.** Create a "Tee" area. Set up targets to hit towards: hoops; flags; ropes; cones
Putt Throw **Demonstrate and practice skills**	**See DPESS Chapter 20 for details.** 10 feet from targets.

Since Frisbee Golf/ Disc Golf evolved from mans natural competitive nature and needs, the early games of this sport used targets of trees, trash cans, light poles, chicken wire baskets, pipes, and coeds. The game was made official when Ed Headrick invented the first Disc Pole Hole, catching devise, consisting of 10 chains hanging in a parabolic shape over an upward opening basket, US Patent 4,039,189, issued 1975. Today we see Frisbee Golf courses in parks.

GAME (5 MINUTES)	
Team Tug-of-War 2 teams; each team on half of the rope. On signal, teams pull rope. First team to pull others over the line wins.	**See DPESS Chapter 18 for details.** Use a "back-to-back" to create two groups.

EVALUATION/REVIEW AND CHEER

Discuss elements of Teeing Off and Putting.
Discuss elements needed for Team Tug-of-War to be successful and safe.

Cheer: Fun, fun, fun … Frisbee's really fun!!!

Frisbee Golf Lesson Plan 4

EQUIPMENT:

1 Hula hoop per student
10 Cones
1 Frisbee per student
Fitness Scavenger Cards

OBJECTIVES:

The student will:

1. Participate in Burpee-Flip-Drill demonstrating agility, and following the instructions described by the instructor.
2. Participate in a Fitness Scavenger Hunt to improve aerobic capacity, strength, endurance, and flexibility during the Fitness section of class.
3. Demonstrate throwing and catching a Frisbee for distance and accuracy as demonstrated by the instructor.
4. Participate in Frisbee 21 demonstrating throwing, catching, and cooperative skills while following the rules presented by the instructor during the closing portion of class.

National Standards Met in this Lesson: **1, 2, 3, 4, 5, 6**

INSTRUCTIONAL ACTIVITIES	TEACHING HINTS
INTRODUCTORY ACTIVITY (2 – 3 MINUTES)	
Burpee-Flip-Drill	**See DPESS Chapter 14 for details.**
FITNESS DEVELOPMENT (8 – 12 MINUTES)	
Fitness Scavenger Hunt	**See DPESS Chapter 16 for details.**
Exercises listed on scavenger cards at stations.	Use whistle mixer to create groups of 3. Assign each group to a starting point.
LESSON FOCUS (15 MINUTES)	
Distance and Accuracy Throwing	**See DPESS Chapter 20 for details.**
Demonstrate proper form for: Thumber throw, overhand wrist flips. Review form for: underhand, side arm, and backhand.	Use management skills to divide the class in half. Use Toe-to-Toe to group students. Direct student to take equipment needed to their area.
Throw into hoops on the ground	Set hoops up at 5', 10' and 20' areas
Rules of Frisbee Golf	**See DPESS Chapter 20 for details.**
GAME (5 – 10 MINUTES)	
Frisbee 21	**See DPESS Chapter 20 for details.**
Game Rules: Throw disk back and forth; 1 point = 1 hand catch; 2 points = 2 hand catch	Use Elbow-to-Elbow to create partners. Identify student to bring Frisbee to partner.

The first formal Disc Golf Course was designed and installed in 1975 in Oak Grove Park, (Pasadena, California), by inventor Ed Headrick and was an instant success. He also founded the Professional Disc Golf Association in 1975.

EVALUATION/REVIEW AND CHEER

What was the most challenging part of the Fitness Scavenger Hunt?
What are points to remember to help make your throwing accurate?
Discuss elements that make throwing, catching, and Frisbee 21 successful.
Review the game rules of Frisbee 21.

Cheer: Hoorah! Hoorah! Frisbee is the best!!!

Frisbee Golf Lesson Plan 5

EQUIPMENT:
15 Cones
CD/ Music for Fitness
1 Fleece ball per student
1 Frisbee per student
CD/ Music player

OBJECTIVES:
The student will:
1. Participate in Mini Pyramids demonstrating agility, and following the instructions described by the instructor.
2. Participate in a Four Corners to improve aerobic capacity, strength, endurance, and flexibility during the Fitness section of class.
3. Play Frisbee Golf demonstrating throwing, catching, and cooperative skills while following the rules presented by the instructor during the closing portion of class.

National Standards Met in this Lesson: **1, 2, 3, 4, 5, 6**

INSTRUCTIONAL ACTIVITIES	TEACHING HINTS
INTRODUCTORY ACTIVITY (2 – 3 MINUTES)	
Mini Pyramids On signal student finds a group to build a partner stunt/ pyramid. On next signal, pyramids safely dismantled and students move around again until signal.	**See DPESS Chapter 18 for details.** Scattered formation. Using Whistle Mixer, create groups of 3 – 5
FITNESS DEVELOPMENT (8 – 12 MINUTES)	
Four Corners Locomotor aerobic activities to direct: Skipping; Jogging; Sliding; Running backwards; Jumping; Leaping; Hopping; Galloping. Follow aerobic work with stretching activities: Lower leg stretch; Achilles tendon stretch; Balance beam stretch; Groin stretch; Cross-legged stretch; twisting; Standing hip bend, etc.	**See DPESS Chapter 18 for details.** Place arms on wall or fence for support. Music directs length of exercise activities. Set up 4 cones creating a square. Each cone should list 2 – 3 locomotor activities. Student executes the movement on the cone until she / he gets to the next cone.
LESSON FOCUS AND GAME (20 MINUTES)	
Play Frisbee Golf Set up Frisbee Golf Course with flags, hoops and cones.	**See DPESS Chapter 20 for details.** Using Whistle Mixer, divide class into several teams.

There are almost 1000 Disc Golf Courses in the United States with around 3,000,000 regular players and over 20,000 professional members of the Professional Disc Golf Association.

EVALUATION/REVIEW AND CHEER

Discuss elements and challenges of the Frisbee Golf Game.

Cheer: 2, 4, 6, 8, Frisbee is always fun!!!

FRISBEE GOLF QUIZ

TRUE/FALSE: Fill in an A on the answer sheet if the answer is **true** and B if the answer is **false.**

1. A Frisbee is said to have "hooked" when it curves off to the right. (false)
2. The throwing hand should be pointing to the target at the end of the follow through. (true)
3. After the drive, the person who's Frisbee is farthest from the hole should play first. (true)
4. One should not play an approach shot to the green until the players ahead have left it. (true)
5. When even a player hits a ball that he feels may hit or come close to another person he should yell "fore". (true)

MULTIPLE CHOICE:
Select the best answer and fill in the letter on your answer sheet.

1. What term is used to refer to the first shot on each hole?
   a. The drive
   b. The pitch and run
   c. The approach
   d. The first shot
   Answer: a

2. In order to best sight the line of a putt, how should a player stand?
   a. With the eyes to the right of the Frisbee
   b. Eyes directly over the Frisbee
   c. With the eyes to the left of the Frisbee
   d. Shoulder to the target and eyes directly over the Frisbee
   Answer: d

3. What is the last stroke necessary to reach the green called?
   a. Approach shot
   b. The drive
   c. The putt
   d. The bomb
   Answer: c

4. Which is common to all stances?
   a. Weight on toes
   b. Weight back towards heels.
   c. Weight on centered over the whole foot
   d. No weight on feet
   Answer: c

5. What term refers to the position of the Frisbee on the ground?
   a. Flat
   b. Lie
   c. Set
   d. Bummer
   Answer: b

Jogging

OBJECTIVES:

The student will:

1. Perform Snowball Tag, Bean Bag Touch and Go, Group Tag, Loose Caboose demonstrating jogging skills, agility, cooperation skills, and following the rules established by the instructor.
2. Execute the Mirroring activity following the movement of her partner, cooperation, and the ability to follow the instructions established by the instructor.
3. Perform the following fitness activities using skills demonstrated by the instructor and following the instructions as stated: Parachute Rhythmic Aerobic Activities; Exercise to Music; Continuity Exercises; Challenge Course and Four Corners Movement.
4. Demonstrate walk-jog-sprint skills during the lesson focus using form demonstrated by the instructor.
5. Perform the Orienteering Run during the lesson focus following the rules established by the instructor.
6. Participate during the Game portion of class in Frisbee 21, Musical Hoops, Triangle Plus One Tag, Parachute activities and Wheel Barrow Relay using form and instructions established by the teacher.

JOGGING BLOCK PLAN
1 WEEK UNIT

Week #1	Monday	Tuesday	Wednesday	Thursday	Friday
Introductory Activity	Snowball Tag	Bean Bag Touch and Go	Mirroring	Group Tag	Loose Caboose
Fitness	Parachute Rhythmic Aerobic Activities	Exercise to Music	Continuity Exercises	Challenge Course	Four Corners Movement
Lesson Focus	Introduction to running form Walk-jog-walk	Walk-Jog-Sprint	Orienteering Run	Cross Country Jog -Walk	Cross Country Jog -Walk
Game	Frisbee 21	Musical Hoops	Triangle Plus One Tag	Parachute Activities	Wheel Barrow Relay

Jogging Lesson Plan 1

EQUIPMENT:

Music CD/music for fitness
1 Frisbee per 2 people
Music player
Parachute

OBJECTIVES:

The student will:

1. Participate in Snowball tag demonstrating cooperative skills, agility, and following the instructions described by the instructor.
2. Participate in Parachute Rhythmic Aerobic Activities to improve strength, endurance, and flexibility during the Fitness section of class.
3. Demonstrate running using form demonstrated by the instructor.
4. Participate in Frisbee 21 as presented by the instructor during the closing portion of class.

National Standards Met in this Lesson: **1, 2, 3, 4, 5, 6**

INSTRUCTIONAL ACTIVITIES	TEACHING HINTS

INTRODUCTORY ACTIVITY (2 - 3 MINUTES)

Snowball Tag	**See DPESS Chapter 14 for details.** Select 2 Its

The game of tag is a fun way to warm-up your muscles for upcoming activities and gets the heart pumping fast.

FITNESS DEVELOPMENT (8 - 12 MINUTES)

Parachute Rhythmic Aerobic Activities	**See DPESS Chapter 16 for details.** Create a CD/Music 8 minutes long Skip both directions, slide both directions, run both directions, jump to center, hop backward, lift parachute overhead, lower parachute to toes, repeat above, run CW with, chute overhead, make a dome.

This parachute fitness activity helps to enhance your fitness level while incorporating rhythm and music into the activity.

LESSON FOCUS (15 - 20 MINUTES)

Introduction to running form **Walk-jog-walk**	**See DPESS Chapter 20 for details.** Identify distance student should walk, jog, walk Allow students to talk quietly while active Explain that jogging is noncompetitive Personal improvement is the goal

Runners should focus their strength training exercises on their shoulders, since runner's actually use quite a bit of their upper body in order to have proper running technique.

GAME (5 MINUTES)

Frisbee 21	**See DPESS Chapter 20 for details.** Use Back-to-Back to create groups of two

As an additional challenge, see how many times you can pass the Frisbee to your partner continuously using your non-dominant arm.

EVALUATION/REVIEW AND CHEER

What muscles were worked during fitness?
What are the main points in correct running form?
What body parts do runners typically forget to work and should work on to improve their form?
What is the goal of jogging and why do people enjoy the activity?

Cheer: 2,4,6, 8, if I jog I'll feel great

Jogging Lesson Plan 2

EQUIPMENT:
1 bean bag per person
1 hoop per person
Music for musical hoops
Music player

OBJECTIVES:
The student will:
1. Participate in Bean Bag Touch and Go demonstrating cooperative skills, agility, and following the instructions described by the instructor.
2. Participate in Astronaut Drills to improve strength, endurance, and flexibility during the Fitness section of class.
3. Demonstrate Walk-Jog-Sprint skills using form demonstrated by the instructor.
4. Participate in Musical Hoops as presented by the instructor during the closing portion of class while demonstrating cooperative skills.

National Standards Met in this Lesson: **1, 2, 3, 4, 5, 6**

INSTRUCTIONAL ACTIVITIES	TEACHING HINTS

INTRODUCTORY ACTIVITY (2 - 3 MINUTES)

Bean Bag Touch and Go

See DPESS Chapter 14 for details.
Scatter formation
On signal, students run to a beanbag, touch it, and resume running. Variation: specify the color of the beanbag and the body part the touch must be made with.

FITNESS DEVELOPMENT (8 - 12 MINUTES)

Astronaut Drills
- Walk throughout the area.
- Run and hurdle.
- Stop, perform push-ups.
- Walk and do arm circles.
- Crab-walk
- Walk and stretch
- Bend and stretch
- Stop and perform curl-ups
- Stop, find a friend, and perform partner strength exercises

See DPESS Chapter 16 for details.
Scatter formation
Students move throughout the area and perform as many exercises as possible.

This type of exercise was performed by the first astronauts in training. The first American astronaut was Alan Shepard.

LESSON FOCUS (15 - 20 MINUTES)

Walk-Jog-Sprint

See DPESS Chapter 20 for details.
This is a continuous movement activity in which the teacher controls the speed of movement with a whistle signal. Three whistles mean sprint, two mean jog, and one means walk. The students start by walking around a given area. The teacher then alternates the periods of walking, jogging, sprinting, for a number of minutes or for a given distance. Progressively build up the time or distance.

People around the world have taken to jogging for to improve their well being and fitness. It's an activity that can be done alone or in groups. It doesn't take equipment, just a good supportive pair of running shoes.

INSTRUCTIONAL ACTIVITIES	TEACHING HINTS
GAME (5 MINUTES)	
Musical Hoops	**See DPESS Chapter 14 for details.** 1 hoop per student on floor Players are given a locomotor movement to do around the hoops while the music is played. When the music stops, the students step inside an empty hoop. Remove 1 hoop each round.

EVALUATION/REVIEW AND CHEER

What muscles and body parts were used in Fitness today?
Describe one of the attractions to jogging that people around the world have discovered.
Are you finding it easier today to jog?
What is the name of the first American astronaut?

Cheer: 1,2,3, jogging is good for me

Jogging Lesson Plan 3

EQUIPMENT:

Music player
Continuity exercise music CD/Music
1 jump rope per person
Orienteering map of school area that you make

OBJECTIVES:

The student will:

1. Participate in Mirroring demonstrating cooperative skills and following the instructions described by the instructor.
2. Participate in Continuity Exercises to improve aerobic endurance, strength, muscular endurance, and flexibility during the Fitness section of class.
3. Demonstrate Orienteering Running skills using form demonstrated by the instructor.
4. Participate in Triangle Plus One Tag as presented by the instructor during the closing portion of class.

National Standards Met in this Lesson: **1, 2, 3, 4, 5, 6**

INSTRUCTIONAL ACTIVITIES	TEACHING HINTS
INTRODUCTORY ACTIVITY (2 - 3 MINUTES)	
Mirroring	**See DPESS Chapter 14 for details.** Use toe-to-toe to make groups of two One person is the leader and makes a quick movement with the hands, head, legs, or body. The partner tries to be a mirror and perform the exact movement.
FITNESS DEVELOPMENT (8 - 12 MINUTES)	
Continuity Exercises These exercises are a type of interval training. Create a CD/Music with 30 - 35 seconds of music and 20 seconds of silence. During the music, the students will jump rope.	**See DPESS Chapter 16 for details.** Scattered formation Direct students to pick up a rope and move to their own space.
During each silence instruct the students to do a different exercise i.e. push-ups; curl ups; reverse push-ups; side leg lifts on each side; coffee grinder, arm circling, crab walks forward and backward, etc.	1 Individual jump rope per student
When the music resumes, the students jump rope again	

INSTRUCTIONAL ACTIVITIES	TEACHING HINTS

Jumping rope is a great form of cardiovascular activity. Try jumping rope continuously for 20 minutes at home; it is sure to give you a great work-out and tire you out!

LESSON FOCUS (15 - 20 MINUTES)

Orienteering Run

See DPESS Chapter 20 for details.
Use Back-to-back to make groups of 2
Distribute Orienteering run map of school area.
Draw map with 10 checkpoints
Emphasize running from point to point on the school grounds. Each checkpoint has a secret clue, such as a letter, word, color, or instructions on where to go next. Students can work with a partner.

GAME (5 MINUTES)

Triangle Plus One Tag

See DPESS Chapter 14 for details.
Use Whistle Mixer to make groups of 4
3 in triangle formation holding hands. One on outside of triangle. Person outside triangle tries to tag leader. Leader and tagger change places when tagged. Triangle rotates to avoid being tagged.

Tag games are great to play with friends at parks or picnics. While having fun, you help improve everyone's aerobic fitness levels.

EVALUATION/REVIEW AND CHEER

What was the focus of the fitness activity today?
What was the most interesting part of the Orienteering Run?
Cheer: Jogging makes me feel so great, yea!

Jogging Lesson Plan 4

EQUIPMENT:

Music CD/Music for challenge course
Challenge course signs
Parachute
Map of campus cross country course you create
Cones to delineate teaching area
Cones for challenge course signs
6 foam balls

OBJECTIVES:

The student will:

1. Participate in Group Tag demonstrating agility, speed, cooperative skills and following the instructions described by the instructor.
2. Participate in the Challenge Course to improve aerobic endurance, strength, muscular endurance, and flexibility during the Fitness section of class.
3. Demonstrate Cross Country Jogging and Walking skills using form demonstrated by the instructor.
4. Participate in Parachute Activities as presented by the instructor during the closing portion of class.

National Standards Met in this Lesson: **1, 2, 3, 4, 5, 6**

INSTRUCTIONAL ACTIVITIES	TEACHING HINTS

INTRODUCTORY ACTIVITY (2 - 3 MINUTES)

Group Tag

See DPESS Chapter 18 for details.
Scatter formation
Designate3 students as "it". They try and tag others, if tagged become a tagger. Last one not tagged wins.

INSTRUCTIONAL ACTIVITIES	TEACHING HINTS

FITNESS DEVELOPMENT (8 - 12 MINUTES)

Challenge Course

Agility run between and around cones
Hop through hula hoops
Hurdle over 3 benches set up with space between them
Leap/jump over ropes set up on a diagonal
Crab walk (feet first) length of a mat
Log roll down the length of a mat
Jump rope 10 times using "Hot Peppers"
Skip around cones set up
Crab walk (hands first) between markers/cones
Curl-ups
Jog around the area
Push-ups
Stretching activities

See DPESS Chapter 16 for details.

Use Whistle Mixer to create groups to begin at designated stations.

Make signs for movement at each station.

Use music to motivate moving through obstacle course. Make a CD/music with 30 seconds of music followed by 5 seconds of silence to change stations. Make the CD/Music for a total of 8 – 9 minutes of playing time.

A Challenge Course is like an obstacle course offering a series of challenging physical obstacles an individual/ team must complete usually while being timed. Obstacle courses can include running, climbing, jumping, crawling and balancing elements with the aim of testing endurance; sometimes a course involves mental tests. Obstacle courses are often included in military boot camp training as a way to familiarize recruits with the kind of tactical movement they will use in combat, as well as for physical training, building teamwork, and evaluating problem solving situations.

LESSON FOCUS (15 - 20 MINUTES)

Cross Country Jog-Walk

See DPESS Chapter 20 for details.

Students work at their own pace

Map out a cross-country course around the school grounds. Ask the students to time themselves on the jog-walk.

Cross Country running is a sport in which individuals and/or teams of runners compete to complete a running course over varying terrain. The goal is to complete the course faster than other teams. In high school competitions, the course is three miles long.

GAME (5 MINUTES)

Parachute Activities

See DPESS Chapter 16 for details.

Delineate two teams around the chute.

Use two to six balls. Try to bounce the balls off the opponents' side, scoring one point for each ball.

EVALUATION/REVIEW AND CHEER

What were the most challenging fitness activities today?
Explain the background of obstacle/ challenge courses.
How did you feel about the cross country jog-walk today?
Remember your time for tomorrow.

Cheer: Cross-country jogging is great, yea!

Jogging Lesson Plan 5

EQUIPMENT:

Four Corners Signs
Cones to delineate teaching area
4 cones for fitness
Map of cross-country course

OBJECTIVES:

The student will:

1. Participate in Loose Caboose demonstrating agility, speed, cooperative skills and following the instructions described by the instructor.
2. Participate in Four Corners to improve aerobic endurance, strength, muscular endurance, and flexibility during the Fitness section of class.
3. Demonstrate Cross Country Jogging and Walking skills using form demonstrated by the instructor.
4. Participate in Wheel Barrow Relay demonstrating cooperative skills and speed as presented by the instructor during the closing portion of class.

National Standards Met in this Lesson: **1, 2, 3, 4, 5, 6**

INSTRUCTIONAL ACTIVITIES | **TEACHING HINTS**

INTRODUCTORY ACTIVITY (2 - 3 MINUTES)

Loose Caboose

Designate one student as the "loose caboose".
Loose Caboose students try to hook onto a train.

See DPESS Chapter 14 for details.
Use Whistle Mixer to make groups of 3 – 4
Create several "trains".
Trains are formed by 3 - 4 students standing in column formation with each person placing their hands on the waist of the person in front of them

A caboose is a manned vehicle/car at the end of a freight train. Although cabooses were once used on nearly every freight train in North America, their use has declined and today they are seldom seen on trains, except on locals and smaller railroads.

FITNESS DEVELOPMENT (8 - 12 MINUTES)

Four Corners

Outline a large rectangle with four cones. Place signs with tasks on both sides of the cones. Students move around the outside of the rectangle and change their movement pattern as they approach a corner sign.
The following movement tasks are suggested:

1. Jogging
2. Skipping/Jumping/Hopping
3. Sliding/Galloping
4. Abdominal strengthening exercises
5. Upper body strengthening exercises
6. Side leg work
7. Full body stretches

See DPESS Chapter 16, 14 for details.
Use Whistle Mixer to create 4 equal groups.

Assign each group a corner to begin at.

These exercises utilize your whole body including what are called your "core muscles." Core muscles refer to your abdominal muscle and your back area/ postural muscles. Keep core muscles strong helps in daily life and helps to prevent injuries.

LESSON FOCUS (15 - 20 MINUTES)

Cross Country Jog-Walk

See DPESS Chapter 20 for details.
Students work at their own pace
Use the same map as yesterday.
Ask the students to time themselves on the jog-walk and see if they improved today.

INSTRUCTIONAL ACTIVITIES	TEACHING HINTS
GAME (5 MINUTES)	
Wheel Barrow Relay Use the wheelbarrow position as the means of locomotion	**See DPESS Chapter 18 for details.** Use Whistle Mixer to create even groups Within each group do Back-to-Back Identify one as the first wheel barrow Line each group up Have relay race in wheelbarrow position Rotate positions before each team is done.

Wheel barrow activities help strengthen the muscles in your entire body and your core muscles.

EVALUATION/REVIEW AND CHEER

What is a caboose?
What are core muscles?
How was jogging the course today versus yesterday? Were you any faster today?
What area of fitness does jogging improve?

Cheer: Wheel Barrow Relays are fun!

Pickleball

This unit has been specifically designed to meet all six components of the NASPE National Standards for Physical Education.

OBJECTIVES:

The student will:

1. Participate in Hoops and Plyometrics; Triangle Tag; Fastest Tag; Blob Tag; and Pickleball Tag demonstrating agility, speed and cooperative skills during the Introductory Activity following rules established by the instructor.
2. Participate in an Aerobic Workout during Fitness to improve strength, flexibility and cardiovascular respiratory and muscular endurance.
3. Participate in Random Running during Fitness to improve muscular strength, flexibility and cardiovascular respiratory endurance.
4. Participate in Interval Training, strengthening and stretching exercises during Fitness to improve cardiovascular respiratory and muscular endurance and flexibility.
5. Participate in the Mini-Challenge Course demonstrating agility, speed, strength, and flexibility to improve fitness levels.
6. Participate in Partner Racetrack Fitness demonstrating agility, speed, strength, and flexibility using form demonstrated by the instructor.
7. Participate in Pickleball balancing ball bouncing drills while locomoting using form demonstrated by the instructor.
8. Demonstrate backhand skills hitting to a partner across the net using form demonstrated by the instructor.
9. Demonstrate lobbing to a partner across the net using form demonstrated by the instructor.
10. Demonstrate forehand, backhand, lobbing, smashing, and serving skills while playing Pickleball following the rules of the game listed on the handout.
11. Participate in Balance Relay demonstrating the skill of balancing the pickleball on a paddle while locomoting across the floor during the game portion of class.
12. Participate in Bouncing Ball Relay demonstrating the skill of balancing the pickleball on a paddle while locomoting across the floor during the game portion of class.
13. Play Hoops on the Ground demonstrating cooperative skills and agility while following the rules of the game during the game portion of class.
14. Participate in Hoops Circle Pass demonstrating cooperative skills and agility while following the instructions established by the instructor during the game portion of class.

PICKLEBALL BLOCK PLAN
1 WEEK UNIT

Week #1	Monday	Tuesday	Wednesday	Thursday	Friday
Introductory Activity	Hoops and Plyometrics	Fastest Tag	Pickleball Tag	Triangle Tag	
Fitness	Interval Training	Aerobic Workout	Random Running	Partner Racetrack Fitness	Mini Challenge Courst
Lesson Focus	Pickleball balancing skills	Pickleball Striking Skills	Forehand, Backhand and Lobbing Skills	Pickleball Game	Pickleball Game
Game	Balancing Relay	Bouncing Ball Relay	Hoops on the Ground	Hoops Circle Pass	

Diagram of Court

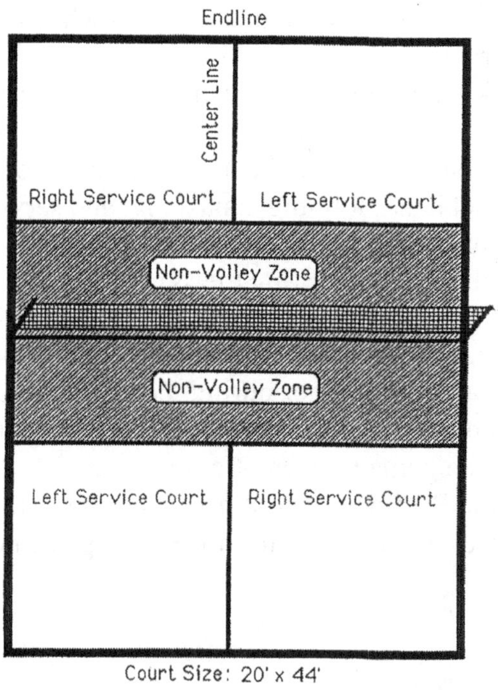

Pickleball Lesson Plan 1

EQUIPMENT:

1 paddle per student
Cones for perimeter
Music/ CD/ Tape for Fitness
1 pickleball per student
1 hoop per person
Music player

OBJECTIVES:

The student will:

1. Participate in Hoops and Plyometrics during the Introductory demonstrating form described by the instructor.
2. Participate in Interval Training, strengthening and stretching exercises during Fitness to improve cardiovascular respiratory and muscular endurance and flexibility.
3. Participate pickleball balancing ball bouncing drills while locomoting using form demonstrated by the instructor.
4. Participate in Balance Relay demonstrating the skill of balancing the pickleball on a paddle while locomoting.

National Standards Met in this Lesson: **1, 2, 3, 4, 5, 6**

INSTRUCTIONAL ACTIVITIES	TEACHING HINTS

INTRODUCTORY ACTIVITY (2 - 3 MINUTES)

Hoops and Plyometrics	**See DPESS Chapter 14 for details.** Scattered formation

FITNESS DEVELOPMENT (8 - 12 MINUTES)

Interval Training Alternate Work Activities with Rest Activities Brisk walking vs. Slow walking Jogging vs. Walking Sprinting vs. Jogging Rope Jumping vs. Walking Jumping in place vs. walking	**See DPESS Chapter 16 for details.** Create a tape with 30 seconds for each Work Activity and leave a blank of 30 seconds for the Rest Activity.
Core strengthening exercises Curl-ups Curl-ups with Twist Reverse curl Pelvis Tilter Push-ups Reverse push-ups/ dips	Continue the use of the same timed tape to indicate a change to the next exercise.
Lower-Back Stretches Back Bender Sitting Toe touch Feet-together stretch	
Lower-Leg Stretches Lower-leg stretch Achilles Tendon Stretch	

Interval training alternates very high intensity exercise for a short period of time followed by a lighter intensity exercise period. This training technique began by gold medal Olympic runners as early as 1912.

INSTRUCTIONAL ACTIVITIES	TEACHING HINTS

LESSON FOCUS (15 - 20 MINUTES)

Go over rules handout

Distribute Rules Handout.

Demonstrate and have students practice skills:

- Balance ball on paddle with non-dominant hand.
- Balance ball on paddle with dominant hand while walking forward.
- Bounce the pickleball on the paddle chest high with your dominant hand while standing in place.
- Bounce the pickleball on the paddle chest high with your dominant hand while walking.
- Bounce ball on paddle chest high with non-dominant hand while walking.

Scattered formation.

Ball Control:

- Balance to ball paddle.
- Rotate ball around the paddles edges.
- Bounce ball on paddle 6" – 1' in air.

Striking the ball:

- Hit ball continuously against wall or fence.
- Vary distance from wall/ fence.

Partner practice:

- Without bouncing the ball first, hit to partner about 6' away.
- Increase distance.
- Drop bounce ball first, then hit to partner.
- Rally with partner.

Use Back-to-Back to create partners.

Pickleball began in a backyard on Bainbridge Island, Washington, in 1965. The game is a cross between Ping Pong, Badminton, and Tennis. It is played with a wood racquet and a wiffle ball. The net is the height of a tennis net, 3 feet high. The game was named after a dog named Pickles who kept stealing the ball and running into bushed to hide it and keep it from the players.

GAME (5 MINUTES)

Balancing Relay:

One by one, each student will balance the ball on the paddle to a cone and return.

Vary the locomotor movement to be used.
(Walking, jogging, backwards walking, etc.)

Use Whistle Mixer to create groups of 4 – 6.
Select leader.
Make a straight line behind each leader.
1 paddle and pickle ball per group.

Students sit when all have completed the relay.

EVALUATION/REVIEW AND CHEER

What type of fitness did you participate in today? How many years ago had this technique been used?
Where do you want your eyes while controlling the pickleball?
When controlling the pickleball, at what angle do you want the paddle?
What is the key phrase to be sure your grip is correct on your paddle? "Shake hands" with the paddle.

Cheer: 2, 4, 6, 8, Pickleball is really GREAT!

PICKLEBALL RULES HANDOUT

Background: Pickleball is a slow-moving racquet game played on a badminton sized court. The net is 3' high. Pickleball is played by either two or four people. Doubles play with four people.

Serving: The ball is served underhand, diagonally without bouncing the ball. Points are earned by the serving side only. Player must keep one foot behind the back line when serving. The serve is made underhand. The server must contact the ball in the air; it cannot be hit after a bounce.

Only one serve attempt is allowed, except if the ball touches the net on the serve and lands in the proper service court. Then the serve may be taken over.

1. A point is scored by the serving team when the receiving team (or player) makes a fault.
2. When the serving team makes its first fault, players will stay in the same courts and turn the ball over to the other team.

Singles Play: All rules apply with one exception; when serving in singles, each player serves from the right hand court when the score is 0 or an even number and from the left hand court when the score is odd numbered.

Determining the Serving Team or Player: Use a coin toss or rally the ball until a fault is made. The winner has the option of serving first or receiving.

VOLLEY: All volleying must be done with player's feet behind the non-volley zone line. It is a fault if the player steps over the line on the volley follow through.

DOUBLE BOUNCE RULE: Each team must play their first shot off the bounce. The receiving team must let the serve bounce and the serving team must let the return of the serve bounce before playing it.

FAULT: It is a fault when:

a. A ball is hit out of bounds. A ball landing on the line is good.
b. The ball does not clear the net.
c. The player steps into the non-volley zone and volleys the ball.
d. A player volleys the ball before it has bounced once on each side of the net.

SCORING: A team may score a point only when serving. A player who is serving shall continue serve until a fault is made by his/her team. The game is played to 11 points. A team must win by 2 points. Keep playing until there is a 2 point spread between teams.

ADDITIONAL RULES:

a. The server may not serve until his opponent is ready, but the opponent shall be deemed "ready" if a return of serve is attempted.
b. If a player is playing a ball that has bounced in the non-volley zone and she/he touches the net with the paddle or any part of the body, it will constitute a fault for that player.
c. A service fault occurs when the server swings the paddle with the intent of striking the ball but misses.
d. Only the player served to may receive the service, but if the ball touches or is hit by his/her partner, the serving side scores a point. Players switch courts only after scoring.

Pickleball Lesson Plan 2

EQUIPMENT:

1 paddle per student
1 Badminton/Pickleball court per 4 students
Music player
1 Pickleball/wiffle ball per student
Music for Aerobic Workout

OBJECTIVES:

The student will:

1. Participate in Fastest Tag s during the Introductory demonstrating cooperative skills and following the rules established by the instructor.
2. Participate in an Aerobic Workout during Fitness to improve strength, flexibility and cardiovascular respiratory and muscular endurance.
3. Demonstrate striking the pickleball to a partner using form demonstrated by the instructor.
4. Demonstrate serving the ball on the court using form demonstrated by the instructor.
5. Participate in Bouncing Ball Relay demonstrating the skill of balancing the pickleball on a paddle while locomoting.

National Standards Met in this Lesson: **1, 2, 3, 4, 5, 6**

INSTRUCTIONAL ACTIVITIES	TEACHING HINTS
INTRODUCTORY ACTIVITY (2 - 3 MINUTES)	
Fastest Tag	**See Chapter 14 for details.** Everyone is "it." Vary the locomotor activities.
FITNESS DEVELOPMENT (8 - 12 MINUTES)	
Aerobic Workout See Racquetball, Lesson 7 for complete details.	**See DPESS Chapter 16 for details.** Scatter formation Use CD/tape to direct exercise
LESSON FOCUS (15 - 20 MINUTES)	
Partner passing: Rally ball to partner continuously allowing ball to bounce on ground before returning 4' apart. Increase distance. Rally ball without a bounce 4' apart. Increase distance.	Use Toe-to-Toe to make partners. Scattered formation/ lines facing partner.
Serving: Use underhand forehand stroke. Do not bounce the ball first. Contact ball at or below the waist. Serve diagonally cross-court clearing the non-volley zone. The Server must keep both feet behind the baseline during the serve with at least one foot on the court surface at the time the ball is hit.	Same partner. Assign courts. 4 people per court.

The server is decided with a coin toss, or a rally until a fault is made. A minimum of three hits must be made for the rally to be valid. The winner has the option of serving or receiving first. At the start of each game in doubles, the first serving team is allowed one fault before giving up the serve to the opponents. Thereafter, both members of each team will serve before the ball is turned over to the opposing team. In singles play the server's score will always be an even number when serving from the right court and an odd number when serving from the left court. Only one serve attempt is allowed, except in the event of a 'let' (the ball touches the net on the serve, and lands on the proper service court) then the serve is taken over.

INSTRUCTIONAL ACTIVITIES	TEACHING HINTS
GAME (5 MINUTES)	
Bouncing Ball Relay Race Run from one end of the relay area to the end and back while hitting the ball up and down on the paddle. Pass paddle and ball to next person. Sit when all in group have completed the relay race.	Use Whistle Mixer to make relay lines of 5 – 6.
EVALUATION/REVIEW AND CHEER	
What muscles were used today during the lesson? What was the most challenging part of class today? Explain serving rules of Pickleball. What was the most challenging part of the relay race? **Cheer: We Love Pickleball.**	

Pickleball Lesson Plan 3

EQUIPMENT:

1 paddle per student
Cones to mark perimeter
Badminton court w/ 3' net 1 per 4 students
1 pickleball per student
1 hoop per student

OBJECTIVES:

The student will:

1. Play Pickleball Tag demonstrating cooperative skills and following the rules established by the instructor.
2. Demonstrate backhand hitting using correct form demonstrated by the instructor.
3. Demonstrate lobbing during the Lesson Focus using form demonstrated by the instructor.
4. Participate in Random Running during Fitness to improve muscular strength, flexibility and cardiovascular respiratory endurance.
5. Play Hoops on the Ground demonstrating cooperative skills and agility while following the rules of the game.

National Standards Met in this Lesson: **1, 2, 3, 4, 5, 6**

INSTRUCTIONAL ACTIVITIES	TEACHING HINTS
INTRODUCTORY ACTIVITY (2 - 3 MINUTES)	
Pickleball Tag Everyone moves around the room while bouncing pickleball on racquet. Taggers try to tag people while also performing the pickleball bouncing on racquet. If tagged, move to outside of area and bounce ball on racquet 10 times. Then, return to game boundaries.	Select 2 - 3 "its"/ taggers. Taggers wear pinnies. Scattered formation.
FITNESS DEVELOPMENT (8 - 12 MINUTES)	
Random Running Students run around at own pace. On signal, students will perform assigned exercise	**See DPESS Chapter 16 for details.** Continuous movement Motivate students with music

INSTRUCTIONAL ACTIVITIES	TEACHING HINTS
LESSON FOCUS (15 - 20 MINUTES)	
Backhand hitting: Skill technique same badminton/ tennis backhand stroke. Drop bounce ball and hit to partner 5' apart. Repeat, increasing distance between players. Continue rallying using backhand only without a bounce. Rally alternating forehand and backhand hitting.	Use Back-to-Back to create pairs of students. **See DPESS Chapter 19 for details on backhand skills in tennis and badminton.**
Lobbing Explain purpose of shot. Partner tosses ball high to partner 5' apart. Partner returns ball with lob shot. Alternate roles.	**See DPESS Chapter 19 for details on lobbing skills for badminton and tennis.**
Overhead Smash Skill technique same badminton/ tennis overhead smash. Explain purpose of shot. Partner tosses ball, receive with a lob, smash back to partner. Change roles. Partner tosses ball, receives with a lob, smash back to partner and continue rallying practicing all strokes.	**See DPESS Chapter 19 for details for badminton and tennis overhead smash techniques.**

When you play Pickleball, you need to look at your opponent's position and racquet head to anticipate where their shot will land. Is the paddle face slightly open for backspin? Is the paddle face slightly closed for a topspin shot? Is the paddle raised above the head for an overhead smash? Is the paddle parallel to the floor, signifying a lob? Watch the position of your opponent's feet. This can also give you an idea where your opponent's general shot will end.

INSTRUCTIONAL ACTIVITIES	TEACHING HINTS
GAME (5 MINUTES)	
Hoops on the Ground Students run around the area where hoops are spread. When the teacher calls a number, that number of students must get inside 1 hoop in 5 seconds or less.	**See DPESS Chapter 14 for details.** Spread hoops around floor. Repeat and vary challenges.

EVALUATION/REVIEW AND CHEER

What was the most challenging part of Pickleball Tag?
What is challenging about Random Running?
When do you use a lob shot?
When do you smash the ball?
Explain Pickleball strategies and how you can "read" your opponent's.

Cheer: (clap while saying cheer) P- I- C- K- L- E- B- A- L- L; Pickle Ball!

OS25061 Photodisc Royalty Free Photograph

Pickleball Lesson Plan 4

EQUIPMENT:

Cones for perimeter
Music player
4 paddles and balls per court
Fitness station task cards you create
Music for fitness
1 hoop per 5 – 7 students
1 court per 4 students

OBJECTIVES:

The student will:

1. Participate in Triangle Tag demonstrating agility, speed and cooperative skills during the Introductory Activity.
2. Participate in Partner Racetrack Fitness demonstrating agility, speed, strength, and flexibility using form demonstrated by the instructor.
3. Demonstrate forehand, backhand, lobbing, smashing, and serving skills while playing Pickleball following the rules of the game listed on the handout.
4. Participate in Hoops Circle Pass demonstrating cooperative skills and agility while following the instructions established by the instructor.

National Standards Met in this Lesson: **1, 2, 3, 4, 5, 6**

INSTRUCTIONAL ACTIVITIES	TEACHING HINTS

INTRODUCTORY ACTIVITY (2 - 3 MINUTES)

Triangle Tag

Form a triangle by holding hands. One person puts flag in pocket. Person with flag is leader. Group tries to keep leader from getting flags pulled. When flag pulled, leader becomes tagger and tagger becomes leader.

See DPESS Chapter 14 for details.
Use whistle mixer, make groups of 3
Choose 3 people to be the taggers

FITNESS DEVELOPMENT (8 - 12 MINUTES)

Partner Racetrack Fitness

10 stations in circular track formation. Each station has task card with exercise to perform. 2 students perform task while other 2 run around track.

See DPESS Chapter 16 for details.
Use whistle mixer, create groups of 4. Use toe-to-toe to make partners. Use music for motivation.

LESSON FOCUS (15 - 20 MINUTES)

Play Pickleball

Use Whistle Mixer to create groups of 4.
Assign courts

The first side scoring 11 points and leading by at least a two-point margin wins. If both sides are tied at ten points, play continues until one side wins by two points.
Match: Best two out of three games or one game to twenty-one points.

GAME (5 MINUTES)

Hoops Circle Pass

See DPESS Chapter 14 for details.
Use whistle mixer, make groups of 5 – 7.
Students work together to help others through the hoop most efficiently.

EVALUATION/REVIEW AND CHEER

What is the most challenging activity today?

Cheer: Circle Pass, Yes!!!

Pickleball Lesson Plan 5

EQUIPMENT:

1 pickleball per court
1 racquet per student
Music for fitness
1 court per 4 students
Instruction task cards for fitness stations

OBJECTIVES:

The student will:

1. Participate in Blob Tag demonstrating agility, speed and cooperative skills during the Introductory Activity.
2. Participate in the Mini-Challenge Course demonstrating agility, speed, strength, and flexibility to improve fitness levels.
3. Demonstrate forehand, backhand, lobbing, smashing, and serving skills while playing Pickleball following the rules of the game listed on the handout.

National Standards Met in this Lesson: **1, 2, 3, 4, 5, 6**

INSTRUCTIONAL ACTIVITIES	TEACHING HINTS
INTRODUCTORY ACTIVITY (2 - 3 MINUTES)	
Blob Tag Last person in the chain tags.	**See DPESS Chapter 14 for details.** Scatter formation Select first taggers
FITNESS DEVELOPMENT (8 - 12 MINUTES)	
Mini-Challenge Course Start lying face down; Run around 2 chairs; Run; Hurdle over 3 benches; High jump over bar; Crab walk length of mat feet first; Agility run around 3 chairs; Forward roll length of mat; Vault 36 over a jumping box.	**See DPESS Chapter 16 for details.** Set up course with space between stations Music makes the challenge course more enjoyable.
LESSON FOCUS AND GAME COMBINED (20 - 25 MINUTES)	
Play Pickleball	Use Whistle Mixer to create groups of 4. Assign courts

Pickleball is played by people all across the U.S. and even in Singapore and Japan. There are tournaments and national competitions in the sport. Enthusiasts hope this will eventually become an Olympic sport.

INSTRUCTIONAL ACTIVITIES	TEACHING HINTS
EVALUATION/REVIEW AND CHEER	

What were the most challenging activities today?
What muscles were used in class today?
Tell me how wide-spread interest is in Pickleball.
How did the name of the game Pickleball originate?

Cheer: Pickleball, pickleball, yea, pickleball!

Rock Climbing

OBJECTIVES:

The student will:

1. Participate in the coffee grinder square as an Introductory Activity.
2. Participate in a Continuity Exercises to improve fitness.
3. Participate in the PACER running activity to improve cardiovascular endurance.
4. Participate in parachute activities for fitness.
5. Participate in a rope jumping fitness activity.
6. Demonstrate how to attach a carabineer to a rope through an ATC.
7. When asked, demonstrate safety procedures for rock climbing.
8. Explain the purpose of a safety harness.
9. Demonstrate tying the following knots used in rock climbing: water knot; bite knot; figure eight; and double figure eight knot.
10. Use the rock climbing equipment safely and properly as demonstrated by the instructor in class.
11. Demonstrate the 5 hand and 5 foot holds demonstrated in class.
12. Tie the double figure eight and follow through knot.
13. Tie the double figure eight with a bite knot.
14. Describe out load why tying knots is important in rock climbing.
15. Demonstrate the skill of belaying using form demonstrated in class.
16. Demonstrate the skill of rappelling using form demonstrated in class.
17. Demonstrate the uses and describe the functions of the safety harness.
18. Participate in partner Tug-of-War activities demonstrating safety and respect for a partner.
19. Participate in the Over and Under Ball Relay.
20. Participate in a Wheelbarrow Relay Race demonstrating strength and cooperative skills.

ROCK CLIMBING BLOCK PLAN
1 WEEK UNIT

Week #1	Monday	Tuesday	Wednesday	Thursday	Friday
Introductory Activity	Move and Perform a Stretch	Weave Drill	Coffee Grinder Square	Flash Drill	Running Weave Drill
Fitness	Aerobic workout	Continuity Exercises	PACER Running	Jog, Walk, Jog	Walk, Jog, Sprint
Lesson Focus	Introduction Rope and Knot Tying	Safety Harness and Knots	Equipment Explanation and Demonstration	Hand and Foot Holds Belaying and Rappelling	Field Trip to Rock Climbing Gym/ Wall
Game	Partner Tug-of-War Activities	Spider Tag	Over and Under Ball Relay	Wheelbarrow Relay	

Rock Climbing Lesson Plan 1

EQUIPMENT:
19 Cones
CD/ music player
1 Continuity music Fitness CD/ music
1 Individual tug-of-war rope per 2 students

OBJECTIVES:
The student will:
1. Participate in Move and Perform a Stretch demonstrating stretching skills, agility, and following the instructions described by the instructor.
2. Participate in the Aerobics Workout to improve aerobic endurance, strength, muscular endurance, and flexibility during the Fitness section of class.
3. Demonstrate rope knot tying using form demonstrated on the videotape/ DVD and by the instructor.
4. Participate in Partner Tug of War activities demonstrating safety rules and activities presented by the instructor during the closing portion of class.

National Standards Met in this Lesson: **1, 2, 3, 4, 5, 6**

INSTRUCTIONAL ACTIVITIES	TEACHING HINTS

INTRODUCTORY ACTIVITY (2 - 3 MINUTES)

Move and Perform a Stretch Students move throughout area in designated manner while the music is playing. When music stops, they stop and perform a stretching activity called out by you.	**See DPESS Chapter 14 for details.** Bring students together in a scattered formation. Use cones to designate activity area.

FITNESS DEVELOPMENT (8 - 12 MINUTES)

Aerobics Workout	**See DPESS Chapter 16 for details.** See Lesson 1, Frisbee Golf for routine.

Aerobic workouts help improve your cardiovascular/ aerobic endurance, muscular strength and endurance and increase the release of endorphins which gives you a boost in attitude.

LESSON FOCUS (15 - 20 MINUTES)

Rock Climbing Introduction Through Videotape/DVD

Rope and Knot Tying Discuss safety issues of knot tying on a harness. Demonstrate tying of: Double figure eight and follow through knot Double figure eight with a bite knot Explain task sheets.	Bring students together in a scattered formation. Have each student get an equipment package and task sheets. Students practice knot tying using the Task Sheet instructions. Check each knot.

Your knowledge of knot tying will help in many activities in the future in addition to rock climbing. Some of these other activities include: sailing, fishing, and camping just to name a few.

GAME (5 MINUTES)

Partner Tug-of-War Activities **Pick-Up and Pull.** On signal, the opponents run to the rope, pick it up, and the tug-of-war ensues. **Different Positions**: Partners can have contests using some of the following positions and activities: facing; back to back; side to side; one handed; two handed; crab position with the rope hooked over the foot; push-up position; on all fours, etc.	**See DPESS Chapter 18 for details.** Use management game to create partners. Use management game to select partner to get rope for the pair. Change partners occasionally.

EVALUATION/REVIEW AND CHEER
Explain a benefit of Aerobic Workouts.
Why is it important to warm up before climbing? Why is it important to be able to properly tie the two knots?
When do you use the double figure eight with a bite?

Cheer: We love rock climbing!

TASK SHEET: DOUBLE FIGURE EIGHT WITH A BITE KNOT

Name: ______________________________ **Period:** ______________

Directions: Read the steps listed below and use the illustrations at the bottom of the page to practice tying the bite knot. Keep practicing until you are told to stop.

1. Double up the length of rope and form a loop with the closed end.
2. Come around open ends with closed ends.
3. Bring closed end back through loop.

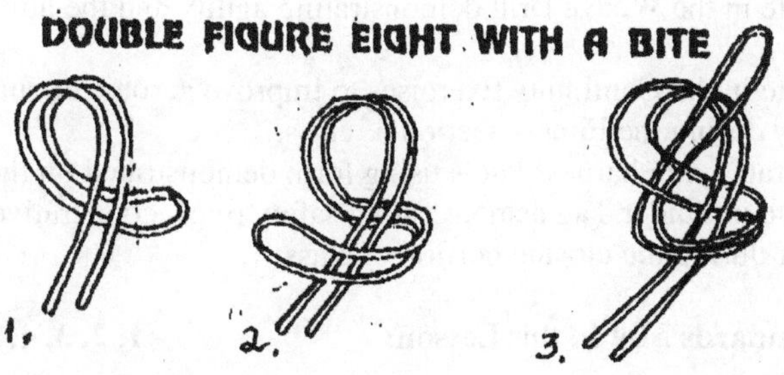

TASK SHEET: DOUBLE FIGURE EIGHT AND FOLLOW THROUGH KNOT

Name: ______________________________ **Period:** ______________

Directions: Read the steps below and use the illustration at the bottom of the page to guide you in tying the knots. Keep practicing the knot tying until you are told to stop.

1. Make a loop near one end of the rope.
2. Bring end of rope behind loop.
3. Bring end of rope around loop and back through between sections of rope.
4. Tighten knot. Figure eight should appear.
5. Extend rope until enough is beyond figure eight to reverse process. Reverse rope between sections.
6. Continue to retrace path of original knot.
7. Complete retracing path and tighten knot.

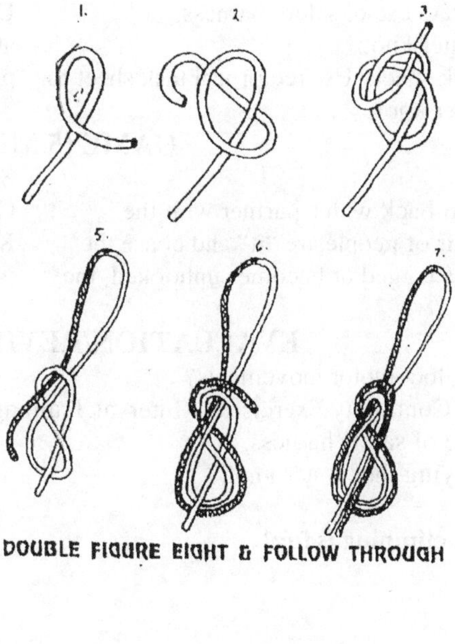

Rock Climbing Lesson Plan 2

EQUIPMENT:

10 Cones
1 Jump rope per student
2 Lengths of ¼" nylon rope per student
1 CD/ music player
1 Fitness CD/ music

OBJECTIVES:

The student will:

1. Participate in the Weave Drill demonstrating agility and the ability to follow the instructions described by the instructor.
2. Participate in the Continuity Exercises to improve aerobic endurance, strength, muscular endurance, and flexibility during the Fitness section of class.
3. Demonstrate tying harness knots using form demonstrated on the videotape/ DVD and by the instructor.
4. Participate in Spider Tag demonstrating safety rules, cooperative skills and following the instructions given by the instructor during the closing portion of class.

National Standards Met in this Lesson: **1, 2, 3, 4, 5, 6**

INSTRUCTIONAL ACTIVITIES	TEACHING HINTS

INTRODUCTORY ACTIVITY (2 - 3 MINUTES)

Weave Drill
Students around cones using a series of movements i.e. skip, slide, jog, gallop, shuffle, carioca, etc.

See DPESS Chapter 14 for details.
Bring students together in a scattered formation.
Use whistle to alert to a new movement command.

Movements such as skipping, jogging, sliding, are all examples of locomotor movements.

FITNESS DEVELOPMENT (8 - 12 MINUTES)

Continuity Exercises
Student's rope jump while music is playing, on silence in direct the following exercises: Have student's jump rope to music until it stops. Give instructions for exercise, for example: Push-ups; Curl-ups; Reverse push-ups; Side leg lifts (both sides); Coffee grinder; Arm circling; Crab walks (forward, sideways, backward).

See DPESS Chapter 16 for details.
Have students get a jump rope and spread around the activity area.
Define activity area with cones.
When music resumes, rope jumping resumes.

Continuity Exercises use the theory of Interval Training to enhance fitness levels in participants. Interval training alternates aerobic work with strength, muscular endurance and flexibility exercises to provide a good workout.

LESSON FOCUS (15 - 20 MINUTES)

Harness and Knots
Display and demonstrate use of safety harness.
Demonstrate tying water knot.
Explain reciprocal task sheet. Use reciprocal task sheet to practice tying the water knot.

Use Toe-to-Toe to create pairs of students. Identify doer and observer. Direct observer to pick up equipment package and reciprocal task sheet.

GAME (5 MINUTES)

Spider Tag
Students stand back-to-back with a partner with the elbows hooked. A pair of people are "it" and chase the other pairs. If a pair is tagged or becomes unhooked, they are "it."

See DPESS Chapter 14 for details.
Create pairs.
Keep the game within the activity area.

EVALUATION/REVIEW AND CHEER

What are examples of locomotor movements?
Describe the value of Continuity Exercises or Interval Training?
Discuss the proper use of safety harness.
Ask questions about tying the "water knot".

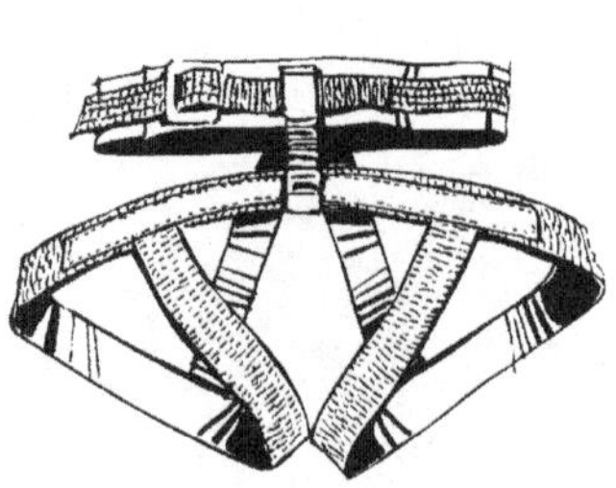

Cheer: 3, 2, 1, Rock climbing is fun!

RECIPROCAL TASK SHEET: WATER KNOT

Doer: ______________________________ **Observer**: ______________________________

Directions: Work in teams of two. One person is the "doer" and the other is the "observer." Print your names on the appropriate line above on this task sheet. The observer reads the instructions to the doer, offers verbal feedback, and places a check in the "yes" or "no" column recording the performance of the doer. You may show the illustrations at the bottom of the page to the doer to aid her or him in performing the task. Complete the task sheet until you are directed to "change roles." Then the doer becomes the observer. Each person has her or his own task sheet.

TYING	**THE WATER KNOT**	**1st Try**		**2nd Try**	
Steps	**Instructions**	**Yes**	**No**	**Yes**	**No**
1	Tie hitch in piece of webbing				
2	Bring in second piece of webbing back along first piece through hole in hitch.				
3	Parallel the first piece of webbing with the second piece.				
4	When parallel is completed, tighten the knot and see if it looks correct.				

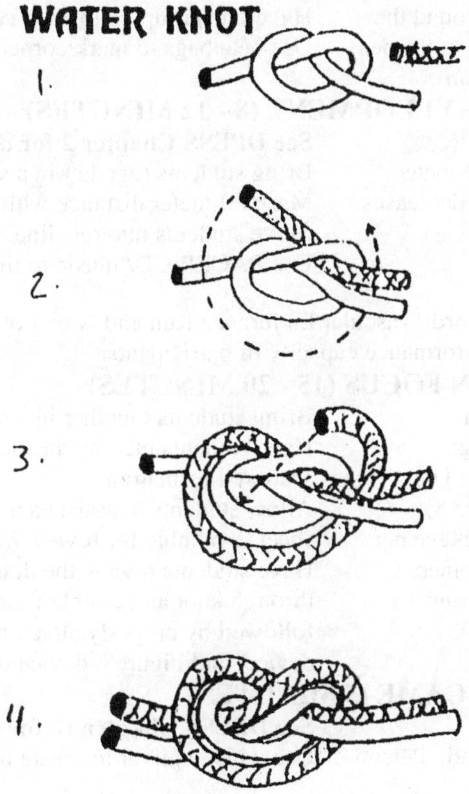

Rock Climbing Lesson Plan 3

EQUIPMENT:

4 Beanbags
20 Cones
PACER running CD/ music
CD/ music player
1 Ball per 5 students
4 Lengths of 1" tubular webbing per 2 students
1 Completed safety harness
1 Ball per five students

OBJECTIVES:

The student will:

1. Participate in the Coffee Grinder Square demonstrating agility and the ability to follow the instructions described by the instructor.
2. Participate in PACER running to improve aerobic endurance during the Fitness section of class.
3. View the videotape/ DVD and demonstrations presented by the instructor during the Lesson Focus.
4. Participate in the Over and Under Ball Relay demonstrating cooperative skills and following the instructions given by the instructor during the closing portion of class.

National Standards Met in this Lesson: 1, 2, 3, 4, 5, 6

INSTRUCTIONAL ACTIVITIES	TEACHING HINTS
INTRODUCTORY ACTIVITY (2 - 3 MINUTES)	
Coffee Grinder Square Students start at one corner of the square, extend the right arm to support the body weight, perform the coffee grinder by having the feet walk 360 degrees around the arm. When a circle is completed, students run to the next corner and reverse arms and do the same motion.	**See DPESS Chapter 14 for details.** Bring students together in a scattered formation. Use management game to create four groups. Have one group go to each corner. Use beanbags to mark corners.
FITNESS DEVELOPMENT (8 - 12 MINUTES)	
PACER Running Students shuttle run back and forth across a 20-meter distance within a specified time that gradually decreases.	**See DPESS Chapter 2 for details.** Bring students together in a scattered formation. Mark 20-meter distance with cones. Move students into one line. Use PACER CD/ music to time runs.

PACER stands for Progressive Aerobic Cardiovascular Endurance Run and is part of the Fitnessgram physical fitness test used nationally. It tests aerobic performance capacity of participants.

INSTRUCTIONAL ACTIVITIES	TEACHING HINTS
LESSON FOCUS (15 - 20 MINUTES)	
Equipment Demonstration and Explanation Demonstrate the use of and show the following: Climbing shoes; Carabiners (Ds, ovals, locking Ds); Belaying and Rappelling Devices (ATC, Figure 8); Camming Devices (quad cam); Equipment package per student: 2 lengths of ¼" nylon rope; 1 D karabiner; 1 oval carabiner; 1 locking D carabiner; 1 ATC; and 1 Figure 8.	Bring students together in a scattered formation. Have students pick up an equipment package and get in scattered formation. Allow students to assist each other. Have Lesson 2 task sheets available for review/instruction. Have students review the double figure eight and follow through knot and double figure eight with a bite knot followed by properly attaching the carabiners, ATC device, and Figure 8 device to the ropes.
GAME (5 MINUTES)	
Over and Under Ball Relay Pass ball to end of row under legs and over head. Person receiving ball at end runs to front of line.	**See DPESS Chapter 18 for details.** Use whistle mixer to create lines of five or six.

EVALUATION/REVIEW AND CHEER

What does PACER stand for and what is the purpose of the test?
What type of knot is used to make the safety harness? Why is a safety harness necessary?

Cheer: 1, 2, 3, rock climbing, yes!

Rock Climbing Lesson Plan 4

EQUIPMENT:

10 Cones
2 Lengths of 1/4" nylon rope per student
1 D carabiner per student
1 Oval carabiner per student
1 Locking D carabiner per student
1 ATC belaying & rappelling device per student
1 Quad cam per student
1 Figure 8 belaying and rappelling device per student

OBJECTIVES:

The student will:

1. Participate in the Flash Drill demonstrating agility and the ability to follow the instructions described by the instructor.
2. Participate in jogging to improve aerobic and muscular endurance during the Fitness section of class.
3. Demonstrate and explain the use of the given rock climbing hand and foot holds: open grip; ring grip; pocket grip; pinch grip and footholds as presented by the instructor during the Lesson Focus.
4. Demonstrate double figure eight tying and attaching a carabiner to a rope.
5. Participate in the Wheelbarrow Relay demonstrating upper body strength, cooperative skills and following the instructions given by the instructor during the closing portion of class.

National Standards Met in this Lesson: 1, 2, 3, 4, 5, 6

INSTRUCTIONAL ACTIVITIES	TEACHING HINTS
INTRODUCTORY ACTIVITY (2 - 3 MINUTES)	
Flash Drill Stutter feet in place. Jump up and return to stuttering feet. Sit on floor and return to stuttering feet. Shuffle right. Shuffle left. Perform a forward roll, stand up stuttering.	**See DPESS Chapter 14 for details.** Bring students together in a scattered formation. Indicate activity area with cones.
FITNESS DEVELOPMENT (8 - 12 MINUTES)	
Jogging Students jog as far as they can. When tired, they can walk until able to resume jogging. Jogging involves cardiovascular endurance, make sure to pace yourself.	**See DPESS Chapter 16 for details.** Indicate activity area with cones.
LESSON FOCUS (15 - 20 MINUTES)	
Rock Climbing Hand and Foot Holds Demonstrate and explain use of: Open grip; Cling grip; Ring grip; Pocket grip; Pinch grip	Have students practice holds after each demonstration. Practice each grip after demonstration.
Foot Holds Demonstrate each of the foot holds and explain when to use each: Smearing; Edging; Back stepping; Rest step	Bring students together in scattered formation. Have students practice foot hold after each demonstration. Students can use a fence to practice.
Belaying and Rappelling: Discuss use of harness and safety when Belaying and Rappelling	Have each student pick up an equipment package.
Demonstrate: 1)Tying a double figure eight and a follow through knot on harness; 2) Attaching a carabiner to a rope through an ATC; 3)Use of guide hand and brake hand for slide; 4)Use of guide hand and brake hand for stopping; 5) Use of belaying commands.	Have students practice after each demonstration. Use management game to make groups of 3.
Videotape demonstrating Belaying & Rappelling	Show videotape to demonstrate belaying.
GAME (5 MINUTES)	
Wheelbarrow Relay All members of each squad must participate in both the carrying position and the floor wheelbarrow position in the race.	**See DPESS Chapter 18 for details.** Use management game to create partners. Combine pairs to create squads of four or six. Identify race area with cones.

EVALUATION/REVIEW AND CHEER

What is the function of a carabiner? What is the function of a camming device?
Which foot hold is used for a slightly rounded hold? Which foot hold uses the leg like a hand
Cheer: Rock climbing is a cool thing to DO!

Rock Climbing Lesson Plan 5

EQUIPMENT:

50 Cones
1 Flag for each student
Field trip permission slips and emergency information

OBJECTIVES:

The student will:

1. Participate in the Running Weave Drill demonstrating agility and the ability to follow the instructions described by the instructor.
2. Participate in Walk, Jog, and Sprint to improve aerobic and muscular endurance during the Fitness section of class.
3. Participate in the Field Trip to the Climbing Gym using skills mastered during the unit and following the instructions given by the instructor.

National Standards Met in this Lesson: **1, 2, 3, 4, 5, 6**

INSTRUCTIONAL ACTIVITIES	TEACHING HINTS

INTRODUCTORY ACTIVITY (2 - 3 MINUTES)

Running Weave Drill
Students run through a maze with a stride determined by the group leader.

See DPESS Chapter 14 for details.
Make four mazes with pairs of cones.
Use a management game to create four groups.
Use a management game to select a group leader.

 Challenge your peers while you are the leader, it will only make them stronger.

FITNESS DEVELOPMENT (8 - 12 MINUTES)

Walk, Jog, Sprint
Three whistles indicates sprint, two whistles indicates jog, and one whistle indicates walk.

See DPESS Chapter 16 for details.
Bring students together in scattered formation.
Establish movement area with cones.

LESSON FOCUS AND GAME OR WHOLE PERIOD (15 - 20 MINUTES)

Field Trip to Climbing Gym or Climbing Wall
Practice all skills by climbing the wall.

GAME (5 MINUTES)

Flag Grab
Students have a flag tucked in belt and attempt to keep others from pulling it out.

See DPESS Chapter 18 for details.
Scattered formation. Identify play area with cones.
Each student has a flag tucked into her/his shorts.

EVALUATION/REVIEW AND CHEER

Discuss experience putting skills into play on the climbing wall.

Cheer: Rock climbing is really great!

References:
Benge, M. and Raleigh, D., Climbing Rock, Carbondale, CO, Elk Mountain Press, 1995.

Long, J., How to Rock Climb, Evergren, CO, Chockstone Press, 1993.

ROCK CLIMBING EXAM

1. Name four good warm up exercises for rock climbing.

   ______________________ ______________________

   ______________________ ______________________

2. Name the three knots covered in this unit.

   ____

   ____

3. Name the piece of equipment that can be made out of 1" tubular webbing.

   ____

4. Name two varieties of carabiners.

   ____

5. Name a type of belaying/rappelling device.

   ____

6. Name two hand holds.

   ______________________ ______________________

7. Name two foot holds.

   ______________________ ______________________

8. Name the procedure for securing a climber by use of a rope.

   ____

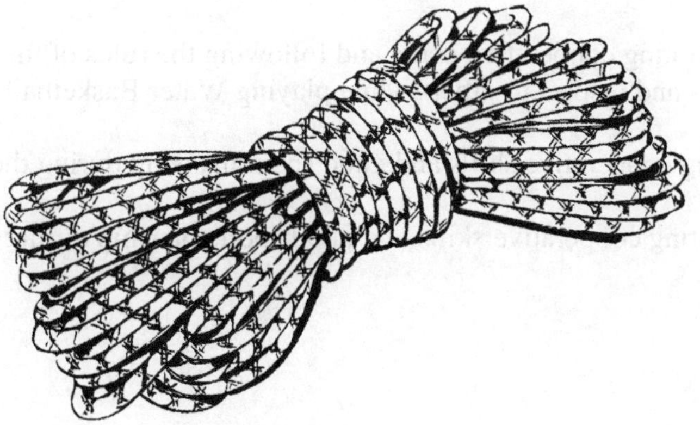

Swimming

This unit has been specifically designed to meet all six components of the NASPE National Standards for Physical Education.

OBJECTIVES:

The student will:

1. When asked, recite the pool rules and Emergency Action Plan governing the swim unit.
2. Rehearse the emergency action plan (EAP) listed on the handout following the instructions of the instructor.
3. Demonstrate entering and exiting the pool correctly using the form demonstrated by the instructor.
4. Participate in Marking during the Introductory Activity demonstrating locomotor skills in the water and cooperative skills.
5. Participate in the Lazy River Introductory activity to warm up the muscles in the body and the core temperature following the instructions directed by the teacher.
6. Perform resistance kicking and running through the shallow end of the pool during the Introductory Activities using form demonstrated by the instructor.
7. Participate in the Water Aerobics activities presented during Fitness to improve cardiovascular respiratory fitness and overall strength and fitness levels.
8. Participate in the Racetrack Fitness in the water to improve overall fitness levels.
9. Participate in Interval Training Treading Water exercises during Fitness to improve overall fitness levels.
10. Demonstrate flutter kicking with breathing while holding the kick board and moving across the width of the pool using form demonstrated by the instructor.
11. Demonstrate the front crawl with breathing the width of the pool using form demonstrated on the videotape and/or instructor.
12. Demonstrate the water safety skills of treading water, breathing, and front floating using form demonstrated by the instructor.
13. Demonstrate the backstroke across the width of the pool using form demonstrated on the videotape and by the instructor.
14. Demonstrate the skills of kicking, breathing, front crawl, back crawl and treading water learned during the semester working cooperatively with a partner to complete the Aquatic Skills Assessment Task Sheet.
15. Play water volleyball demonstrating cooperative skills and following the rules of the game.
16. Demonstrate cooperative skills and respect to others while playing Water Basketball during the game portion of class.
17. Play Five Passes demonstrating cooperative skills and good sportsmanship during the game portion of class.
18. Play Water Frisbee demonstrating cooperative skills and good sportsmanship during the game portion of class.

SWIMMING BLOCK PLAN 1 WEEK UNIT

Week #1	Monday	Tuesday	Wednesday	Thursday	Friday
Introductory Activity	Pool Rules Emergency Action Plan (EAP) Pool Entry/ Exit	EAP Practice	Marking	Partner Resistance Kicking	Lazy River
Fitness	Lazy River	Flutter Kick	Aqua Aerobics	Treading-Water Intervals	Racetrack Fitness in the Water
Lesson Focus	Water Safety: Treading Water Breathing Back Floating	Front Crawl Skills	Breathing Technique Front Crawl	Backstroke Skills	Partner Task Assessment Sheet
Game	Water Volleyball	Team Relay: Kicking with Boards	Water Basketball	Five Passes	Water Frisbee

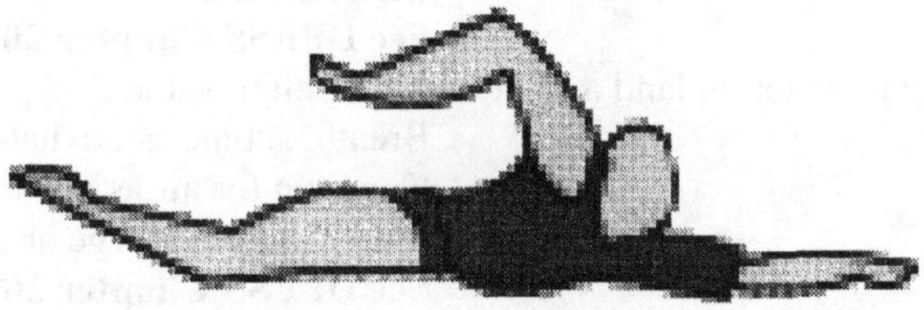

Lesson Plan 1

EQUIPMENT:

Emergency Action Plan information sheets 1 per student
Pool rules information sheets 1 per student
2 beach balls for Water Volleyball
Volleyball net and standards to stretch over pool shallow area

OBJECTIVES:

The student will:

1. Read and recite the pool rules and Emergency Action Plan governing the swim unit.
2. Demonstrate the proper method to enter and exit the shallow water.
3. Demonstrate the water safety skills of treading water, breathing, and front floating using form demonstrated by the instructor.
4. Play water volleyball demonstrating cooperative skills and following the rules of the game.

National Standards Met in this Lesson: **1, 2, 3, 4, 5, 6**

INSTRUCTIONAL ACTIVITIES	TEACHING HINTS
INTRODUCTORY ACTIVITY (2 - 3 MINUTES)	
Pool Rules, Emergency Action Plan (EAP)	**See DPESS Chapter 20 for details.**
FITNESS DEVELOPMENT (8 - 12 MINUTES)	
Lazy River Students walk slowly in the shallow end of the pool, as if they are wading through a river. Students walk in their own personal space.	**See DPESS Chapter 20 for details.** Teacher calls out new directions every 30–60 seconds. Examples of student walking directions: normal steps, short steps, long steps, backward steps, side steps, and leg crossovers.
LESSON FOCUS (15 - 20 MINUTES)	
Entering and exiting the pool Demonstrate proper method to enter and exit pool	**See DPESS Chapter 20 for details.**
Water Safety Skills—Treading Water, Breathing, Front Floating	**See DPESS Chapter 20 for details.**
Treading Water Demonstrate leg movements on land and in the water. Show video of skill.	**See DPESS Chapter 20 for details.** Practice first in chest-deep water. Keep body upright. Legs move in rhythmic motion. Hands cupped using sculling motion. Two leg styles: Bicycle leg pumping Scissors kick
Breathing Demonstrate breathing with face in water on land and in water.	**See DPESS Chapter 20 for details.** Waist-high water. Breath, submerge, exhale, blow bubbles under water. Come up for air as needed. Students resubmerge and repeat the process.
Front Float Demonstrate front floating in waist-deep water. Face in water, arms out to side, body supported in water. Demonstrate recovery from front float.	**See DPESS Chapter 20 for details.** Use Back-to-Back to create pairs. Waist deep water. Recovery: Student brings knees to chest, hands to sides.

You float because you are buoyant. Buoyancy is the phenomenon (discovered by Archimedes) that an object less dense than a fluid will float in the fluid.

INSTRUCTIONAL ACTIVITIES	TEACHING HINTS
GAME (5 MINUTES)	
Water Volleyball Focus on noncompetitive rallying.	Shallow water. Use Back-to-Back to create pairs. Use management skills to divide into two groups: 1 has hands on head; 1 has hands on waist Identify the side to move to if hands on head or waist.

EVALUATION/REVIEW AND CHEER

What was most difficult for you today?
What muscles did you use in class today?
Who discovered buoyancy?
Recite one pool rule.
Describe the emergency plans for the pool area.

Cheer: We can float. Thank you Archimedes!

Lesson Plan 2

EQUIPMENT:

1 kick board per student
Videotape/DVD of front crawl stroke

OBJECTIVES:

The student will:

1. Rehearse the emergency action plan (EAP) listed on the handout following the instructions of the teacher.
2. Demonstrate entering and exiting the pools correctly as demonstrated by the instructor.
3. Demonstrate flutter kicking with breathing while holding the kick board and moving across the width of the pool.
4. Demonstrate the front crawl arm stroke and breathing techniques using form demonstrated by the instructor.
5. Play the Kicking with Boards Relays game demonstrating cooperative skills, flutter kicking and following the rules set by the instructor.

National Standards Met in this Lesson: **1, 2, 3, 4, 5, 6**

INSTRUCTIONAL ACTIVITIES	TEACHING HINTS
INTRODUCTORY ACTIVITY (2 - 3 MINUTES)	
Practice EAP	**See DPESS Chapter 20 for details.**
FITNESS DEVELOPMENT (8 - 12 MINUTES)	
Walk/ Run through shallow water	Point what direction students should run.
Flutter Kick	**See DPESS Chapter 20 for details.** Show video/ DVD of today's skills.
Flutter kick repetitively	Students in shallow end holding edge of pool.
Flutter Kick with breathing	Place face in water and blow bubbles and breathe.
Flutter kick width of pool shallow end with kick board	Comment on improvement techniques when student reaches side of pool.
Flutter kick and breathing going width of pool	Use kick board. If necessary, have one student flutter kick across pool with kickboard and alternate students kick at wall.
LESSON FOCUS (15 - 20 MINUTES)	
Front Crawl Stroke	**See DPESS Chapter 20 for details.** Waist deep water Show videotape/ DVD on front crawl
Demonstrate skill while standing and bent at hip	Use wall for support. While standing and holding wall, practice arm stroke. Use kickboard hands extended to practice arm stroke. Move across width of pool kicking, holding kickboard, and using arm stroke. Move across width of pool kicking, holding kickboard, using arm stroke, and breathing.

INSTRUCTIONAL ACTIVITIES | **TEACHING HINTS**

The front crawl has been in use since ancient times. The front crawl was first reported observed in a competition held in 1844 in London, where it was swum by South American Indians, who easily defeated the British breaststroke swimmers. In the late 1800's, John Trudgen, combined the side stroke scissors kick with the front crawl arms. That became known as the Trudgen crawl and it is still used today in Lifesaving.

GAME (5 MINUTES)

Team Relay: Kicking with Boards

See DPESS Chapter 20 for details.
Use Whistle Mixer to create groups of 4 - 6
Perform flutter kick to wall and back. Pass off kickboard to next team member.
Alternate method: Divide each group in ½ and position ½ group across from the rest of the group. Each person flutter kicks with board one width only.

EVALUATION/REVIEW AND CHEER

What muscles were used in class today?
What is the history of the front crawl stroke?
What was the most challenging part of class today?

Cheer: Swimming makes me safe and cool!

Lesson Plan 3

EQUIPMENT:

Music for Water Aerobics 110 - 120 beats per minute
1 kickboard per person
2 floating basketball hoops
1 water polo ball

OBJECTIVES:

The student will:

1. Participate in Marking during the Introductory Activity demonstrating locomotor skills in the water and cooperative skills.
2. Participate in the Water Aerobics activities presented during Fitness to improve cardiovascular respiratory fitness and overall strength and fitness levels.
3. Demonstrate the front crawl with breathing the width of the pool using form demonstrated on the videotape and/or instructor.
4. Demonstrate cooperative skills and respect to others while playing Water Basketball during the game portion of class.

National Standards Met in this Lesson: **1, 2, 3, 4, 5, 6**

INSTRUCTIONAL ACTIVITIES | **TEACHING HINTS**

INTRODUCTORY ACTIVITY (2 - 3 MINUTES)

Marking

Partners walk through water, trying to lose his/ her partner. On the signal, both stop. The chaser must try to reach out and touch their partner to mark them. If the partner can be touched/ marked, that player receives 1 point. If the chaser cannot mark their partner, the walking partner receives a point. Partners then switch, with the chaser becoming the leading walker.

See DPESS Chapter 20 for details.
Use Elbow-to-Elbow to make pairs of students.
Shallow end of pool.
Identify one chaser and one runner in each pair.

INSTRUCTIONAL ACTIVITIES	TEACHING HINTS
FITNESS DEVELOPMENT (8 - 12 MINUTES)	
Water Aerobics Alternate aerobic movements with standing stretches, leg swings, twisting, bending. Aerobic movement ideas: walk forward, walk backward, jog forward, jog backward, march in place, jumping jacks, treading water, scissor kicks, jumping in place, side-to-side ski jumping.	**See DPESS Chapter 20 for details.** **See Casten, <u>Aqua Aerobics Today</u>, for in depth details on Aqua Aerobics workouts.** Play music alternating 30 seconds with 30 seconds of silence. During music, direct each locomotor movement. During silence direct the axial movements, stretching, leg swings, etc.
LESSON FOCUS (15 - 20 MINUTES)	
Front Crawl Stroke Review Review front crawl with a demonstration and practice.	**See DPESS Chapter 20 for details.** Start students on 1 wall in shallow end. Use kickboard to review. Direct distance across width of pool to practice the front crawl. Attempt without kickboard.
Breathing coordination with arm stroke Review stroke with breathing standing in shallow. Demonstrate and practice across width of pool.	**See DPESS Chapter 20 for details.** May use kick board again to introduce skill.
Breathing, arm stroke, and kicking	Demonstrate combined stroke. Practice combining breathing, arm stroke and kicking.

Swimming has been around since the beginning of time. Ancient wall drawings estimated to be about 6,000 years old depict men swimming. The Bible, the Iliad, the Odyssey all contains references to swimming.

GAME (5 MINUTES)	
Water Basketball A student cannot hold the ball longer than 3 seconds. A team must make three passes before attempting to shoot a basket.	**See DPESS Chapter 20 for details.** Use Elbow-to-Elbow to make pairs. Use management technique of one hand on head, one on waist and direct those with hands on head to go to one side of shallow end, the other group to other side pool. Place floating baskets at each end of shallow. Play non-contact Basketball.

EVALUATION/REVIEW AND CHEER

What muscles were used today in class?
What is challenging about the front crawl with breathing?
What was the most challenging about the game of Water Basketball?

Cheer: 1, 3, 4, Swimming floats my boat!

Lesson Plan 4

EQUIPMENT:

Fitness tape/CD/music 15 - 20 seconds' music, 10 - 15 seconds silence
Music player — 1 kickboard per student
Beach ball/ water polo ball

OBJECTIVES:

The student will:

1. Perform resistance kicking and running through the shallow end of the pool during the Introductory Activities using form demonstrated by the instructor.
2. Participate in Interval Training Treading Water exercises to improve fitness levels.
3. Demonstrate the backstroke using form demonstrated on the videotape and by the instructor.
4. Play Five Passes demonstrating cooperative skills and good sportsmanship.

National Standards Met in this Lesson: **1, 2, 3, 4, 5, 6**

INSTRUCTIONAL ACTIVITIES	TEACHING HINTS
INTRODUCTORY ACTIVITY (2 - 3 MINUTES)	
Resistance Kicking	**See DPESS Chapter 20 for details.** Student sits on side of pool and kicks feet up through water.
Run through shallow end	Run through shallow end pool following teacher directional arm signals.
FITNESS DEVELOPMENT (8 - 12 MINUTES)	
Interval Training Treading Water Treat water 15- 20 seconds, 10- 15 seconds to recover and stretch	**See DPESS Chapter 20 for details.** Scattered formation, shallow end of pool. Music directs timing of exercises.
LESSON FOCUS (15 - 20 MINUTES)	
Back Float Demonstrate back float	**See DPESS Chapter 20 for details.** Use Back-to-Back to create pairs. Shallow end of pool. One person stands next to other to help floating position.
Demonstrate push-off from wall and back float.	Hold kick board overhead and back float. Add push-off.
Backstroke Demonstrate arms out of water.	**See DPESS Chapter 20 for details.** Show videotape of backstroke. Practice arms out of water.
Demonstrate in water.	Practice push-off back float and add arms.
Demonstrate with kicking.	Hold on to side of wall and kick on back Hold kickboard overhead, back float, push-off, and flutter kick on back. Add backstroke arms to back float with flutter kick.

Backstroke is an ancient style of swimming, recorded before 1587. It was first included at the Olympic Games in 1900.

INSTRUCTIONAL ACTIVITIES	TEACHING HINTS
GAME (5 MINUTES)	
Five Passes Object of the game: First team to make five consecutive passes to five different players using a flotation ball, without losing possession of the ball. Players may not hold the ball longer than 3 seconds. If a team successfully makes five consecutive passes, they score 1 point, and possession goes to other team. If defense takes possession of ball, they begin their five passing attempts.	**See DPESS Chapter 20 for details.** Use management game to create 2 teams Scattered formation in shallow end of pool.

EVALUATION/REVIEW AND CHEER

What is challenging about running through water?
What muscles were used today?
Describe the back stroke movements.

Cheer: Splish, splash, swimming makes me dash!

Lesson Plan 5

EQUIPMENT:

1 Task Sheet per person
Music for Fitness
1 Frisbee per 2 people
1 Clipboard and pen per 2 people
Music Player

OBJECTIVES:

The student will:

1. Participate in the Lazy River Introductory activity to warm up the muscles in the body and the core temperature following the instructions directed by the teacher.
2. Participate in the Racetrack Fitness in the water to improve fitness levels.
3. Demonstrate the skills learned during the semester working cooperatively with a partner on Aquatic Skills Assessment Task Sheet.
4. Play Water Frisbee demonstrating cooperative skills and good sportsmanship.

National Standards Met in this Lesson: **1, 4, 5, 6**

INSTRUCTIONAL ACTIVITIES	TEACHING HINTS
INTRODUCTORY ACTIVITY (2 - 3 MINUTES)	
Lazy River Walk slowly through the water, as if wading through a river. Use arms to help pull you through water. Alternate walking with jogging.	**See DPESS Chapter 20 for details.** Shallow water. Scattered formation. Use music timed with 30 seconds for jogging, 30 second silence for walking. You can vary locomotors to leaping, carioca, etc.
FITNESS DEVELOPMENT (8 - 12 MINUTES)	
Racetrack Fitness in Water	**See DPESS Chapter 20 for details.**
LESSON FOCUS (15 - 20 MINUTES)	
Partner Task Assessment Sheet	**See DPESS Chapter 20 for details.** Task sheet below

Plato once declared that anyone who could not swim lacked a proper education, and Julius Caesar was known for his swimming prowess.

GAME (5 MINUTES)	
Water Frisbee **Cheer: Swimming keeps me safe!**	**See DPESS Chapter 20 for details.** Use management game to create 2 teams

Partner Task Assessment Sheet
Aquatics Skills

Student Name: ____

Student is a: ____ nonswimmer ____ beginning swimmer ____ experienced swimmer

Partner/ScorerName:____

Pool entry and exit: ______ Enters shallow end using feet first ______ Ensures no students are in path ______ Exits shallow end using two hands	**Emergency Action Plan response:** ______ Exits pool; goes to bleachers quickly ______ Sits in bleachers quietly ______ Remains calm and follows directions
Floating on back: ______ Holds head back and comfortably maintains a floating position. ______ Is able to limit arm and leg movement while floating	**Breathing technique for front crawl stroke**: ______ With face in water, can exhale, blowing bubbles ______ Turns head to side to take a breath, keeping side of head in water
Level of participation during fitness component: ______ Participates fully ______ Participates with reservations	**Treading water**: ______ Able to tread water comfortably for 30 seconds ______ Keeps body upright while treading
Front crawl skills: ______ Flutter kick movement starts from hips ______ Arms alternate using power phase and recovery	**Backstroke skills**: ______ Flutter kick movement from hips ______ Brings thumb out of the water first and submerges pinkie first

Table Tennis

This unit has been specifically designed to meet all six components of the NASPE National Standards for Physical Education.

OBJECTIVES:

The student will:

1. Participate in Move and Change Directions demonstrating quickness and pivoting skills
2. Practice Juggling 3 Scarves as instructed during the Introductory Activity.
3. Demonstrate agility while participating in Leap Frog, Seat Roll and Jog.
4. Demonstrate the ability to follow instructions and creativity during the Hoops and Plyometrics Introductory activity.
5. Participate in Circuit Training, Continuity Exercises, Fitness Scavenger and Aerobic workout to improve fitness.
6. Execute the forehand and backhand shots using form demonstrated by the instructor.
7. Execute the forehand and backhand serves using form demonstrated by the instructor.
8. Play Table Tennis following the rules in the class Round Robin Tournament.

TABLE TENNIS BLOCK PLAN
1 WEEK UNIT

Week #1	Monday	Tuesday	Wednesday	Thursday	Friday
Introductory Activity	Move and Change Directions	Juggling Scarves	Seat Roll and Jog	Hoops and Plyometrics	Leap Frog
Fitness	Circuit Training	Aerobic Workout	Fitness Scavenger Hunt	Partner Racetrack Fitness	Continuity Exercises
Lesson Focus	Forehand and Backhand Shots	Forehand and Backhand Serves Rules of the Game	Review all Skills Rally Describe Tournament	Round Robin Tournament	Round Robin Tournament
Game	Triangle Plus One Tag	Spider Tag	Entanglement		

Table Tennis Lesson Plan 1

EQUIPMENT:

Station cones and signs
Music/ CD and music player
1 table tennis/ ping pong ball per student
Music for Circuit Training
1 Ping pong racket per student
1 Table Tennis table per 4 students

OBJECTIVES:

The student will:

1. Participate in Move and Change Direction demonstrating agility, jogging skills, cooperative skills and following the instructions described by the instructor.
2. Participate in Circuit Training to improve their strength, endurance, and flexibility during the Fitness section of class.
3. Demonstrate forehand, backhand and ball control using form demonstrated by the instructor.
4. Participate the Triangle Plus 1 Tag game demonstrating cooperative skills as presented by the instructor during the closing portion of class.

National Standards Met in this Lesson: **1, 2, 3, 4, 5, 6**

INSTRUCTIONAL ACTIVITIES	TEACHING HINTS
INTRODUCTORY ACTIVITY (2 - 3 MINUTES)	
Move and Change Direction Students will jog towards each other and give high fives to the other group. Skip the other direction, return giving high fives as the students meet the other group again.	**See DPESS Chapter 14 for details.** Divide the student into two groups using Toe- to-Toe and then separating into two halves.
FITNESS DEVELOPMENT (8 - 12 MINUTES)	
Circuit Training When the music starts, each group will perform the exercise described on each labeled cone. When the music stops, students walk counter-clockwise to the next station performing arm circles.	**See DPESS Chapter 16 for details.** Using Whistle Mixer, make groups of 5 - 6 to begin at each station.
Exercises listed at **stations**: Push-ups, knee-lifts, jumping jacks, trunk twisters, sit-ups, arm extensions, single crab kicks, arms up and down, jog in place, triceps push- ups.	Place instructions for each station on cones set-up to identify location of station. Use illustrations to assist in understanding of the activities.
LESSON FOCUS (15 - 20 MINUTES)	
Racket and Ball Control **Demonstrate different ways of bouncing** the ball on the paddle in the air: forehand side of racket; backhand side; alternating hands; alternating forehand and backhand; bounce ball on table or floor.	Scattered formation. 1 racket and ball per student.
Open and Closed Racket Forehand and Backhand Student will use open and closed racket position to hit the ball over the net. Each student will hit five times and rotate counter clockwise.	Demonstrate at Table Tennis table. Student roles are: ball chasers, catcher, feeder and hitter.

Table tennis, also known as Ping Pong, originated in England in the 1880's as an after-dinner activity for upper-class Victorians. In the early 1900's the sport spread to China, Japan and Korea.

INSTRUCTIONAL ACTIVITIES	TEACHING HINTS
GAME (5 MINUTES)	
Triangle Plus 1 Tag Person outside triangle tries to tag leader. Leader and tagger change places when tagged.	**See DPESS Chapter 14 for details.** Create groups of 4 using management game. 3 make triangle formation holding hands. Select leader in group.

EVALUATION/REVIEW AND CHEER

What parts of the body did fitness cover today? What muscles were used?
Were there any activities you learned today that were particularly challenging
What is the history of Table Tennis?
Cheer: P.E. is fun!

Table Tennis Lesson Plan 2

EQUIPMENT:
3 Juggling Scarves per student
Music / CD and music player
1 Table Tennis ball per student
Aerobic workout music/CD
1 Table Tennis Racket per student

OBJECTIVES:
The student will:
1. Juggle 1, 2, and 3 scarves demonstrating concentration, eye-hand coordination and following the instructions described by the instructor.
2. Participate in Aerobic Workout to improve aerobic endurance, strength, muscular endurance, and flexibility during the Fitness section of class.
3. Demonstrate forehand, backhand serves and ball control using form demonstrated by the instructor.
4. Participate in the Spider Tag game demonstrating creativity, cooperative skills as presented by the instructor during the closing portion of class.

National Standards Met in this Lesson: 1, 2, 3, 4, 5, 6

INSTRUCTIONAL ACTIVITIES	TEACHING HINTS
INTRODUCTORY ACTIVITY (2 - 3 MINUTES)	
Juggling Scarves	**See DPESS Chapter 18 for details.**
Column juggling; Cascading juggling	Scattered formation; 3 scarves per student
FITNESS DEVELOPMENT (8 - 12 MINUTES)	
Aerobic Workout	**See DPESS Chapter 16 for details.**
	See Lesson 7, Racquetball Unit for details
LESSON FOCUS (15 - 20 MINUTES)	
Demonstrate the Forehand Drive stance, open and closed racket position.	Scattered formation
Each student hits ball 5 times using open and closed racket face position.	Rotate around the table clockwise.
Demonstrate Serves Forehand and Backhand	Ball placed in palm of hand for serve
Each student serves forehand 5 times. Rotate clockwise.	Stand side to target to serve
Each student serves backhand 5 times. Rotate clockwise.	5 balls per table
	Receivers catch balls for next person
Describe Table Tennis Rules	

Table tennis is the second-most popular sport in the world (after soccer).

GAME (5 MINUTES)	
Spider Tag	**See DPESS Chapter 14 for details.**
Pairs work together to tag other pairs	Using a management game, create partners
When tagged, they become "its"	Select on pair to be the "its"

EVALUATION/REVIEW AND CHEER
Review Table Tennis Rules.
Are there any questions about the Forehand or Backhand Serve that I taught you today?
Are there any questions about the Forehand or Backhand shot?
How popular is Table Tennis?

Cheer: PE (clap clap), PE (clap clap), PE (clap clap), yea!

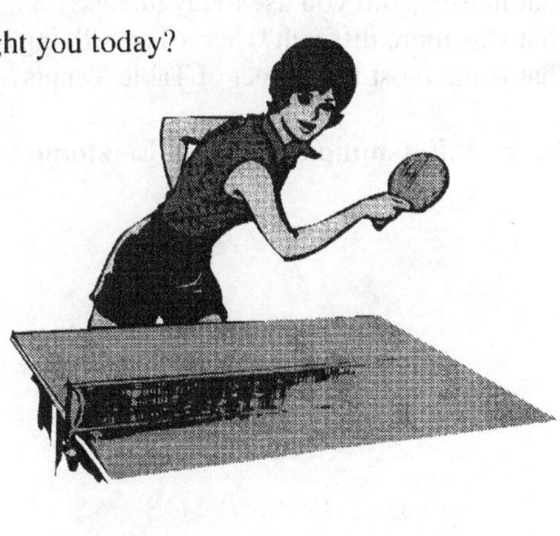

Table Tennis Lesson Plan 3

EQUIPMENT:
Fitness Scavenger Hunt Cards Music for Fitness (optional)
1 Table Tennis ball per student 1 Table Tennis Racket per student

OBJECTIVES:
The student will:
1. Participate in the Seat Roll and Jog demonstrating agility, jogging skills and following the instructions described by the instructor.
2. Participate in the Fitness Scavenger Hunt to improve aerobic endurance, strength, muscular endurance, and flexibility during the Fitness section of class.
3. Demonstrate forehand, backhand serves, rallying and ball control using form demonstrated by the instructor.
4. Participate in Entanglement demonstrating creativity and cooperative skills as presented by the instructor during the closing portion of class.

National Standards Met in this Lesson: **1, 2, 3, 4, 5, 6**

INSTRUCTIONAL ACTIVITIES	TEACHING HINTS
INTRODUCTORY ACTIVITY (2 - 3 MINUTES)	
Seat Roll and Jog	**See DPESS Chapter 14 for details.**
Direct students to seat roll right/left with hand signal.	Scattered formation.
Alternate rolls with jogging in place.	Student begins on "all fours" with head up looking at teacher for instructions.
FITNESS DEVELOPMENT (8 - 12 MINUTES)	
Fitness Scavenger Hunt	**See DPESS Chapter 16 for details.**
Exercises listed on scavenger cards at stations.	Use whistle mixer to create groups of 3. Assign each group to a starting point.
LESSON FOCUS (15 - 20 MINUTES)	
Review serves, forehand and backhand drives	Scattered around demonstration table
Rally using serves, forehand and backhand drives	Use Whistle Mixer to create groups of 4. Assign tables.

Modern table tennis at national and international levels is a very fast and rigorous sport requiring high levels of skill, physical fitness, and mental concentration.

GAME (5 MINUTES)	
Entanglement	**See DPESS Chapter 18 for details.**
Each group makes a tight circle with their arms.	Use Whistle Mixer to make several groups.

EVALUATION/REVIEW AND CHEER

What muscles did you use today in class?
What was more difficult? Serves or rallying? Why?
What is the most fun aspect of Table Tennis?

Cheer: P.E. (stomp feet 2 x), P.E. (stomp feet 2 x), P.E. (stomp feet 2 x), yea!

Table Tennis Lesson Plan 4

EQUIPMENT:

Round Robin Tournament Chart
Station cone markers and station signs for Fitness
1 Hoop per student

OBJECTIVES:

The student will:

1. Participate in the Hoops and Plyometrics demonstrating agility and following the instructions described by the instructor.
2. Participate in the Partner Racetrack Fitness to improve aerobic endurance, strength, muscular endurance, and flexibility during the Fitness section of class.
3. Participate in the Round Robin Table Tennis Tournament in class demonstrating good sportsmanship and using table tennis form demonstrated by the instructor.

National Standards Met in this Lesson: **1, 2, 3, 4, 5, 6**

INSTRUCTIONAL ACTIVITIES | **TEACHING HINTS**

INTRODUCTORY ACTIVITY (2 - 3 MINUTES)

Hoops and Plyometrics

Each student rolls the hoop while running. On signal, the hoops are dropped. Challenge students to move in and out of a given number of hoops specified by color. State locomotor movement to use. Student then picks up the hoop and resumes rolling it.

See DPESS Chapter 14 for details.
Scatter formation.
Each student has a hoop and listens for instructions..

Plyometric exercise is defined as a special type of strength training where the muscles are trained to rapidly contract. It is designed to improve your explosive strength.

FITNESS DEVELOPMENT (8 - 12 MINUTES)

Partner Racetrack Fitness

On signal 1 partner begins the first activity on station card while other jogs around perimeter. Switch roles, then perform next task alternating positions until they complete all tasks at the station. Rotate to next station. Task suggestions: Strengthening and stretching exercises i.e. sit-ups, push-ups, upper and lower body stretches, etc.

See DPESS Chapter 16 for details.
Use Back-to-Back to create partners.
Assign partners to a station to begin.
Explain station rotation.

LESSON FOCUS AND GAME (20 MINUTES)

Create Round Robin Table Tennis Tournament

Have teams determined ahead of time or use Whistle Mixer to determine teams.

See DPESS Chapter 13 for details.
Assign teams to tables for tournament play.

EVALUATION/REVIEW AND CHEER

During Fitness today, you participated in Plyometric activities. Define Plyometrics and what it is designed to improve. What was the most challenging aspect of the Tournament play? Are you ready to continue tomorrow? Are there any questions about the rules of the game?

Cheer: Table Tennis, yes!

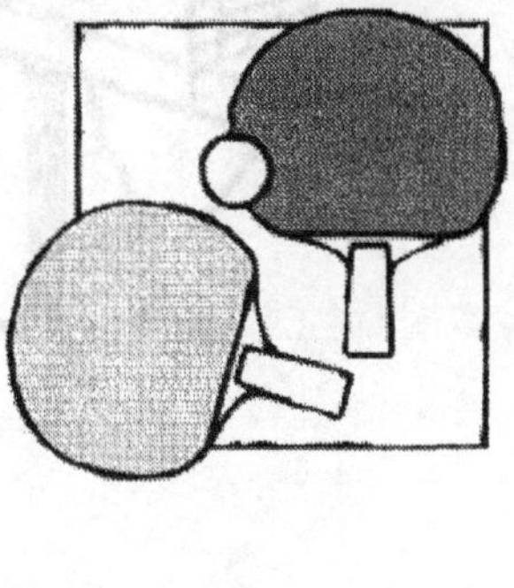

Table Tennis Lesson Plan 5

EQUIPMENT:

Continuity exercise music/ CD
1 Paddle per person
Round Robin Tournament Chart
CD/ Music player
2 Table Tennis balls per table

OBJECTIVES:

The student will:

1. Participate in Leap Frog demonstrating agility, cooperative skills and following the instructions described by the instructor.
2. Participate in Continuity Exercises to improve aerobic endurance, strength, muscular endurance, and flexibility during the Fitness section of class.
3. Participate in the Round Robin Table Tennis Tournament in class demonstrating good sportsmanship and using table tennis form demonstrated by the instructor.

National Standards Met in this Lesson: **1, 2, 3, 4, 5, 6**

INSTRUCTIONAL ACTIVITIES	TEACHING HINTS

INTRODUCTORY ACTIVITY (2 - 3 MINUTES)

Leap Frog
See Badminton, Lesson 11 for details

See DPESS Chapter 18 for details.
Using Whistle Mixer, create groups of 5.

FITNESS DEVELOPMENT (8 - 12 MINUTES)

Continuity Exercises

See DPESS Chapter 16 for details.

When you perform Continuity Exercises you are participating in a type of resistance training whereby your own body weight provides resistance. The goal of resistance training, according to the American Sports Medicine Institute (ASMI), is to "gradually and progressively overload the musculoskeletal system so it gets stronger."

LESSON FOCUS AND GAME (20 MINUTES)

Create Round Robin Table Tennis Tournament
Continue play with teams from yesterday

See DPESS Chapter 13 for details.

EVALUATION/REVIEW AND CHEER

Explain how Continuity Exercises help you.
What was the most challenging aspect of the Tournament play today?

Cheer: Table Tennis rocks!

NAME:________________________________ **CLASS PERIOD:**________

TABLE TENNIS EXAM

1. Select the correct order of techniques for a table tennis serve in a doubles match.
   a. Toss the ball 10 inches in the air, bounce the ball on the table, hit on the - opponents side of the table.
   b. Using the palm of the hand toss the ball up 6 inches; hit the ball on the way down. Player must be behind the end of the table; the ball must bounce once on the server's side of the table and go over the net on the diagonal to the opponent's side of the table.
   c. Using the forefinger and the thumb toss the ball in the air, hit the ball on the way down, standing behind the end of the table, the ball must bounce once on the servers side and go over the net on the diagonal to the opponents side.

Use key below for questions 2 & 3

a. A netball b. A let ball
c. The first fault d. A good serve

2. If the serve strikes the top of the net and still goes in. This is called a...

3. If the serve goes into the net and comes back over to the server's side of the table. This is called

4. How many times does a player serve before the other player gets a turn to serve?

   a. One b. Two
   c. Four d. Five

5. The server must toss the ball
   a. At least 4 inches in the air b. At least 5 inches in the air
   c. 6 inches in the air d. 10 inches in the air

6. A game is played to how many points?
   a. 21 b. 15
   c. 11 d. 13

7. If a game is tied 20-20, by how many points do you need to win?
   a. One point b. Two points
   c. Three points d. Five

8. Table Tennis is a high paying professional sport in some countries. True/ False

9. Is it legal to volley in Table Tennis? True/ False

10. If the ball hits the edge of the table is it considered good?
   a. Yes b. No
   c. Sometimes d. Never

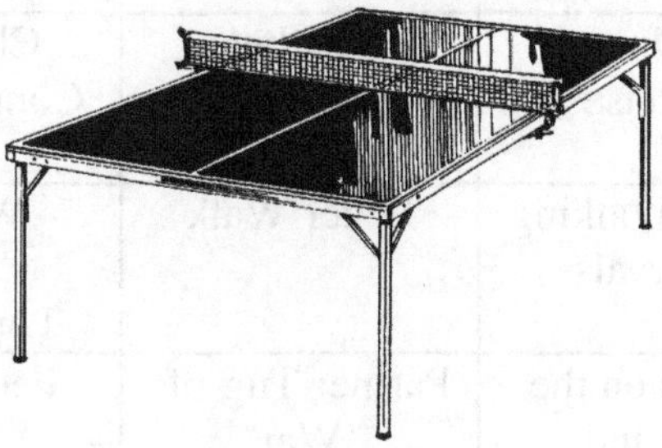

Walking

This unit has been specifically designed to meet all six components of the NASPE National Standards for Physical Education.

OBJECTIVES:

The student will:

1. Demonstrate agility, starting, stopping and stretching skills during the Move and Stretch Activity.
2. Demonstrate quickness and teamwork during Run and Lead and Vanishing Beanbags.
3. Demonstrate safety skills explained by the instructor while participating in Individual Stunts.
4. Demonstrate agility and dodging skills during the introductory activities.
5. Participate strengthening and stretching exercises, jump roping activities, during the Fitness Challenge Course Circuit, Parachute Rhythmic Activities, Four Corners Fitness activities, Continuity Exercises, and Squad Leader Exercises to improve their overall fitness levels.
6. Play Tug-of-War challenges with a partner.
7. Participate in Wand Whirl, Hoops on the Ground, Fetch Relay and Over and Under Relays demonstrating cooperation and good sportsmanship.
8. Follow all instructions in the use of the Pedometers as explained in class by the instructor.
9. Participate in Speed Walking Intervals using full speed as directed.
10. Continuously walk as instructed during the Poker Walk activity.
11. Follow the rules of the Walking "Golf" Tournament during class and demonstrate courtesy to other class members.
12. Complete the "I Spy" Walking Challenge card as directed by the instructor.
13. Play Wand Whirl demonstrating focus and quickness.
14. Play Hoops on the Ground following the instructions described by the instructor.
15. Participate in Individual Tug-of-War activities carefully following the safety rules.
16. Play Fetch Relay running as quickly as possible.
17. Play Over and Under Relay while passing the ball as carefully and quickly and demonstrating agility.

WALKING BLOCK PLAN
1 WEEK UNIT

Week #1	Monday	Tuesday	Wednesday	Thursday	Friday
Introductory Activity	Square Drill	Run and Lead	Individual Stunts	Move and Stretch	Vanishing Bean Bags
Fitness	Squad Leader Exercises	Continuity Exercises	Parachute Rhythmic Activity	Challenge Course Circuit	Four Corners
Lesson Focus	Pedometer Introductory Activities	Speed Walking Intervals	Poker Walk	Walking "Golf" Tournament	"I Spy" Walking Challenge
Game	Wand Whirl	Hoops on the Ground	Partner Tug-of-War	Fetch Relay	Over and Under Relay

Walking Lesson Plan 1

EQUIPMENT:

1 pedometer per student
Cones to mark perimeter
Music for fitness
1 wand per student
Cones on which to put Squad Leader Exercise Cards
Music player

OBJECTIVES:

The student will:

1. Participate in Square Drill demonstrating agility, shuffling skills, cooperative skills and following the instructions described by the instructor.
2. Participate in Squad Leader Exercises to improve their strength, endurance, and flexibility during the Fitness section of class.
3. Demonstrate the proper use of pedometers as demonstrated by the instructor.
4. Participate in Wand Activities demonstrating creativity and cooperative skills as presented by the instructor during the closing portion of class.

National Standards Met in this Lesson: **1, 2, 3, 4, 5, 6**

INSTRUCTIONAL ACTIVITIES	TEACHING HINTS
INTRODUCTORY ACTIVITY (2 - 3 MINUTES)	
Square Drill	**See DPESS Chapter 14 for details.** The class forms several 10-yard squares with boundary cones. Students stand in the middle of each side of the square and face the center. On signal, they shuffle around the square to the left or right, depending on the signal of the teacher. A student can be in the center of the square to give a direction signal.
FITNESS DEVELOPMENT (8 - 12 MINUTES)	
Squad Leader Exercises **Exercises for Upper-Body Development** • Push-Ups • Reclining Partner Pull-Ups • Rocking Chair • Crab Walk **Exercises for the Midsection** • Reverse Curl • Pelvis Tilter • Knee Touch Curl-Up • Curl-Up with Twist • Leg Extension	**See DPESS Chapter 16 for details.** Squad leaders take their squad to a designated area and put the squad through a fitness routine that you have written on a station card. Background music can be used.

Core exercises are an important part of a well-rounded fitness program. The Squad Leader Exercises work your core muscles as well as your upper body. Your body's core is the area around your trunk and pelvis. When you have strong core muscles and good core stability, the muscles in your pelvis, lower back, hips and abdomen work in harmony. Strong core muscles make it easier to do most physical activities.

INSTRUCTIONAL ACTIVITIES	TEACHING HINTS

LESSON FOCUS (15 - 20 MINUTES)

Demonstrate and explain the use of pedometers
Direct students to:
On signal, students move to their assigned container, pick up a pedometer and put it on while walking. As soon as the pedometer is in place, students should reset the pedometer and keep walking. As soon as they have completed putting on their pedometers on the move, freeze the class and ask them to reset their pedometers.

See DPESS Chapter 15 for details.
Organize class into small groups of 5-6 students using Whistle Mixer.
Pedometers (6) are placed in containers around the area.
Reinforce students who accumulate the most activity time (they will have been the quickest to get their pedometers in place).

Walk as fast as possible for 30 seconds.
After 30 seconds, drop down to an easy pace for 30 seconds. Repeat the 30 seconds speed and 30 second rest 8-12 times. Cool down with a 10-minute easy pace walk.

Identify the perimeters of a walking course

Notice how many steps were taken during the 30 seconds.

Estimation How Many Steps does it Take? Measure off a distance that is exactly one-eighth or one-fourth mile in length.

Reset pedometer at the starting line and walk at a normal pace to the end of the distance. Depending on whether they walked a one-eighth or one-fourth-mile distance, they multiply the number of steps they accumulated by 8 or 4. That is the number of steps it takes them to walk one mile.

Have students record on a task sheet how many steps they took during the lesson focus and how many steps a mile will take.

GAME (5 MINUTES)

WAND ACTIVITIES
Wand Whirl
Stand wand in front of body. Balance it with 1 finger. Release, turn, and catch the wand.

See DPESS Chapter 18 for details.
Scattered formation

Wand Balance and Change

Work with a partner.
Each person holds wand in vertical position.
On signal, run across to where partner's wand is and try to catch it before it falls.

Wand Kick over Begin same as Whirl, but leg kick over the wand before turning.

Wand Wrestle
Goal: move the wand to a horizontal plane.

EVALUATION/REVIEW AND CHEER

Explain the importance of core exercises.
Have students record how many steps they took in class
Ask students how many steps they found it takes to walk a mile.
Were there any problems using the pedometer?
What was the most challenging fitness activity?
What muscles were used in fitness?
What was the most challenging Wand activity?
Cheer: Pedometers count my steps, yea!

Walking Lesson Plan 2

EQUIPMENT:

Cones to mark perimeter of teaching area
Continuity fitness music CD/tape
1 pedometer per student
Music player
1 hoop per student
Pedometer storage box

OBJECTIVES:

The student will:

1. Participate in Run and Lead demonstrating jogging skills, cooperative skills and following the instructions described by the instructor.
2. Participate in Continuity Exercises to improve strength, endurance, and flexibility during the Fitness section of class.
3. Demonstrate walking and checking pedometers as demonstrated by the instructor.
4. Participate in Hoops on the Ground demonstrating cooperative skills as presented by the instructor during the closing portion of class.

National Standards Met in this Lesson: **1, 2, 3, 4, 5, 6**

INSTRUCTIONAL ACTIVITIES	TEACHING HINTS

INTRODUCTORY ACTIVITY (2 - 3 MINUTES)

Run and Lead (Similar to File Running)
Students jog in formation. Last person sprints to front of line to become leader.

See DPESS Chapter 16 for details.
Line or circle formation

FITNESS DEVELOPMENT (8 - 12 MINUTES)

Continuity Exercises
See Badminton Unit, Lesson 3 for complete details.

See DPESS Chapter 18 for details.
Scattered formation

Continuity Exercises help you develop aerobic endurance, upper body strength and core strength. Core exercises help you strengthen your core muscles. Any exercise that uses the trunk of your body without support will develop your core. Think squats, push-ups and abdominal crunches to work on your core muscles.

LESSON FOCUS (15 - 20 MINUTES)

Checking pedometer
Show students how to gently move it up and down (ceiling to floor) to see if it is counting correctly. Ask students to reset their pedometer and practice comparing shakes with the pedometer step counts. Ask students to hold the pedometer with the display parallel to the floor. Now shake it up and down. Note that it won't count steps or time when it is in this position.

- Have students put pedometer on by taking it from their assigned container. As soon as the pedometer is in place, students should reset the pedometer and keep walking.
- Shaking the pedometer too hard will prevent the pedometer from counting accurately. The pedometer measures very small up and down movement.

Speed walking intervals
Walk fast for 8 minutes.
Then slow down to an easy pace for 2 minutes.
Repeat this for 2 repetitions. Cool down for 2 minutes at an easy pace.

- Have students record how many steps they took during the Speed Walking intervals.
- Replace the pedometers in the proper containers after they have been reset.
- Record steps on a task sheet you create.

GAME (5 MINUTES)

Hoops on the Ground
Spread hoops around the area and give directions to move around using locomotor movements and freeze inside a hoop.

See DPESS Chapter 14 for details.
Scattered formation.

EVALUATION/REVIEW AND CHEER

Did you take more steps during the lesson focus today than yesterday?
What part of the lesson focus was the most enjoyable today? Why?
What muscles did you work during fitness?
What did fitness focus on today?
Cheer: Pedometers help me count my steps!

Walking Lesson Plan 3

EQUIPMENT:

Several decks of cards for Poker Walk
Cones to mark teaching area
1 Individual tug-of-war rope per two students
Parachute
Music CD/tape for fitness

OBJECTIVES:

The student will:

1. Participate in Individual Stunts cooperative skills and following the instructions described by the instructor.
2. Participate in Parachute Rhythmic Aerobic Activity to improve endurance and flexibility during the Fitness section of class.
3. Participate in the Poker Walk as demonstrated by the instructor.
4. Participate in Partner Tug-of-War demonstrating cooperative skills and safety skills as presented by the instructor during the closing portion of class.

National Standards Met in this Lesson: **1, 2, 3, 4, 5, 6**

INSTRUCTIONAL ACTIVITIES	TEACHING HINTS
INTRODUCTORY ACTIVITY (2 - 3 MINUTES)	
Individual Stunts Leg dip; Behind Back Touch; Double Heel Click	**See DPESS Chapter 18 for details.** Scattered formation Explain stunts and student practices
FITNESS DEVELOPMENT (8 - 12 MINUTES)	
Parachute Rhythmic Aerobic Activity • Skip both directions • Slide both directions • Run both directions • Jump to center • Hop backward • Lift parachute overhead • Lower parachute to toes • Repeat above • Run CW with chute overhead • Make a dome • Strengthening and stretching exercises	**See DPESS Chapter 16 for details.** Direct locomotor movements while holding parachute. Use music to motivate. Alternate locomotor movements with seated strength and stretching exercises.
LESSON FOCUS (15 - 20 MINUTES)	
Put pedometer on. **Poker Walk** Students walk to the areas and pick up one card without looking at the card. They walk to as many areas as possible within a time limit and then add up the points.	**See DPESS Chapter 15 for details.** **Distribute pedometers** • Pre-arrange several decks of cards at set areas around walking area • Have a prize for high- and low-point totals and then change the rules each time. Set it up so anyone can win by just walking to the card areas, picking up the card, and then adding up the points at the end of the time limit.
GAME (5 MINUTES)	
Partner Tug-of-War Pull facing partner Pull with backs to partners and between legs Pull on foot in crab walk position Other foot	**See DPESS Chapter 18 for details.** Use management game to create pairs. 1 rope per 2 students

EVALUATION/REVIEW AND CHEER

Check pedometer steps for the day and compare to previous days
What was the hardest tug-of-war activity?
Cheer: Walking keeps me fit!

Walking Lesson Plan 4

EQUIPMENT:

1 pedometer per student
Cones to mark perimeters of teaching area
Hoops for Walking Tournament
1 tennis ball per student
Cones to mark fitness Challenge Course Circuit
4 mats for fitness
Signs for Challenge Course
Wands for fitness course
Music for fitness
Music player for fitness
Balance bench
6 individual jump ropes

OBJECTIVES:

The student will:

1. Participate in Move and Stretch demonstrating locomotor and stretching skills while following the instructions described by the instructor.
2. Participate in the Challenge Course Circuit to improve endurance and flexibility during the Fitness section of class.
3. Participate in the Walking Golf Tournament following rules described by the instructor.
4. Participate in the Fetch Relay game demonstrating agility and cooperative skills as presented by the instructor during the closing portion of class.

National Standards Met in this Lesson: **1, 2, 3, 4, 5, 6**

INSTRUCTIONAL ACTIVITIES	TEACHING HINTS

INTRODUCTORY ACTIVITY (2 - 3 MINUTES)

Move and Stretch

See DPESS Chapter 14 for details.

- Students run within set perimeter and perform stretches upon designated signal. Use flash cards to signal stretches.
- Both Arms Up: stretch high
- Touch Toes
- Hamstring Stretch: Right leg forward left back with heal on ground. Hold 30 seconds and switch.
- Standing Hip Bend: Both sides. Hold 20 seconds each side.
- Wishbone Stretch: Hands clasped behind back and lean forward.

Scattered formation

Teacher calls instructions

FITNESS DEVELOPMENT (8 - 12 MINUTES)

Challenge Course Circuit

See DPESS Chapter 16 for details.

Set up 3-4 parallel (side-by-side) courses in one-half of the area.

Movement should be continuous.

Course 1. Crouch jumps; pulls, or scooter movements or balance down a bench; agility hop through two hoops on floor. Skip, slide, or jog to a cone.

Arrange three or four courses with a group at each course.

Course 2. Weave in and out of four wands held upright by cones; Crab walk between two cones: lead with feet once, hands once. Gallop to a cone.

Students perform the challenges from start to finish and jog back to repeat the course. On signal, groups move to a new course.

Course 3. Do a tumbling activity length of mat; agility run through hoops; Leap frog over partner alternating roles between cones.

Rotate groups to each course after a specified time. Music can be used for motivation and to signal changes.

Course 4. Curl-ups and push-ups on a mat. Sitting stretches. Jump rope in place.

INSTRUCTIONAL ACTIVITIES | **TEACHING HINTS**

Flexibility is defined as the range of motion at a given joint. Having good flexibility allows you to increase your physical performance, allowing the joint the ability to move further with less energy. If we don't work on flexibility one day, be sure to work on it on your own.

LESSON FOCUS (15 - 20 MINUTES)

Walking "golf" tournament

Students throw the ball into a hoop and then walk with their group to a hoop. Students use a scorecard to keep track of the number of throws for each hole.

See DPESS Chapter 15 for details.
Put on pedometers
Use hula hoops for holes
Set the course up around your teaching space with cones for the tees
Each student has an old tennis ball
Play Whistle Mixer to create even groups
Provide scorecard

GAME (5 MINUTES)

Fetch Relay

Squads line up and place 1 member at the other end of the playing area, 10 to 20 yards away. This person runs back to the squad and fetches the next person. The person who has just been fetched in turn runs back and fetches the next person. The pattern continues until all members have been fetched to the opposite end of the playing area.

See DPESS Chapter 18 for details.

Use Whistle Mixer to create groups of 4-5.

Create lines/squad formation with each group.

Identify first player to go to opposite end of playing area.

EVALUATION/REVIEW AND CHEER

How many steps did you take in class today? How did that compare to previous lessons?
What was challenging about the Walking Tournament?
What areas of the body did fitness work on today?
How many steps did you take today in comparison to the steps you took yesterday?
Collect pedometers

Cheer: We always do our best, and soar above the rest!

Walking Lesson Plan 5

EQUIPMENT:

Challenge cards for "I Spy"
1 Beanbag per person
4 cones for Four Corners
1 rubber ball per 4 students for game
Cones to outline teaching area
Signs for each corner

OBJECTIVES:

The student will:

1. Participate in Vanishing Bean Bags demonstrating locomotor and cooperative skills while following the instructions described by the instructor.
2. Participate in Four Corners to improve strength, endurance and flexibility during the Fitness section of class.
3. Participate in the I Spy Walking Challenge following rules described by the instructor.
4. Participate in the Over and Under Ball Relay game demonstrating agility and cooperative skills as presented by the instructor during the closing portion of class.

National Standards Met in this Lesson: **1, 2, 3, 4, 5, 6**

INSTRUCTIONAL ACTIVITIES | **TEACHING HINTS**

INSTRUCTIONAL ACTIVITIES | **TEACHING HINTS**

INTRODUCTORY ACTIVITY (2 – 3 MINUTES)

Vanishing Bean Bags

Spread beanbags throughout the area to allow 1 per student. Students move around the area until a signal is given. On the signal, they find a beanbag and sit on each. Each round, direct a new locomotor movement task and take away a beanbag.

See DPESS Chapter 14 for details.

Scatter formation

FITNESS DEVELOPMENT (8 – 12 MINUTES)

Four Corners

Outline a large rectangle with four cones. Place signs with tasks on both sides of the cones. Students move around the outside of the rectangle and change their movement pattern as they approach a corner sign.

The following movement tasks are suggested:

1. Jogging
2. Skipping/Jumping/Hopping
3. Sliding/Galloping
4. Abdominal strengthening exercises
5. Upper body strengthening exercises
6. Side leg work
7. Full body stretches

See DPESS Chapter 16 for details.

Use Whistle Mixer to create 4 equal groups.

Assign each group a corner to begin at.

LESSON FOCUS (15 – 20 MINUTES)

"I Spy" Walking Challenge

Challenge Cards:

Identify all of the makes of cars you see on your walk.
Identify all of the colors of the cars you see.
List as many different birds you see on the walk.
List as many different animals you see on the walk
How many people did you walk by?

See DPESS Chapter 15 for details.

Distribute pedometers
Distribute "I Spy" Challenge Cards
Explain perimeters of walking course
Use whistle mixer to make ever groups

A recent study showed that a moderate level of physical activity, such as walking 30 minutes a day, lengthened life by 1.3 years and added 1.1 more years without cardiovascular disease, compared with those with more sedentary lifestyles.

GAME (5 MINUTES)

Over and Under Ball Relay

Distribute 1 ball per group

See DPESS Chapter 17 for details.

Use Whistle Mixer to create lines/squads of 5-6.
Assign spaces for lines leaving room between lines.

EVALUATION/REVIEW AND CHEER

What is the value of walking for health?
Have one student from each group report on what they wrote on their challenge cards.
Was there a common car most people saw?
What was the main animal passed on the walk?
How did your steps compare today to the number you took yesterday during the lesson focus?

Cheer: 10,000 steps is my goal!

Walking Golf Tournament Score Card

Directions: Work with your group. Place all of your names on the scorecard. Record how many throws it takes each person to make a hole. Do not try more than 3 times. 3 would be the maximum anyone would score. You are striving for a low team score.

Begin the course on the hole number assigned by your teacher and complete the course progressing to each hole. Walk as briskly as possible between holes.

NAME	HOLE NUMBER							
	1	2	3	4	5	6	7	8
1.								
2.								
3.								
4.								
5.								
6.								

"I Spy" Walking Scorecard

Directions: Work with your group in the area designated by your teacher. Place all of your names on the scorecard. Record how many of the following you see on your walk:
Identify all of the makes of cars you see on your walk.
Identify all of the colors of the cars you see.
List as many different birds you see on the walk.
List as many different animals you see on the walk
How many people did you walk by?

NAME	"I Spy" the items listed below							
	Makes of Cars		Birds		Animals		People	
		color	#	type	#	type	# M	# F
1.								
2.								
3.								
4.								
5.								
6.								

Aerobics

This unit has been specifically designed to meet all six components of the NASPE National Standards for Physical Education.

OBJECTIVES:

The student will:

1. Participate in the introductory games of Hospital Tag and Vanishing Bean Bags while demonstrating agility, the ability to follow instructions and cooperation as described by the instructor.
2. Participate in the standing Aerobics routine during the fitness and lesson focus sections of class using form and movements demonstrated by the instructor.
3. Participate in the stretch, isolation and strengthening movements using form and movements demonstrated by the instructor.
4. Play Triangle plus One Tag and Balance Tag using movements described by the instructor while demonstrating cooperation and good sportsmanship with classmates.

AEROBICS BLOCK PLAN
2 DAY UNIT

Two Day Unit Plan	Day One	Day Two
Introductory Activity	Hospital Tag	Vanishing Bean Bags
Fitness	Combine fitness and lesson focus today to focus on Aerobics Routine	Combine fitness and lesson focus today on Aerobics Routine
Lesson Focus		
Game	Triangle plus one Tag	Balance Tag

Aerobics Lesson Plan 1

EQUIPMENT:

Aerobic Music/ CD

CD/ Music player

OBJECTIVES:

The student will:

1. Play Hospital Tag demonstrating speed, agility, cooperation and following the rules established by the instructor.
2. Participate in the standing Aerobics routine during the fitness and lesson focus sections of class using form and movements demonstrated by the instructor.
3. Play Triangle plus One Tag using movements described by the instructor while demonstrating cooperation and good sportsmanship with classmates.

National Standards Met in this Lesson: **1, 3, 4, 5, 6**

INSTRUCTIONAL ACTIVITIES	TEACHING HINTS
INTRODUCTORY ACTIVITY (2–3 MINUTES)	
Hospital Tag	**DPESS pages 312–313** Select several students to be the "medics."
COMBINE FITNESS AND LESSON FOCUS TODAY (20–25 MINUTES)	
Aerobic Workout Routine	**Casten, C. and Jordan, P.** ***Aerobics Today, 2nd Ed.*** **Wadsworth, 2002.**
Walk in place while moving arms from hips to overhead.	32 counts
Step to the right and touch your left toe to the right, then step to the left and touch the left toe next to the left foot	8 times
Hop on the left foot 4 times while pointing and tapping the right foot forward and then to the side (for example, forward, side, forward, feet together on count 4, jump/change sides).	Repeat the entire phrase while hopping (bouncing) on the right foot 4 times and tapping the left foot forward and to the side as described. Repeat the phrase again on each side.
Run in place 8 times, clap on each run.	
Do 8 jumping jacks using full arm movements.	
Slide to the right 8 times, clap on the 8th slide.	Repeat to the left.
Jump in place 8 times while hitting the sides of your thighs with straight arms.	
Run in place 8 times while lifting your feet high in the rear.	
Run in place 8 times while lifting your knees high in front.	Repeat the two running in place phrases
Perform 8 jumping jacks, moving your arms down and up in coordination with the leg movements.	
Perform 8 jumping jacks, moving your arms down and only half way up (to the shoulder level) in coordination with each leg movement.	
Mountain Climber	With your feet separated, jump and land forward and backward a distance of about one foot. Alternate feet as you land in front and in back on each jump. Your arms can swing high in opposition to the leg movements.
Pony: "Hop, step, step." Hop on the right foot to the side, and then quickly step with the left foot and then the right foot.	Repeat on the other side.
Heel, toe, slide, slide: Hop on the left foot while tapping the right heel to the right side. While hopping again on the left foot, swing the right foot to the front and touch the toe on the floor. Perform 2 slides to the right.	Repeat the entire phrase by hopping on the right foot and sliding to the left.
Hop on one foot and lift up the opposite knee.	Reverse.

INSTRUCTIONAL ACTIVITIES	TEACHING HINTS
Hop on one foot, and swing kick the opposite foot forward.	Reverse.
Charleston Bounce Step: Use a very bouncy step throughout this phrase. Step right, kick the left foot forward, step back on the left foot, and touch the right toe back.	Repeat 8 times. Reverse with opposite foot leading.
Can-Can Kick: Hop on the right foot, and simultaneously bring the bent left knee up high in front. Hop again on the right foot, lightly touch the left foot on the floor next to the right, and kick the left foot into the air forward and up.	Repeat 4 times and then repeat on the other side. A more advanced version involves alternating sides after each kick.
Walk in place while moving arms from hips to overhead.	32 counts
Walk in place. While staying near the hips, hands are flexed, and move away from the body and back towards the hips.	32 counts
STRETCHES AND ISOLATIONS	
Head isolations	Repeat the set 4 to 8 times.
Lift head up and down. Turn head to the right and then the left.	Caution: All head and neck exercises should be performed smoothly and in a relaxed manner. If the neck is allowed to arch or roll back, unnecessary tension could be placed on the cervical vertebrae.
Shoulder Circles	Reverse the direction of the roll, and repeat it 8 times.
In a slow, smooth manner, circle shoulders forward, up, back, and around 8 times.	
Rib Isolations	Repeat by reversing the direction of the rib isolations.
While standing with good posture, place hands on hips (this helps keep hips from moving). Move ribs forward, back to center, to the side, back to center, to the back, back to center, to the other side, and back to center.	
Rib Circles	Perform them several times in each direction.
Perform rib circles the same way as the rib isolations, but in a continuous manner.	
Hip Isolations	Repeat 8 times.
While standing with good posture, slightly bend the knees. Now smoothly tilt the pelvis forward and then backward.	
Hip Swings	Repeat 8 times. Be sure to execute these movements in a smooth, sustained manner.
Tilt hips and pelvic area to the right and then the left.	
Hip Circles	Reverse the direction and perform the hip circles the same number of times. Keep movements smooth and sustained. Jerking movements should be avoided.
While standing with good posture, slightly bend knees. Smoothly circle hips forward, to the side, to the back, and to the other side. Continue circling hips at least 8 times.	
Deep Lunge	Hold this position for 20 seconds.
Begin in a standing position with good posture. With feet parallel, take a large step forward on one foot. Assume a deep lunge position, place hands on each side of the knee. The heel of the forward foot must remain on the floor, and the knee should be directly above the foot. Keep the extended back leg straight, with the toes of the foot pushing against the floor.	You may want to repeat the entire exercise for each leg.
Now, straighten your forward bent leg and lift the toe up. Gently, without pulling, try to have your head touch your knee. This exercise will stretch your quadriceps, hamstrings, and the Achilles' tendon. Perform the exercise on your other leg.	

INSTRUCTIONAL ACTIVITIES	TEACHING HINTS
Side lunge Begin in a wide straddle position, with legs and feet turned out. Bend one knee, and keep the other leg straight. Be sure to keep the knee over the toes and the feet flat while in the lunge position. Lift the toes of the straight leg, and let the hips sink as low as possible to get a nice stretch. Keep hands/fingertips on the floor for balance. Hold this position for 15 to 30 seconds, and then perform it on the other side.	Repeat the exercise on each side. This exercise stretches the muscles in the inside of the hip flexor muscles.
Hamstring Stretch While lying on back with feet parallel, bend one leg and keep the other foot on the ground for support. Lift the straight leg up and try to keep the knee straight. Place hands under the thigh of the lifted leg. Hold the lifted leg under the thigh for a minimum of 15 seconds, preferably for 30 to 60 seconds.	This exercise stretches the hamstrings. Repeat on the other side. Perform another set.
Quadriceps Stretch Stand up with good posture. Keeping the supporting leg slightly bent, grasp the lower leg near the foot and gently pull foot toward buttocks.	Proceed carefully, as this exercise can place stress on your knee joint. Repeat on each leg.
Calf Stretches Perform either or both of the following calf exercises: Perform a standing lunge by stepping forward with one foot so that both feet are approximately 1 to 2 feet apart. The front leg is bent, the back leg is straight with the toes facing forward.	Hold this position for 20 seconds. Repeat on the other leg. Repeat the set again.
Stand facing a wall, approximately 2 feet away from it. Keep the body in a straight line and lunge forward, place both hands on the wall about shoulder level. In the lunge position, the forward leg is bent, and the back leg is straight. There should be a stretch in the calf of the straight leg. If not, adjust the position until a stretch is felt.	Repeat the exercise on the other leg.
Ankle Circles While standing or sitting, circle each ankle 10 times in each direction.	Repeat on other foot.
Ankle Raises From a standing position in good posture, raise up on the balls of both feet. Hold for 4 counts, and then lower back to the floor in 4 counts.	Repeat 10 times. Do another set, holding for 2 counts in each position.
Heel Walking Lift toes up and walk around the room on both heels.	This strengthens the tibialis muscles.
Sitting Straddle Side Stretch Sit on the floor in a wide straddle position, with legs straight and toes pointed. Hold arms overhead, and stretch to the side. Hold this position for 10 seconds. Variation 1: If the knee hurts, bend one leg so the foot faces the body as shown, and stretch over the extended leg. Variation 2: Instead of holding both arms overhead, stretch one arm overhead and the other one toward the toes.	Repeat on the other side. Repeat the total exercise several times.
Sitting Straddle Forward Stretch Sit on the floor in a wide straddle position. Let gravity pull the torso down, and lean the upper body forward. Be sure to bend from the hips.	Hold this position for 10 seconds. Sit up, and repeat the exercise.

INSTRUCTIONAL ACTIVITIES	TEACHING HINTS

STRENGTHENING EXERCISES

Push-Up

Perform the maximum number of push-ups.

Repeat as many times as possible.

Reverse Push-Ups

Begin with weight supported on hands and feet with the back parallel to the floor. Fingers must point toward the heels. Shift most weight toward the shoulders. Lower the body halfway to the floor, and then straighten the elbows to return to the starting position.

This exercise strengthens triceps muscles.
Repeat as many times as possible.

Abdominal Curl-Ups

Donkey Leg Lifts

Begin on hands and knees, with weight supported on forearms. Keep head looking between hands. Lift a bent leg up to hip level. Lift leg in this position several inches, and then lower it to hip level. Keep hips parallel to the floor, and be sure not to lean to one side.

Repeat this exercise at least 20 times on each leg. This exercise strengthens your gluteal muscles in the buttocks.

Side Leg Lifts

Begin lying on side. Have the arm closest to the floor supporting the head and have the top arm bent in front of the chest, with the palm on the floor. Lift the top leg straight up toward the ceiling, keeping it on a forward diagonal between 30°– 45° from the body. Point the toe slightly towards the floor. Slowly lower the leg.

This exercise works the abductor muscles located on the upper outside thigh.

Repeat this exercise at least 20 times on each leg.

Bent Side Leg Lifts

Begin lying on side. Bend both legs. Bring the top leg up toward the chest, and place the knee and lower leg on the floor for support. Lift the top leg up, hold it there, then slowly lower it to the floor.

Repeat this 20 times on each side. This exercise strengthens the abductor muscles.

Pelvic Lifts/Buttocks Exercise

Lie on back with knees bent, the soles of the feet on the floor, and hands by the sides. Keeping the lower back close to the floor, contract the abdominal muscles and gluteal muscles to tilt and lift the pelvis approximately 1 to 2 inches toward the ceiling.

Repeat approximately 20 to 30 times.

Caution: Do not lift the lower and middle back off the floor.

Stand up and stretch and take deep breathes.

Aerobic workouts are an effective way to control your weight, exercise your heart, strengthen your muscles and make you feel good. After such a workout, people have a sense of well being. Aerobic workouts are any exercise that helps your body use oxygen more efficiently. This is done by increasing your heart rate and breathing more heavily than usual for an extended period of time.

GAME (5 MINUTES)

Triangle plus 1 Tag

Triangle moves around to avoid getting leader tagged.
Tagger tries to tag leader.

DPESS page 312

Use Whistle Mixer to make groups of 4.
Identify leader and tagger.
3 make triangle and hold hands.

EVALUATION/REVIEW AND CHEER

What muscles were worked today?
What areas need more flexibility work?
What part of the Aerobic Routine did you enjoy the most?
Cheer: Aerobics takes my breath away!

Aerobics Lesson Plan 2

EQUIPMENT:

Aerobics Music/ CD
One bean bag per student
Music Player

OBJECTIVES:

The student will:

1. Play Vanishing Bean Bags demonstrating speed, agility, cooperation and following the rules established by the instructor.
2. Participate in the standing Aerobics routine during the fitness and lesson focus sections of class using form and movements demonstrated by the instructor.
3. Play Balance Tag using movements described by the instructor while demonstrating balance skills, cooperation and good sportsmanship with classmates.

National Standards Met in this Lesson: **1, 2, 3, 4, 5, 6**

INSTRUCTIONAL ACTIVITIES	TEACHING HINTS
INTRODUCTORY ACTIVITY (2–3 MINUTES)	
Vanishing Bean Bags Take away bean bags after each episode.	**DPESS page 309** Scattered formation
COMBINE FITNESS DEVELOPMENT AND LESSON FOCUS (20–25 MINUTES)	
Aerobic Workout Routine	**Casten, C. and Jordan, P.** ***Aerobics Today, 2nd Ed.*** **Wadsworth, 2002.**
Walk in place while moving arms from hips to overhead.	32 counts
Step to the right and touch your left toe to the right, then step to the left and touch the left toe next to the left foot.	8 times
Hop on the left foot 4 times while pointing and tapping the right foot forward and then to the side (for example, forward, side, forward, feet together on count 4, jump/change sides).	Repeat the entire phrase while hopping (bouncing) on the right foot 4 times and tapping the left foot forward and to the side as described. Repeat the phrase again on each side.
Run in place 8 times, clap on each run.	
Do 8 jumping jacks using full arm movements.	
Slide to the right 8 times, clap on the 8th slide.	Repeat to the left.
Jump in place 8 times while hitting the sides of your thighs with straight arms.	
Run in place 8 times while lifting your feet high in the rear.	
Run in place 8 times while lifting your knees high in front.	Repeat the two running in place phrases
Perform 8 jumping jacks, moving your arms down and up in coordination with the leg movements.	
Perform 8 jumping jacks, moving your arms down and only half way up (to the shoulder level) in coordination with each leg movement.	
Mountain Climber	With your feet separated, jump and land forward and backward a distance of about one foot. Alternate feet as you land in front and in back on each jump. Your arms can swing high in opposition to the leg movements.
Pony: "Hop, step, step." Hop on the right foot to the side, and then quickly step with the left foot and then the right foot.	Repeat on the other side.

INSTRUCTIONAL ACTIVITIES	TEACHING HINTS
Heel, toe, slide, slide: Hop on the left foot while tapping the right heel to the right side. While hopping again on the left foot, swing the right foot to the front and touch the toe on the floor. Perform 2 slides to the right.	Repeat the entire phrase by hopping on the right foot and sliding to the left.
Hop on one foot and lift up the opposite knee.	Reverse.
Hop on one foot, and swing kick the opposite foot forward.	Reverse.
Charleston Bounce Step: Use a very bouncy step throughout this phrase. Step right, kick the left foot forward, step back on the left foot, and touch the right toe back.	Repeat 8 times. Reverse with opposite foot leading.
Can-Can Kick: Hop on the right foot, and simultaneously bring the bent left knee up high in front. **Hop** again on the right foot, lightly touch the left foot on the floor next to the right, and kick the left foot into the air forward and up.	Repeat 4 times and then repeat on the other side. A more advanced version involves alternating sides after each kick.
Twist the body while using a bounce landing, and swing the arms in opposition overhead on each twist. The arms can also be swung from side to side at chest level.	
Skiers' jump: Jump to the right while twisting the body toward the left diagonal. Perform 8 times.	Reverse on the other side. For variety, jump twice on each side before changing directions.
Walk in place while moving arms from hips to overhead.	32 counts
Walk in place while stay near the hips, hands are flexed, and move away from the body and back towards the hips.	32 counts
Stretches and Isolations	
Head isolations Lift head up and down. Turn head to the right and then the left.	Repeat the set 4 to 8 times Caution: All head and neck exercises should be performed smoothly and in a relaxed manner. If the neck is allowed to arch or roll back, unnecessary tension could be placed on the cervical vertebrae.
Shoulder Circles In a slow, smooth manner, circle shoulders forward, up, back, and around 8 times.	Reverse the direction of the roll, and repeat it 8 times.
Rib Isolations While standing with good posture, place hands on hips (this helps keep hips from moving). Move ribs forward, back to center, to the side, back to center, to the back, back to center, to the other side, and back to center.	Repeat by reversing the direction of the rib isolations.
Rib Circles Perform rib circles the same way as the rib isolations, but in a continuous manner.	Perform them several times in each direction.
Hip Isolations While standing with good posture, slightly bend the knees. Now smoothly tilt the pelvis forward and then backward.	Repeat 8 times.
Hip Swings Tilt hips and pelvic area to the right and then the left.	Repeat 8 times. Be sure to execute these movements in a smooth, sustained manner.
Hip Circles While standing with good posture, slightly bend knees. Smoothly circle hips forward, to the side, to the back, and to the other side. Continue circling hips at least 8 times.	Reverse the direction and perform the hip circles the same number of times. Keep movements smooth and sustained. Jerking movements should be avoided.

INSTRUCTIONAL ACTIVITIES	TEACHING HINTS
Deep Lunge Begin in a standing position with good posture. With feet parallel, take a large step forward on one foot. Assume a deep lunge position, place hands on each side of the knee. The heel of the forward foot must remain on the floor, and the knee should be directly above the foot. Keep the extended back leg straight, with the toes of the foot pushing against the floor. Now, straighten your forward bent leg and lift the toe up. Gently, without pulling, try to have your head touch your knee. This exercise will stretch your quadriceps, hamstrings, and the Achilles' tendon. Perform the exercise on your other leg.	Hold this position for 20 seconds. You may want to repeat the entire exercise for each leg.
Hamstring Stretch While lying on back with feet parallel, bend one leg and keep the other foot on the ground for support. Lift the straight leg up and try to keep the knee straight. Place hands under the thigh of the lifted leg. Hold the lifted leg under the thigh for a minimum of 15 seconds, preferably for 30 to 60 seconds.	This exercise stretches the hamstrings. Repeat on the other side. Perform another set.
Quadriceps Stretch Stand up with good posture. Keeping the supporting leg slightly bent, grasp the lower leg near the foot and gently pull foot toward buttocks.	Proceed carefully, as this exercise can place stress on your knee joint. Repeat on each leg.
Calf Stretches Perform either or both of the following calf exercises: Perform a standing lunge by stepping forward with one foot so that both feet are approximately 1 to 2 feet apart. The front leg is bent, the back leg is straight with the toes facing forward. Stand facing a wall, approximately 2 feet away from it. Keep the body in a straight line and lunge forward, place both hands on the wall about shoulder level. In the lunge position, the forward leg is bent, and the back leg is straight. There should be a stretch in the calf of the straight leg. If not, adjust the position until a stretch is felt.	Hold this position for 20 seconds. Repeat on the other leg. Repeat the set again.
Ankle Circles While standing or sitting, circle each ankle 10 times in each direction. Repeat	Repeat the exercise on the other leg.
Ankle Raises From a standing position in good posture, raise up on the balls of both feet. Hold for 4 counts, and then lower back to the floor in 4 counts.	Repeat 10 times. Do another set, holding for 2 counts in each position.
Heel Walking Lift toes up and walk around the room on both heels.	This strengthens the tibialis muscles.
Sitting Straddle Side Stretch Sit on the floor in a wide straddle position, with legs straight and toes pointed. Hold arms overhead, and stretch to the side. Hold this position for 10 seconds. Variation 1: If the knee hurts, bend one leg so the foot faces the body as shown, and stretch over the extended leg. Variation 2: Instead of holding both arms overhead, stretch one arm overhead and the other one toward the toes.	Repeat on the other side. Repeat the total exercise several times.

INSTRUCTIONAL ACTIVITIES	TEACHING HINTS
Sitting Straddle Forward Stretch Sit on the floor in a wide straddle position. Let gravity pull the torso down, and lean the upper body forward. Be sure to bend from the hips.	Hold this position for 10 seconds. Sit up, and repeat the exercise.
Strengthening Exercises	
Push-Up Perform the maximum number of push-ups.	Repeat as many times as possible.
Reverse Push-Ups Begin with weight supported on hands and feet with the back parallel to the floor. Fingers must point toward the heels. Shift most weight toward the shoulders. Lower the body halfway to the floor, and then straighten the elbows to return to the starting position.	This exercise strengthens triceps muscles. Repeat as many times as possible.
Abdominal Curl-Ups	
Donkey Leg Lifts Begin on hands and knees, with weight supported on forearms. Keep head looking between hands. Lift a bent leg up to hip level. Lift leg in this position several inches, and then lower it to hip level. Keep hips parallel to the floor, and be sure not to lean to one side.	Repeat this exercise at least 20 times on each leg. This exercise strengthens your gluteal muscles in the buttocks.
Side Leg Lifts Begin lying on side. Have the arm closest to the floor supporting the head and have the top arm bent in front of the chest, with the palm on the floor. Lift the top leg straight up toward the ceiling, keeping it on a forward diagonal between 30°–45° from the body. Point the toe slightly towards the floor. Slowly lower the leg.	This exercise works the abductor muscles located on the upper outside thigh. Repeat this exercise at least 20 times on each leg.
Bent Side Leg Lifts Begin lying on side. Bend both legs. Bring the top leg up towards the chest, and place the knee and lower leg on the floor for support. Lift the top leg up, hold it there, then slowly lower it to the floor.	Repeat this 20 times on each side. This exercise strengthens the abductor muscles.
Pelvic Lifts/Buttocks Exercise Lie on back with knees bent, the soles of the feet on the floor, and hands by the sides. Keeping the lower back close to the floor, contract the abdominal muscles and gluteal muscles to tilt and lift the pelvis approximately 1 to 2 inches toward the ceiling.	Repeat approximately 20 to 30 times. Caution: Do not lift the lower and middle back off the floor.
Slowly sit up.	Take deep breaths once sitting up.
Slowly stand up.	Take deep breaths while lifting the arms from by the sides to overhead.
Stretch the arms overhead.	8 counts alternating arms
Open the feet to "second position," feet parallel.	
Stretch one arm overhead and towards the diagonal.	Repeat on the other side.
Take a full deep breath and exhale.	Repeat several times.

COOL-DOWNS, consisting of deep breathing, slow walking and stretching, are performed after aerobic exercise for a duration of 5-7 minutes. The purpose of cool-downs is to gradually return your heart rate and blood pressure to resting or pre-exercise levels.

GAME (5 MINUTES)

INSTRUCTIONAL ACTIVITIES	TEACHING HINTS
Balance Tag	**DPESS page 312** Select several "its." Rotate positions frequently. Select a balance position in which one is safe.

INSTRUCTIONAL ACTIVITIES	TEACHING HINTS

EVALUATION/REVIEW AND CHEER

Was the Aerobic Routine easier for you today since this was your second day?
What muscles were worked today?
What do you need to continue working on?

Cheer: 2, 4, 6, 8, Aerobics makes me feel great!

Juggling

This unit has been specifically designed to meet all six components of the NASPE National Standards for Physical Education.

OBJECTIVES:

The student will:

1. Run, change directions, pivot, evade other students, and assume poses during Rubber Band and Run and Change Direction Introductory Activities as directed by the instructor.
2. Demonstrate cooperation in Triangle plus 1 Tag and Foot tag activities following the instructions established by the instructor.
3. Participate in Parachute Fitness and Jump and Jog Fitness activities to improve their overall fitness.
4. Demonstrate Cascading, Reverse Cascading, and Column Juggling skills while using one, two, and three scarves and using form demonstrated by the instructor.

JUGGLING BLOCK PLAN
2 DAY UNIT

Week #1	Day One	Day Two
Introductory Activity	Run and Change Direction	Rubber Band
Fitness	Jump and Jog Fitness	Parachute Fitness
Lesson Focus	Cascading Reverse Cascading Column Juggling	Review Juggling Additional challenges in Juggling
Game	Triangle plus 1 Tag	Help Me Tag

Juggling Lesson Plan 1

EQUIPMENT:

3 juggling scarves per student	Jump ropes for half the number of students
5–6 cones	Music/ CD for fitness
Instructional signs	Music player

OBJECTIVES:

The student will:

1. Run, change directions, pivot, evade other students, and assume poses during the Run and Change Direction Introductory Activity following the directions given by the instructor.
2. Participate in Jump and Jog Fitness activities to improve their overall fitness.
3. Demonstrate Cascading, Reverse Cascading, and Column Juggling skills while using one, two, and three scarves and using form demonstrated by the instructor.
4. Demonstrate cooperation in Triangle plus 1 Tag game following the instructions established by the instructor.

National Standards Met in this Lesson: **1, 2, 3, 4, 5, 6**

INSTRUCTIONAL ACTIVITIES	TEACHING HINTS
INTRODUCTORY ACTIVITY (2–3 MINUTES)	
Run and Change Direction	**DPESS page 308**
Students run in any direction, changing directions on signal.	Scattered formation Specify type of angle, i.e., right, obtuse, 45-degree.
FITNESS DEVELOPMENT (8–12 MINUTES)	
Jump and Jog Fitness	**DPESS page 357**
One partner jumps rope at the cone, other jogs around the circle. Change roles. Variations in moving around circle: • Slide • Carioca • Power Skip	Use continuity music /CD to signal activity change. Set up 5–6 cones in a circle in gym or field area. 3 jump ropes at each cone
LESSON FOCUS (15–20 MINUTES)	
Tossing One Scarf at a time	**DPESS pages 392–394**
Demonstrate tossing straight up and catching with one scarf in each hand.	
Cascading	
Demonstrate with 1, then 2 scarves. Demonstrate **Three-scarf cascading.**	Proceed to 3 scarves only when 2 are mastered
Reverse Cascading	
Demonstrate with 1, then 2 scarves. Demonstrate **Three-scarf reverse cascading.** Demonstrate with 1, then 2 scarves. Demonstrate **Three-scarf reverse cascading again.**	Proceed to 3 scarves only when 2 are mastered
Column Juggling	
Demonstrate with 3 scarves.	To perform three-scarf column juggling, begin with two scarves in one hand and one in the other hand

People who juggle regularly state that if you juggle for 30 minutes straight, you will breath hard, perspire, and enjoy a good workout. It is said that juggling invigorates one's spirit.

INSTRUCTIONAL ACTIVITIES	TEACHING HINTS

GAME (5 MINUTES)

Triangle plus 1 Tag
Triangle moves around to avoid getting leader tagged.

DPESS page 312

Use Whistle Mixer to make groups of 4.
Identify leader and tagger.
3 make triangle and hold hands.
Tagger tries to tag leader.

EVALUATION/REVIEW AND CHEER

What activity was the most challenging during fitness today?
Which juggling skills were the easiest to master?
Which juggling skills do you need to work on more and why?
What is the most important skill to practice in Triangle plus 1 Tag?

Cheer: 3, 2, 1, Juggling is fun!

Juggling Lesson Plan 2

EQUIPMENT:

3 juggling scarves per student
Parachute
Stuffed animal/chicken
Music/ CD player
Fitness music /CD

OBJECTIVES:

The student will:

1. Perform a locomotor movement, jump, hop and change directions during the Rubber Band Introductory Activity following the directions given by the instructor.
2. Participate in Parachute Fitness activities to improve their overall fitness.
3. Demonstrate Cascading, Reverse Cascading, Column and Showering Juggling skills while using one, two, and three scarves and using form demonstrated by the instructor.
4. Demonstrate cooperation in Help Me Tag game following the instructions established by the instructor.

National Standards Met in this Lesson: **1, 2, 3, 4, 5, 6**

INSTRUCTIONAL ACTIVITIES	TEACHING HINTS

INTRODUCTORY ACTIVITY (2–3 MINUTES)

Rubber Band
Students move away from instructor performing a locomotor movement (jump, hop, slide, etc.). On signal, students run back to instructor.

DPESS page 309
Scattered formation
Use whistle for signals

INSTRUCTIONAL ACTIVITIES	TEACHING HINTS

FITNESS DEVELOPMENT (8–12 MINUTES)

Parachute Fitness	**DPESS page 351**
Jog: hold chute in right hand; Change directions, switch hands. Slide, hold chute with both hands.	Use music to make fitness fun and exciting.
Skip: hold chute with right hand. Change directions, switch hands. Freeze and shake chute.	Use signal to change task.
Sit with bent legs under chute for curl-ups. Lay on right side, lift left leg up. Reverse.	Keep all movements under control.
Stand up and shake chute. Jog and lift chute up and down. Repeat.	

LESSON FOCUS (15–20 MINUTES)

Review: • **Cascading** • **Reverse Cascading** • **Column Juggling**	**DPESS pages 392–394**
Demonstrate Showering	Showering is more difficult than cascading because of the rapid movement of the hands. Start with two scarves; one in the right hand and one in the other
Additional Cascading Juggling Challenges	While cascading, toss a scarf under one leg. While cascading, toss a scarf under one leg. While cascading, instead of catching one of the scarves, blow it upward with a strong breath of air. Begin cascading by tossing the first scarf into the air with a foot. Lay the scarf across the foot and kick it into the air. Try juggling three scarves with one hand. Do not worry about establishing a pattern; just catch the lowest scarf each time. Juggle three scarves while standing side by side with inside arms around each other.
Additional Column Juggling Challenges	While doing column juggling, toss up one scarf, hold the other two, and make a full turn. Resume juggling.

The American Heritage Dictionary defines juggle first as "To keep (two or more) objects in the air at one time by alternately tossing and catching them." That is the definition of what is known as toss juggling.

GAME (5 MINUTES)

Help Me Tag	**DPESS page 312**
Students touching stuffed animal are safe.	Use Whistle Mixer to create groups of 3–5.
Can be 3 people touching animal	You need 3–5 taggers.
Must pass animal in 30 seconds	You need 3 people in center of area holding a stuffed animal in safe area.
Students about to be tagged call for help and the animal needs to be passed to them for safety.	

EVALUATION/REVIEW AND CHEER

What muscles were used during fitness?
Which juggling skills were the most challenging today?
Which juggling skills were easier to master today than yesterday?
Cheer: 5, 4, 2, Juggling is cool!

Kickboxing

OBJECTIVES:

The student will:
1. Demonstrate agility and listening skills while participating in the Move and Change Direction Introductory Activity.
2. Participate in the Circuit Training Fitness activities following directions and using form demonstrated by the instructor.
3. Demonstrate the Boxer's stance placing the dominant foot to the rear of the front foot and using form demonstrated by the instructor.
4. Demonstrate the Boxer's center jog stance using form demonstrated by the instructor.
5. Demonstrate the Jab, Cross, Uppercut, Hook, Block and Flutter Jabs using the right and left hand and form demonstrated by the instructor.
6. Demonstrate the basic kicks of front, side, and roundhouse leading with both the right and left foot and using form demonstrated by the instructor.
7. Demonstrate the routine presented by the instructor to the music provided and use form demonstrated by the instructor.
8. Participate in the Wheelbarrow relay games demonstrating cooperation and good sportsmanship while following directions.

KICKBOXING BLOCK PLAN
2 DAY UNIT

Two Day Unit Plan	Day One	Day Two
Introductory Activity	Move and Change Directions	Bean Bag Challenges
Fitness	Circuit Training	Squad Leader Exercises
Lesson Focus	Stance Punches and Blocks Kicks	Review Basic Moves Teach Kickboxing Routine
Game	Wand Activities	Addition Tag

Kickboxing Lesson Plan 1

EQUIPMENT:

Cones for each station
Jump ropes at each required station
CD/ Music player
Signs for each station
Fitness music /CD with timing as listed
1 wand per person

OBJECTIVES:

The student will:

1. Demonstrate agility and listening skills while participating in the Move and Change Direction Introductory Activity.
2. Participate in the Circuit Training Fitness activities following directions and using form demonstrated by the instructor.
3. Demonstrate the Boxer's stance placing the dominant foot to the rear of the front foot and using form demonstrated by the instructor.
4. Demonstrate the Boxer's center jog stance using form demonstrated by the instructor.
5. Demonstrate the Jab, Cross, Uppercut, Hook, Block and Flutter Jabs using the right and left hand and form demonstrated by the instructor.
6. Demonstrate the basic kicks of front, side, and roundhouse leading with both the right and left foot and using form demonstrated by the instructor.
7. Participate in the Wand activities demonstrating cooperation and good sportsmanship while following directions.

National Standards Met in this Lesson: **1, 2, 3, 4, 5, 6**

INSTRUCTIONAL ACTIVITIES	TEACHING HINTS

INTRODUCTORY ACTIVITY (2–3 MINUTES)

Move and Change Direction
Scattered formation

DPESS page 308
Students run in any direction, and change direction on signal given by the instructor.

FITNESS DEVELOPMENT (8–12 MINUTES)

Circuit Training
Jump rope station
Upper body stretching
Jump rope station
Lower body stretching
Jogging in place station
Push-up and reverse push-up station
Jumping jacks and mountain climber station
Curl-up station
Run around the area station
Side leg lifts
Jump rope station
Leg and back flexibility station
Stuttering/quick running in place station
Sit and reach station
Backwards running around the area station

DPESS page 348
Create a music CD/cassette tape with 30–40 seconds of music followed by 5–10 seconds of silence CD/tape to change stations.

Create signs for each circuit training station clearly indicating expectations.

INSTRUCTIONAL ACTIVITIES	TEACHING HINTS

LESSON FOCUS (15–20 MINUTES)

Basic Skill Introduction & Demonstrations	**DPESS page 361**
Boxer's stance Hands held chin high. Dominant hand slightly behind the opposite hand. Weight on balls of the feet. dominant foot to the rear of the front foot.	Scattered formation so students see demonstrator. Most punches require a weight transfer and a pivot off the rear foot.
Boxer's center jog stance	Bounce on both feet with the hands up to the chin. Feet even, parallel, and shoulder width apart.
Punches and blocks:	
• **Jab**	Lead arm snaps forward and back.
• **Cross**	Rear arm used with a shoulder turn and a pivot on the rear foot.
• **Uppercut**	Uppercut involves dropping the knee and starting a circular windmill motion with the arm followed by rotating the hips and extending the knee upward as the punch comes up and forward.
• **Hook**	Performed with either arm. Involves a slight drop of the arm and a rounded hooking motion to hit the side of the target.
• **Blocks**	Involve moving either arm upward in an L shape to block a punch.
• **Flutter jabs**	Flutter jabs are done from the center jog stance and involve a burst of continuous jabs.
Basic Kicks	
• **Front**	Involves a step with the opposite foot followed by bringing the knee up with a flexed ankle and extending the kick forward.
• **Side**	Right side kick: Step sideways on R foot, cross over L foot. Bring up R knee, and extend kick to the side.
• **Roundhouse**	Step forward with opposite foot, raise kicking leg to a flexed position, pivot on rear foot, and explode the kick forward with the toes pointed.

Muscle and Fitness magazine rated aerobic kickboxing as the number one calorie burner of all fitness activities with around 800 calories burned per hour. Comparatively, regular aerobics/dance classes burn around 500 calories per hour.

GAME (5 MINUTES)

Wand Activities	**DPESS 402**
Wand Whirl Wand Kick over Wand Walk Down Wand Reaction Time	Everyone has a Wand.

EVALUATION/REVIEW AND CHEER

Ask the students questions to review the elements of the stance, punches and blocks and basic kicks.
Ask review questions discussing the challenges of the Circuit Training and Wand activities.
Ask which activities were the most challenging and why they were challenging.
About how many calories per hour are you burning performing aerobic kickboxing?

Cheer: 3, 6, 9, Kickboxing is fine!

Kickboxing Lesson Plan 2

EQUIPMENT:

CD/ Music player
Fitness music /CD with timing as listed
Instructional cards with exercises listed for Squad Leaders
1 bean bag per student

OBJECTIVES:

The student will:

1. Demonstrate agility, tossing and catching skills while participating in the Bean Bag Challenges Introductory Activity.
2. Participate in Squad Leader Exercises following directions and using form demonstrated by the instructor/ leader.
3. Demonstrate the boxer's stance, Jab, Cross, Uppercut, Hook, Block and Flutter Jabs using the right and left hand and form demonstrated by the instructor.
4. Demonstrate the basic kicks of front, side, and roundhouse leading with both the right and left foot and using form demonstrated by the instructor.
5. Participate in the boxing routine using form demonstrated by the instructor.
6. Participate in Addition Tag demonstrating speed, cooperation and good sportsmanship while following directions.

National Standards Met in this Lesson: **1, 2, 3, 4, 5, 6**

INSTRUCTIONAL ACTIVITIES	TEACHING HINTS
INTRODUCTORY ACTIVITY (2–3 MINUTES)	
Bean Bag Challenges	**DPESS page 360**
Toss the bean bag overhead and catch it	
Try catching on different body parts, such as shoulder, knee, and foot.	
Toss the bean bag, make a half-turn, and catch it.	
Try making a different number of turns (full, double).	
Toss, clap the hands, and catch. Try clapping the hands a specified number of times.	
Clap the hands around different parts of the body.	
FITNESS DEVELOPMENT (8–12 MINUTES)	
Squad Leader Exercises	**DPESS page 346**
Plan exercises covering the following:	Provide squad leaders with instructional cards listing the exercises you would like them to lead.
Two exercises for the arm-shoulder girdle area	Play aerobics music /CD during fitness.
Two for the abdominal region	
One exercise for the legs	
Three exercises for flexibility	The leader can add additional exercises that you have taught in class previously.
Two–three minutes of continuous movement	

INSTRUCTIONAL ACTIVITIES	TEACHING HINTS

LESSON FOCUS (15–20 MINUTES)

Review Basic Movements from Lesson 1: • Stances • Punches and jabs • Basic Kicks	**DPESS page 361** Scattered formation
Routine: • Boxer's jog with bobbing, weaving, jabs and blocks. • Left jabs and right jabs • Left hooks and right hooks • Left uppercuts and right uppercuts • Left side kicks and right side kicks • Left roundhouse kicks and right roundhouse kicks • Left combo kicks and right combo kicks	Use an Aerobics Music CD/cassette tape.

Kick-boxing aerobics classes combine Kick-boxing and Karate skills with aerobic exercise to provide a fast paced combination of flexibility, strength, endurance, and cardio-vascular exercise with the added benefit of self-defense skills. It is a high-energy workout where the body and the mind must work together.

GAME (5 MINUTES)

Addition Tag	**DPESS page 312** Select several "its." Play the game 2–3 times.

EVALUATION/REVIEW AND CHEER

What body parts were worked today during the Fitness section?
Which challenges were the most difficult with the Bean Bag Introductory Activities?
Which activities are the most challenging in Kickboxing?
What is fun about Addition Tag?
Cheer: Kickboxing, yeah!

Pilates Mat

OBJECTIVES:

The student will:

1. Participate in the Move and Change Locomotion introductory activity following the instructions given by the instructor.
2. Participate in the Move and Perform a Stretch introductory activity following the instructions given by the instructor.
3. Participate in the Walk and Jog fitness activity continuously moving to the best of her ability.
4. Participate in the Pilates mat movements presented in class using form demonstrated by the instructor.
5. Participate in the game Zipper demonstrating cooperation and good sportsmanship while following the rules of the game.
6. Participate in the game Musical Hoops demonstrating cooperation and good sportsmanship while following the rules of the game.

PILATES MAT BLOCK PLAN
2 DAY UNIT

Two Day Unit Plan	Day One	Day Two
Introductory Activity	Move and Change Locomotion	Move and Perform a Stretch
Fitness	Walk and Jog	Combine fitness and lesson focus today to focus on Pilates movements
Lesson Focus	Basic Beginner Pilates Mat Movements	Review Basic Beginner mat movements and continue with additional Pilates movements
Game	Zipper	Musical Hoops

Pilates Mat Lesson Plan 1

EQUIPMENT:

1 individual mat/towel per student
Aerobics music / CD
Music/ CD player

OBJECTIVES:

The student will:

1. Participate in the Move and Change Locomotion introductory activity following the instructions given by the instructor.
2. Participate in the Walk and Jog fitness activity continuously moving to the best of her ability.
3. Participate in the Pilates mat movements presented in class using form demonstrated by the instructor.
4. Participate in the game Zipper demonstrating cooperation and good sportsmanship while following the rules of the game.

National Standards Met in this Lesson: **1, 2, 3, 4, 5, 6**

INSTRUCTIONAL ACTIVITIES	TEACHING HINTS
INTRODUCTORY ACTIVITY (2–3 MINUTES)	
Move and Change the Type of Locomotion	**DPESS page 308**
Students move using a specified locomotor movement. On signal, they change to another type of movement.	Scattered formation Specify the locomotor movements. Challenges can be given to do the movements forward, backward, sideways, or diagonally.
FITNESS DEVELOPMENT (8–12 MINUTES)	
Walk and Jog	**DPESS page 347**
Walk and jog continuously for 5–8 minutes.	Use an Aerobics music CD/cassette tape to motivate the walking and jogging. Allow student to move at his/her own pace.
LESSON FOCUS (15–20 MINUTES)	
Basic Beginner Movements	
Posture and arms	**DPESS page 363**
Lift and straighten the spine as though resting against an imaginary wall Bend the elbows at a 90-degree angle to protect the shoulder in "its" socket Lift shoulders in a circular motion up and back, move arms back and down as shoulders move down, so it feels as if shoulder blades are sliding down the spine. Raise the bent arms overhead and end with arms in starting position. Repeat.	Scattered formation Each student on towel/mat Sit cross-legged in good posture. Inhale. Exhale.
Roll Up Lie on back, legs straight, arms stretched above head, shoulders down.	Lie on back with legs straight and arms stretched above head, shoulders down.
While breathing out, slowly roll forward, lifting the spine off the mat one vertebra at a time.	Lie on back with legs straight and arms stretched above head, shoulders down. Keep back flat on the floor, slowly lift arms toward the ceiling as breathe in. Breathe out and slowly roll up and forward, lifting spine off mat one vertebrae at a time. Head remains straight, eyes focused forward. Stomach remains taut, not crunched.
Breathe in again, stretch spine and arms over legs, hands toward toes. Breathe out while slowly rolling back down to the floor.	Breathe in again while stretching out over legs. Breathe out while slowly rolling back down to the floor. While breathing in, roll up again to begin the second repetition. Repeat several times.

INSTRUCTIONAL ACTIVITIES	TEACHING HINTS
	Keep back flat on floor; slowly lift arms toward the ceiling while breathing in. Head remains straight, eyes focused forward, arms move forward toward feet. Stomach remains taut, not crunched. Without a pause, breathe in, roll up again, to begin the second repetition. Repeat several times.
Spinal rotation Slowly rotate upper body to the left and then right.	Sit in slight straddle position with the legs extended and arms out to sides.
The Hundred On back with legs between a 90-degree to 120-degree angle. Lift shoulders and arms up slightly, exhale 5 times pressing the hands down and then 5 times pressing the hands upward with palms down.	Increase until this sequence can be done 10 times for one hundred breaths.
Abdominal strengthener Lie on back with hands behind the head and knees flexed or hands on thighs sliding up during the movement. Exhale and curl-up slowly using just the abdominal muscles.	Repeat several times. Keep chin tucked.
Single-leg stretch Lie back with one leg extended about 12 inches off the floor. Flex the other leg and bring the knee to the chest. Hold the flexed leg at the tibia and raise the shoulders slowly.	Hold the position while rotating the position of the legs and changing the hand touch from tibia to tibia.

Joseph Pilates developed the now popular form of exercise in the 1920's. His interest in physical fitness stemmed from a determination to strengthen his own body and improve his health after being a sickly child. With a background in yoga, Zen meditation, martial arts and other ancient fitness techniques plus some success as a gymnast, diver and boxer, Joseph Pilates devised a sequence of movements that worked the mind and muscles in harmony. It is very popular today.

GAME (5 MINUTES)

Zipper Players make a single-file line. Each student bends over, reaches between the legs with the left hand, and grasps the right hand of the person to the rear. On signal, the last person in line lies down, the next person backs over the last person and lies down until the last person lies down, and then immediately stands and reverses the procedure.	**DPESS page 407** Use Whistle Mixer to create several groups. The first team to zip and unzip the zipper is declared the winner.

EVALUATION/REVIEW AND CHEER

Which Pilates mat movements were the most challenging?
What muscles were used during class today?
Was there anything about the game Zipper that was difficult to accomplish? If so, what?
Cheer: Pilates does a body good!

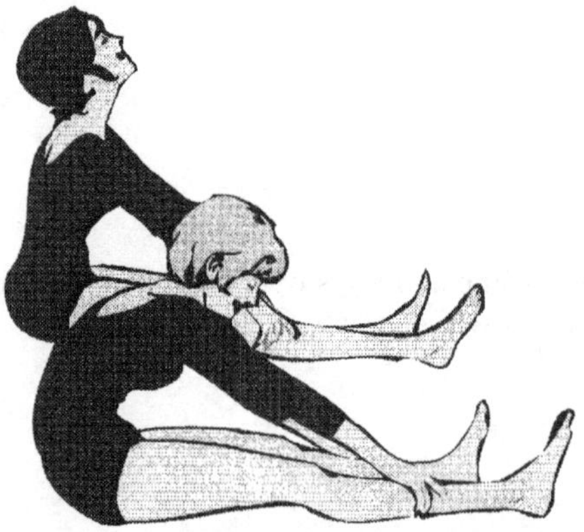

Pilates Mat Lesson Plan 2

EQUIPMENT:

One hoop per student	Music/ CD for Musical Hoops
Music player	1 mat per person

OBJECTIVES:

The student will:

1. Participate in the Move and Perform a Stretch introductory activity following the instructions given by the instructor.
2. Participate in the Pilates mat movements presented in class using form demonstrated by the instructor.
3. Participate in the game Musical Hoops demonstrating rhythmical awareness, cooperation and good sportsmanship while following the rules of the game.

National Standards Met in this Lesson: **1, 2, 3, 4, 5, 6**

INSTRUCTIONAL ACTIVITIES	TEACHING HINTS
INTRODUCTORY ACTIVITY (2–3 MINUTES)	
Move and Perform a Stretch Run throughout the area. On signal, stop and perform a designated stretching activity.	**DPESS page 308** See Chapter 16 for a comprehensive list of stretching exercises. A list of stretches that covers all body parts can be posted, and students can perform a different stretch after each signal.
COMBINE FITNESS DEVELOPMENT AND LESSON FOCUS TODAY (20 MINUTES)	
Review all of the basic beginner movements from Day 1.	**DPESS page 363**
Add the following movements: **Double straight leg** Lie on back with hands behind head and legs pointed toward the ceiling while held tight together. Lift the chin and shoulders slightly off the mat and lift the legs about one foot. Keep the lower back tight to the floor. Lower chin, shoulders, and legs.	Repeat 5–6 times.
Forward spine stretch and roll-ups Sitting position with legs and arms extended forward. Stretch forward and exhale. Add the roll-up by slowly going backward to the mat with the arms extended forward.	Repeat 5–6 times Gently roll down to the floor and back up to the extended position.
Pelvic Tilt Lie on back with the arms extended, palms down, and knees bent. Lift the pelvic girdle upwards using the abdominal and gluteal muscles.	Take 4 counts to lift the pelvis, hold for 4 counts. Repeat several times.
Back strengthener All-fours position. Lift and extend the opposite arm and leg and hold the position several seconds and then switch arms and legs.	Repeat several times.
Total rest pose All-fours position. Push the hips to heels, stomach to thighs, head down on floor. Slowly extend arms forward with palms down and flat on the floor.	Hold for a 4–6 counts. Sit up onto knees then repeat.

INSTRUCTIONAL ACTIVITIES **TEACHING HINTS**

Pilate's exercises can be done on a mat, on a ball and mat, or in a studio with specialized resistance equipment. Mr. Pilates worked as an orderly at an infirmary during World War I. He engineered a way to rig springs on hospital beds to offer light resistance exercises to bedridden patients, and thus developed the first type of Pilate's resistance equipment.

GAME (5 MINUTES)

Musical Hoops

Hoops are spread over the floor space with each student standing inside a hoop. The locomotor movement can be changed each round.

This activity is similar to musical chairs. Hoops are spread over the floor space with each student putting one foot or two feet in a hoop (depending on how many hoops are available). Play a musical CD/tape with random pauses. The teacher collects some of the hoops during the music so that some students will be eliminated when the music stops.

DPESS page 310

Play a musical CD/cassette tape with random pauses. The teacher collects some of the hoops during the music so that some students will be eliminated when the music stops. The eliminated students go to the perimeter and perform a designated stretch or some type of exercise until the music stops and then get back in the game.

EVALUATION/REVIEW AND CHEER

Were there any activities that were particularly challenging today? Which ones? Why?
In what way do Pilate's movements make you feel good?
What is the history of the Pilates exercise machine?
What was fun about musical hoops?

Cheer: Pilates makes me strong. Yeah!